INTRODUCTORY ACCOUNTING, FINANCE AND AUDITING FOR LAWYERS

Seventh Edition

■ ■ ■

Lawrence A. Cunningham

Henry St. George Tucker III Research Professor of Law
The George Washington University Law School
and
Founding Faculty Director
George Washington in New York (GWinNY)

AMERICAN CASEBOOK SERIES®

WEST
ACADEMIC
PUBLISHING

American Casebook Series is a trademark registered in the U.S. Patent and Trademark Office.

Printed in the United States of America

ISBN: 978-1-63460-410-9

For my late Mother and Father—

for my daughters' sake,
I hope the apples
don't fall
far from the tree.

PREFACE

Lawyers need familiarity with basic principles of accounting, finance and auditing, three pillars of private-sector ordering. Concepts from each area arise routinely in a business law practice and creep into many other law practices. This book introduces lawyers to the basic principles of each subject, with greatest emphasis on accounting and the remainder about equally divided between finance and auditing.

Accounting is a centuries-old discipline concerned principally with measuring, classifying and reporting on economic activity; finance, in its current form, is a decades-old discipline concerned principally with measuring financial value and financial risk by using accounting information; and financial auditing, likewise a relatively young discipline, is concerned principally with assessing and opining upon the veracity of accounting information prepared by others. In brief, accounting is about the past, finance is about prospects, and auditing is the bridge that enables using historical data to gauge the future.

Policymakers and citizens depend upon principles and professionals in all three areas to do critical jobs. These include allocating capital effectively and promoting accountability among those responsible for administering the engines of economic activity. Lawyers are involved in both allocation and accountability. Law has come to rely upon principles and professionals in these fields with increasing significance.

Part I consists of this Preface and Chapter 1, introducing all three subjects. Chapter 1 presents the ground rules and goals of accounting, highlighting the concept of generally accepted accounting principles (GAAP) and how these principles become generally accepted. It also summarizes the basic components of financial statements—the balance sheet, income statement, statement of changes in owners' equity, and statement of cash flows, as well as footnotes. It introduces basic auditing functions, including the auditor's report, and comments on the use of resulting information by financial analysts. The Chapter concludes with a brief historical perspective on the evolution of accounting, auditing, and finance.

Part II is devoted to accounting, along with the bookkeeping mechanisms that underlie it. Chapters 2 through 5 introduce basic concepts of accounting, with an emphasis on how accounting records are developed and financial statements derived. These Chapters begin with an examination of the core building block, the fundamental equation. It specifies that assets are always equal to liabilities plus owners' equity(Chapter 2). The Part then explains the accrual system of accounting and recognition principles (Chapter 3) and furnishes in-depth treatment of two central exercises in accounting: inventory and the cost of goods sold (Chapter 4) and fixed assets and depreciation (Chapter 5).

Chapter 6 goes beyond basics by introducing a variety of other kinds of assets and liabilities and more advanced principles of accounting. Topics include receivables, intercompany ownership, financial instruments, intangible assets, leases, employee matters, loss contingencies, and going concern disclosure. Here breadth of subject is given precedence over in-depth treatment to broaden the scope of this introduction to accounting. Chapter 7 rounds out the discussion of the basic financial statements by examining owners' equity or capital accounts.

Chapters Eight and Nine shift the focus from basic principles of accounting to various ways to analyze the condition and performance of a business using accounting tools. Chapter 8 discusses financial statement analysis, introducing a variety of analytical ratios that can be applied to financial statements to answer questions about liquidity, activity, and value. Chapter 9 examines the statement of cash flows, a central component of financial statements that addresses liquidity and solvency.

Part III sharpens the shift from preparing accounting information to its interpretation. It introduces finance. The basic principles of valuation are presented, including the time value of money and the operational principles necessary to make basic valuation calculations (Chapter 10). This introduction is followed by an extended discussion of techniques used in valuing businesses (Chapter 11). This material builds on all preceding materials in discussing valuation techniques based on assets, income, and cash flow. Finance theory complements this introduction to fundamental valuation techniques, along with some perspectives on passive versus active investing (Chapter 12).

Part IV moves to auditing, a profession charged with promoting the integrity of accounting information. It begins with a deep, introductory look at audit practice, including illustration of the standard statistical sampling techniques applied in the engagement (Chapter 13).This introduction includes discussion of internal control and assessing control effectiveness. The role of auditing in corporate governance and the concept of auditor independence are considered, along with legal duties and liability risks of auditors (Chapter 13).

The lawyer's role is considered, including advising on loss contingencies, dealing with the attorney-client privilege, and forensic accounting (Chapter 15). Highlighting principles introduced throughout the book, the final Chapter draws a series of lessons from a potpourri of financial reporting scandals and audit failures (Chapter 16).

Throughout the book, the principles are accompanied by Illustrations and each Chapter contains Problems to test understanding of the principles. Those studying these subjects for the first time should note that material and Problems are cumulative so that an understanding of principles discussed in earlier Chapters is usually necessary to an understanding of principles discussed later. Solutions to Problems are provided to professors using this book as both an Appendix to the accompanying Teacher's Manual and in PowerPoint slide format. Students should use solutions to prior Problems as they proceed to solve succeeding Problems.

Most Chapters conclude with a set of Conceptual Questions designed to provoke deeper thought and assessment of these subjects, including how they relate to one another and to public policy and law. Chapters Three through Nine also contain concluding notes highlighting some ways that generally accepted accounting principles in the United States, on which the book concentrates, differ from the international alternative, called International Financial Reporting Standards.

Excerpts from corporate financial statements appear throughout for illustration and analysis. Readers are urged to expand the learning experience by going to the Internet (or elsewhere) and perusing additional examples of financial statements, to which they can apply principles discussed in this book.

The book balances technical accuracy with accessibility to the fundamental principles of accounting, finance and auditing. Targeted readers are law students, including those taking the basic course in corporate law (whether called corporations, business associations or other designation) as well as those taking a separate course on accounting for lawyers(whether called accounting for lawyers, law and accounting, accounting and finance or other designation). The book can also serve as a reference for the legal profession and has been used successfully in training programs for law firms and governmental agencies, such as the Internal Revenue Service and Securities and Exchange Commission.

The book is designed so that readers may profit, whatever their background and whether they revel in its subjects or have related phobias. Based on two decades of teaching the materials at four universities as part of the basic corporations course and as a stand-alone course, the book is written to appeal to students with varied backgrounds. At many schools, these range from the MBA who has educated financial journalists to the Ph.D. in Art History who eschews business news.

The objective of the materials and of the related exercises is to acquaint readers with the vocabulary of the subjects covered and to offer an opportunity to consider some basic problems that arise in everyday settings, both business and otherwise. The objective is not to train readers as accountants, financial analysts or auditors, but to enable them to be more effective lawyers.

Indeed it is not possible for any single textbook to train anyone to be an accountant, financial analyst or auditor. While reading and studying are necessary, training for these professions requires hands-on experience. It is in this spirit that each Chapter includes Illustrations and concludes with one or more Problems and Conceptual Questions.

Moreover, these subjects command vast territories. Related curriculum at undergraduate and graduate levels includes scores of courses going far beyond the basics given here. Examples in accounting include entire books and courses devoted to Financial Statement Analysis introduced here in a single Chapter; in finance entire books and courses are devoted to Valuation, covered here in two Chapters; and in auditing, entire books and courses are devoted to Audit Practice, again covered here in a single Chapter.

The book's title suggests the scope. It is introductory and for lawyers. It encapsulates three subjects operating in the financial reporting process: the preparation (accounting), use (finance) and testing (auditing) of financial statements.

L.A.C.

September 14, 2017

ACKNOWLEDGMENTS

I owe much gratitude to numerous people whose assistance contributed to this book and previous editions. Thanks to Ronald Ricci (Duquesne) for preparing a full set of accompanying PowerPoint slides that I have updated for this edition, which are available free from the publisher. Thanks also to Elliott Weiss (Arizona) who wrote some of the problems that appear in modified form.

The historical perspective on financial reporting that concludes Chapter 1 is based upon original research and writing by Laura Ford for graduate work in Columbia University's School of International & Public Affairs (SIPA). It draws extensively on the monumental work, *A History of Accountancy in the United States: The Cultural Significance of Accounting,* by Gary John Previts and Barbara Dubis Merino (Ohio St. U. Press 1998).

Professor Weiss, along with Jeffrey Bauman (Georgetown) and Alan Palmiter (Wake Forest), kindly granted me permission to use the valuation parable appearing in Chapter 11, revised for this book. That valuation story originally was written by the late Don Schwartz (Georgetown). Some discussion in Chapter 12 draws on materials originally prepared by Professor Palmiter; I thank him for allowing me to adapt them for inclusion. Some other valuation discussion adapts materials in my book *What Is Value Investing?,* published by McGraw-Hill and the casebook *Corporate Finance and Governance* prepared with Jeff Haas (New York), published by Carolina Academic Press

In Chapter 16, discussion of the Big Four Frauds (Section C) is adapted from my 2002 article published in the *Connecticut Law Review* (The Sarbanes-Oxley Yawn: Heavy Rhetoric, Light Reform (And It Might Just Work); the Satire (Section D) is adapted from a chapter in my 2001 book published by McGraw-Hill *(How To Think Like Benjamin Graham and Invest Like Warren Buffett);* and the perorational commentary called Lawyers as Part-Time Accountants (Section E) is adapted from my 2002 article published in *The Business Lawyer* (Sharing Accounting's Burden: Lawyers in Enron's Dark Shadows). The periodic Chapter notes on International Financial Reporting Standards are adapted from my 2009 article, with William Bratton (Georgetown), in *Virginia Law Review* (Treatment Differences and Political Realities in the GAAP-IFRS Debate).

Helpful feedback was provided by many people to whom I am grateful.

Teachers include: Bernard Black (Northwestern), Steve Bradford (Nebraska), William Bratton (Penn), Zuzana Colaprete (California Western), Mitch Engler (Cardozo), Theresa Gabaldon (George Washington), Gerry Grant (Mississippi College), Monty Gray (Seattle), Jeff

Haas (New York), Barbara Hauser (Minnesota), Mark Kaplan (California Western), Doug Litowitz (Ohio Northern), the late Lewis Lowenstein (Columbia), Jim MacDonald (Idaho), David Mason (Boston College), Hilal Maximan (Cardozo), Dale Oesterle (Ohio State), Allan Samansky (Ohio State), George Van Cleve, Frank White (Boston College), and Zuzana Colaprete (Cal. Western).

Practicing lawyers include those from my days serving as of counsel to the New York law firm of Roberts, Sheridan & Kotel (now Dickstein Shapiro Morin & Oshinsky), especially Todd Roberts and Muna Farid, as well as Tom Riesenberg (Ernst & Young).

Students include, from Boston College: Justin Belair and Beth Fitzpatrick; Cardozo Law School: Harley Goldstein, Benjamin Gruberg, Jon Hutton, Eric Ovitz, and Andrew White; George Washington University: Rick Dolcetti, Christa Laser, Jodi Le Bolt, and Saima Jalal Zuberi; and Vanderbilt University: Yaw Awah, Rachael Crews, Jenny Hayes, and Kathryn Virginia Whitfield.

Valuable source materials drawn upon in preparing this book include the voluminous publications of the ABA, AICPA, FASB, PCAOB and SEC, as well as the references listed in the Bibliography.

For institutional and financial support, thanks to The Samuel and Ronnie Heyman Center on Corporate Governance at the Benjamin N. Cardozo School of Law and to the Deans of the following law schools: Boston College, Cardozo, George Washington and Vanderbilt.

Special thanks to the wonderful professionals at West Academic Publishing past and present, including James Cahoy, Staci Herr, Pat Heinz, Heidi Hellekson, Louis Higgins, Laura Holle, Bonnie Karlen, Greg Olson, Tim Payne, Ryan Pfeiffer, Owen Shaffer, Pam Siege and James Vculek. Without their confidence and support, this book would not have been possible.

TABLE OF CONTENTS

PART III. FINANCE

INTRODUCTORY ACCOUNTING, FINANCE AND AUDITING FOR LAWYERS

Seventh Edition

PART I

FIRST PRINCIPLES

■ ■ ■

CHAPTER 1

THREE PILLARS

■ ■ ■

A. INTRODUCTION

Suppose a clause in your client's contract entitles him to compensation in an amount equal to a stated percentage of the "net profits" earned from a product he helped to create. The other party to the contract informs him that the amount of net profits on the product has been negative and so claims it owes him nothing. Your client is dismayed, because he had been led to understand from reports in the news media that the product had been a spectacular success, with tens of millions of people lining up for it and paying a total of nearly $200 million to enjoy it.

On behalf of your client, you request the other party to send you documentary evidence defending its claim that net profits had been negative. The other party sends you a one-page document, captioned "Financial Statement," which contains a list of numbers. Lo-and-behold, at the bottom of the page on a line called "net profits," there it is in black-and-white—net profits on the product were negative $18 million. The document is signed by an independent "auditing" firm, as called for by the contract. You compare the definition of the term net profits in the contract with the list of numbers and find that they are in accord with each other. You do what may seem the obvious thing—you call your client and comfort him because, alas, his case is easy and over. He has no claim.

But wait. Suppose that the contract or the financial statement you have been given is not what it seems. Suppose that the term "net profits" as used in the contract and followed scrupulously in the financial statement is distorted in some way. What if the term net profit in the contract implied to an ordinarily intelligent reader of the English language that your client would be paid a percentage of the amount by which revenues fairly attributable to the product were greater than expenses fairly incurred to create and market it? And what if the net profits reported on the financial statement you have been furnished were computed according to some other method that departed from that ordinary understanding? Would your client have some claim after all, either under his contract or otherwise?

To be more concrete, suppose your client were well-known humorist and writer Art Buchwald and the contract was with the movie studio, Paramount Pictures. Suppose the contract granted Paramount the rights to the idea for the film *Coming to America*, starring Eddie Murphy, in exchange for Mr. Buchwald's right to payment equal to a stated percentage of that film's net profits. And suppose finally that the film had been a blockbuster hit, generating $160 million in worldwide box-office receipts, and that it had been widely reported in film-industry trade publications that the film cost a fraction of that to make. Further suppose that upon release, the producer calculated estimated total audience, projected resulting cash flows, and valued those flows (the motion picture business routinely does this in setting rental charges) and estimated value to exceed $100 million. Any claim now?

At stake in this case is your client's claim. But more broadly, at stake is the manner in which events in the real world are reported in terms of summary, numerical statements about that reality. In the case of *Coming to America*, Mr. Buchwald sued Paramount. Mr. Buchwald's lawyers argued in part that the contract's clause concerning determining "net profits" was substantively unconscionable. In particular, the argument ran, the way net profits were to be calculated under the contract understated revenues reasonably attributable to the film and overstated expenses reasonably associated with producing it. Although cases holding contract terms to be substantively unconscionable are rare, a California court agreed with Mr. Buchwald's lawyers that this was such a case. How did Mr. Buchwald's lawyers know that this strategy might have a chance of legal success and what enabled them to make the winning argument? They knew accounting.

Problems like this are not limited to that one film, or to Hollywood. They arise in virtually every context raising financial issues. Those contexts include not only film-making, but royalty agreements on intellectual property of all kinds, divorce settlements, child custody agreements, collective bargaining agreements, employment agreements, sports franchise and partnership agreements, loan agreements, bankruptcy plans of reorganization, the purchase or sale of a business entity, and virtually every other situation in which money is at stake. To be frank (if slightly overstated): almost every situation worth negotiating about or litigating over!

In all these matters, lawyers play a role. And of course explicit legal issues must be resolved in the course of negotiating and resolving such matters—the definition of a property right, the requirements of contract formation, the allocation of risk of tort liabilities, and so on. But important as they are, these issues are less likely to dominate discussions. The focus of negotiation or disputation will likely be on financial issues. In terms of your training during the first year of law school, the "facts" at the center of discussion will be financial, and in terms of relative importance in the universe you undoubtedly know that the facts dominate the law. To be an effective advocate on your client's behalf, therefore, an understanding of financial issues and how they are reported and described is crucial. This book is an introduction to the world defined by the facts in these terms.

To begin the introduction, consider the following hypothetical problem of how to report a series of very basic events concerning a new business operation.

Problem 1—An Introduction

Annie and Marta formed KFC (Hungary), Inc. ("KFC") to operate a Kentucky Fried Chicken franchise in Budapest. Annie and Marta invested $600,000 in KFC. During Year 1, KFC engaged in the following transactions:

1.   KFC spent $50,000 training a Hungarian staff to operate the planned store in the manner required by KFC's franchise agreement.

2.   KFC ordered equipment from German manufacturers, agreeing to pay the equivalent of $150,000 on delivery. At the time the equipment was delivered, its market value had increased to $180,000, due to changes in exchange rates and to inflation.

3.   KFC's bank added $40,000 to KFC's account, representing interest earned by KFC on the amount on deposit in its account.

Assuming KFC engaged in no other transactions in Year 1, what would you say was the value of KFC at the end of Year 1? How much would you say KFC earned (or lost) in Year 1? What additional information, if any, would you need to answer these questions? Consider the following additional questions posed by these general ones.

First, how does one treat the initial investment of $600,000? One impulse might be to treat it as *earnings* and an alternative would be to characterize it as a cash *investment* (capital investment—common stock).

Second, how does one treat $50,000 spent training employees? Several possibilities seem plausible: as a one-time expense (that reduces *earnings now*); as an expense to be recognized periodically over time (called amortizing, which would reduce *earnings over time*); or to treat it as an asset (by recognizing that it offers continuing *value* to the business over time).

Third, how does one treat the equipment that was bought and delivered? Again several possibilities seem plausible: to *value it at cost* ($150,000); to *value it at market* ($180,000); or to *reduce its value for depreciation* (say to $140,000).

Fourth, how does one treat interest earned from the bank? It could be treated as *revenue* like payments received from customers; or it could be considered as a *special kind of revenue* since it does not arise from managing the franchise's central and ongoing operations—frying and selling chicken.

Finally, confer with classmates. Ask if they would be willing to attest to the veracity of your conclusions. Would they do so if you modified some of your assumptions?

B. INTRODUCTION TO GAAP

While the various treatments suggested for each event in Problem 1 seem plausible, they lead to different answers for what the company earned and what its year-end value is. As a result, the reports of earnings and of value are not meaningful without a thorough understanding of the choices that were made to reach them. If the reports are to have meaning, it would seem desirable to establish "answers" for how to treat each event. That way, the bottom line numbers can be a reliable basis for understanding how well or poorly the entity is doing compared to prior periods, compared to expectations about it, or compared to others. This is a major purpose of accounting, pursued through the promulgation and use of a body of principles designed to deal with the infinite variety of transactions with which accounting must contend. Despite this pursuit, these principles leave discretion concerning the classification and measurement of various transactions.

GAAP and FASB.

Generally accepted accounting principles)

Those principles are embodied in a set of accounting guidelines called *generally accepted accounting principles* (which are referred to by the acronym "*GAAP*" and pronounced gap). The leading principles contained in GAAP are the product of agreement among leading accounting professionals, a group called the *Financial Accounting Standards Board* (which is referred to by the acronym "*FASB*" and pronounced *faz-bee*). GAAP are set forth in FASB's "Accounting Standards Codification" which, since 2009, FASB has declared the "single source of authoritative" GAAP in the United States. The Codification organizes the subject of accounting into some 90 topics, drawing on scattered sources that historically contributed to the subject.

FASB was formed in 1973 as an independent body composed of board members drawn from certified public accountants, corporate executives, financial analysts and academics. It has issued its pronouncements in various forms. The central organizing principles were set forth in a series of seven Statements of Financial Accounting Concepts (SFAC) expressing broad frameworks on which FASB built nearly 200 particularized pronouncements called Statements of Financial Accounting Standards (SFAS), supplemented by periodic Staff Interpretations, Technical Bulletins and other releases, including those of a specially-designated Emerging Issues Task Force (EITF).

Many accounting pronouncements result from years of disagreement, negotiation, controversy, and compromise. GAAP are thus the result of choices FASB made among competing principles they could have adopted. There is no reason to believe that the choices are the product of any scientific process that can be verified *a priori*. GAAP are best understood as conventions, the primary purpose of which is to facilitate the comparability of financial statements among business entities and with respect to a particular business entity over time.

One important consequence that follows from these observations is that it is possible that there can be more than one "right" way of accounting for a certain kind of financial event. In many such cases, FASB has elected to permit alternative ways of handling the matter, but only so long as the chosen way is both one of those accepted under GAAP and is fully disclosed in the financial statements. Much of this book is concerned with trying to understand GAAP basics.

As a private organization, FASB's promulgation of GAAP does not *ipso facto* bind accountants in a legal sense. On the other hand, as promulgated by the accounting profession's lead rulemaking body, GAAP does define standards of practice and professional conduct that bear on the reasonableness of an accountant's performance. GAAP therefore influences the legal definition of professional negligence for accountants. As a practical matter, moreover, GAAP is the grammar of business and persons with whom an entity deals—especially lenders and trade creditors—often insist on receiving and reviewing financial statements that are prepared in accordance with GAAP before investing, lending money or otherwise extending credit.

AICPA.

Important supplemental sources of GAAP are principles articulated by the American Institute of Certified Public Accountants (AICPA). It is the national, professional organization for all Certified Public Accountants (CPAs). Before FASB's founding in 1973, various AICPA arms performed the lead standard setting function for GAAP. Among these arms were the AICPA's Committee on Accounting Procedures (1953–1959), which issued a series of Accounting Research Bulletins (ARBs) (51 in all); its Committee on Terminology (1953–1957), which issued a short series of Accounting Terminology Bulletins and its Accounting Principles Board (APB, 1962–1973), which issued some 31 APB Opinions. The AICPA has published a variety of other standards through numerous Accounting Guidelines, Practice Bulletins and Statements of Position.

The AICPA's mission is to provide members with the resources, information, and leadership that enable them to provide services in a professional manner to benefit the public as well as employers and clients. In fulfilling its mission, the AICPA works with state CPA organizations and gives priority to those areas where public reliance on CPA skills is most significant.

The AICPA is in part an advocacy group for the accounting profession, by representing the interests of CPAs before governments, regulatory bodies and other organizations in advancing members' interests. It promotes uniform certification and licensing standards and the CPA designation. It also generates public awareness and confidence in the integrity, objectivity, competence and professionalism of CPAs and monitors the needs and views of CPAs. The AICPA encourages highly qualified individuals to become CPAs and supports the development of academic programs. It also establishes professional standards; assists members in improving their professional conduct, performance and expertise; and monitors such performance to enforce current standards and requirements. Lawyers might recognize the AICPA's professional counterpart in the American Bar Association.

The SEC.

Apart from indirect legal and practical consequences of FASB and the AICPA, the primary legal authority having jurisdiction over accounting rules and practice is the Securities and Exchange Commission (SEC), a federal agency charged with administering the body of federal securities laws. These laws center on prescribing the manner and timing of disclosure concerning the financial condition and performance of entities that issue securities to the public (called *public companies* or *SEC registrants*). Much of that disclosure is in turn driven by accounting rules and practice. So the SEC has a distinct interest in participating in the process of promulgating accounting rules, including GAAP. In general, however, the SEC has adopted a strong deferential stance towards the rulemaking power of FASB and tends to sanction, as a matter of law, the GAAP rules FASB promulgates. As a matter of practice, this has entailed cooperative effort between FASB and the SEC in developing accounting principles.

The SEC has power not only to specify accounting rules that govern entities subject to its jurisdiction, but to review resulting financial statements and to bring legal proceedings against those who fail to comply. Private rights of action also can be maintained under the federal securities laws for violations of those laws. Two of the most significant grounds for making claims under the federal securities laws are Section 11 of the Securities Act of 1933, 15 U.S.C. § 77k and Section 10(b) of the Securities Exchange Act of 1934, 15 U.S.C. § 78j(b), and related rules promulgated by the SEC. These provisions generally prohibit material misrepresentations in, or omissions from, informational documents required to be prepared by SEC registrants. The entity issuing the securities is subject to liability for violating these provisions. When acting as primary participants, liability may also be imposed on advisors such as accountants, auditors, lawyers, and underwriters.

Multiple Sources, Hierarchy and Codification.

FASB, the AIPCA, and the SEC, as well as numerous other professional accounting organizations ranging from the American Accounting Association (a professional association of academic accountants) to the Financial Executives Institute, regularly opine on the proper accounting treatment of a wide variety of issues and do so using numerous forms of pronouncements. Historically, the multiple sources of authority were classified according to a "GAAP hierarchy." It gave priority to FASB statements, then APB opinions, followed by a list running down various other FASB or AICPA publications. For SEC registrants, moreover, all these could be superseded by accounting regulations imposed by the SEC.

This complex model with its multiplicity of sources created the need for practitioners and their advisors to consult numerous bodies of pronouncements rather than one. *Cf. Shalala v. Guernsey Memorial Hospital*, 514 U.S. 87, 101 (1995) (Kennedy, J.) (lamenting that "there are 19 different GAAP sources, any number of which might present conflicting treatments of a particular accounting question"). To reduce complexity, FASB embarked on a codification project to consolidate and restate all GAAP authority in a unified topical arrangement. Completed in 2009, FASB's Accounting Standards Codification, referenced above, ordains GAAP contained within it as authoritative and classifies all else as non-authoritative. The result is that there is no distinction, as there once was, among various forms of FASB pronouncements or those of predecessor bodies.

Accordingly, in addition to SEC regulations, the Codification is the source of GAAP in the United States. All else is non-authoritative. According to FASB, it will henceforth issue Accounting Standards Updates, which will not *ipso facto* bear authoritative weight, but "serve only to update the Codification." As a result, the erstwhile GAAP hierarchy is gone and there are "only two levels of GAAP: authoritative and non-authoritative," FASB says.

Contemporary Accounting Standard Setting.

The Sarbanes-Oxley Act of 2002 directed the SEC in determining how accounting principles become generally accepted, at least for public companies. Until this Act, FASB was funded by private contributions, including from reporting entities and their outside auditors. To continue its standard-setting function, Sarbanes-Oxley requires it (or any other such body) to be funded from issuers of public securities, through so-called annual accounting support fees.

Making it clear that Sarbanes-Oxley does not limit the SEC's pre-existing authority to establish accounting principles and standards applicable to SEC registrants, the statute permits the SEC to recognize as "generally accepted" those accounting principles established by standard-setting bodies possessing detailed characteristics, including funding as Sarbanes-Oxley directs from annual accounting support fees.

To qualify as a standard-setter under Sarbanes-Oxley, bodies must be private entities serving the public interest and comprised of a majority of persons unassociated for at least two years with a registered public accounting firm (discussed further below). Bodies must have procedures to promptly consider needed accounting changes by majority vote. They must consider the need to keep standards current and to achieve international convergence. Each body must submit annual reports to the SEC that are made publicly available.

International Financial Reporting Standards.

Outside the US, neither the SEC, FASB nor the AICPA has power to promulgate accounting standards. That responsibility is reposed in various regulatory and professional organizations in each country. However, as cross-border transactions proliferated, increasing pressure emerged to harmonize GAAP with accounting standards accepted in other countries. The National Securities Markets Improvements Act of 1996, for example, required the SEC to report to Congress on progress in developing international accounting standards.

Since then, the SEC has worked with the International Accounting Standards Board (IASB, formerly known as the International Accounting Standards Committee (IASC)) to promulgate a core set of accounting pronouncements constituting a comprehensive basis of international GAAP. The IASB calls these International Financial Reporting Standards (IFRS). The effort has been encouraged by a range of governmental ministers, including the Finance Ministers and Central Bank Governors of leading industrial countries, as well as the World Bank and the International Organization of Securities Commissioners (IOSCO).

Enthusiasm for a single global set of accounting standards is widespread. IFRS has many backers. It is adopted as the primary basis of accounting in some 100 countries, including Canada, members of the European Union and India. Since 2008, the SEC has allowed non-US entities to file financial statements with it using IFRS instead of GAAP. The SEC also has pushed for a process that would lead the US to shift from GAAP to IFRS. However, IFRS is not yet adopted in the US, where GAAP remains the standard.

The scale and complexity of fashioning a single set of global standards produces critics. They note that, despite substantial progress in forging IFRS into a universal set of standards, significant limitations exist. These arise because accounting is partly a cultural phenomenon, reflecting national traditions concerning entrepreneurship, markets, risk-taking and the role of the state. Cultural differences may make it difficult to establish a single set of global standards to which all nations subscribe and adhere.

Yet there is considerable convergence between GAAP and IFRS. FASB and IASB have undertaken dozens of joint projects to hasten the process of convergence between the two sets of standards. Many projects have succeeded, including one on the fundamental question of revenue recognition effective in 2018; others, such as on the advanced topic of lease accounting, ended in the two bodies adopting quite different approaches. Most persistent deviations between the two involve advanced accounting topics, although a few reflect philosophical differences or stances on trade-offs accounting confronts.

Despite differences, the two systems share an underlying orientation as to many introductory matters. In this book, some salient differences are highlighted in "IFRS Notes" ending Chapters Three through Nine. It is worth considering how these differences, sometimes subtle but usually important, reflect the judgments inherent in both accounting applications and standard setting.

Objectives and Foundational Principles.

In promulgating principles of general application or for particular circumstances, FASB is guided by the following objectives that financial accounting and reporting seeks to meet (set forth in Statement of Financial Accounting Concepts, No. 1, Nov. 1978):

1. To provide information useful to present and potential external users—primarily investors and creditors and their advisors and representatives so that they may make rational economic decisions;

2. To provide information relating to an entity's cash inflows and outflows since these flows eventually trickle down to creditors (in payment of debt) and investors (in payment of dividends); and

3. To provide information relating to assets, liabilities, and equity and changes in them during each reporting period.

Each of these objectives is united by a few overarching qualitative characteristics that accounting information should possess. Primary qualities are relevance and reliability. *Relevance* requires that information be recorded and presented on a timely basis, so that it may be used both to forecast future performance and to aid in understanding past performance. *Reliability* means that the information should be free from error and bias, which requires that the numbers in terms of which transactions are reported be accurate, and that those reports can be verified by independent parties.

Secondary qualities are comparability and consistency. *Comparability* means that users should be able to compare accounting information of one entity with that of other similar entities using the same accounting methods and with statements of the same entity over succeeding periods of time. *Consistency* means that the entity should use the same accounting methods and procedures from year to year or, if a change is to be made, it be made only for justified reasons that are disclosed as part of the financial reporting process.

In seeking to achieve the fundamental objectives of financial accounting and reporting and to attain the foregoing qualities of accounting information, FASB is in turn guided by a series of foundational principles or assumptions on which the entire architecture of GAAP ultimately rests. Chief among these foundational principles or assumptions are the following:

separate entity assumption: the reporting entity is regarded as distinct from those who own it, whether or not it is a separate entity for legal purposes;

going concern assumption: the entity being reported on is assumed to be continuing in operation for an indeterminate period, as a going concern, and is not expected to terminate operations or liquidate its business;

time period assumption: the entity's activities can be divided into discrete time periods (such as monthly, quarterly and annually);

monetary transactions principle: the transactions to be reported must be capable of measurement in money based on some observable transaction;

realization principle: items of revenue should be recognized only when the entity has completed or virtually completed the exchange that generates them;

matching principle: items of expense should be allocated to the period in which the benefit from them will contribute to generating revenue;

conservatism principle: a preference for understating earnings, values, and cash flows, rather than for overstating them;

cost principle: assets are to be reported at their historical cost (and not at higher market prices);

consistency principle: within a set of financial statements, one must apply principles consistently—a preference against picking and choosing to apply different conventions to the same transactions being reported in financial statements; and *materiality principle*: information to be reflected in financial statements should be meaningful to users and not trivial.

Throughout your study of accounting, keep in mind the objectives accounting seeks to achieve, the qualities that should characterize accounting information, and the foundational principles on which GAAP rests. The foundational principles will be referred to repeatedly throughout this book as the basics of GAAP are presented. As you study those basic principles of accounting, and GAAP, it may occasionally occur to you that the rules FASB has chosen do not always seem to be the product of logic, intuition, fairness, or reality! When that occurs to you, return to the foregoing list of foundational principles and assumptions on which GAAP rests, the objectives it seeks to meet, and the qualities it seeks to promote. Then ask yourself whether the principle that is troubling you is defensible in terms of those ideas.

C. COMPONENTS OF FINANCIAL STATEMENTS

An important minimum requirement to achieve the objective of comparability between financial statements of different enterprises is that the format of the presentation be the same. Accountants have devised four basic forms for the presentation: the balance sheet, the income statement, the statement of owners' equity, and the statement of cash flows. These are the main documents that compose what is usually meant by *financial statements*.

These four documents report the financial and other information necessary for shareholders, creditors, and anyone else who deals with the business to evaluate the entity's financial condition and performance. The financial statements are prepared from the entity's internal day-to-day records by its employees and managers. The day-to-day records are maintained by recording the financial transactions in which the entity engages each day. Those daily transactions are periodically summarized, usually at the end of each month, then quarterly, and then cumulatively at the end of each year. It is on the basis of those daily records and the periodic summaries that the financial statements are ultimately prepared. Annual financial statements are prepared with respect to a *fiscal year*, which may be the calendar year (ending on December 31) or may be defined to end on some other date depending on the nature of the entity's business operations.

The annual financial statements in turn usually form a part of an annual report that also includes a narrative commentary on the entity's financial condition and performance for the year and summary reports of other statistical data. Selected examples from a full set of financial statements appear periodically in the book. Readers are urged to peruse additional real-world examples of such statements. The richest resource is the SEC's data base of company filings, available on Westlaw and on the Internet and generally.

The Balance Sheet.

The balance sheet is like a snapshot of an entity at a specific date. It is intended to reflect the *financial condition* of that entity *as of that specific date*. It lists the entity's assets as of a specified date and the entity's liabilities as of that date and then shows the difference between these totals.

Assets are defined by FASB as "probable future economic benefits obtained or controlled by an entity resulting from past transactions or events."

Liabilities are defined by FASB as "probable future sacrifices of economic benefits arising from present obligations to transfer assets or render services in the future."

Equity is defined by FASB as "the residual interest in assets of an entity after subtracting its liabilities" from its assets. Equity represents the net ownership interest in the entity, and for that reason is often called *"owner's equity"* It represents both the initial investments made by the entity's owners as well as the entity's increases in income that it reinvests in the business.

As a matter of convention, assets are listed on the balance sheet in the order of their *liquidity*, beginning with cash (the very definition of liquid), and going through to such relatively illiquid assets as real property, and other things not expected to be converted into cash for a significant period of time. Similarly, liabilities are listed on the balance sheet beginning with obligations having the shortest due date (such as accounts payable, usually due in 30 days) through those with the longest due date (such as long term bonds, often not due for 10 or more years). The owners' equity is listed next and it will always equal total assets minus total liabilities.

Financial statements usually include a balance sheet for two succeeding reporting periods, such as two succeeding months or two succeeding years, so that users can compare changes in the entity's financial condition from one period to the next. We will consider the balance sheet in some detail beginning in the next Chapter and throughout the book.

The Income Statement.

The income statement is like a motion picture of the enterprise over a defined period of time, such as one year, and is intended to reflect the *financial performance* of the entity *during that period of time*. It lists the total revenues generated by the entity during the period and the total expenses incurred by the entity during that period and then shows the difference between these totals.

> *Revenues* are defined by FASB as "increases in equity resulting from asset increases and/or liability decreases from delivering goods or services or other activities that constitute the entity's ongoing major or central operations." Revenues therefore "cover sales of merchandise, rendering of services, sales of securities by a securities dealer, sales of buildings and land by a real estate developer, rentals of commercial buildings and land by real property owners, and dividends and interest earned by financial institutions—all of which represent the entity's major or central operations."

Note that revenue is not necessarily cash—for example, it includes sales made on credit.

> *Expenses* are defined by FASB as "decreases in equity from asset decreases and/or liability increases from delivering goods or services, or carrying out any activities which constitute the entity's ongoing major or central operations." Expenses therefore "cover cost of goods manufactured and sold, selling and administrative expenses, and interest expense of financial institutions."

The difference between revenues and expenses during each reporting period is called the entity's *net income* for the period (or, when expenses exceed revenues, the net loss). Either way, it is a measure of the entity's financial performance during the period. Net income is also referred to as *earnings* and can be broken down according to the portion allocable to each ownership interest in the entity, a breakdown called *earnings per share*. Items included in net income are sometimes displayed in various classifications, including income from continuing operations, income from discontinued operations, extraordinary items, or income due to the cumulative effect of changes in accounting principles.

Income (or loss) ultimately leads to changes in owners' equity. This reflects a key relationship between the income statement and the balance sheet. The amount of net income, calculated in the income statement, equals the amount of increase in owners' equity, calculated in the balance sheet. The statements are measured in the same terms. Accountants refer to such a relationship as *articulation*.

Owners' equity can also change due to other transactions or events (in addition to new investments by owners or distributions to owners). These items are collectively called *other comprehensive income* and together with net income constitute *comprehensive income*. Examples of other comprehensive income include unrealized gains (or losses) on investments in certain marketable securities, on positions in certain financial "hedging" arrangements, and from changes in an entity's employee pension plan liabilities (all are discussed further in Chapter 6), as well as from the effects of foreign currency translation adjustments for an entity operating internationally (discussed in Chapter 7).

Financial statements usually include an income statement for three succeeding reporting periods, so that users can evaluate changes in the entity's financial performance over several periods. We will consider the income statement in some detail beginning in the next Chapter and throughout the book.

The Statement of Changes in Equity.

An entity can choose to allocate its net income with respect to any reporting period between distributions to owners, as by the declaration and payment of dividends, or to reinvestment in the business. To keep track of the historical allocation between these uses, entities prepare a separate financial statement called a statement of owners' equity (often also called a *statement of shareholders' equity* or *statement of retained earnings*). In addition to serving as the historical record of the portion of net income—or equivalently, earnings—not paid out to owners, this statement typically is used to show accumulated changes in each category of other comprehensive income. We will consider the statement in some detail in Chapter 7, after we explore the balance sheet and income statement.

The Statement of Cash Flows.

The cash flow statement is also like a motion picture of the entity over the same period covered by the income statement, only the camera's lens camera is more focused. It lists the total cash that flowed into the entity during the period and the total cash that flowed out of the entity during the period. These cash amounts may be different from the revenue and expense amounts listed on the income statement because not all items of revenue or expense are paid for in cash (for example, some customers may buy goods from the entity on credit). The difference between cash inflows and cash outflows gives a measure of an entity's ability to pay its debts as they come due. We will consider this statement in some detail in Chapter 9, also after we have thoroughly explored the balance sheet and the income statement, as well as the statement of changes in owners' equity.

Footnotes.

Most information necessary to understanding the financial condition of a business at a moment in time, its financial performance over a period of time, and its ability to pay its debts as they come due can be reflected in (and therefore gleaned from) the balance sheet, the income statement, and the cash flow statement, respectively. But not all of it. When other information is important, it can be presented in a number of supplementary formats as part of these three basic financial statements.

Chief among these are explanations and elaborations of the presentation in the basic financial statements in the form of footnotes accompanying them. As lawyers know, sometimes the most important information in any document is contained in footnotes, and the financial statements are no exception. The footnotes are the place to disclose which choice a reporting entity has made when GAAP permits more than one method of accounting for a particular event. We will consider the significance of footnote disclosure in financial statements in Chapter 6 and in other parts of this book.

D. INTRODUCTION TO GAAS

To obtain some objective assurance that the financial statements are relevant and reliable, an independent accounting firm can be hired to "audit" the financial statements. The *audit* takes the form of a general review of the financial statements and the underlying day-to-day records and periodic summaries on which they are based. As such, it is a kind of monitoring mechanism and is an important device that can lend credibility to the financial statements.

Though many treat auditing as a branch of accounting, it is most useful to appreciate it as a distinct subject. Auditing is the professional activity of reviewing and opining upon assertions made by another party. Financial auditing involves such a review and opinion concerning financial statement assertions by management. Financial auditors need to know accounting, and GAAP, but they also must have additional knowledge relating to conducting these attestation services. This knowledge base is known as *generally accepted auditing standards* (GAAS) (pronounced *gas*).

It is easy to conflate accounting and auditing because auditors are usually accountants. In fact, among accountants, most of them are auditors first and accountants second. Internal managers make the accounting decisions (and are effectively accountants) and external accountants check those decisions (and in this capacity are called auditors).

GAAS and PCAOB.

For generations, establishing GAAS had been the province of the American Institute of Certified Public Accountants (AICPA). (Notice the dual role AICPA has played, participating in establishing both GAAP and GAAS; further history is provided in the last section of this Chapter). AICPA used various arms and structures to exercise this authority, often reconfiguring committees following periodic audit failures that produced public calls and SEC pressure for reform. Through the late 1990s, AICPA's Auditing Standards Board led the effort. It was, in turn, supervised by another AICPA arm: the SEC Practice Section's independent Public Oversight Board (POB). The POB, ultimately, was overseen by the SEC. But it remained funded by AICPA, a structure that threatened the independence and objectivity of the entire process of promulgating GAAS and supervising the public auditing profession.

The Sarbanes-Oxley Act of 2002 changed this structure. It created the Public Company Accounting Oversight Board (PCAOB). A self-regulatory organization, the SEC appoints and oversees the PCAOB's five-member board. The PCAOB's duties include reviewing audit procedures and policies; establishing audit standards; registering public accounting firms engaged in auditing SEC registrants; and overseeing, disciplining and sanctioning such public accounting firms.

Auditors and Independence.

Virtually all entities of any significant size have their annual financial statements audited, and all public entities are required by federal securities law to do so. Those laws, and SEC regulations promulgated under them, require that the auditor of a public company be "independent" of the entity in accordance with rules we will consider in Chapter 14. Other businesses are not required by law to have their financial statements audited, but often it is necessary for them to do so as a practical matter in order to attract investors into the business or to establish other relationships with third parties.

A number of large accounting firms, as well as many other firms of various smaller sizes, are engaged in the business of auditing financial statements. Substantial consolidation in the auditing industry occurred in recent decades, reducing the number of these large organizations from eight to four. The four largest firms, which command annual revenue in the range of $25–40 billion, are Price Waterhouse Coopers (called PWC); Deloitte & Touche; Ernst & Young; and KPMG (Klynveld Peat Marwick Goerderler). The next largest, which command annual revenue in the range of $5–8 billion, include BDO International; RSM (formerly McGladrey& Pullen); and Grant Thornton. In 2007, these firms and others formed, along with the AICPA, the Center for Audit Quality, as a forum to contribute views on public policy concerning accounting and auditing.

The Auditor's Report.

An audit conducted by an independent firm does not change the fact that an entity's management prepares the financial statements and is responsible for them. The audit is a review of those statements made in accordance with GAAS. The auditor's responsibility in connection with its review and analysis of the financial statements is summarized in a letter, called the *auditor's report*. It accompanies the financial statements when finally released for use by investors, creditors, and other constituents.

A standard auditor's report explains that auditors conducted their audit in accordance with GAAS and how that requires planning and performing an audit to obtain "reasonable assurance" about whether the financial statements are "free of material misstatement." This, in turn, involves examining evidence, on a test basis, assessing the accounting principles and estimates management used and evaluating the overall presentation. The auditor's report then expresses an opinion as to whether the financial statements "present fairly" the entity's financial position and results of operations and cash flows for the periods the financial statements cover "in conformity" with GAAP.

Unqualified Audit Reports.

An auditor's report is called "unqualified" when it expresses an opinion that financial statements present fairly the entity's financial position and results of operations and cash flows for the periods the financial statements cover in conformity with GAAP. That is the equivalent of a clean bill of accounting health. However, if during an audit, auditors find that the financial statements do not so "present fairly" or are not "in conformity" with GAAP, auditors must state those conclusions in their report. Such auditor reports that are not "unqualified" fall into three categories.

Non-Standard Audit Reports.

If the auditor is unable to say the statements were prepared in conformity with GAAP, but that they nevertheless constitute a fair presentation, then the auditor would issue a *qualified opinion*, stating the particular area of nonconformity with GAAP. A more severe situation arises where for whatever reason, whether due to nonconformity with GAAP or otherwise, the auditor cannot opine that the statements present fairly the entity's financial performance or condition. In that case, the auditor would issue a *disclaimer*, indicating that inability. The most severe situation arises where the auditor finds that the financial statements do not fairly present the financial position or results in conformity with GAAP. In that case, the auditor would issue an *adverse opinion*. An adverse audit report is seen by anyone dealing with the entity as a red flag of caution and therefore carries potentially grave consequences for the entity.

Change in Accounting Principles.

A variation on the standard form of audit report that also constitutes a clean audit report is a statement that discloses that the reporting entity made changes in the principles of accounting it applied during the reporting period. As we shall see, GAAP permits, and sometimes requires, that certain changes be made in the accounting principles applied from time to time. A change in the accounting principles an entity applies often has significant consequences for the presentation of its financial statements. When this happens, the audit report seeks to call attention to the change. It does not mean that an adverse opinion is being given.

Critical Audit Matters (CAM).

In 2017, the PCAOB amended the standard form of audit report, effective in 2019–2020, to require discussion of "critical audit matters" (CAMs). These are matters communicated or required to be communicated by the auditor to the company's audit committee that: "(1) relate to accounts or disclosures that are material to the financial statements; and (2) involved especially challenging, subjective, or complex auditor judgment."

The PCAOB explained, after a six-year period of outreach to its constituents, that the audit report otherwise conveyed "little of the information obtained and evaluated by the auditor as part of the audit." Shareholders and other financial statement users would benefit from more detail, the PCAOB reasoned, on matters such as significant estimates, peculiar risks, unusual transactions, or major changes.

Skeptics of the reform expressed concern that the new disclosure could expose auditors to additional legal liability for misrepresentation when accounting misstatements go undetected. The PCAOB responded by clarifying that the auditor's disclosure would continue to be presented as opinion, not fact, mitigating related liability risk (as we will explore in Chapter 14). It said such risks were slight compared to the vastly greater benefits to investors of the additional insight auditor discussion of CAMs will provide.

Internal Control.

Internal controls are processes or mechanisms designed to provide reasonable assurance regarding the achievement of an organization's objectives and its compliance with laws and, most importantly for our purposes, the adequacy of financial reporting. Internal financial reporting controls consist of mechanisms designed to assure that transactions are executed in accordance with management policy and are recorded properly in the accounting records and to assure that assets are deployed only in accordance with management policy. They include mechanisms ranging from requiring records to be updated daily and reviewed periodically by others, to procedures for review of various accounting judgments, to the expression and periodic review of risk management policies and so on. Some such mechanisms are required for public entities under federal securities laws.

Within a corporation, both boards of directors and managers play a role in defining, implementing and evaluating internal controls. In principle, however, ultimate responsibility for internal controls rests with the board of directors, both as a matter of sense and as a matter of policy. This is because boards have a comparative informational advantage and greater motivation to police managerial opportunism than managers themselves do. The obligation entails supervising the design of internal control systems and supporting their administration. Internal controls are then implemented and reviewed by a team of internal auditors within the entity.

Apart from the practical benefits internal controls can generate through promoting the integrity of financial statements and deterring and detecting aggressive or irregular practices, there are also legal benefits. These include (a) limiting legal exposure of companies under the Foreign Corrupt Practices Act, which can expose businesses to legal liability under federal securities laws for failing to maintain adequate accounting records; (b) benefiting from sentencing reductions for organizational wrongdoing under the Federal Sentencing Guidelines; and (c) helping a corporate entity's board of directors discharge its fiduciary duties. *See Graham v. Allis-Chalmers Manufacturing Co.*, 188 A.2d 125 (Del.1963); *In re Caremark International, Inc.*, 698 A.2d 959 (Del.Ch.1996); *Stone v. Ritter*, 911 A.2d 362 (Del. 2006).

In addition, the Sarbanes-Oxley Act of 2002 enhanced the role of internal control in the financial disclosure process for public companies. This builds on a requirement that a company's top executives (chief executive officer, CEO, and chief financial officer, CFO) certify periodic reports as containing financial statements that "fully comply" with Section 13(a) or 15(d) of the Exchange Act and that reports "present fairly, in all material respects, the financial condition and results of operations of the company."

These certifications also say that the CEO and CFO designed corporate internal controls to ensure that information flows to senior management and that they evaluated internal control effectiveness within the preceding 90 days. These officers must affirm that they disclosed any control deficiencies or weaknesses to their outside auditors, as well as any fraud, material or not, involving employees with significant internal-control roles. The auditing firm attesting to the financial statements also must express an opinion on the effectiveness of the entity's internal control over financial reporting.

PCAOB has developed an elaborate set of procedures auditors must use when auditing internal control over financial reporting and related financial statements. These procedures draw heavily on traditional methods for conducting control audits, the basis for which was established in 1985 by an expert committee sponsored by various organizations interested in reliable financial reporting. That committee is called the

Committee of Sponsoring Organizations (COSO) or, sometimes, the Treadway Commission, after its chairman, James C. Treadway, Jr., a Washington lawyer with the firm of Dickstein, Shapiro & Morin and an SEC Commissioner. COSO published authoritative guidelines for auditor responsibilities relating to internal control over financial reporting. These are discussed in detail in Chapter 13.

Management Letters.

Based on an auditor's assessment of internal controls, the auditor issues a separate letter to the entity's management, called a *management letter*. The management letter advises the entity's management of any weaknesses discovered in the internal control mechanisms, or if true, indicates that none appeared. These letters are then reviewed by the entity, usually by senior executives in the entity but in cases where serious weaknesses are found, also with the entity's board of directors or at least a standing board committee, called the *audit committee*.

Management then issues a response to the management letter and, depending on the seriousness of reported weaknesses, may agree with the auditors on a plan for improving the internal controls. Finally, to the extent the auditor discovers and reports material weaknesses in internal controls, it must issue an *adverse* opinion on internal control and it is usually necessary to expand the scope of substantive testing during the financial statement audit in light of those weaknesses. In extreme cases, inadequate internal controls may constrain the auditor to issue an adverse or qualified opinion on an entity's financial statements.

Audit Firm Tenure.

In 2017, the PCAOB amended its standard form of audit report to require disclosure of the auditor's service length or tenure: "the year in which the auditor began serving consecutively as the company's auditor." In general, this requirement is due to longstanding debate about how auditor independence may degrade with successive audits.

Imposing term limits might solve this problem, but an auditor's experience is also valuable in an audit and many companies are so large or specialized that reliance on just one auditor from among the oligopoly of major firms is a practical necessity.

By 2017, about half of the largest public companies routinely disclosed their auditors' tenure voluntarily. PCAOB's mandatory disclosure was therefore intended to bring the rest into line with common practice while providing incremental value at scant cost.

Text of Combined Auditor's Report.

Thanks to the PCAOB, for SEC registrants, the auditor's report can seem elaborate. Auditors of SEC registrants must report both on the entity's financial statements and on its internal control over financial reporting. PCAOB authorizes auditor's reports to combine both matters in a single report. PCAOB's standard prescribed form follows.

Auditor's Report

To the shareholders and the board of directors of W Company:

Opinions on the Financial Statements and Internal Control over Financial Reporting

We have audited the accompanying balance sheets of W Company (the "Company") as of December 31, 20X8 and 20X7, and the related statements of [titles of the financial statements, e.g., income statement, balance sheet, cash flows] for each of the years in the three-year period ended December 31, 20X8, and the related notes [and schedules] (collectively referred to as the "financial statements"). We also have audited the Company's internal control over financial reporting as of December 31, 20X8, based on [identify control criteria, such those issued by the Committee of Sponsoring Organizations of the Treadway Commission (COSO).].

In our opinion, the financial statements referred to above present fairly, in all material respects, the financial position of the Company as of December 31, 20X8 and 20X7, and the results of its operations and its cash flows for each of the years in the three-year period ended December 31, 20X8 in conformity with accounting principles generally accepted in the United States of America (U.S. GAAP). Also in our opinion, the Company maintained, in all material respects, effective internal control over financial reporting as of December 31, 20X8, based on [identify control criteria as above].

Basis for Opinion

The Company's management is responsible for these financial statements, for maintaining effective internal control over financial reporting, and for its assessment of the effectiveness of internal control over financial reporting, included in the accompanying management's report. Our responsibility is to express an opinion on these the Company's financial statements and an opinion on the Company's internal control over financial reporting based on our audits. We are a public accounting firm registered with the Public Company Accounting Oversight Board (United States) ("PCAOB") and are required to be independent with respect to the Company in accordance with the U.S. federal securities laws and the applicable rules and regulations of the Securities and Exchange Commission and the PCAOB.

We conducted our audits in accordance with the standards of the PCAOB. Those standards require that we plan and perform the audits to obtain reasonable assurance about whether the financial statements are free of material misstatement, whether due to error or fraud, and whether effective internal control over financial reporting was maintained in all material respects.

Our audits of the financial statements included performing procedures to assess the risks of material misstatement of the financial statements, whether due to error or fraud, and performing procedures that respond to those risks. Such procedures included examining, on a test basis, evidence regarding the amounts and disclosures in the financial statements. Our audits also included evaluating the accounting principles used and significant estimates made by management, as well as evaluating the overall presentation of the financial statements. Our audit of internal control over financial reporting included obtaining an understanding of internal control over financial reporting, assessing the risk that a material weakness exists, and testing and evaluating the design and operating effectiveness of internal control based on the assessed risk. Our audits also included performing such other procedures as we considered necessary in the circumstances. We believe that our audits provide a reasonable basis for our opinions.

Definition and Limitations of Internal Control Over Financial Reporting

A company's internal control over financial reporting is a process designed to provide reasonable assurance regarding the reliability of financial reporting and the preparation of financial statements for external purposes in accordance with generally accepted accounting principles. A company's internal control over financial reporting includes those policies and procedures that (1) pertain to the maintenance of records that, in reasonable detail, accurately and fairly reflect the transactions and dispositions of the assets of the company; (2) provide reasonable assurance that transactions are recorded as necessary to permit preparation of financial statements in accordance with generally accepted accounting principles, and that receipts and expenditures of the company are being made only in accordance with authorizations of management and directors of the company; and (3) provide reasonable assurance regarding prevention or timely detection of unauthorized acquisition, use, or disposition of the company's assets that could have a material effect on the financial statements.

Because of its inherent limitations, internal control over financial reporting may not prevent or detect misstatements. Also, projections of any evaluation of effectiveness to future periods are subject to the risk that controls may become inadequate because of changes in conditions, or that the degree of compliance with the policies or procedures may deteriorate.

Critical Audit Matters

[Include disclosure as appropriate; PCAOB prescribes no standard language for this portion of the auditor report.]

Auditor Tenure

We have served as the Company's auditor since [year].

Auditing is treated in greater detail in Part IV of this book, with particular attention to internal control over financial reporting in Chapter 13.

E. FINANCE AND USING FINANCIAL INFORMATION

Finance boasts no equivalent to GAAP or GAAS. It is instead a body of learning dedicated to developing tools to appraise financial value and assess risk. It also is a more general framework for analyzing financial systems and how people allocate scarce resources. Introductory materials in this book concentrate on the first two contributions. In this context, finance relies upon both accounting information and the meaning of audit attestations in analyzing or interpreting financial information necessary to estimate value and risk.

Of particular interest to lawyers are the contributions finance makes to determining the time value of money, valuing businesses or interests in them, and evaluating the risk of alternative investments and how to manage this risk. While no codified body of principles underlies finance, most basic principles are not in dispute. However, many advanced principles are hotly contested.

The basic principles deal with calculating the present value or future value of money. More advanced principles grapple with appropriate techniques to value businesses or interests in them. In this area, analysts generally agree that a variety of alternative approaches used in combination is the optimal way to draw conclusions about value.

Leading debates in finance concern theorizing about how markets place values on businesses and interests in them. Learning in this area has been prodigious, with pioneers in the field having won Nobel Prizes in economics for their contributions. For example, the 1990 Nobel Prize in economics was shared by Harry Markowitz and William Sharpe. Markowitz's contributions were made in a 1952 paper explaining how to trade off risk and reward in choosing investments. Sharpe won for a 1964 article that developed a theory of asset pricing that related risk and reward along the lines Markowitz's analysis suggested. These topics are considered in Chapter 12.

Finance research and theory prompted reassessment of accounting data's relevance. A simple view would suggest that financial analysts begin their work using accounting data and this implies a critical role for accounting information. The opposite view suggests that since financial analysts reconfigure accounting data to enable them to make value and risk estimates, that accounting information, as presented in financial statements, does not matter. These analysts will arrive at substantially the same value and risk estimates without regard to the form in which accounting information is presented. This range of views contributes to friction or jealousy between professionals in accounting and finance. Whichever view one holds, some familiarity with both disciplines is critical to lawyers.

F. HISTORICAL PERSPECTIVE

The preceding introductory discussion, and most discussion in this book, is descriptive. It reports upon the concepts and principles underlying accounting, finance and auditing, with critical assessment mostly in the background (though the Conceptual Questions concluding each Chapter provoke this more consciously). The descriptive bias is designed to facilitate delivering basic knowledge. Despite this approach, it is useful to recognize at the outset that the content of these disciplines is neither inevitable nor uncontested. Advanced treatments of these subjects delve deeply into related debates. While this book generally stops short of such debates, a useful flavor of the landscape can be imparted by a brief historical perspective on financial reporting and the uses of accounting information.

Deep Roots.*

Some form of financial record-keeping can be traced to the earliest civilizations. The first use of accounts to classify records of transactions is generally attributed to the medieval commercial republics of Italy. In 1494, a Franciscan friar, Luca Pacioli, published a treatise describing these practices as they existed in Venice, which came to be known as the "Italian method" or the "Method of Venice." This method spread across Europe in the 15th and 16th centuries and was exported to America early in colonial history.

By the late 19th century, these tools had been supplemented by more elaborate financial reporting and accompanying narrative disclosure. Investors began to regard accounting data (primarily composed of balance sheets) as providing important information and analytical content for assessing alternatives. Business leaders began to advocate expert accounting analysis and certification of financial information as a means to publicize financial results. Rudimentary information-control structures were being developed in response to the growing complexity of business

---

*   This section adapts material prepared by Laura Ford for graduate work in Columbia University's School of International & Public Affairs (SIPA), which in turn draws extensively on Gary John Previts & Barbara Dubis Merino, *A History of Accountancy in the United States: The Cultural Significance of Accounting* (Ohio St. U. Press 1998).

enterprise and the diffusion of ownership from sole proprietors to widely-held corporations.

Legal requirements emerged in this period. In 1848, New York State adopted legislation requiring annual financial reports of companies to be published in newspapers, signed by the company's president and its board, though the content was limited to the amount of shareholder investment and the amount of debt. A Congressionally-established Commission published in 1902 a report recommending requiring corporations to publish annual financial statements—including balance sheet and income statement—that would also be audited. The New York Stock Exchange in 1913 began to impose reporting obligations as a condition of listing on the exchange.

Modern Accounting's Roots.

It was not until after the stock market crash of 1929 and ensuing Great Depression, however, that a more elaborate financial reporting system emerged. Leading commentators of the era, including Louis Brandeis and Felix Frankfurter, participated in developing the federal securities laws that formally created a system of mandatory accounting and financial disclosure for public companies. Primary goals of these statutes, such as those adopted in 1933 and 1934, were to promote shareholder monitoring and to enhance the market's ability to value public securities.

These developments would not have been possible without an accounting profession, which had begun to professionalize during the 19th century and blossomed during the 1890s. The Institute of Accounts of New York was formed in 1882 and is the first known example of a professional accounting organization in the US. In 1887, the American Association of Public Accountants was incorporated, partly in response to the lack of public/legal recognition of accountants as a professional class. In 1896, New York State became the first state to legislatively recognize a class of professionals, the "certified public accountants," and mandate that only accountants with this certificate be employed to examine accounts, or serve as expert accountants or auditors. By the mid-1920s comparable legislation was in place in all 48 states.

In 1916, in response to increasing criticism of the accounting profession as exclusive and ineffective, arising out of substantial infighting between various state accounting organizations, the American Association of Public Accountants was reorganized and became the American Institute of Accounts ("AIA"). This reorganization was intended to quell criticism of the profession and avert federal legislation. The AIA's bylaws empowered it to prohibit and punish "acts discreditable to the profession." Partly due to an understanding that accountants bear direct responsibilities to third parties (financial statement users), and possibly as a result of disappointment over the educational system for accountants in the early

1900s, the accounting profession interpreted this phrase as referring to areas of technical competence as well as personal conduct.

At the same time, accountants were calling for a "science of accounts," by which they meant systematic guidelines to direct accountants to uniform and correct conclusions in like cases. The hope was to keep these guidelines informal so that uniformity in all cases would not produce dogma and destroy the profession, or turn accountants into clerks. As politicians and business leaders called for uniform rules, accountants resisted, arguing that accountants could never have a strict rule book, if they were to remain professionals.

In 1917, the Federal Reserve Board published a document called "Uniform Accounting," proposing to establish uniform accounting standards. It included rules for measuring assets and liabilities, with verification of statements to be rendered by accountants registered with a federal agency, such as the Federal Reserve Board. In response to this federal threat, the accounting profession, through the AIA, published "Uniform Accounting," written by an accountant at the prominent public accounting firm of Price Waterhouse (predecessor to today's Price Waterhouse Coopers). While the AIA managed to circumvent federal registration of accountants, it did so at a cost to the profession in terms of internal disagreement.

The complexity of the accountant's role rose during the early 1920's. Accountants increasingly were called upon to advise corporations, particularly concerning federal taxes. This tended to diminish their role of providing independent audits, and a sense of obligation to third parties. A rising belief during the 1920's in the ability of the corporate structure to provide sufficient investor protection also diminished the accountant's role as external auditor. On the other hand, the 1929 market crash created public outcry for oversight, and the general preference of managers and politicians was to provide this through external auditing, not government regulation.

Between 1932 and 1934, the AIA and the New York Stock Exchange (NYSE) engaged in wide-ranging discussion concerning the accounting profession's responsibilities. The NYSE was particularly concerned about corporations using undisclosed accounting methods. In 1932, the AIA crafted five broad accounting principles, which were endorsed by the NYSE and became the first "accepted principles of accounting." This was the first formal attempt at articulating "generally accepted accounting principles."

Following the 1933 Act, the atmosphere of accounting-standards creation underwent significant change. The 1933 Act gave the Federal Trade Commission authority to prescribe accounting standards; the 1934 Act gave this power to the newly-created Securities and Exchange Commission (SEC). On the other hand, by focusing on consistency, as a weaker form of "uniformity," the 1933 and 1934 Acts arguably lightened the responsibilities of accountants. Rather than independently determining whether a particular accounting approach was preferable, accountants needed only agree that it was an accepted practice and had been properly applied. Accountants began to insist that management was responsible for determining the propriety of accounting principles selected.

In 1938, the SEC formally (but not irrevocably) delegated its authority to determine financial reporting standards to the AIA and its Committee on Accounting Procedure (CAP) in Accounting Series Release No. 4. That Release provided that where *substantial authoritative support* exists for a company's accounting and the SEC had not taken a position on a matter, the SEC would not dispute the practices. The substantial authoritative support would come from private standard-setting bodies, including CAP which in 1939 began to issue Accounting Research Bulletins (ARBs) and emerged as the first official rule-making body for accounting pronouncements in the United States.

Modern Auditing's Roots.

The AIA/NYSE discussion also included an exchange addressing the accountant's role in an external audit. The accountants' view was that auditors are responsible for the expression of "an informed and independent judgment on the question of whether the accounts which he approves are a full and fair presentation." The position went on to state that accountants "commonly and rightly" rely on an "adequate system of internal check" in making this determination. Discussion considered whether a disclaimer stating that auditors do not perform a comprehensive examination would help the public to understand the nature of the audit process; the general consensus was that such a statement would probably not mean much, although it would likely limit auditor liability.

The securities acts of the 1930s did not give the SEC direct responsibility for auditing standards. As a result, the SEC periodically criticized the cautious, liability-averse pronouncements auditors published. In 1936, in response to Congressional threats of a federal licensing regime for auditors, the AIA issued a bulletin entitled "Examination of Financial Statements," which tended to state the role of auditors negatively (*i.e.*, it limited the responsibility of auditors). The general perception was that auditing was not operating effectively. The AIA tried to respond and foreclose federal intervention through promulgation of generally accepted auditing standards (GAAS).

In 1946, the SEC indicated dissatisfaction with the financial reporting of over-the-counter-traded companies and criticized the accounting profession for not taking a more active role in preventing the alleged misleading accounting techniques. In conjunction with the American Accounting Association (AAA), a professional association of academic accountants, the SEC began to call for a comprehensive framework for financial reporting. The AIA responded through CAP by issuing several Statements on Auditing Procedure (SAP 23 and 24) in order to require auditors to clarify their audit reports.

In 1948, CAP issued a field-work standard requiring that auditors evaluate and study the internal control of a company in order to determine the degree of reliance that could be placed on such internal control and to structure requisite audit procedures. However, the standard was perceived as being too general to be very effective. It also did not require auditors to effectively document the relationship between their internal control assessment and the actual audit procedures used.

Modern Links Between Accounting and Auditing.

In 1957, the AIA was renamed the American Institute of Certified Public Accountants (AICPA). The next year it created the Accounting Principles Board to develop rules for financial reporting. This body adopted authoritative pronouncements that addressed both accounting (GAAP) and auditing (GAAS). In particular, it prohibited auditors under GAAS from furnishing unqualified audit opinions on any financial statements that departed from GAAP.

As the accounting profession moved into the 1970's, computer technology used for accounting vastly increased the complexity of audits. This fueled an explosion in number of accountants and expanded their legal liability. Through numerous Accounting Series Releases, the SEC emphasized that auditors are responsible to third parties in addition to clients; a series of judicial decisions held that accountants and auditors are not protected from liability solely as a result of following GAAP or GAAS. *E.g., United States v. Simon*, 425 F.2d 796 (2d Cir. 1969) (Friendly, J.), *cert. denied*, 397 U.S. 1006 (1970) (concerning GAAP); *S.E.C. v. Arthur Young & Co.*, 590 F.2d 785, 788–89 (9th Cir. 1979) (concerning GAAS) (dicta).

Auditing ventured into non-financial territories. These included attesting to the effectiveness of systems designed to ensure corporate compliance with an exploding array of laws and regulations. They included more general examinations of internal control systems, as well as certifying a variety of managerial assertions concerning matters ranging from product qualities to the operation of governmental lottery drawings. The massive increase in scope of auditors' responsibilities created renewed focus on auditor independence (a subject addressed more fully in Chapter 14).

The 1970s were also a period of perceived rapid change. The accounting profession underwent strenuous efforts to reform itself internally. For example, in 1971 the AICPA formed the Wheat Committee (chaired by Francis M. Wheat) to reassess the process of establishing accounting standards and the Trueblood Committee (chaired by Robert M.

Trueblood) to elaborate the purposes of financial reporting. Their joint work led to FASB's creation in 1973.

FASB was initially composed of seven full-time members, and charged with establishing a due-process form of private-sector accounting standard-setting (*i.e.*, fully open to the public following the model of our federal administrative agencies). In 1973, the AICPA adopted Rule 203 of its *Code of Professional Conduct*, requiring AICPA members to follow FASB pronouncements (unless doing so would result in a material misstatement). In 1982, in order to permit FASB to respond more quickly to emerging issues, it established an Emerging Issues Task Force to articulate less formal responses.

On the auditing side, in 1974, in the wake of several large financial reporting scandals, the AICPA formed the Cohen Commission, chaired by Manuel F. Cohen, a Washington lawyer with the law firm Wilmer, Cutler & Pickering, a Commissioner of the SEC, and Adjunct Professor at George Washington University Law School. The Cohen Commission examined the role of accountants as auditors. A chief finding was the existence of a gap between what users of financial statements expect and what the accounting and auditing professions deliver (since then dubbed the *expectations gap*, and seemingly an enduring feature of our world).

In 1985, the AICPA the Treadway Commission (the "committee of sponsoring organizations" or COSO), referenced earlier. It examined accountants' roles in financial reporting broadly, focusing on responsibilities of auditors and the expectations gap. The Treadway Commission published a set of guidelines, called the COSO Guidelines, relating to internal control over financial reporting that constitute the definitive treatment of the subject. It is commonly used by auditors of SEC registrants when providing opinions on internal control over financial reporting that PCAOB prescribes.

In all, several dozen committees and commissions have examined numerous aspects of accounting and auditing in the last few generations, in addition to those mentioned above. The aggregate effect of these modern professional examinations was to complete the move begun in the 1930s from accounting and auditing focused narrowly on the preparation of financial statements to a broader focus on financial reporting and disclosure. This movement dovetailed with parallel movements in the world of modern finance theory.

Link to Modern Finance.

Modern finance theory traces its roots to the research of financial economists in the mid-1950s. Researchers developed models of risk and return that showed how rational investors would make investment decisions and how resulting prices should reflect specific kinds of risk. The field blossomed in the 1960s when theorists developed the idea of efficient capital markets. This is a view of asset pricing in which market participants digest fundamental information as soon as it becomes available and translate this information into market prices.

Prior to this period, financial analysts tended to examine value by reference to age-old accounting data, chiefly the balance sheet and income statement. Contemporary approaches began to emphasize cash flows, stock prices and stock trading activity. In this world accounting's emphasis on the other two financial statements and its historical perspective appeared to some as obsolete. Analysts needed data to forecast the future and accounting data didn't have it, critics held. In this view, when accounting information was useful, it was only useful in limited ways. Analysts had to reinterpret it. Even so, most users of financial information understand that accounting is the starting point for business evaluation. Accounting is not an end, but an essential beginning.

PART II

ACCOUNTING

■ ■ ■

Introduction

Accounting is interesting, important and challenging, even while detractors have been known to say it is mystifying, boring, or heavily mathematical. Among reasons some aspiring law students cite for choosing law as a profession is an aversion to business and financial matters, such as seem to be at the heart of accounting. But such perceptions and aversions probably arise from misunderstandings.

First, accounting reports tell a story about an entity and that story, although presented largely in numerical form, will be as fascinating and interesting as the entity itself. What is more, the very idea that the financial condition and performance of a complex entity—whether a multinational conglomerate or a medium-size law firm—can be depicted in a few pages of numerical data is itself remarkable. (And this remains true even though, as we shall see, efforts to do so can never succeed perfectly.)

Second, lawyers are one of the most important audiences for whom financial accounting is relevant. Accounting seeks to describe and report an entity's financial condition and performance that would be difficult to ascertain by physical inspection. Numerous people with whom that entity deals need to evaluate the accounting reports in order to make all sorts of decisions, virtually all of which pose legal consequences. For any significant decision, therefore—such as a bank deciding to lend to the entity, an investor considering an investment, or even a customer seeking a long-term relationship—lawyers are likely to be involved in the process.

Finally, the principles of accounting resemble legal principles in several challenging but often overlooked ways. Among these are the purposive, the critical, and the analogical. The principles of accounting are selected not by a scientific process of deduction but with a view toward the purpose for which the process is designed, much as the common law. The promulgation of these principles, as well as the selection of appropriate principles when more than one could apply, require the exercise of good judgment, also much as the common law.

In turn, therefore, the process of selecting and applying principles is subject to critical evaluation by both those who employ them and those who seek to understand and use the results. In the process of promulgating, and indeed studying, these principles, strong analogical links appear between

33

particular principles used in different contexts. Similarities to law should not be stressed too much, however, for there are also many significant differences in the ways professionals in each discipline approach their subjects.

CHAPTER 2

THE FUNDAMENTAL EQUATION

● ● ●

The objective of accounting is to present relevant and reliable financial statements that are meaningful to users by providing a consistent basis for comparing the performance of an entity over time and with other entities from time to time. To meet that objective, all transactions during a period must be recorded in a format that can be reflected in the financial statements. That daily recording is the process called *double-entry bookkeeping* and is dedicated to facilitating preparation of the balance sheet and income statement, as well as the statements of retained earnings and cash flows.

A.   ASSETS, LIABILITIES AND EQUITY

There is one governing law that enables accountants to prepare the financial statements from the underlying bookkeeping records in a form that reliably states the entity's financial condition at a point in time and its financial performance over a period of time. It is called the *fundamental equation* and is written as follows:

Assets = Liabilities + Owners' Equity

Recall the FASB definition of assets from Chapter 1—"probable future economic benefits obtained or controlled by an entity resulting from past transactions or events." Less formally, *assets* are the properties, resources, and claims owned or controlled by an entity.

Recall also the FASB definition of liabilities from Chapter 1—"probable future sacrifices of economic benefits arising from present obligations to transfer assets or render services in the future." Also less formally, *liabilities* are the amounts owed by an entity to others, in the form of debts, accounts payable, and other obligations. Recall finally, that *owner's equity* (which is also sometimes called simply "equity" or "net worth") represents the amount of the owners' interest in the enterprise.

Owners can increase or decrease equity by contributing assets to or withdrawing assets from the entity. Equity also increases when the entity earns a profit from its operations and decreases when the entity incurs a loss from its operations.

Double-Entry Bookkeeping.

By definition, the fundamental equation is an equation. That means the left side of the equation must always equal the right side of the equation. In other words, the amounts on the left must balance with the amounts on the right. And here we can see the meaning of the term "balance sheet." The fundamental equation is simply the balance sheet in its most elementary form. The intuition should be obvious: the rights and claims an entity holds against others (its assets) must equal the rights and claims others hold against it (its creditors with respect to its liabilities and the owners as residual claimants with respect to the equity).

To keep the fundamental equation always in balance at every moment in time, accountants developed an ingenious system called *double-entry bookkeeping*. Here is another point of linguistic purity: the idea behind double-entry bookkeeping is that, to keep the fundamental equation in balance, there will be *two entries* for every transaction to be accounted for.

Debits and Credits.

Double-entry bookkeeping is implemented by two mechanisms whose labels are not only of no use to us but whose very names have been the source of endless agonizing by students new to the art of the project. The terms are "*debits*" and "*credits*." Before your anxiety heightens, let us put out into the open what continues to be to many a secret. When used to describe accounting steps in double-entry bookkeeping, and for every purpose of this book, these terms have no other meaning except the following: **debit means left-side entry** and **credit means right-side entry**. That is the secret. They have absolutely no other meaning. And from now on, we will ordinarily talk about double-entry bookkeeping by using left-side entry and right-side entry and largely dispense with the jargon of debit and credit.

Having said that, however, you should also know that accountants have not dispensed with those terms and you can expect to hear accountants use them. Indeed you may hear accountants use these terms as verbs: to record an increase in the Cash account, for example, accountants do not say "record an increase in the Cash account;" they say "debit Cash." You may benefit from learning these terms but your understanding will not be diminished if you do not master them.

You may also observe accountants using the abbreviations Dr. for debit and Cr. for credit. The designation may seem obvious as to Cr. for credit but curious as to Dr. for debit. The roots of these abbreviations help explain some contemporary confusion about the meaning of the words. They derive from kindred Italian words, *debitore* and *creditore*, though these words mean literally debtor and creditor. While the origins of today's debit and credit trace back to debtor and creditor, today's meanings are decoupled from those origins.

Confusion about the meanings of debit and credit also arises from everyday speech. Credit sometimes means good; debit sometimes means bad. The terms often appear on bank statements that way, as when a bank indicates your balance has increased by an "interest credit" or decreased by a "service fee debit." But in accounting they have no such meanings. In the case of the bank statement, they are used that way because the bank is speaking from its side of the transaction: when it credits your account it is taking its cash and giving it to you; when it debits your account with a service fee it is taking cash from you and allocating it to itself.

The key function of these concepts of debit and credit is that the total of the debit and credit entries for any transaction must always equal each other. In other words, left-side entries always equal right-side entries. This makes it easy to check the accuracy of recordkeeping. In fact, an old joke among accountants quips that there is only one hard-and-fast rule in accounting—debits always equal credits—and beyond that everything is judgment.

Accounts and Their Names.

To keep track of the wide variety of transactions an entity enters into over time, accountants have defined a number of accounts, as suggested by the foregoing depiction of the fundamental equation. Table 2-1 shows examples of the main types of each of the three categories of accounts depicted above: asset accounts, liability accounts, and owner's equity accounts. Note that these three categories of accounts are collectively called *balance sheet accounts* because they appear directly on the balance sheet.

Table 2-1	
Balance Sheet Accounts—Some Examples	
Asset Accounts	Liability Accounts
Cash	Accounts Payable
Supplies	Notes Payable
Notes Receivable	
Equipment	Owners' Equity Accounts
Land	Common Stock

Before illustrating the fundamental equation in operation, a note on the titles of accounts is in order. It is important to know whether some account is an asset account, a liability account or an owner's equity account, and also to know that all these accounts are balance sheet accounts. It is less important what names are given to the accounts within those categories. For example, we could call the account "Land" by the name "Property" if we wanted to or we could call the account "Supplies" by the name "Office Supplies" if we wanted to.

We could also condense some of the accounts if we thought that it was not very important to treat them separately (remember the materiality principle from Chapter 1). So instead of having an account called "Equipment" and another account called "Factory Plant," we could have a single account called "Equipment & Factory Plant." For that matter, we could also decide that, although we have used separate accounts for "Equipment" and "Factory Plant" in our financial records for previous periods, the accounts can now safely be condensed together.

What is important in naming the accounts, and either separating or condensing them, is that the account title give some indication of what activity it is being used to record and that activities that are important to keep track of separately be given their own account. You will develop the judgment necessary to make these decisions as your study proceeds. You may find it helpful to consult this book's Glossary periodically.

Finally, note that Table 2-1's illustration of various accounts lists under Owner's Equity only one account, which is named, rather redundantly, "Owner's Equity." We will use only that one account, for the sake of simplicity, for owner's equity in the next few Chapters, deferring until Chapter 7 a further discussion and breakdown of the various kinds of owner's equity accounts.

B. JOURNAL ENTRIES

The daily recording of each transaction in which an entity engages is made to books called *journals*, in form not unlike the check register found in every checkbook. The entries in those books are called *journal entries*. Technically, there are a number of different, specialized, journals used to record different sorts of transactions by transaction type, such as those involving cash or those involving sales of goods on credit. Indeed, many such journals are automated on-line computer systems rather than manual hand-recorded books. For illustrative purposes, however, this text limits the discussion to a single, *general journal*, with all entries being made in it by hand.

Three Questions.

To make the appropriate double-entries in the general journal to record any transaction, you should ask yourself three separate questions. First, *what has happened*? That is, restate the transaction being described from the entity's perspective (remember the separate entity assumption from Chapter 1)—what has come into the entity, what has gone out of the entity? Second, *which accounts are affected* by what has happened? That is, what accounts should be used to reflect this thing moving in to or out of the entity? Third and finally, *in which direction are the affected accounts moving* by what has happened—are they increasing in amount or decreasing in amount? After answering these three questions in this order, you may use the "map" of the fundamental equation depicted in Table 2-2 to determine the bookkeeping entries required to record the transaction. The "map" of the fundamental equation shows how the action of right side and left side entries can be worked to keep it in balance.*

Table 2-2
Fundamental Equation Map: Balance Sheet

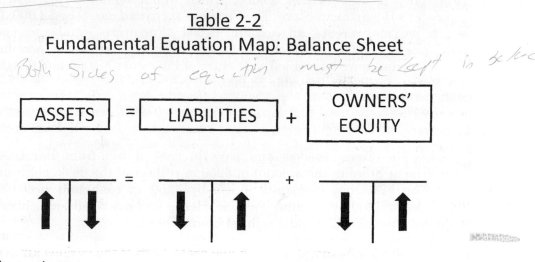

Illustrations.

Let us now put the fundamental equation to work, showing how we always keep it balanced, by making double entries—left side and right side—for a series of hypothetical transactions of a new business.

1.   Larry the Lawyer ("Larry") opens a new law office (the "Firm") and contributes to it $10,000 cash. From the Firm's point of view, it has *increased assets* by $10,000 in cash and *increased owner's equity* by $10,000, in the form of capital that has been invested in it. Cash is an asset account that is increasing in amount, calling for a left-side entry, and Owner's Equity is an owner's equity account that is increasing in amount, calling for a right-side entry. Hence we have a left-side entry of Cash $10,000 and a right-side entry of Owner's Equity $10,000:

Cash	$10,000	
Owner's Equity		$10,000

2.   The Firm has elegant legal stationery printed at a cost of $500, for which it paid cash. The Firm has *decreased assets* by $500 in cash and *increased assets* by $500, for which we may create an account and call it "Office Supplies." Hence we have a left-side entry of Office Supplies $500 and a right side entry of Cash $500.

---

*   You may find it helpful to develop a more elaborate version of this chart, adding to it the specific additional accounts discussed throughout this book.

| Office Supplies | $500 | |
| Cash | | $500 |

3. The Firm buys a Steelcase cherry desk and chair and a Martin Brattrud sofa at a cost of $3,000, which it put on its credit card at Barrister's Department Store. The Firm has *increased assets* by $3,000, for which we may create an account called "Furniture," and *increased liabilities* by $3,000, for which we may create an account called "Accounts Payable." Hence we have a left-side entry of Furniture $3,000 and a right-side entry of Accounts Payable $3,000.

| Furniture | $3,000 | |
| Accounts Payable | | $3,000 |

4. The Firm receives and pays in cash a bill from Barrister's Department Store in the amount of $250 in respect of the desk, chair and sofa. The Firm has *decreased assets* by $250 in cash and *decreased liabilities* by $250 in Accounts Payable. Hence we have a left-side entry of Accounts Payable $250 and a right-side entry of Cash $250.

| Accounts Payable | $250 | |
| Cash | | $250 |

5. Larry decides he needs the sofa more at home than at the office so the Firm lets him take the sofa home. The Firm has *decreased assets* by the cost of the sofa (say $800) and *decreased owner's equity* by the same amount ($800). Hence we have a left-side entry of Owner's Equity $800 and a right-side entry of Furniture $800.

| Owner's Equity | $800 | |
| Furniture | | $800 |

6. Barrister's Department Store has decided to terminate all its credit card accounts and insists that all its customers instead execute promissory notes for all outstanding debts or future debts. The Firm cooperates. The Firm has *decreased liabilities* by the outstanding balance on its account with Barrister's of $2,750 and *increased liabilities* by the same amount, for which we may create an account called "Notes Payable." Hence we have a left-side entry of Accounts Payable $2,750 and a right-side entry of Notes Payable $2,750.

| Accounts Payable | $2,750 | |
| Notes Payable | | $2,750 |

7. The Firm is sued for malpractice and agrees to settle the claim, which it believes is unfounded, by paying the ungrateful former client $500 over time. The Firm has *increased liabilities* by $500, for which we may create an account called "Lawsuit Obligation," and *decreased owner's equity*

by the same amount (since the Firm has gained nothing of tangible value in return for its promise to pay). Hence we have a left-side entry of Owner's Equity $500 and a right-side entry of Lawsuit Obligation $500.

Owner's Equity	$500	
Lawsuit Obligation		$500

8. The ungrateful former client from the previous transaction realizes her claim was all a big mistake and wants to forgive the Firm (which again cooperates, of course). The Firm has *decreased liabilities* by $500 in Lawsuit Obligation and *increased owner's equity* by the same amount. Hence we have a left-side entry of Lawsuit Obligation $500 and a right-side entry of Owner's Equity $500.

Lawsuit Obligation	$500	
Owner's Equity		$500

C. CREATING THE BALANCE SHEET

Now that we have a bundle of transactions recorded on a daily basis in the general journal as they arise, we want at the end of the period to summarize them. Accountants do this by *posting* each journal entry to a *ledger* organized by account type. For each account, the ledger contains what is called a "*T-Account*" because it looks like a capital T—see how it looks:

Cash	
Left	Right

Each part of every journal entry will be reported in an appropriate ledger T-Account. Each posting to the T-Account should also identify the transaction number to which it relates in the general journal so that all transactions can be traced back to the original entry in the general journal. (You can consider this a form of internal control.) After all posting is done, the balance in each account is determined by subtracting the lesser amount in each T-Account from the greater amount in each T-Account. This is the final step before reporting those balances as separate line items on the balance sheet.* The following T-Accounts show the results of posting the foregoing eight transactions from the general journal to the ledger T-Accounts:

---

* Technically, there is an intermediate step involving preparation of what is called the "trial balance" which is essentially a listing of the balances in the T-Accounts. It presents the balances as left side and right side entries and that is the only difference between the trial balance and the final statements—the balance sheet and income statement—that are the central object of the exercise. We have therefore omitted use or discussion of the trial balance as a step in the process. Nevertheless you may find it helpful to prepare trial balances to visualize how double-entry bookkeeping's rules of making left-and right-side entries (debits and credits) in equal amounts means that the fundamental equation always balances.

ASSETS

Cash				Office Supplies			Furniture			
(1)	10,000	500	(2)	(2)	500		(3)	3,000	800	(5)
		250	(4)							
	10,000	750								
	9,250				500			2,200		

LIABILITIES

Accounts Payable				Notes Payable			Lawsuit Obligation			
(4)	250	3,000	(3)			2,750	(6)	(8)	500	500	(7)
(6)	2,750									
		0				2,750				0

OWNER'S EQUITY

Owner's Equity			
(5)	800	10,000	(1)
(7)	500	500	(8)
	1,300	10,500	
		9,200	

From these T-Accounts, the balance sheet is prepared by reporting the balance in each T-Account in the appropriate place on the balance sheet. The balance sheet for Larry's Firm as of the end of the period in which the foregoing transactions occurred would be as follows:

Larry's Law Firm
Balance Sheet
(as of end of period)

Assets		Liabilities	
Cash	$9,250	Notes Payable	$2,750
Office Supplies	500		
Furniture	2,200		
		Owner's Equity	
		Owner's Equity	9,200
	$11,950		$11,950

Order of Assets.

Notice that, as discussed in Chapter 1, the assets on the balance sheet are reported in the order of their liquidity: beginning with Cash, then Office Supplies, then Furniture. If additional assets such as Buildings or Land were also listed, they would come next in order, following Furniture. It is customary to distinguish between two categories of assets based on the degree of their relative liquidity: current assets and long-term assets. *Current assets* are those assets that are reasonably expected to be realized in cash or otherwise sold or consumed within a reasonably short period of time, usually one year. Long-term assets are those not expected to be turned into cash within that time. Current assets are by definition more liquid than long-term assets and are therefore listed first on the balance sheet.

Notice also that each entry on the balance sheet—each "*line item*"—reports precisely the T-Account balance for that item and indeed is taken directly from the respective T-Account. That balance marks the beginning balance in that T-Account—and for that *line item* on the balance sheet—for the next period. Notice finally that in the case of the liability accounts Lawsuit Obligation and Accounts Payable no entry is made on the balance sheet. This is because, even though activity occurred in those accounts during the period, as of the end of the period each account carried a zero balance. So there is nothing to report about them on the balance sheet.

Now that you understand how to report a financial transaction in the general journal on a daily basis, how to post the journal entries to the ledger T-Accounts at the end of each period, and how to prepare the balance sheet, try taking all these steps with respect to the following Problem.

Problem 2A

Jack and Jill are two entrepreneurial lovebirds who agree to form a corporation, J&J, Inc. ("J&J"), to operate a bicycle repair shop in a bucolic region of the western United States. They begin business on July 1. The following transactions occur during the month of July. Prepare journal entries, T-Accounts, and a balance sheet as of July 31 for J&J.

1. (a) Jack pays $5,000 to J&J in exchange for 100 shares of J&J stock. (b) Jill transfers to J&J title to land, valued at $5,000, in exchange for 100 shares of J&J stock.

2. J&J buys tools, supplies and a large tent from ABC Supplies for $1,200, charging the purchase to its account. (The lovebirds are also nature lovers and they are going to operate the business outdoors during the summer months.)

3. J&J orders $5,000 in used equipment from Xenon Products, that it expects will last until next Spring. The terms of the order permit J&J to cancel the order without any obligation whatsoever up until the time of delivery.

4. J&J borrows $6,000 from Citybank, giving Citybank a one year note at 10% interest per year. The parties agree that interest will begin to accumulate as of September 1 and is to be paid, along with the principal amount, on the note's maturity date.

5. Xenon Products delivers the equipment J&J ordered. J&J pays Xenon for the equipment when it is delivered.

6. J&J pays ABC $400 on its account.

7.   J&J decides it ordered one repair stand too many from Xenon. It sells the extra repair stand to Sam, a friend of Jill's, for $500, which is what J&J paid for it. Sam gives J&J a note, payable by Sam to J&J in 30 days.

D. REVENUES AND EXPENSES

You may have noticed that in both our example of Larry the Lawyer and his Firm and in the foregoing Problem concerning J&J we dealt only with transactions that impacted the balance sheet. None of the transactions involved the rendering of services or the selling of goods that would generate revenue and none involved incurring costs that would constitute expenses. Let us now add such transactions involving revenue and expense.

You may have an intuitive sense that increases in revenue will lead directly to increases in owner's equity and that is right. As well, increases in expenses also lead directly to decreases in owner's equity. Given that, then one could imagine a bookkeeping process in which items of revenue and expense were recorded directly as increases or decreases in owner's equity. But since items of revenue and expense are one of the core bases for assessing the financial performance of an entity over time, it would be more helpful to show those items in a separate format. That is the purpose of the income statement.

As a matter of bookkeeping, therefore, we treat items of revenue and expense separately and reflect them as sub-categories of the owner's equity portion of the fundamental equation. Table 2-3 expands the map of the fundamental equation set forth in Table 2-2 to reflect how transactions affecting revenue and expense relate to it.

Table 2-3
Fundamental Equation Map:
Balance Sheet with Income Statement

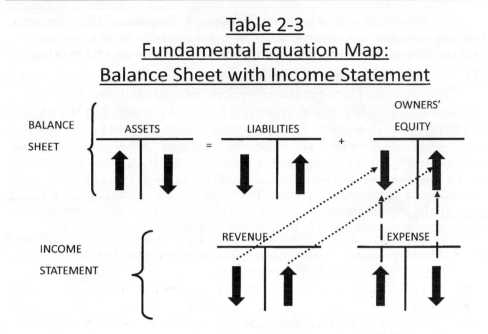

Table 2-3 shows also how the income statement relates to the balance sheet. It shows that expenses and revenues are income statement accounts and that changes in the balances in those accounts will affect the owner's equity portion of the balance sheet. To understand that relationship, notice that transactions which generate revenue will imply an increase in the owner's equity. As such, revenue-generating transactions call for a right-side entry. Conversely, expense-incurring transactions will imply a decrease in owner's equity. So expense-incurring transactions call for a left-side entry.

Recall the FASB definition of revenue from Chapter 1—"increases in equity resulting from asset increases and/or liability decreases from delivering goods or services or other activities that constitute the entity's ongoing major or central operations." Less formally, *revenue* consists of amounts generated by the entity upon the sale of goods it is in the business of selling and fees from the rendition of services it is in the business of rendering.

Recall also the FASB definition of expenses from Chapter 1— "decreases in equity from asset decreases or liability increases from delivering goods or services, or carrying out any activities which constitute the entity's ongoing major or central operations." Less formally, *expenses* consist of costs incurred by the entity in order to generate its revenue and for which the entity does not receive in return any equivalent asset.

Put another way, revenues are increases and expense are decreases in equity. As such, changes in revenue and expense accounts could be recorded directly in the owner's equity account. But since items of revenue and expense are the determinants of net income, and net income is a central measure of economic performance, separate presentation of revenue and expense is desirable.

To enable that presentation requires records that are functionally identical to those that would be created by direct recording in the owner's equity account. Thus, since an increase in expense reduces equity and that would call for a left-side entry in the owner's equity account, it will call for a left-side entry to the expense account; an increase in revenue increases equity and that would call for a right-side entry, so it will call for a right-side entry to the revenue account. To summarize in terms captured by the map of the fundamental equation in Table 2-3, if expense and revenue items were recorded directly to owner's equity they would result in:

expense account increases ....equity decreases (left, left)
expense account decreases ....equity increases (right, right)
revenue account decreases ....equity decreases (left, left)
revenue account increases ....equity increases (right, right)

In the same way that Table 2-1 above suggested a series of examples of the basic kinds of balance sheet accounts, Table 2-4 suggests some of the basic kinds of income statement accounts, categorized as either expense accounts or revenue accounts.

Table 2-4	
Income Statement Accounts—Some Examples	
Expense Accounts	**Revenue Accounts**
Cost of Goods Sold	Sales
Research Expense	Fee Revenue
Library Expense	Interest Income
Rent Expense	

Names Given to Accounts (Amplified).

As emphasized in the discussion about the balance sheet accounts, what is important for one to master is which accounts are balance sheet accounts (asset, liability, and owner's equity accounts) and which accounts are income statement accounts, and whether a particular income statement account is an expense account or a revenue account. It is usually less important what names are given to the accounts. For example, as far as revenues are concerned, we could call Service Revenue by the name Fee Revenue if we wanted to and we could even condense various miscellaneous accounts into a single account called Other or Miscellaneous (such as the cost of coffee and tea for the office).

Assigning names to accounts is often a matter of judgment or context, possible because many accounting terms are synonyms. For example, profit, earnings and income all have the same meaning. On the other hand, some accounting terms have specific meanings so that terms must be chosen to reflect specific meanings. For example, revenue is distinct from profit, earnings and income (each of these is the difference between revenue and expense). Accounting vocabulary also includes homonyms (the word loss has different usages, for example, as the Glossary notes). Moreover, terms used in accounting often have different meanings used in other fields (such as tax, commercial, or corporate law). As a result, when entities prepare financial records and publish accounting reports, they frequently define names assigned to particular accounts and transactions. Lawyers do the same when drafting agreements using accounting terms (some definitions are heavily negotiated).

Further Illustrations.

Let us take a few examples, by following up on further transactions engaged in by Larry the Lawyer and his Firm. Remember the three sorts of questions you must ask yourself in seeking to use double-entry bookkeeping for recording transactions.

9.   Larry's Firm represents Hugo Ace in negotiating and closing the purchase of a distinctive vacation property for a fee of $5,000, which the client pays in cash at the closing. The Firm has *increased assets* by $5,000 in cash and generated an *increase in revenues* of $5,000 from fees. Hence we have a left-side entry of Cash $5,000 and a right-side entry of Fee Revenue $5,000.

Cash	$5,000	
Fee Revenue		$5,000

10.   Larry's Firm buys a used set of Corbin on Contracts from a lawyer who is retiring from practice for a price of $500, which is paid in cash. The Firm has *increased assets* by $500, for which we may create an account "Library," and *decreased assets* by $500 in cash. Hence we have a left-side entry of Library $500 and a right-side entry of Cash $500.

resale value.

Library	$500	
Cash		$500

11. Larry's Firm signs up for Westlaw's computerized research database, and pays a fee for one month of $250. The Firm has *incurred an expense* of $250, for which we may create an account "Research Expense," and *decreased assets* by $250 in cash. Hence we have a left-side entry of Research Expense $250 and a right-side entry of Cash $250.

no resale value

Research Expense	$250	
Cash		$250

Suppose that during a period clients paid for services provided by Larry's Firm partly in cash and partly using credit accounts the Firm extends to them. In transaction 9, for example, suppose clients paid $3,000 in cash and $2,000 in newly-opened accounts. The entries would be as follows:

Cash	$3,000	
Accounts Receivable	$2,000	
Fee Revenue		$5,000

This slight refinement divides the form of consideration generated from rendering these services into the two different asset accounts. Note that the sum of the left-side entries still equals the sum of the right-side entries. This is the key to "double-entry" bookkeeping—equal entries on each of two sides. It does not mean there is only one entry on each side. When multiple entries are made on one side, as in this example, it is called a *compound entry*.

E. CREATING THE INCOME STATEMENT

As the foregoing discussion and "map" emphasize, there is a direct link between the income statement and the balance sheet. Whatever profit an entity generates in a period will have the effect of increasing the owner's equity for that period (and correspondingly any loss an entity generates in a period will have the effect of decreasing owner's equity for that period). It is therefore necessary to have a mechanism to implement this consequence or, more precisely, to formalize this link between the income statement and the balance sheet.

This is done by a process called making "closing entries." The objective is to calculate the total profit or loss during the period—which can then be reported on the income statement as the "bottom line" earnings for the period and also reflected on the balance sheet as the increase or decrease in owner's equity for the period. To do this, we first need to summarize the revenues and expenses during the period. This is done by creating a special account called the *profit and loss account,* which is usually abbreviated as the *P&L Account.* (It is sometimes called, equivalently, the *income and expense summary*.) The P&L Account is neither a balance sheet account nor an income statement account. Instead it is a *nominal* account, created and used solely for the administrative purpose of calculating the profit or loss during a period.

The calculation of profit or loss using the P&L Account is governed by the same rules that govern preparing journal entries reflecting actual transactions. The difference is that each closing entry will be performed for the purpose of reducing to zero the balance in each revenue account and each expense account and reporting a balancing entry to the newly-created

P&L Account. The result will be that we have in one single place a summary of all revenues and all expenses during the period, and in that one place we may then compute the profit or loss for the period. And, to repeat, this amount is our quest, for it will be displayed on the income statement for the period, and reflected as an increase or decrease in owner's equity on the balance sheet as of the end of the period.

Before putting this method of closing entries to work, a crucial point should be emphasized. The process of closing entries is performed solely with respect to income statement accounts—that is, revenue accounts and expense accounts. The revenue and expense accounts are closed because they are the determinants of net income. Balance sheet accounts, in contrast, are never closed. The balance in each balance sheet T-Account is *posted* to the balance sheet and that balance constitutes the balance for the beginning of the next period. With that distinction in mind, let us put the closing entries process to work by performing it for the period in which transactions 1 through 11 occurred for Larry's Firm. Preliminarily, we should update the T-Accounts to reflect all transactions during that period, as follows:

ASSETS

Cash				Office Supplies		Furniture			Library	
(1) 10,000	500	(2)		(2) 500		(3) 3,000	800 (5)		(10) 500	
(9) 5,000	250	(4)								
	500	(10)								
	250	(11)								
15,000	1,500									
13,500				500		2,200			500	

LIABILITIES

Accounts Payable				Notes Payable		Expenses Payable		
(4)	250	3,000	(3)	2,750	(6)	(8) 500	500	(7)
(6)	2,750							
	3,000	3,000						
		0		2,750			0	

OWNER'S EQUITY

Owner's Equity			
(5)	800	10,000	(1)
(7)	500	500	(8)
	1,300	10,500	
		9,200	

REVENUES AND EXPENSES

Fee Revenue			Research Expense	
	5,000	(9)	(11)	250

Closing Entries Reduces revenue + expenses to 0 → "closed"

We need to make two closing entries because two of the transactions during the reporting period involved revenue or expense accounts (transactions 9 and 11). The effect of making each of these closing entries is to reduce the balance in the revenue and expense accounts to zero—in technical terms, those accounts will be *closed*. Indeed, they will be "*closed into the P&L Account*" in that the closing entry with respect to each of those accounts is made by a balancing entry to the P&L Account. The closing entries will therefore result in all the balances for revenue and expenses during the period to be contained solely in the P&L Account. For convenience, we can use lower case letters to identify each closing entry, to distinguish the closing entries from daily general journal entries, and enable us to tie back our final results to each entry.

Closing Entries for Revenue Accounts.

The closing entries for the revenue account, Fee Revenue, would be as follows:

Closing Entry

a.	Fee Revenue	$5,000	
	P&L		$5,000

Notice that the closing entry for Fee Revenue is a left-side entry. There are two ways to understand why. First, the balance in the Fee Revenue T-Account before making this entry had been a right-side balance. To reduce it to zero—to close it out—therefore requires a left-side entry. Second, Fee Revenue is a revenue account. In this step, we are reducing its balance to zero, and therefore according to the map of the fundamental equation given above, a left-side entry is required.

Conversely, the balancing closing entry for the P&L Account with respect to Fee Revenue is a right-side entry. Again there are two ways to understand why. First, since we know that the closing entry for the Fee Revenue account is a left-side entry, we must have a right-side entry. Second, we can conceptualize the P&L Account as representing a proxy for changes in owner's equity—profits will increase it and losses will decrease it. With that conception in mind, we can again refer to the map of the fundamental equation given above, which shows that entries that increase owners' equity require right-side entries.

Closing entries for Revenue Account

The foregoing principles will hold true for closing entries for all revenue accounts. Closing revenue accounts into the P&L Account requires (1) left-side closing entries to the revenue accounts and (2) right-side closing entries to the P&L Account.

Closing Entries for Expense Accounts.

For expense accounts, things are exactly the other way around, precisely because they have exactly the opposite effect on profit or loss for the period (and on owner's equity). Thus our closing entry for the expense account Research Expense will be as follows:

b.	P&L	$250	
	Research Expense		$250

Again there are two ways to understand why the closing entry for the expense account Research Expense must be a right-side entry. First, the balance in the Research Expense T-Account before making this entry had been a left-side balance. To reduce it to zero—to close it out—therefore requires a right-side entry. Second, Research Expense is an expense account. In this step, we are reducing its balance to zero, and therefore according to the map of the fundamental equation given above, a right-side entry is required.

Conversely, the balancing closing entry for the P&L Account with respect to Research Expense is a left-side entry. Again there are two ways to understand why. First, since we know that the closing entry for the Research Expense account is a right-side entry, we must have a left-side entry. Second, we can again conceptualize the P&L Account as representing a proxy for changes in owners' equity—profits will increase it and losses will decrease it. With that conception in mind, we can again refer to the map of the fundamental equation given above, which shows that entries that decrease owners' equity require left-side entries.

Once again, the foregoing principles will hold true for closing entries for all expense accounts. Closing expense accounts into the P&L Account requires (1) right-side closing entries to the expense accounts and (2) left-side closing entries to the P&L Account.

Closing the T-Accounts.

Having made the appropriate closing entries for each revenue account and each expense account, it remains to reflect those closing entries in their respective T-Accounts so they can be closed. The T-Accounts for Fee Revenue and Research Expense would be closed by recording the respective closing entry in them, as follows:

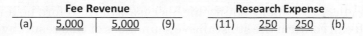

	Fee Revenue				**Research Expense**		
(a)	5,000	5,000	(9)	(11)	250	250	(b)

The P&L Account.

Similarly, having made the appropriate closing entries for each revenue account and each expense account, we <u>must prepare a T-Account</u> for the P&L Account. This is done in a methodologically identical way to the preparation of T-Accounts for each of the other accounts we have previously considered. The P&L T-Account for Larry's Firm would appear as follows (and notice how the closing entries designated as (a) and (b) in the P&L Account tie back to the closing entry designated as (a) in the Fee Revenue T-Account and as (b) in the Research Expense T-Account):

[handwritten: Combines the Revenue & expenses]

	P&L Account		
(b)	250	5,000	(a)
		$4,750	

Voila.

[handwritten: Balance in P&L account Net income"]

The balance in the P&L Account is the profit or loss during the period. In this example, the profit for the period is $4,750. That profit is reported in the income statement as *"net income."* The full income statement of Larry's Law Firm is set forth below, and displays the revenue accounts, the expense accounts, and the net income:

Larry's Law Firm
Income Statement
(for the period)

Fee Income	$5,000
Research Expense	250
Net Income	$4,750

One More Thing.

We have accomplished half of our objective—calculating the profit (or loss) and reporting it as net income on the income statement. The other half of our objective is to reflect that profit (or loss) as an increase (or decrease) in owner's equity as of the end of the period. In other words, the final step is to record the profit (or loss) on the balance sheet. To do so, we follow the now-familiar step of closing out the P&L Account. And since we want to get that profit (or loss) reflected in owner's equity, our balancing entry will be to the owner's equity account. Which will be the left-side entry and which will be the right-side entry?

The easiest way to answer that is to determine on which side the final P&L Account balance stands and make the closing-entry on the opposite side. In the current example, the balance in the P&L Account stands on the right side and so to close it out we will need to make a left-side entry. The balancing entry to owner's equity in this case will therefore be a right-side entry. You can confirm the substantive soundness of this result by referring again to the map of the fundamental equation. The owner's equity account is being increased to reflect the profit during the period and calls for a right-side entry. Accordingly, our final closing entry would be as follows:

P&L	$4,750	
Owner's Equity		$4,750

Notice that had there been a loss during the current period, all these steps would go the opposite way: the balance in the P&L Account would have appeared on the left side; a right-side closing entry to the P&L Account would have been necessary; and the balancing entry to owner's equity would have been to the left-side, which is precisely what is necessary to show the decrease in owner's equity that such a loss would entail.

Returning to our actual example, the P&L T-Account is now closed and the Owner's Equity account is increased by $4,750, an increase that will be reflected in the owner's equity portion of the balance sheet. The full balance sheet would appear as follows:

Larry's Law Firm
Balance Sheet
(as of end of period)

Assets		Liabilities	
Cash	$13,500	Note Payable	$2,750
Office Supplies	500		
Furniture	2,200	Total Liabilities	2,750
Library	500		
		Owner's Equity	
		Owner's Equity	13,950
		Total Liabilities	
Total Assets	$16,700	& Owner's Equity	$16,700

F. NINE POSSIBLE PAIRS

Here is an alternative way to understand all the basic bookkeeping set forth above. The fundamental equation and journal entries used to sustain it and to prepare balance sheets and income statements can be captured by a total of nine different pairs of double entries as depicted in the following graphic. It shows the three categories of balance sheet accounts and how increases or decreases in them are entered as left or right side entries along with increases or decreases in the others. All income statement accounts in turn relate indirectly to these movements in balance sheet accounts and thus amount to variations on these nine possibilities.

	Asset		Liability		Equity	
	Left	*Right*	*Left*	*Right*	*Left*	*Right*
1	⇑	⇓				
2	⇑					⇑
3	⇑			⇑		
4		⇓	⇓			
5		⇓			⇓	
6			⇓	⇑		
7			⇓			⇑
8				⇑	⇓	
9					⇓	⇑

Rows 1, 2 and 3 show how *increases in an asset* can affect other accounts, either: (1) a balancing decrease in an asset (say increasing cash upon the sale of a piece of land); (2) an increase in owner's equity (say increasing cash upon an investment by the owner); or (3) an increase in a liability (say increasing cash by borrowing $10,000).

Rows 4 and 5 show how *decreases in an asset* can affect other accounts, in addition to the way already shown (in Row 1, a balancing increase in an asset account), either: (4) a decrease in a liability (say decreasing cash upon repaying a loan); or (5) a decrease in owner's equity (say decreasing cash upon an owner withdrawing a previous investment).

Rows 6, 7 and 8 show how other changes in a liability can affect remaining accounts: (6) a decrease in a liability balanced by an increase in a liability (say borrowing from lender Peter to repay lender Paul); (7) a decrease in a liability balanced by an increase in owner's equity (say Peter forgives his loan to the entity); and (8) an increase in a liability balanced by a decrease in owner's equity (say Peter changes his mind and insists on being repaid).

Row 9 completes the picture by showing the final possibility, that a decrease in owner's equity can be balanced by an increase in owner's equity. The possibilities here are somewhat complex, as you will see in Chapter 7. For now, consider as an example the exchange of an existing class of common stock for a replacement class of common stock bearing different legal rights.

G. DATA MANAGEMENT

In this book, bookkeeping and most accounting matters involve the manual entry, aggregation and presentation of data. For most businesses, these steps are done using computers. A specialized computer language, called extensible business reporting language (XBRL), is increasingly available to present accounting information tagged with classifications (taxonomies) that enable users to read and manipulate the information in more useful ways than traditional formats.

Computers and XBRL offer numerous advantages over manual data-entry and aggregation, including speed, reduced risk of error due to transposition and computation, ease of making multiple uses of input data, and bearing safe-guards against deliberate errors or fraud. On the other hand, accountants must design these systems and no computer can prevent people from deliberate error or fraud. Moreover, the best way to learn about the financial reporting process, as you are now doing, is through manual exercises.

Problem 2B

Put to work your knowledge of bookkeeping as it relates to both the balance sheet and the income statement. The following Problem is an extension of Problem 2A, reporting new transactions occurring in month 2 (August).

On August 1, J&J opens for business. Prepare an income statement for the month of August and a balance sheet as of August 31 (and supporting journal entries and T-Accounts), taking account of the following transactions and adding new account titles as necessary. (Do not forget to include in your financial statements those transactions that occurred in July.)

8.   (a) During the month of August, J&J does bicycle repairs, priced at $6,200, for its customers. Customers pay J&J $4,800 in cash for these services and charge $1,400 to accounts that J&J allows them to open. (b) At the end of August, customers have paid $200 of the amounts they have charged and $1,200 in charges are outstanding.

9.   J&J pays Jack and Jill each a salary of $1,500 for the month of August.

10.   J&J sponsors a local bicycle race at a cost of $350. J&J pays $250 of that amount in cash and charges the remaining $100, representing the cost of beverages provided to competitors.

11.   J&J pays the balance of $800 it owes to ABC Supplies.

12.   Sam pays off the $500 note he gave to J&J.

Conceptual Questions 2A

Is the income statement necessary? Why not report all transactions only in the balance sheet? Is the balance sheet necessary? Why not report all transactions in the income statement? The same measurements are used in both reports (they articulate): the difference between revenues and expenses constitutes earnings and this amount is equivalent to the period's change in owners' equity. Consider two views of the conceptual underpinnings. The balance sheet view sees revenues and expenses as resulting from changes in assets and liabilities (revenues are asset increases and/or liability decreases while expenses are asset decreases and/or liability increases). The income statement view sees earnings as the key, with assets and liabilities as residual holding places for the results of operating activities driving revenues and expenses. Which view does FASB take? Do you concur?

Conceptual Questions 2B

Accounting nomenclature is replete with synonyms. Take the following clusters of terms that for a business entity usually have identical meanings: (1): book value, owners' equity, and net worth; (2) earnings, profit, and net income; and (3) accounts payable, payables, current obligations, and current liabilities. Is this due to lack of a single codification? Does it matter? Would it help people's understanding of accounting to have a single set of unique definitions (would it help you)? Peruse this book's Glossary now and as you read further. Does this help you grasp the subject?

CHAPTER 3

THE ACCRUAL SYSTEM AND RECOGNITION PRINCIPLES

■ ■ ■

The choice to place asset account increases on the left side of the journal and liability and equity increases on the right are products of convention. The convention could have been the other way around. (In Hebrew, where one reads from right to left, accounting is done this other way around!) Though there is nothing inevitable about the choice of conventions, once the choice is made it must be adhered to. Otherwise, you will have problems akin to those you would face if instead of driving on the right side of the road in the US, you adopted the British custom of driving on the left side of the road.

The reason for following through may not be immediately obvious but will become clear. Assets and expenses are directly related. Any expense paid in advance creates an asset; when used up, the asset becomes an expense. Likewise, assets are almost always pre-paid expenses—they will be used in the business somehow or another and sooner or later. This is why the balance sheet—which lists assets—is a set of *permanent accounts*, *as of* a moment in time, whereas the income statement—which lists expenses—is a set of *periodic accounts*, *for a* particular and limited stretch of time. The judgment concerns when a permanent item should be recorded as partly used up—when an asset should become an expense, when a resource is spent. These principles are the subject of this Chapter.

Things are relatively simple to keep track of when all transactions during a period are paid in full when they occur. For a service that is paid in full when it is rendered we have simultaneously an increase in cash and an increase in revenue for that period; when a utility bill is received and paid in a single period we have simultaneously an increase in expense and a decrease in cash for that period.

Sometimes these moments are separated in time however, as where we render the service in one month but are not paid for it until a later month or where we receive the benefit of some utility in one month but do not pay for it until a later month. Accounting divides activities into time periods, such as the calendar month or fiscal year, and yet also assumes (realistically) that most entities continue as going concerns indefinitely. These two points create one of the most difficult problems in accounting.

How should this separation in time between the occurrence of an economic event and the payment of cash in respect of it be treated?

A. CASH VERSUS ACCRUAL ACCOUNTING

One approach is simply to keep track of all transactions strictly in terms of when cash is received or paid with respect to any transaction. This way of doing things is called *cash basis accounting*. It is probably the method that you use, even if informally, in conducting your personal affairs. Neither you, nor the cash basis of accounting, are concerned with keeping track by time period of when economic activity generates revenue or when incurring expenses generates earning power. Nor is this cash basis of accounting concerned with measuring changes in equity. Instead you, and the cash basis of accounting, just keep track of things as cash comes in and as cash goes out. This method of accounting is often used by individuals and small businesses and for federal income tax purposes. However, it is not a method recognized under GAAP.

Reconsider a few transactions from the previous Chapter concerning Larry's Firm. Larry contributed $10,000 cash as an equity investment in Larry's Firm (transaction 1). This increased cash and equity but had no effect on revenue. Larry's Firm paid cash to buy a used set of *Corbin on Contracts* (transaction 11). This increased one asset and decreased another, having no effect on expense. The Firm rendered services for which clients promised to pay a portion of the fee in the future (transaction 12). This increased revenue but had no effect on cash. These examples highlight two complementary points: (1) revenue and expense are not necessarily directly related to changes in cash and (2) changes in cash are not necessarily coupled with changes in revenue or expense. The cash basis system of accounting does not care about these distinctions; the accrual system's distinguishing characteristic is that it does.

GAAP is concerned with tracking both income (the difference between revenue and expenses) and changes in equity (resulting from income). On the revenue side, this gives rise to the concept of *revenue recognition* driven by the conservatism principle. Under it, increases in equity as through revenue are recognized only when they are *reasonably certain*, while decreases in equity as through expense are recognized when they are *reasonably possible*. This gives rise to an important principle: revenue is recognized in the period when goods or services are delivered (called the *realization principle*). On the expense side, it implicates the *matching principle*. Under it, costs associated with the revenues of a period are expenses of that period.

To implement these principles, accountants devised the concepts of accrual and deferral. It may be useful to think of this *accrual system of accounting* in the following terms. We want to *burden the income statement* with all expenses that were incurred to generate revenue on a period-by-period basis (without regard to when they were paid for in cash) and we want to *benefit* the income statement with revenues that were earned on a period-by-period basis (without regard to when they were paid for in cash).

The Accrual Concept.

Accrual and deferral are two sides of the same coin. Accrual is the idea that some event should be recognized during a current period even though the cash in respect of that event will not be paid or received until some future period. For example, if Larry the Lawyer writes a will in March for which the client pays him cash in April, accountants recognize the event in March when the services were done, not in April because of the fortuity that the cash arrived that month. In other words, they want to *benefit the income statement* of any period to reflect the work done in that period. More formally, accruals are revenues that have been earned and expenses that have been incurred by the end of a given accounting period, but will not be collected or paid until a subsequent accounting period.

The Deferral Concept.

Deferral is the idea that some event should not be recognized until some later period even though the cash in respect of that event is paid or received in the current period. This is the opposite of the situation just described and can be shown by the opposite example: if Larry the Lawyer is paid an advance fee in March by a client for a service to be rendered in April, accountants recognize the event in April when the services are to be done, not in March because of the fortuity that the cash arrived in that month. In other words, they do not want to benefit the income statement of any period unless the work is done in that period. More formally, deferrals are assets, liabilities, revenues or expenses that must be adjusted at the end of an accounting period to reflect earned revenues or incurred expenses.

B. REVENUE AND EXPENSE RECOGNITION

The preceding discussion mentioned the concept of recognition. It suggested the importance to accounting of a basis for determining when revenue and expense are recognized. These are central issues in accounting because revenue and expense determine net income. More accounting errors, irregularities and fraud are associated with revenue and expense recognition than with any other accounting subject.

FASB and IASB pursued a joint project on revenue recognition for more than a decade, culminating in new guidance from both bodies effective in the United States in 2018. Both standard setters perceived weaknesses in their historical models, along with differences between them. IFRS yielded wide variation in practice due to a lack of comprehensive guidance. For instance, it did not address handling revenue on contracts with multiple elements, such as whether to treat installment sales contracts as a single deal or a series of divisible transactions. GAAP varied greatly in application due to a proliferation of industry-specific standards that ended up treating economically equivalent transactions differently. To put the new GAAP standard in context, therefore, a brief look back at GAAP's traditional approach is helpful.

Historical Approach.

Traditionally, revenue was recognized when the earnings process associated with the underlying activity was complete or substantially complete. Recall, from Chapters One and Two, FASB's conception of revenues: "an entity's revenue-earning activities involve delivering or producing goods, rendering services, or other activities that constitute its ongoing major or central operations." FASB stated that "revenues [were] considered to have been earned when the entity has substantially accomplished what it must do to be entitled to the benefits represented by the revenues." This required meeting one of two conditions: that they are *realized* or are both *realizable and being earned.*

FASB said those two conditions were "usually met by the time product or merchandise is delivered or services are rendered to customers, and revenues from manufacturing and selling activities . . . are commonly recognized at time of sale (usually meaning delivery)." For transactions that extend over multiple periods (like paying rent or interest), reliable grounds for determining when revenue should be recognized could be found in contractual provisions governing the exchange.

Determining when these broad revenue recognition standards were met could vary with the type of earnings process, such as involving service contracts, merchandise sales or construction contracts. GAAP provided particular guidance to govern some of these categories of revenue generating activity. Consider three examples.

First, revenues from service contracts, such as providing consulting advice to a business client over a period of years, were generally recognized ratably over the service period, even if advance or delayed payments are received. Second, revenues arising from contracts involving multiple elements, such as installment sales contracts, were deferred until the transaction was complete if non-delivery of subsequent installments entitled the customer to a refund. Third, revenues under construction contracts were approached in a variety of authorized ways, depending on specific characteristics, including based on the percentage of the job that was completed or only when the entire contract was performed.

Prevailing Approach.

FASB's updated approach establishes one comprehensive framework to govern revenue recognition. The core principle holds that vendors recognize revenue to reflect the transfer of promised goods or services to customers in amounts measured by the consideration expected in exchange. So revenue is recognized when control over the subject matter is transferred to the customer. *[handwritten: → Revenue Recognition]*

FASB directs applying the core principle through a five-step analysis: (1) identify the contract; (2) identify any separate performance obligations; (3) determine the transaction price; (4) allocate the transaction price to respective performance obligations; and (5) recognize revenue when each performance obligation is satisfied. *[handwritten: 5 steps for rev. rec.]*

These steps have strong intuitive and analytical appeal to most business people, and will likely resonate with law students having taken the law school course on contracts. Experience suggests the frequent general feasibility of contract identification—devices that create enforceable rights and duties between a vendor and customer. "Performance obligations" are the vendor's promises to transfer goods or render services, which may be distinct or combined, and the transaction price is allocated accordingly. In effect, revenue is recognized when the promise is discharged.

The SEC has longed used similar terminology to elaborate a more comprehensive standard of revenue recognition: "revenue generally is realized or realizable and earned when all of the following criteria are met: (1) persuasive evidence of an arrangement exists; (2) delivery has occurred or services have been rendered; (3) the seller's price to the buyer is fixed or determinable; and (4) collectability is reasonably assured." SEC Staff Accounting Bulletin No. 101. *[handwritten: SEC standard of revenue recognition]*

[handwritten margin: a.k.]

Expenses are recognized in accordance with the matching principle. This is usually more straightforward than revenue recognition, though determining whether a disbursement is an expense or the exchange of one asset for another can be difficult. One nettlesome area of expense recognition concerns costs of restructuring an enterprise or business units. In general, these are recognized when little discretion to avoid them exists, usually meaning when most of them have been incurred. Another thorny problem concerns costs of overhauling an enterprise or units. In general, major overhaul costs are treated as expenses when incurred, not as exchanging one asset (like cash) for another (the resulting overhaul). (This distinction is pursued more technically and closely in Chapter 5.) *[handwritten: Expense rec]*

[handwritten at bottom: costs associated w/ revenues of a period are expenses of that period (they match)]

C. FOUR TIMING MATTERS

Suppose you are paid a $2,000 signing bonus in May ahead of a summer associate job. In a cash basis system you would have revenue (you may call it income) in May and that would be the end of it (this is the approach of the federal income tax system for individuals). In an accrual system, we want to defer recognizing that as revenue until August, after you have earned it.

To do so while still taking account of the payment, we can use a balance sheet account—a liability account, say Deferred Bonus Revenue—to indicate that you have assumed an obligation to work in return for that up-front payment. When August comes, we can treat the $2,000 as earned, indicate it as revenue in the income statement and balance that with an entry reducing the liability account.

More generally, to implement the accrual system of accounting to allocate events to periods other than those when cash changes hands, the bookkeeping mechanism is to store the transaction on the balance sheet between the occurrence of the event and the time the event is to be reported in the income statement. This is an illustration of how the double-entry bookkeeping system provides a bridge between the balance sheet and the income statement.

The circumstances implicated by the accrual system of accounting boil down to four: work before pay; pay before work; using before paying; and paying before using. Let's see how each is handled.

Accrual in Action.

An accrual can be required in respect of either revenue or expense. Take the following examples in the case of Larry's Firm for an accrual in respect of revenue (numbers 12a & 12b) and an accrual in respect of expense (numbers 13a & 13b). (The numbers used to identify the transactions in these examples continue the numbering system begun in the examples of the Firm in Chapter 2.)

12a. Larry's Firm represents the young rock group Victoria in negotiating a music recording contract with a major record label. The total fee for the services is $10,000, to be paid over time, and Larry sends a bill to the rock stars. We have rendered the service giving rise to the future right to be paid the cash, so we recognize that income now (even though the cash is not to be paid until the future). The Firm has *increased assets* by $10,000 in accounts receivable and generated an *increase in revenues* of $10,000 in fee revenue. Hence we have a left-side entry of Accounts Receivable $10,000 (to which we can append the designation Victoria for the convenience of enabling us to keep track of each client account separately) and a right-side entry of Fee Revenue $10,000.

Accounts Receivable		
(Victoria)	$10,000	
Fee Revenue		$10,000

12b. Six months later, Larry's Firm receives a cash payment of $5,000 from Victoria (whose record is selling very well Larry was happy to know). This is the receipt of cash for services rendered in a prior period and requires the second step of the accrual mechanism. The Firm has *increased assets* by $5,000 in cash and *decreased assets* by $5,000 in accounts receivable. Hence we have a left-side entry of Cash $5,000 and a right-side entry of Accounts Receivable (Victoria) $5,000.

Cash	$5,000	
Accounts Receivable		
(Victoria)		$5,000

Notice the consequence of the combination of transactions 12a and 12b. Revenue earned in a given month is allocated to that month by an entry to the Fee Revenue account. Since that is an income statement account, each month's income statement will be benefited, as it should be, by that amount of revenue. To facilitate that objective while keeping the fundamental equation in balance, we have simply kept track of the right to receive cash in respect of that month by building up the Accounts Receivable (Victoria) account, which is a balance sheet account. When the payment is actually received, only the balance sheet accounts of Cash and Accounts Receivable (Victoria) are affected.

13a. Larry's Firm leases its office under a lease agreement calling for quarterly payments of $6,000 in arrears (that is, every three months at the end of the three months). Although a cash payment in respect of any month is not made until the end of each quarter, the use of the office under the lease facilitates generating revenue that month. Accordingly, each month's income statement should be burdened with its share of the total, here $2,000 per month. For each month, therefore, the Firm has *increased liabilities* by $2,000 in lease payable and *incurred an expense* of $2,000 in lease expense. Hence we have a left-side entry of $2,000 Lease Expense and a right-side entry of Lease Payable $2,000.

Lease Expense	$2,000	
Lease Payable		$2,000

13b. At the end of the quarter, Larry's Firm pays $6,000 in cash under its lease agreement. This is the disbursement of cash in respect of resources used in the prior months and requires the second step of the accrual mechanism. The Firm has *decreased liabilities* by $6,000 in Lease Payable

and *decreased assets* by $6,000 in Cash. Hence we have a left-side entry of
Lease Payable $6,000 and a right-side entry of Cash $6,000.

Lease Payable	$6,000	
Cash		$6,000

Notice the consequence of the combination of transactions 13a and 13b
and how it is the mirror image of the consequence of the combination of
transactions 12a and 12b. Each month has been allocated the portion of the
lease payment allocable to it by the Lease Expense entry for that month.
Since each such entry is to an income statement account each month's
income will be burdened, as it should be, by that amount. To facilitate that
objective while keeping the fundamental equation in balance, we have
simply kept track of the obligation to pay cash in respect of that month by
building up the Lease Payable Account, which is a balance sheet account.
When the payment is actually made, only the balance sheet accounts of
Lease Payable and Cash are affected.

Deferral in Action.

As with accruals, deferrals can be required in respect of either revenue
or expense. For either, and in an analogous way to accruals, the cash
exchange is recorded when paid or received and the related activity
recorded subsequently when earned or incurred. Take the following
examples in the case of Larry's Firm for a deferral with respect to revenue
(numbers 14a & 14b) and a deferral with respect to expense (numbers 15a
& 15b).

14a. Larry's Firm is retained by Rudy Red to advise her concerning
estate planning. Red does not want the Firm to do any work for another
couple of months because she is not ready to evaluate her overall financial
position. But to assure that the Firm will be there when she needs it, Red
pays the Firm an advance fee of $5,000.

The Firm *increased assets* by $5,000 in cash. That is the left-side entry.
What's the right-side entry? Since the services have not been rendered, the
Firm has not earned the fee. It would therefore be premature to recognize
the fee as revenue. Instead, the Firm has become obligated to render the
services. It bears a liability. The deferral concept is used to reflect this. To
classify it, notice that when the services are rendered and the fee is
therefore earned, it will then count as revenue. So we can label this new
liability account "Deferred Revenue" (some call it "Deferred Income").
Hence we have a left-side entry of Cash $5,000 and a right-side entry of
Deferred Revenue $5,000.

Cash	$5,000	
Deferred Revenue		$5,000

14b. A few months later, Larry's Firm prepares all documents and gives appropriate legal advice to Red in connection with her estate planning. Thus completing the rendition of services, it has earned the full $5,000 she previously paid in advance. It is time to recognize the revenue. The Firm has *decreased liabilities* by $5,000 in Deferred Revenue and *increased revenue* by $5,000 in Fee Revenue. Hence we have a left-side entry of Deferred Revenue $5,000 and a right-side entry of Fee Revenue $5,000.

Deferred Revenue	$5,000	
Fee Revenue		$5,000

Notice the consequence of the combination of transactions 14a and 14b and how it is analogous but opposite to the accrual of income set forth above (12a & 12b). We achieve the same objective here as we achieved using the accrual device: benefiting the income statement for the period in which the work was done. We once again achieve that goal by using only balance sheet accounts in respect of the cash payment and then using income statement accounts when the work is actually done. The only difference is the chronological sequence and that is driven simply by the fact that here the cash payment precedes the work, whereas in the case of accruals the work (or use) preceded the cash payment.

15a and 15b. Let's reverse the situation referred to in example 13a above by assuming that Larry's Firm leases its office under a lease agreement calling for quarterly payments of $6,000 in *advance* (that is, every three months at the *beginning* of the three months). All the matching principles we discussed in 13a remain applicable, except we reverse the approach, as follows. Although a cash payment in respect of any month is made before that month begins, each month's use of the office under the lease facilitates generating revenue that month. Accordingly, each month's income statement should be burdened with its share of the total, here again $2,000. At the end of any month, the portion remaining unallocated is an asset available for future use.

Bookkeepers record this type of transaction in one of three alternative ways, though all of them will put the books in the same place. The three ways differ in the initial records by treating the disbursement as (1) the acquisition of an asset (subsequently adjusted), (2) the incurrence of an expense (also subsequently adjusted), or (3) a combination (not requiring subsequent adjustment). So a bookkeeper could:

　　(1)　record the prepayment of rent as the acquisition of an asset (called "*prepaid lease*")

Prepaid Lease	$6,000	
Cash		$6,000

(2)   record the prepayment of rent as the incurrence of an expense (called "*lease expense*"):

Lease Expense	$6,000	
Cash		$6,000

or

(3)   split it up to reflect which portion is an expense this month and which portion remains as an asset available to be consumed in the future:

Lease Expense	$2,000	
Prepaid Lease	$4,000	
Cash		$6,000

All these ways of recording the transaction are acceptable. There is some appeal to approach 3's direct compound-entry, since it puts the books in the position we end up in. The other two require a further adjustment to split the disbursement between the expense piece (this period's use of the property) and the asset piece (for future period use). In these approaches this adjustment is taken at the end of the period during the closing process. In each case, an "*adjusting entry*" is made. These would be as follows.

In the case of having recorded the disbursement as an asset (example 1), we need an adjusting entry to create an expense for the $2,000 used this month and reduce the asset to its remaining future amount. So there is an increase in an expense account (a left-side entry) and a decrease in an asset account (a right-side entry):

Adjusting Entry

Lease Expense	$2,000	
Prepaid Lease		$2,000

The opposite would need to be done in the case of having recorded the disbursement as an expense (example 2). We need an adjusting entry for the $4,000 of the resource not used up. So we reduce the initially recorded expense (a right-side entry) and increase a newly created asset (a left-side entry):

Adjusting Entry

Prepaid Lease	$4,000	
Lease Expense		$4,000

Whichever approach is used, in subsequent periods adjusting entries must be made. These will reflect that period's allocable expense (a left-side entry) with a balancing entry to reduce the asset (a right-side entry). In this example, each month's allocable portion of expense increase and asset decrease is $2,000. Accordingly, the adjusting entry for each subsequent month until the asset is fully consumed and expensed would be as follows:

Adjusting Entry

Lease Expense	$2,000	
Prepaid Lease		$2,000

Which of these 3 alternatives bookkeepers choose often turns on the intuitive rather than technical character of the transaction. The common approach to disbursements relating to prepaid rent, for example, is to record it as an expense with a subsequent adjusting entry to create the asset. There is a modest advantage to using an adjusting entry rather than making the direct compound entry. It is to build into the bookkeeping system a record of transactions calling for periodic asset reductions through expense transactions that could otherwise be hidden. That can be helpful because in some cases at period-end determining how much of an asset has been consumed and thus to be expensed requires judgment that an accountant rather than a bookkeeper must make.

In each case, notice the consequence of the combination of entries for transaction 15 (and related adjusting entries) and how each implements the matching principle that we have been illustrating. Each month has been allocated the portion of the lease payment allocable to it by the Lease Expense entry for that month. Since each such entry is to an income statement account each month's income will be burdened, as it should be, by that amount.

To facilitate that objective while keeping the fundamental equation in balance, we have simply kept track of the prepayment of cash in respect of that month by first creating an account for the purpose (Prepaid Lease, which is a balance sheet account) and then reducing that account as the periods pass and burdening the Lease Expense account, which is an income statement account, each month.

D. ADJUSTING ENTRIES

In transaction 15 above we introduced the need for adjusting entries to implement aspects of the accrual system of accounting. All adjusting entries are based on the accrual system but there are many more types of adjusting entries than those introduced in that discussion. In the closing process, dozens of adjusting entries are typically required for a business of even modest complexity.

All adjusting entries fall into three categories. The first concerns *apportionment*, of the type in transaction 15. Apportionment may be required in connection with either a *recorded cost* or an *unearned revenue*.

A cost that benefits more than one period is apportioned between the benefited periods. Examples include prepaid insurance or prepaid rent. An advance collection of cash for services not yet rendered calls for a subsequent adjusting entry in the period or periods in which the services are rendered.

The second category of adjusting entries is to record *unrecorded expenses* or *unrecorded revenues*. Expenses incurred in a current period for which no invoice is received and no payment is planned still must be recorded this period. An adjusting entry does the trick. An example is interest that accrues on an outstanding debt or an obligation arises to pay managerial salaries and bonuses.

Likewise, revenue earned this period may go unbilled and uncollected this period, yet must be recorded. A good example is the case of a law firm offering continuing services to a client and for whom bills are sent in accounting periods subsequent to the one in which services are rendered. Again, the adjusting entry can be used to record this otherwise unrecorded revenue.

The third category of adjusting entries relates to adjustments to the balance sheet carrying amount of various assets, including accounts receivable and securities. These topics are discussed in Chapter 6.

E. CONVERSION EXERCISE

The cash basis of accounting is commonly used by small businesses whose operations for various reasons do not warrant the expense and expertise demanded to comply with GAAP and its rules relating to accrual system accounting. Examples of such businesses include those whose operations are best gauged by cash flows rather than income, such as physician groups that distribute profits based on cash-earnings. Companies with few shareholders and lenders and therefore a small number of users of their financial statements might use the cash basis as well, as might companies whose operations are straightforward.

Even these businesses whose simplicity and scale justify using the cash basis may from time to time have a need for accrual statements, however. This will arise most often when the business seeks additional financing from other equity investors or from lenders. When the need arises, the cash-basis business may need to convert its records to an accrual basis system. To do so requires converting to an accrual basis both cash received from customers and cash paid for operating expenses. An example of this exercise will be instructive.

Suppose Larry's Firm kept its records on a cash basis. This year the Firm received $300,000 cash from its clients and paid $170,000 cash for rent, utilities and other operating expenses. So it enjoyed net cash flows of $130,000. What was net income on an accrual basis?

Suppose further that at the start and end of the year, the Firm's records showed the following:

	January 1	December 31
Accounts Receivable	15,000	9,000
Unearned Fee Revenue	0	5,000
Accrued Liabilities	4,000	11,000
Prepaid Expenses	1,500	3,200

Revenue Conversion.

To convert the amount of cash received from clients of $300,000 to accrued fee revenue, adjustments must be made to the Accounts Receivable and Unearned Fee Revenue items. January 1 Accounts Receivable are revenues earned last year to be collected this year while December 31 Accounts Receivable are revenues earned this year but to be collected next year. Thus to convert the cash receipts of $300,000 to revenue on an accrual basis calls for (a) subtracting January 1 Accounts Receivable (earned last year) and (b) adding December 31 Accounts Receivable (earned this year though with no cash yet in hand).

Likewise, January 1 Unearned Fee Revenue is cash received last year for revenues earned this year and December 31 Unearned Fee Revenue is cash received this year for revenue to be recognized next year. Thus to convert the cash receipts of $300,000 to revenue on an accrual basis calls for (a) adding January 1 Unearned Fee Revenue (we earned it this year!) and (b) subtracting December 31 Unearned Fee Revenue (cash but not yet earned!). Putting these two steps of the cash-to-accrual conversion process together would look like this:

Cash receipts from clients		$300,000
Less Beginning Accounts Receivable	(15,000)	
Plus Ending Accounts Receivable	9,000	
Plus Beginning Unearned Fee Revenue	0	
Less Ending Unearned Fee Revenue	(5,000)	
		(11,000)
Service Revenue (Accrual)		289,000

Expense Conversion.

The other half of the cash-to-accrual conversion process addresses cash paid for operating expenses, here of $170,000. January 1 Prepaid Expenses are recognized as expenses this year for cash payments that were made last year while December 31 Prepaid Expenses represent cash outlays this year for expenses to be recognized next year. Accordingly, (a) January 1 Prepaid Expenses must be added to the cash outlay in computing accrual-based expenses (the burden is this year's!) and (b) December 31 Prepaid Expenses must be subtracted from the cash outlay (the burden is next year's!).

Likewise, January 1 Accrued Liabilities arise from expenses recognized last year that call for cash outlays this year while December 31 Accrued Liabilities arise from expenses recognized this year that call for cash outlays next year. Accordingly, (a) January 1 Accrued Liabilities must be subtracted from the cash outlay and (b) December 31 Accrued Liabilities must be added to the cash outlay. Putting these steps together gives the following:

Cash paid for operating expenses		$170,000
Plus Beginning Prepaid Expenses	1,500	
Less Ending Prepaid Expenses	(3,200)	
Less Beginning Accrued Liabilities	(4,000)	
Plus Ending Accrued Liabilities	11,000	5,300
Operating Expenses (Accrual Basis)		175,300

Combining the information, the accrual income for the period is therefore the accrual basis revenue of $289,000 less the accrual basis operating expenses of $175,300, for a net income of $113,700.

Table 3-1 summarizes the relationship between elements in converting from a cash basis of accounting to an accrual basis of accounting.

Table 3-1: Converting from a Cash to Accrual Basis	
Revenue Side	
	(when cash > revenue, subtract; when cash < revenue, add)
Opening 1/1 Accounts Receivable	this year's cash but last year's services (so subtract)
Ending 12/31 Accounts Receivable	next year's cash but this year's services **so add**
Opening 1/1 Advance Fees	last year's cash but this year's services **so add**
Ending 12/31 Advance Fees	this year's cash but next year's service (so subtract)
Expense Side	
	(when cash > expense, add; when cash < expense, subtract)
Opening 1/1 Pre-Paid Expenses	last year's cash but this year's expense **so add**
Ending 12/31 Pre-Paid Expenses	this year's cash but next year's expense (so subtract)
Opening 1/1 Accrued Liabilities	this year's cash but last year's expense (so subtract)
Ending 12/31 Accrued Liabilities	next year's cash but this year's expense **so add**

Problem 3

In addition to the transactions reported in Problems 2A and 2B, assume that in August the following transactions of J&J also occurred. Prepare a revised balance sheet for J&J as of August 31 and a revised income statement of J&J for August to reflect all the transactions of J&J through August 31 (in the case of the balance sheet) and during August (in the case of the income statement). Also prepare supporting journal entries and T-Accounts.

13. (a) J&J subscribed for cellular telephone services from Verizon and paid Verizon a refundable security deposit of $150 in respect of the cell-phone. (b) During August, J&J incurred telephone charges of $50, for which it is billed on September 10, with payment due October 10.

14. J&J and Citybank renegotiated the loan terms, now agreeing that interest on the note accumulates as of August 1. Accordingly, account for the interest accrued on this note (originated in Chapter 2, Problem 2A, transaction 4).

15. J&J purchased a liability insurance policy, paying a premium of $1,200 for coverage from August 1 through the following January 31.

16. J&J became obligated to pay Jack and Jill bonuses of $300 and $400, respectively, pursuant to their employment agreements, which J&J intends to pay in cash in a future accounting period.

17. J&J agreed to provide repair services to the members of a local bicycle racing club, beginning September 1, at a monthly fee of $200. The club paid J&J $200 in advance as its fee for September.

18. J&J paid $1,000 for bicycle tires and tubes that it plans to resell. The tires and tubes were delivered to J&J.

Conceptual Questions 3

The accrual system's theoretical basis includes the stewardship function of accounting information. Financial reports should reflect how well managers are operating a business. The matching principle pushes this by insisting that expenses burden the income statement in the period they contribute to revenue generation (or earlier if this cannot be determined, under the conservatism principle). But isn't cash at least as critical? The exercise of converting a cash system to an accrual system is required in reverse under an accrual system, as expressed in the statement of cash flows (Chapter 9 discusses it). Why not just go to cash in the first place?

IFRS Note 3

In 2014, FASB and IASB issued jointly a converged standard on revenue recognition which drastically improved comparability of the top line in financial statements globally. FASB stated in its press release:

> Revenue is a vital metric for users of financial statements and is used to assess a company's financial performance and prospects. However, the previous requirements of both IFRS and U.S. GAAP were different and often resulted in different accounting for transactions that were economically similar. Furthermore, while revenue recognition requirements of IFRS lacked sufficient detail, the accounting requirements of U.S. GAAP were considered to be overly prescriptive and conflicting in certain areas.

> Responding to these challenges, the boards have developed new, fully converged requirements for the recognition of revenue in both IFRS and U.S. GAAP—providing substantial enhancements to the quality and consistency of how revenue is reported while also improving comparability in the financial statements of companies reporting using IFRS and U.S. GAAP.

> The core principle of the new standard is for companies to recognize revenue to depict the transfer of goods or services to customers in amounts that reflect the consideration (that is,

payment) to which the company expects to be entitled in exchange for those goods or services. . . .

Among differences between GAAP and IFRS concerning topics addressed in this Chapter are the following,

- Under GAAP, costs associated with restructuring of an enterprise or its business units are recognized when little discretion to avoid the costs exists, usually meaning when most of them have been incurred; IFRS contemplates recognition of restructuring costs when the restructuring is announced or begun.

- Major overhaul costs are expensed when incurred under GAAP, but may be treated as the exchange of one asset for another under IFRS (the technical term for this treatment is to capitalize the disbursement as an asset rather than treat it as an expense, a topic pursued in Chapter 5).

CHAPTER 4

INVENTORY AND THE COST OF GOODS SOLD

...

Chapter 3's illustrations involved companies rendering services. In this Chapter we add illustrations involving goods. Special accounting rules apply to transactions involving goods. Differences between accounting for services and accounting for goods may explain why invoices you may have received from automotive repair shops distinguish between "parts" and "labor."

Goods purchased or produced and held for sale are called *inventory*—in J&J's case, tubes and tires. Businesses engaged in buying goods and then selling them for profit are called *merchandising businesses*. (Those engaged in rendering services are called *service businesses*.) Inventory is central for any merchandising business because it is the process of buying inventory at a relatively lower *cost* and selling it at a relatively higher *price* that generates profits in the business. Measuring the amount of profits a firm generates from sales of goods requires determining revenues generated from selling the goods and the cost of purchasing those goods. Similar analysis applies to businesses engaged in producing goods from raw materials and selling them for profit (called *manufacturing businesses*).

Revenues generated from selling goods are called *sales* and are recorded in a revenue account called Sales. Expenses incurred in the purchase or production of goods are called the *cost of goods sold* and are recorded in an expense account called Cost of Goods Sold (abbreviated as "*COGS*"). Sales are recorded in the journal when made, usually upon delivery of the goods to the customer, and are in an amount equal to the price the customer is charged for them.

Recording and measuring the COGS are more complicated exercises because of two issues. The first is a bookkeeping question of when COGS should be recorded in the journal—when the goods are sold or at the end of each accounting period. The second is a computational question of how to determine the COGS, whether the journal entries are made at the time of sale or at the end of each period. In this Chapter, we take up each issue in turn. The Chapter concludes by noting additional inventory issues concerning, among other things, subtle differences in determining COGS associated with merchandising businesses compared to manufacturing businesses.

A. RECORDING COGS

Consider the following hypothetical. Larry's Law Firm publishes an "Individual's Guide to Legal Problems," that addresses in simple but practical ways a wide range of legal problems, such as how to prepare one's own will, how to file one's own divorce, how to handle one's own personal bankruptcy, and so on. On January 1, the Firm produces 100 books at a total cost to it in cash of $1,000 and on January 7 it sells 50 books at a sales price of $40 each (for a total of $2,000). How should the Firm account for the production and sale of this merchandise? There are two acceptable approaches, called the perpetual inventory system and the periodic inventory system.

Perpetual Inventory System.

In a perpetual inventory system, all elements of every merchandising transaction are recorded when they occur—the accounting records with respect to merchandising activities are constantly being updated during the reporting period to reflect all merchandising activities. When goods are purchased or produced, whether by the payment of cash or on credit, a left-side entry is made to an asset account called Inventory and a right-side entry is made to Cash or Accounts Payable, as appropriate. In the case of Larry's Firm, the production of books on January 1 would be recorded on that day as follows:

Inventory	$1,000	
Cash		$1,000

Notice that the amount being recorded to the Inventory account is equal to the amount that it cost to produce this inventory. Cost is always used to record the purchase or production of inventory, under all inventory bookkeeping systems. It follows from GAAP's cost principle, which requires that assets be recorded at their historical cost.

When goods are sold, whether for cash or on credit, a left-side entry is made to increase the related asset account, either Cash or Accounts Receivable, and a right-side entry is made to the revenue account Sales. In the case of Larry's Firm, the sale of books on January 7 would be recorded on that day as follows:

Cash	$2,000	
Sales		$2,000

In addition, upon the sale of goods, another entry is made according to the matching principle (match expenses to the revenue they generate). For sales of inventory, an entry is made to reflect the cost of goods being sold. For that purpose, a left-side entry is made to the expense account Cost of Goods Sold and a right-side entry is made to the asset account Inventory. Continuing with our example, the entry to reflect the cost of goods sold on January 7 would be as follows:

| COGS | $500 | |
| Inventory | | $500 |

Notice that this entry for both COGS and Inventory is based upon the cost of books to Larry's Firm, not the price for which they have been sold. This is necessary and appropriate for two reasons: it is that cost that we are trying to record in the COGS, and we are reporting amounts in the Inventory account at cost, as described above.

In addition to making the foregoing entries as each merchandising transaction occurs under a perpetual inventory system, it is also customary to indicate the quantity of goods (*e.g.*, the number of books) being added to inventory or sold out of inventory. That step usually is taken by the preparation of a *special inventory journal* for that purpose. During the course of the year, therefore, one might expect to be able to determine at any moment in time from these records the *physical quantity* of goods on hand in inventory. But also during the course of a typical year for a typical entity, some merchandise it purchases or produces will go to waste. A merchandiser of fine china, for example, will usually experience breakage and almost all merchandisers suffer some inventory losses through spoilage and employee theft.

As a result, merchandising businesses conduct a *physical inventory* at the end of the accounting period to reconcile the physical count of goods actually in inventory with the count that would be expected based on the journal entries. Any discrepancy is called *inventory shrinkage* and is reflected by an increase to the COGS account (a left-side entry) and a decrease to the Inventory account (a right-side entry). (During an accounting period, estimates of inventory shrinkage are made and recorded using more advanced techniques of a type considered in the next Chapter.)

Finally, in a perpetual inventory system, at the end of each reporting period closing entries must be made for the revenue and expense accounts. This is performed in the same way discussed in previous Chapters, with the Sales account being closed to the P & L Account in the same way all other revenue accounts are closed, and the COGS account being closed to the P & L Account in the same way all other expense accounts are closed. A T-Account for the asset Inventory is also prepared. It will reflect all entries that affected the asset account Inventory during the life of the business (*i.e.*, it is a permanent account, which is never closed). The ending inventory during each period will be reported on the balance sheet along with all other assets.

Periodic Inventory System.

A periodic inventory system differs from a perpetual inventory system principally in that neither the Inventory account nor the COGS account is kept up-to-date during a reporting period. Instead, those accounts are both brought up to date "*periodically*"—at the end of reporting periods.

With respect to the purchase or production of inventory during a period under the periodic inventory system, rather than making an entry directly to the asset account Inventory, a different account is used. It is called *Purchases* in the case of inventory bought from others and *Production* in the case of inventory produced internally by the entity. In the example of Larry's Firm, the production of books on January 1 would be recorded on that day as follows:

Production	$1,000	
Cash		$1,000

Notice that in using the asset account Production rather than the account Inventory, the entry's amount is still equal to the amount it cost to produce this inventory, just as in the perpetual inventory system. Again, this is necessary to comply with GAAP's cost principle.

With respect to sales of inventory during the period under the periodic inventory system, an entry is still made to the revenue account Sales when they occur (just as in the perpetual inventory system), but no separate entry is made to COGS as sales are made. This is the primary bookkeeping difference between the two inventory systems. For the example of Larry's Firm, the sale of books on January 7 would be recorded on that day as follows:

Cash	$2,000	
Sales		$2,000

The main consequence of the different bookkeeping approaches under the perpetual versus periodic inventory system concerns *closing entries*. By recording merchandising transactions to Inventory and COGS as they occur in the perpetual inventory system, no special closing entries are required at period end. But in the periodic inventory system, since no journal entries are made to those accounts during the period, both accounts must be brought up-to-date at period end. This requires some additional steps during the process of making closing entries.

A preliminary step is to conduct a physical inventory, which is also required in the perpetual inventory system as noted above. The difference is that the physical inventory called for when using the perpetual inventory system was necessary primarily to determine the extent of any inventory shrinkage during the period. In the periodic inventory system, the end-of-period physical inventory is also necessary to determine the ending balance to be reported in the Inventory account. That is equal to the cost of inventory determined to be on hand at period end. It is called *ending inventory*.

Once we have determined ending inventory, which we can abbreviate as "EI" for convenience, we can then calculate the COGS. The COGS for any period is equal to the total cost of goods available for sale during the period minus the total cost of goods left unsold at period end. In other words, COGS is equal to the cost of beginning inventory (which we can abbreviate as "BI" for convenience), plus the cost of purchases or production during the period (which we can abbreviate as "P" for convenience), minus the cost of ending inventory (EI). In symbols:

$$COGS = BI + P - EI$$

This formula is all that is necessary to make an arithmetic calculation of COGS in a periodic inventory system. The beginning inventory (BI) would be read off the balance sheet from the prior period, all purchases or production (P) would be summarized from the journal entries, and the ending inventory (EI) would be based on the physical count of inventory.

The formula's arithmetic is fine, but we also need to conduct this exercise in bookkeeping terms. In particular, we need to prepare an account for the COGS. To do so, we can prepare a series of closing entries, relating in each entry the COGS to each other account depicted in the foregoing equation, BI, P, and EI. Let's do so.

The first closing entry will transfer BI to COGS. This is done by *posting* the asset account, Inventory, from the prior period to the expense account, Cost of Goods Sold (COGS). This posting is necessary to reflect that inventory has a *dual character*. It is an asset and therefore a balance sheet account. But since the cost of inventory becomes the cost of goods sold as goods are sold, it also represents an expense, an income statement account. It is to reflect this dual aspect of inventory that we post the beginning inventory to the COGS account.

To illustrate the mechanics, assume that the beginning inventory was $5,000. In posting that account to the COGS, we are increasing the COGS account. Since the COGS is an expense account, being increased in amount, it calls for a left-side entry. The Inventory account, an asset account, is being decreased in amount so calls for a right-side entry. Our entry would therefore be as follows:

a. COGS $5,000

    Inventory $5,000

The posting entry with respect to P, purchases or production, follows the same logic. The COGS account (an expense account) is being increased in amount and so calls for a left-side entry and the Production account, an asset account, is being decreased in amount and so calls for a right-side entry. Our entry would therefore be as follows:

b. COGS $1,000

    Production $1,000

The entries with respect to ending inventory are the reverse of that in the foregoing examples. Here, we are reporting in the asset account Inventory the balance as of the period's end. Before making this entry, the balance in the Inventory account will have been zero (as a result of the posting in entry a above). We are now increasing the balance in Inventory to reflect the ending inventory. Accordingly, we will make a left-side entry to the asset account Inventory for the cost of Inventory left unused as of the period's end. Since the amount of that ending inventory represents goods not sold during the period, that portion of goods *does not* represent the cost of goods that were sold during the period. For that reason, we are effectively reducing the expense account COGS, therefore requiring a right-side entry to that account. Assuming that the ending inventory was $500, the entry would therefore be as follows:

c. Inventory $500

    COGS $500

These three closing entries are then used to prepare the T-Account for COGS, which would appear as follows.*

	COGS		
(a)	5,000	500	(c)
(b)	1,000	___	
	5,500		

Notice that the result of computing the COGS using the T-Account for COGS is the same result as would be obtained by simple mathematical application of the formula for COGS presented above:

---

* In connection with each entry to the COGS T-Account, it is also customary to note the quantity of goods being referred to, the cost per unit associated with them, and any inventory shrinkage during the period.

$$COGS = BI + P - EI$$

$$= 5,000 + 1,000 - 500$$

$$= \underline{5,500}$$

Having made these special closing entries in the periodic inventory system to compute the COGS, as well as the ending inventory, we have reached the point to which we were led in the perpetual inventory system without all these special closing entries. We are at the point, in other words, where we have a COGS expense account that can be closed out into the P & L Account with all other expense accounts as part of the ordinary closing process and we are also at the point where we have a balance in our asset account Inventory that can be reported on the balance sheet. We would also prepare closing entries for the Sales account, which will be closed out into the P & L Account like all other revenue accounts.

Which Is Better—the Perpetual or the Periodic Inventory System?

The perpetual inventory system and the periodic inventory system lead to the same ultimate results for the financial statements at the end of a period—Sales, the COGS, and the ending Inventory are all reported at the same amounts. The difference between the systems resides in how the books arrive at those results. In the perpetual system, the level of inventory and the cost of goods sold are known at every moment in time—perpetually—throughout the period (subject to shrinkage). In the periodic system, the level of inventory and the cost of goods sold are not known except at period end—periodically.

From a management perspective, this makes the perpetual system more advantageous because it can help make more efficient use of inventory flows. For example, it can enable inventory managers to minimize the amount of stock sitting idle in factories or warehouses at any moment in time. After all, it costs money to leave inventory sitting idle compared to keeping the flow up at a continuous pace. *Just-in-time inventory* is a name widely given to the strategy of managing inventory in a way that maximizes its flow—inventory stocking time is minimized. As a result, product cost will be lower, enabling the entity either to charge lower prices to its customers or to continue to charge the same price but generate more profit!

From a bookkeeping perspective, the advantage of a periodic system is that it does not require keeping track during the period of the cost of various goods being sold. Historically, for many businesses it was unduly burdensome to try to keep track of all goods sold according to cost. Consider a major department store selling thousands of different kinds of goods every day. Keeping track of the cost of all goods sold in the store could be time-consuming, at least if the tracking was all done by hand by sales clerks within the store.

Point-of-sale terminals and the price bar codes that you see on many consumer goods (and on the outside back cover of this book) are ways of implementing this technology and facilitating the maintenance of a perpetual inventory system at relatively low cost. As a result, most businesses of any substantial size use the perpetual inventory system, although smaller businesses continue to rely on the periodic inventory system. In either case, businesses must also adopt a convention to determine the cost of goods sold.

B. DETERMINING COGS

In the preceding discussion, we have assumed that the cost with respect to all items of inventory was constant over time and on that basis were able to distinguish between the two systems of recording COGS. Additional complexity arises, however, when the cost of producing or purchasing inventory is not constant over time but varies. For example, assume that on Monday a business pays $10 per unit for some goods and on Tuesday it pays $12 per unit for some goods of the same kind. Then on Friday it sells some of those goods for $20. What was the cost of the goods that it sold? Were the goods that were sold on Friday from the lot purchased on Monday, on Tuesday, or on some other previous day? Or, does it matter? There are two kinds of methods of determining the cost of goods sold for a period when those costs vary.

Specific Identification Method.

The first method of relating the cost of goods sold to the goods that are sold is called the *specific identification method*. Under this method, the actual cost of each item of inventory is specifically identified to the goods during the merchandising process—that is, from the time they are purchased or produced through the time they are sold. In the preceding example, the goods purchased on Monday would be tagged as "Goods Purchased on Monday at a cost cost per unitof $10" and the goods purchased on Tuesday would be tagged as "Goods Purchased on Tuesday at a cost per unit of $12" and so would all other goods purchased or produced at any time. When goods are sold, we would know exactly when they were purchased and at what cost. Similarly, when we count up goods on hand, we would also know which ones were sold and at what cost.

The specific identification method of tracking inventory costs implements the matching principle precisely by relating the cost of generating revenue to that revenue. The burden of doing this varies with the type of business and the type of inventory. For a dealer in fine arts—a seller of paintings and what not—this may be easy and also necessary to implement the matching principle. Indeed, GAAP requires businesses with that kind of inventory to use the specific identification method. But for the seller of huge volumes of essentially *fungible goods*—like the Firm's Legal Guide—the specific identification method may be both impracticable and also too time consuming. For these types of businesses, making some sort of cost flow assumption may be more desirable, and GAAP permits this.

Cost Flow Assumption Methods.

The cost flow assumption method recognizes that it may not be practicable to keep track of the actual cost of each item of inventory being sold by tagging goods purchased in lots. There are three alternative assumptions about cost flows that can be made in determining COGS.

The first alternative cost flow assumption is *FIFO*. FIFO is an acronym standing for "First-In, First-Out." It defines as an assumption for purposes of calculating COGS that the *first goods* in inventory to be purchased or produced are also the first goods in inventory sold. It is common to conceptualize this assumption by the image of a *pipeline*. Inventory is assumed to move through the production and sale process much as oil gushes through a pipeline—the first elements put in at one end are the first elements to emerge from the other end. In our Monday/Tuesday/Friday example, this assumption would mean that the goods sold on Friday were those purchased on Monday—the COGS for the Friday sale would be $10 per unit.

[handwritten margin note: FIFO first goods purchased, first goods sold]

The second alternative cost flow assumption is *LIFO*. LIFO is an acronym standing for "Last-In, First-Out." In opposition to FIFO, it defines as an assumption for purposes of calculating COGS that the *last goods* in inventory to be purchased or produced are the first goods in inventory sold. It is common to conceptualize this assumption by the image of a *barrel*. Inventory is assumed to be put into a barrel and sold off the top of the barrel—the first elements into the barrel stay in the longest and the goods that are sold first are the goods that are put in the barrel more recently (or last). In our Monday/Tuesday/Friday example, this assumption would mean that the goods sold on Friday were those purchased on Tuesday—the COGS for the Friday sale would be $12 per unit.*

[handwritten margin note: LIFO last goods purchased → first goods to be sold]

The third alternative cost flow assumption is based on neither discrete image associated with LIFO and FIFO but instead takes an *average*. The idea is that neither a barrel nor a pipeline nor any other heuristic image properly captures the flow. The gas station is an easy example, where the inventory is resupplied weekly at potentially different prices but the gas obviously all mixes together and cannot be specifically identified nor can it be seen purely as either a barrel or a pipeline. In this context, the best thing to do is to take an average of the cost of each purchase of inventory,

---

*   FIFO and LIFO also go by other acronymous nicknames, less commonly used and more informal. FIFO's alias is LISH, which stands for "Last-In-Still-Here" and LIFO's alias is FISH, which stands for "First-In-Still-Here."

weighted according to the various quantities purchased at different times. In our Monday/Tuesday/Friday example, this assumption would mean that the goods sold on Friday were taken evenly from those purchased on Monday and on Tuesday—the COGS for the Friday sale would be $11 per unit.

Assumptions Are Not Reality.

None of the cost flow assumptions used to determine the COGS pretends to reflect the actual COGS, in the way that the specific identification method does. They are chosen instead to avoid the burden of keeping track of reality so closely. And just as GAAP permits an entity selling fungible goods to choose to employ either the specific identification method or a cost flow assumption method, it also permits an entity opting for a cost flow assumption to choose which sort of cost flow assumption it will make. But notice from our Monday/Tuesday/Friday example that the resulting COGS will be very different under each assumption: the COGS for the Friday sale would be either $10, $11 or $12, depending on the assumption made.

The consequence for the financial statements of choosing between alternative cost flow assumptions can therefore be significant and an understanding of those consequences becomes crucial. To illustrate the sorts of consequences that follow from these choices, let us take an example of how financial statements would be affected by a choice between the FIFO or the LIFO cost flow assumption. We will illustrate the difference first in terms of the consequence in determining the ending inventory (the balance sheet consequence) and then in determining the expense COGS, which in turn affects gross profit (the income statement consequence).

Balance Sheet Consequences.

Assume that Larry's Firm begins the year on January 1 with 200 books in stock ("BI" in Table 4-1), which cost $10 each to produce ("unit" in Table 4-1). Assume also that the Firm produces 200 books each on three separate occasions during the current year, but at an increasing cost per unit (noted in Table 4-1), and ends the year on December 31 with 300 books in stock ("EI" in Table 4-1). This information is depicted in Table 4-1.

Table 4-1. Inventory-COGS Exercise			
Date	Units	Unit Cost	Total Cost
BI 1/1	200	$10	$2,000
3/15	200	11	2,200
6/15	200	12	2,400
9/15	200	13	2,600
EI 12/31	300		?

The balance sheet question is: what is the cost of the ending inventory? The consequences of choosing between LIFO and FIFO as the cost flow assumption will become clear if we calculate the ending inventory using each method.

Recall that **FIFO** assumes those books produced *first* are the books sold first. As a result of this assumption, we are also assuming that the 300 books in stock at the end of the year are composed of books that were produced later in the year (last in) rather than earlier in time (first in). Accordingly, the cost to be placed on those 300 books for inventory purposes is the cost of producing the *last* 300 books during the year. In particular, the 300 in stock at year end would be deemed to consist of all 200 produced on 9/15 plus 100 of those produced on 6/15.

Looked at this another way. When reporting inventory using FIFO and the tabular presentation of yearly inventory flow, count *up from the bottom* of the table until you reach the total ending inventory quantity and report each quantity at its unit cost. In this example, therefore, the ending inventory would be equal to the sum of 200 x 13 plus 100 x 12 for a total of $3,800. This method and result can be depicted graphically:

Balance Sheet Consequence Using FIFO

Date	Units		Unit Cost	Total Cost	
BI 1/1	200		$10	$2,000	
3/15	200		11	2,200	
6/15	200	100	12	2,400	1,200
9/15	200		13	2,600	
EI 12/31	300			3,800	

Under LIFO, alternatively, recall that the assumption is that the books produced *last* are the books that are sold first. As a result of this assumption, we are also assuming that the 300 books in stock at the end of the year are composed of books that were produced earlier in time (first in) rather than later (last in). Accordingly, the cost to be placed on those 300 books for inventory purposes is the cost of producing the *first* 300 books during the year. In particular, the 300 in stock at year end would be deemed to consist of all 200 produced in prior periods (what we began with as beginning inventory) plus 100 of those produced on 3/15.

Again, look at this another way. When reporting inventory using LIFO and the tabular presentation of yearly inventory flow, count *down from the top* of the table until you reach the total ending inventory quantity and report each quantity at its unit cost. In this example, therefore, the ending inventory would be equal to the sum of 200 x 10 plus 100 x 11 for a total of $3,100. This method and result can also be depicted graphically:

Balance Sheet Consequence Using LIFO

Date	Units		Unit Cost	Total Cost	
BI 1/1	200		$10	$2,000	
3/15	~~200~~	100	11	~~2,200~~	1,100
~~6/15~~	~~200~~		~~12~~	~~2,400~~	
~~9/15~~	~~200~~		~~13~~	~~2,600~~	
EI 12/31	300			3,100	

Notice the significant difference, in the report of ending inventory, of using LIFO versus FIFO. The difference arises precisely because during the period under consideration prices of production have been rising. As a result, in such periods of rising prices (sometimes called *inflationary periods*) the ending inventory under FIFO will be higher than the ending inventory under LIFO. This difference obviously has a significant impact on the balance sheet because the reported amount of the asset Inventory will vary depending on whether LIFO or FIFO has been used—it will be higher under FIFO and lower under LIFO. There will also be significant follow-through effects on the income statement.

Income Statement Consequences.

Start with a statement of what *gross profit on sales* is. It is the amount by which Sales exceeds COGS (the price charged to customers for sales of goods less the cost to the entity of purchasing or producing those goods). More formally, this can be written as follows, where GP stands for gross profit on sales, S stands for sales and COGS stands for the cost of goods sold:

$$GP = S - COGS$$

Let's continue with the preceding example to calculate the expense, COGS, first under FIFO and then under LIFO. Recall from Table 4-1 that the Firm's beginning inventory ("BI") was $2,000 and that the cost of its purchases ("P") during the year totaled $7,200 (*i.e.*, the sum of the purchases on 3/15 of $2,200, plus 6/15 of $2,400, plus 9/15 of $2,600). We then calculated its ending inventory ("EI") using *FIFO* to be $3,800 and using *LIFO* to be $3,100. We emphasized that this calculation implied a significant consequence for the balance sheet—ending inventory reported on the balance sheet using LIFO was lower than under FIFO.

Now we can plug these numbers into the formula for calculating the expense, COGS, and we will see the first consequence for the income statement of choosing FIFO versus LIFO. Recall from the preceding section that the cost of goods sold is calculated by the formula:

$$COGS = BI + P - EI$$

Under *FIFO* in this example, the cost of goods sold calculation would therefore be as follows:

$$COGS_{FIFO} = \$2,000 + \$7,200 - \$3,800$$
$$COGS_{FIFO} = \underline{\$5,400}$$

Under *LIFO*, the cost of goods sold calculation would look like this:

$$COGS_{LIFO} = \$2,000 + \$7,200 - \$3,100$$
$$COGS_{LIFO} = \underline{\$6,100}$$

This comparison shows that with respect to the expense COGS, using LIFO implies a higher amount for that expense than FIFO does. And this simply follows from our earlier determination that the EI under LIFO was lower than under FIFO.

Any change in the level of an expense account will of course also have the effect of changing the bottom line income amount. In the context of inventories, this can be seen clearly if we proceed to calculate the *gross profit on sales* in this example, using the formula:

$$GP = S - COGS$$

Assume that sales during the period totaled $10,000. Then under *FIFO* in this example, the gross profit calculation would be as follows:

$$GP_{FIFO} = \$10,000 - \$5,400$$
$$GP_{FIFO} = \underline{\$4,600}$$

Under *LIFO* in this example, the gross profit calculation would look like this:

$$GP_{LIFO} = \$10,000 - \$6,100$$

$$GP_{LIFO} = \underline{\$3,900}$$

This comparison shows that with respect to gross profits, using LIFO implies a lower amount of gross profit than FIFO does. And this simply follows from the foregoing determination that the expense COGS is higher under LIFO (which, at the risk of belaboring things, in turn simply followed from our earlier determination that the EI under LIFO was lower than under FIFO).

While all this may follow "simply" as the foregoing text has said several times, it remains for many people difficult to follow. Two possible ways of coping with that difficulty may be helpful.

The first is a mnemonic: when thinking of LIFO versus FIFO and their consequences in an inflationary period, one could emphasize that the *L* in LIFO stands for *L*ower bottom *L*ines. That is, the bottom line report on the balance sheet for ending inventory will be *lower under LIFO* and the bottom line report of gross profit on the income statement will be *lower under LIFO*. What will not be lower under LIFO is the COGS, and to keep the mnemonic helpful, one could for this purpose emphasize that COGS is not a "bottom line" number but is an intermediate one (it is, after all, an expense account).

The second way of conceptualizing the relationship between FIFO and LIFO and the elements of the inventory equation is graphic. Consider the following chart.

Inflationary Period (Rising Purchase Prices or Costs)			
	EI	COGS	GP
FIFO	Higher	Lower	Higher
LIFO	Lower	Higher	Lower

To summarize, in an inflationary period, using FIFO rather than LIFO will result in reporting the asset inventory on the balance sheet at a higher level; and since this means that the COGS (an expense) for that period is accordingly lower, using FIFO rather than LIFO will also result in reporting income on the income statement at a higher level. (Note: all that we have said above about the impact of using FIFO versus LIFO was with respect to inflationary periods; in deflationary periods, the effects are exactly the opposite.)

Evaluation.

FIFO presents inventory costs on the balance sheet more accurately, but presents expenses on the income statement less accurately. The former is true because FIFO records inventory at current costs—so balance sheets are up-to-date. The latter is true because FIFO does not match current COGS with current sales—the COGS is based on the costs of the oldest items in inventory while sales are being made and reported at current prices. As such, during inflationary periods FIFO tends to understate the COGS and thus report artificially high profit levels.

In contrast, LIFO is generally more accurate in the income statement (for it reflects current COGS) and less accurate in the balance sheet (for it reflects historical costs). Since the inaccuracies in the balance sheet tend to err on the side of understating costs of inventory (and hence carrying amounts) it is more in harmony with GAAP's principle of conservatism. On the other hand, the degree of accuracy in the income statement depends on the entity continuing to maintain quantities of inventory at least equal to the quantities reflected on the balance sheet.

If an entity using LIFO begins to sell inventory in greater quantities than the amount listed on the balance sheet, then its reported income in respect of those sales will be burdened by those outdated costs—producing artificially high reported income. This phenomenon is referred to as a *LIFO liquidation*, and the degree to which it is done is measured by what are called *LIFO layers* (*i.e.*, the degree to which the LIFO-based historical costs are "eaten into" as the basis of the COGS). LIFO liquidations should be disclosed in the footnotes to the financial statements. To prepare for them, moreover, and to reconcile LIFO and FIFO's trade-offs somewhat, it is also desirable to maintain records of the difference LIFO creates between current costs of inventory replacement and the historical costs shown on the balance sheet (called *LIFO reserves*).

C. LOWER OF COST OR MARKET

We have emphasized that inventories are recorded and reported at cost. We said that was necessary to comply with GAAP's *cost principle*. But recall again GAAP's *principle of conservatism*. What if inventory that cost $10 per unit declines in value to $8 per unit, because of obsolescence for example? Under GAAP's principle of conservatism, there is a preference for understating asset amounts rather than overstating them. To implement that principle in the case of inventories (as well as other assets to be discussed in later Chapters), accountants devised a subsidiary principle, called the principle of *lower of cost or market*. It is abbreviated as "*LCM*" and requires that inventories (and such other assets) be reported at cost, or at market value if that market value is lower. Adjustments to report inventory at market, when it is lower than cost, cannot be reversed.

Market values and costs may depart from one another for a variety of reasons. In the retailing industry, for example, market values of goods in the ordinary course are usually higher than cost because of the margin retailers impose in the course of selling. On the other hand, slow-moving or obsolete inventory often sells for less than cost. To the extent that inventory market value has declined below its cost, the account balance is adjusted at period in a manner similar to the way inventory shrinkage is recorded. As discussed above, the asset account inventory is reduced (by a right-side entry) and the expense account COGS is increased (by a left-side entry).

Determining market value for inventory accounting purposes is somewhat complex. In principle, market value is what it would cost the company at current prices to replace the inventory (called *replacement cost*). But GAAP imposes two constraints. First, the market value amount cannot exceed the inventory's *net realizable value* to the entity (that is, its selling price less its selling costs). This is called the *ceiling*. Second, the market value amount cannot be less than the *net realizable value minus a normal profit* (that is, the selling price less selling costs and minus a normal profit). This is called the *floor*.

Consider the following data as an example of hitting a ceiling:

Inventory at cost	$10
Replacement cost	10
Selling price	14
Selling costs	6

In this example, inventory at cost and replacement cost are the same, $10, so it appears the lower of cost or market rule isn't implicated. But since inventory will sell for $14 with associated selling costs of $6, the net realizable value is $8. That is the market value and since that is less than inventory at cost, the inventory should be carried at that amount.

Consider this example of hitting a floor:

Inventory at cost	$15
Replacement cost	10
Selling price	20
Selling cost	5
Normal selling profit	2

Measured as replacement cost, market appears to be $10. But the second constraint means market cannot be lower than net realizable value minus a normal profit. Here, that means a selling price of $20, less selling costs of $5, giving net realizable value of $15. Then subtract from that $15 the normal selling profit of $2 and you get $13, which is the floor (the lowest amount at which to carry the inventory).

A rule of thumb emerges in determining market for purposes of implementing the LCM principle applied to inventory. Calculate replacement cost, net realizable value, and net realizable value minus a normal profit. Market is the median (middle) of the three figures. In the immediately preceding example, the figures were replacement cost = $10, net realizable value = $15, and net realizable value minus a normal selling profit = $13. Market was $13.

Though the LCM is defended under the conservatism principle, notice a tension. When market is below cost it would be conservative to use market rather than cost, yielding a lower reported ending inventory and a lower net income for that period. But remember that lower ending inventory in one period implies higher net income for the succeeding period. This is not conservative. The tension has produced some debate among accounting theorists concerning the LCM principle as applied to inventory.

D. COST ACCOUNTING

We assumed in this Chapter's illustration of Larry's Firm that we knew what the production costs for its books were. Indeed, for retailers and other pure merchandisers the cost of goods sold and the carrying amount of inventory can be readily determined by inspecting invoices the entity receives from its suppliers. For entities like Larry's Firm that convert raw materials into finished goods there is an additional complexity in measuring *production costs* (also known as *conversion costs*).

Production costs consist of the cost of materials, the cost of labor and a fair share of related overhead (general costs of an operation such as administrative costs). The process of assigning production costs to goods is called *cost accounting*. Production costs are first classified into either product costs or period costs. *Product costs* are those directly associated with the goods, such as direct materials and direct labor, and are treated in the way discussed in this Chapter—as part of inventory during the production process and as part of cost of goods sold when the product is sold. Cost accounting systems are designed to track the link between these costs and particular goods.

Period costs are those associated with the general manufacturing and sales effort and are expensed as incurred. *Overhead* can be partly a period cost and partly a product cost. The heating bill for the sales office would be a period cost (expensed as incurred) while the heating bill for the plant would be a product cost (included in inventory and eventually therefore in cost of goods sold). Overhead costs treated as product costs are added to the direct materials and direct labor costs to determine the total amount to be added to the inventory account (and eventually included in cost of goods sold).

E. DISCLOSURE AND TAX MATTERS

Entities with inventory must disclose in the footnotes to their financial statements the method they use to determine the cost of goods sold—that is the specific identification method or a cost flow assumption, and, if a cost flow assumption, whether LIFO, FIFO, or an average. In addition, any change that is made in the method of determining the cost of goods sold must be disclosed, as well as its balance sheet and income statement effects.

Distinguishing Sub-Categories of Inventory.

In the foregoing discussion, we have treated inventory as a single category, without considering the possibility that many goods involve assembly from a number of component parts. For example, a bicycle consists of numerous parts, such as tires, a seat, handle bars, and a chain. For purposes of inventory counting and reporting of cost, how should these component parts be treated? It would be a mistake to count and record only those goods that have been completely assembled—only completed bicycles—because all these component parts must be bought or manufactured and they will contribute to the final product sold.

Accordingly, the component parts are also treated as part of inventory, and to do so all the principles discussed above remain applicable, and the consequence is that they are tracked and recorded separately on the entity's internal books. In addition, supplemental data breaking down the components of inventory are usually presented separately in the notes to the financial statements, breaking the categories down into such elements as raw materials (tires and tubes, for example), work-in-progress (the bicycle in stages of the production process), and finished goods (the bicycle ready for the showroom floor).

Tax Matters.

Tax policy makers understand the consequences, for income tax liabilities, that choosing between LIFO and FIFO present. One benefit of LIFO's tendency to report lower income is that this means a lower income tax obligation. The awareness is illustrated by two rules that are intended to limit an entity's ability to manage its taxable income according to the choice. First, an entity must use the same approach to inventory for purposes of both its financial statements prepared in accordance with GAAP (which are provided to investors) and its financial statements prepared for purposes of calculating its income tax liability (which are provided to the government). (In other areas, different statements are permitted to be used, as we shall see in the next Chapter.)

Second, an entity can only change inventory flow assumptions one time—it cannot shift back and forth between LIFO and FIFO depending on forecasts about inflation or any other factors. Tax law also has special rules dealing with LIFO reserves and LIFO liquidations, but those complexities are beyond the scope of this book. In addition, tax policy makers periodically consider disallowing using LIFO for federal income tax purposes entirely.

Illustration 4-1.

Look at Illustration 4-1, an excerpt from a full set of financial statements. It discloses in Note 1 that the company reports inventories, following the principle of lower of cost or market, according to the FIFO method. It discloses in Note 2 the breakdown of inventory in two categories, raw materials as well as "Work in process, finished stock and packaging materials."

Illustration 4-1 also provides an example of the income statement presentation of Sales, COGS, and the resulting Gross Profit on Sales. From the income statement, the first line item reports "Net Sales." This is a slightly refined category of what we have been calling Sales. The refinement is reflected by the addition of the word "Net" and means that the amount being reported has been reduced by the amount of all returns, refunds, and similar adjustments impacting the original, gross, sales total. The next line item reports the COGS, as we have been discussing it, and subtracts that amount from Net Sales to give the Gross Profit.

The word "Gross" is used here to denote that this is the amount of profit generated by the company's sales of inventory less only the amounts that it cost to acquire or produce the inventory—the COGS. Other expenses that went into the activity of selling the inventory as such, as well as the other expenses of running the business, are not yet reflected in this figure—hence the term Gross. Those items are subtracted in succeeding line items on the income statement.

The largest category of other expenses of operating a business entity is often collectively referred to as (and pronounced) "*SG & A*", which stands for the expenses of "*Selling, General, and Administrative.*" In Illustration 4-1, that category is slightly broader, and includes, as the account title announces, the costs of *Advertising, Marketing, and Research and Development.* Were any of these separate expenses deemed sufficiently material, they would be given their own separate account and reported separately on the income statement. For this company, a manufacturer of low-cost consumer products, it appears that management regards the amount spent on research and development over time as not sufficiently material to warrant separate presentation.

ILLUSTRATION 4–1

BIC CORPORATION AND SUBSIDIARIES

NOTES TO CONSOLIDATED FINANCIAL STATEMENTS

1. SUMMARY OF SIGNIFICANT ACCOUNTING POLICIES: A summary of significant accounting policies for BIC Corporation and its subsidiaries (the "Corporation"), manufacturers and distributors of high-quality, low-cost consumer products, is as follows: . . .

Inventories Inventories are valued at the lower of cost (determined on the first-in, first-out basis) or market.

* * * * *

2. INVENTORIES: Inventories consist of the following (in thousands):

	This Year	Last Year
Work in process, finished stock and packaging materials	$46,503	$49,363
Raw materials	7,860	10,063
Total	$54,363	$59,426

* * * * *

BIC CORPORATION AND SUBSIDIARIES

STATEMENTS OF CONSOLIDATED INCOME
FOR THE LAST THREE FISCAL YEARS
(In thousands, except for per share data)

	This Year	Last Year	Year Before
Net Sales	$475,118	$439,311	$417,377
Cost of Goods Sold	242,457	235,820	225,806
Gross Profit	232,661	203,491	191,571
Advertising, Selling, General & Administrative, Marketing & Research and Development Expenses	121,694	112,851	110,742

Problem 4A

Based on the following assumed data with respect to the inventory of a merchandising business with no other source of revenue, make the following calculations first under FIFO and then under LIFO: (a) the ending inventory, (b) the cost of goods sold, and (c) the gross profit on sales.

Date	Units	Unit Cost	Total Cost
BI	100	$20	$2,000
1/15	200	21	4,200
6/15	200	25	5,000
8/15	100	30	3,000
EI	200		?

Assume that net sales were $12,000.

Problem 4B

In September, J&J begins to sell tires and tubes, and to provide repair services. Prepare an income statement for September and a balance sheet as of September 30 (and supporting journal entries, T-Accounts, adjusting entries, inventory entries and closing entries), taking account of the following transactions.

J&J has not yet developed a computerized system to enable it to track its cost of goods sold as they are sold, and it will therefore use a *periodic inventory system*. On the other hand, Jill thinks it will be very easy at the end of each month to determine which tubes and tires still in inventory were bought at what times and at what costs because J&J's supplier tags all the goods it sells to J&J by date and price. J&J will therefore use the *specific identification method* rather than any cost flow assumption.

19. (a) During the month of September, J&J provided repair services valued at $8,400 to its customers. In the course of the month, $1,900 in services were charged, and the rest were paid in cash. (b) At the end of September, $1,600 of these charges were outstanding and $300 had been paid.

20. J&J received $1,000 in payments from customers who charged services during August.

21. J&J provided the promised services to the bicycle club (not included in services noted in transaction 19); at the end of the month, though, the club terminated the arrangement with J&J because its members preferred to arrange their own repairs. (*See* Transaction 17, Problem 3.)

22. (a) J&J paid Jack and Jill each a salary of $1,500 for the month; (b) it made no payment with respect to the bonuses they earned in August,

but incurred an obligation to pay additional bonuses of $450 and $500, respectively.

23. J&J established a line of credit with its supplier and purchased, for resale, additional tubes and tires at a total cost of $1,300, all paid for on credit.

24. J&J sold $2,500 in tubes and tires during the month, $1,800 in cash and $700 on credit.

25. As part of a promotional campaign, Verizon waived J&J's phone charges in respect of September.

Finally, though not a transaction, J&J conducted a physical inventory on September 30 and determined that it had on hand quantities of tubes and tires that had cost it a total of $1,250.

Conceptual Questions 4

During inflationary periods, FIFO is more faithful to economic reality in the balance sheet and LIFO is more faithful to economic reality in the income statement. In which statement should we seek to promote greater faithfulness? Should you be able to use LIFO in the income statement and FIFO in the balance sheet? As it exists, GAAP calls for articulation between the two reports. That is, revenues minus expenses equals earnings and this amount determines changes in owners' equity. So the same method of determining the cost of goods sold and inventory must be used in both statements. Why not allow the two to bear different measurements (that is, to allow for non-articulation)?

IFRS Note 4

Among differences between GAAP and IFRS concerning topics addressed in this Chapter are the following:

- GAAP allows choice of measuring inventory using LIFO or FIFO (plus other methods); IFRS prohibits LIFO.

- GAAP measures inventory at the lower of cost or market, using a fairly complicated formulaic approach to determining what market value is for that purpose; IFRS measures inventory at the lower of cost or "net realizable value," a concept that may often, but not inevitably, yield measurements identical or similar to GAAP measurements.

- Whereas GAAP adjustments to lower of cost or market cannot be reversed, IFRS adjustments to lower of cost or net realizable value must be reversed in some cases.

CHAPTER 5

FIXED ASSETS AND DEPRECIATION

■ ■ ■

Most business enterprises acquire and use in their operations assets that have an expected useful life of an extended period of time, measured in years. [Assets that have an expected useful life in excess of one year are called *fixed assets*.] Decisions about how to account for the acquisition and use of such assets are governed by the *matching principle*. Given that the asset will be used for periods exceeding one year, it therefore will also contribute to the enterprise's earning power during that time. Accordingly, under the matching principle the cost of acquiring the asset should also be allocated over that time. In other words, they should not be "expensed" entirely in the period in which the outlay was made.

Accountants have devised several alternative methods for making this allocation of cost over time, all of which go generically under the label of [*depreciation*.] That label captures the general idea of allocating the cost of a fixed asset over its expected useful life. The depreciation rules do not apply to land, on the theory that it has an infinite useful life.

This Chapter introduces the alternative depreciation methods. It shows how this concept relates to other concepts we have developed, identifies a series of judgments that go into the exercise, presents the bookkeeping underlying the exercise, and shows the consequences of the choices. Concluding sections address additional matters, including how GAAP depreciation differs from tax depreciation and how it eludes effects of inflation.

A.   RELATIONSHIP TO OTHER CONCEPTS

As you consider the technique of allocating the cost of a fixed asset over time, notice some conceptual similarities between the accountant's approach to depreciation and the concept of the accrual system of accounting (Chapter 3) and accounting for inventories (Chapter 4). The similarities arise because each device seeks in some way to respect the matching principle—each raises a timing problem of allocating economic events to discrete accounting time periods.

Recall from our discussion of the accrual system of accounting, for example, how the pre-payment of a lease becomes an asset—called prepaid lease—that is reduced over its term of enjoyment and a corresponding expense is recorded for each period the lease (the premises it governs) was enjoyed—called lease expense. In bookkeeping terms, this was recorded as follows:

Lease Expense	$x,xxx	
Prepaid Lease		$x,xxx

Recall from the previous Chapter that inventory—an asset—becomes an expense—a part of COGS—over time. In the perpetual inventory system that dual character of inventory was reflected in the accounting records throughout reporting periods, by making ongoing entries to Inventory and the COGS. In the periodic inventory system, we made closing entries specifically to reflect this dual character. In particular, to transfer beginning inventory into cost of goods sold, we made a closing entry in the following form:

COGS	$x,xxx	
Beginning Inventory		$x,xxx

Conceptually, the accounting approaches to fixed assets parallel these approaches. Fixed assets are "consumed" by the business in a conceptually similar way to inventory or prepaid expenses—they are employed in the business to generate revenue from period to period. Following the matching principle, which also drives the system of accruals and inventory accounting, the financial statements of a business will more accurately reflect the financial condition and performance of the business if the cost of fixed assets are allocated as an expense over all the periods during the asset's useful life. In slightly more technical language, depreciation enables entities to charge against revenue on a regular and periodic basis the cost of the fixed assets it uses to produce its revenue.

Recall also that for inventory accounting GAAP allows alternative conventions for recording the cost of goods sold (the perpetual or periodic inventory systems) and for determining the cost of goods sold (the specific identification method or a cost flow assumption, whether LIFO, FIFO, or an average). Similarly, GAAP allows alternative conventions for allocating the cost of fixed assets to different accounting periods and thus for reporting the fixed asset at any point in time. Also as with inventory conventions, which are not necessarily concerned with tracing actual cost flow, these conventions do not seek to show the actual physical wearing out of the fixed asset over time. It is not practicable given many different fixed assets and given the difficulty and subjectivity associated with conducting periodic or continuous appraisals.

The absence of a conscious effort to link depreciation expense with physical erosion of fixed assets should not be mistaken to mean that depreciation expense is a phantom expense that can be ignored. On the contrary, the amount of depreciation remains a useful proxy for the level of outlays to buy or expand fixed assets (called *capital expenditures*) likely to be required for the business to maintain its current business and financial performance and competitive position. The proxy may be imperfect, but the amounts are real.

B. REQUIRED JUDGMENTS

Several preliminary judgments are necessary to allocate the cost of a fixed asset over time. All these judgments have significant consequences for the income statement and balance sheet over time.

Historical Cost.

The first judgment required for the depreciation exercise is to determine the asset's *historical cost*. In many cases this will be easy. If an entity pays the seller of some machinery $20,000 for the machinery, the historical cost is obviously $20,000. But what if the entity thereafter pays an additional $2,000 to have the machinery installed and adapted slightly for its particular production processes? The question is whether the $2,000 should be deemed part of the fixed asset's historical cost and therefore allocated to its useful life over time or whether it should be treated as a one-time expense. The answer GAAP gives is that the amount paid for installation and adaptation is a part of the cost of acquisition and not an expense and is therefore included in the historical cost of the fixed asset to be allocated over time.

installation —> historical cost.

Trickier decisions arise with respect to maintaining and improving fixed assets. For example, should the cost to replace a gasket on a machine's motor be deemed part of the historical cost of the fixed asset or treated as an expense? Here GAAP's bright-line rules blur and judgment becomes necessary. The operative test is one of reasonableness and involves considering whether the outlay in respect of some asset extended its useful life, or was simply a necessary repair incidental to its ordinary operation.

Scrap Value and the Depreciable Base.

The second judgment required in the cost allocation exercise concerns deciding what portion of any fixed asset will not be used up as such during its life. Suppose, for example, that the machinery referred to above will still have some punch even after the entity will have withdrawn it from the production process. The thing can be sold, let us assume, at the end of its life for $1,500, to be welded into scrap metal and recycled. The $1,500 is called the fixed asset's *scrap value* (or, equivalently, *salvage value* or *residual value*). It means that the historical cost to be allocated over time should exclude that amount. It is an amount that is not consumed during the course of usage. The judgment required, therefore, is estimating the scrap value of the fixed asset, a judgment that must be made at the outset in order to decide how much of the historical cost is to be allocated over time. This amount to be allocated is referred to as the *depreciable base* of the fixed asset (or, equivalently, the *net cost* or *depreciable cost*).

Expected Useful Life. $DB = HC - SV$

The third judgment necessary concerns how long the fixed asset will remain in use in the production process. Colloquially, the question is how long will it last; in accounting terms, the question is what is the fixed asset's *expected useful life* (or, equivalently, its *service life*). One could compare the historical experience of similar types of assets to make an educated guess about the expected useful life of a particular asset. If a machine very similar to the one being purchased has just been retired after 20 years of service, perhaps deciding that the expected useful life of the new machine is 20 years also makes sense.

We could extrapolate in general terms about the expected useful life of categories of assets, a practice widely followed by accountants. As a matter of convention, for example, it is customary to start with the proposition that the expected useful life of a building is 30 years. In any event, the estimate of expected useful life must be made bearing in mind the objective of the exercise, which is to match outlays to the periods in which they will contribute to the revenue generating power of the entity over time. Accountants often draw on guidelines contained in the Internal Revenue Code to determine appropriate estimates of expected useful lives of fixed assets (refer to Section E below).

Time of Acquisitions (and Dispositions).

A final question concerns when an asset is acquired or deemed acquired. Several conventions exist. The first is straightforward: depreciation exercises are applied based upon when an acquisition (or disposition) actually occurs. Others are conventions to make computations easier when assets are acquired or disposed of in the middle of an accounting period. One convention calls for rounding to the nearest whole month, so that assets bought before the 16th are treated as if acquired on the first of that month and those acquired then or after are treated as if acquired on the first of the following month. Another, called the *half-year convention*, calls for recording six months' of depreciation on all assets acquired in any given year, on the grounds that randomness of acquisitions throughout the year will average out. In each of these conventions, similar treatments are applied to asset dispositions.

Significance of Judgments.

The foregoing preliminary judgments required for depreciation exercises have significant consequences for both the balance sheet and the income statement over a period of years. For example, the more costs associated with the acquisition of an asset—its purchase price plus its installation costs for example—the more spread out will be their treatment as an expense. Depreciating these costs over time rather than expensing them when incurred therefore increases reported income in the period of actual outlay and decreases reported income in the later periods to which the outlay is charged. As well, the lower the scrap value placed on a fixed asset, the greater its depreciable base and therefore the greater the burden on reported income. Likewise, the longer the period of time over which the allocation is made the less the impact on reported income will be in any given period. Thus, the longer the expected useful life placed on a fixed asset, the less impact on reported income it will have in any given year, but such impact as there is will extend over a longer period of time.

All these effects will be most acute, of course, to an entity for which depreciation expense is a substantial portion of total expenses. The more *asset intensive* a business is, in other words, the more sensitive its earnings will be to judgments that go into the depreciation exercise.

C. DEPRECIATION BOOKKEEPING

With these initial judgments made, we can discuss the bookkeeping steps required to account for a fixed asset. There are three temporal phases of the exercise: upon acquisition of the asset; during its life; and upon disposition. In each step, bear in mind that two GAAP principles are implicated by the depreciation exercise: the cost principle requires that we record and report the fixed asset at its historical cost, and the matching principle requires that we record an allocable portion of that cost as a burden to net income during the fixed asset's useful life.

Upon Acquisition.

Upon acquisition of a fixed asset, we want to get the asset reflected in the appropriate balance sheet account for that asset or that asset type. To do so, we record the asset at its cost—remember the cost principle—as a left-side entry under that asset category. For example, if Larry's Firm bought a copier machine at a cost of $10,000, plus $1,000 to install it, the asset has a cost of $11,000. Assuming we paid cash for the machine and its installation, we would make the following journal entry:

	L	R
Copier	$11,000	
Cash		$11,000

During Asset's Life.

Under the matching principle, each year during a fixed asset's expected useful life, a portion of the cost will be allocated as an expense. That expense is called *depreciation expense* for that asset. Assume that we have determined that the Firm's new copier has an expected useful life of

4 years, and a projected scrap value at the end of 4 years of $3,000. This means we want to allocate the net cost of $8,000 over that four-year period. Assume for the moment that we want to allocate that $8,000 evenly over each year of the copier's expected useful life. That means we want to expense $2,000 per year. To do so, at the end of each of the 4 years we would have a left-side entry for depreciation expense equal to $2,000. What is our right-side entry?

One possibility is to reduce the reported cost of the asset being depreciated so that we would have a right-side entry to the asset Copier. That would be theoretically coherent but it also would not fully respect the cost principle and the matching principle. The cost principle requires that the financial statements report fixed assets at historical cost, so we should not make a direct reduction to the fixed asset. The matching principle suggests that the financial statements should depict the cumulative effect of the expensing of the fixed asset over time.

To achieve both these objectives of reporting fixed assets at historical cost and reporting cumulative depreciation expense over time, accountants use a special account called a *contra account*. Unrelated to the valiant rebels in 1980s Nicaragua, this account is simply a marker, a place, to keep track of the depreciation expense that accumulates with respect to a fixed asset over time. The contra account for this purpose is called *accumulated depreciation* (or sometimes, equivalently, *allowance for depreciation*). It is used instead of making a right-side entry to the asset being depreciated. For our copier example, the end-of-the-year adjusting entry for each of years 1 through 4 would be as follows:

Adjusting Entry
Depreciation Expense	$2,000	
Accumulated Depreciation		$2,000

The left-side entry is an increase in the expense account Depreciation Expense and the right-side entry is in effect a decrease in the fixed asset copier. It is written in a way that enables us to show the historical cost of the copier on the balance sheet, together with its accumulated depreciation over time. As a result, on the balance sheet at the end of each period the cost of the copier will be listed and then separately, immediately below it, the accumulated depreciation with respect to it will be shown. In our example of the copier for the Firm, at the end of year 1 the portion of the balance sheet depicting this information would appear as follows:

Long-Term Assets
Copier	$11,000
Less Accumulated	
Depreciation	2,000
	9,000

This approach enables us to present the fixed asset at its historical cost on the balance sheet, $11,000, and enables us to reflect what is called *the book value of that asset*—its historical cost less the depreciation that has been accumulated on it and expensed in the accounting process, $9,000.

As a matter of presentation in the financial statements, however, one is not required to report the amount of the accumulated depreciation separately directly on the balance sheet. Instead it is permissible to report the fixed asset (or more precisely the total of all fixed assets), net of the total amount of accumulated depreciation, on the balance sheet and report separately in the notes to the financial statements the amount of accumulated depreciation.

Illustration 5-1.

Look at Illustration 5-1, an excerpt from a full set of financial statements. It shows a line item on the balance sheet for all the company's fixed assets under the label "Property, Plant and Equipment—Net." The Company is reporting the historical cost of all its fixed assets less an amount equal to the accumulated depreciation thereon. From the income statement, Depreciation Expense is shown for the last three years. (Don't get excited about how the change in the balance sheet amount of the fixed assets is not as great as the annual expense for depreciation, which reflects that the company acquired some Property, Plant and Equipment during the period that increased the amount in this fixed asset account.) Illustration 5-1 also excerpts additional disclosure about the company's depreciation of fixed assets from note 3 to its financial statements. It breaks down into several categories the various fixed assets summarized in the line item of the balance sheet for Property, Plant, and Equipment— Net. It also reports the total amount of accumulated depreciation on all fixed assets as a whole.

ILLUSTRATION 5–1
BIC CORPORATION AND SUBSIDIARIES
CONSOLIDATED BALANCE SHEETS
(Dollars in thousands, except per share amounts)

	This Year	Last Year
ASSETS:		
* * * * *		
Property, Plant and Equipment—Net	132,553	140,317
* * * * *		

STATEMENTS OF CONSOLIDATED INCOME
(In thousands, except for per share data)

	This Year	Last Year	Prior Year
Depreciation Expense	23,801	20,881	15,703

* * * * *

NOTES TO CONSOLIDATED FINANCIAL STATEMENTS

3. PROPERTY, PLANT AND EQUIPMENT—NET: Property, plant and equipment—net consists of the following (in thousands):

	This Year	Last Year
Land	$2,706	$2,841
Buildings and improvements	57,722	57,428
Machinery and equipment	204,556	193,234
Construction in progress	18,934	24,742
Total	283,918	278,245
Less accumulated depreciation	151,365	137,928
Total	132,553	140,317

After Asset's Life.

The approach of using the contra account Accumulated Depreciation in the bookkeeping process has a couple of consequences for how to account for the fixed asset when its life is ended. Both the asset account Copier and the contra account Accumulated Depreciation in respect of it will be affected. As of the end of year four, the balance sheet with respect to the copier would appear as follows:

Long Term Assets	
Copier	$11,000
Less Accumulated	
Depreciation	8,000
	3,000

(Notice that the book value of the copier is $3,000, which is simply what we declared and assumed its scrap value would be at this time—the end of four years).

Now assume that the copier is sold at the end of year four for $3,000 cash. What journal entries are necessary to account for this transaction? We have a decrease in the asset Copier of the full amount at which that account stands on the balance sheet of $11,000. So we make a right-side entry of Copier $11,000. We also have an increase in the asset account Cash of $3,000, so we make a left-side entry of Cash $3,000.

We have of course one more thing to do to keep things in balance, however, and that is to deal with the Accumulated Depreciation account. We need to reduce that account by its full $8,000 balance. Decreases in a contra account are handled in the opposite way from which the account it is representing would be handled. A depreciation contra account is representing an asset, so decreases in it call for a left-side entry (since decreases in an asset account call for a right-side entry). So we have the following:

Cash	$3,000	
Accumulated Depreciation	$8,000	
Copier		$11,000

To make this more intuitive, notice that if we had not been using the Accumulated Depreciation device to keep track of historical cost and accumulated depreciation separately, we would have been reducing the asset account Copier each year instead of accumulating the amount of depreciation. In that case at the end of its last year we would just enter $3,000 for the copier on the right side. But since we have been keeping track of Accumulated Depreciation separately we must treat it separately here, though of course the net effect is the same—the asset's book value of $11,000 less its accumulated depreciation equals $3,000.

Gain or Loss on Disposition.

In the preceding example we assumed that the copier was sold for a price equal to its book value. What if instead it were sold for some greater or lesser amount? If a fixed asset is sold for a price greater than its book value, there is said to be a *gain on sale*; if a fixed asset is sold for a price less than its book value, there is said to be a *loss on sale.* Either way, an additional journal entry must be made to reflect the difference.

How should this be treated in bookkeeping terms? It would be possible, presumably, to treat gains as revenue and losses as expenses. But that treatment would then obscure the objective of reporting on the performance of the financial operations of a business during a period when gains or losses were incurred. To avoid that, FASB distinguishes from the idea of revenue the concept of *gain* and distinguishes from the idea of expense the concept of *loss.*

For FASB, *gains* are "increases in equity generally from nonowner sources, which result from peripheral or incidental transactions" and *losses* are "decreases in equity generally from nonowner sources, which result from peripheral or incidental transactions." Gains and losses therefore cover incidental interest received or paid; profit or losses on incidental sales of investments, property, plant, and equipment; and profits or losses resulting from litigation and casualties. Gains also include dividends received on investments.

In bookkeeping terms, therefore, a gain on sale is treated separately from items of revenue and a loss on sale is treated separately from expenses. On the other hand, however, gains will have the effect of boosting income during a period and losses will have the effect of reducing it.

To illustrate, assume that the copier was sold for $5,000 cash at a time when its book value was $3,000. We therefore have a gain on sale of $2,000. The journal entries would therefore be as follows:

Cash	$5,000	
Accumulated Depreciation	$8,000	
Copier		$11,000
Gain on Sale		$2,000

Conversely, if the copier had been sold for $2,000 cash at a time when its book value was $3,000, we would have a loss on sale of $1,000. The journal entries would therefore be as follows:

Cash	$2,000	
Accumulated Depreciation	$8,000	
Loss on Sale	$1,000	
Copier		$11,000

Mid-Course Changes and Impairment Tests.

What happens if during the course of a fixed asset's actual life, it is discovered that one or more of the judgments required for the depreciation exercise turn out to be materially incorrect? For example, suppose machinery believed at purchase to have an expected useful life of 20 years becomes obsolete after three years. GAAP permits changes to be made in the depreciation calculations based on such mid-course changes in the original assumptions. The issue is whether when such a change is made, the historical financial statements must be restated to reflect the changes or not.

The answer is no: prior financial statements need not be restated, although obviously current and future financial statements will be prepared on the basis of the changed information. To do this, the same formulas for depreciation are used, the only difference being that we now use the cost not yet depreciated, any changed information about scrap value, and the current information concerning the asset's remaining expected useful life. The changes should be disclosed in the footnotes to the financial statements.

On the other hand, periodic tests must be applied to fixed assets to verify that their value is not *impaired*. For this purpose, impairment is suggested when a fixed asset's book value exceeds the amount of gross future cash flows the asset is expected to generate. If that occurs, the amount of impairment is measured using recognized techniques that involve forecasting probable future cash flows from the asset and estimating their present value. (This valuation method, discussed in Chapters Ten and Eleven, is called discounted cash flow analysis). The effects of any such impairment are recognized in current income. Once impairment losses are recognized, they cannot be reversed. ?

D. DEPRECIATION METHODS

We assumed in the preceding example that we desired to allocate the net cost of a fixed asset evenly over its expected useful life. That is one way to approach the depreciation exercise, and it is called the *straight line method* of depreciation. There is an alternative approach one could choose, which is called the *accelerated method* of depreciation. Rather than allocate the net cost evenly over a fixed asset's expected useful life, the allocations are accelerated in earlier years and decline in later years. There are in turn a number of alternative accelerated methods of depreciation, which we will illustrate below.

Recall that to calculate depreciation expense, one needs to determine the total historical cost, the salvage value, and the expected useful life. Assume that Larry's Firm has purchased a limousine to be used in the business, at a total cost of $100,000; with a salvage value of $20,000; and an expected useful life of 10 years. Let's calculate the annual depreciation expense for this fixed asset and the consequences for its book value under each of these methods.

Straight Line Method.

Under the straight line method of depreciation, an equal portion of the fixed asset's cost, less its scrap value, is allocated to each year of its expected useful life. For an asset with a 5-year expected useful life, 1/5 of the net cost is expensed each year. The formula for doing so is as follows:

$$\text{Depreciation Expense} \;=\; \frac{\text{Cost} - \text{Scrap Value}}{\text{Useful Life}}$$

In our Firm's limousine example, we would apply the straight-line method formula to compute annual depreciation expense as follows:

$$\frac{\$100,000 - 20,000}{10} = \$8,000$$

Armed with the amount of the annual depreciation expense, we can present all the financial data relating to this fixed asset in a single table, as in Table 5-1, and call it a depreciation schedule.

	A		B	C	D
Table 5-1 Larry's Firm Limousine Depreciation Schedule Straight Line Method					
Year	Total Historical Cost	Formula	Annual Depreciation Expense	Accumulated Depreciation [∑ all Bs]	Book Value [A – C]
1	100,000	1/10 x 80,000	8,000	8,000	92,000
2	100,000	1/10 x 80,000	8,000	16,000	84,000
3	100,000	1/10 x 80,000	8,000	24,000	76,000
4	100,000	1/10 x 80,000	8,000	32,000	68,000
5	100,000	1/10 x 80,000	8,000	40,000	60,000
6	100,000	1/10 x 80,000	8,000	48,000	52,000
7	100,000	1/10 x 80,000	8,000	56,000	44,000
8	100,000	1/10 x 80,000	8,000	64,000	36,000
9	100,000	1/10 x 80,000	8,000	72,000	28,000
10	100,000	1/10 x 80,000	8,000	80,000	20,000

Table 5-1 shows in Column A the total historical cost of the asset, which would be reported on the balance sheet, and in Column B the annual depreciation expense, which would be reported on the income statement. It also shows in Column C the accumulated depreciation and in Column D book value, which would be reflected on the balance sheet in one of two alternative ways, at the reporting entity's option. Either the asset would be reported directly at book value on the balance sheet with a footnote disclosing historical cost and accumulated depreciation, or it would be reported at the historical cost less the accumulated depreciation. From this table, it will also be easy to determine upon the sale of the asset whether any gain or loss would occur.

Finally, notice that the book value at the end of the ten-year estimated useful life is equal to the scrap value that we assigned to this asset. That is because we have excluded the scrap value from the depreciable base, and this is required in all depreciation methods: one does not depreciate the scrap value of any fixed asset. Put differently, a fixed asset may not be depreciated below its scrap value.

Sum of the Years' Digits Method.

The term <u>accelerate</u> in the context of depreciation means that we seek to allocate and expense larger amounts of a fixed asset's net cost in the earlier years of the asset's expected useful life and smaller amounts in later years. We therefore increase the portion of the net cost of the asset to be expensed in earlier years and decrease it for later years. Mathematically, we want to increase the fraction used to allocate cost to earlier periods and decrease that fraction for later periods.

One approach employs the method called the *sum-of-the-years' digits.* Each year's depreciation expense is a varying fraction of the asset's net cost. The fraction in the earlier years is greater than the fraction that would apply using the straight line method and in later years lower than that.

The fractions are determined by summing the years' digits, beginning with the number of years of the asset's expected useful life. For example, if the expected useful life is 5 years, then the digits to be summed are these: 5 + 4 + 3 + 2 + 1. The sum of those digits is 15. That means that in each year the fraction will be based on a denominator of 15. The numerator for each year is the next digit in line: year one's fraction would be 5/15; year two's 4/15; year three's 3/15; year four's 2/15; and the last year's, year five's, 1/15. In each case the fraction is applied to the asset's net cost. (A short-cut formula for summing the digits for n years is $n\,(n{+}1)\,/\,2$.)

Let's see how this works for the example of the Firm's limousine. Recall that the cost was $100,000, the scrap value is $20,000, and the expected useful life is 10 years. The digits to be summed are: 10 through 1, which sum to 55 (using the formula, $10(10{+}1)/2 = 110/2 = 55$). Therefore our schedule of depreciation over the 10 years, in chronological order, is 10/55, 9/55, 8/55, 7/55, 6/55, 5/55, 4/55, 3/55, 2/55 and 1/55. Those fractions are applied to the net cost of the asset, which is the cost of $100,000 minus the scrap value of $20,000 for a net cost of $80,000. The results are presented in the depreciation schedule shown in Table 5-2. Notice that the book value at the end of year 10 is equal to $20,000, which reflects our assumption that the limousine's scrap value is $20,000.

Table 5-2
Larry's Firm
Limousine Depreciation Schedule
Sum-of-the-Years' Method

	A		B	C	D
Year	Total Historical Cost	Formula	Annual Depreciation Expense	Accumulated Depreciation [∑ all Bs]	Book Value [A – C]
1	100,000	10/55 x 80,000	14,545	14,545	85,455
2	100,000	9/55 x 80,000	13,091	27,636	72,364
3	100,000	8/55 x 80,000	11,636	39,272	60,728
4	100,000	7/55 x 80,000	10,181	49,453	50,547
5	100,000	6/55 x 80,000	8,727	58,180	41,820
6	100,000	5/55 x 80,000	7,273	65,453	34,547
7	100,000	4/55 x 80,000	5,818	71,271	28,729
8	100,000	3/55 x 80,000	4,364	75,635	24,365
9	100,000	2/55 x 80,000	2,909	78,544	21,456
10	100,000	1/55 x 80,000	1,456	80,000	20,000

Declining Balance Method.

An alternative method of accelerated depreciation, also well named, is the declining balance method. It seeks precisely the same objective of allocating more expense to earlier years and less to later years. It therefore also involves increasing the fraction in the earlier years and decreasing it for the later years. The magnitude of the acceleration is determined by the rate at which the declining balance is determined. The most common rate is double and that method called the *double-declining balance method*. The operative word is *double*. It means that to operate the method one *doubles* the fraction or percentage that applies under the straight line method. For example, if the fraction (or percentage) applicable under the straight line method were 1/5 (20%), then the fraction (or percentage) applicable under the double-declining balance method would be 2/5 (40%).

There is one twist with this method: the scrap value component of the depreciation exercise is picked up on the back-end rather than the front-end. That is, while the other methods compute the depreciable base as the historical cost minus the scrap value (up-front), the declining balance method begins depreciation allocations based on the full historical cost, then halts the allocations once the accumulated depreciation reaches the point of the scrap value. (Hence the term back-end). In other words, the percentage applied under the declining balance method is applied *not* to the net cost of the asset but to its remaining book value, subject, however, to the golden rule of depreciation that it is not permissible to depreciate the asset below its scrap value. In the declining balance method, therefore, once accumulated depreciation has reached the depreciable base, no more depreciation expense is recognized.

For an asset with a useful life of 5 years, the straight line method allocates 1/5 in each of five years (20%). So under double declining balance, what percentage would we apply? Answer: 40%, the percentage equivalent of the fraction 2/5 (which in turn is double the fraction 1/5).

Following through on our limousine example, the straight line method allocates 1/10 each year, so under double declining balance the fraction will be 2/10, which is 20% (rather than 10% as under straight line method). The results are set forth in the depreciation schedule shown in Table 5-3.

Table 5-3
Larry's Firm
Limousine Depreciation Schedule
Double Declining Method

	A	B	C	D	E
Year	Total Historical Cost	Opening Balance	Annual Depreciation Expense [20%xB]	Accumulated Depreciation [∑ all Cs]	Book Value [A – D]
1	100,000	100,000	20,000	20,000	80,000
2	100,000	80,000	16,000	36,000	64,000
3	100,000	64,000	12,800	48,800	51,200
4	100,000	51,200	10,240	59,040	40,960
5	100,000	40,960	8,192	67,232	32,768
6	100,000	32,768	6,554	73,786	26,214
7	100,000	26,214	5,242	79,028	20,972
8	100,000	20,972	972*	80,000	20,000
9	100,000	20,000	0*	80,000	20,000
10	100,000	20,000	0*	80,000	20,000

The asterisks (*) in Table 5-3 highlight that in this example under the declining balance method, accumulated depreciation reaches the amount of the depreciable base (and equivalently, book value reaches scrap value) during the calculation of depreciation expense for year 8. In that year, depreciation expense is equal to only the remaining portion of the depreciable base (and equivalently, the amount by which book value had exceeded scrap value), rather than the full amount of depreciation that the formula would otherwise have yielded that year. In this example, that amount was $972.

An anomaly arises. Under double-declining-balance, a fixed asset in the later years of its expected useful life may remain in service, contributing to revenue, but not carry any depreciation expense. This result poses some tension with the matching principle, purely applied.

Other Methods.

Numerous other methods of depreciation exist and may be attractive for particular asset classes. For example, the *units-of-output* method of depreciation bases net cost allocations on estimates of useful output rather than estimates of useful life. A car rental company might choose this method to depreciate its fleet of cars based on expected miles driven rather than expected years used. The accountant still needs to estimate expected miles. Suppose these are 100,000 for a car that cost $17,000 and has an assumed scrap value of $2,000. The depreciation rate would be expressed as cents per mile of operation as follows:

$$\frac{\text{cost} - \text{scrap value}}{\text{estimated units of output}}$$
$$\text{(miles)}$$

$$\frac{17,000 - 2,000}{100,000 \text{ miles}}$$

$$\$.15 \text{ per mile}$$

Depreciation expense for each period would be the actual miles driven times $.15. Notice that while depreciation expense calculated this way remains an imperfect measure of actual wearing out, the wear on a car is probably better measured by miles than age.

E. TAX DEPRECIATION DISTINGUISHED

Recall from Chapter 4 that management must employ the same method of determining the cost of goods sold for federal income tax purposes that it uses for financial reporting purposes. In contrast, management may choose to employ one method of depreciation for federal income tax purposes and a different method for financial reporting purposes. As a result, for financial reporting purposes, the most commonly used method of depreciation is the straight line method because it allows the entity to report relatively higher earnings. For tax reporting purposes, however, accelerated methods of depreciation are commonly used because they allow the entity to report relatively lower earnings and therefore reduce its federal income tax liabilities.

In fact, US tax law provides an innovative approach to depreciation known as the Modified Accelerated Cost Recovery System (MACRS). It functionally jettisons all elements of the depreciation exercise under GAAP. With MACRS, the concepts of useful life and salvage value are effectively abandoned; the system generally contemplates defining specified accelerated methods of depreciation during most of an asset's presumed life based on the declining balance method (except for assets with useful lives exceeding 25 years), applied beginning in the asset's second year of use.

MACRS classifies all fixed assets into eight categories and then defines the allowable percentage of each asset's fixed cost to be taken annually. The system allows for double-declining balance (DDB) for most asset classes and 1.5 declining balance (1.5DB) for others, in each case with a mid-point switch from that accelerated method to the straight-line method. Table 5-4 indicates the property classes and Table 5-5 indicates the cost recovery periods.

Table 5-4: MACRS Tax Classifications

Property Class in Years and Depreciation Method	Useful Life (in Years)	Examples
3-year, DDB	≤ 4	Small tools
5-year, DDB	$> 4 < 10$	Cars, trucks, computers, copiers, lab equipment
7-year, DDB	$\geq 10 < 16$	Furniture, fixtures, production machinery and equipment
10-year, DDB	$\geq 16 < 20$	Heavy machinery and equipment
15-year, 1.5 DB	$\geq 20 < 25$	Infrastructure (sewage treatment plants, telephone, electric distribution facilities)
20-year, 1.5 DB	≥ 25	Service stations
27.5-year, SL	NA	Residential rental property
31.5-year, SL	NA	Commercial rental property

MACRS creates a systematic opportunity for accelerated depreciation, producing higher depreciation deductions from taxable income in an asset's early years of service. This is intended to encourage investment in fixed assets. Under MACRS, it is possible for a company to opt for the straight-line method nevertheless, which may be attractive to companies boasting little or no income that could be offset by the increased tax deductions MACRS offers.

Table 5-5: MACRS Tax Depreciation Schedule

Year	3-year	5-year	7-year	10-year	15-year	20-year
1	33.3%	20.0%	14.3%	10.0%	5.0%	3.8%
2	44.5	32.0	24.5	18.0	9.5	7.2
3	14.8*	19.2	17.5	14.4	8.6	6.7
4	7.4	11.5*	12.5	11.5	7.7	6.2
5		11.5	8.9*	9.2	6.9	5.7
6		5.8	8.9	7.4	6.2	5.3
7			8.9	6.6*	5.9*	4.9
8			4.5	6.6	5.9	4.5*
9				6.5	5.9	4.5
10				6.5	5.9	4.5
11				3.3	5.9	4.5
12					5.9	4.5
13					5.9	4.5
14					5.9	4.5
15					5.9	4.5
16					3.0	4.4
17						4.4
18						4.4
19						4.4
20						4.4
21						2.2
Total	100%	100%	100%	100%	100%	100%

* Indicates year of changeover to straight-line depreciation.

Substantial complexities arise from differences between depreciation methods used for financial reporting under GAAP on the one hand and tax reporting on the other. As noted, companies often use one depreciation method for GAAP and another for tax. Their goal is to decrease taxes currently payable and thus preserve cash on a current basis. The tax obligation gets deferred. For GAAP, this gives rise to a concept known as [*deferred taxes.*] Determining the amount involves calculating the difference between theoretical taxable income before and after giving effect to the tax depreciation. Associated complexities are beyond the scope of this introductory book.

F. CONSISTENCY, DISCLOSURE AND CHANGING PRICES

GAAP permits an entity's management to decide which method of depreciation to apply to its fixed assets. The choice is not dictated by the degree to which one or the other methods accurately reflects the wearing out of any fixed asset over time. On the contrary, none of the conventions themselves even pretend to do so. The choice is instead driven primarily by the impact on reported earnings that the alternative methods entail.

The Consistency Principle.

Recall from Chapter 1 GAAP's principle of consistency. It requires that accounting principles be consistently applied. In the context of depreciation, that means that an entity generally should avoid changing its method of depreciating a particular asset from period-to-period. Indeed, GAAP prohibits changing the depreciation method used with respect to a particular asset from the straight line method to any accelerated method (although it permits changes from an accelerated method to the straight-line method). However, the consistency principle does not require that all assets of an entity be depreciated according to the same method. The consistency principle also does not require that an entity use the same depreciation method in its financial statements as in its tax returns.

Disclosure.

The method an entity chooses to depreciate its fixed assets should be disclosed in the footnotes to its financial statements. A reader of the financial statements must know what method is being used in order to evaluate the meaning of those statements. Accelerated methods of depreciation allocate the cost of fixed assets to expenses more rapidly than the straight-line method. They therefore result in reporting lower earnings and lower asset values sooner than under the straight-line method.

Illustration 5-2.

Look at Illustration 5-2, an excerpt from a full set of financial statements. From note 1 to those financial statements under the heading "Property, Plant and Equipment," it discloses the methods the company uses for depreciating its assets and some of the judgments applied in the exercise. It says that the depreciation is usually performed according to the double declining balance method. It also reports the range of useful lives applicable to categories of fixed assets (10–50 years for buildings and improvements and 3–12 years for machinery and equipment). It also discloses information with respect to how the depreciable base is calculated, stating that the expenditures for maintenance and repairs are not included but instead are charged to operations as they are incurred— that is, they are *expensed*. On the other hand, expenditures for betterments and major renewals are added to the depreciable base—that is what is meant by the term *"capitalized"* in this context. Finally it discloses, in accordance with the principles discussed in this Chapter, the method of treating fixed assets upon disposition.

ILLUSTRATION 5–2

BIC CORPORATION AND SUBSIDIARIES

NOTES TO CONSOLIDATED FINANCIAL STATEMENTS

1. **SUMMARY OF SIGNIFICANT ACCOUNTING POLICIES:** A summary of significant accounting policies for BIC Corporation and its subsidiaries (the "Corporation"), manufacturers and distributors of high-quality, low-cost consumer products, is as follows:

Property, Plant and Equipment Property, plant and equipment is recorded at cost. Depreciation, principally on the double-declining balance method, is provided over the estimated useful lives of the assets as follows:

Buildings and improvements	10–50 years
Machinery and equipment	3–12 years

Expenditures for maintenance and repairs are charged to operations as incurred. Expenditures for betterments and major renewals are capitalized. Costs of assets sold or retired and the related amounts of accumulated depreciation are eliminated from the accounts in the year of disposal and any resulting gains or losses are included in income.

Changing Prices.

In periods of changing prices, the historical cost principle applied to fixed assets diminishes the utility of reported amounts. Suppose a company bought an acre of land 20 years ago for a cost of $100,000 and a contiguous functionally identical acre today for $1 million. Its balance sheet would show a total for these of $1.1 million (recall that land is not subject to depreciation exercises). But the figures suggest a total current value for them of $2 million. The historical cost principle thus carries an embedded assumption that currency amounts are a stable unit of measurement like gallons, tons, or miles. This assumption is false whenever average price levels change.

For short periods of relatively stable prices the stable-currency assumption may not matter much. But over short periods with rapidly changing price levels or long periods with modest period-to-period changes, the assumption renders comparisons difficult. In the aftermath of the hyper-inflationary period of the 1970s, FASB flirted with rules that would reflect inflationary effects on fixed asset carrying amounts. It experimented with requiring large entities to report supplementary data concerning the effects of inflation on current values and current replacement costs. The experiment revealed that the costs of computing and supplying such data outweighed associated benefits and the requirement was repealed. One can expect accounting standard-setters to revisit the issue if hyper-inflationary periods return or deflation occurs.

G. DEPLETION AND AMORTIZATION

We have used the term depreciation throughout this Chapter to capture the idea of allocating the cost of a fixed asset over time. Technically, the term *depreciation* and the conventions described above apply to fixed assets having a *physical existence*, such as machinery, equipment, vehicles and buildings, and that are not literally consumed over their lives. For other kinds of assets, the conventions differ, though only slightly.

Depletion is the equivalent of depreciation for assets that are *literally consumed* in a physical sense over time, such as mineral resources and oil and gas. The significant accounting difference between depletion and depreciation is that the cost of the asset is allocated based on the number of units the asset represents, such as the number of barrels of oil. Also, with depletion a common convention is to write the asset's carrying value down directly rather than use an accumulated depletion account. *Amortization* is the equivalent of depreciation for *intangible assets*—those lacking physical existence except on paper, such as patents and trademarks. The chief accounting differences between amortization and depreciation are introduced in the next Chapter.

Problem 5

With the cold weather fast approaching, J&J is planning to move operations indoors. It is considering buying a customized work trailer and having it installed permanently on J&J's land. A friend of Jack's has offered to sell them her trailer for a price of $28,000, plus a $2,000 installation fee. J&J wants to evaluate alternative methods of accounting for the trailer over time before proceeding with the purchase. J&J estimates that the trailer's useful life is 5 years and its estimated salvage value is $5,000. The company proposes recording the acquisition (and eventual disposition) of the trailer using the actual dates, recording acquisition and disposition when they occur.

a. Assume that J&J were to pay cash for the trailer and its installation (despite not having sufficient cash available now for the purpose). Prepare the appropriate journal entry to reflect the acquisition.

b. Prepare three separate depreciation schedules along the lines of Tables 5-1, 5-2, and 5-3 of this Chapter, showing for years 1 through 5 the annual depreciation expense, the accumulated depreciation, and the book value of the trailer under (i) the straight line method, (ii) the sum-of-the-years' digits method, and (iii) the double-declining balance method.

c.   Assume that J&J were to sell the trailer at the end of year 4 for $8,000 in cash. Prepare the appropriate journal entries to reflect that disposition under (i) the straight line method, (ii) the sum-of-the-years' digits method, and (iii) the double-declining balance method.

d.   Restate the depreciation schedule determined in question (b) under the straight-line method using the following alternative assumptions: (i) useful life of 3 or 7 years (keeping the assumption that salvage value is $5,000) and (ii) salvage value of $3,000 or $7,000 (keeping the assumption that useful life is 5 years). Please interpret your results.

Conceptual Questions 5

GAAP has long prescribed measuring fixed assets at historical cost, subject to periodic depreciation expense. It also has long prescribed measuring inventory at its acquisition cost, subject to the lower of cost or market principle. Since inventory is a current asset, it is possible that inventory measurements approximate current fair values of inventory. For that matter, accounting principles often prescribe or allow measuring certain kinds of assets at their fair values as of the time financial statements are prepared. Concluding sections of this Chapter mentioned how FASB considered applying fair value accounting to fixed assets but abandoned the effort. The following IFRS Note mentions that IFRS authorizes doing so. The next Chapter pursues fair value accounting and its relative appeal in some detail. Consider, preliminarily, whether you would favor applying fair value accounting to fixed assets. In doing so, consider what effect this would have on the utility of accumulated depreciation.

IFRS Note 5

Among differences between GAAP and IFRS concerning topics addressed in this Chapter are the following:

- When testing for fixed-asset impairment, GAAP considers impairment to be suggested when book value exceeds gross expected future cash flows; it then measures the amount of impairment using discounted cash flow analysis. In contrast, IFRS considers impairment to occur when book value exceeds the greater of the asset's value in use (based on discounted cash flows) or its fair value less the cost to sell it.

- Under GAAP, effects of impairment are recognized in current income and cannot be reversed. In general, under IFRS, similar impairment is treated as a balance sheet adjustment of the asset, not part of income, and recognized impairments are reversed in certain cases.

- Perhaps the most salient difference between GAAP and IFRS on accounting for fixed assets concerns initial measurement. Under GAAP, fixed assets are recorded at cost, and subject to annual depreciation charges. Under IFRS, this cost and capitalization method is authorized, but IFRS also allows fixed assets to be recorded at current fair market value.

CHAPTER 6

OTHER ASSET AND LIABILITY ISSUES

∎ ∎ ∎

We have so far focused our attention on some of the basic assets and liabilities as a way of introducing the fundamental principles of accounting and bookkeeping. We turn our attention in this Chapter to discuss some of the[wider variety of assets and liabilities one encounters.]In doing so, the fundamental principles discussed in previous Chapters reappear in new forms and additional principles and issues posed by these other assets and liabilities are presented. In addition, attention is given to the degree to which financial statements must be accompanied by footnote disclosure about those principles to make the statements meaningful to users.

An important issue to notice in materials discussed in this Chapter is the basis used to measure assets. In previous Chapters, especially Chapter 4 (Inventory) and Chapter 5 (Fixed Assets), we saw the principle of asset measurement based on *cost* (for Inventory, subject to the lower of cost or market principle and, for Fixed Assets, subject to periodic depreciation expense). For many assets discussed in this Chapter (especially Section B, Intercompany Ownership and Section C, Financial Instruments), the principle of asset measurement is based on an asset's *fair value* at the time financial statements are prepared, not historical cost.

The choice to measure assets at cost or fair value entails a struggle to determine which approach more faithfully reflects economic reality. This implicates two accounting objectives, relevance and reliability, that can be in tension. Cost is a reliable asset measure but, with the passage of time, its relevance may decline; current fair value may be more relevant but, given market vicissitudes, may be less reliable.[In general, cost is deemed more suitable for assets lacking an organized trading market, such as inventory and buildings, and fair value for those enjoying an organized trading market, such as investments in common stock of public companies and certain financial instruments.]

A. RECEIVABLES

Most businesses sell at least a portion of their goods and services on credit. From the entity's point of view, amounts due from customers in respect of such sales on credit constitute an asset called *accounts receivable*. The terms of accounts receivable vary but they typically call for payment within a short period of time, usually 30, 60, or 90 days. Accounts receivable can typically be paid at any time until the end of such period without penalty. All such receivables are considered to be current assets.

Credit Policies.

Most entities that sell on credit have a credit department charged with evaluating the creditworthiness of customers and continuously assessing each customer's compliance with payment obligations. Before extending credit, a customer's creditworthiness can be ascertained from credit-reporting agencies such as Dun & Bradstreet and Trans Union for individuals and Standard & Poor's and Moody's for businesses.* For individuals and businesses, credit quality can also be gleaned from analyzing the customer's financial statements. After extending credit, accounts receivable on which the customer complies with the payment obligations are said to be *current*. Accounts receivable on which a required payment is not made are called *delinquent* and usually will prompt a computer signal that results in the business sending a dunning letter to the customer seeking prompt payment. If that does not do the trick, and the payment is still not made within the next two periods or so, the account will be deemed *uncollectible*.

Charge-Offs.

Accounts receivable that are deemed uncollectible are no longer assets of the entity but instead represent expenses as part of the cost of doing business by extending credit. Those uncollectible accounts are called *charge-offs*. Under GAAP's matching principle, the expense with respect to accounts receivable that are deemed uncollectible must be allocated to the period in which the related sales on credit occurred. For example, a sale made on credit in January determined to be uncollectible in July must be charged-off in January in order to burden the income statement with the expense that month. To implement the matching principle with respect to uncollectible accounts expense therefore requires an estimate at the end of each month of what portion of the accounts receivable generated that month will eventually be deemed uncollectible. The estimate of charge-offs is based on past experience, considered together with current economic conditions. Under GAAP's conservatism principle, moreover, that estimate should err on the side of overestimating charge-offs rather than underestimating them.

Adjusting Entry.

In bookkeeping terms, an adjusting entry is made at the end of the month to reflect the estimated amount of accounts receivable charge-offs.

---

*   The Fair Credit Reporting Act allows credit-reporting agencies to list negative credit and public record information for 7 years from the date of the adverse event or 10 years from the date of a person's bankruptcy filing. You can obtain a copy of your own credit report, along with a summary of applicable consumer protection laws, by writing to one of the consumer credit-reporting agencies.

The <u>left-side entry is made</u> to an expense account called *Uncollectible Accounts Expense* (or, equivalently, *Bad Debt Expense*). That expense account will be closed out into the P & L Account along with all other expense accounts at the end of that month.

What is the right-side entry? One possibility is to reduce the asset, Accounts Receivable, directly by the amount of estimated charge-offs. But note that at the end of each period we are only estimating total charge-offs in the aggregate rather than reducing the actual balance in any given customer's account receivable. Therefore, if we reduced the Accounts Receivable balance directly, then the sum of all the individual accounts receivable would not equal the total amount of Accounts Receivable reported. To avoid that imbalance, rather than reducing the balance in the Accounts Receivable asset account directly, a separate account is used. It is called the *Allowance for Doubtful Accounts*. It is a *contra account*, similar to the one we employed in recording accumulated depreciation (see Chapter 5).

To illustrate, assume that during January Larry's Firm generated $100,000 in accounts receivable but it knows from past experience that approximately 4% of its accounts receivables are ultimately deemed uncollectible. An adjusting entry of the following form would be made during the closing process:

Uncollectible Accounts Expense	$4,000	
Allowance for Doubtful Accounts		$4,000

Both the income statement and the balance sheet will be affected by this adjusting entry. The income statement will reflect the expense, Uncollectible Accounts Expense, and will be burdened by the amount of that expense. The balance sheet will report the balance in the asset account, Accounts Receivable, as well as the balance in the contra account, Allowance for Doubtful Accounts. As an example, consider the following hypothetical portion of Larry's Firm's balance sheet:

Current Assets		
Cash		$200,000
Accounts Receivable	$100,000	
Less: Allowance for Doubtful Accounts	4,000	96,000
Inventory		80,000
Total Current Assets		376,000

The effect of this presentation is to show the *net realizable value* of the Accounts Receivable, which is equal to the balance in the Accounts Receivable account, less the balance in the contra account, Allowance for Doubtful Accounts. (Notice the similarity to the presentation of fixed assets that are depreciated over time from Chapter 5.)

Write Offs.

Once a specific account receivable is determined to be uncollectible, it is no longer an asset. That customer's balance is written off to zero. In the journal, this transaction affects only the balance sheet, as estimated expenses for uncollectible accounts have already been taken. It is recorded as a reduction in the asset account Accounts Receivable (a right-side entry) and a reduction in the contra account Allowance for Doubtful Accounts (a left-side entry). So a $1,000 receivable determined to be worthless would be written off by the following journal entry:

Allowance for Doubtful Accounts	$1,000	
Accounts Receivable		$1,000

Note the parallel to the entries made upon disposing of a fixed asset such as the copier discussed in Chapter 5. The asset account for the fixed asset is reduced, calling for the right-side entry to the asset account Copier as here with Accounts Receivable; and the related contra account is being reduced, in that case Accumulated Depreciation and here Allowance for Doubtful Accounts, calling for a left-side entry.

Note also that this pair of entries to the balance sheet does not affect the net carrying value of accounts receivable. They have not changed. This is because the expense has already been taken. Indeed, the expense was allocated, as the matching principle requires, to the period in which the accounts receivable now written off were originally generated.

This process of estimating losses upon creating receivables and taking an expense at that time with subsequent adjustments to the balance sheet accounts is almost always imperfect. That is, the estimated losses vary from the ultimate write offs. The trends in differences call for constantly reviewing and revising the estimates of charge offs each period.

A variety of techniques are available to aid the estimation process. The most common looks to the aging of receivables and focuses on the balance sheet carrying amount of net receivables; another looks to the income statement to estimate probable losses as a percentage of sales on credit.

Direct Write-Off Method and Tax Accounting.

As in other areas, financial reporting and income tax regulations vary. Income tax rules relating to receivables jettison the matching principle implemented by the allowance method altogether and instead use the *direct write-off method*. This means a receivable is only written off when it is determined to be worthless. A receivable generated in January and determined to be worthless in July would be treated as an expense in July rather than in January. Some companies also employ the direct write-off method for financial reporting purposes as well, though most large companies appear to use the allowance method.

Illustration 6-1.

Look at Illustration 6-1, an excerpt from a full set of financial statements. From the balance sheet under the heading current assets there is an entry entitled "Receivables—Trade and Other (Net of Allowance for Doubtful Accounts)." That line item does not separately state the dollar amount of the allowance for doubtful accounts. The receivables balance is reported after subtracting that amount. It is also customary to disclose additional data about the Allowance for Doubtful Accounts. Illustration 6-1 also excerpts disclosure from a schedule customarily accompanying the financial statements called "Consolidated Allowance Accounts." It discloses additional detail about the allowance for doubtful accounts over time. (The next section discusses the meaning of "Consolidated" as it applies to financial statements.)

ILLUSTRATION 6–1

BIC CORPORATION AND SUBSIDIARIES

CONSOLIDATED BALANCE SHEETS

(LAST TWO YEARS)

(Dollars in thousands, except per share amounts)

	12/31 This Year	12/31 Last Year
ASSETS:		
Current Assets:		
Cash and Cash Equivalents	$48,091	$24,094
Receivables—Trade and Other (Net of		
Allowance for Doubtful Accounts)	62,867	52,019
Inventories	54,363	59,426
Deferred Income Taxes	18,549	16,809
Other	10,575	13,637
Total Current Assets	194,445	165,985

* * * * *

CONSOLIDATED ALLOWANCE ACCOUNTS

FOR LAST THREE FISCAL YEARS ENDED

(in thousands)

Classification

Allowance for

Doubtful Accounts:

	Balance at Beginning of Year	Additions Charged to Profit and Loss	(Additions) Deductions from Reserves(1)	Balance at End of Year
This Year	$4,084	$1,467	$1,021	$4,530
Last Year	5,076	85	1,077	4,084
Year Before	2,420	2,286	(370)	5,076

(1) Principally accounts written off, less recoveries.

B. INTERCOMPANY OWNERSHIP

In addition to investing resources in the operations of its own business, an entity can also invest in the business of other entities. Investments in other entities can take the form of debt instruments or equity securities. Investments in debt are subdivided into three categories for accounting purposes: *held-to-maturity securities* are debt instruments the holder intends to hold until they mature; *trading securities* are debt instruments bought and held solely for the purpose of resale; and *available-for-sale* securities are instruments that are neither held-to-maturity nor trading securities.]

Investments in equity securities are divided into categories based on the level of influence the position enables the holder to exert, ranging from none or little (less than 20% ownership), to meaningful (20% to 50%), to full control (more than 50%). Equity securities representing less than 20% of an investee are further distinguished between those with and without readily determinable fair values, and the former designated as either trading securities or available-for-sale securities under the same definitional approach used for debt securities. ?

Debt Securities.

Debt securities consist of a wide variety of instruments that are privately issued, such as bank certificates of deposit, commercial paper, and notes as well as those that trade in public capital markets, such as corporate and municipal bonds. They are contractual commitments of the issuer to repay specified amounts of principal along with interest at designated times, ranging from 30 days to 10 or more years, and perhaps to abide by other restrictions.

Held-to-maturity securities are so classified if the holder has the positive intent and ability to hold the securities until maturity. They are accounted for on the investor's balance sheet *at cost* (subject to adjustment to the extent purchased at a discount or for a premium), without regard to periodic fluctuations in their market value. Interest on held-to-maturity securities is recognized as part of net income when earned. Gains or losses are recorded in net income when the securities are sold. Unrealized gains or losses are not recognized.

Investments in debt securities not classified as held-to-maturity are measured at *fair value* on the balance sheet and classified as *trading securities* if bought and held mainly for short-term resale and *available-for-sale* securities otherwise. Unrealized gains and losses on trading securities are included in net income but unrealized gains and losses on available-for-sale securities are excluded from net income and reported instead as "other comprehensive income" (a separate category about which more is said in the next Chapter). As with held-to-maturity debt securities, interest on these categories of debt investments is recognized as part of net income when earned.

For debt securities classified as available-for-sale or held-to-maturity, if fair value declines below cost, the holder must determine whether the decline is "other than temporary." If it is, the carrying amount is reduced from cost to value and that change reflected in net income as a *realized* loss. The new cost basis cannot be adjusted based on later recovery in the asset's fair value.

Equity Securities.

Equity securities represent an ownership interest in an entity, by giving the holder not a fixed contractual claim to the issuer's assets but a residual claim to those assets remaining after all other claimants are paid. Equity securities customarily are entitled to vote in the election of directors of the issuer and on certain extraordinary matters. The voting rights give the holder of substantial voting percentages the power to influence or control the issuer. Returns on equity securities arise in part through the declaration of dividends and in part through value appreciation. Accounting for equity securities depends primarily on the level of control the holder's ownership interest represents.

Cost or Fair Value Method for Less than 20%. Investments in the stock of another entity amounting to less than 20% of the total voting power of that other entity are accounted for using either the cost or fair value method, depending on whether they are listed for trading on an organized capital market. This affects whether there is a readily determinable fair value. For example, common stock issued by a corporation with few stockholders and not listed on a public stock exchange may lack readily determinable fair values whereas common stock issued by a large publicly-traded corporation would ordinarily have readily determinable fair values.

Under the *cost method*, the investor records its investment at cost. Most dividends received are treated as income (special rules apply for dividends exceeding the issuer's earnings, which are accounted for by reducing the investment's carrying amount). Under the *fair value method*, the investor adjusts the carrying amount of the investment based on the market value of the investee's stock. It recognizes both dividends received and changes in market prices of the stock in income, as earnings or losses from investment.

To illustrate the bookkeeping (generally applicable to investments in both equity and debt securities), suppose that on May 1 Larry's Firm buys, for $10,000 cash, shares of IBM stock. To account for that investment, the following entries would be made:

IBM Stock	$10,000	
Cash		$10,000

Now assume that on May 31, the market price of IBM stock is $6,000. Under the cost method, no entry or change would be made. Under the fair value method, the carrying amount should be reflected as lower. We could do this by making a right side entry to the asset account IBM Stock for $4,000. Indeed, that is precisely what we would do if we were to sell the stock. But since we are not selling it, we need a mechanism to show the historical cost of the shares and their current fair value. To do this, we draw again on the *contra account* concept discussed above in connection with Accounts Receivable charge offs and in Chapter 5 concerning accumulated depreciation.

The contra account used to track changes in the fair value of investments in debt and equity securities is called a *Valuation Account*. To reflect reduction in the market value below the previous carrying amount (below cost), we would make a left side entry to charge the amount of the decline ($4,000) to income and a right side entry to reduce the asset IBM Stock.

Unrealized Loss on IBM Stock	$4,000	
Valuation Account (IBM Stock)		$4,000

Note that the left side entry is characterized as an *unrealized* loss to reflect that no *actual* loss has occurred because no sale of the asset has occurred. When the securities are sold, any gain or loss at that time will be reflected directly in the IBM Stock account.

Equity Method for 20% to 50%. When an investment of from 20% to 50% of the voting stock of another entity is made, the other entity is called an *investee* and the investing entity is called the *investor*. Under the equity method of accounting, the investor reports the initial investment in the investee at cost. The investment is then adjusted each period to reflect changes in the owners' equity of the investee. When the investee generates earnings (or incurs losses), its owners' equity increases (or decreases), and the investor's proportionate share of that increase (or decrease) is reflected in the investment's carrying amount. Receipts of cash dividends on the investment are treated as converting a part of the investment from an interest in the investee's owners' equity into cash.

Consolidation Method for More than 50%. Different rules apply when an investment of more than 50% of the voting power of another entity is made. When the other entity is a corporation, it is called a *subsidiary* and the investing entity is called the *parent*. Ownership of a majority of the voting power of another entity gives the investing entity the legal power to direct its affairs. In the case of a corporation, this power arises through the power to elect the board of directors. There are many advantages to a parent corporation of operating its overall business through numerous subsidiaries, including operational and organizational benefits as well as insulating a parent's assets from the reach of the subsidiary's creditors. As a result, most United States corporations of any substantial size operate through a number of subsidiaries.

As separate legal entities, the parent and the subsidiaries each prepares their own financial statements. But because of the parent's control over the subsidiaries, the parent will, in addition, prepare a set of *consolidated financial statements*. The statements show the aggregate financial condition and performance of the entire group of separate entities as a whole. In particular, the parent's consolidated financial statements will present the sum of the line items of all accounts (cash, sales, earnings, and so on) of itself, and all its subsidiaries.

When preparing consolidated financial statements, all revenues and expenses that result from transactions between members of the consolidated group are eliminated for reporting purposes. This is because such transactions within the group do not affect the consolidated group's overall financial condition or performance. For example, rent paid by a subsidiary to its parent should be eliminated because neither the expense to the subsidiary nor the revenue to the parent affects the results of operations or financial condition of the consolidated entity as a whole. Other examples of intercompany eliminations include sales to affiliated entities, cost of goods sold regarding sales between affiliated entities and interest expense or revenue on loans between affiliated entities.

Similarly, the ownership interest of the parent in the subsidiary is eliminated in combining their financial statements. That interest is eliminated from both the asset and the owners' equity components of the balance sheet (as well as the retained earnings component of the statement of changes in owners' equity, discussed in the next Chapter). In cases where the parent's ownership interest is less than 100%—say an outside investor owns a 10% stake—the portion owned by the outsider will not be so eliminated. It appears in the owners' equity portion of the balance sheet on a line item called *non-controlling interest* (in financial statements prepared before 2008, the term *minority interest* was used).

One consequence of the consolidation method of accounting for investments is that the particular contributions of subsidiaries to a parent's overall financial condition and performance may be obscured. Indeed, GAAP does not require that a parent and subsidiary apply the same accounting policies to their respective accounts. It is therefore prudent, and may even be required by federal securities laws discussed in Chapter 8, to include with a parent's consolidated financial statements a narrative discussion of any subsidiaries whose performance could have a material effect on the parent's overall performance. *See* In re Caterpillar, Inc., Exchange Act Release No. 34–30,532 (Mar. 31, 1992), 50 S.E.C. 903, 1992 WL 71,907 (S.E.C.).

Illustration 6-2.

Look at Illustration 6-2, an excerpt from a full set of financial statements. From note 1 to those financial statements under the heading "Consolidation," it indicates that the financial statements report the company's investments in "affiliated companies" using the equity method. It also discloses that the financial statements are "consolidated" by including the accounts of the parent entity as well as its subsidiaries.

Finally, the disclosure notes that all significant intercompany transactions have been eliminated.

ILLUSTRATION 6–2
BIC CORPORATION AND SUBSIDIARIES
NOTES TO CONSOLIDATED FINANCIAL STATEMENTS

1. **SUMMARY OF SIGNIFICANT ACCOUNTING POLICIES**: A summary of significant accounting policies for BIC Corporation and its subsidiaries (the "Corporation"), manufacturers and distributors of high-quality, low-cost consumer products, is as follows:

Consolidation The consolidated financial statements include the accounts of BIC Corporation and its subsidiaries. An investment in an affiliated company is accounted for on the equity method. All significant intercompany balances and transactions have been eliminated.

Off-Balance Sheet Arrangements.

The intercompany ownership rules relating to equity securities often tempt managers to exploit the seemingly bright line between the equity and consolidation methods set at greater than 50% ownership. Managers may be tempted, for example, to negotiate investments in investees at exactly 50% rather than greater. That enables using the equity method (which calls for a single line item on the investor's balance sheet showing "equity investments" at adjusted cost) rather than the consolidation method (which requires full inclusion on the parent's financials of all line items of the subsidiary, including debt).

This is an example of a broader category of techniques called "off-balance sheet financing." The label reflects that using investees of 50% or less as investment vehicles can enable a party to fund substantial operations through that vehicle without burdening its own balance sheet with that funding. Table 6-1 shows how substantial the differences can be.

Table 6-1
Off-Balance Sheet Financing
Comparison of Equity Method and Consolidation Method

	Equity Method		Consolidation Method
	Parent	Sub	Consolidated
Current assets	$50,000	$100,000	$150,000
Long term assets	100,000	40,000	140,000
Equity in investee	5,000		
TOTAL	155,000	140,000	290,000
Current Liabilities	10,000	10,000	20,000
Long term liabilities	20,000	120,000	140,000
Minority interest			5,000
Owners' equity	125,000	10,000	125,000
TOTAL	155,000	140,000	290,000

Parent shows a lean (unleveraged) balance sheet using the equity method: total liabilities of $30,000 versus equity of $125,000. Sub is highly leveraged: total liabilities of $130,000 versus equity of $10,000. Using the equity method, the investor gets to continue to sport its leanness; using the consolidated method, it must reveal that it is leveraged: total liabilities of $160,000 versus equity of $125,000. While these differences should strike an intuitive significance, Chapter 8 discusses further these sorts of ratios, which are broadly referred to as debt-to-equity ratios.

The substantial differences and the resulting temptation explain why accounting principles for investments in equity securities are in fact written as presumptions rather than as bright line rules. That is, ownership of greater than 50% of the voting power of another entity presumptively indicates control requiring using the consolidation method but control can arise at lower levels that would require using the consolidation method as well.

Conversely, consolidation treatment can be negated even at more than 50% ownership in unusual circumstances when the parent nevertheless lacks control (say the subsidiary is in receivership or operates in a politically unstable foreign country) or where the minority interest is also heavily concentrated (say 45% is owned by a single entity). When consolidation otherwise would apply but for such negating circumstances, the equity method is used. The equity method likewise applies to ownership positions of less than 20% when effective control or significant influence nevertheless exists.

A company may enter into a wide variety of contractual relationships with unconsolidated but related parties (sometimes called *special purpose entities* or *SPEs*). These relationships constitute *off-balance sheet* financing arrangements when the company has some level of obligation with respect to them. Obligations may arise under guarantee contracts such as indemnification commitments or letters of credit supporting the other entity's borrowings; financial instruments not otherwise appearing on the company's financial statements but fluctuations in the value of which nevertheless affect it (*see* Section C below); or asset transfers between the company and the other entity used to support either's credit, liquidity or market risk. GAAP requires the company to disclose all such arrangements bearing effects on the company's financial position or performance. For SEC registrants, these disclosures must be made in narrative form as part of management's discussion and analysis (MD&A, a subject discussed in Chapter 8).

C. FINANCIAL INSTRUMENTS

Business managers face a variety of risks in managing an entity's affairs, and some of these risks can be reduced by using specialized financial instruments. For example, assume an entity has outstanding debt of $50,000 it previously borrowed at a fixed interest rate of 9% pursuant to a loan agreement that carries a substantial penalty for prepayment. Current interest rates have fallen to 5%. If the entity believes that interest rates will remain below 9% during the remaining term of the loan, then it would be desirable to take advantage of the lower rate. How can it do this without incurring the prepayment penalty under the loan agreement?

One way is to enter into an agreement with another party that has different beliefs about the direction of interest rates or a different appetite for the risk of adverse changes in those rates. The entity can agree to pay a floating rate of interest on the $50,000 debt in exchange for the other party's agreement to pay the 9% fixed rate on that amount of debt. This device is called an *interest rate swap*. It is one example of a wide variety of financial instruments that are often collectively referred to as *derivatives* because the value of the instrument is *derived from* some other benchmark—in this case, the relationship between the fixed rate of interest and the floating rate of interest over time.

At a conceptual level, everything is a derivative since value exists ultimately only in relation to something other than the thing being valued. This label is given to a sub-class of the universe of things, however, that reflect innovation in ability to identify, measure and hedge certain kinds of financial risk. Another typical example of a derivative of this sub-class of the universe is an executory contract to buy some commodity (say oil) at the prevailing price today for delivery at some future time (say in one year). The value of that contract is derived from the prevailing price of oil at all times between today and one year from today. This device is often called a *futures contract.*

These simple examples are just two of a multitude of derivatives that proliferated in recent decades. They include risk hedging with respect to fluctuations in the prices and values of a whole range of underlying things including oil and other commodities, interest rates, foreign currency exchange rates, equity and debt securities, and just about any other financial benchmark you can think of.

In general, entities must recognize all derivatives as either assets or liabilities on the balance sheet and measure them at fair value. Yet the fair value of such a financial instrument can change over time with market conditions, alternately representing an asset of the entity (when the value is positive to it) or a liability to it (when the value is negative to it). These changes in value of the instrument have the effect of generating gains or losses. The changing market value therefore needs to be reflected by recording gains or losses on the investment in the income statement in accordance with the matching principle.

Yet, the complexity of many derivative financial instruments makes accounting for them correspondingly complex. FASB has struggled to provide suitable accounting for the wide variety of derivative financial instruments. An example appears in its distinction between various objectives derivative financial instruments may be designed to achieve. *Fair value hedges* address exposure to changes in asset or liability values (such as an interest rate swap intended to hedge the risk that rising interest rates will decrease the fair value of a debt investment) and gains or losses on such contracts are recognized as part of net income when they occur. In contrast, *cash flow hedges* address exposure to variable cash flows of a forecasted transaction (such as a currency swap calling for one party to pay in US dollars and its counterparty to pay in Euros). Gains or losses on these are recorded as part of other comprehensive income when they occur and later reclassified into net income when the related (hedged) transaction affects earnings.

Difficulties can arise in assuring that accounting for the financial instrument coheres with accounting for the related hedged transaction. Suppose, for example, an entity invests in the debt of another entity promising a fixed 5% interest rate for five years and intends to hold it to maturity. If interest rates rise to 6% in those years, the debt's relative value decreases, but if rates fall to 4%, the debt's relative value increases. To hedge against such fluctuations in interest rates, suppose the investor also enters into a financial instrument whose value changes inversely with the changing relative value of the debt investment. So if rates rise, the instrument's value increases and if rates fall, its value decreases.

Under traditional accounting applicable to held-to-maturity debt securities (discussed in the previous section), fluctuations in the debt's value are not recognized; yet, under accounting applicable to financial instruments, fluctuations in the instrument's value may be recognized. That is an odd result: if interest rates fall, the debt instrument increases in value but that is not recognized whereas the financial instrument decreases in value and that is recognized. Struggles like this have increasingly led FASB to consider expanding the scope of fair value accounting to a wider variety of asset classes than traditionally has been the case, to promote more coherent accounting.

A more comprehensive strategy of accounting policy to capture these complexities is simply to require extensive narrative disclosure concerning the use, value fluctuation and accounting treatment of financial instruments and related hedged transactions. Accordingly, apart from direct inclusion of fair values of derivatives on the balance sheet and associated recognition of gains and losses on both the derivative and the hedged asset or liability on the income statement, GAAP calls for considerable footnote disclosure.

Entities must disclose their objectives in holding or issuing derivative instruments, the context needed to understand those objectives, and their strategies for achieving the objectives. This disclosure must distinguish between fair value hedges, cash flow hedges, as well as various types of analogous foreign currency hedges. This disclosure must also describe the entity's risk management policy for each type of hedge, including a description of the types of transactions that are hedged. More generally, accounting for financial instruments requires extensive disclosures concerning how and why an entity uses them and details concerning related accounting treatment, including how the treatment affects the entity's financial position, results of operations and cash flows.

Illustration 6-4.

Look at Illustration 6-4, an excerpt from a set of full financial statements. From note 14 of the financial statements, it discloses information about the company's use of financial instruments of various kinds.

ILLUSTRATION 6-4
BIC CORPORATION AND SUBSIDIARIES
NOTES TO CONSOLIDATED FINANCIAL STATEMENTS

14. FINANCIAL INSTRUMENTS.

The estimated fair values of other financial instruments, including debt, equity and risk management instruments, have been determined using available market information and valuation methodologies. These estimates require considerable judgment in interpreting market data, and changes in assumptions or estimation methods may significantly affect the fair value estimates. Fair values of all derivative instruments are reported on the balance sheet. The Company is exposed to market risks, such as changes in interest rates, currency exchange rates and commodity pricing. To manage the volatility relating to these exposures, the Company nets the exposures on a consolidated basis to take advantage of natural offsets. For the residual portion, the Company enters into various derivative transactions.

Interest Rate Hedging The Company's policy is to manage interest cost using a mix of fixed and variable-rate debt. To do so, the Company enters into interest rate swaps in which it agrees to exchange, at specified intervals, the difference between fixed and variable interest amounts calculated by reference to an agreed-upon notional principal amount. The Company has swaps with a fair value of $125 million designated as *fair value hedges* of underlying fixed-rate debt obligations and recorded as long-term assets. The values of both the fair value hedging instruments and the underlying debt obligations are recorded as equal and offsetting gains and losses in the interest expense component of the income statement. All existing fair value hedges are 100% effective. As a result, there is no impact to earnings due to hedge ineffectiveness.

Currency Rate Hedging The Company manufactures and sells its products in many countries and thus is exposed to movements in foreign currency exchange rates, with major exposures in Western and Eastern Europe. The purpose of the Company's foreign currency hedging activities is to manage the volatility associated with foreign currency purchases of materials. The Company uses purchased foreign currency options, forward exchange contracts and cross currency swaps which qualify as *cash flow hedges*. These are intended to offset the effect of exchange rate fluctuations on forecasted sales, inventory purchases and royalties. The fair values of these instruments are recorded as $94 million in assets and $101 million in liabilities. Gains and losses on these instruments are deferred in other comprehensive income (OCI) until the underlying transaction is recognized in earnings. The earnings impact is reported in either net sales, cost of goods sold, or marketing research and administrative expenses, to match the underlying transaction being hedged. These amounts will be reclassified into earnings as the underlying transactions are recognized.

Commodity Price Management Raw materials used by the Company are subject to price volatility caused by weather, supply conditions, political and economic variables and other factors. To manage the volatility related to anticipated inventory purchases, the Company uses futures and options with maturities generally less than one year and swap contracts with maturities up to five years. These market instruments are designated as *cash flow hedges*. Gain or loss is included in OCI to the extent effective, and reclassified into cost of goods sold in the period during which the hedged transaction affects earnings.

Historical Cost Versus Fair Value Accounting.

As noted in this Chapter's introduction, there are two long-recognized approaches to measure assets that are not sold and may be difficult to value. The first is historical cost. As Chapters Four and Five explored, this measures assets based on cost and then adjusts the carrying amount in specified ways, such as through annual depreciation for fixed assets. Recall that depreciation is recognized without regard to market values. That does not mean the exercise is arbitrary. The exercise commits to the result that, upon full depreciation, the asset will be reported at its salvage value. Periodic market value changes are essentially deferred until the asset is disposed of.

The second approach to asset measurement is fair value. This approach came into widespread use following a financial crisis that plagued the savings and loan industry in the 1980s. Critics said the industry used historical cost accounting to disguise the fact that asset values of its loans were falling in the market place. To prevent such schemes, fair value accounting was prescribed to require periodic revaluation of certain financial assets. This approach requires entities to assign values to assets they hold based on prevailing fair market values. (This explains why it also often is called "mark to market" accounting, a term usually used in the law and literature on tax accounting rather than financial accounting.)

Why measure some assets based on historical cost and others based on fair value? Use of different bases of measurement for different classes of assets is sometimes referred to as characteristic of a *mixed attribute* model of accounting. Such a model reflects that different measurements are justified depending on how one or the other optimizes two of accounting's fundamental objectives, reliability and relevance. Historical cost may be more reliable because it is based on an actual exchange transaction, but as time passes an asset's historical cost may become less relevant; prevailing fair values may be more relevant, but can sometimes be less reliable, as they are not based on an actual exchange transaction.

Accurate use of fair value measures requires the existence of a readily available market with observable prices or at least observable inputs. When an active market does not exist for an asset, it may be more prudent to measure it using historical cost, not fair value. Yet temptation is strong to conceptualize certain assets, including financial instruments, as best represented by fair value, even if that requires making assumptions based on models and expectations rather than actual market conditions. This approach, sometimes informally called "mark to model" accounting, involves developing a model of what a market would look like and to imagine what a willing buyer and willing seller would trade the asset for in an orderly market transaction. GAAP allows for this in certain circumstances, requiring extensive disclosure of the model's details and related assumptions.

D. INTANGIBLE ASSETS

Intangible assets are non-monetary assets that lack physical substance in that they cannot be seen or touched or physically measured.

Readily imaginable examples include legal interests such as copyrights, patents, trademarks and franchise arrangements. They also include more complex concepts described as goodwill and in-process research and development. The latter raise special problems in the context of business acquisitions.

Accounting Goodwill.

In acquiring a majority equity interest in another entity, GAAP at one time permitted two alternative approaches for the accounting. If only stock was used in the takeover and other restrictions were met, the acquisition could be treated as if nothing other than a business marriage had occurred. Under this *pooling method*, the assets and liabilities of the two entities were pooled and the entries of the resulting entity's balance sheet were basically the sum of those items beforehand.

If these restrictions were not met, the acquisition had to be treated as a purchase of one entity by the other. Under this *purchase accounting* for a business combination, the acquisition of one entity (the target) by another (the buyer) is treated just as the buyer's acquisition of any other resource would be: the cost of the acquisition is recorded on the buyer's balance sheet. The cost is equal to the purchase price. That price is allocated to each line item of the target's balance sheet at the respective fair market values of the target's various assets and liabilities. The carrying amounts listed on the target's balance sheet become functionally irrelevant (*e.g.*, historical costs net of accumulated depreciation for fixed assets and the lower of cost or market for all assets are jettisoned).

In many acquisitions, the purchase price exceeds the net fair market value of the target's balance sheet. The premium paid may reflect synergy gains and/or cost-savings the two entities may enjoy when combined. These can arise by eliminating back-office costs or teaming up a great brand with a great distribution system and so on.

When such a premium is paid, pooling accounting ignores it as irrelevant. Purchase accounting characterizes it as a new asset account called "goodwill." That asset would subsequently be treated in substantially the same way that other fixed assets are treated—its cost allocated over future periods, up to 40 years, as an expense. Since goodwill is an intangible asset, this cost allocation technique is called amortization. Goodwill amortization under the purchase method of accounting for business combinations thus had the effect of reducing net income over a period up to 40 years, as a result of the expense.

Under the pooling method, such a premium is irrelevant as an accounting matter since all line items on the constituent firms' financial statements are added together to form the combined firm's statements. No adjustments from historical cost to market value occur and no separate account is made for any difference between the purchase price and the fair value of the assets acquired. No goodwill account exists to be amortized.

Managers tended to prefer pooling because it liberated them from the perennial drag on earnings that goodwill amortization entailed. Deals were structured to meet the pooling requirements and paid for in stock whenever possible. Accounting purists argued that purchases were simply being disguised.

Each side had a point. The pro-pooling party's best argument was that in most acquisitions goodwill (the premium paid) did not decline in value in the years after the acquisition. So imposing an annual charge to earnings did not make sense. It was less like depreciating the price paid for other long term assets that wear out with time, and more like land which does not wear out and which GAAP does not require to be amortized or depreciated. The pro-purchase party's best argument was that most acquisitions are not conceptually equivalent to a marriage, but are instead exactly like any other asset acquisition an entity makes, and should be accounted for similarly.

A compromise rule now applies. Acquisitions are treated as purchases so that a goodwill account must be created to record any premium purchase price. But that amount does not automatically have to be amortized. As long as the goodwill value does not decline in the years after the acquisition, it does not have to be written off. So there is no charge to earnings. Only when the assessed value of goodwill is less than the carrying amount of goodwill will a hit to earnings occur, treated as an "impairment loss" to be recorded on the income statement.

The value of the goodwill account must be examined annually to determine whether it has been impaired. (Part III discusses valuation techniques useful in such exercises.) The annual review must be supplemented by periodic reviews if circumstances arise that suggest possible permanent impairment (ranging from major legal problems to adverse economic environments to plans to dispose of the related business by sale or otherwise). This approach is akin to the lower of cost or market in that implied goodwill values greater than carrying values do not justify writing up the goodwill account.

In-Process Research and Development.

The special accounting rules governing business acquisitions include special treatment of particular classes of assets that accompany them. A leading example concerns the treatment of research and development projects that the acquired entity has in process on the acquisition date. Ordinarily, costs of research and development are treated as expenses when incurred. For many years, that same standard also applied to the acquisition of such in-process research and development. In 2007, however, FASB modified this standard to require buyers to account for such in-process research and development in substantially the same way GAAP treats acquired goodwill. Acquiring entities record in-process research and development as an asset, at its fair value on the acquisition date. It is tested annually for impairment until the related projects are completed or abandoned.

Economic Goodwill.

The term goodwill is sometimes used in a non-accounting sense to refer to the value a business possesses above and beyond its asset base that enables it to perform better than its peers with similar asset bases. This *economic goodwill* can be due to the characteristics of the business as a going concern, and can include brand name recognition, customer loyalty, and other intangible reputation benefits arising in product markets as well as markets for labor and capital. Economic goodwill in this sense may be an intangible asset, but is never recorded on a balance sheet.

Other Intangible Assets.

Other types of intangible assets sometimes do appear on a balance sheet. These intangible assets are resources lacking physical substance but furnishing probable future economic benefits and arising in connection with an economic exchange. Examples include patents, trademarks, franchises and copyrights. Intangible assets such as these are an increasingly important economic resource for many entities.

In general, the main accounting issue relating to such intangible assets concerns whether associated costs are to be treated as one-time expenses or capital assets whose cost is allocated to expense over time (amortized). Costs incurred to acquire intangible assets from third parties are invariably required to be treated as capital assets. These are amortized following principles that parallel the principles of depreciation applicable to fixed (tangible) assets described in Chapter 5. GAAP offers special guidance to determine the expected useful lives of various categories of intangible assets, especially to take into consideration the possibility of extensions or renewals of their useful lives.

In contrast, costs associated with developing intangible assets internally are ordinarily treated as expenses when incurred. Research and development leading to the award of a patent or to the creation and marketing of a trademarked product are good examples. So are advertising and similar disbursements. As noted, these are expensed when incurred.

Fees paid to obtain a franchise or copyright are treated as expenses if they are minor in relation to the acquirer's size. When a large publishing house pays a new author to buy a first novel for $5,000 that is usually treated as an expense when incurred. For fees that are substantial in relation to the publisher's size, the matching principle is implicated. When an entrepreneur starts a sole proprietorship established to own and operate a McDonald's franchise, the franchise's cost would be treated as an asset.

Should it be amortized? Unlike tangible assets, such as equipment and buildings, many intangible assets tend not to decline in value or wear out or require reinvestment to maintain. A McDonald's franchise may increase in value over time, as might the Coca-Cola trademark. To reflect this difference, acquired intangible assets with indefinite lives are not subject to automatic amortization but instead are treated like acquired goodwill and acquired in-process research and development are treated. They must be tested at least annually for impairment by comparing the fair values of those assets with their recorded amounts.

Acquired intangible assets with finite lives, however, must be amortized over their estimated useful lives. Patents, for example, are exclusive rights for the manufacture, use and sale of a particular product, granted by law for a period of years, typically 20 years in the United States and Europe (though this varies). That patent term would be the maximum useful life, and the amortization period cannot exceed that length. It could be shorter. If the patent is likely to lose its value in fewer years, that shorter time is the period of amortization.

GAAP also requires footnote disclosure of information about goodwill and other intangible assets. This includes (a) information about the changes in the carrying amount of goodwill from period to period (in the aggregate and by reportable segment), (b) the carrying amount of intangible assets by major intangible asset class for those assets subject to amortization and for those not subject to amortization, and (c) the estimated intangible asset amortization expense for the next five years.

Illustration 6-3.

Look at Illustration 6-3, an excerpt from a full set of financial statements. From note 1, the summary of significant accounting policies, it discloses how the company treats goodwill and other intangible assets, distinguishing between indefinite-lived intangible assets and others and summarizing its approach to the impairment test. (Portions detailing the carrying amount and amortization of goodwill are not included.)

ILLUSTRATION 6-3
BIC CORPORATION AND SUBSIDIARIES
NOTES TO CONSOLIDATED FINANCIAL STATEMENTS

1. **SUMMARY OF SIGNIFICANT ACCOUNTING POLICIES . . .**

Goodwill and Other Intangible Assets. In accordance with recent FASB pronouncements, the Company has eliminated the pooling-of-interests method of accounting for business acquisitions and eliminated the amortization of goodwill for indefinite-lived intangible assets and initiates an annual review for impairment. Identifiable intangible assets with a determinable useful life continue to be amortized. The Company will annually perform an impairment test based on a fair value concept of all its non-amortizable intangible assets, including goodwill. The annual review will be supplemented when events or circumstances indicate a possible inability to recover the carrying amount. Such evaluation is based on various analyses, including cash flow and profitability projections that incorporate the impact of the Company's existing businesses. The analyses necessarily involve significant management judgment to evaluate the capacity of an acquired business to perform within projections. No goodwill impairment has resulted to date.

E. LEASES AND OTHER LONG-TERM OBLIGATIONS

Leases: History and Challenges.

A lease is a contract that conveys the right to control the use of identified property for a period of time in exchange for consideration. There are an infinite variety, ranging from simple short-term arrangements like vacation car rentals to complex long-term mechanisms that more resemble a sale, as when an aircraft manufacturer leases planes to an airline for 25-year terms.

The wide variety of arrangements—and their ubiquity in business—has long made lease accounting a more intricate topic than you might expect. One result of the challenges was an ongoing tension between what GAAP sought to produce and how GAAP was being applied in practice. Most recently, FASB overhauled GAAP lease accounting in standards taking effect in 2019. The great practical and intellectual significance of this warrants discussion of both the historical treatment and the new approach.

Accountants traditionally distinguished between two kinds of leases, the *operating lease* and the *capital lease*. An operating lease is the thing that comes to mind when one speaks of a lease in generic terms. It authorizes a lessee (tenant) to use some property for a defined period of time in exchange for rental payments called for periodically over that time. Since the property is owned by the lessor and only rented by the lessee, it is an asset of the lessor and does not appear as an asset on the lessee's balance sheet. Nor does the lessee's obligation under an operating lease appear as a liability to it on the balance sheet, but instead the lease payments are treated as expenses as and when they are paid (subject of course to the rules governing accrual of lease obligations studied in Chapter 3).

A capital lease was treated very differently. It was treated as if the lessee had acquired the leased property and as if it belonged to it. The property therefore appeared as an asset on the lessee's balance sheet and the payment obligations as a liability on its balance sheet. The liability is reduced over time by the full amount of the lease payments less some portion thereof deemed to constitute an appropriate amount of interest given the context of the transaction.

The significance of the difference between these types of leases was therefore the impact they had on the assets and liabilities a lessee would report when engaging in the transaction. There may be good reasons for an entity to desire to include on (or exclude from) its balance sheet some asset or some liability. To the extent such balance sheet management could be achieved through structuring a lease transaction as either an operating lease or a capital lease, it may have been desirable to do so.

Such an effort is another example of the more general strategy of *off-balance sheet financing* to avoid any direct impact on the balance sheet, whether to the level of assets or to the level of liabilities. For example, an entity may be operating its business subject to various contractual arrangements with lenders or others that put limits on the relationship between its assets and its liabilities.

An example of a common form of such a restriction is a covenant in a loan agreement or a bond indenture to maintain assets at a level at least twice as high as the level of liabilities. Faced with that sort of restriction, the entity may be precluded from buying outright some new asset it desires. Assume an airline operating under such a covenant had an assets to liabilities ratio of exactly two-to-one and sought to purchase additional aircraft by making a 10% downpayment in cash and financing the other

90%. Doing so could violate the covenant, however, by reducing the ratio of assets to liabilities below 2:1.*

To circumvent the restriction, one could structure the deal as a lease rather than a purchase. The entity could lease the planes for say 20 years, with no downpayment, annual rental payments set approximating the economic terms of the outright purchase, and with the final caveat that the planes become theirs at the end of the term. The result of achieving characterization as a lease would be that the aircraft does not appear as an asset nor does the payment obligation appear as a liability.

But can (or should) the alternative structure be characterized and treated in these different ways, given that the economic substance of the two alternative deals is the same? Traditionally, this is where the distinction between operating leases and capital leases was implicated. The lease in the foregoing circumvention hypothetical, if characterized as a capital lease, would prevent the circumvention and in effect force the economically equivalent transaction to be accounted for as creating an asset and a liability for the entity.

The challenge, then, was how to distinguish between transactions properly characterized as operating leases versus capital leases. Traditionally, GAAP provided four bright line rules, *if any one of which applied*, the transaction was deemed to be a capital lease and not an operating lease. These four rules were stated in terms of characteristics of the transaction to divine the degree to which the transaction gave the lessee the functional equivalent of ownership in the property. These were the bright line rules:

- If the lessee ended up owning the property under the terms of the lease at the end of the lease term;

- If the lessee had the right to purchase the property under the terms of the lease at or near the end of the lease term for an option price that amounts to what accountant's call a "*bargain price*"—that is some price so dramatically below any possible sense of the asset's market value that only a fool would fail to buy;

---

* To illustrate, suppose assets = 200, liabilities = 100 and the plane costs 50. Entries would be:

Plane	50	
Cash		5
Debt		45

Now assets = 245 and liabilities = 145, for an asset-to-liability ratio of about 1.7.

- If the term of the lease covered a period of time equal to or greater than 75% of the useful life of the property upon inception of the lease; *or*

- If the present value of the total of payments to be made under the lease amounted to 90% or more of the fair market value of the property.

If any of these traits characterized the deal, then the deal was a capital lease and not an operating lease. FASB ultimately found this approach unsatisfactory, observing that a great many leases with a very large aggregate market value, were being treated as operating leases that probably should have appeared on the balance sheet.

Leases: Contemporary Approach.

FASB undertook a lengthy project to revise GAAP on lease accounting. As a result, lessees must record all long-term leases (those with terms exceeding 12 months) on the balance sheet. They recognize both an asset—the right of use—and a liability—the present value of contractual payments for that right.

On the income statement, the lessee's accounting still depends on whether the lease is an operating lease or not. Substantially the same determinations are made as under the traditional guidance, though without treating any of the factors as bright line rules. For operating leases, lessees recognize lease expense allocating the total lease payments on a straight-line basis over the term of the lease; otherwise, lessees recognize interest expense on the lease liability and amortization expense on the right-of-use asset.

For many companies whose business involves significant leasing activity—perhaps as many as half of all sizable companies—these changes are momentous. As companies work through the transition, many are providing disclosure such as the following in footnotes to their annual financial statements:

> In February 2016, the FASB issued accounting standard update (ASU) No. 2016–02, Leases (Topic 842). This new lease guidance requires that an entity should recognize assets and liabilities for leases with a maximum possible term of more than 12 months. A lessee would recognize a liability to make lease payments (the lease liability) and a right-of-use asset representing its right to use the leased asset (the underlying asset) for the lease term. Leases would be classified as either Type A leases (generally todays capital leases) or Type B leases (generally todays operating leases).

> For certain leases of assets other than property (for example, equipment, aircraft, cars, trucks), a lessee would classify the lease

as a Type A lease and would do the following: (1) recognize a right-of-use asset and a lease liability, initially measured at the present value of lease payments and (2) recognize the unwinding of the discount on the lease liability as interest separately from the amortization of the right-of-use asset.

For certain leases of property (that is, land and/or a building or part of a building), a lessee would classify the lease as a Type B lease and would do the following: (1) recognize a right-of-use asset and a lease liability, initially measured at the present value of lease payments and (2) recognize a single lease cost, combining the unwinding of the discount on the lease liability with the amortization of the right-of-use asset, on a straight-line basis. This new lease guidance is effective for our Company beginning in 2019. We are currently evaluating the impact of the adoption of this guidance in our consolidated financial statements.

Long-Term Debt.

There are a wide variety of other long-term liabilities, including long-term borrowing in the form of bonds and bank loans, as well as mortgages on fixed assets.

The principal amount of long-term debt that is payable in future accounting periods (usually measured in years) is set forth as a long-term liability on the balance sheet. The portion of any long-term debt that is payable within the next succeeding accounting period (usually the next year), whether for interest or for principal, is separately set forth as a current liability under the heading "Current Portion of Long-Term Debt."

The substantive terms of long-term debt—with respect to whether it is secured by the assets of the entity or unsecured, whether it enjoys senior status or subordinated status with respect to other debt, the interest rate, penalties for prepayment and other material terms—must be set forth in the footnotes to the financial statements.

Apart from disclosure associated with particular debt issues and related accounting treatment, additional disclosure should be made about debt containing material covenants. Some covenants restrict a borrower's rights to incur additional debt, limit the aggregate amount of interest obligations the borrower may commit to, and maintain various characteristics of financial health (these are discussed in Chapter 8).

Disclosure should be made when a company is in breach of those covenants, or reasonably likely to be in breach of them. Appropriate disclosure goes beyond the terms of the covenants to include steps taken to avoid or cure the breach (or have it waived), the impact of failure to achieve these results (including consequences such as triggering defaults on other obligations), and alternate sources of funding to repay the obligation and generate replacement funds. Disclosure should also be made concerning the impact of debt covenants on the entity's ability to obtain additional financing.

When a borrower is in default on debt otherwise classified as long-term, the lender may have the right to accelerate the debt's maturity date, meaning the debt would properly be classified as short-term. If the borrower obtains a waiver of default from the lender, however, GAAP allows continuing to treat the debt as long-term rather than short-term. This is true for any waiver obtained through the date the borrower issues its financial statements.

F. EMPLOYEE MATTERS

Most compensation payments to employees call for straightforward accounting and bookkeeping exercises. Cash paid weekly as salary to clerks at Larry's Firm, for example, are recorded as paid (or as earned in the case of accruals). More difficult accounting issues arise, however, concerning additional features of many compensation packages, including the following.

Pensions.

In the years following World War II, many business entities established *pension plans*, primarily as a means to circumvent limitations on the amount of compensation business entities could pay to employees. Early plans were called *defined-benefit plans* and obligated an employer to make specified pension payments to employees during their retirement. The employer would fund those future payments by periodic investment of resources in a pension fund. In more recent years, many business entities have redesigned their pension plans and have begun to provide a different sort of plan, called the *defined-contribution* plan. Largely driven by tax considerations, these plans usually require (or allow) an employee to make specified contributions to a retirement fund during the time she is employed, and some of them also obligate the employer to make matching contributions to the fund, also during the time of employment. Payments made to retired persons are drawn from that fund, and the employer has no separate obligation to make payments during retirement.

The assets in pension funds are managed by a third-party trustee on behalf of the entity sponsoring them and are usually invested in a variety of debt and equity securities. As a consequence of the investment of such funds, the total value of the assets in a plan fluctuates over time, not only by reason of new contributions but also because of changes in the rate of return on the invested assets over time. Also changing over time is the expected value of the payout the plan will be required to make as employees retire or otherwise become eligible for pension plan payments and as compensation levels change.

To ascertain the relationship between the value of the plan assets and the amount of the plan liabilities therefore requires making a number of estimates and judgments. On the investment side, estimates of the rates of return on invested assets are necessary, for example; and on the liability side, actuarial estimates of the rate and number of employee retirements or deaths are required. As a result of the fluctuations in such variables, at any moment in time, it is possible—indeed likely—that there will be a mismatch between the assets and liabilities in a pension plan.

When assets exceed liabilities a plan is said to be *overfunded*; when liabilities exceed assets a plan is said to be *underfunded*. In general, entities must recognize the overfunded or underfunded status of defined benefit pension plans as an asset or liability, respectively, on the balance sheet. Measurement is based on the difference between the fair value of plan assets and projected benefit obligations. The latter are estimated using a complex combination of inputs, including assumptions about employee longevity and inflation rates. Periodic changes in the net measurement are recorded as part of other comprehensive income (a concept explored in the next Chapter).

These notes on pension plan accounting are short because the rules are so complex that a full treatment would extend far beyond the scope of this book. Complexities arise not so much due to the nature of pension plans—which are fairly intuitive—but to the actuarial bases for estimating future liabilities and the dynamics that result in virtually daily changes to the integrity of those estimates.

Illustration 6-5.

Look at Illustration 6-5, an excerpt from a full set of financial statements. From note 7, it contains extensive disclosure with respect to the funded status of the company's pension plans. Note in particular the assumptions on which the calculations are based and the manner in which the plan assets were invested.

```
┌─────────────────────────────────────────────────────────────────┐
│                      ILLUSTRATION 6–5                             │
│                 BIC CORPORATION AND SUBSIDIARIES                  │
│              NOTES TO CONSOLIDATED FINANCIAL STATEMENTS           │
│                          * * * *                                 │
```

7. EMPLOYEE BENEFIT PLANS: . . . The following table sets forth the funded status at of the Corporation's defined benefit pension plans (in thousands):

	12/31 This Year		12/31 Last Year	
	Over-Funded	Under-Funded	Over-Funded	Under-Funded
Fair value of plan assets	$30,924	$24,923	$33,491	$27,425
Projected benefit obligation for services rendered to date	(26,319)	(31,593)	(28,150)	(32,173)
Excess of plan assets over projected benefit obligation (excess of projected benefit obligation over plan assets)	4,605	(6,670)	5,341	(4,748)
Unrecognized net (gain) loss	472	2,747	(252)	2,595
Prior service costs not yet recognized in net periodic pension costs	384	1,014	682	20
Unrecognized net asset	(2,239)	(533)	(2,666)	(666)
Prepaid pension (pension liability)	$3,222	$(3,442)	$3,105	$(2,799)
Actuarial present value of benefit obligations:				
Vested benefit obligation	$20,832	$31,395	$21,822	$31,908
Accumulated benefit obligation	$21,691	$31,476	$22,662	$31,933

```
                          * * * * *
```

The following assumptions were used in developing the above benefit obligation amounts:

	12/31 This Year	12/31 Last Year
Assumed discount rate	8.0%	7.0%
Assumed rate of compensation increase	4.0%	4.0%
Expected rate of return on plan assets	10.0%	10.0%

The plan assets were invested as follows:

	12/31 This Year	12/31 Last Year
Equity securities	63.9%	65.0%
United States Government securities	12.7	13.7
Cash equivalents and debt securities	23.4	21.3
Total	100.0%	100.0%

Contributions under the employees share purchase plans, the 401(k) Savings and Investment Plans and the Group Registered Retirement Plan were approximately $857,000, $728,000 and $406,000 in each of the last three years, respectively.

Other Retirement Benefits.

Another aspect of employee benefits that raises difficult accounting issues relates to retirement benefits, such as retiree medical and dental care and life insurance. In earlier eras these benefits were accounted for on a cash basis, treated as expenses when claims or premiums were paid. More recently, accountants moved to require these obligations to be approached from an accrual perspective. This requires recognition of liabilities in respect of retirement benefits. Determining the proper amount of such liabilities poses a number of significant problems of estimation, akin to those required in calculating pension benefits, with twists.

For example, determining the amount of payment obligations with respect to non-pension retirement benefits such as medical care depends on the nature of the medical care that will be required or offered in the distant future and healthcare costs at that time. Unlike the payment obligations under pension plans, moreover, payments for medical care will not ordinarily involve a steady stream of payments. Further, while early retirement will usually reduce benefits under typical pension plans, it usually will increase them under typical retired-employee benefit plans because more years will be covered and less expenses will be paid by Federal assistance such as Medicaid.

Illustration 6-6.

Look at Illustration 6-6, an excerpt from a set of full financial statements. It shows the Noncurrent Liabilities section of the company's balance sheet, which lists an account called Postretirement Benefits Other Than Pensions. From note 8 to those financial statements, it also shows the manner of calculating that noncurrent liability.

ILLUSTRATION 6–6
BIC CORPORATION AND SUBSIDIARIES
(LAST TWO YEARS)
CONSOLIDATED BALANCE SHEETS
(Dollars in thousands, except per share amounts)

	12/31 This Year	12/31 Last Year
Noncurrent Liabilities:		
Postretirement Benefits Other		
Than Pensions	19,882	17,854
Other	4,259	2,921
Total Noncurrent Liabilities	24,141	20,775

* * * * *

NOTES TO CONSOLIDATED FINANCIAL STATEMENTS

8. POSTRETIREMENT BENEFITS OTHER THAN PENSIONS: The Corporation provides certain postretirement medical and life insurance benefits for qualifying retired and active unionized and non-unionized employees in the United States. Most retirees outside the United States are covered by government sponsored and administered programs. Postretirement benefits are not pre-funded and are paid by the Corporation as incurred . . . .

The following table sets forth the status of postretirement benefits (in thousands):

	12/31 This Year	12/31 Last Year
Accumulated postretirement benefit obligation:		
Retirees	$ 9,088	$ 9,590
Fully eligible active plan participants	2,404	3,507
Other active plan participants	7,399	8,568
	18,891	21,665
Unamortized net gain (loss)	991	(3,811)
Total	$19,882	$17,854

For measurement purposes, a 14.0% annual rate of increase in the per capita cost was assumed for the last two years. The rate was assumed to decrease gradually to 5.5% over the next 15 years and remain at that level thereafter. The discount rate used in determining the accumulated postretirement benefit obligation was 8.0% at 12/31 this year and 7.0% at 12/31 last year. The unamortized net gain will be amortized over future periods.

A 1% increase in the assumed health care cost trend rate for each year would increase the accumulated postretirement benefit obligation as of 12/31 this year by $2.6 million and the net periodic postretirement benefit cost by $523,000.

Stock Option Compensation.

Stock options are a sizable portion of compensation at many business organizations. A typical stock option gives its holder the right (but not the duty) to buy stock in the entity during a future specified period such as 6 months or 3 years (called the *option period*) for a specified price (called the *exercise price*). It is typical for the exercise price to be set at an amount that is higher than the stock price when the option is issued. The motivation for such compensation is said to be to provide additional incentives for the recipient to manage the entity well—if he or she does, the stock price should rise and if it rises to an amount above the exercise price within the option period, then the recipient makes a profit by exercising the option.

Since 2004, GAAP has required recording stock option compensation as an expense on the income statement. Doing so entails numerous judgments based on alternative valuation models developed to measure the fair value of a stock option. In a widely-used model, stock option value is a function of its duration, its exercise price, prevailing interest rates, the price volatility of the related stock, and the dividends expected. Though most of these variables require some degree of judgment, the judgments are not harder than many other judgments accounting poses, such as determining the proper annual depreciation expense for a fixed asset like Larry's Limousine. (An old-fashioned method of valuing stock options, called the intrinsic value method, is simply the difference between the market price of the stock and exercise price of the options when granted.)

G. LOSS CONTINGENCIES

Uncertainties are pervasive in the business world, as elsewhere. For example, insurance companies may face potential losses from time to time as a result of changes in the regulations to which they are subject, and financial concerns may be subject to potential losses with respect to obligations to fund margin accounts in respect of positions they take in securities markets. Most generally, there is the uncertainty surrounding potential legal claims that most companies of any substantial size must contend with.

Even though no loss has yet occurred and so no monetary transaction cognizable under GAAP has transpired, GAAP's conservatism principle requires that such uncertainties be disclosed in the financial statements. These uncertainties are collectively called *loss contingencies* and reference is made to them as a line item on the balance sheet. The line item for loss contingencies does not usually state a monetary amount, but instead makes a cross-reference to the footnotes to the financial statements that contain a narrative discussion of the nature of the loss contingencies, management's assessment of their relative uncertainty, and the probable amount of any loss that it reasonably estimates will result from its actual occurrence.

Disclosure of loss contingencies alone is inadequate, however, once a loss becomes probable (rather than merely possible) and its amount can reasonably be estimated (rather than only broadly guessed). At that point, the loss must be recorded. A good parallel example would be the allowance for doubtful accounts concerning receivables discussed in Section A of this Chapter.

The cost of warranty coverage issued by a manufacturer is another example. These costs are typically handled by recording, when a sale is made, a warranty expense and a warranty liability, both in estimated amounts (much as with receivables). The liability is called an *estimated liability*.

At the other extreme, losses that are remote need not be disclosed at all. Determining whether a loss is remote, possible or probable is not always easy and calls for professional judgment from managers, accountants, auditors and lawyers. The subject is discussed further in Chapter 15.

Illustration 6-7.

Look at Illustration 6-7, an excerpt from a full set of financial statements. From note 12, it contains disclosure concerning contingencies and commitments not presently required to be reported on the company's balance sheet. As noted, companies carrying such disclosure will also include on the face of their balance sheet under the heading Noncurrent Liabilities an entry "Contingencies and Commitments." This line item often does not list any dollar amounts but instead makes a cross-reference to the note disclosing the matter.

ILLUSTRATION 6-7
BIC CORPORATION AND SUBSIDIARIES
NOTES TO CONSOLIDATED FINANCIAL STATEMENTS

* * * * *

12. CONTINGENCIES AND COMMITMENTS: The Corporation has significant contingent liabilities with respect to pending litigation, claims and disputes, principally relating to its lighters, which arise in the ordinary course of its business.

In July of last year, the U.S. Environmental Protection Agency ("EPA") issued its final volumetric ranking of Potentially Responsible Parties ("PRPs") for the Solvents Recovery Service of New England ("SRSNE") Superfund Site in Southington, Connecticut.

The Corporation has been notified that it is a PRP at the site and has been ranked, by the EPA, number 192 of a total of 1,659 PRPs. This ranking represents less than 1% of the total volume of waste disposed at the SRSNE Site, with the first 191 PRPs representing 90% of the total volume.

The Corporation cannot predict with certainty the total costs of cleanup, the Corporation's share of the total costs, the extent to which contributions will be available from other parties, the amount of time necessary to complete the cleanup, or the availability of insurance coverage. Based on currently available information, the Corporation believes that its share of the ultimate cleanup costs at this Site will not have a material adverse impact on the Corporation's financial position or on its results of operations, if such operations continue at the present level.

In November of the prior year, a state court jury in Creek County, Oklahoma, in a 9 to 3 verdict, awarded $11 million in actual damages and $11 million in punitive damages against the Corporation in connection with a case involving a cigarette lighter. On May 3, this year, the Court of Appeals of Oklahoma reduced the amount of punitive damages by $8 million. On May 23, the Corporation filed a petition for writ of certiorari with the Oklahoma Supreme Court and on July 13, the Oklahoma Supreme Court denied the Corporation's petition, thereby concluding this matter. This decision did not have a significant effect on the Corporation's consolidated financial position or on its results of operations.

While the ultimate liability with respect to the above matters, including any additional liability not provided for, is not presently determinable, it is the opinion of management, after consultation with counsel to the Corporation, that any liabilities resulting therefrom will not have a material adverse effect on the Corporation's consolidated financial position or on its results of operations if such operations continue at the present level.

H. GOING CONCERN DISCLOSURE

An important assumption underlying GAAP is that an entity will continue as a going concern. In that case, the ordinary principles of accounting concerning assets and liabilities, as well as revenues and expenses, remain relevant and reliable. But when a company faces imminent insolvency or becomes insolvent, GAAP envisions applying a specialized set of "liquidation accounting" principles instead. These alter many measurement and timing rules. Even when insolvency is not imminent, however, circumstances may jeopardize a company's ability to operate as a going concern. In such cases, GAAP requires the company to analyze the circumstances and, in some situations, disclose information about associated conditions and events.

Until 2016, GAAP provided scant guidance on this subject, whereas GAAS and federal securities law require that an auditor evaluate whether there is substantial doubt about an entity's ability to continue as a going concern for a reasonable period of time (not to exceed one year); GAAS further requires auditors to consider the possible financial statement effects. Effective in 2016, FASB requires *management* to evaluate whether there is substantial doubt about an entity's ability to continue as a going concern and to provide related footnote disclosures.

Specifically, management evaluates whether there are conditions or events, considered in the aggregate, that raise substantial doubt about the entity's ability to continue as a going concern within one year after the date financial statements are issued. "Substantial doubt" about an entity's ability to continue as a going concern exists when relevant conditions and events, considered in the aggregate, indicate that it is probable that the entity will be unable to meet its obligations as they become due within one year after the date its financial statements are issued. The term *probable* is taken to have the same meaning as that concerning loss contingencies, discussed in Section G above.

When management identifies and addresses such conditions or events, it should consider whether its plans to mitigate the effect will alleviate the substantial doubt. The mitigating effect is to be considered only to the extent that (1) it is probable that the plans will be successfully implemented and, if so, (2) it is probable that the plans will alleviate the conditions or events that raise the substantial doubt.

If the substantial doubt is alleviated as a result of management's plans, the entity should disclose information that enables users of the financial statements to understand the following: conditions or events that raised the substantial doubt; management's evaluation of their significance in relation to the entity's ability to meet its obligations; and the plans that alleviated the substantial doubt. But if substantial doubt is not alleviated, the entity should include a statement in the footnotes so indicating.

Companies of all sizes and ages can face going concern problems, though they are not common overall and tend to occur more often in smaller and younger ones. Among the first large companies to act on these new going concern warnings was the struggling retailer, Sears Holding Corp. Notably, its mitigation plans were apparently sufficient such that its outside auditor, Deloitte, did not reference any going concern problems in its auditor report. Some found it incongruous that GAAP would compel a company to disclosure going concern risks while GAAS and federal securities laws permit its auditor to give a clean audit report without mentioning the going concern question. Others stressed that this simply meant the system was working: the company both flagged the problem and proposed a solution, and the auditor indicated that the mitigation plan removed the doubt.

Problem 6

The summer gone, J&J move operations indoors in October, and the following things happen that month. Prepare an income statement for October and a balance sheet as of October 31 (and supporting journal entries, T-Accounts and closing entries), taking account of them. (Do not forget to include in your financial statements any impact that transactions occurring in prior periods have on this period.) In addition, prepare appropriate brief notes to accompany the financial statements with respect to transactions you believe call for such disclosure.

26. On October 1, J&J purchased the trailer discussed Problem 5 and had it installed on its land. The invoice for the trailer indicates a purchase price of $30,000 plus a separate installation charge of $2,800. J&J paid $5,000 of the total in cash; it borrowed the balance from Capital Bank, giving Capital Bank a mortgage on the trailer and promising in a loan agreement to repay the loan over 5 years by making monthly payments beginning November 1 covering principal and interest at an 8% annual rate. Assume that total payments due within the succeeding accounting period amount to $6,000. As of October 1, J&J had not decided how to depreciate the trailer.

27. On October 2, J&J bought 100 shares of BIC Corporation common stock at a per share price of $30. These shares represent less than 1% of BIC's total equity.

28. (a) During the month of October, J&J provided repair services valued at $10,500 to its customers. For those services, customers paid cash of $4,500 and charged the rest. (b) At the end of October, $2,200 of these charges were outstanding and $3,800 had been paid in cash.

29. (a) J&J received $200 in payments from customers who had charged services during August or September. (b) It decided that it was unlikely that it was going to be paid by customers that had charged a total of $400 in services on credit in October.

30. (a) J&J paid the phone bill it had received in September (transaction 13) and (b) during October J&J incurred telephone charges of $75, for which it is billed on October 10, with payment due November 10.

31. On October 15, one of the racers in the bike race J&J had organized filed a complaint against J&J in state court, alleging unspecified damages for injuries he sustained in an accident he suffered during the race that he claims are due to J&J's failure to warn him that he should have been wearing a bicycle helmet during the race. J&J has formed the

belief, after consulting with counsel (Larry's Firm, of course), that the lawsuit is frivolous and plans to defend it vigorously. J&J also mailed a copy of the complaint to its insurance company.

32. On October 25, the local newspaper ran a feature story about J&J characterizing it as one of the "most important new businesses in the area," press coverage that Jack and Jill believe will lead to substantial increases in demand for their services in the next couple of months.

33. On October 31, the closing price per share of BIC Corporation common stock on the public markets was $28.

34. On October 31, J&J made its judgment that the useful life of the trailer purchased and installed on October 1, is 5 years and J&J estimated its salvage value to be $4,000. J&J has decided to depreciate the trailer using the straight line method.

In preparing J&J's October financial records, please note that the foregoing transaction summary provides no information concerning inventory or salary/bonus expense. Since related transactions appear in J&J's previous financial statements, you would need to inquire about these and (1) assure proper accounting if transactions occurred or (2) prepare footnote disclosure explaining why if they had not. In addition, to the extent J&J has earned taxable income, it would be necessary for it to accrue related tax liabilities and disclose information concerning its tax rate.

Conceptual Questions 6A

A debate in accounting theory concerns the degree to which the ideal system is based mostly on detailed rules or mostly on general standards. Some believe that as business transactions grow more sophisticated and complex, accounting concepts follow suit. Compared to general accounting standards, detailed accounting rules may be more difficult to use, costly to implement and allow for structuring transactions to meet literal requirements while ignoring intent and spirit. Advocates of a standards-based approach argue it facilitates better reporting while pro-rules advocates caution that this could reduce the comparability of financial information and leave too much room for judgment by companies and auditors. Do the accounting principles discussed so far give you a basis for a preliminary opinion? Consider GAAP governing the subjects considered in this Chapter; are these rules or standards? How would you make them more of one or the other?

Conceptual Questions 6B

GAAP contemplates measuring assets either at historical cost (less depreciation for fixed assets) or fair value. It prescribes the method for some assets, such as historical cost for a building and fair value for most financial instruments. It is said that this mixed attribute model enables optimizing among two accounting objectives, relevance and reliability. Historical cost measures may be more reliable than market measures while market measures may be more relevant than cost measures. Different assets may more faithfully be measured using one than the other. One observes an increasing tendency in recent decades to apply fair value accounting to a broader range of asset classes than traditionally. Do you regard that trend as desirable? How important is the existence of an active functioning market to support fair value accounting, in general or as extended to more asset classes?

IFRS Note 6

Chapter 1 noted that persistent differences between GAAP and IFRS tend to involve advanced accounting topics. This is reflected in how many differences between the two arise in the advanced subjects discussed in this Chapter. It would require considerable space to detail all the ways the two standards differ on this Chapter's potpourri of topics. There are both formal and practical differences in application in many areas, including as to receivables, financial instruments, employee matters and loss contingencies. Highlighted below are some more discrete and salient formal differences concerning the Chapter's other topics.

- Under GAAP, the classifications of trading, available-for-sale, and held-to-maturity are used solely with respect to investment securities, such as debt and equity; under IFRS, all financial instruments, including securities, are classified into those three categories.

- For securities not listed on a public capital market, GAAP prescribes the cost method (not the fair value method); IFRS allows using fair value if a reliable measure is available.

- Whereas GAAP prescribes the equity method of accounting for investee positions, IFRS allows using the equity method, cost or fair value.

- GAAP bases the test for consolidation primarily on majority ownership, requiring consolidation of majority-owned subsidiaries unless the parent does not exercise control; under IFRS, the consolidation test is based primarily on control, requiring controlled entities to be consolidated. IFRS further provides an exception to this requirement for interests in subsidiaries classifiable as available-for-sale.

- Under GAAP, it is not necessary for parent and consolidated subsidiary accounting policies to be in conformity with one another; under IFRS, they must conform.

- Research and development costs are expensed as incurred under GAAP; under IFRS, they are capitalized and amortized.

- GAAP lease accounting distinguishes for income statement purposes between operating leases (lease expense allocated on a straight-line basis) and financing leases (allocated between interest expense and amortization expense). IFRS dispenses with the distinction and requires all long-term leases to be accounted for alike. Lease accounting is one area of significant persistent divergence between GAAP and IFRS.

- Under GAAP, disclosures are required when there is substantial doubt about an entity's ability to continue as a going concern or when substantial doubt is alleviated as a result of consideration of management's plans, with an outlook period up to one year. Under IFRS, disclosures are required when management is aware of material uncertainties that may cast significant doubt about an entity's ability to continue as a going concern. The IFRS time frame is at least one year from the financial statement date, with no outer time limit.

CHAPTER 7

CAPITAL ACCOUNTS

. . .

We have until now investigated in detail the asset and liability accounts, as well as the sub-categories of owners' equity, revenue, and expense. Our goal has been to compute net income by journal entries, T-Accounts and closing entries, and then to transfer net income to owners' equity on the balance sheet. In making that transfer to owners' equity, we have used a single owners' equity account. In this Chapter, we add greater detail to the owners' equity portion of the balance sheet, refining the category into a series of owners' equity accounts, or *capital accounts* as they will be called henceforth.

Capital accounts are neither assets nor liabilities—they are accounts in which the owners' interest in the entity is represented. The sum of the balances in all the capital accounts for any entity at any moment in time is equal to the entity's total assets minus total liabilities. $CA = A - L$

It is helpful to categorize capital accounts into three groups of accounts, reflecting the portion of owners' equity that is (1) contributed to the entity directly by owners; (2) generated by operations over time; and (3) subject to adjustment due to events designated as contributing to other comprehensive income.

The capital accounts for an entity differ depending on the legal form in which the entity is organized, as a corporation, a partnership, a sole proprietorship, or a limited liability company, to take the major examples. In this Chapter, the focus is on the capital accounts of corporations, and the others are briefly mentioned at the end.

A. CONTRIBUTED CAPITAL AND DISTRIBUTIONS

Amounts of capital invested by the shareholders of a corporation could simply be recorded in the corporation's books by listing the amount of consideration invested and the number of shares of stock issued in respect of it. In bookkeeping terms, a left-side entry could be made to reflect the increase in the corporation's assets as a result of the investment, and a right-side entry could be made to reflect the increase in the owner's equity as a result of the investment. If the corporation were to return any such invested amounts to a shareholder, opposite entries could be made in the appropriate amounts. But what if creditors of the corporation had made loans to the corporation between the time of the initial investment and the time of the return, and in making the loan had relied for some reason—however reasonable or unreasonable that might be—on the amount of the invested capital?

To deal with this perceived problem, in the early development of the corporate form of business organization, state legislatures created a system, called the *legal capital regime,* to protect creditor reliance. Here is how it worked. The shares of stock issued in respect of any investment in those shares were assigned a *par value* and the amount of consideration invested by a shareholder was divided into two parts. One part was equal to the total par value of the shares issued and was called *legal capital* (or *stated capital*), and the other part was equal to the rest of the consideration paid. A corporation could not issue shares for less than the par value and it could not return capital to shareholders out of the legal capital. In this way, so it was thought, creditors could rely on the amount of legal capital invested in the corporation.

Over time, this legal capital regime and the motivation to protect creditors came to be regarded as very naive. First, the assignment of a par value to shares of stock is entirely arbitrary. It would be set by the corporation's organizers and could be set equal to a penny, a nickel, a dime, a dollar, or any other amount. It was therefore meaningless as a substantive matter. Second, creditors are not interested in the amount of capital that was invested in the corporation at a prior point in time, but what the level of invested capital is compared to the earnings and cash flows a business generates over time. (Later Chapters furnish more details on these matters of measuring business performance and position.)

Most state legislatures have by now acknowledged that the legal capital regime does not serve the purposes for which it was originally designed. Indeed, the Model Business Corporation Act, adopted by some forty states, has substantially dismantled the legal capital regime and gives each corporation wide latitude in determining the proper method of accounting for contributions of invested capital from shareholders. However, some states, including Delaware (a leading state of incorporation for large corporations), retain significant vestiges of the legal capital regime. It remains necessary, therefore, to understand the basic features of that regime.

Continuing Legal Significance of Legal Capital Regime.

There are essentially three features of the legal capital regime that are significant as a matter of law. First, stock cannot be issued *by the corporation* for an amount of consideration less than the par value of the share (a shareholder can sell her stock for whatever consideration she likes). Any stock issued in violation of this rule is called "watered" stock and means that the corporation's shareholders can be held liable to the corporation's creditors for the deficiency amount, despite the usual rule that the liability of shareholders of corporations is limited to their equity investment in the corporation ("*limited liability*").

Second, the discretion of a board of directors to declare and pay dividends on stock or make other distributions to shareholders is constrained by the amount of legal capital. This constraint is a direct consequence of the historical belief that the balance in that account provided protection to creditors and distributions to shareholders could not be made from that account.

The third feature of the legal capital regime limits the kinds of consideration that can lawfully be paid for shares issued by a corporation, usually limiting it to cash and other tangible property and usually excluding promissory notes and promises to render future services. These limitations stemmed from a similarly primitive view about what sorts of assets qualified as valuable for purposes of the legal capital regime, reflecting again the mistaken belief that the idea of legal capital protected creditors somehow and that only consideration having unquestionable value could count in computing it.

To appreciate the operation of these rules and the degree to which many modern legislatures have come to regard them as anachronistic, consider the following provisions of the Model Business Corporation Act ("MBCA"), and the Official Comments thereto.*

Model Business Corporation Act

§ 6.21. Issuance of Shares

(a) The powers granted in this section to the board of directors may be reserved to the shareholders by the articles of incorporation.

(b) The board of directors may authorize shares to be issued for consideration consisting of any tangible or intangible property or benefit to the corporation, including cash, promissory notes, services performed, contracts for services to be performed, or other securities of the corporation.

(c) Before the corporation issues shares, the board of directors must determine that the consideration received or to be received for shares to be issued is adequate. That determination by the board of directors is conclusive insofar as the adequacy of consideration for the issuance of shares relates to whether the shares are validly issued, fully paid, and nonassessable.

---

*   These excerpts are for pedagogical rather than reference purposes and therefore deleted portions have not been indicated with ellipses or other punctuation.

(d) When the corporation receives the consideration for which the board of directors authorized the issuance of shares, the shares issued therefor are fully paid and nonassessable.

OFFICIAL COMMENT

The financial provisions of the Model Act reflect a modernization of the concepts underlying the capital structure and limitations on distributions of corporations. This process of modernization began with amendments in 1980 to the 1969 Model Act that eliminated the concepts of "par value" and "stated capital," and further modernization occurred in connection with the development of the revised Act in 1984. Practitioners and legal scholars have long recognized that the statutory structure embodying "par value" and "legal capital" concepts is not only complex and confusing but also fails to serve the original purpose of protecting creditors and senior security holders from payments to junior security holders. Indeed, to the extent security holders are led to believe that it provides this protection, these provisions may be affirmatively misleading. The Model Act has therefore eliminated these concepts entirely and substituted a simpler and more flexible structure that provides more realistic protection to these interests.

Section 6.21 incorporates not only the elimination of the concepts of par value and stated capital from the Model Act in 1980 but also eliminates the earlier rule declaring certain kinds of property ineligible as consideration for shares.

Since shares need not have par value, under section 6.21 there is no minimum price at which specific shares must be issued and therefore there can be no "watered stock" liability for issuing shares below an arbitrarily fixed price. The price at which shares are issued is primarily a matter of concern to other shareholders whose interests may be diluted if shares are issued at unreasonably low prices or for overvalued property. This problem of equality of treatment essentially involves honest and fair judgments by directors and cannot be effectively addressed by an arbitrary doctrine establishing a minimum price for shares such as "par value" provided under older statutes.

Section 6.21(b) specifically validates contracts for future services (including promoters' services), promissory notes, or "any tangible or intangible property or benefit to the corporation," as consideration for the present issue of shares. The term "benefit" should be broadly construed to include, for example, a reduction of a liability, a release of a claim, or benefits obtained by a corporation by contribution of its shares to a charitable organization or as a prize in a promotion. In the realities of commercial life, there is sometimes a need for the issuance of shares for contract rights or such intangible property or benefits. And, as a matter of business economics, contracts for future services, promissory notes, and intangible property or benefits often have value that is as real as the value of tangible property or past services, the only types of property that many older statutes permit as consideration for shares. Thus, only business judgment should determine what kind of property should be obtained for shares, and a determination by the directors [made in good faith and with due care] to accept a specific kind of valuable property for shares should be accepted and not circumscribed by artificial or arbitrary rules.

Accounting principles are not specified in the Model Act, and the board of directors is not required by the statute to determine the "value" of noncash consideration received by the corporation (as was the case in earlier versions of the Model Act). In many instances, property or benefits received by the corporation will be of uncertain value; if the board of directors determines that the issuance of shares for the property or benefits is an appropriate transaction that protects the shareholders from dilution, that is sufficient under section 6.21. The board of directors does not have to make an explicit "adequacy" determination by formal resolution; that determination may be inferred from a determination to authorize the issuance of shares for a specified consideration.

Section 6.21 also does not require that the board of directors determine the value of the consideration to be entered on the books of the corporation, though the board of directors may do so if it wishes. Of course, a specific value must be placed on the consideration received for the shares for bookkeeping purposes, but bookkeeping details are not the statutory responsibility of the board of directors. The statute also does not require the board of directors to determine the corresponding entry on the right-hand side of the balance sheet under owner's equity to be designated as "stated capital" or be allocated among "stated capital" and other surplus accounts. The corporation, however, may determine that the owners' equity accounts should be divided into these traditional categories if it wishes.

The second sentence of section 6.21(c) describes the effect of the determination by the board of directors that consideration is adequate for the issuance of shares. That determination, without more, is conclusive to the extent that adequacy is relevant to the question whether the shares are validly issued, fully paid, and nonassessable. Section 6.21(c) provides that shares are fully paid and nonassessable when the corporation receives the consideration for which the board of directors authorized their issuance. Whether shares are validly issued may depend on compliance with corporate procedural requirements, such as issuance within the amount authorized in the articles of incorporation or holding a directors' meeting upon proper notice and with a quorum present. The Model Act does not address the remedies that may be available for issuances that are subject to challenge. This somewhat more elaborate clause replaces the provision in earlier versions of the Model Act and many state statutes that the determination by the board of directors of consideration for the issuance of shares was "conclusive in the absence of fraud in the transaction."

§ 6.22. Liability of Shareholders

(a) A purchaser from a corporation of its own shares is not liable to the corporation or its creditors with respect to the shares except to pay the consideration for which the shares were authorized to be issued (section 6.21) or specified in the subscription agreement.

(b) Unless otherwise provided in the articles of incorporation, a shareholder of a corporation is not personally liable for the acts or debts of the corporation except that he may become personally liable by reason of his own acts or conduct.

OFFICIAL COMMENT

With the elimination of the concepts of par value and watered stock in 1980, the sole obligation of a purchaser of shares from the corporation, as set forth in section 6.22(a), is to pay the consideration established by the board of directors (or the consideration specified in the subscription, in the case of preincorporation subscriptions). The consideration for the shares may consist of promissory notes, contracts for future services, or tangible or intangible property or benefits, and, if the board of directors so decide, the delivery of the notes, contracts, or accrual of the benefits constitute full payment for the shares. See the Official Comment to section 6.21. Upon the transfer to the corporation of the consideration so determined or specified, the shareholder has no further responsibility to the corporation or its creditors "with respect to the shares," though the shareholder may have continuing obligations under a contract or promissory note entered into in connection with the acquisition of shares.

§ 6.40. Distributions to Shareholders

(a) A board of directors may authorize and the corporation may make distributions to its shareholders subject to restriction by the articles of incorporation and the limitation in subsection (c).

(c) No distribution may be made if, after giving it effect:

(1) the corporation would not be able to pay its debts as they become due in the usual course of business; or

(2) the corporation's total assets would be less than the sum of its total liabilities plus (unless the articles of incorporation permit otherwise) the amount that would be needed, if the corporation were to be dissolved at the time of the distribution, to satisfy the preferential rights upon dissolution of shareholders whose preferential rights are superior to those receiving the distribution.

(d) The board of directors may base a determination that a distribution is not prohibited under subsection (c) either on financial statements prepared on the basis of accounting practices and principles that are reasonable in the circumstances or on a fair valuation or other method that is reasonable in the circumstances.

OFFICIAL COMMENT

The reformulation of the statutory standards governing distributions is another important change made by the 1980 revisions to the financial provisions of the Model Act. It has long been recognized that the traditional "par value" and "stated capital" statutes do not provide significant protection against distributions of capital to shareholders. While most of these statutes contained elaborate provisions establishing "stated capital," "capital surplus," and "earned surplus" (and often other types of surplus as well), the net effect of most statutes was to permit the distribution to shareholders of most or all of the corporation's net assets—its capital along with its earnings—if the shareholders wished this to be done. However, statutes also generally imposed an equity insolvency test on distributions that prohibited distributions of assets if the corporation was insolvent or if the distribution had the effect of making the corporation insolvent or unable to meet its obligations as they were projected to arise.

The financial provisions of the Model Act, which are based on the 1980 amendments, sweep away all the distinctions among the various types of surplus but retain restrictions on distributions built around both the traditional equity insolvency and balance sheet tests of earlier statutes.

Section 6.40 imposes a single, uniform test on all distributions. Many of the old "par value" and "stated capital" statutes provided tests that varied with the type of distribution under consideration or did not cover certain types of distributions at all.

EQUITY INSOLVENCY TEST

As noted above, older statutes prohibited payments of dividends if the corporation was, or as a result of the payment would be, insolvent in the equity sense. This test is retained, appearing in section 6.40(c)(1).

In most cases involving a corporation operating as a going concern in the normal course, information generally available will make it quite apparent that no particular inquiry concerning the equity insolvency test is needed. While neither a balance sheet nor an income statement can be conclusive as to this test, the existence of significant owners' equity and normal operating conditions are of themselves a strong indication that no issue should arise under that test. Indeed, in the case of a corporation having regularly audited financial statements, the absence of any qualification in the most recent auditor's opinion as to the corporation's status as a "going concern," coupled with a lack of subsequent adverse events, would normally be decisive.

It is only when circumstances indicate that the corporation is encountering difficulties or is in an uncertain position concerning its liquidity and operations that the board of directors or, more commonly, the officers or others upon whom they may place reliance, may need to address the issue. Because of the overall judgment required in evaluating the equity insolvency test, no one or more "bright line" tests can be employed. However, in determining whether the equity insolvency test has been met, certain judgments or assumptions as to the future course of the corporation's business are customarily justified, absent clear evidence to the contrary.

These include the likelihood that (a) based on existing and contemplated demand for the corporation's products or services, it will be able to generate funds over a period of time sufficient to satisfy its existing and reasonably anticipated obligations as they mature, and (b) indebtedness which matures in the near-term will be refinanced where, on the basis of the corporation's financial condition and future prospects and the general availability of credit to businesses similarly situated, it is reasonable to assume that such refinancing may be accomplished.

To the extent that the corporation may be subject to asserted or unasserted contingent liabilities, reasonable judgments as to the likelihood, amount, and time of any recovery against the corporation, after giving consideration to the extent to which the corporation is insured or otherwise protected against loss, may be utilized. There may be occasions when it would be useful to consider a cash flow analysis, based on a business forecast and budget, covering a sufficient period of time to permit a conclusion that known obligations of the corporation can reasonably be expected to be satisfied over the period of time that they will mature.

In exercising their judgment, the directors are entitled to rely, as noted above, on information, opinions, reports, and statements prepared by others. Ordinarily, they should not be expected to become involved in the details of the various analyses or market or economic projections that may be relevant. Judgments must of necessity be made on the basis of information in the hands of the directors when a distribution is authorized. They should not, of course, be held responsible as a matter of hindsight for unforeseen developments. This is particularly true with respect to assumptions as to the ability of the corporation's business to repay long-term obligations which do not mature for several years, since the primary focus of the directors' decision to make a distribution should normally be on the corporation's prospects and obligations in the shorter term, unless special factors concerning the corporation's prospects require the taking of a longer term perspective.

BALANCE SHEET TEST

Section 6.40(c)(2) requires that, after giving effect to any distribution, the corporation's assets equal or exceed its liabilities plus (with some exceptions) the dissolution preferences of senior equity securities. Section

6.40(d) authorizes asset and liability determinations to be made for this purpose on the basis of either (1) financial statements prepared on the basis of accounting practices and principles that are reasonable in the circumstances or (2) a fair valuation or other method that is reasonable in the circumstances. The determination of a corporation's assets and liabilities and the choice of the permissible basis on which to do so are left to the judgment of its board of directors. In making a judgment under section 6.40(d), the board may rely upon opinions, reports, or statements, including financial statements and other financial data prepared or presented by public accountants or others.

Section 6.40 does not utilize particular accounting terminology of a technical nature or specify particular accounting concepts. In making determinations under this section, the board of directors may make judgments about accounting matters, giving full effect to its right to rely upon professional or expert opinion.

In a corporation with subsidiaries, the board of directors may rely on unconsolidated statements prepared on the basis of the equity method of accounting as to the corporation's investee corporations, including corporate joint ventures and subsidiaries, although other evidence would be relevant in the total determination.

a.   Generally accepted accounting principles

The board of directors should in all circumstances be entitled to rely upon reasonably current financial statements prepared on the basis of generally accepted accounting principles in determining whether or not the balance sheet test of section 6.40(c)(2) has been met, unless the board is aware that it would be unreasonable to rely on the financial statements because of newly-discovered or subsequently arising facts or circumstances. But section 6.40 does not mandate the use of generally accepted accounting principles; it only requires the use of accounting practices and principles that are reasonable in the circumstances. While publicly-owned corporations subject to registration under the Securities Exchange Act of 1934 must, and many other corporations in fact do, utilize financial statements prepared on the basis of generally accepted accounting principles, a great number of smaller or closely-held corporations do not. Some of these corporations maintain records solely on a tax accounting basis and their financial statements are of necessity prepared on that basis.

Others prepare financial statements that substantially reflect generally accepted accounting principles but may depart from them in some respects (*e.g.*, footnote disclosure). These facts of corporate life indicate that a statutory standard of reasonableness, rather than stipulating generally accepted accounting principles as the normative standard, is appropriate in order to achieve a reasonable degree of flexibility and to accommodate the needs of the many different types of business corporations which might be subject to these provisions, including in particular closely-held corporations. Accordingly, the Model Business Corporation Act contemplates that generally accepted accounting principles are always "reasonable in the circumstances" and that other accounting principles may be perfectly acceptable, under a general standard of reasonableness.

b. Other principles

Section 6.40(d) specifically permits determinations to be made under section 6.40(c)(2) on the basis of a fair valuation or other method that is reasonable in the circumstances. Thus the statute authorizes departures from historical cost accounting and sanctions the use of appraisal and current value methods to determine the amount available for distribution. No particular method of valuation is prescribed in the statute, since different methods may have validity depending upon the circumstances, including the type of enterprise and the purpose for which the determination is made.

Accounting Significance of the Legal Capital Regime.

For corporations that have issued stock having a par value, two capital accounts are necessary to reflect shareholder contributions to capital. Accountants call these (1) the capital stock account or common stock account and (2) the additional paid-in-capital account or paid-in-capital in excess of par value account. State corporate law calls these accounts the stated capital and capital surplus accounts, respectively. The *capital stock account* reflects the number of shares outstanding times the par value of the shares. The *additional paid-in-capital account (APIC)* reflects the amount paid by shareholders to the corporation for stock over and above the par value of the shares. For example, a corporation that issues 100 shares of common stock, having a par value of $1 per share, for a total consideration of $500 in cash, the bookkeeping entries would be as follows:

Cash	$500	
Capital Stock		
(Common Stock, 100 shares, par value $1)		$100
Additional Paid-in-Capital		$400

For corporations that issue stock without par value, as the MBCA contemplates, there are two approaches that can be used to account for the issuance of stock. The first retains the mechanical aspects of the par value regime by having the board of directors state that some portion of the consideration received for shares sold by the corporation be allocated to an account called stated capital and the rest allocated to additional paid-in-capital. If the stock in the foregoing example had not been assigned any par value, then the bookkeeping entry could still be approached using the traditional form, as follows:

Cash	$500	
Capital Stock		
(Common Stock, 100 shares, no par value)		$100
Additional Paid-in-Capital		$400

The other approach is to dispense with any stated capital account and instead to report, in a single account called Common Stock, all amounts paid to the corporation in exchange for stock by shareholders. Under this approach, the foregoing example would be accounted for as follows:

Cash	$500	
Common Stock (100 shares, no par value)		$500

For corporations that have authorized or issued more than one class of stock, a separate account for each such class could be used. It is customary, for example, for a corporation that has authorized or issued preferred stock as well as common stock, to maintain a separate capital account called Preferred Stock.

B. RETAINED EARNINGS AND DIVIDEND BOOKKEEPING

To be distinguished from capital accounts that seek to reflect capital contributed by shareholders is an account that seeks to reflect amounts earned by the corporation over time. Accountants call this the *retained earnings account* (corporate law refers to it as the *earned surplus account*). This account states the cumulative amount of earnings the corporation has generated over time, minus the cumulative amount of such earnings that have been paid out to shareholders in the form of dividends. To vary the point, the account reflects that a corporation may choose to deploy earnings generated in the course of business in two ways. It can either distribute the earnings to shareholders (subject to the statutory restrictions referred to above) or it can reinvest earnings in the business. Portions of earnings reinvested are called *retained earnings.*

The label "retained earnings" may be slightly misleading, however. The only sense in which the earnings so reflected are "retained" is in the sense that they are not given over to shareholders. The amounts are not retained in the sense of sitting idly around and not being used. On the contrary, they are redeployed in the business, invested in the enterprise's operations in order to generate more revenue in the future.

In bookkeeping terms, net earnings generated during a period are therefore recorded in the retained earnings account. Assume an entity generated $10,000 in earnings during an accounting period. The P & L Account would be closed into the Retained Earnings account as part of the closing entries process, as follows:

P & L	$10,000	
Retained Earnings		$10,000

Dividends to shareholders may be made in a variety of forms authorized by state statute. All states permit the payment of cash dividends or dividends in the form of new stock. All state statutes also impose limits on the extent to which distributions (of any kind, in dividends or otherwise) can be made to shareholders. Such statutes often limit such distributions to the prevailing balance in the retained earnings account or, as in the MBCA excerpted above, subject to satisfying financial tests concerning the entity's dividend-paying capacity. The further technical aspects of those limitations are quite involved and are beyond the scope of this book, but may be studied by reference to any basic textbook or casebook on corporate law. What we take up next are the accounting and bookkeeping consequences of paying dividends in cash versus stock from the perspective of both the corporation and the shareholder. This distinction, you should note, reflects GAAP's *separate entity assumption*.

Cash Dividends—Corporation's Perspective.

There are two moments of bookkeeping significance in connection with any dividend. The first is at the time of declaration of the dividend by a corporation's board of directors; the second is at its time of actual payment. With respect to a cash dividend, from the corporation's perspective, it will have the effect upon declaration of committing the payment of cash and upon payment of reducing the asset Cash. Assume a corporation has 100 shares of stock outstanding and its board of directors declares a cash dividend equal to $1 per share. The corporation's bookkeeping entries upon declaration are as follows:

Retained Earnings	$100	
Cash Dividend Payable		$100

Upon actual payment of the dividend in cash, the bookkeeping entries are as follows:

Cash Dividend Payable	$100	
Cash		$100

Notice that this pair of entries is the conceptual equivalent of our approach to accrual discussed in Chapter 3. Retained Earnings is reduced upon the declaration of the dividend and therefore calls for a left-side entry. But since the asset Cash is not reduced until the cash dividend is paid, the right-side entry to Cash will be made only when paid. To facilitate this, a Cash Dividend Payable account is used, first as an increase in the liability upon declaration (Cash Dividend Payable, a balance sheet account) and second as a decrease in that account upon payment.

Stock Dividends—Corporation's Perspective.

In contrast to a cash dividend, a stock dividend does not reduce any asset of the corporation—no asset is being disbursed. Instead, from the corporation's perspective, a stock dividend calls only for a rearrangement of the capital accounts. This is because changing the number of shares in this way is not a substantive economic event but is instead artificial in the sense that it leaves unchanged the corporation's total equity and therefore leaves unchanged each shareholder's proportionate interest in it. For example, assume an entity had outstanding 100 shares of stock which were valued in the market at $4 per share. If the corporation pays a dividend in stock equal to one full share for each share already outstanding, then after the issuance there will be 200 shares outstanding. But because no substantive economic event has occurred, one would suppose that the market value of each of the 200 shares is now $2. The size of the pie has not changed at all; only the size of the slices has changed.

Two other differences between a cash dividend and a stock dividend should be noted. First, the declaration of a cash dividend represents the creation of a liability of the corporation during the period prior to its payment. The declaration of a stock dividend does not create such a liability. Second, neither the declaration nor the payment of a cash dividend will have any effect on a corporation's charter document (its articles of incorporation or its certificate of incorporation). In contrast, the declaration of a stock dividend may require amending the corporation's charter to provide sufficient authorized shares to pay the stock dividend. In addition, specialized forms of stock dividends—called splits—made in respect of stock with a par value require changing the stock's par value, also requiring a charter amendment. The bookkeeping treatment of stock dividends differs depending on their type, which we can classify into the following four categories: large stock dividends, small stock dividends, stock splits, and reverse stock splits.

Large Stock Dividends.

For stock dividends involving the issuance of a number of shares equal to 20% or more of the shares outstanding immediately prior to the dividend (called large stock dividends), the bookkeeping entries rearrange the capital accounts based on the par value or stated value of the dividend shares. To illustrate, assume that the stock in the foregoing example has a par value (or stated value) of $1. This is a 100% stock dividend (one dividend share for each outstanding share). The bookkeeping entries for the stock dividend of one share for each of the 100 shares outstanding upon declaration would be as follows:

Retained Earnings	$100	
Stock Dividend to be Distributed		$100

Upon actual delivery of the dividend in stock, the bookkeeping entries are as follows:

Stock Dividend to be Distributed	$100	
Capital Stock		$100

In this example, retained earnings are once again being reduced as a formal matter and so require a left-side entry. But instead of reducing Cash as a cash dividend would, the stock dividend entails no disbursement of cash, only a recognition that more shares are now outstanding. Those shares carry a par value (of $1 in our example) and so cause an increase in the capital stock account equal to the par value times the number of new shares being paid in the stock dividend.

Small Stock Dividends.

For stock dividends involving the issuance of a number of shares equal to less than 20% of the shares outstanding immediately prior to the dividend (called small stock dividends), the bookkeeping entries rearrange the capital accounts not based on the par value or stated value of the dividend shares but instead based on the market value of those shares (deemed for this purpose to be the prevailing trading price for stock actively traded on a public market). To illustrate, change the assumption in the preceding example and assume instead that the stock dividend is 10% (1/10 of one share for each share outstanding) and its market price is $20 per share. So 10 new shares are to be issued, with an aggregate market value of $200 and an aggregate par value of $10. The bookkeeping entries for the stock dividend of 1/10 of one share for each of the 100 shares outstanding upon declaration would be as follows:

Retained Earnings	$200	
Stock Dividend to be Distributed		$10
Additional Paid-in-Capital		$190

Upon actual delivery of the dividend in stock, the bookkeeping entries are as follows:

Stock Dividend to be Distributed	$10	
Capital Stock		$10

Stock Splits.

A variation on the stock dividend theme is a device called the *stock split*. It consists of splitting the existing number of outstanding shares into a new number of shares. A two-for-one stock split, for example, means that the number of shares outstanding is going to be doubled—each prior share is split into two shares. This resembles a 100% stock dividend and it would be identical except there is one distinguishing feature of a stock split, at least for stock having a par value: in addition to changing the number of shares outstanding, the par value of all shares is also changed, in proportion to the change in the number of shares. Thus in a two-for-one stock split, the par value of all shares is cut in half. The only effect in bookkeeping terms of a stock split is therefore to recognize in the description of the stock on the balance sheet the new number of shares outstanding and, for stocks having a par value, the new par value.

Some company boards may judge it better optics for their stock to be high-priced. They would oppose stock splits. Context may determine a director's appetite. During the late 1990s and early 2000s, stock splits were common, but became rarer in the decade beginning with the financial crisis of 2008–09. In the earlier period, average share prices were within $25 to $40 while two decades later they ran to $100—with some popular stocks such as Amazon and Alphabet (parent of Google) exceeding $1,000 per share. Several factors seemed to drive change.

Back then, before the development of online trading, shares were traded in lots of 100. It was one thing for an individual investor to buy 100 shares at $25 for a total order of $2,500 and quite another to buy them at $1,000—a total order price of $100,000. In today's market, individuals can trade single shares at a time, so the high price is insignificant. In addition, over recent decades, the portion of shares held by individuals fell substantially compared to institutions, such as index funds, and the latter oppose increased costs associated with lower-priced shares, especially due to higher aggregate trading volumes. Finally, in the earlier period, splitting signaled pending prosperity, while in the later period, a high price became a sign of success. That was particularly true after the 2008 financial crisis, when pervasive low-pricing was a stigma to be overcome, not a sign of good times ahead.

Reverse Stock Splits.

After a stock split, the total number of shares outstanding increases. It is also possible to do the opposite—to effect a reduction in the number of shares to be outstanding following a split. This device is called a reverse stock split. A one-for-two reverse stock split, for example, means that the number of shares outstanding is cut in half; the price should double

For stock having a par value, the par value of the shares would also be changed in proportion to the change in the number of shares outstanding.

In addition, although the number shares authorized in the corporation's charter will not need to be increased, some statutes suggest that a charter amendment should be effected in connection with a reverse stock split to reduce the number of authorized shares (*e.g.*, MBCA § 6.23, Official Comment).

One objective of the reverse stock split is to eliminate minority shareholders. It is accomplished by setting the ratio high enough so that the shares held by minority shareholders become fractions (less than one) which may be eliminated for cash pursuant to most state statutes. *E.g.*, MBCA § 6.04; Del. Gen. Corp. L. § 155. N.Y. Bus. Corp. L. § 509. For public companies, another objective is to produce a share price above the minimum required by some stock exchanges to continue to list a stock.

Cash Dividends—Shareholder's Perspective.

Shareholders may enjoy income from investments in common stock in two forms. One way is through the receipt of cash dividends on the stock. From a shareholder's perspective, therefore, a cash dividend is a taxable event because it represents income to the shareholder when paid.

The other way a shareholder enjoys income from investments in common stock arises when the stock is sold at a profit—that is for an amount greater than the amount at which it was purchased. The amount of income is equal to the excess of the sale price of any share over the amount that for tax purposes the stock was purchased for—this amount is called the *basis*. The basis is initially equal to the actual purchase price paid for the stock but this amount can change over time depending on a whole series of events that for tax purposes are deemed to affect that initial cost. One reason an adjustment can be required is the payment of a stock dividend.

Stock Dividends—Shareholder's Perspective.

From the shareholder's perspective, a stock dividend is not usually a taxable event, but only calls for a reallocation in the way the stock will at some future time be treated for tax purposes. In particular, the effect of the stock dividend is to increase the number of shares a shareholder owns. But this increase does not require the payment of any consideration. In effect, whatever consideration the shareholder originally paid for her original number of shares of stock is now the price she has effectively paid for the new total number of shares she has.

For example, if an investor bought 10 shares originally at a price of $3, the total cost for those shares was $30. If the investor now is given 10 new shares in the form of a stock dividend she has a total of 20 shares but still has only paid a total of $30 for them. For purposes of calculating the amount of income she gains on the sale of the stock, subtract the sale price of the stock from the basis. In this example, the basis in each share after the stock dividend would now be equal to $1.50 (the total original purchase price of $30 divided by the now existing total number of shares of 20).

C. OTHER COMPREHENSIVE INCOME

Most activity affecting owners' equity can be depicted readily in the capital accounts relating to contributed capital and retained earnings. Accountants have struggled with what to do with various items that are not seen as significant to the measurement of an entity's economic or financial performance but nevertheless impact owners' equity.

There are two polar choices: (1) run them through the income statement anyway as with events and transactions that do reflect such performance and affect owners' equity (called the *clean surplus position*) and (2) by-pass the income statement and make direct adjustments to the owners' equity account (called the *current operating performance position*). GAAP has taken a middle position: to create a separate concept called *other comprehensive income* to capture these events and transactions and to record them separately in the income statement and present them separately on the balance sheet and as part of the statement of changes in equity.

Consider an example of the kinds of events or transactions being considered. Suppose a United States corporation operates a subsidiary in a foreign country in which the local currency is radically devalued during a reporting period. That subsidiary's earnings during the period as derived from its journal entries do reflect its operating performance during the period but the resulting contribution from net income to the interest of the parent company's shareholders will not be an accurate indicator of their economic punch—of their purchasing power in the local currency, for example.

Accordingly, putting such figures on the income statement as part of net income does not seem satisfactory but they must go on the owner's equity portion of the balance sheet. Likewise, they do bear on performance and therefore perhaps should be run through the income statement. Hence the compromise: putting them in a special place in the financial statements in a group of events or transactions called other comprehensive income. Other members of this class include examples given in Chapter 6: unrealized gains (or losses) on certain investment securities and on financial hedging transactions, as well as periodic changes involving pensions plans.

No specific format is prescribed to present other comprehensive income, the significance of which varies across companies and across time, ranging from *de minimis* to substantial. Possible styles of presentation include listing other comprehensive income on the income statement directly (and calling the document statement of comprehensive income) or incorporating it into the statement of changes in equity.

D. HYBRID INSTRUMENTS

This Chapter highlights capital accounts appearing in the owners' equity portion of the balance sheet. Chapter 6 included discussion of debt obligations an entity may incur to others that appear in the liability portion of the balance sheet. It is possible to imagine a clear distinction between these two kinds of instruments: an entity's owners contribute capital and enjoy capital appreciation as the entity generates net income that increases shareholders' equity; an entity's lenders extend capital resources and enjoy interest payments as the entity repays the contractual obligation over time.

Yet it is also possible to design investment securities with attributes of both equity and debt. For example, an entity may issue debt securities that are convertible into equity securities. Or an entity may issue equity securities that it contractually commits to redeem in the future. A wide variety of such *hybrid instruments* can be imagined, posing complexities about how to account for them. For instance, proceeds from the sale of a convertible debt security or a contractually redeemable equity security could be apportioned between a liability account and an owners' equity account. In general, however, the tendency is for GAAP to treat all such instruments wholly as liabilities, rather than as equity to any extent, although there can be complex exceptions to this treatment.

E. NON-CORPORATE ENTITIES

The preceding discussion introduced the capital accounts for a corporation. For other forms of business organization, the owners' equity accounts are treated differently to reflect the form of organization (although the other principles discussed in this book apply equally to such other forms of business organization). Other forms of business organization include the sole proprietorship, the partnership, and the limited liability company ("LLC"). In a sole proprietorship, there is only one owner and only one owner's equity account.

Partnerships and LLCs have more than one owner and a separate capital account is used for each one to reflect each owner's equity investment in the enterprise. Owners of partnerships and LLCs can also lend money to their businesses, and such loans are designated in the financial records and statements as loans from the owner, identified by name. That treatment is required for two reasons. First, such liabilities would take priority over the return of capital upon dissolution or winding-up of the enterprise. Second, such liabilities to partners would usually be junior in order of priority to the claims of other creditors.

Profits (or losses) from operations are allocated to each owner's account according to the agreement of the participants or according to applicable state law if no agreement is made. Profits (or losses) may be allocated according to specified percentages agreed upon (say 20% to Partner A, 30% to Partner B, and 50% to Partner C) or according to the balance in each owner's capital account. Another way, very common for law firms and accounting firms, is to divide the firm into units, according to seniority or revenue-generating histories, and assign each owner a number of units. Consider the following example of a 60-partner law firm consisting of 10 senior partners, 20 middle-level partners, and 30 junior partners.

	Senior Partners	Middle Partners	Junior Partners
Units Each	3	2	1
Total Partners	10	20	30
Total Units	30	40	30

Each senior partner has a 3/100 or 3% profit interest, each middle partner has a 2/100 or 2% profit interest, and each junior partner has a 1/100 or 1% profit interest. Suppose each year the firm promotes new partners from the ranks of associates and this year adds five new junior partners. Then each existing partner's profit interest declines—to 3/105 for senior partners, 2/105 for each middle partner, and 1/105 for each junior partner. The hope is, obviously, that the new junior partner will contribute sufficient additional profits to the firm so that the smaller fractions do not mean shrinking per partner profits.

When profits generated in operating the firm are paid to partners or members of LLCs, those payments are reflected in accounts called drawing accounts. Each owner has his or her own drawing account.

Problem 7A

Suppose Bandit Inc. has the following balance sheet:

Assets	This Year	Last Year	Year Before
Cash	200,000	300,000	400,000
Accounts Receivable	1,900,000	1,700,000	1,400,000
Inventory	1,235,000	1,002,000	980,000
Total Current	3,335,000	3,002,000	2,780,000
Long-Term Securities	100,000	100,000	100,000
Property, Plant and Equipment (Net)	3,565,000	4,000,000	4,435,400
TOTAL ASSETS	7,000,000	7,102,000	7,315,400
Liabilities & Equity			
Notes Payable	2,650,000	2,700,000	2,750,000
Long Term Debt	3,750,000	4,000,000	4,250,000
Total Liabilities	6,400,000	6,700,000	7,000,000
Common Stock (5000 shares)	5,000	5,000	5,000
Retained Earnings	595,000	397,000	310,400
Total Equity	600,000	402,000	315,400
TOTAL LIABILITIES & EQUITY	7,000,000	7,102,000	7,315,400

Could Bandit Inc.'s board lawfully declare and pay a cash dividend on its common stock, This Year, in the aggregate amount of $200,000 under the MBCA? What bearing do the trends in accounts receivable and inventory over the past few years have on this question?

Problem 7B

Assume that J&J's common stock has a par value of $1 per share.

(A) In light of the additional concepts discussed in this Chapter concerning owners' equity accounts, return to the following transactions from Problems 2A, 2B, 3 and 4B. Restate the indicated entries involving capital accounts, using the new account titles, capital stock, additional paid-in-capital and retained earnings:

(a) From Problem 2A, transaction 1;

(b) From Problem 2B, the closing entry required to close out the P & L Account to a capital account;

(c) From Problem 2B, the owners' equity portion of the balance sheet as of August 31;

(d) From Problem 3, the closing entry required to close out the P & L Account to a capital account;

(e) From Problem 3, the owners' equity portion of the balance sheet as of August 31;

(f) From Problem 4B, the closing entry required to close out the P & L Account to a capital account; and

(g) From Problem 4B, the owners' equity portion of the balance sheet as of September 30.

(B) Assume the board of directors of J&J decides to declare and pay a cash dividend of $2 per share to its stockholders during the month of October. Prepare bookkeeping entries to account for that dividend, at the time of declaration and at the time of payment.

(C) Assume instead the board of directors of J&J decides to declare and pay a stock dividend of 1 share of stock for each share outstanding to its stockholders during the month of October. Prepare bookkeeping entries to account for that dividend, at the time of declaration and at the time of payment.

(D) Under what circumstances involving bookkeeping for dividends would it be necessary to know the market value of the shares of the corporation paying the dividend? Was it necessary in either problem (B) or (C) to know the market value or market price of J&J stock?

Conceptual Questions 7

Should the MBCA or particular state corporate codes direct that firms use a particular accounting method? Would GAAP be appropriate? The SEC, a federal agency, requires GAAP for corporations. Should it? Given the choice under the MBCA, could a company adopt one set of rules for its income statement and a different set for its balance sheet? Suppose this scenario for an entity: (1) if the balance sheet rules it adopted were applied to its income statement it would fail the solvency test for shareholder distributions and (2) if the income statement rules it adopted were applied to its balance sheet it would fail the balance sheet test but (3) in each case it passes otherwise.

IFRS Note 7

A principal difference between GAAP and IFRS concerning topics addressed in this Chapter concerns the classification of certain hybrid instruments. In general, GAAP classifies convertible debt as a liability; IFRS classifies convertible debt as both a liability and equity based on relative fair values.

CHAPTER 8

FINANCIAL STATEMENT ANALYSIS

● ● ●

A. INTRODUCTION

Preceding Chapters considered steps and conventions that go into preparing financial statements. Now when you read a set of financial statements, you will understand some of the choices necessary in preparing them and limits those choices imply for interpreting information presented. Accordingly you should know that an understanding of those issues is necessary not only to prepare financial statements, but to use them once prepared. In this Chapter, discussion centers more directly on how to read financial statements, in terms of both what went into their preparation and what the resulting presentation tells us about an entity's financial condition and performance.

What do financial statements tell us? Sometimes all they tell us is what questions must be asked to understand them. If inventory levels seem to have been changing materially over time, can this be explained in terms of inventory accounting conventions or is something more substantive being revealed? If accounts receivable have been building, is this because sales have increased or collections have been slowing? More generally, what does the information tell us about the ability of an entity to pay its debts as they come due? What is the entity's capacity to incur and service additional debt? In this Chapter, we consider methods to evaluate such questions, or, perhaps more precisely, of using financial statements to determine what questions they leave unanswered about a particular entity.

A series of conventions can be used to analyze the financial condition and performance of an entity, generally characterized as ratio analysis. These conventions involve comparisons of bits of information on the financial statements designed to investigate trends in aspects of a business and the entity's capacity to operate the business over time.

Before discussing these ratios, the usefulness and limits of them must be emphasized. The ratios are working tools for analysis, not absolutes. They cannot be interpreted in a vacuum and cannot be applied dogmatically. Rather, every ratio must be evaluated principally with an understanding of the unique characteristics of the business in mind and then compared against the same ratio for the same entity at different periods in time and compared to other entities in the same industry or possessing economic characteristics similar to the entity under study. Rules of thumb emerge and may be of some use, but the phrase itself should be taken at face value (to mix the metaphor): a rule of thumb is only a starting point. It can never be the end point of any analysis.

With that in mind, let's "read" the following financial statements. They are abbreviated for ease of exposition to include only the balance sheet and income statement as well as some information from the statement of changes in owners' equity. Also for convenience, the data and discussion refer to the periods covered by the financial statements as this year (TY), last year (LY), and the prior year (PY), whereas actual statements would designate the year by a figure (2015, 2014, 2013, and so on). The company on which these financial statements are based is BIC Corporation, maker of low-cost consumer goods such as lighters, shavers, and pens.

BIC CORPORATION AND SUBSIDIARIES
CONSOLIDATED BALANCE SHEETS
(In thousands, except per share amounts)

	12/31/TY	12/31/LY
ASSETS:		
Current Assets:		
Cash and Cash Equivalents	$48,091	$24,094
Receivables—Trade and Other (Net of Allowance for Doubtful Accounts)	62,867	52,019
Inventories	54,363	59,426
Deferred Income Taxes	18,549	16,809
Other	10,575	13,637
Total Current Assets	194,445	165,985
Property, Plant and Equipment—Net	132,553	140,317
Other Assets	31,689	29,914
Total	$358,687	$336,216
LIABILITIES AND SHAREHOLDERS' EQUITY:		
Current Liabilities:		
Bank Borrowings		$6,731
Accounts Payable—Trade and Other	$18,915	21,179
Accrued Expenses:		
Federal and State Income Taxes	8,526	8,085
Insurance	23,261	22,739
Payroll and Payroll Taxes	7,200	6,108
Other	28,727	23,911
Total Current Liabilities	86,629	88,753
Noncurrent Liabilities:		
Postretirement Benefits Other Than Pensions	19,882	17,854
Other	4,259	2,921
Total Noncurrent Liabilities	24,141	20,775
Contingencies & Commitments (See Notes)		
Shareholders' Equity:		
Preferred Shares ($1 Par Value; Authorized—1,000,000; No Shares Issued or Outstanding)		
Common Shares ($1 Par Value; Authorized—50,000,000; Outstanding—23,559,244)	23,559	23,559
Retained Earnings	238,076	205,902
Foreign Currency Translation Adjustment	(13,718)	(2,773)
Total Shareholders' Equity	247,917	226,688
Total	$358,687	$336,216

BIC CORPORATION AND SUBSIDIARIES

STATEMENTS OF CONSOLIDATED INCOME

FOR THE LAST THREE FISCAL YEARS

(In thousands, except for per share data)

	This Yr.	Last Yr.	Prior Yr.
Net Sales	$475,118	$439,311	$417,377
Cost of Goods Sold	242,457	235,820	225,806
Gross Profit	232,661	203,491	191,571
Advertising, Selling, General & Administrative, Marketing & Research and Development Expenses	145,495	133,732	126,445
Income from Operations	87,166	69,759	65,126
Other Income—Net	41	4,227	2,152
Income Before Income Taxes and Cumulative Effect of Changes in Accounting Principles	87,207	73,986	67,278
Provision for Income Taxes	35,563	29,206	27,243
Income Before Cumulative Effect of Changes in Accounting Principles	51,644	44,780	39,935
Cumulative Effect of Changes in Accounting Principles for:			
Postemployment Benefits, Net of Taxes of $410	(623)		
Postretirement Benefits Other Than Pensions, Net of Taxes of $6,384		(9,816)	
Net Income	$51,021	$34,964	$39,935
Earnings Per Common Share:			
Income Before Cumulative Effect of Changes in Accounting Principles	$2.19	$1.90	$1.70
Cumulative Effect of Changes in Accounting Principles	(0.02)	(0.42)	
Net Income	$2.17	$1.48	$1.70

B. LIQUIDITY AND ACTIVITY

The financial health of a business over the short term can be stated in terms of an entity's ability to pay its debts as they come due. At any moment in time, an entity will have assets that will generate cash in the ordinary course and liabilities that will require payment of cash in the ordinary course. By definition these are short-term assets and short-term liabilities. A significant mismatch between these two categories can create short-term liquidity problems. Several tests can be applied to gauge relative liquidity. A series of related tests concerning business activity provide additional insight about liquidity.

Working Capital.

The first test focuses on the concept of *working capital*. This is a measure of the resources an entity has available to operate its business on a day-to-day basis. Technically, working capital is the amount by which current assets exceed current liabilities. It is a measure, in a sense, of the fuel in the business at a moment in time. Too little working capital poses a threat to the ability of an entity to operate in the ordinary course over the immediate future. It threatens an entity's ability to pay its debts as they come due. On the other hand, too much working capital can mean that resources are not being deployed in optimal ways. But how can one tell whether working capital is too high or too low?

A simple calculation of subtracting current liabilities from current assets gives us a raw number. For example, BIC Corporation's working capital, as of 12/31 this year, was $107,816,000. Is that good or bad? It is hard to tell. As a raw dollar amount, the level of working capital gives us little to go on analytically, for it does not say anything about how much working capital is needed.

One way to determine how much working capital is needed and to assess its adequacy is to compare the working capital to sales. Typically, a retailing business that generates substantial sales of low-cost items such as a supermarket needs less working capital per dollar of sales (perhaps around 10–15%) than does an industrial manufacturer of high-ticket items such as airplanes (perhaps around 25–35%). A manufacturer of consumer goods such as BIC might require some level in between these sorts of entities.

In BIC's case, its $107,816,000 working capital at the end of this year compared to its sales this year of $475,118,000 gives a working capital to sales ratio of about 23%, which looks adequate using these rules of thumb. In testing that adequacy, however, it would be important to compare it to other entities in the same line of business. It can also be helpful to compare working capital to other financial baselines, such as an entity's fixed assets, total debt, and owner's equity and to compare those with the ratios of other entities as well.

Current Ratio.

A more general way to evaluate the working capital position is to compare the relationship between current assets and current liabilities in relative terms. Called the *current ratio*, this gauge of working capital management is obtained by calculating the ratio of current assets to current liabilities. Look at BIC's balance sheet and note the total amount of current assets and the total amount of current liabilities. Using those amounts, BIC's current ratio as of the end of this year and last year would be calculated as set forth in Table 8-1.

Table 8-1
BIC Corporation: Current Ratio

$$\frac{\text{Current Assets}}{\text{Current Liabilities}}$$

This Year	Last Year
$\dfrac{194{,}445}{86{,}629}$	$\dfrac{165{,}985}{88{,}753}$
= 2.24	= 1.87

BIC's current ratio of 2.24 as of the end of this year means that for every dollar of liabilities coming due in the next year, there are $2.24 in relatively liquid assets to cover them. Similarly, the current ratio of 1.87 as of the end of last year means that for every dollar of liabilities coming due in the ensuing year, there are $1.87 in relatively liquid assets to cover them. As a matter of intuition, both these ratios may seem to imply that there is some cushion in the entity's ability to pay its debts as they come due. And in evaluating current ratios, intuition plays a significant role. These current ratios would be deemed to be within the range of satisfactory. As a rule of thumb, for most entities the optimal current ratio is around 2.

A current ratio substantially higher—say 3 or 4 or more—is a sign of potential problems, though not with respect to liquidity but with respect to efficiency. It implies that current assets may not be being deployed in their most productive manner but are instead sitting idle, not producing profits. At the other extreme, a current ratio of 1 or less is a warning signal that an entity may face difficulties in paying its debts as they come due in the short term. As the ratio falls below 2 and approaches 1 or goes below 1, a user of financial statements should investigate the liquidity question further.

Quick Ratio.

One way to refine the current ratio to get a more precise gauge of liquidity is to limit the sorts of current assets included in the calculation. In particular, recall that current assets are all those that are expected to be realized in cash within the operating cycle, usually one year. For any entity about whom there is any question regarding liquidity, however, we could limit the liquidity test to those assets expected to be converted into cash more quickly than one year—say six months or so. For this purpose, therefore, we would exclude such current assets as inventory and prepaid expenses. This would leave us with such assets as cash, which we would obviously include (because it is liquidity itself), as well as accounts receivable that are due in shorter periods (say within three months). This more refined test is known as the *quick ratio* and sometimes (equivalently) as either the "*liquidity ratio*" or the "*acid test ratio*." In the case of BIC, the quick ratio would be calculated as shown in Table 8-2.

Table 8-2
BIC Corporation: Quick Ratio

$$\frac{\text{Current Assets} - [\text{Inventory} + \text{Deferred Income Taxes} + \text{Other}]}{\text{Current Liabilities}}$$

This Year	Last Year
$\dfrac{194{,}445 - [54{,}363 + 18{,}549 + 10{,}575]}{86{,}629}$	$\dfrac{165{,}985 - [59{,}426 + 16{,}809 + 13{,}637]}{88{,}753}$
$= 1.28$	$= 0.86$

Rules of thumb again apply. A minimum quick ratio of 1 is desirable, and higher ratios are generally better. This is useful to know because of what it can tell us about the relative level of the current ratio. For example, a current ratio may be within the range of satisfactory—not dramatically below 2—but it could be due to high inventory levels. And since one cannot pay debts with inventory, there is reason to worry about an entity's ability to pay its debts as they come due if it has a low quick ratio while it has a high current ratio. In the case of BIC as of the end of last year, the current ratio and the quick ratio both suggested reasons to be concerned about liquidity. However, the higher ratios of each test for this year suggest that the company corrected any liquidity problems it had.

Of course, one can also not pay debts with accounts receivable and one must rely on the entity's ability to collect those debts in a timely manner.

It becomes important therefore to consider ways of measuring more precisely the relative liquidity of non-cash current assets, particularly inventory and accounts receivable. Doing so will also reveal something about the entity's *operating cycle*, which is the average period of time over which its cash is converted into inventory, the inventory into accounts receivable, and the accounts receivable into cash again.

Inventory Turnover.

Inventory is considered a current asset under the definition that it is expected to be realized in cash within a reasonably short time, usually one year. It is possible to be more precise about the expected, relative liquidity of inventory by measuring the speed at which inventory is sold over time—that is, the speed of inventory turnover. To do this involves calculating what is called the *inventory turnover ratio*. To measure how often a stock of inventory turns over—is sold during a period—we can examine the relationship between the cost of goods sold during the period and the average level of inventory during that period. That relationship will give us a measure of inventory turnover because all variables in it are recorded in terms of cost—the COGS is of course cost itself, and recall that all inventories are also recorded at cost (subject to the lower of cost or market rule).

More formally, inventory turnover for any year is the cost of goods sold (COGS) for that year divided by the average inventory over that year (which in turn is usually determined by adding the beginning inventory to the ending inventory and dividing by two). In formula terms, it is this:

$$\frac{\text{Current Year's Cost of Goods Sold}}{[\text{Beginning Inventory} + \text{Ending Inventory}] / 2}$$

In the case of BIC, the inventory turnover ratio for this year would be as shown in Table 8-3. (Note that we lack sufficient information to calculate BIC's inventory turnover ratio for last year because we do not have the amount for ending inventory for the prior year. If this metric was important for our purposes, we would request that information from the company.)

Table 8-3

BIC Corporation: Inventory Turnover Ratio

$$\frac{\text{Current Year's Cost of Goods Sold}}{[\text{Beginning Inventory} + \text{Ending Inventory}] / 2}$$

$$\frac{242{,}457}{[59{,}426 + 54{,}363] / 2}$$

$$= \underline{4.26}$$

This means that BIC's inventories turned over an average of 4.26 times this year. Dividing this ratio into the number of days in a year (usually 365), in turn, tells us that BIC's inventory turned over this year about once every 86 days (that is, 365/4.26). This inventory is therefore relatively liquid. *→ the smaller the #, the faster, the more liquid*

Apart from liquidity, we could also use the inventory turnover ratio to assess how well inventory levels are being managed. After all, the longer inventory sits around without being sold, the less value that inventory is adding to the business, since the cash into which it could be converted could be deployed to more productive uses. Large inventory levels can also cause other problems, such as increasing the risk of its obsolescence or spoilage, requiring large amounts of bank borrowings to finance it, absorbing large amounts of cash, or posing the risk of loss if the market price at which it can be sold declines materially. Once again, for purposes of critical examination of a particular entity's inventory turnover ratio, a comparison to other businesses selling the same kind of goods is appropriate and may be meaningful. After all, milk moves or should move at a different velocity than used cars, for example.

In making such comparisons, moreover, you would also need to be careful to consider the effects of inventory accounting conventions used by that particular entity and the entities with which it is being compared. Recall from Chapter 4, for example, that an entity using LIFO rather than FIFO will, all other things being equal, report inventory at lower amounts on its balance sheet and this would imply a higher apparent inventory turnover ratio. So when analyzing the performance of two otherwise comparable companies, with one using LIFO and the other FIFO, the analyst must adjust respective inventory amounts or be misled.

Analytical tailoring must also be done for seasonable businesses. Retailers, for example, tend to generate a disproportionate amount of sales volume in the fourth calendar quarter amid Christmas gift-giving season; confectioners increase sales volume around Valentine's Day; sellers of swimming pool paraphernalia more in the summer and so on. For seasonable businesses, inventory turnover rates (as well as other ratio analyses) should be focused on the seasonality. This would mean examining beginning and ending inventory at more frequent intervals than annually, such as monthly, for example.

Accounts Receivable Turnover.

The same insights that motivate and make meaningful the inventory turnover ratio can also be applied to the current asset accounts receivable. The speed with which accounts receivable are collected during a period indicate by definition their relative liquidity and also give a basis for appraising the integrity of the entity's credit and collection policies.

The mechanism for the measurement of accounts receivable turnover ratios is the dollar amount of sales made on credit during the period divided by the average accounts receivable outstanding during the period. The formula is as follows:

$$\frac{\text{Credit Sales}}{[\text{Beginning Accounts Receivable} + \text{Ending Accounts Receivable}] / 2}$$

You will note that many income statements (including those in our example) report sales in aggregate terms without distinguishing between sales for cash and sales on credit. When this is the case, it is not possible from the income statement alone to calculate a precise accounts receivable turnover ratio. Depending on the purpose for which the calculation is being made, it may remain useful, as a proxy for the accounts receivable turnover ratio, to use total sales. In the case of BIC, assuming all sales reported were sales on credit, the accounts receivable turnover ratio this year would be as shown in Table 8-4.

Table 8-4
BIC Corporation: Accounts Receivable Turnover Ratio
$\dfrac{475,118}{[62,867 + 52,019] / 2}$
= <u>8.27</u>

After computing the accounts receivable turnover ratio in this manner, it can be compared to other entities in the same way the inventory ratio was. Also, as with the inventory ratio, we can determine the speed of collection of accounts receivable. To do so, divide the number of days in a year by the accounts receivable turnover ratio. The result expresses the average number of days the receivables are outstanding (called *days sales uncollected*). In the case of BIC, this is equal to 365/8.2711 or 44. This implies that BIC's accounts receivable are relatively liquid. Before concluding that it is good, however, one should also compare this velocity to the terms of the accounts. If payments are due within 60 days, then this

↳ CHECK WHEN
     PAYMENTS ARE DUE!

record is fine; but if payments are due within 30 days, then this raises questions about the entity's credit-extension and debt-collection practices.

Debt-to-Equity.   *-- review*

The debt-to-equity ratio, introduced in Chapter 6, measures the entity's borrowing capacity or, in more practical terms, the level of comfort a lender or potential lender can have in the entity's ability to repay indebtedness. As the name *debt-to-equity ratio* may imply, the components of the calculation can vary depending on the purpose for which the calculation is being made and the capital structure of the entity being considered. For example, "debt" may be defined expansively to include all liabilities, be narrowly limited to long-term obligations owed to lenders, or involve some other combination. The choice will depend, as noted, on the purpose for which the calculation is being made. If you are comparing ratios across entities within an industry, you may be led to one test or the other to insure that the various ratios are comparable—that the comparisons are between entities having similar debt structures, for example.

A slightly different formulation of this ratio, sometimes referred to as the debt-to-capital ratio, is determined by dividing long-term debt by the sum of owners' equity plus long-term debt. The term capital in this formulation of the ratio does not refer to the accounting concept of capital but to a more general sense of capital encompassing long-term investments, and so includes long-term debt. By whatever formulation, the ratio indicates how many dollars of equity (or capital, as the case may be) are invested in the entity for every dollar of indebtedness (whether long-term or both long-term and short).

A comparison of the ratio across entities within an industry gives some measure of the entity's relative borrowing capacity and debt-paying over the long term. Entities with relatively high debt-to-equity ratios are characterized as "highly-leveraged," meaning that the debt level in relation to the investment level of the owners in the business (the shareholders) is very high. What levels of debt-to-equity ratios are normal has varied historically, in accordance with economic conditions and collective beliefs about credit. Notice that BIC Corporation has no debt outstanding and therefore its debt-to-equity ratio is zero! It is common to characterize such a debt-free business as having a very "clean" balance sheet.

C. PROFITABILITY AND PERFORMANCE

Most liquidity/activity ratios concentrate on how an entity is managing its assets and liabilities, which can also reveal information about its prospective ability to meet its obligations as they come due. The next level of analysis concerns the entity's profitability and performance.

Profit Margin.

A principal method of evaluating the performance of a business is to consider how well it is meeting its basic financial objective, which is to generate a profit in operating its business in the ordinary course. BIC's operating income this year was $87,166,000. That is a lot. But as a raw dollar amount, it does not tell us much in terms of business performance. In particular, it does not tell us what went in to generating that amount of operating income.

To pursue the more critical inquiry about how efficiently the business is being managed, we should investigate the relationship of the operating income generated to the sales level that generated it. In other words, is the entity getting a lot or a little out of its sales effort? The relationship between operating income and sales is called the *profit margin*. To calculate it, divide operating income by net sales for the period and express the result as a percentage. In BIC's case for this and last year, the calculation is shown in Table 8-5. (Incidentally, an alternative calculation at a more general level called the *gross profit margin* does a similar thing by dividing gross profit on sales by net sales.)

Table 8-5
BIC Corporation: Profit Margin

Operating Income	
Net Sales	

This Year	Last Year
87,166	69,759
475,118	439,311
= 0.1834	= 0.1587
= 18.3%	= 15.9%

These two ratios show that the company's profit margin increased from last year to this year. That is a good sign—it is a positive trend. The trend of the profit margin may reveal important information about the entity's direction and how well it is being managed. Positive trends in the profit margin suggest that the business is constantly improving the efficiency of its operations and its sales efforts. But a positive trend in profit margin should not be taken at face value. It could be due to other factors that either have nothing to do with efficient operations or which may be counterproductive long term. Perhaps it is the consequence of favorable market conditions that are benefiting all businesses and reveals nothing special about the particular entity.

Two points are implied: first, an entity's profit margin and its trend should be compared to those of comparable entities, and second, a study should be made of all line items on the particular entity's income statement that go into determining sales and profit calculations. That kind of investigation is called *variation analysis*.

Variation Analysis.

Variation analysis examines changes in items of financial data between periods with a view toward determining trends in an entity's financial condition and performance. Variation analysis (sometimes called *line item trend analysis*) can reveal significant information about how an entity is being managed. In particular, the level of expenses in every income statement expense account over the comparison years should be examined. A significant reduction in an expense for research and development, for example, would have the effect of significantly increasing operating income in a period. But growth in operating income due to the reduction in such an expense would not mean the entity is being managed more efficiently, and could mean there are reasons to worry about growth prospects.

Moreover, we noted above the utility of comparing the average number of days required to collect accounts receivable with the entity's credit policies. Suppose that the average number of collection days during a period has been increasing in relation to the credit terms. Maybe part of any growth in sales during the period is due to a relaxation in credit collection policies, rather than business efficiency. If those accounts are more likely to go uncollected, the growth in sales may be adverse for the business in the long run.

Finally, all line items on the income statement could also be analyzed in each period as a percentage of sales and then those percentages could be compared over time. In particular, one could compute COGS as a percentage of sales, earnings before interest and taxes (called and pronounced as *EBIT*) as a percentage of sales, and net income as a percentage of sales. Those percentages in any given period could then be compared to the percentages in prior periods to determine what trends are taking place in the business. Those percentages could also be compared to other businesses during the same time periods to gauge how well the subject business is being managed compared to those other businesses. In the case of BIC, the variation analysis from two years ago to this year would appear as in Table 8-6.

Table 8-6 BIC Corporation: Variation Analysis (Selected Income Statement Line Items as a Percentage of Net Sales) (000s omitted)			
	This Year	**Last Year**	**Prior Year**
Net Sales	475,118	439,311	417,377
COGS	242,457	235,820	225,806
% of Sales	51.03%	53.68%	54.10%
EBIT	87,207	73,986	67,278
% of Sales	18%	17%	16%
Net Income	51,021	34,964	39,935
% of Sales	11%	8%	9.6%

This variation analysis reveals that COGS as a percentage of sales has been decreasing steadily and EBIT as a percentage of sales has been increasing steadily. While net income as a percentage of sales increased this year from the level two years ago, it fell last year from the prior year. The question is why.

The answer can be seen by looking at BIC's income statement. It shows that the company took a one-time, extraordinary, charge to net income last year of $9,816,000. That extraordinary item explains the decline in net income as a percentage of sales. So the decline depicted in this variation analysis should not be regarded as indicating anything adverse about the manner in which the business was being operated last year.

Presentation.

It is possible for an entity to adopt a modified presentation of the income statement to facilitate applying ratio and variation analysis. It is a common practice to prepare interim reports—reports as of the end of fiscal quarters as opposed to year-end—on a condensed basis to highlight variations. Consider Table 8-7, a condensed statement of income for a recent two-year period of Gap Inc. (the clothing store company, which happens to report its financial statements in accordance with GAAP). It highlights in a separate column the percentage increases (or decreases) in critical line items, and also states pretax earnings as a percentage of sales and net earnings as a percentage of sales.

Table 8-7
Gap Inc. Condensed Income Statement Data
(dollars in thousands, except per share amounts)

	This Year	Last Year	Percentage Increase (Decrease)
Net Sales	$3,015,125	$2,617,457	15.2%
Costs & Expenses			
COGS	1,999,238	1,642,146	
Operating Expenses	677,585	595,802	
Interest Expense (Net)	4,503	2,830	
Earnings Pre-tax	333,799	376,679	(11.4%)
Percentage of Sales	11.1%	14.4%	
Income Taxes	126,844	142,468	
Net Income	206,955	234,211	(11.6%)
Percentage of Sales	6.9%	8.9%	
Weighted Average Number of Shares	144,050,824	142,453,420	
Earnings Per Share	$1.44	$1.65	

This format of presentation makes it easier to compare an entity's performance with that of other entities without regard to the relative size of the entities. This is useful because the raw dollar amounts of various line items of entities of dramatically different sizes would not make the comparison meaningful. For example, Gap Inc. reports sales of about $3 billion during this fiscal year. It also reports net income of about $207 million. Try to compare that data to BIC's sales this year of about $475 million and net income of about $51 million. Comparing raw amounts does not tell us very much.

But when we also consider that for Gap Inc. net income as a percentage of sales was 6.9% that year and for BIC net income as a percentage of sales was 11%, we are getting somewhere. In particular, that comparison tells us that BIC is generating more earnings from its sales effort as compared to Gap Inc. This approach enables comparing the performance of businesses adjusted for their relative size. The general approach is referred to as the computation of *common size ratios*. The numbers in raw terms that vary so greatly because of differences in business size are adjusted or scaled so that the data are comparable.

Assorted Coverage Ratios.

A ratio whose function is similar to the balance sheet ratio of debt-to-equity is the *interest coverage ratio*. This is sometimes also referred to as the *times interest earned ratio* (*TIER*). TIER compares earnings to interest payment obligations. The ratio expresses the number of times interest obligations are covered by earnings.

A slightly more conservative variation on the interest coverage ratio is called the *fixed charge coverage ratio*. In addition to interest coverage, this ratio also tests for earnings coverage of fixed charges such as lease obligations.

Note that these coverage ratios can be applied either on an overall basis or with respect to particular classes (or issues) of debt instruments. If an entity proposes to issue debt securities that will rank senior upon liquidation to some existing "junior" debt, then the calculation can be made without regard to interest obligations on junior debt. For example, the senior debt holder in a company with EBIT of $100 annually and facing annual senior interest debt of $40 and annual junior interest debt of $20 can safely consider only the 100:40 times-interest-earned of 2.5-to-1 (not bad).

A similar analysis can be applied to evaluate the coverage of dividends, particularly on preferred stock. Where no debt ranks higher than the preferred stock, the calculation is simply earnings divided by the number of preferred shares outstanding. If senior debt exists, however, the earnings available for payment of dividends on the preferred stock must be first be reduced by the interest obligations on that debt.

Earnings Per Share.

Beyond these line item analyses that can offer an understanding of an entity's relative efficiency in a period and over time, a different sort of question can be analyzed by looking at the earnings of an entity. This is the more general proposition about what results the entity is producing for its shareholders, usually expressed in terms of *earnings per share* (*EPS*). EPS is total earnings during the period (after giving effect to interest and taxes) divided by the average number of equity shares outstanding during that period. It expresses the portion of earnings mathematically allocable to each equity share and provides a useful element in valuing that share (a subject pursued in Part III).

The first issue in calculating earnings per share is determining the number of shares outstanding. The number outstanding can vary throughout an accounting period due to stock being issued or repurchased. The total outstanding is adjusted for these changes weighted according to the length of time given numbers were outstanding. For example, suppose on January 1, a corporation has 10,000 shares outstanding and on April 1, the corporation repurchases 2,000 of these and no other changes occur. The weighted-average common stock outstanding is:

$$\left(10{,}000 \times \frac{3}{12}\right) + \left(8{,}000 \times \frac{9}{12}\right) = 8{,}500$$

A second issue in calculating and evaluating EPS is determining which shares are to be included in calculating average shares outstanding. It would obviously include at least the average number of common shares outstanding, but what about other instruments that are convertible into common shares or which provide an option to elect to purchase common shares? Those rights upon exercise will have the effect of diluting the portion of earnings mathematically allocable to each common share prior to that exercise. To address this, EPS is calculated in two ways: basic EPS and diluted EPS.

Basic EPS is computed by dividing income available for distribution to common stockholders by the weighted average number of common shares outstanding during the reporting period. For purposes of determining such shares outstanding, certain contingently issuable shares must also be counted. Such shares include those that will be issued in the future upon satisfaction of specific conditions, those that have been placed in escrow when all or part must be returned if specified conditions are not met, and those that have been issued but the holder must return if specified conditions are not met.

Diluted EPS is computed by also including in the weighted number of shares deemed outstanding other common shares issuable upon certain other events or pursuant to other instruments or plans to the extent they would, upon issuance, affect the calculation of basic EPS. These instruments or plans include options and warrants, stock-based compensation arrangements, written put options, convertible securities, and contracts that may be settled in cash or in stock.

In the case of BIC this year, net income was $51,021,000 and the weighted average number of common shares outstanding was 23,559,244. Its basic EPS was therefore $2.17 (determined by dividing net income by that number of shares). There would be no difference in BIC's diluted EPS because the financial statements do not disclose the existence of any outstanding warrants or options convertible into common stock, or any outstanding preferred stock.

The Price-Earnings Ratio.

A common way of making comparisons between the performances, or at least the perceived performances, of entities is drawn from the way public markets price common stocks for entities with various earnings. It compares the market price per share of common stock with the earnings per share of that common stock. Called the *price-earnings ratio* (the "*P/E ratio*"), it is computed by dividing the market price of a share of common stock by the entity's earnings per share.

This year, BIC's common stock had been trading at prices in the range of between $26 and $32 per share. Its earnings per share this year were $2.17. Its P/E ratio during that period therefore ranged from about 12 to nearly 15.

In general, higher P/E ratios suggest that investors are more optimistic about an entity's prospects than comparable entities with lower P/E ratios. However, the relative levels of P/E ratios also vary according to an entity's growth outlook, its industry, its relative maturation (whether it is a start-up entity or an established business), and the accounting policies used by the entity in arriving at its calculation of net income. We will consider the P/E ratio further in Chapter 11.

Return on Equity, Investment and Assets.

"Returns" are a measure of what bang a business gets for its buck. The bang is invariably measured in terms of earnings. There are several bases against which to measure the bang. We mention three: equity, investment, and assets.

In each measure, it is smart to gauge the return over a relatively long period of time—say five to ten years—rather than over short periods. This enables a perspective that tracks an entity's ability to weather the downsides, and reap the upsides, of the ever-fluctuating economic environment in which it operates.

Return on equity is the amount the business earned on the capital owned by its shareholders (owners' equity). Owners' equity is equal to total assets minus total liabilities. If a business earns $10 million on equity of $100 million, then its return on equity is 10%. In periods of economic exuberance, returns on equity have been around 22% while in more contracted periods they may range below 10%.

Return on investment is the amount a business earned on both the equity held by its shareholders and the capital supplied by lenders on a long term (over one year) basis. A business might borrow capital rather than issue equity if it needs funds and believes it will generate greater returns on borrowed funds than what it costs to borrow them.

Suppose a business with $100 million in owners' equity borrows $50 million from long-term lenders and then generates earnings before interest and taxes (EBIT) of $15 million on that total capital. (EBIT is used in this calculation since interest is the return on debt.) Its return on investment would be 10% (15/150). But this leveraging boosts the business's return on equity—earnings of $15 million on owners' equity of $100 million means a return on equity of 15%.

Return on assets is the amount a business earned on all its resources— not only owners' equity and long term borrowing but short term resources generated by effective management of working capital. (The sum of these is of course equal to total assets under the fundamental equation, so it is customary to denominate this measure of return as return on assets.) A business may seek short term, low-rate loans or buy goods on credit that it resells for cash, thus increasing assets available for deployment at low or no cost. Those assets contribute to incremental increases in earnings, boosting both return on equity and return on investment.

Suppose a business maintains an average amount of short term assets of $20 million over a year (by continually repaying related obligations as they come due and incurring new ones as roll-overs). That could increase incremental annual earnings by say $2 million. So a company with owners' equity of $100 million, long-term debt of $50 million, carrying that additional $20 million in short-term assets, and earning $17 million generates a return on assets of 10% (17/170). This deployment boosts return on investment to 11.3% (17/150) and return on equity to 17% (17/100).

Return on assets is the toughest measure of performance based on returns, as it reveals the results of deploying all resources at management's disposal. Starting with a high return on assets should yield a high return on investment and hence on equity. Some analysts calculate a *financial leverage index* equal to the return on equity divided by the return on assets.

Think back to the fundamental equation that assets equal liabilities plus owners' equity (A = L + OE). The three measures of return can be decomposed in terms of the fundamental equation. Return measures express an income statement figure divided by one of the following balance sheet concepts: (a) owners' equity (return on equity or ROE); (b) owners' equity plus long-term liabilities (return on investment or ROI); and (c) owners' equity plus long-term liabilities plus current liabilities which, given the fundamental equation, is equivalent to total assets (so return on assets or ROA). Table 8-8 captures the measurements.

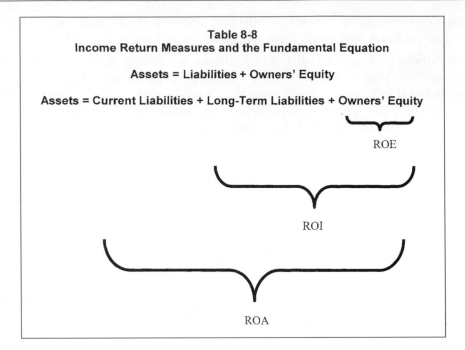

Table 8-8
Income Return Measures and the Fundamental Equation

Assets = Liabilities + Owners' Equity

Assets = Current Liabilities + Long-Term Liabilities + Owners' Equity

ROE

ROI

ROA

In calculating return on equity, investment and assets, note that the income statement measure for any period is compared to the balance sheet measure as of the beginning of that period. In formula terms, for example:

$$\text{Return on Equity} \quad = \quad \frac{\text{Net Income (Current Year)}}{\text{Equity (End of Prior Year)}}$$

To calculate BIC's return on equity (ROE) for this year, compare its net income this year to its equity as of the end of last year. Accordingly BIC's ROE this year would be calculated as set forth in Table 8-9. This ROE of 22.5% is respectable. Note that in BIC's case its return on equity and return on investment are the same, because it has no debt. Finally, its return on assets is 15.2%: this year's income of $51,021 divided by last year-end total assets of $336,216.

For BIC, these are fine results, and suggest both solid performance and very prudent (highly cautious) management not interested in boosting returns with leverage, but rather letting operations do the work. (This is unusual in corporate America; most companies use substantial debt financing.)

Table 8-9
BIC Corporation: Return on Equity

$$\frac{\text{Net Income (This Year)}}{\text{Equity (End of Last Year)}}$$

$$\frac{51,021}{226,688}$$

$$=0.2251$$

$$=\underline{22.51\%}$$

If return on equity is an ultimate performance measure, note that the other analytics drive it. For example, the faster a company turns over its assets, the higher its return on equity will be. So higher inventory and receivables turns drive higher returns on equity. Likewise, higher profit margins drive higher returns on equity as they express how much of every sales dollar turns into profit. Finally, the more debt compared to equity is used the higher the return on equity will be (subject of course to risks of overleveraging that prevent a company from repaying debt when due).

Noting these drivers of returns on equity enables appreciating the various ways a company can enhance returns on equity. These include: speeding inventory and receivables turnover and shedding less productive assets; increasing sales volume or price and decreasing expenses; and increasing borrowing or buying back shares. Advantages of this analytical decomposition include both transparency of manifestation and precision. One can focus explicitly on asset management, sales, or leverage, and also see the possibility of trading off benefits in one metric for those of another. For example, to improve ultimate results managers can improve margin and/or improve turnover.

Other Measures.

The ratios discussed above and summarized in Table 8-10 are just some of the leading methods employed to analyze financial statements. Some can be calculated or approached in slightly different ways than set forth above. For example, an entity's ratio of interest expense (or all fixed charges) to gross revenues may be helpful in evaluating its debt capacity. The amount of an entity's annual depreciation expense also may be of interest in evaluating its future needs for capital expenditures. These are all potentially helpful tools that will be more or less significant depending on the purpose for which the analysis is being conducted.

Table 8-10: Ratio Analysis Summary		
Liquidity and Activity		
	Numerator	*Denominator*
Current Ratio	Current Assets	Current Liabilities
Quick Ratio	Speedy Assets	Current Liabilities
Inventory Turnover Ratio	COGS	Average Inventory
Inventory Speed	365	Inventory Turnover Ratio
A/R Turnover Ratio	Credit Sales	Average A/R
A/R Speed	365	A/R Turnover Ratio
Debt-to-Equity	Total Debt	Equity
Debt-to-Capital	Total Debt	Total Debt + Equity
Profitability and Performance		
	Numerator	*Denominator*
Profit Margin	Operating Income	Net Sales
Gross Profit Margin	Gross Profit on Sales	Net Sales
Interest Coverage Ratio	EBIT	Interest Expense
Earnings Per Share	Earnings	Average Shares
Price-to-Earnings	Market Price per Share	EPS
Return On Equity	Earnings	Owners' Equity
Return on Investment	EBIT	Total Capital
Return on Assets	Earnings	Total Assets or L + OE

For that matter too, all the income statement ratios are driven by reported earnings, and a whole set of analogous ratios can be developed and applied to learn about an entity from its statement of cash flows, which we will consider in the next Chapter. In addition, advanced measures of particular use by auditors in reviewing and opining upon the fairness of financial statements are discussed in Chapter 13.

A user of financial statements can learn a lot from conducting a rigorous ratio analysis of those statements along the lines suggested above. But often that analysis raises as many questions as it answers. In light of this, the federal securities laws require that the financial statements of public companies be accompanied by a narrative discussion and analysis of trends management sees the financial statements to reveal (or to obscure). That narrative is called the Management's Discussion and Analysis ("MD&A").

D. MANAGEMENT'S DISCUSSION AND ANALYSIS (MD&A)

Reading the income statement and balance sheet, along with the statement of cash flows (discussed in the next Chapter), and footnotes to all of them, and conducting ratio analysis will reveal a lot about the business and financial condition and performance of an entity. Yet it is unlikely that the whole story can be told that way. Indeed, it would be an extraordinary feat if any set of financial statements, reporting as they do a huge variety of financial transactions, could be complete in the full sense of that word.

To fill in between the line items, as it were, all public entities are required by federal securities laws to provide supplemental disclosure explaining the financial statements. That disclosure is an important source of information to users of financial statements, including lawyers, but it is also of special interest to lawyers for another reason: the disclosure is often written by lawyers, and almost always reviewed by them.

The federal securities laws requiring disclosure were promulgated under the broad philosophy underlying the mandatory disclosure system of the federal securities laws—that a compulsory disclosure system enables investors to make informed decisions about investment alternatives. The detailed structure of those rules is beyond the scope of this book, and is usually taken up in a separate course in the law school curriculum called Securities Regulation. This brief overview is intended to suggest ways in which part of the structure seeks to elaborate on the accounting and other financial data presented in disclosure documents, many of which are required to be filed with the federal regulatory agency charged with administering the federal securities laws, the Securities and Exchange Commission (the SEC), under laws and regulations prescribing the contents of such disclosure documents.

Chief among these is the section called "Management's Discussion and Analysis," usually abbreviated and referred to as the "MD&A." The MD&A rules are motivated by the notion that a narrative assessment of the meaning of the numerical and footnote presentation in financial statements is necessary for investors to understand those financial statements fully. The MD&A is designed to provide investors with an insider's view of an entity's financial condition, performance, and prospects.

The MD&A must address an entity's liquidity, capital resources, results of operations, and information relating to trends in and uncertainties about aspects of the business. The MD&A must also address under a separate caption any material off-balance sheet arrangements (that is, contractual relationships with unconsolidated but related parties under which the company has some level of obligation, as discussed in Chapter 6).

Although the MD&A rules are comprehensive, they are also intentionally open-ended and seek to elicit particularized disclosure about the specific situation of individual entities, rather than general, boilerplate discussion. Their purpose is to provide—in a few pages in one place—material historical and prospective textual disclosure enabling users of financial statements to assess an entity's financial condition and performance with particular emphasis on its prospects for the future.

The MD&A's emphasis on prospects for the future has proven controversial. The impulse for that emphasis follows from a distinction that is made between "hard information" and "soft information." Hard information purports to be that which is reflected by the numerical presentation in the financial statements. Soft information purports to be that which only an insider could see in those numbers. In other words, the basis for the distinction reflects that the preparation and presentation of the hard financial data entails a substantial amount of judgment.

What makes this distinction and the resulting emphasis on future prospects controversial is that even the most honest and rigorous insider conducting an analysis of the soft information in light of the hard information (or the hard information in light of the soft) can turn out to be wrong when the future unfolds. When that happens, should legal liability result from the picture painted in the MD&A that 20/20 hindsight shows was wrong?

Consider the following excerpt from the MD&A portion of BIC Corporation's SEC filing accompanying its financial statements excerpted in the beginning of this Chapter. Consider the extent to which the discussion, especially the references to various ratios discussed above, improves your understanding of BIC's financial condition, performance, and prospects.

BIC Corporation
Management's Discussion and Analysis
of Financial Condition and Results of Operations
[Selected Portions Concerning Liquidity and Capital Resources]

The cash required by the Corporation for working capital, capital expenditures and dividend payments was generated primarily from operations. The Corporation expects to continue to satisfy most of its cash requirements through internally generated funds. The Corporation's current ratio was 2.24 this year and 1.87 last year, reflecting the Corporation's highly liquid position and ability to finance its current operations without significant short-term borrowings.

Trade and other receivables, net of allowance for doubtful accounts, were $62.9 million at year end, as compared with $52.0 million at year end last year. The increase is primarily due to a 16.7% increase in net sales for the fourth quarter of last year, as compared to the same period in the prior year.

As reflected in the Consolidated Balance Sheets, inventories decreased by $5.1 million this year. This decrease was largely attributable to a reduction in the inventory valuation of the Corporation's Mexican subsidiary due to the translation effect of the peso devaluation. Average inventory turnover was 4.3 times this year and 4.0 times last year.

At year end, the Corporation had no bank borrowings, while at year end last year, bank borrowings totaled $6.7 million. The prior year's bank borrowings primarily reflected borrowings by the Corporation's United States operations.

Accounts payable and accrued expenses increased by $9.0 million this year and decreased by $2.8 million last year. This year's increase is largely due to an increase in accrued advertising and promotion cost and accrued income taxes in the United States. The increase also includes an increase in the Corporation's Mexican subsidiary's accounts payable balance. Last year's decrease was primarily due to the timing of income tax payments by the Corporation's subsidiary.

Capital spending decreased in this year and last. Purchases of property, plant and equipment were $21.7 million this year and $41.2 million last year. Capital spending this year included purchases of machinery and equipment for the new child-resistant lighter manufacturing process, and a new ink dye manufacturing process in stationery products (the Corporation previously purchased ink dye from Societe BIC S.A., the Corporation's majority shareholder). This year's spending was also for capacity, productivity and product quality improvements in stationery products, and productivity increases and improvements in shavers.

Spending last year included purchases of machinery and equipment for productivity increases and quality improvements in stationery products and lighters; capacity increases in stationery products and new stationery products; expansions of the Duncan, South Carolina; Fountain Inn, South Carolina; Clearwater, Florida and Cuautitlan, Mexico facilities and building improvements for the Gaffney, South Carolina facility.

In July of last year, the U.S. Environmental Protection Agency ("EPA") issued its final volumetric ranking of Potentially Responsible Parties ("PRPs") for the Solvents Recovery Service of New England ("SRSNE") Superfund Site in Southington, Connecticut. The Corporation has been notified that it is a PRP at the Site and has been ranked, by the EPA, number 192 of a total of 1,659 PRPs. This ranking represents less than 1%

of the total volume of waste disposed at the SRSNE Site, with the first 191 PRPs representing 90% of the total volume.

The Corporation cannot predict with certainty the total costs of cleanup, the Corporation's share of the total costs, the extent to which contributions will be available from other parties, the amount of time necessary to complete the cleanup, or the availability of insurance coverage. Based on currently available information, the Corporation believes that its share of the ultimate cleanup costs at this Site will not have a material adverse impact on the Corporation's financial position or on its results of operations, if such operations continue at the present level.

At year end this year and last year, the Corporation carried no long-term debt. At year end this year, unused lines of credit were $113.0 million and standby letters of credit were $29.6 million, which management believes is more than adequate to meet the Corporation's current or future requirements if operations continue at the present level.

In January of last year, the Corporation concluded negotiations with its unionized employees, local utilities and local taxing authorities. Concessions received through these negotiations will result in a modest, but important, reduction in future operating costs at its Milford, Connecticut facility. In addition, the Corporation has accepted from the State of Connecticut a $9 million grant and financing package to offset capital spending for its Milford, Connecticut facility.

The Corporation self-insures against some risks. The Corporation also has in place risk management programs other than insurance to minimize exposure to loss. The programs remained relatively unchanged from the prior year. Management believes its overall risk management and insurance programs are adequate to protect its assets and earnings against significant loss, provided that its results of operations continue at the present level.

This year, the Corporation's net sales increased by $35.8 million to $475.1 million due to increased sales of stationery products of $23.5 million, lighters of $6.6 million and shavers of $6.8 million, partially offset by a decline in sport products of $1.1 million. The increase in stationery products reflects an increase in the number of units sold and higher average selling prices of approximately 5% by its North American operations. The Corporation's Special Markets Division made significant contributions to these improvements. The improvement in lighters primarily represents an increase in units sold and higher average selling prices for the BIC fixed flame lighter in the United States. The shaver improvement is attributable to an increase in the number of BIC twin blade shaver units sold and higher average selling prices.

Last year, the Corporation's net sales increased by $21.9 million to $439.3 million due to increased sales of stationery products of $17.1

million, lighters of $1.3 million and shavers of $4.0 million, partially offset by a decline in sport products of $0.5 million. The increase in stationery products primarily represented an increase in average selling prices of approximately 9% by its North American operations. The increase in lighters primarily reflected an increase in units sold of approximately 3% by its United States operations. The shaver increase was attributable to higher average selling prices of approximately 10% in North America. This shaver increase was partially offset by a slight decline in units sold.

Net sales of sport products decreased by $1.1 million this year and by $0.5 million last year. These reductions primarily reflect decreases in the number of units sold. Income (loss) before income taxes and cumulative effect of changes in accounting principles for sport products was $(0.9) million this year and $1.6 million last year. The $2.5 million decrease in income is primarily due to adjustments in the provision related to sailboard litigation.

Foreign sales increased by approximately 4% this year, while remaining relatively flat last year. The increase this year is primarily due to improvements in sales by the Corporation's Canadian subsidiary, and also to increased export sales by the United States operations. The Corporation's other foreign operations also contributed to the sales improvements.

The Corporation's purchases from Societe BIC, S.A., the Corporation's majority shareholder, and from other affiliated companies were $41.1 million this year and $42.2 million last year. The Corporation purchases from Societe BIC, S.A. and other affiliated companies, products that it does not presently manufacture, certain component parts and machinery and equipment. Information concerning the Corporation's transactions and balances with Societe BIC, S.A. and other related parties is contained in Note 13 of Notes to Consolidated Financial Statements.

Gross profit as a percentage of net sales increased by 2.7 percentage points this year and 0.4 percentage points last year. This year's increase primarily reflects improvements in the United States and Mexican operations. In the United States, higher average selling prices in each of the Corporation's core operations (stationery products, lighters and shavers) contributed to the gross profit increase. Lower unit costs in stationery products and shavers also contributed to this increase. These improvements were partially offset by slightly higher unit costs in lighters. The lower unit costs in stationery products were principally due to manufacturing efficiencies. In shavers, the reduction was the result of manufacturing efficiencies and favorable foreign exchange rates associated with imports. Higher unit costs in lighters were due to the conversion to BIC Lighter with Child Guard. The improvements in the Mexican operations were largely due to higher average selling prices and manufacturing efficiencies in stationery products.

Advertising, selling, general and administrative, marketing and research and development expenses increased by $11.8 million to $145.5 million this year and by $7.3 million to $133.7 million last year. This year's increase primarily reflects higher selling expenses, a 9% increase in marketing expenses and an increase in bad debt expense. The increase in selling expense is related to higher sales levels. The higher marketing costs are attributable to an increase in consumer promotions in the United States, and to the launch of the twin blade shaver in Mexico. Last year's increase reflected higher selling expenses and an 18% increase in marketing expenses. These increases were partially offset by an 8% decrease in general and administrative expenses. The increase in selling expense was attributable to higher sales levels. The increase in marketing was related to the costs associated with the promotion of the Corporation's line of twin blade shavers. The decrease in general and administrative expenses reflected a decrease in the provision for general liability and workers' compensation insurance, relocation costs and bad debt expense. These decreases were partially offset by an increase in the amortization of intangibles associated with the purchase of Wite-Out Products, Inc.

Income before cumulative effect of changes in accounting principles increased by $6.9 million and by $4.8 million this year and last year, respectively. This year's increase primarily reflects improvements in stationery products and shavers in the United States. The Corporation's foreign operations also contributed to this year's profit increases. Last year's increase was primarily due to improvements in core operations (stationery products, lighters and shavers) in the United States.

In response to numerous financial reporting scandals that focused national attention on the limitations of accounting information, the SEC issued a formal interpretation of MD&A requirements. Excerpts from this interpretation follow (another excerpt appears in Chapter 9). Footnotes are omitted and section headings abbreviated.

**Securities and Exchange Commission
Release Nos. 33–8350; 34–48960
Interpretation: Guidance Regarding MD&A
(December 22, 2003)**

Key Indicators.

. . . [O]ne of the principal objectives of MD&A is to give readers a view of the company through the eyes of management by providing both a short and long-term analysis of the business. To do this, companies should . . . address those key variables and other qualitative and quantitative factors which are peculiar to and necessary for an understanding and evaluation of the individual company. . . .

Financial measures generally are the starting point in ascertaining these key variables and other factors. However, financial measures often tell only part of how a company manages its business. Therefore, when preparing MD&A, companies should consider whether disclosure of all key variables and other factors that management uses to manage the business would be material to investors, and therefore required. These key variables and other factors may be non-financial, and companies should consider whether that non-financial information should be disclosed.

Many companies . . . disclose non-financial business and operational data. Academics, authors, and consultants also have researched the types of information, outside of financial statement measures, that would be helpful to investors and other users. Such information may relate to external or macro-economic matters as well as those specific to a company or industry. For example, interest rates or economic growth rates and their anticipated trends can be important variables for many companies. Industry-specific measures can also be important for analysis, although common standards for the measures also are important. Some industries commonly use non-financial data, such as industry metrics and value drivers. Where a company discloses such information, and there is no commonly accepted method of calculating a particular non-financial metric, it should provide an explanation of its calculation to promote comparability across companies within the industry. Finally, companies may use non-financial performance measures that are company-specific.

. . . MD&A should provide a frame of reference that allows readers to understand the effects of material changes and events and known material trends and uncertainties arising during the periods being discussed, as well as their relative importance. To satisfy the objectives of MD&A, companies also should provide a balanced view of the underlying dynamics of the business, including not only a description of a company's successes, but also of instances when it failed to realize goals, if material. Good MD&A will focus readers' attention on these key matters.

Trends and Uncertainties.

One of the most important elements necessary to an understanding of a company's performance, and the extent to which reported financial information is indicative of future results, is the discussion and analysis of known trends, demands, commitments, events and uncertainties. . . .

One of the principal objectives of MD&A is to provide information about the quality and potential variability of a company's earnings and cash flow, so that readers can ascertain the likelihood that past performance is indicative of future performance. Ascertaining this indicative value depends to a significant degree on the quality of disclosure about the facts and circumstances surrounding known material trends and uncertainties in MD&A. Quantification of the material effects of known material trends and uncertainties can promote understanding. Quantitative disclosure should be considered and may be required to the extent material if quantitative information is reasonably available. . . .

Analysis.

. . . Identifying the intermediate effects of trends, events, demands, commitments and uncertainties alone, without describing the reasons underlying these effects, may not provide sufficient insight for a reader to see the business through the eyes of management. A thorough analysis often will involve discussing both the intermediate effects of those matters and the reasons underlying those intermediate effects. For example, if a company's financial statements reflect materially lower revenues resulting from a decline in the volume of products sold when compared to a prior period, MD&A should not only identify the decline in sales volume, but also should analyze the reasons underlying the decline in sales when the reasons are also material and determinable. The analysis should reveal underlying material causes of the matters described, including for example, if applicable, difficulties in the manufacturing process, a decline in the quality of a product, loss in competitive position and market share, or a combination of conditions.

Similarly, where a company's financial statements reflect material restructuring or impairment charges, or a decline in the profitability of a plant or other business activity, MD&A should also, where material, analyze the reasons underlying these matters, such as an inability to realize previously projected economies of scale, a failure to renew or secure key customer contracts, or a failure to keep downtime at acceptable levels due to aging equipment. Whether favorable or unfavorable conditions constitute or give rise to the material trends, demands, commitments, events or uncertainties being discussed, the analysis should consist of material substantive information and present a balanced view of the underlying dynamics of the business.

If there is a reasonable likelihood that reported financial information is not indicative of a company's future financial condition or future operating performance due, for example, to the levels of subjectivity and judgment necessary to account for highly uncertain matters and the susceptibility of such matters to change, appropriate disclosure in MD&A should be considered and may be required. For example, if a change in an estimate has a material favorable impact on earnings, the change and the underlying reasons should be disclosed so that readers do not incorrectly attribute the effect to operational improvements. In addition, if events and transactions reported in the financial statements reflect material unusual or non-recurring items, aberrations, or other significant fluctuations, companies should consider the extent of variability in earnings and cash flow, and provide disclosure where necessary for investors to ascertain the likelihood that past performance is indicative of future performance. Companies also should consider whether the economic characteristics of any of their business arrangements, or the methods used to account for them, materially impact their results of operations or liquidity in a structured or unusual fashion, where disclosure would be necessary to understand the amounts depicted in their financial statements.

Critical Accounting Estimates.

Many estimates and assumptions involved in the application of GAAP have a material impact on reported financial condition and operating performance and on the comparability of such reported information over different reporting periods. [A] company should address material implications of uncertainties associated with the methods, assumptions and estimates underlying the company's critical accounting measurements. . . .

When preparing disclosure under the current requirements, companies should consider whether they have made accounting estimates or assumptions where [1] the nature of the estimates or assumptions is material due to the levels of subjectivity and judgment necessary to account for highly uncertain matters or the susceptibility of such matters to change; and [2] the impact of the estimates and assumptions on financial condition or operating performance is material. [Either way], companies should provide disclosure about those critical accounting estimates or assumptions in their MD&A.

Such disclosure should supplement, not duplicate, the description of accounting policies . . . disclosed in the notes to the financial statements. The disclosure should provide greater insight into the quality and variability of information regarding financial condition and operating performance. While accounting policy notes in the financial statements generally describe the method used to apply an accounting principle, the discussion in MD&A should present a company's analysis of the uncertainties involved in applying a principle at a given time or the variability that is reasonably likely to result from its application over time.

A company should address specifically why its accounting estimates or assumptions bear the risk of change. The reason may be that there is an uncertainty attached to the estimate or assumption, or it just may be difficult to measure or value. Equally important, companies should address the questions that arise once the critical accounting estimate or assumption has been identified, by analyzing, to the extent material, such factors as how they arrived at the estimate, how accurate the estimate/assumption has been in the past, how much the estimate/assumption has changed in the past, and whether the estimate/assumption is reasonably likely to change in the future. Since critical accounting estimates and assumptions are based on matters that are highly uncertain, a company should analyze their specific sensitivity to change, based on other outcomes that are reasonably likely to occur and would have a material effect. Companies should provide quantitative as well as qualitative disclosure when quantitative information is reasonably available and will provide material information for investors.

For example, if reasonably likely changes in the long-term rate of return used in accounting for a company's pension plan would have a material effect on the financial condition or operating performance of the company, the impact that could result given the range of reasonably likely outcomes should be disclosed and, because of the nature of estimates of long-term rates of return, quantified.

———————

The foregoing interpretation followed an SEC statement of "cautionary advice" concerning critical accounting policies that MD&A should address. Excerpts from this pronouncement follow (footnotes are omitted).

Securities and Exchange Commission
Release Nos. 33–8040; 34–45149
Cautionary Advice Regarding
Disclosure about critical Accounting Policies
(December 12, 2001)

[I]nvestors increasingly demand full transparency of accounting policies and their effects. Reported financial position and results often imply a degree of precision, continuity and certainty that can be belied by rapid changes in the financial and operating environment that produced those measures. As a result, even a technically accurate application of generally accepted accounting principles ("GAAP") may nonetheless fail to communicate important information if it is not accompanied by appropriate and clear analytic disclosures to facilitate an investor's understanding of the company's financial status, and the possibility, likelihood and implication of changes in the financial and operating status.

Of course, public companies should be mindful of existing disclosure requirements in GAAP and our rules. Accounting standards require information in financial statements about the accounting principles and methods used and the risks and uncertainties inherent in significant estimates. Our rules governing Management's Discussion and Analysis ("MD&A") currently require disclosure about trends, events or uncertainties known to management that would have a material impact on reported financial information.

We have observed that disclosure responsive to these requirements could be enhanced. For example, environmental and operational trends, events and uncertainties typically are identified in MD&A, but the implications of those uncertainties for the methods, assumptions and estimates used for recurring and pervasive accounting measurements are not always addressed. Communication between investors and public companies could be improved if management explained in MD&A the interplay of specific uncertainties with accounting measurements in the financial statements. . . .

We encourage public companies to include in their MD&A this year full explanations, in plain English, of their "critical accounting policies," the judgments and uncertainties affecting the application of those policies, and the likelihood that materially different amounts would be reported under different conditions or using different assumptions. The objective of this disclosure is consistent with the objective of MD&A.

Investors may lose confidence in a company's management and financial statements if sudden changes in its financial condition and results occur, but were not preceded by disclosures about the susceptibility of reported amounts to change, including rapid change. To minimize such a loss of confidence, we are alerting public companies to the importance of employing a disclosure regimen along the following lines:

1. Each company's management and auditor should bring particular focus to the evaluation of the critical accounting policies used in the financial statements. As part of the normal audit process, auditors must obtain an understanding of management's judgments in selecting and applying accounting principles and methods. Special attention to the most critical accounting policies will enhance the effectiveness of this process. Management should be able to defend the quality and reasonableness of the most critical policies, and auditors should satisfy themselves thoroughly regarding their selection, application and disclosure.

2. Management should ensure that disclosure in MD&A is balanced and fully responsive. To enhance investor understanding of the financial statements, companies are encouraged to explain in MD&A the effects of the critical accounting policies applied, the judgments made in their application, and the likelihood of materially different reported results if different assumptions or conditions were to prevail.

3. Prior to finalizing and filing annual reports, audit committees should review the selection, application and disclosure of critical accounting policies. Consistent with auditing standards, audit committees should be apprised of the evaluative criteria used by management in their selection of the accounting principles and methods. Proactive discussions between the audit committee and the company's senior management and auditor about critical accounting policies are appropriate.

4. If companies, management, audit committees or auditors are uncertain about the application of specific GAAP principles, they should

consult with our accounting staff. We encourage all those whose responsibility it is to report fairly and accurately on a company's financial condition and results to seek out our staff's assistance. We are committed to providing that assistance in a timely fashion; our goal is to address problems before they happen.

E. CRITICAL ACCOUNTING POLICIES

Critical accounting policies are emphasized in the foregoing SEC cautionary advice and related estimates in the last section of the preceding SEC interpretation of MD&A requirements. Particulars vary by industry, sector, company and specifics. Generalizations are therefore difficult. Nevertheless, a pattern shows that discussion and analysis includes an introduction to this section of the following type. Consider whether the summary introduction satisfies the prescriptions of the foregoing SEC releases or whether it is mere boilerplate.

> Our discussion and analysis of the company's financial condition and results of operations are based upon our consolidated financial statements, which have been prepared in accordance with accounting principles generally accepted in the United States. Preparing these financial statements requires us to make estimates and judgments that affect the reported amounts of assets, liabilities, revenues and expenses, and related disclosure. In doing so, we have identified significant accounting policies that, as a result of the estimates and judgments, as well as uncertainties, uniqueness and complexities of the underlying accounting standards and operations involved, could result in material changes to the company's financial condition or results of operations under different conditions or using different assumptions. These significant accounting policies are described in note 1 of our accompanying financial statements and summarized further below. In general, we base our estimates on historical experience and on various other assumptions that are believed to be reasonable under the circumstances. We also review these estimates and assumptions each year. Nevertheless, actual results may differ from these estimates under different assumptions or conditions.

After such an introduction, critical accounting policies are presented. The range of accounting topics that count as critical varies. Common examples include inventories, fixed assets, and accounts receivable. Other topics regularly identified as critical accounting policies are revenue recognition, goodwill and other intangible assets, investments in marketable securities, derivative instruments, loss contingencies (especially environmental liabilities) and defined benefit retirement plans. A few illustrative MD&A concerning the most common critical accounting policies follow. Consider whether they satisfy the prescriptions in the foregoing SEC releases or whether they are mere boilerplate.

Inventories. Inventories are predominantly finished goods. They are measured at the lower of cost or market. Cost is determined using the first-in, first-out (FIFO) method. A detailed analysis of inventory is performed on a periodic basis throughout the year. This evaluation includes analyses of inventory levels, historical write-off trends, expected product lives, sales levels by product and projections of future sales demand. Year-end inventory is further evaluated for obsolescence and excess quantities. If actual market conditions are less favorable than those projected by management, additional write downs may be required. Inventory purchases and commitments are based upon future demand forecasts for our products and our current level of inventory. If there is a sudden and significant decrease in demand for our products or there is a higher risk of inventory obsolescence because of rapidly changing technology and requirements, we may be required to write-down inventory. This would be reflected in an increase in our cost of goods sold, resulting in adverse effects on our gross profit margin.

Fixed Assets. The Company routinely considers whether there is evidence of impairment of its property, plant and equipment (fixed assets). The Company reviews the carrying values of its fixed assets whenever events or changes in circumstances indicate that such carrying values may not be recoverable. Unforeseen events, changes in circumstances, market conditions, and changes in estimates of future cash flows could negatively affect the fair value of the Company's fixed assets and result in an impairment charge. Fair value is the amount at which the asset could be bought or sold in a current transaction between willing parties. Fair value is determined by discounted estimated future cash flows, appraisals or other methods deemed appropriate. When fair value is less than carrying value, the Company determines whether to withdraw the asset from service and sell it or retain it. If retained, an impairment loss is recognized equal to the difference. The asset's fair value becomes the asset's new carrying value, which we depreciate over the asset's remaining estimated useful life. The asset's fair value could differ using different estimates and assumptions.

Allowance for Doubtful Accounts Receivable. The Company maintains an allowance for doubtful accounts for estimated losses resulting from the inability of our customers to make required payments, which are charged to bad debt expense. Management determines the adequacy of this allowance by regularly reviewing our accounts receivable aging and evaluating individual customer receivables, considering customers' financial condition, credit history and current economic conditions. In addition, management analyzes the age of receivable balances, historical bad debts write-off experience, industry and geographic concentrations of customers, general customer creditworthiness and current economic trends when determining its allowance for doubtful accounts. Significant management judgments and estimates must be made and used in connection with establishing these allowances. Actual results could be different from the Company's current estimates, possibly resulting in increased future charges to earnings. While we believe that our allowance for doubtful accounts is adequate and that the judgment applied is appropriate, if there is a deterioration of a major customer's credit worthiness or actual defaults are higher than our previous experience, recoverability would be adversely affected.

In addition to referencing particular critical accounting policies, related MD&A disclosure might include discussion and analysis of the probable lengths of time required for changes in areas identified as critical accounting policies to manifest. Consider the following example:

Accounting policies considered critical require that we make estimates in preparing our financial statements as of a given date. However, since our business cycle is relatively short, actual results related to these estimates are generally known within the six-month period following the financial statement date. Thus, these policies generally affect only the timing of reported amounts across two to three quarters. Within the context of these critical accounting policies, we are not currently aware of any reasonably likely events or circumstances that would result in materially different amounts being reported.

F. SEGMENT REPORTING

Useful financial statements of a complex business entity need to reveal how the various component parts of the entity are performing and how capital is being allocated among them. GAAP uses the highly pragmatic "management approach": operating segments on which separate reporting must be furnished are "components of an enterprise about which separate financial information is available that is evaluated regularly by the chief operating decision maker in deciding how to allocate resources and in assessing performance."

The central required information concerning each such operating segment includes the segment assets and segment profit or loss (and certain items that go into that calculation), each as used internally for evaluating performance and making capital allocation decisions. However, GAAP does not require segment cash flow data to be presented. In addition, information concerning products and services, geographic areas and major customers is also required.

To give a full understanding of this disclosure's meaning, entities must also describe the way the operating segments were determined, their respective products and services, differences between the measurements used in reporting segment information and those used in the entity's general financial statements, and changes in segment amounts from period to period.

Evaluating a large business with attention to its segments is useful in understanding how overall operations interact. It also enables the user of financial statements to focus on strengths and weaknesses. That can otherwise be difficult when a powerful segment offsets a weak one, for example.

G. RATIO CATEGORIES

The admonition at the outset that these ratio analytics furnish rules of thumb for guidance can be broadened a bit. Now that you have a feel for them, you should recognize that there is nothing inevitable about organizing the techniques as this Chapter has according to the headings "liquidity/activity" or "performance/profitability." Other possible classifications include efficiency, coverage, and value. They also could be classified according to the sources where the information is found: balance sheet ratios and income statement ratios.

Many financial institutions and services compute and present business ratios, and do so using a variety of different descriptive headings. These are often published on the Internet. One Web site organizes the ratios as presented in Table 8-11. It gives examples of average ratios in the categories, for a consumer products company, along with that company's broader industry and its sector within it, and the Standard & Poor's index of 500 leading businesses.

Note also that ratios in addition to those discussed in this Chapter are presented. Among them are: revenue, sales, or net income per employee and asset turnover (akin to receivables and inventory turnover). Visit a few financial Web sites, compare the various styles of presentation, and develop an opinion concerning which are better and worse. Note also how these metrics are likely to vary with underlying economic, business and credit conditions, including the markets for initial public offerings (IPOs) and mergers and acquisitions (M&A).

Table 8-11
Consumer Products Company

	Company	Industry	Sector	S&P 500
Efficiency				
Inventory Turnover	6.3	5.2	6.8	10.0
Receivables Turnover	12.4	10.0	13.0	9.0
Financial Strength				
Current Ratio	1.1	1.4	1.2	1.7
Quick Ratio	.6	.6	.6	1.2
Debt to Equity	1.0	1.4	1.1	1.0
Interest Coverage	6.0	7.0	9.6	9.0
Profitability				
Gross Margin	44.2	48.3	47.5	48.5
Operating Margin	15.0	14.0	14.5	18.3
Net Margin	9.2	8.5	8.8	11.5
Effectiveness				
Return on Equity	32.7	32.1	33.0	22.4
Return on Investments	16.0	15.6	16.7	13.2
Return on Assets	11.3	10.4	10.8	8.3

These data can be used as comparative rules of thumb. Apart from comparability, key issues in so using them include assessment of various statistical qualities that are discussed in the next Chapter. Among these are the statistical integrity of the averages (whether they are weighted or not for example) and techniques such as standard deviation used to assess the relative degree of normalcy or extremes.

Problem 8

J&J has been operating its business successfully for five years and has generated substantial amounts of cash that it has determined it could more profitably use to purchase another business than it could by reinvesting that cash in its own existing business. A business that is particularly attractive to J&J is MountainView, Inc. ("MVI"), a corporation that manufactures and distributes a line of mountain bikes. Selected pages from MVI's financial statements are set forth below.

a. *Liquidity/Activity.* Calculate the following financial ratios for MVI as of 12/31/Y3: current ratio; quick ratio; inventory turnover ratio; accounts receivable turnover ratio (assume all net sales were made on credit); and debt-to-equity ratio (using total liabilities and total owners' equity). Consider the following issues with respect to these ratios:

(1)   What does the relationship between the current ratio and the quick ratio suggest?

(2)   How liquid is MVI's inventory?

(3)   If MVI's credit policy calls for payment within 30 days, how well is its credit collection practice being managed?

(4)   If the industry in which MVI operates has an average debt-to-equity ratio of 3:1, what does this suggest about MVI's capacity to attract additional debt financing?

b. *Profitability/Performance.* Calculate and identify trends and reasons for trends in the following financial ratios for MVI (for Years 3 and 2 in the case of the operating profit margin and for Years 3, 2 and 1 for the others):

(1)   operating profit margin;

(2)   COGS as a percentage of sales;

(3)   pre-tax earnings as a percentage of sales; and

(4)   net income as a percentage of sales.

What explains the trends (if any) in the foregoing ratios?

c. *Further Questions; MD&A.* What further questions do the foregoing ratios and issues suggest J&J should ask of MVI's management? What issues raised by MVI's financial statements would you expect to see addressed by MVI in an MD&A section if MVI were required or chose to prepare one?

d.   What is MVI's Year-3 return on equity? How does this compare with returns on equity summarized in Table 8-11?

MountainView, Inc.—Balance Sheet

Assets	12/31/Y3	12/31/Y2
Current Assets		
Cash	150,000	275,000
Accounts Receivable (Net)	1,380,000	1,145,000
Inventory	1,310,000	1,105,000
Prepaid Expenses	40,000	35,000
Total Current Assets	2,880,000	2,560,000
Fixed Assets		
Land	775,000	775,000
Buildings	2,000,000	2,000,000
Machinery	1,000,000	935,000
Office Equipment	225,000	205,000
Total Property, Plant & Equipment	4,000,000	3,915,000
(Less Accumulated Depreciation)	1,620,000	1,370,000
Net Fixed Assets	2,380,000	2,545,000
Total Assets	5,260,000	5,105,000
Liabilities and Owners' Equity		
Current Liabilities		
Accounts Payable	900,000	825,000
Notes Payable	600,000	570,000
Accrued Expenses	250,000	235,000
Total Current Liabilities	1,750,000	1,630,000
Long-Term Liabilities		
Notes Payable, 12.5%, Due 12/15/Y6	2,000,000	2,000,000
Notes Payable, 11%, Due 7/10/Y3	———	355,000
Total Liabilities	3,750,000	3,985,000
Owners' Equity		
Common Stock (100,000 shares, par value $1)	100,000	100,000
Additional Paid-in-Capital	100,000	100,000
Retained Earnings	1,310,000	920,000
Total Owners' Equity	1,510,000	1,120,000
Total Liabilities & Owners' Equity	5,260,000	5,105,000

MountainView, Inc.—Income Statement

	Year 3	Year 2	Year 1
Net Sales	7,500,000	7,000,000	6,800,000
Operating Expenses			
Cost of Goods Sold	4,980,000	4,650,000	4,607,000
Depreciation	250,000	240,000	200,000
Selling, General & Administrative	1,300,000	1,220,000	1,150,000
Research & Development	50,000	125,000	120,000
Operating Income	920,000	765,000	723,000
Interest Expense	320,000	375,000	375,000
Earnings Before Income Taxes	600,000	390,000	348,000
Income Taxes	210,000	136,000	122,000
Net Income	390,000	254,000	226,000

Conceptual Questions 8

Why the narrative (MD&A) on top of the numerical? Why not leave the narrative to the footnote disclosure accompanying the financial statements proper? Should GAAP require MD&A? For external users such as investors (as compared to internal uses for managerial decision-making), why not jettison the statements and put all accounting information in narrative form? Or why not require an additional Statement of Ratios, capturing the dozen or so standard ratios users routinely apply to financial statements? Finally, why not dispense with the conceit of computing a single number for earnings and a single number for owners' equity and instead report a range of reasonable figures for each?

IFRS Note 8

Financial statement analysis requires attention to the accounting policies an entity applies, including changes from period to period and differences with those otherwise-comparable entities apply. To the extent that IFRS and GAAP standards differ, comparing entities applying the respective standards requires adjustment to affected line items, ratios and other analysis. Recall some of the examples of differences summarized in IFRS Notes at the end of previous Chapters that may bear on financial statement analysis:

- Revenue and expense recognition principles (Chapter 3).

- Inventory, particularly how GAAP allows the LIFO method that IFRS prohibits (Chapter 4).

- Measuring fixed assets (using cost under GAAP but either cost or fair value under IFRS) and testing and accounting for their impairment (Chapter 5).

- Accounting for intercompany ownership, intangible assets (particularly how research and development costs are expensed under GAAP and capitalized under IFRS) (Chapter 6).

- Distinguishing between operating and capital leases (Chapter 6).

- Classification of convertible debt as a liability under GAAP and as both a liability and equity under IFRS (Chapter 7).

Such differences do not prevent comparative financial analysis of an entity applying GAAP with one applying IFRS. But they require adjustments to render the respective financial statements comparable. Accompanying narrative disclosure and managerial analysis of financial information can help pinpoint differences. Yet also appreciate that disclosure may differ, with the SEC's US federal law disclosure regime potentially differing from law applicable to non-US companies applying IFRS. For example, the SEC's focus on critical accounting policies may be particularly helpful but similar disclosure may not accompany IFRS financial statements filed in other countries.

CHAPTER 9

THE STATEMENT OF CASH FLOWS

▪ ▪ ▪

The balance sheet, income statement, and statement of changes in equity do not depict the flow of cash through a business during any accounting period. These statements keep track of an entity's overall operations by recording and reporting a whole range of transactions without regard to the inflow or outflow of cash (other than as one among many assets being tracked). Indeed under the matching principle and the accrual method of accounting that seeks to implement it, the actual inflow and outflow of cash is affirmatively obscured. Economic events are allocated to periods in which they contributed to revenue generation (as expenses) or constituted revenue generation (as revenue) without regard to when cash flowed in or out of the business.

While this accrual method of accounting has advantages for reflecting the *financial performance* of the operation of an entity over time, it has the potential to hide what may be a more significant issue concerning the *financial viability* of an entity. This is the question of an entity's ability to meet its debts as they come due, which depends in major part on how cash in the business is managed and how it flows through the business. This can be very important because an entity with high income may appear to be successful based upon an examination of its income statement but, if it lacks cash to pay its debts as they come due, belief in that apparent success can have devastating consequences.

To keep track of cash as a separate feature of an entity's position, GAAP requires an entity to prepare a statement of cash flows as part of its financial statements. In part, this statement seeks to reverse the consequences of the accrual system of accounting and permit a user of financial statements to evaluate directly the way the entity manages cash. (Compare the opposite exercise in Chapter 3, Section D of converting from a cash system to an accrual system.) In this Chapter we consider the methodology of preparing the statement of cash flows. The Chapter also presents various analytical and interpretive tools that can be applied to evaluate an entity's cash flow position.

Before doing so, however, a preliminary question should be addressed: what is cash? You may imagine that cash is legal tender sitting in a vault or in a till or stuffed in a wallet or a mattress. That is true. But for financial accounting purposes, it also includes so-called cash equivalents, such as amounts on deposit in bank accounts. For example, a typical note in financial statements would appear under the heading "Cash and Cash Equivalents." It would disclose that the company's cash management policy is "to invest in highly liquid, short-term financial instruments." It then defines cash equivalents as consisting of "U.S. Government obligations, time deposits, overnight securities and other short-term, highly liquid securities with original maturities of three months or less."

A cautionary note about this seemingly simple set of propositions is in order. Difficulties can arise in determining whether a financial instrument is functionally equivalent to cash. For example, some instruments that nominally enable a holder to convert to cash within a short period, such as one year, depend on circumstances, such as an active liquid market and willing buyers, that may not be reliably assumed. These difficulties may cast doubt on the utility of the concept of cash equivalents for accounting purposes. At minimum, they warrant careful attention to the terms of instruments purporting to be cash equivalents.

A. RATIONALE AND ORGANIZATION

The statement of cash flows is intended primarily to provide relevant information about the cash receipts and cash payments of an entity during an accounting period. It is intended in particular to enable users of financial statements to assess the entity's ability to generate positive cash in the future, to assess its ability to pay its debts as they come due, to pay dividends, to obtain financing, to understand the reasons for differences between net income and cash flows, and to assess the effects of investing and financing activities on an entity's overall business and financial condition. To do all of this, the statement of cash flows separately reports transactions involving cash flows according to three categories: operating, investing, and financing. The content of these categories is not entirely intuitive, and results from principles articulated by FASB. Also, if cash flow applies to more than one classification (operating, investing or financing), it is classified to the category constituting the main activity (not divided among categories).

Operating activities are transactions arising in connection with the daily operation of the business in the ordinary course. They can be thought of as the activities that generate items of revenue and expense. Obvious examples are making sales to customers and paying suppliers and employees. Another good example is research and development costs, which GAAP classifies as operating cash flows, reflecting how it requires them to be expensed when incurred (Chapter 6). Taxes are also classified as operating cash flows.

One type of transaction included in this category of operating activities that could have been put elsewhere is the receipt of interest and dividends and the payment of interest. These could be considered to be investing or financing activities but FASB has deemed them too closely connected with revenues and expenses for such treatment and therefore considers them to be operating activities for purposes of the statement of cash flows.

Investing activities are those transactions arising in connection with the purchase and sale of items for purposes of generating returns not directly related to the daily operations of the business in the ordinary course. These would include purchases and sales of such things as marketable securities, investments in other entities and loans made to other entities (and of course the receipt of cash in repayment of such loans). The category also includes, under the FASB declaration, the purchase and sale of fixed assets, such as property, plant, and equipment. Although used in the ordinary course of operating the business, these types of assets are also investments in a real sense and their impact on revenue and expense is sufficiently attenuated to treat them as investments.

Financing activities are transactions in which the entity borrows money (and all transactions in which it repays the borrowings). These activities include borrowings from banks and other lenders, as well as the issuance of common stock and other equity securities and also debt securities. Repayments of principal in respect of all such activities, as well as payment of dividends on equity, are all considered financing activities. (And note why putting the payment of dividends in the financing category rather than the operating category makes sense in terms of this three-fold scheme: the payment of dividends is not an expense so it is not an operating activity; it is a return to shareholders on their investment, which from the entity's point of view is a source of funding and therefore a financing activity.)

The statement of cash flows is prepared after the balance sheet and income statement are finalized. Remember that all the plusses and minuses on the income statement net out to equal net income, the bottom line on the income statement, and that bottom line is reflected on the balance sheet in owners' equity. Remember also that the balance sheet always balances, which means that if cash has increased, something else has decreased and vice versa.

B. DIRECT METHOD

The statement of cash flows can be prepared in one of two ways: the direct method or the indirect method. True to its name, the direct method of preparing and presenting the statement of cash flows calls for reporting directly each account in which a change in cash occurred during the period. All journal entries during the period are reviewed and each entry that affected the cash account is allocated to one of the three categories of activities referred to above. For example, reconsider the transactions in which Larry's Firm engaged from Chapter 2 (transactions 1 through 11). The transactions affecting cash were these: transactions 1, 2, 4, 9, 10, and 11. Each such transaction is organized into sub-categories within each of the three separate categories of operating, investing, and financing activities. The result of this process for Larry's Firm as of the end of the period referred to in Chapter 2 would be as shown in Table 9-1.

Table 9-1 Larry's Firm Statement of Cash Flows (for the period ending in Chapter Two) [DIRECT METHOD]		
Cash Flows from Operating Activities		
Collections from Customers (9)		5,000
Payments to Suppliers (2)		(500)
Payments for Research (11)		(250)
Net Cash Provided by Operating Activities	4,250	
Cash Flows from Investing Activities		
Payments for Investment in Furniture (4)		(250)
Payments for Investment in Library (10)		(500)
Net Cash Used by Investing Activities	(750)	
Cash Flows from Financing Activities		
Receipts upon Issuance of Common Stock (1)		10,000
Net Cash Provided by Financing Activities	10,000	
NET INCREASE (DECREASE) IN CASH	13,500	

Notice that in Table 9-1's illustration each entry is accompanied by a reference number denoting the underlying transaction to which it relates. This has been done in this illustration so that you can follow it; in actual statements of cash flows, the transactions are not tied back directly to the journal entries in this way.

Presentation Using Parentheses.

More importantly, notice that for amounts that reflect an outflow of cash (all entries called "Payments" in this example), the amount is placed in parentheses. This is a standard signal in accounting and finance to denote that the amount being reported is in effect a negative amount. In this context, those payments are a reduction in cash flow because they involve the disbursement of cash by the entity and so are shown as having the effect of decreasing cash flow. Receipt of cash on the other hand has the effect of increasing cash flow during the period and this is signaled by listing these amounts without parentheses. Note also that the last line, the bottom line, on this statement is expressed as "Net Increase (Decrease) in Cash," and the use of the parentheses around the word (Decrease) signals the same thing. Finally, note the convention that the summary of cash flows by activity category states either the "Net Cash Provided by" that activity when that flow was positive; or "Net Cash Used by" that activity when negative.

C. INDIRECT METHOD

GAAP permits the statement of cash flows to be prepared and presented using the direct method or the indirect method. The difference between the direct and indirect method relates only to the portion of the statement of cash flows concerning operating activities—the preparation and presentation of the other two categories of activities affecting cash (financing and investing) remain the same under both methods.

The difference between the methods with respect to operating activities relates to the perspective from which those operating activities are regarded. Whereas the direct method tracks each of those operating activities that affect cash directly, the indirect method approaches the problem from a different perspective: it starts from the proposition that a major purpose of the statement of cash flows is to show the relationship between cash flows during the period to net income during the period. So it takes as its starting point the net income during the period and then identifies the types of transactions that would impact net income in a way that differs from the impact of those transactions on cash flows.

Accounting Effects Requiring Reconciliation.

Recall the numerous ways in which the accrual system of computing net income and the other principles discussed in preceding Chapters obscure the cash flow through the business during the period.

- In Chapter 3 we saw that the accrual system of accounting allocates economic events to discrete time periods and reports their effect on net income without regard to when cash in respect of those activities is paid or received.

- In Chapter 4 we saw that the conventions for inventory accounting view inventory as having a dual aspect—it is an asset account so far as the goods are on hand but then becomes an expense (the COGS) as the goods are sold. This dual aspect of inventory implies that there will be a mismatch in any one period between cash expended to create the asset and the COGS recognized as an expense to burden net income.

- In Chapter 5 we saw that the principles of depreciation require allocating the net cost of a fixed asset over its expected useful life and that this allocation burdens net income in those periods even while no cash is actually spent in respect of the fixed asset in those periods.

All these transactions therefore affect net income in ways that differ from their effect on cash flows.

Start with Net Income.

The indirect method of preparing and reporting the statement of cash flows seeks to reflect these sorts of differences between net income and cash flows. The starting point for preparing the portion of the statement of cash flows concerning operating activities under the indirect method is to list net income for the period. Next, a separate entry is made for each sort of transaction that entails different effects for net income than for cash flows. The magnitude of these differences, whether causing net income to be higher than cash flows or causing net income to be lower than cash flows, are reported and then added together. The entire process seeks, in short, to reconcile net income to net cash flows for the period.

To see the simplicity of the difference between the direct and indirect methods, reconsider the example of Larry's Firm just used. Under the indirect method, we start with the net income for the period of $4,750 from the income statement (Chapter 2, section E). We then examine the income statement and balance sheet for changes in accounts that relate to operating activities (recall that these are accounts that involve revenue or expense) and in which activity affecting cash occurred. These would ordinarily consist of the sorts of transactions just mentioned in the bullet-points above under the heading "Accounting Effects Requiring Reconciliation"—accruals/deferrals, inventory/cost of goods sold and fixed assets/depreciation.

In the case of Larry's Firm for the period ending in Chapter 2, there is only one such account, the supplies account, which increased during the period by $500. The cash used to fund that purchase produced no reported effect on net income. That means cash compared to net income is lower to the extent of the cash purchase. This calls for subtracting that amount from the net income figure in computing net cash flows. The portion of the statement of cash flows that would be different from the direct method given in the previous example is the following:

Cash Flows from Operating Activities	
Net Income	4,750
Increase in Current Assets	(500)
Net Cash Provided by Operating Activities	4,250

Take another example, using the financial statements of J&J from September (Chapter 4). To prepare the statement of cash flows of J&J for September using the direct method, first review all the journal entries to determine which of those affected cash. You will see that the transactions in September affecting cash were 19a, 19b, 20, 22a, and 24. Also note that all those transactions related to operating activities. Armed with that information, the statement of cash flows using the direct method would appear as in Table 9-2.

Table 9-2		
J & J		
Statement of Cash Flows, Sept.		
[DIRECT METHOD]		
Cash Flows from Operating Activities		
Collections from Customers		
(19a, 19b, 20, 24)		9,600
Payments to Employees (22a)		(3,000)
Net Cash Provided by Operating Activities	6,600	
Cash Flows from Investing Activities		
None		0
Cash Flows from Financing Activities		
None		0
NET INCREASE IN CASH	6,600	

Collections from customers that provided cash from operating activities were recorded as transactions 19a, 19b, 20, and 24. The sum of those amounts is reflected directly on the first line of the statement of cash flows prepared using the direct method. Similarly, all outflows of cash in respect of operating activities are listed directly—in this case, transaction 22a, involving the payment of cash to employees. (Note again that while the example in Table 9-2 identifies all the relevant transaction numbers parenthetically for illustrative purposes, a final statement of cash flows would not.)

Using the indirect method, J&J's September statement of cash flows would appear as in Table 9-3. It depicts the balances in the relevant accounts as of the end of the preceding period and as of the end of the current period. The change in the balance in each account gives the indirect measure of cash flows in or out of the entity in respect of that account.

		Table 9-3	
		J & J	
		Statement of Cash Flows, Sept.	
		[DIRECT METHOD]	
Cash Flows from Operating Activities			
		Net Income	5,850
8/31	9/30		
1200	2500	(Increase) in Accounts Receivable	(1,300)
1000	1250	(Increase) in Inventory	(250)
1000	800	Decrease in Prepaid Insurance	200
750	1700	Increase in Expenses Payable	950
50	100	Increase in Interest Payable	50
100	1400	Increase in Accounts Payable	1,300
200	0	(Decrease) in Deferred Income	(200)
Net Cash Provided by Operating Activities		6,600	
Cash Flows from Investing Activities			
None			0
Cash Flows from Financing Activities			
None			0
NET INCREASE IN CASH		6,000	

Typical Reconciliation Steps.

Most businesses will be significantly more complex than Larry's Firm and J&J's, although the basic principles underlying the statement of cash flows remain the same. They would invariably include the following categories and steps.

Start with non-cash charges to income. Depreciation and amortization expense will be the most obvious. They burden net income. But they are non-cash expenses. So the effect of depreciation or amortization expense is to cause net income to be lower than net cash flows. Hence, the amount of those expenses is added to the net income figure on the way toward calculating the net cash flow figure. The same is true for charge-offs on accounts receivable. When a provision for losses on receivables is made, the income statement takes a hit, but no cash has changed hands.

For each current asset account—accounts receivable, inventory and so on—if the current asset rises from the prior period, it is a use of cash. Suppose the balance sheet shows an increase in accounts receivable. When customers owe the company more now than they did a year ago, they are holding its cash. It has not received the cash, even though it has reported a sale. This then is a use of cash on the statement of cash flows.

Put another way, this means the company has taken into income sales on credit to customers, not yet paid for in cash. That creates a difference between net income (based on those credit sales) and net cash flow (for which cash has not come in). The reconciliation therefore calls for decreasing the net income amount by this level of receivables, on our way toward computing net cash flow. If receivables had declined, the opposite would be called for.

Suppose the balance sheet shows a decrease in inventory during the period. This means that the entity has sold more inventory than it has produced or purchased during the period. When the entity sells more inventory than it produces or purchases, that excess is an expense (COGS) but does not involve the disbursement of cash. So we have to add back to net income that amount of expense to come up with our net cash flow number.

Consider the reverse situation, where inventories have increased. That means the entity purchased or produced more inventory than it sold, but note that such extra inventory on hand is not yet an expense (it won't be until it is eventually included in COGS). Nevertheless, if cash was expended in the purchase or production of the inventory, we would have to subtract from net income that amount of extra inventory to come up with our net cash flow number. If paid on credit rather than in cash (as is common), inventory increases still need to be reversed to reconcile net income with cash flows, and the same steps just taken will do it, so long as similar reconciliations are made to accounts payable, as discussed next.

For working capital components on the liability side—short term obligations such as accounts payable—if the account rises from the prior year, it means the entity still has the money in its pocket. It has not paid a supplier, for example. So this is functionally a source of cash to the entity. Suppose for example that accounts payable increased. The effect of an increase in accounts payable is to reduce net income but without involving the disbursement of an equivalent amount of cash. As a result, the net income figure is understated compared to net cash flows and therefore the reconciliation calls for an increase in the net income figure on our way to computing the net cash flow for the period.

Note, finally, that amounts treated as part of other comprehensive income that would otherwise in principle call for a reconciliation to net cash flows are not required to be so reconciled. In other words, the cash flow statement reconciliation between cash flows and net income is a reconciliation to net income—not to comprehensive income. FASB's judgment was that while noncash items that are part of other comprehensive income would become additional reconciling items in the cash flow statement, adding them would not add meaningful informational content.

Graphical Illustration of Relationships Requiring Reconciliation.

To try to simplify things, the objective of the reconciliation must be borne in mind: we recognize that accounting principles under the accrual method dedicated to calculating net income deliberately obscure cash flows. But we also know that most of those accounting principles can be traced and that we can in effect reverse out their effects on net income to come up with a figure showing net cash flow. Conceptually, things can remain easy and intuitive, although implementing them according to the discussion just presented can be mind-numbing. Perhaps we can simplify things not in words but in Table 9-4. It depicts the relationship between net income and net cash flow for increases and decreases in various account categories.

Table 9-4 Reconciling Net Income to Net Cash Flow		
	Effect on Net Income	Reconciliation Necessary to Compute Net Cash Flow
A. Depreciation Expense	(Reduces)	Add Back
B. Other Non-Cash Charges	(Reduces)	Add Back
C. Increases in Assets	Raises	(Subtract Out)
D. Decreases in Assets	(Reduces)	Add Back
E. Increases in Liabilities	(Reduces)	Add Back
F. Decreases in Liabilities	Raises	(Subtract Out)

A.   Table 9-4 depicts that depreciation expense burdens net income (*reduces it*) but does not involve cash outlays; so we have to *add back* the amount of that expense to net income when calculating cash flows.

B.   Table 9-4 also depicts that other non-cash expenses burden net income (*reduce it*) but do not involve cash outlays. Examples include the establishment or increase in an allowance for doubtful accounts or a reserve for loss contingencies (both of which are discussed in Chapter 6). In each case, as with depreciation expense, we have to *add back* the amount of each such expense to net income when calculating cash flows.

C. Table 9-4 also depicts that an increase in asset accounts benefits net income (*raises it*) but does not involve cash receipts; so we have to *subtract out* the amount of that increase from net income when calculating cash flows. For *accounts receivable* this follows because sales on credit increase net income but do not generate cash; for *inventory* this follows because increases in it do not entail an expense until sold but could require cash to produce or purchase.

D. In contrast, a decrease in an asset account does not generate net income but does involve the receipt of cash (*e.g.*, *accounts receivable* taken into income last year that are paid this year will not be reported in income this year but do involve the receipt of cash; *inventory* sold this year is reported as an expense through the COGS but it was purchased or produced with cash expended in prior periods). This burdens net income (*reduces it*) but does generate cash; so we must *add back* that amount to net income in calculating net cash flow.

E & F. The situation with liabilities is just the reverse of the situation for assets. That is, (a) an increase in a current liability requires that the net income amount be adjusted to a cash basis by *adding* to it and (b) a decrease in a current liability requires that the net income amount be adjusted to a cash basis by *subtracting* from it.

Note that for asset-intensive companies the depreciation-reconciliation adjustment to convert net income to net cash flows is large compared to the net effect of the reconciliation adjustment in working capital accounts. This leads many analysts to a shortcut for such businesses of adding depreciation expense to net income as a rough estimate of net operating cash flow. This can lead to the false and erroneous impression, however, that depreciation expense is a source of cash, which it is not.

Users of financial statements must understand these relationships between net income and net cash flow but need not memorize them. Cash flow statements show the net effects that are summarized in Table 9-4.

D. ASSESSMENT

Accountants debate whether the direct or indirect method is superior. While most financial statement users seem to prefer the direct method, most preparers tend to provide the indirect method. One helpful practice when using the direct method would be for preparers to use the same headings in it as they use in the income statement, which is neither required nor routinely done.

Some financial statement users prefer the direct method because it more nearly reflects real-world events such as the receipt of cash from customers and the payment of cash to suppliers, employees, and others. This facilitates understanding the entity's business. Likewise, the classification of cash flows into these general categories is not available or revealed by the indirect method. As the next section shows, it can better equip the user to assess the "quality" of an entity's income—that is, the portion of income generating current cash flows—by enabling a line by line comparison of income to cash flow based on equivalent line items.

Perhaps the strongest argument against the indirect method is an evident lack of congruency between the balance sheet line items and the cash flow statement figures (called, in the parlance of accounting specialists, "non-articulation"). That is, changes in the current asset and liability account balances on the balance sheet are often reported in the statement of cash flows at significantly different amounts. A common example arises for companies recently completing acquisitions of other companies having used different depreciation conventions, which must be adjusted in the indirect but not in the direct method.

These arguments suggest that FASB might find it desirable to require the direct method (it does encourage the direct method). Many financial statement users appear to believe that both are desirable—that is, they prefer a direct method statement along with an indirect reconciliation of income to operating cash flows. Not everyone agrees of course, with many suggesting that the information about cash received from customers and paid to suppliers and employees is not worth much.

The objective and result of the reconciliation is crucial: the relationship between net income and net cash flows from operating activities, and for what reasons they differ, is considered to be so important that whether one uses the direct method or the indirect method, the statement of cash flows must include a reconciliation of net income to net cash flows. Let's consider ways to put this information to use.

E. ANALYZING CASH FLOW

The cash flow statement aids in assessing a company's liquidity and solvency. A variety of tools can be used to glean insights into these questions, including adaptations of the ratio analyses discussed in Chapter 8 related to the balance sheet and income statement. Illustrative ratios are considered below, after first introducing two more general observations about analyzing cash flow.

Working Capital Changes.

Consider the net effect of working capital changes. An increase in non-cash current assets means more cash inflow is tied up in accounts receivable, inventory and other non-cash current assets with a corresponding decrease in cash. This implies that when cash is low, managers try to *minimize* current asset levels (for example by speeding inventory sales and receivables collections). Conversely, an increase in current liabilities means more cash is freed up, with suppliers given promises instead of cash. This implies that when cash is low, managers try to *maximize* current liability levels (for example by procuring inventory on credit and extending accounts and notes payable). Therefore if net working capital rises (driven by non-cash current asset increases and/or current liabilities decreases) operating cash flow is *lower* than net income because cash is tied up in other current assets. If net working capital falls (driven by non-cash current asset decreases and/or current liabilities increases) operating cash flow is *higher* than net income because cash is released from other current assets.

Free Cash Flow.

As a business grows, its current asset accounts such as accounts receivable and inventory will grow and this indicates a need for more cash to finance them. Growth may bring future profits, but getting there requires more cash. As a business faces difficulties, a significant rise in current liabilities compared to current assets may signal cash flow problems, posing higher risks for lenders and owners. A barometer of an entity's solvency is its *free cash flow*. This is equal to net operating cash flow less (a) required reinvestment in the business to maintain current operational levels, (b) required payments on long-term debt coming due and (c) any normal cash distributions to owners. Free cash flow thus indicates cash available to cushion against economic adversity and/or to exploit opportunities arising from economic fortune.

Cash Interest Coverage Ratio.

Moving on to ratio analysis, the income statement-based interest coverage ratio considered in Chapter 8 is affected by the accrual system of accounting. It is based on income that includes many items that do not generate cash flows. But since one cannot pay interest, or any other obligation, with accrual income, a more refined statement of an entity's interest coverage capacity is the *cash interest coverage ratio*, which can complement the (general) interest coverage ratio.

The ratio is calculated by dividing cash flow provided by operating activities by the total interest expense for the period, as follows:

$$\frac{\text{Cash Flow Provided by Operating Activities}}{\text{Total Interest Expense}}$$

It thus expresses the number of times cash outflows for interest are covered by cash inflows from operations. It too can be compared with that of other entities or the industry norm to suggest an entity's ability to meet interest commitments (or the risk of default on instruments requiring interest payments).

Cash Dividend Coverage Ratio.

A test looking strictly from a shareholder's perspective could examine the relationship between operating cash flow and historical levels of cash dividend payments to give a measure of the entity's ability to make cash dividend payments in the future. The ratio is often calculated as cash flow provided by operating activities divided by total cash dividend payments in the most recent year.

$$\frac{\text{Cash Flow Provided by Operating Activities}}{\text{Cash Dividends Paid}}$$

To calculate the Cash Dividend Coverage for common stock, one might subtract from cash flow provided by operating activities all cash dividends paid to preferred stockholders or to minority stockholders in subsidiary companies. The level of historical dividends to be used would depend on that historical pattern: if dividends have been steady over time, that steady amount would be used; if they have been increasing at regular intervals, then that rate of increase would be applied.

Quality of Income Ratio.

As noted, the relationship between net income and net cash flow is so crucial that the statement of cash flows must include a reconciliation of these amounts. The relationship between these amounts can also be used to evaluate the *quality of an entity's income*, expressed as the ratio of cash flows provided by operating activities to net income:

$$\frac{\text{Cash Flow Provided by Operating Activities}}{\text{Net Income}}$$

This ratio can be important because it can reveal the degree to which income is being generated without corresponding cash generation, as where income is driven by increasing volumes of sales on credit without a steady inflow of cash on the receivables. Variations in this very sensitive ratio over time would be a red flag calling for further investigation of reasons for the change.

Cash Flow Per Share.

A highly controversial measure sometimes used, but which GAAP prohibits from inclusion as part of the statement of cash flows, is Cash Flow Per Share. It is equal to cash available for distribution to common stockholders divided by the weighted average number of common shares outstanding during the period:

$$\frac{\text{Cash}}{\text{Outstanding Shares}}$$

The cash flow per share ratio is controversial largely because cash dividends on common stock are declared and paid only at the discretion of the entity's board of directors and discretion not to pay dividends or to pay very low dividends can be exercised without regard to the levels of cash available for distribution. Accordingly, it would be a serious mistake to believe that cash flow per share is any indication at all of what cash dividends are likely to be. Subject to that caution, however, cash flow per share can inform the analysis of dividend paying capacity by comparing that number to the historical manner in which the entity has paid out earnings to shareholders or retained them for reinvestment in the business.

Cash Return on Assets.

The final ratio we consider is the cash return on assets. It is intended to give a measure of an entity's ability to generate cash flows available for investment in new assets. The cash return used in this ratio is the increase (or decrease) in cash during the current period and the base against which that change in cash position is measured is usually the entity's total assets as of the end of the prior period:

$$\frac{\text{Net Increase (Decrease) in Cash (Current Period)}}{\text{Total Assets (Prior Period)}}$$

F. INTERPRETING CASH FLOW

The cash flow statement is a relative newcomer to accounting. Its predecessor was called the funds flow statement; it dates to the 19th century, but became more common in the 1970s and 1980s. The funds flow statement focused on working capital, whereas the cash flow statement encompasses all cash activities.

Each category in the cash flow statement—operating, investing, and financing—provides differential information. Information utility can vary with a company's life-cycle stage. For example, investing and financing cash flows add particularly valuable information concerning start-up and rapidly-growing businesses (those with fewer assets) whereas operating cash flows add particularly valuable information concerning mature or declining companies (those with more assets).

Cash flow analysis has assumed increasing importance in recent decades. Theory and practice increasingly focus on cash generation as the ultimate result of productive activity. Cash management demonstrates relative managerial prowess. Cash flow statements enable users to assess cash flow generation and absorption. That enables users to compare the present value of probable future cash flows across different businesses, subjects pursued in Finance, the next Part of this book.

Chapter 8 included excerpts from SEC interpretations of rules requiring public companies to accompany their financial statements with a narrative Management's Discussion and Analysis (MD&A). The MD&A must address specifically liquidity and resources, matters tied directly to the information presented in the cash flow statement. Accordingly, the following additional excerpts from the SEC's interpretation of cash-related MD&A requirements are enriching. Footnotes are omitted and section headings abbreviated.

Securities and Exchange Commission
Release Nos. 33–8350; 34–48960
Interpretation: Guidance Regarding MD&A
(December 22, 2003)

A company is required to include in MD&A the following information, to the extent material:

- historical information regarding sources of cash and capital expenditures;

- an evaluation of the amounts and certainty of cash flows;

- the existence and timing of commitments for capital expenditures and other known and reasonably likely cash requirements;

- discussion and analysis of known trends and uncertainties;

- a description of expected changes in the mix and relative cost of capital resources;

- indications of which balance sheet or income or cash flow items should be considered in assessing liquidity; and

- a discussion of prospective information regarding companies' sources of and needs for capital, except where otherwise clear from the discussion.

Discussion and analysis of this information should be considered and may be required to provide a clear picture of the company's ability to generate cash and to meet existing and known or reasonably likely future cash requirements.

In determining required or appropriate disclosure, companies should evaluate separately their ability to meet upcoming cash requirements over both the short and long term. Merely stating that a company has adequate resources to meet its short-term and/or long-term cash requirements is insufficient unless no additional more detailed or nuanced information is material. In particular, such a statement would be insufficient if there are any known material trends or uncertainties related to cash flow, capital resources, capital requirements, or liquidity.

Cash Requirements.

In order to identify known material cash requirements, companies should consider whether the following information would have a material impact on liquidity (discussion of immaterial matters, and especially generic disclosure or boilerplate, should be avoided):

- funds necessary to maintain current operations, complete projects underway and achieve stated objectives or plans;

- commitments for capital or other expenditures; and

- the reasonably likely exposure to future cash requirements associated with known trends or uncertainties, and an indication of the time periods in which resolution of the uncertainties is anticipated.

One starting point for a company's discussion and analysis of cash requirements is tabular disclosure of contractual obligations, supplemented with additional information that is material to an understanding of the company's cash requirements. For example, if a company has incurred debt in material amounts, it should explain the reasons for incurring that debt and the use of the proceeds, and analyze how the incurrence of that debt fits into the overall business plan, in each case to the extent material. Where debt has been incurred for general working capital purposes, the anticipated amount and timing of working capital needs should be discussed, to the extent material.

Companies should address, where material, the difficulties involved in assessing the effect of the amount and timing of uncertain events, such as loss contingencies, on cash requirements and liquidity. Any such discussion should be specific to the circumstances and informative, and companies should avoid generic or boilerplate disclosure. In addition, because of these difficulties and uncertainties, companies should consider whether they need to make or change disclosure in connection with quarterly as well as annual reports.

Sources and Uses of Cash.

[A] company's discussion and analysis of cash flows should not be a mere recitation of changes and other information evident to readers from the financial statements. Rather, MD&A should focus on the primary drivers of and other material factors necessary to an understanding of the company's cash flows and the indicative value of historical cash flows.

In addition to explaining how the cash requirements identified in MD&A fit into a company's overall business plan, the company should focus on the resources available to satisfy those cash requirements. Where there has been material variability in historical cash flows, MD&A should focus on the underlying reasons for the changes, as well as on their reasonably likely impact on future cash flows and cash management decisions. Even where reported amounts of cash provided and used by operations, investing activities or financing have been consistent, if the underlying sources of those cash flows have materially varied, analysis of that variability should be provided. The discussion and analysis of liquidity should focus on material changes in operating, investing and financing cash flows, as depicted in the statement of cash flows, and the reasons underlying those changes.

Operations.

The discussion and analysis of operating cash flows should not be limited by the manner of presentation in the statement of cash flows. Alternate accounting methods of deriving and presenting cash flows exist, and while they generally yield the same numeric result in the major captions, they involve the disclosure of different types of information. When preparing the discussion and analysis of operating cash flows, companies should address material changes in the underlying drivers (*e.g.*, cash receipts from the sale of goods and services and cash payments to acquire materials for manufacture or goods for resale), rather than merely describe items identified on the face of the statement of cash flows, such as the reconciling items used in the indirect method of presenting cash flows.

For example, consider a company that reports an overall increase in the components of its working capital other than cash with the effect of having a material decrease in net cash provided by operations in the current period. If the increase in working capital was driven principally by an increase in accounts receivable that is attributable not to an increase in sales, but rather to a revised credit policy resulting in an extended payment period for customers, these facts would need to be addressed in MD&A to the extent material, along with the resulting decrease in cash provided by operations, if not otherwise apparent. In addition, if there is a material trend or uncertainty, the impact of the new credit policy on cash flows from operations should be disclosed.

While a cash flow statement prepared using the indirect method would report that various individual components of working capital increased or decreased during the period by a specified amount, it would not provide a sufficient basis for a reader to analyze the change. If the company reports negative cash flows from operations, the disclosure provided in MD&A should identify clearly this condition, discuss the operational reasons for the condition if material, and explain how the company intends to meet its cash requirements and maintain operations. If the company relies on external financing in these situations, disclosure of that fact and the company's assessment of whether this financing will continue to be available, and on what terms, should be considered and may be required.

A company should consider whether, in order to make required disclosures, it is necessary to expand MD&A to address the cash requirements of and the cash provided by its reportable segments or other subdivisions of the business, including issues related to foreign subsidiaries, as well as the indicative nature of those results. A company also should discuss the effect of an inability to access the cash flow and financial assets of any consolidated entities. For example, an entity may be consolidated but, because the company lacks sufficient voting interests or the assets are legally isolated, the company may be unable to utilize the entity's cash flow, cash on hand, or other assets to satisfy its own liquidity needs.

Financing.

To the extent material, a company must provide disclosure regarding its historical financing arrangements and their importance to cash flows, including, to the extent material, information that is not included in the financial statements. A company should discuss and analyze, to the extent material:

- its external debt financing;

- its use of off-balance sheet financing arrangements;

- its issuance or purchase of derivative instruments linked to its stock;

- its use of stock as a form of liquidity; and

- the potential impact of known or reasonably likely changes in credit ratings or ratings outlook (or inability to achieve changes).

In addition to these historical items, discussion and analysis of the types of financing that are, or that are reasonably likely to be, available (or of the types of financing that a company would want to use but that are, or are reasonably likely to be, unavailable) and the impact on the company's cash position and liquidity, should be considered and may be required. For example, where a company has decided to raise or seeks to raise material external equity or debt financing, or if it is reasonably likely to do so in the future, discussion and analysis of the amounts or ranges involved, the nature and the terms of the financing, other features of the financing and plans, and the impact on the company's cash position and liquidity (as well as results of operations in the case of matters such as interest payments) should be considered and may be required.

Cash Management.

Companies generally have some degree of flexibility in determining when and how to use their cash resources to satisfy obligations and make other capital expenditures. MD&A should describe known material trends or uncertainties relating to such determinations. For example, a decision by a company in a highly capital-intensive business to spend significantly less on plant and equipment than it has historically may result in long-term effects that should be disclosed if material. Material effects could include more cash, less interest expense and lower depreciation, but higher future repair and maintenance expenses.

G. CASH FLOW VARIABILITY

Notice the references in the foregoing SEC release to "variability in historical cash flows" and the need in certain circumstances for the MD&A to provide "analysis of that variability." Analyzing a company's cash flow variability aids in assessing trends and uncertainties. Such variability analysis can also be applied to other financial statement items, particularly earnings, as well as specific line items, such as sales.

In this section, useful tools for this exercise are presented, using cash flow as the example. Simple tools include calculating average cash flow over a meaningful period such as five years or the average pessimistic cash flow, meaning the minimum cash flow a company can reasonably be expected to generate under worst-case scenarios. More advanced tools include the standard deviation of cash flow and the coefficient of variation in cash flow.

Averages.

The term *mean*, in statistics, designates the average of a given data set, also known as its *central value*. There are three measures of this central value: arithmetic mean, weighted mean, and geometric mean.

The *arithmetic mean* is a simple average. Calculate it by adding the value of each item in the data set and then dividing by the number of items in the data set. Suppose a company's cash flows were as follows:

Year	Cash Flow
1	3.00
2	3.10
3	2.95
4	3.25
5	3.30

The arithmetic mean of these cash flow data is:

$$\frac{3.00 + 3.10 + 2.95 + 3.25 + 3.30}{5}$$

$$= \$3.12$$

The arithmetic mean is a simple average in the sense that it treats each item in the data as having equal significance. The *weighted mean* captures circumstances in which the individual items bear different relative importance. For example, an analyst may form an opinion that a company's most-recent cash flow experience is more relevant than its earlier cash flow experience. Suppose she decides, in the foregoing example, that Year 5's cash flows are entitled to greatest weight, then those of year 4, 3, 2, and 1, in that order and proportionately. Armed with this supplemental data we can calculate the weighted mean as follows.

Year	Cash Flow	Weight	Result
1	3.00	1	3.00
2	3.10	2	6.20
3	2.95	3	8.85
4	3.25	4	13.00
5	3.30	5	16.50
		15	$47.55

The weighted mean of these cash flow data is:

$$\frac{\$47.55}{15}$$

$$= \$3.17$$

The *geometric mean* is used to gain insight into the average rate of change in a data set over time. By how much did cash flow grow, on average, during this 5-year period? We could determine the arithmetic rate of change year-to-year as follows:

Year	Cash Flow	Change	Percent
1	3.00	–	–
2	3.10	+ .10	+ 3.33%
3	2.95	– .15	– 4.84%
4	3.25	+ .30	+10.17%
5	3.30	+ .05	+ 1.50%

The arithmetic mean of these changes in cash flow is 2.54%. That is determined as follows:

$$\frac{3.33 - 4.84 + 10.17 + 1.50}{4}$$

$$= 2.54\%$$

This is a potentially misleading figure in that if you apply that rate of 2.54% to each year, in succession from year 1 through Year 5, the Year 5 cash flow figure would be $3.32. In fact, it is $3.30.

The rate of change that will yield exactly $3.30 is the geometric mean. Its formula is as follows:

$$= \sqrt[n]{(1 + x_1)(1 + x_2)(1 + x_3)...(1 + x_n)} - 1$$

where:

x = the percentage rate of change

n = the number of observations (here, 4 years of data)

Applying this we get:

$$= \sqrt[4]{(1 + .0333)(1 - .0484)(1 + .1017)(1 + .015)} - 1$$

$$= \sqrt[4]{1.099} - 1$$

$$= 1.024 - 1$$

$$= 2.4\%$$

When you apply this rate of 2.4% to each of the years in succession, the result for Year 5 is $3.30.

For a more striking proof that the arithmetic and geometric means tell different stories, consider this simplified example. You buy an investment for $100. After Year 1 it is worth $200 and after Year 2 it is worth $100 again. Your return for Year 1 was 100% (generating $100 in return on $100 principal amount invested) and for Year 2 was –50% (suffering $100 in decline on $200 principal amount at stake). Your arithmetic mean return is 100% – 50% / 2 = 25%. But this investment clearly did not return 25% after 2 years; in fact, it returned nothing: you bought it for $100 and as of Year 2 it is still worth $100—it gave a 0% return. The geometric mean gives this answer. In the formula:

$$= \sqrt[2]{(1 + 1)(1 - .5)} - 1$$

$$= \sqrt[2]{(2)(.5)} - 1$$

$$= \sqrt[2]{1} - 1$$

$$= 1 - 1$$

$$= 0$$

The key conceptual difference between arithmetic and geometric means concerns suppositions concerning the relationship between data in a series. The arithmetic mean assumes that all data points are independent of one another; the geometric mean assumes the observations are linked. In other words, the arithmetic mean gives all possible future states equal weighting (it treats data points as independent of one another); the geometric mean treats the series as an integrated path. Two other points for any given data set: (1) arithmetic means are higher than geometric means and (2) the difference between the two increases as the data set contains more variation, a subject standard deviation measures.

Standard Deviation.

Standard deviation is a basic tool of statistics, used to measure the dispersion within a data set. It can be applied to an infinite variety of data sets, from test scores among students in a class, to characteristics of a nation's population, to the cash flow or earnings of a company or the financial ratios of a sample of companies selected for comparison (it can also be used to measure the risk associated with a share of common stock, an application discussed in Chapter 12).

Here's an intuitive account of standard deviation. A set of data will have some tendency to spread out. How much spreading there is can provide a basis for inferences about the chances that a particular future instance will differ from its expected amount. The expected amount can be traced back to the foregoing paragraphs on averages—the expected amount is the mean or average of past observations (arithmetic, weighted or geometric). How much the population spreads out above and below that average is a measure of how much variability (or stability) there is. These intuitions are formalized in the standard deviation, and its cousin the coefficient of variation.

The formula below shows a basic calculation of standard deviation, traditionally denoted by the Greek letter *sigma*, σ:

$$\sigma = \sqrt{\frac{\sum (y_t - \bar{y})^2}{n - 1}}$$

If you think of this as applied to a cash flow-variability exercise, you would define the variables in this formula as follows:

y = cash flow for each given period, designated as t

$\bar{y}$ = mean cash flow of the entire data set

n = number of years

Calculate standard deviation by the following steps:

1. Calculate the mean of the data set ($\bar{y}$)
2. From each observation (y_t), subtract the mean ($y_t - \bar{y}$)
3. * Square each result ($y_t - \bar{y}$)^2
4. Sum the squares (Σ)
5. Divide the sum by $n - 1$
6. Take the square root of the foregoing $\sqrt{}$

Using the cash flow data assumed in the previous discussion of averages, we can elaborate the foregoing steps. We already took step 1 when we calculated the arithmetic mean cash flow as $3.12, so that will be $\bar{y}$ in this standard deviation exercise. Step 2 calls for taking each observation and subtracting that mean, as follows:

Year	Cash Flow		Mean		Result
1	3.00	−	3.12	=	−.12
2	3.10	−	3.12	=	−.02
3	2.95	−	3.12	=	−.17
4	3.25	−	3.12	=	.13
5	3.30	−	3.12	=	.18

---

*	Squaring the difference eliminates effects of negative numbers when summing the results. Squaring also implies it does not matter whether one subtracts the observed cash flow from the mean or subtracts the mean from the observed cash flow.

Step 3 calls for squaring each result, a step that converts all negative numbers to positive numbers and thus enables aggregating the information to capture departures above and below the mean:

Year	Cash Flow		Mean		Result	Squared
1	3.00	−	3.12	=	−.12	.0144
2	3.10	−	3.12	=	−.02	.0004
3	2.95	−	3.12	=	−.17	.0289
4	3.25	−	3.12	=	.13	.0169
5	3.30	−	3.12	=	.18	.0324

Step 4 is to sum those squares: .0144 + .0004 + .0289 + .0169 + .0324 = .093. Step 5 is to divide this sum by $n - 1$, which here means $5 - 1 = 4$. That is: .093/4 = .02325. The final Step, 6, is to take the square root of that figure. That is,

$$\sqrt{.02325}$$

So the standard deviation is .15 or 15%. Standard deviation is an absolute measure of variability. High standard deviations indicate greater variability. In the case of standard deviations of cash flow, this means greater instability in cash flow. Variability can be understood ultimately as an expression of associated risk in the item under consideration.

Standard deviation can be used to take a relative measure of variability or risk. This measure relates the standard deviation of a data set to the mean of the data set. It is called *coefficient of variation*. It is expressed by the following formula:

$$= \frac{\sigma}{\bar{y}}$$

In this cash flow data set, that is .15 / 3.12 = 4.9%.

A number of additional mathematical tools can help to assess cash flow variability (as well as variability or risk associated with a wide variety of data set types such as earnings). For example, a cash flow or earnings trend can be plotted and a straight line drawn that best fits the relationship between actual results and the trend. The slope of the resulting line expresses a measure of risk.

———————

Problem 9A

Prepare a statement of cash flows of J&J for October, using (a) the direct method and (b) the indirect method by comparing the financial statements of October 31 with those of September 30.

Problem 9B

Consider the financial statements of MVI set forth in Chapter 8, now supplemented by the statement of cash flows that follows. For MVI in Years 3 and 2, calculate cash interest coverage and the quality of income ratio. What do these reveal? What MD&A disclosure would be appropriate?

MountainView, Inc.—Statement of Cash Flows

	Year 3	Year 2
From Operating Activities		
Net Income	390,000	254,000
Decrease (Increase) in Accounts Receivable	(235,000)	(34,000)
Decrease (Increase) in Inventory	(205,000)	(28,000)
Decrease (Increase) in Prepaid Expenses	(5,000)	(3,000)
Increase (Decrease) in Accounts Payable	75,000	25,000
Increase (Decrease) in Accrued Expenses	15,000	7,000
Depreciation	250,000	240,000
Cash Provided by Operating Activities	285,000	461,000
From Investing Activities		
Sales (Purchases) of Machinery	(65,000)	(378,000)
Sales (Purchases) of Office Equipment	(20,000)	(27,000)
Cash (Used by) Investing Activities	(85,000)	(405,000)
From Financing Activities		
Increase (Decrease) in Short-Term Borrowings	30,000	(40,000)
Increase (Decrease) in Long-Term Borrowings	(355,000)	———
Cash (Used by) Financing Activities	(325,000)	(40,000)
Increase (Decrease) in Cash	(125,000)	16,000

Conceptual Questions 9A

How does the cash flow statement relate to debate concerning the relative supremacy of the income statement and balance sheet (Conceptual Questions, Chapters Two and Four)? How does it interface with the debate concerning the merits of the accrual system of accounting (Conceptual Questions, Chapter 3)? How does it relate to conceptual challenges concerning the principle of historical cost driving the reporting of fixed assets on the balance sheet (Conceptual Questions, Chapter 5)? Does it contribute anything to the debate over rules versus standards in accounting (Conceptual Questions, Chapter 6)? In other words, where does the cash flow statement rank? Evaluate the following assertion: ultimately, cash flow is a fact, while earnings are an opinion.

Conceptual Questions 9B

The statement of cash flows distinguishes activity into categories of operating, investing and financing. Other financial statements (the balance sheet and income statement) do not. Can the cash flow statement's distinctions be adapted to improve the usefulness of the balance sheet and income statement? Could those be organized using similar activity classifications? So organizing an income statement would facilitate easier reconciliation of net income to cash flows. All three statements could further disaggregate activity into cash transactions, accrual transactions and changes arising from fair value fluctuations.

Along the same lines, given that the balance sheet and income statement are prepared using what is essentially a direct method, should the direct method of preparing the statement of cash flows be required? If the foregoing renovations were made, wouldn't that requirement make absolute sense? Finally, to what extent could such a redesign of financial statement presentation enable discarding traditional measures of financial performance, such as net income itself? Would it be useful in this format simply to present the disaggregated information without expressing an ultimate bottom line?

IFRS Note 9

Among differences between GAAP and IFRS concerning topics addressed in this Chapter are the following:

- GAAP treats research and development costs as part of operating cash flows, which also reflects how GAAP requires them to be expensed when incurred (Chapter 6); IFRS classifies research and development costs as investing cash flows, which likewise reflects how IFRS treats them as capital assets.

- GAAP classifies interest paid and dividends received as operating cash flows and dividends paid as financing cash flows; IFRS allows choices in classifying: (1) dividends paid or received and interest paid or received as operating cash flows or (2) interest or dividends paid as financing cash flows and interest or dividends received as investing cash flows.

PART III

FINANCE

■ ■ ■

Introduction

Finance has contributed substantial theory concerning how accounting information should be used. While lawyers will detect limited methodological affinities between finance and law, lawyers need to understand finance basics both for their practices and to appreciate the mechanisms used to measure value and risk and allocate resources. Accountants must know finance, especially valuation principles and techniques, often used in many accounting exercises, such as testing the impairment of fixed assets or goodwill.

The value of any productive asset, including companies and shares of their stock, is the present value of its future net cash flow. Determining value thus requires estimating the cash flows and applying a present value factor to them. The concepts and operation of present and future values are introduced in Chapter 10. Ensuing Chapters take up two debates on this seemingly straightforward proposition.

The first debate concerns techniques for fundamental valuation. The issue here is principally how best to estimate future cash flows. Analysts could use date from balance sheets, income statements, and cash flow statements to aid the exercise. The most conservative fundamental analysts treat current earnings as the most reliable estimate of future cash flows. The former group prefers not to assume any growth in future cash flows. These alternatives are covered in Chapter 11.

The other debate concerns the role markets play in solving valuation challenges. One school believes markets do so for publicly traded shares better than any other approach. This school is called modern finance theory. Its key hypothesis is that markets are efficient in the sense of accurately pricing asset values, at least for shares of publicly traded companies. This is the dominant school of thought in academic finance and among the majority of financial analysts. It is covered in Chapter 12.

Opponents are efficiency skeptics. They doubt markets have the power to make value transparent. They favor conducting independent fundamental valuation analysis making their own estimates and judgments. This minority of fundamental analysts—often dubbed *value investors*—then compare their conclusions with the market's conclusions and try to buy shares or companies priced below value. They believe this offers higher returns on investments than the average market. A key difference between efficiency devotees and fundamental analysts is determining the appropriate rate at which to discount future cash flows to present values.

Before proceeding, note that financial analysts are important consumers of accounting information. They seek to measure financial value by analyzing accounting information. But accounting is a record-keeping system entailing classification, measurement and aggregation for the purpose of presenting fairly financial position and performance. It is not designed to report value. Accounting reports are essential to valuation but must be interpreted and sometimes reconfigured. Part of this process includes understanding the basis upon which a set of financial statements was prepared.

Examples of what financial analysts must understand (and by now so should you) include: preparation in accordance with GAAP (a cash or accrual basis for example); inventory accounted for using FIFO, LIFO or another method and how these affect the income statement, balance sheet, and inventory turnover ratio; depreciation judgments as to historical cost, expected useful life, and salvage value and the method and its effects (straight-line or accelerated basis); the relation between accumulated depreciation and probable required reinvestment in the business; and reserving accounts receivable for bad debt allowance and whether credit terms match receivables turnover.

Additional consideration would be given to more advanced topics in certain cases, including whether investments are carried properly; if lease rates differ from current market rates, whether that difference has been valued; the extent to which debt is used to fund operations; the relation between debt service and income generation and debt service and cash generation; the degree to which pension plans are over-funded or under-funded; and whether there are any unrecorded or contingent liabilities, such as for environmental claims, retiree obligations, product warranties, and the like.

Previous Chapters encountered many of these examples, and there are many more that this book does not cover. The key point concerns the relationship between accounting and finance. Accounting figures are the starting point in financial analysis, including valuation. They are indispensable components of business analysis. However, they must be adjusted for the job and their limits understood.

CHAPTER 10

VALUATION PRINCIPLES

■ ■ ■

Finance is based upon a set of underlying valuation principles. The bedrock of these is the time of value of money. A dollar held today is worth more than a dollar promised tomorrow. The principles of valuation enable measuring how much more. The time value of money looks in two directions: the present value of a future dollar and the future value of a present dollar. It also captures two fact patterns: a single dollar or a stream of dollars. Pivotal to these valuation principles are the drivers of time value differences, known as interest rates or discount rates. These are a function of different risk characteristics, such as between specifically-promised dollars (say, on debt instruments) and residual rights to potential dollars (say, on equity securities). This Chapter moves through this sequence: laying the bedrock of the time value of money and finishing by conceptualizing interest rates or discount rates for debt and for equity.

A. THE TIME VALUE OF MONEY

Any amount of money in hand today is worth more than the same amount to be paid at any future time. Suppose your professor were to offer you $1,000 in exchange for reading this book (setting aside the legal problem of past consideration) and gave you the choice of being paid immediately upon completing reading or being paid one year later. Which would you choose? Presumably you, like most people, would choose immediate payment. But what if the offer were for either $1,000 paid upon completing reading or $1,100 one year later? Or $1,500 one year later?

Two questions arise. First, why should people generally prefer earlier payment of money to deferred payment of money? Second, in terms of our example, at what amount of money to be paid in the future would you, or most people, opt for the future sum instead of the present sum? With respect to why people should generally prefer earlier payment of money to deferred payment of money, there are three sorts of reasons: utility, risk and opportunity cost.

Utility is the notion that things of value satisfy desire and immediate possession of the thing can satisfy immediate desire. With the payment of $1,000 upon reading this book, you could throw a party for your classmates or buy a share in a ski house or a beach house. If this satisfies your desires more than getting even a larger sum when you enter the third year of law school or are about to graduate from law school, then you may opt for earlier payment rather than later payment. But your friends may have a different set of preferences, or different utility, for entertainment and gratification now as opposed to deferring entertainment and gratification until a year on. Despite these different preferences, however, in order to be indifferent about payment now and payment in the future, most people would insist on a greater amount in the future.

Risk. In choosing between your professor's offer to pay $1,000 upon completing reading this book (say this semester) and to pay $1,100 one year later, you will be concerned about the possibility of breach. That is, in thinking about opting for the future payment, you will be concerned about the possibility of not getting it. Perhaps you will have graduated from law school and are so busy doing deals and making money that you forget all about it. Or perhaps your professor will be running the law school's Oxford program next year and forget all about it. Or (heaven forbid) your professor may declare personal bankruptcy during the year and simply not have the $1,100 to pay you then.

All these situations pose the problem of *risk*—the risk of nonpayment of the future sum, for whatever reason. What emerges is the hackneyed adage that a bird in hand is worth two in the bush. But, as with utility, there will be some amount of additional money to be paid in the future that will induce you to accept the risk of nonpayment. If the choice is $1,000 to be paid this semester versus $1,500 to be paid a year later, perhaps you are willing to take your chances on forgetfulness or bankruptcy. Once again, your willingness to take that risk may differ from that of your classmates. But also in the same vein, whatever you or your classmates' appetite for risk is, the promised future payment will have to be greater than the present payment to compensate you or your classmates for taking that risk.

Opportunity cost is a fundamental concept in economic theory. It recognizes that people have all sorts of opportunities available to them but that some of these are mutually exclusive. In choosing one opportunity, other opportunities are foreclosed. In the context of the time value of money, the idea is that you may have available to you the opportunity to invest the $1,000 paid this semester and earn interest on that amount. For example, you could deposit the $1,000 in your savings account. Assuming your bank is paying an annual interest rate of 5% on that account, then you could earn $50 during the year while the $1,000 is on deposit.

On these facts, you would be indifferent between receiving $1,000 upon completing reading and receiving $1,050 one year hence, subject of course to the question of risk. But if your savings account is insured by the federal government so that your investment and the earnings thereon are in effect risk free, you would remain indifferent. In any event, if you considered the risk of losing the $1,000 investment in your insured savings account to be equivalent to the risk of your professor not paying you the $1,050 in one year's time, then you would again be indifferent as between these opportunities. In this example, the opportunity cost of foregoing the payment now is $50 and you would insist on being paid in the future that additional amount in order to be indifferent between these choices.

Our second question—what amount of money to be paid in the future would lead you, or most people, to opt for the future sum instead of the present sum—can be answered by investigating more fully the meaning of the time value of money concept. For an intuitive introduction, consider the following excerpt from a characteristically lucid and witty essay by Warren E. Buffett, the Chairman of Berkshire Hathaway Inc. and one of the most successful investors in the history of finance and investing (it is taken from a letter Mr. Buffett wrote to his investment partners in 1963, when Mr. Buffett was 32 years old):

> I have it from unreliable sources that the cost of the voyage Isabella originally underwrote for Columbus was approximately $30,000. This has been considered at least a moderately successful utilization of venture capital. Without attempting to evaluate the psychic income derived from finding a new hemisphere, it must be pointed out that . . . the whole deal was not exactly another IBM. Figured very roughly, the $30,000 invested at 4% compounded annually would have amounted to something like $2 trillion.

The time value of money generally is expressed in terms of the concept of *present value*. Present value tells us what the right to receive a certain sum at some point in the future is worth to us today. Similarly, present value allows us to determine the rate of return we will receive on our investment if we anticipate receiving a particular sum of money in the future. By determining the present value of an investment, we can thus compare it not only with the right to receive a sum of money today, but with the present value of other investments that are available to us. To understand present value, it is first useful to understand the related concept of *future value*. The following discussion first defines future value, shows a formula for calculating it under various conditions, and then does the same for present value.

B. FUTURE VALUE

Assume you have $100 that you decide to deposit in a savings account that is paying 8% interest annually. What will your account balance be at the end of the year (assuming no deposits or withdrawals)? It will be $108. You may have been able to calculate that result in your head. How did you do it? Probably by multiplying $100 by .08 to determine the interest and then adding that to the $100 balance you started with. How would you respond if asked what your balance would be at the end of two years? You would repeat the foregoing calculation and then in addition add to your new balance of $108 an amount equal to 108 times .08 to reflect the interest to be earned during the second year. That would be *108 + (108 x .08)* and would equal $116.64. If you were asked, what about for three years, four years, five years and so on, you would probably just keep doing the series of calculations. That is fine, but there is an easier and less time consuming way. You could use a single formula:

$$FV_n = x \, (1 + k)^n$$

This formula says that your balance (abbreviated as *FV*, standing for the phrase "future value") at the end of some future year (denoted by *n*) is equal to the amount you started with (which we have called *x*) times a function of the interest rate (which we have called *k*) and the number of years in the future we are considering. That is, the term *(1 + k)^n* (which is called the *future value factor*) is a way of avoiding the problem of repeating a series of calculations by instead just doing one calculation. Let's try this for the two examples we just did. Your account balance at the end of one year would be:

$$F = 100(1+.08)^1 = \$108$$

Your account balance at the end of two years would be:

$$FV_2 = 100(1+.08)^2 = \$116.64$$

Continuing, your account balance at the end of three years would be:

$$FV_3 = 100(1+.08)^3 = \$125.97$$

Using this formula makes things clearer and also makes the calculation simpler because it can be done very easily using a basic calculator. Things are even simpler than that, you may be happy to know. Look at Table 10-1. It shows the results of using the future value formula for $1 for time periods at various interest rates.

In the table, each "cell" is defined by an interest rate and a period of time. For the future value of $100 at an annual interest rate of 8%, at the end of 3 years, use Table 10-1 as follows: go down the year row to 3, go across the percentage column to 8% and the cell gives you the future value of $1. It is equal to $1.2597. Multiply that by the $100 you are interested in and you get the same result we just got in our calculation: $125.97.

(Tables like these were developed in the mid-1950s, before calculators capable of making requisite computations became widely available. You can do computations using either a calculator or applicable tables, though doing both may maximize learning. Perusing the tables will develop your sense of the relationship between future and present value; using a calculator will develop your sense of the arithmetic relations.)

CALCULATION

TABLE.

Table 10-1: Future Value of Lump Sums

	4%	5%	6%	7%	8%	9%	10%	11%	12%	13%	14%	15%
1	1.0400	1.0500	1.0600	1.0700	1.0800	1.0900	1.1000	1.1100	1.1200	1.1300	1.1400	1.1500
2	1.0816	1.1025	1.1236	1.1449	1.1664	1.1881	1.2100	1.2321	1.2544	1.2789	1.2996	1.3225
3	1.1249	1.1576	1.1910	1.2250	1.2597	1.2950	1.3310	1.3676	1.4049	1.4429	1.4815	1.5209
4	1.1699	1.2155	1.2625	1.3108	1.3605	1.4116	1.4641	1.5181	1.5735	1.6305	1.6890	1.7490
5	1.2167	1.2763	1.3382	1.4026	1.4693	1.5386	1.6105	1.6851	1.7623	1.8424	1.9254	2.0114
6	1.2653	1.3401	1.4185	1.5007	1.5869	1.6771	1.7716	1.8704	1.9738	2.0820	2.1950	2.3131
7	1.3159	1.4071	1.5036	1.6058	1.7138	1.8280	1.9487	2.0762	2.2107	2.3526	2.5023	2.6600
8	1.3686	1.4775	1.5938	1.7182	1.8509	1.9926	2.1436	2.3045	2.4760	2.6584	2.8526	3.0590
9	1.4233	1.5513	1.6895	1.8385	1.9990	2.1719	2.3579	2.5580	2.7731	3.0040	3.2519	3.5179
10	1.4802	1.6289	1.7908	1.9672	2.1589	2.3674	2.5937	2.8394	3.1058	3.3946	3.7072	4.0456
11	1.5395	1.7103	1.8983	2.1049	2.3316	2.5804	2.8531	3.1518	3.4785	3.8359	4.2262	4.6524
12	1.6010	1.7959	2.0122	2.2522	2.5182	2.8127	3.1384	3.4985	3.8960	4.3345	4.8179	5.3503
13	1.6651	1.8856	2.1329	2.4098	2.7196	3.0658	3.4523	3.8833	4.3635	4.8980	5.4924	6.1528
14	1.7317	1.9799	2.2609	2.5785	2.9372	3.3417	3.7975	4.3104	4.8871	5.5348	6.2613	7.0757
15	1.8009	2.0789	2.3966	2.7590	3.1722	3.6425	4.1772	4.7846	5.4736	6.2543	7.1379	8.1371
16	1.8730	2.1829	2.5404	2.9522	3.4259	3.9703	4.5950	5.3109	6.1304	7.0673	8.1372	9.3576
17	1.9479	2.2920	2.6928	3.1588	3.7000	4.3276	5.0545	5.8951	6.8660	7.9861	9.2765	10.7613
18	2.0258	2.4066	2.8543	3.3799	3.9960	4.7171	5.5599	6.5436	7.6900	9.0243	10.5752	12.3755
19	2.1068	2.5270	3.0256	3.6165	4.3157	5.1417	6.1159	7.2633	8.6128	10.1974	12.0557	14.2318
20	2.1911	2.6533	3.2071	3.8697	4.6610	5.6044	6.7275	8.0623	9.6463	11.5231	13.7435	16.3665
21	2.2788	2.7860	3.3996	4.1406	5.0338	6.1088	7.4002	8.9492	10.8038	13.0211	15.6676	18.8215
22	2.3699	2.9253	3.6035	4.4304	5.4365	6.6586	8.1403	9.9336	12.1003	14.7138	17.8610	21.6447
23	2.4647	3.0715	3.8197	4.7405	5.8715	7.2579	8.9543	11.0263	13.5523	16.6266	20.3616	24.8915
24	2.5633	3.2251	4.0489	5.0724	6.3412	7.9111	9.8497	12.2392	15.1786	18.7881	23.2122	28.6252
25	2.6658	3.3864	4.2919	5.4274	6.8485	8.6231	10.8347	13.5855	17.0001	21.2305	26.4619	32.9190
26	2.7725	3.5557	4.5494	5.8074	7.3964	9.3992	11.9182	15.0799	19.0401	23.9905	30.1666	37.8568
27	2.8834	3.7335	4.8223	6.2139	7.9881	10.2451	13.1100	16.7386	21.3249	27.1093	34.3899	43.5353
28	2.9987	3.9201	5.1117	6.6488	8.6271	11.1671	14.4210	18.5799	23.8839	30.6335	39.2045	50.0656
29	3.1187	4.1161	5.4184	7.1143	9.3173	12.1722	15.8631	20.6237	26.7499	34.6158	44.6931	57.5755
30	3.2434	4.3219	5.7435	7.6123	10.0627	13.2677	17.4494	22.8923	29.9599	39.1159	50.9502	66.2118

($1 at the end of *n* periods)

Compounding Frequency and Future Values of Lump Sums.

Notice that the key operation in the foregoing calculations turns on the future value factor. In particular, what is crucial in the formula is that we are adding to your account balance interest earned at the end of each year and then using that new balance to calculate the interest to which you are entitled in the next year and so on.Type equation here. This process is called *compounding*. It means that you in effect earn interest on interest over time. We have assumed that you are getting the interest payments added to your balance at the end of each year and not more frequently. This is called *compounding annually*.

Some bank accounts and other investments make the interest calculations and payments more often than each year, however. For example, your bank may make the calculation and add it to your account balance every six months rather than every year. When they do that, it is called *compounding semi-annually* (every six months). It has the effect of letting you earn interest on your interest more frequently. Hence the future value of your initial deposit under semi-annual compounding will be greater than under annual compounding. To calculate by how much, we can work with the same formula we just used with one refinement.

If you are getting 8% compounded semi-annually, that means that at the end of every six months your balance will be paid interest for that six months equal to 4% and then that additional interest amount will be added to your balance. To reflect this idea in our formula, we just indicate the frequency of compounding in the *(1 + k)ⁿ* term by dividing the *k* term by the number of times per year that interest will be paid (*m*) and keeping track of the frequency for the number of periods by modifying *n*, the exponent. So the formula becomes the following:

$$FV_n = x\left(1 + \frac{k}{m}\right)^{mn}$$

This modification to the formula means that the interest you are paid, *k*, will be calculated and added to your balance *m* times per year. In other words, the exponent "*m* times *n*" is equal to the number of times compounding will occur—the number of times interest will be calculated. So if your bank is giving you semi-annual compounding, then *m* in the formula will equal 2. (Note that if your bank were giving you annual compounding, then *m* = 1 and has no effect on the result of the computation—we would be back to the basic formula for annual compounding.)

Let's see how this works for the examples we just did. Your account balance at the end of the first 1/2 year would be:

$$FV_{1/2} = 100\left(1 + \frac{.08}{2}\right)^1 = \$104$$

Your account balance at the end of one year would be:

$$FV_1 = 100\left(1 + \frac{.08}{2}\right)^2 = \$108.16$$

Confirm using Table 10-1: this payout is for 2 periods at 4% and Table 10-1's 2 period/4% cell shows a future value factor of 1.0816.

Notice the consequence on the future value of your $100 of semi-annual compounding as compared to annual compounding. At the end of one year with semi-annual compounding your $100 balance is now $108.16 whereas with annual compounding it was only $108. Thus, more frequent compounding results in higher future values.

What would be the future value at the end of one year of your $100 deposit if your bank were to pay 8% interest compounded quarterly (every three months)? (Solve this problem on your own before consulting the following solution.) Your account balance at the end of one year would be:

$$FV_1 = 100\left(1 + \frac{.08}{4}\right)^4 = \$108.24$$

Repeat this problem to calculate the future value of your $100 at the end of three years.

Comparing annual compounding with more frequent compounding reveals why you often see consumer finance companies such as credit card issuers quote both an annual percentage rate and an annual percentage yield. The rate is the nominal rate as if interest were compounded annually; the yield is the actual rate given the more frequent compounding. Thus an advertisement might read:

18% interest for a limited time only! (annual effective yield is 19.56% due to monthly compounding)

You can compute the annual effective yield (AEY) of a nominal rate using the following formula:

$$AEY = \left(1 + \frac{k}{m}\right)^m - 1$$

In the preceding example of an 18% nominal rate and monthly compounding (12 times per year), applying the formula gives:

$$AEY = \left(1 + \frac{.18}{12}\right)^{12} - 1$$

$$= (1 + .015)^{12} - 1$$

$$= 1.1956 - 1$$

$$= .1956$$

$$= 19.56\%$$

A final note is that compounding is not necessary, whether annually or more (or less) frequently. Instead, it is possible to use the *simple interest method*. This means no compounding at all. To determine the amount of interest accrued using the simple interest method, multiply the principal amount by the term of the arrangement (number of years of a loan, say) by the annual interest rate. So the interest due on a $1,000 face amount note paying 7% annual interest in 5 years is (1,000 x 5 x .07) = $350. Compounded annually, the same loan would yield interest of 402.60 (see Table 10-1's cell for 5 periods at 7%).

C. PRESENT VALUE

Now that you understand how to calculate future values, we can perform the opposite procedure to work from future values to present values. Here we ask not how much will our money today grow to in the future (what is its future value) but rather how much is some amount to be paid in the future worth today (what is its present value). This question can be asked of both some lump sum amount that you expect to receive in the future and also of some lump sum amount that you will be obligated to pay in the future. Of the first sort of questions you may ask what some investment with a fixed payment such as a bond is worth today; of the second sort of questions you may ask how much you need to set aside today to make a payment of a certain amount in the future.

Present Values of Lump Sums.

You may have an intuitive sense that determining present values is the opposite of determining future values. To confirm that intuition, ask yourself this question: If you need to make a payment of $116.64 exactly two years from today, how much would you have to deposit in your savings account (bearing interest of 8% compounded annually) to have that amount at that time? Answer: $100. (See the discussion above of this point from the other perspective.) This relationship between future values and present values is the whole idea of the time value of money.

Just as we formalized the method of calculating future values, let us now formalize the method of calculating present values. The formula for determining the present value (*PV*) of a lump sum (which we call *x*) to be paid at the end of some future year (which we again call *n*) is:

$$PV_n = \frac{x}{(1+k)^n}$$

Notice that this is a mathematical confirmation of your intuition about the relationship between future values and present values. That is, in the future value formula we *multiplied x* by the *(1 + k)ⁿ* term and here in the present value formula we *divide x* by the *(1 + k)ⁿ* term. And now that term is called the *present value factor*. The result is that future values are reciprocals of present values.

A notable terminology difference between the future value and the present value formula is how we characterize *k*. In the future value formula and related discussion we called *k* the interest rate. It was the amount of interest your bank was going to pay you. In the case of present values, we call k the discount rate rather than the interest rate. Despite the different labels, they are both taking account of the three factors discussed in the previous essay concerning why people prefer earlier payment of a sum of money to later payment of the same sum: utility, opportunity cost and risk.

More particularly, each incorporates two discrete factors. The first is the pure time value of money. It is the idea that if you had the money today you could invest it profitably in a federally-insured savings account or other risk-free instrument. The second is the risk that you will fail to receive all or a portion of the money you expect to receive at the end of the period. The discount rate and interest rate are intended to compensate for each of these elements: the risk-free time value of money and the additional risk of the particular investment being considered.

Take an example of how the present value formula works. What is the present value of $100 to be received at the end of year two, assuming a discount rate of 8% compounded annually?

$$PV_2 = \frac{100}{(1+.08)^2} = \$85.73$$

As with the future value calculations, there are tables that show the present value of lump sums to be paid in the future under various discount rates. Look at Table 10-2. All you need to do is select a discount rate and the number of periods in the future until payment, and multiply this rate by the amount of money to be received. (As with the future value table, the present value table gives the present value of $1.00 for each discount rate and time period.) For example, the present value of $100 to be received in five years discounted using an 8% annual rate is: $100 x .6806 (the discount rate for $1 discounted at 8% for five years), or $68.06.

Table 10-2: Present Value of a Lump Sum

	4%	5%	6%	7%	8%	9%	10%	11%	12%	13%	14%	15%
1	0.9615	0.9524	0.9434	0.9346	0.9259	0.9174	0.9091	0.9009	0.8929	0.8850	0.8772	0.8696
2	0.9246	0.9070	0.8900	0.8734	0.8573	0.8417	0.8264	0.8116	0.7972	0.7831	0.7695	0.7561
3	0.8890	0.8638	0.8396	0.8163	0.7938	0.7722	0.7513	0.7312	0.7118	0.6931	0.6750	0.6575
4	0.8548	0.8227	0.7921	0.7629	0.7350	0.7084	0.6830	0.6587	0.6355	0.6133	0.5921	0.5718
5	0.8219	0.7835	0.7473	0.7130	0.6806	0.6499	0.6209	0.5935	0.5674	0.5428	0.5194	0.4972
6	0.7903	0.7462	0.7050	0.6663	0.6302	0.5963	0.5645	0.5346	0.5066	0.4803	0.4556	0.4323
7	0.7599	0.7107	0.6651	0.6227	0.5835	0.5470	0.5132	0.4817	0.4523	0.4251	0.3996	0.3759
8	0.7307	0.6768	0.6274	0.5820	0.5403	0.5019	0.4665	0.4339	0.4039	0.3762	0.3506	0.3269
9	0.7026	0.6446	0.5919	0.5439	0.5002	0.4604	0.4241	0.3909	0.3606	0.3329	0.3075	0.2843
10	0.6756	0.6139	0.5584	0.5083	0.4632	0.4224	0.3855	0.3522	0.3220	0.2946	0.2697	0.2472
11	0.6496	0.5847	0.5268	0.4751	0.4289	0.3875	0.3505	0.3173	0.2875	0.2607	0.2366	0.2149
12	0.6246	0.5568	0.4970	0.4440	0.3971	0.3555	0.3186	0.2858	0.2567	0.2307	0.2076	0.1869
13	0.6006	0.5303	0.4688	0.4150	0.3677	0.3262	0.2897	0.2575	0.2292	0.2042	0.1821	0.1625
14	0.5775	0.5051	0.4423	0.3878	0.3405	0.2992	0.2633	0.2320	0.2046	0.1807	0.1597	0.1413
15	0.5553	0.4810	0.4173	0.3624	0.3152	0.2745	0.2394	0.2090	0.1827	0.1599	0.1401	0.1229
16	0.5339	0.4581	0.3936	0.3387	0.2919	0.2519	0.2176	0.1883	0.1631	0.1415	0.1229	0.1069
17	0.5134	0.4363	0.3714	0.3166	0.2703	0.2311	0.1978	0.1696	0.1456	0.1252	0.1078	0.0929
18	0.4936	0.4155	0.3503	0.2959	0.2502	0.2120	0.1799	0.1528	0.1300	0.1108	0.0946	0.0808
19	0.4746	0.3957	0.3305	0.2765	0.2317	0.1945	0.1635	0.1377	0.1161	0.0981	0.0829	0.0703
20	0.4564	0.3769	0.3118	0.2584	0.2145	0.1784	0.1486	0.1240	0.1037	0.0868	0.0728	0.0611
21	0.4388	0.3589	0.2942	0.2415	0.1987	0.1637	0.1351	0.1117	0.0926	0.0768	0.0638	0.0531
22	0.4220	0.3418	0.2775	0.2257	0.1839	0.1502	0.1228	0.1007	0.0826	0.0680	0.0560	0.0462
23	0.4057	0.3256	0.2618	0.2109	0.1703	0.1378	0.1117	0.0907	0.0738	0.0601	0.0491	0.0402
24	0.3901	0.3101	0.2470	0.1971	0.1577	0.1264	0.1015	0.0817	0.0659	0.0532	0.0431	0.0349
25	0.3751	0.2953	0.2330	0.1842	0.1460	0.1160	0.0923	0.0736	0.0588	0.0471	0.0378	0.0304
26	0.3607	0.2812	0.2198	0.1722	0.1352	0.1064	0.0839	0.0663	0.0525	0.0417	0.0331	0.0264
27	0.3468	0.2678	0.2074	0.1609	0.1252	0.0976	0.0763	0.0597	0.0469	0.0369	0.0291	0.0230
28	0.3335	0.2551	0.1956	0.1504	0.1159	0.0895	0.0693	0.0538	0.0419	0.0326	0.0255	0.0200
29	0.3207	0.2429	0.1846	0.1406	0.1073	0.0822	0.0630	0.0485	0.0374	0.0289	0.0224	0.0174
30	0.3083	0.2314	0.1741	0.1314	0.0994	0.0754	0.0573	0.0437	0.0334	0.0256	0.0196	0.0151

($1 due at the end of *n* periods)

Present Values of Annuities.

Now that you have mastered the basic concept of present value with respect to a lump sum to be paid in the future, consider the slightly more complicated problem of determining the present value of a stream of payments over time. For example, what is the present value of the right to receive $10 at the end of each of the next five years?

The payment of a constant sum at fixed intervals over a period of years is called an *annuity*. It should be evident that determining the present value of an annuity requires calculating the present values of each payment. You could therefore determine the present value of an annuity by applying the basic present value formula as follows:

$$PV = \frac{x_1}{(1+k)^1} + \frac{x_2}{(1+k)^2} + \frac{x_3}{(1+k)^3} + \dots \frac{x_n}{(1+k)^n}$$

This formula determines the present value for each individual payment and then adds them together. We could then express the formula more simply, using the summation (capital Sigma) symbol:

$$PV = \sum \frac{x_n}{(1+k)^n}$$

Alternatively, you could determine the present value of each payment using Table 10-2 and add them together. Once again, lucky us, tables have been developed to give us the present value factor to apply to annuity payments. As a result, the easiest way to calculate the present value of an annuity is to use Table 10-3. It sets forth the present value of annuity payments in much the same way that Table 10-2 sets forth the present value of lump sum payments.

To use Table 10-3, all you need to do is select a discount rate and the number of periods over which the future payments are to be made, and multiply this rate by the amount of money to be received. For example, the present value of $10 to be received at the end of each of the next five years discounted using an 8% annual rate is: $10 x 3.993 (the present value factor for $1 to be paid at the end of each of the next five years, discounted at 8%), or $39.93.

Table 10-3: Present Value of Annuities

	4%	5%	6%	7%	8%	9%	10%	11%	12%	13%	14%	15%
1	0.962	0.952	0.943	0.935	0.926	0.917	0.909	0.901	0.893	0.885	0.877	0.870
2	1.886	1.859	1.833	1.808	1.783	1.759	1.736	1.713	1.690	1.668	1.647	1.626
3	2.775	2.723	2.673	2.624	2.577	2.531	2.487	2.444	2.402	2.361	2.322	2.283
4	3.630	3.546	3.465	3.387	3.312	3.240	3.170	3.102	3.037	2.974	2.914	2.855
5	4.452	4.329	4.212	4.100	3.993	3.890	3.791	3.696	3.605	3.517	3.433	3.352
6	5.242	5.076	4.917	4.767	4.623	4.486	4.355	4.231	4.111	3.998	3.889	3.784
7	6.002	5.786	5.582	5.389	5.206	5.033	4.868	4.712	4.564	4.423	4.288	4.160
8	6.733	6.463	6.210	5.971	5.747	5.535	5.335	5.146	4.968	4.799	4.639	4.487
9	7.435	7.108	6.802	6.515	6.247	5.995	5.759	5.537	5.328	5.132	4.946	4.772
10	8.111	7.722	7.360	7.024	6.710	6.418	6.145	5.889	5.650	5.426	5.216	5.019
11	8.760	8.306	7.887	7.499	7.139	6.805	6.495	6.207	5.938	5.687	5.453	5.234
12	9.385	8.863	8.384	7.943	7.536	7.161	6.814	6.492	6.194	5.918	5.660	5.421
13	9.986	9.394	8.853	8.358	7.904	7.487	7.103	6.750	6.424	6.122	5.842	5.583
14	10.563	9.899	9.295	8.745	8.244	7.786	7.367	6.982	6.628	6.302	6.002	5.724
15	11.118	10.380	9.712	9.108	8.559	8.061	7.606	7.191	6.811	6.462	6.142	5.847
16	11.652	10.838	10.106	9.447	8.851	8.313	7.824	7.379	6.974	6.604	6.265	5.954
17	12.166	11.274	10.477	9.763	9.122	8.544	8.022	7.549	7.120	6.729	6.373	6.047
18	12.659	11.690	10.828	10.059	9.372	8.756	8.201	7.702	7.250	6.840	6.467	6.128
19	13.134	12.085	11.158	10.336	9.604	8.950	8.365	7.839	7.366	6.938	6.550	6.198
20	13.590	12.462	11.470	10.594	9.818	9.129	8.514	7.963	7.469	7.025	6.623	6.259
21	14.029	12.821	11.764	10.836	10.017	9.292	8.649	8.075	7.562	7.102	6.687	6.312
22	14.451	13.163	12.042	11.061	10.201	9.442	8.772	8.176	7.645	7.170	6.743	6.359
23	14.857	13.489	12.303	11.272	10.371	9.580	8.883	8.266	7.718	7.230	6.792	6.399
24	15.247	13.799	12.550	11.469	10.529	9.707	8.985	8.348	7.784	7.283	6.835	6.434
25	15.622	14.094	12.783	11.654	10.675	9.823	9.077	8.422	7.843	7.330	6.873	6.464
26	15.983	14.375	13.003	11.826	10.810	9.929	9.161	8.488	7.896	7.372	6.906	6.491
27	16.330	14.643	13.211	11.987	10.935	10.027	9.237	8.548	7.943	7.409	6.935	6.514
28	16.663	14.898	13.406	12.137	11.051	10.116	9.307	8.602	7.984	7.441	6.961	6.534
29	16.984	15.141	13.591	12.278	11.158	10.198	9.370	8.650	8.022	7.470	6.983	6.551
30	17.292	15.372	13.765	12.409	11.258	10.274	9.427	8.694	8.055	7.496	7.003	6.566

($1 per period for *n* periods)

Many investments contain both the promise of a lump sum payment and the promise of an annuity. To calculate the present value of such instruments, one values the lump sum component using the present value Table 10-2 as described above and then separately values the annuity component using the present value Table 10-3 as described above. Then the two present values are added together.

Continuing with our assumption that the appropriate annual discount rate prevailing at the time is 8%, for example, a $100 bond with a maturity date of five years that pays interest of $10 per year at the end of each of the next five years has a present value equal to the sum of $68.06 (the present value of the lump sum component) plus $39.93 (the present value of the annuity component) or a total of $107.99.

Compounding Frequency and Present Values of Lump Sums.

Recall that the future value of a lump sum today will be greater if compounding occurs more frequently than annually. Similarly, but with opposite effect, the present value of a lump sum to be paid in the future will be lower if compounding occurs more frequently than annually. To calculate by how much, we can modify the present value formula (in an analogous way to the way we modified the future value formula). In particular, we modify the *(1 + k)ⁿ* term by adding a term, *m*, to the formula to denote the number of times per year interest is compounded, as follows:

$$PV_n = \frac{x}{\left(1 + \dfrac{k}{m}\right)^{mn}}$$

Let's try another example. What is the present value of a lump sum of $100 to be received at the end of year two, assuming a discount rate of 8% compounded semi-annually?

$$PV_2 = \frac{\$100}{\left(1 + \dfrac{.08}{2}\right)^{2 \times 2}} = \$85.48$$

Confirm using Table 10-2: this payout is for 4 periods at 4% and Table 10-2's 4 period/4% cell shows a present value factor of 0.8548.

Notice the consequence for present values of semi-annual compounding as compared to annual compounding. The present value of a lump sum payment of $100 at the end of two years was $85.73 under annual compounding (discussed above) but with semi-annual compounding it declines to $85.48. As we would expect, this is the opposite of the effect when future values are compounded more often than annually.

Compounding Frequency and Present Values of Annuities.

When compounding is non-annual, determining the present value of annuities involves an additional refinement. It requires using as the interest rate the annual effective yield (AEY), mentioned above. Recall that this is calculated by the following formula:

$$AEY = \left(1 + \frac{k}{m}\right)^m - 1$$

For example, if the annual interest rate is 8%, and compounding is semi-annual (2 times per year), then the annual effective yield is 8.16%. That is:

$$AEY = \left(1 + \frac{.08}{2}\right)^2 - 1 = 8.16\%$$

For annuities compounded more frequently than annually, the AEY is used as the k term in the present value formula. (Note that the tables use rates rounded to whole numbers whereas the AEY is often not a whole number. In this case, it is possible to make rough present value estimates using Table 10-3 by locating the AEY between whole figures; but for precise results, a calculator is required.)

Annuities Due.

Most annuities follow the assumptions used above, specifically a payment made at the end of each period. These are called *ordinary annuities*. Some annuities are structured so that payment is made at the beginning of each period. These are called *annuities due*. The key difference is that for otherwise identical annuities, annuities due are discounted for one less period compared to ordinary annuities. This means that the present values differ by one period. This difference can be captured by calculating the present value of the ordinary annuity then multiplying that result by *(1 + k)* to determine the instrument's value as an annuity due.

Note on the Tables.

Finally, as noted several times above, the tables are for "periods" rather than "years." This means they can be used to calculate present and future values for any frequency (days, weeks, months and so on). Just be sure the discount rate being used covers the same time period. For example, the present value of an annuity paying 8% annually compounded annually converted to one paying the same compounded semi-annually can be recalculated using 4% and a six month period. This insight can also be useful in calculating present values of instruments issued at odd times during a year (requiring, for example, valuing an instrument with a life of 4.3 years instead of an even 4 years).

D. RULE OF 72s

Differences that seem like pocket change—like that between $85.48 and $85.73 in the preceding discussion—can become quite significant over time. Recall Warren Buffett's point about Queen Isabella's investment in the New World: if you think a quarter today does not amount to a hill of beans, consider how much it will grow to over time! Maybe it would also be helpful to know the title Mr. Buffett gave to that essay: "The Joys of Compounding." The intuitions are powerful: (1) the more often your money compounds, the more it will grow (its future value is greater); and (2) the more often your money could compound but doesn't because you don't have it yet, the more you give up in waiting (its present value is lower).

A tool for the joys of compounding is a numerical "yearstick" to gauge how long it takes a given amount of money to double at varying compounded rates of return (or interest rates). Called the *Rule of 72s*, it says dividing 72 by the rate of return (ignoring the decimal) gives the approximate number of years it takes for an amount of money to double. Put differently, a sum of money doubles when the product of the return and the horizon equals about 72. This metric approximates (a) the requisite horizon given some return or (b) the requisite return given some horizon. So for a sum to double over an 8-year horizon requires a 9% annual return (9 x 8 = 72). A 6% annual return requires a 12-year horizon (6 x 12 = 72). (Make yourself a full list.)*

The Rule of 72s is a rule-of-thumb. For example, it doesn't work for one-year periods (doubling money in a single year is a 100% return for 1 year, for a product of 100). It is only an approximation for other periods. Suppose your money has doubled in 5 years (say you bought a house for $250,000 cash and 5 years later sold it for $500,000 cash). Using the Rule of 72s indicates a return of 14.4% (5 x 14.4 = 72), though using a formal calculation yields 14.87%. (Note that the Rule of 72s operates using geometric averages; in this case the arithmetic average is 100% divided by 5 = 20%. The geometric average is also known as the *compound annual growth rate*, or CAGR.)

You can use the Rule of 72s to calculate all sorts of variations on the relationship between money in hand and money in the future. For example, you can determine what rate of return is necessary for a certain sum to grow to a desired sum in the future. Or, if you know what rate of return is available, you can determine how much money someone needs today in order for it to grow to a desired level at some future time.

Take an example: if the available average annual rate of return on money from now until 40 years from now is 9%, then how much money does a 25-year old person need today in order to retire as a millionaire at age 65 without saving another cent over that time? Work backwards from ending up with $1,000,000 at age 65. Since money earning a compound annual rate of return of 9% doubles approximately every 8 years, at age 57 she'd need to have $500,000; at age 49 she'd need to have $250,000; at age 41 she'd need to have $125,000; at age 33 she'd need to have $62,500; and today at age 25 she'd need to have (only!) $31,250.

If this illustrates the joy in compounding, take another use of the Rule of 72s to illustrate the joy of slightly higher rates of return. Assume instead of being able to earn about a 9% annual rate of return over the next 40 years, our 25-year old can only reasonably expect a 6% annual rate of return. Now her money will double approximately only every 12 years

---

* Your list could be more precise if you use 69 or 70 rather than 72 but the computations are easier using 72. The reason 69 or 70 would be more precise is that these estimating tools are linked to the natural logs of numbers and the natural log of 2 (doubling) is 0.69315. A parallel estimating tool is the rule of 110s, drawing on roughly the log of 3 to determine how long it takes for a sum to triple at a given interest rate. Thus a sum roughly triples when the product of the return and horizon equals 110—for example, with a 10% compound annual return a sum triples in about 11 years.

rather than every 8. So 12 years hence at age 37 she'd have $62,500; at age 49 she'd have $125,000; at age 61 she'd have $250,000; at age 73 she'd have $500,000; and she'd have to reach the ripe age of 85 to end up with a million!

E. INTEREST RATES, TAX EFFECTS, AND INFLATION

Interest rates play a pivotal role in the value of assets. US Treasury instruments provide a risk-free rate of interest. That benchmark interest rate is a major determinant of the value of any other asset in the economy, including the value of whole businesses and shares of stock in them. The risk-free rate sets the standard of value of assets with risk. The higher the risk-free rate, the lower the values of riskier assets; the lower the risk-free rate, the higher the values of risky assets.

When the risk-free rate was very high in the late 1960s and 1970s, for example, the average price of stocks was depressed. The Dow Jones Industrial Average, a bellwether of American economic performance based on the composite stock prices of 30 leading corporations, hardly moved at all from the early 1960s to the late 1970s because to get investors to buy stocks they had to get a return that exceeded the sky-high risk-free interest rate. When the risk-free rate was very low from the mid-1980s to the early 2000s, in contrast, average stock prices hiked. The Dow enjoyed the greatest bull market in history because the risk-free rate was so low it was relatively easy for investors to get a risk premium (returns above the risk-free rate).

Taxes also affect the long-term value of investments. Suppose you buy an investment that pays 15% per year for 30 years and you keep that investment compounding yearly until the end of that time without being obligated to pay taxes on it. Suppose also that you are taxed on your income from that investment at the end of that 30th year at a rate of 35%. This means your after tax annual rate of return on that investment was about 13.3%. Hard to beat.

Suppose instead that your 15% per year investment for 30 years pays you that 15% annually and subjects you to tax of 35% each year you get it. Your annual after-tax return suddenly shrinks to about 9.75%. Not a bad net return you say, but that is over 3.5% less than the tax-deferred position. And now we are talking about huge sums, with that 3.5% difference compounding over periods like 30 years.

The same is true at every level of return differentials, and remains quite substantial even at lower rates of return. A 10% pre-tax return with taxes due only at the end of 30 years gives you an after tax return of about 8.3%, compared with about a 6.5% after-tax return if you had paid taxes on that income each year. Again, that kind of 2% difference compounded over a few decades works out to be lots of dollars.

Inflation is a final factor to consider. It often differs from returns and returns differ from each other. Annual inflation of 4% means that a basket of goods that can be bought for $100 on January 1 costs $104 on December 31. But if during that same year you put $100 in a savings account paying 8%, your balance at the end of that year would be $108. Left uninvested, that $100 would decline in purchasing power to about $96, whereas the invested amount gives you purchasing power of about $104 (the $108 you have less the impact on its buying power of the 4% inflation).

Inflation thus erodes the purchasing power of money. A 20-year old who invests $100 earning 8% compound annual interest ends up with $3,192 at age 65. But suppose during that 45-year period the cost of living grows too (*i.e.*, there is inflation). If inflation bore the same 8% as the return, then the $3,192 45-years later is in a real sense exactly the same as the $100 at the outset. *Nominal* rates must therefore be corrected for the effects of inflation to produce *real* rates.

You might have an intuitive sense that the real rate of return is simply the difference between the nominal rate and the inflation rate. That is, if the nominal rate is 8% and the inflation rate is 5% you might suppose the real rate is 3%. This is correct if both rates are *continuously* compounded. For returns compounded periodically (such as annually or quarterly), computation is a bit more involved. You must divide what you'll have in the future by what that future amount will get you in real terms.

Use these figures assuming annual compounding. At 8%, the $100 will grow to equal $108 in one year and this will produce the equivalent of $105 worth of purchasing power. The real value of the money is therefore equal to $108/$105, which is 1.02857. That is, for every basket of goods you defer today you will be able to buy 1.02857 baskets a year later. So the real return is 2.857% (close to 3% but not quite).

The general formula for computing real rates based on nominal rates and inflation is:

$$= \frac{R - I}{1 + I}$$

where R is the nominal rate and I is the inflation rate. Completing the foregoing example gives 2.857%:

$$= \frac{.08 - .05}{1 + .05} = .02857$$

These insights can be applied to determine the real future value of $100 earning a nominal 8% compound annual return over the next 45 years. There are two ways to adjust this future value for inflation. The first is simply to use the real interest rate instead of the nominal rate. That is, using the formula $FV_n = x(1+k)^n$ the real future value of $100 bearing real interest of 2.857% over 45 years is: $100(1.02857)^{45}= 355.

The other way is to work back from the nominal future value we computed of $3,192 and *deflate* it by adjusting its purchasing power. The price level 45 years from now given 5% inflation is: $1.05^{45} = 8.985$. Divide the nominal future value of $3,192 by this deflator of 8.985 to get $355 in real terms.

Similar alternatives work to adjust present values for inflation. Suppose a person wants to have $10,000 in four years to buy some good so priced today. What amount must she set aside today? Using the formula:

$$PV_n = \frac{x}{(1+k)^n}$$

and assuming a discount rate of 8%, then in nominal terms she needs:

$$\frac{10,000}{(1.08)^4} = \$7,350$$

That is: the nominal present value of $10,000 four years hence assuming an 8% discount rate is $7,350.

But whatever she wants to buy will cost more in four years too. To adjust for this, first figure what that $10,000 item today will cost in four years. Again assuming a 5% inflation rate, the item would cost $10,000 x $1.05^4 = $12,155$. The same alternatives apply. First, compute the present value of $10,000 using the real rate of 2.857%. That is: $10,000/1.0257^4 = $8,934$. The other is to deflate the nominal future cost of $12,155 by the nominal discount rate: $12,155/1.08^4 =$8,934$.

Study the Tables.

It will pay to study the accompanying tables to get a feel for the relationship between future values and changes in interest rates, the relationship between present values and changes in discount rates, and the relationship between present values and future values. For example, notice that the future values given in Table 10-1 are the reciprocals of the present values given in Table 10-2. For another example, notice that the higher the discount rate, the lower the present value; and the higher the interest rate, the greater the future value. Select any "Period" line on the present value table and look across at the present value of $1 at different discount rates. The higher the discount rate, the lower the present value. The reason, again, is that discount rates reflect your opportunity cost of capital. The higher the rate of return available to you today, the more value you have sacrificed by waiting to receive your payment. Finally, relate the tables to the Rule of 72s. Skim Table 10-1 to see cells showing a future value factor of about 2 and notice how the product of the related horizon and rate is about 72; skim Table 10-2 to see combinations where the product of the horizon and rate is about 72 and notice how the related present value factor is about 0.5.

F. VALUING BONDS

These valuation principles can be applied to value a wide range of instruments, including bonds. Bonds can be thought of as IOUs, with an issuer promising to repay the borrowed amount (principal) along with periodic payments of interest. They are issued pursuant to often-elaborate contracts called indentures (IOUs can also be in the form of bank loans issued by private lenders pursuant to contracts called credit agreements). Bonds are issued by corporations, governmental agencies, and other entities.

The structuring and sale of bonds is an involved process that can take from a few weeks to many months. For bonds to be sold to the public, a company hires underwriters to help negotiate and market the bonds to investors, auditors to examine the financial statements that must be furnished to investors considering buying the bonds, and lawyers to document the transaction and assure compliance with disclosure and other laws. Public bonds are listed on a secondary market, such as the New York Stock Exchange, where investors trade them.

When a bond offering is ready to be sold to the public, the conditions in world credit markets and the creditworthiness of the issuer determine the price—the interest rate on the debt. Applying the valuation principles just discussed, the value of a bond is equal to the present value of its future cash flows, which consist of (1) the periodic interest payments promised to be made plus (2) the principal to be repaid at maturity. The rate used to compute these values is a rate that produces an acceptable rate of return on the funds given the issuer's credit risk and prevailing market conditions such as those discussed earlier in this Chapter.

Traditionally, bonds issued to the public were represented by thick pieces of bond paper expressing the issuer's promise to repay the principal amount of the bond (also called its *face amount* or *par value*) plus make a series of interest payments. The interest payments were represented by pieces of strippable perforated paper alongside the instrument's edge and resembled coupons. The bondholder would clip a coupon and turn it into the issuer to collect each interest payment when due. While most bonds today are issued and records kept in electronic form, this history continues to lead people to refer to the interest rate on bonds as the "coupon."

The coupon on a bond is expressed as a percentage of the bond's face amount or par value. So a bond with a 10% coupon and a face amount of $1,000 promises to pay $100 per year. The value of the bond may change as the investment community revises assessments of the issuer's creditworthiness and as conditions in the credit market change.

If the issuer's creditworthiness declines (say its debt-to-equity ratio rises substantially or its liquidity is materially impaired) or the overall credit market becomes pessimistic about finance (interest rates rise), investors may select a higher discount rate to value the bond's cash flows. Conversely, if the issuer's creditworthiness or market conditions improve, a lower rate could be applied. Either way, the face value of the bond differs from the present value of its cash flows. The difference is either a *premium* (when the bond sells for more than face value) or a *discount* (when the bond sells for less than face value).

As the market value of the bond changes with changes in interest rates, the yield to holders of the bond changes as well. The return to bondholders is called the *effective yield* or *market rate*. For bonds selling at a discount, the effective yield is higher than the coupon. For bonds trading at a premium, the effective yield is lower than the coupon.

These relationships can be summarized in broader terms: there is an inverse relationship between the value of a bond and prevailing market interest rates. As interest rates rise, the value of bonds outstanding falls and vice versa. Consider a bond with a coupon of 10%. If market rates fall to 5%, that bond is worth more than newly issued bonds (better to get 10% than 5% after all); if rates rise to 15%, it is worth less (you can get superior returns investing in newly issued bonds).

To determine the value of a bond requires computing the present value of both the interest flow and the maturity repayment of principal. In other words, we must compute the present value of an annuity (for the interest stream) and add to that the present value of a lump sum (the principal component). Take a bond with a face value of $100,000, due in 5 years, with a 9% annual coupon (thus paying $9,000 interest per year). Suppose that today, given credit conditions for the bond issuer and the general market, the appropriate discount rate applied to this issuer is 11%. What is the value of the bond?

To determine the present value of the principal, use Table 10-2 (or the related formula). In Table 10-2's cell for the present value of $1 at the end of 5 years using a discount rate of 11%, the Table indicates a present value factor of .5935. Applied to the $100,000 face value of this bond gives us $59,350. To determine the present value of the interest stream, use Table 10-3 (or the related formula). The 5-year/11% cell in Table 10-3 for a $1 annuity shows a present value factor of 3.696, indicating a value for these cash flows of $33,264 (that is, 3.696 x $9,000). The value of the bond is the sum of these two pieces, giving a total of $92,614.

Notice that this means this bond should sell at a discount to its face value (confirming the inverse relationship between bond prices and prevailing interest rates). In market parlance, the bond's price would be stated as a percentage of the par value—in this case, 92.6% of par. Prices on bonds are quoted in "points" (with each point equal to $10) and 1/8 increments of points (so each 1/8 is equal to $1.25), using $1,000 as the base (the common face value denomination in which bonds are issued). So a bond quoted at 95 1/2 sells for $955 and one quoted at 105 7/8 sells for $1058.75. A bond, as in our example, trading at $926 (per $1,000) would be quoted at 92 5/8; one trading at $1,100 would be quoted at 110.

G. THE COST OF EQUITY

In the foregoing discussion of valuing bonds, the investment carried the issuer's promise to pay interest and repay principal. The promise enables defining a stream of cash flows and the interest rate enables settling upon a discount rate (subject to ensuing adjustments to reflect changes in market interest rates and the issuer's credit quality).

In valuing equity securities, neither the cash flows nor an interest rate can be so readily ascertained. Common stock, for example, does not carry a promise to pay interest or principal (dividends are payable in the board's discretion). To value common stock, therefore, requires estimating both the cash flows and the discount rate. We will consider tools for estimating both in ensuing Chapters. As an introduction, however, note that from an issuer's perspective just as surely as the debt it issues bears a cost (the interest rate, less associated tax deductions), equity also bears a cost.

Equity is riskier than debt, so the discount rate for a given company's equity securities (called the *cost of equity*) will be some increment above the prevailing rates at which any debt it has outstanding is discounted. The challenge is determining how much greater. Conceptually, the cost of equity is the rate of return a prudent investor would require for allocating equity capital to the subject company.

The key reference is what other capital market participants are paying investors to attract equity financing for enterprises of comparable risk. To estimate the cost of equity capital for high-risk venture capital projects, for example, one could consult the returns offered by venture capitalists in such enterprises. For low-risk enterprises, underwritten secondary public offerings of blue-chip companies can be examined.

Most generally, the practice is to estimate the returns investors are insisting upon for companies bearing like qualities (in terms of industry, capital structure, maturation, size, competitive outlook, and so on). For companies with long records of sustained earnings, low rates are indicated, perhaps just a few points above the risk-free rate. For newer more volatile operations, a larger premium is required.

The estimate requires exercising practical judgment based on learning what compensation is given to investors bearing comparable business and financial risks. What special business and financial risks do common stockholders face? What are the debt levels? What is the likelihood that high debt would throw the company into bankruptcy? What is the company's financial strength and industry leadership? Is its market expanding or contracting? Is there room for growth that will add value?

In short, assessing risk relevant to the cost of equity implicates the sorts of questions analysts ask when applying ratio analytics to a set of financial statements, interpreting the financial data in light of footnote disclosure, and studying relevant portions of an accompanying annual report such as the MD&A. *See* Chapter 8.

There are more elaborate methods for estimating the cost of equity. One will be presented in the context of discounted cash flow analysis, discussed in Chapter 11, and another will be presented in the context of modern finance theory, discussed in Chapter 12.

Problem 10

Most of the following problems can be answered by direct reference to the Tables discussed in this Chapter, although some require additional calculations using the formulas discussed in this Chapter. In each case, make your calculations without regard to any potential effect of inflation or taxes.

a.   Rebecca is a 35-year-old lawyer who has just been informed by her precocious 6-year-old son Josh that he wishes to attend Yale when he graduates from high school ten years from now. Assume Rebecca now has $10,000 in a savings account, paying 10% interest compounded annually. (i) What will her balance be when Josh graduates, assuming no deposits or withdrawals? (ii) What would her balance be if interest were compounded semi-annually instead of annually?

b.   Sarah received a letter from Fred McCann notifying her that she has just won third prize in a major sweepstakes. Fred gives Sarah a choice of two prizes: $15,000 in cash awarded immediately or $1,800 in cash paid at the end of each year for the next ten years. Assume that Sarah would deposit the $1,800 annual payments in a bank account earning 12% compounded annually. Which prize should Sarah choose?

c.   Assume that you have just won $1,000,000 in the New York State lottery. The $1,000,000 will be paid to you in 20 annual installments of $50,000 each, with the first installment to be paid one year from today and each additional installment to be paid on that date in the 19 following years. If New York State 20-year bonds currently pay an interest rate of 7%, what is the present value of the amount you have won in the lottery? (Assume for purposes of making this calculation that the New York State Lottery Commission is part of New York State and that the payments would not be taxable. Why are these assumptions important?)

d.   Assume you are able to generate a rate of return on investment of 8% compounded annually. Calculate what amount of money you would need to invest on your birthday this year to reach $1,000,000 on your 65th assuming no other future savings (for those older than 65 or just curious, assume you are going to give the money to me, a 38-year-old, to assure that I can retire as a millionaire at age 65).

e.   What is the greatest amount a rational investor would pay for a $1,000 ten-year bond that pays $120 interest annually, assuming that the appropriate discount rate for valuing the bond is 8%? (What is the meaning of "rational investor" in this problem?)

f.   An investment opportunity you are considering is expected to pay $400 a year for the first 10 years, $600 a year for the 15 years thereafter, and then nothing. Assume the appropriate discount rate is 8%. What is its present value?

g.   The yield on 10-year US Treasury securities is 5%. Company A is a start-up venture attempting to develop a single unproven biotechnology product. It has no financial or operating history. Company B is a long-established manufacturer of well-known household products with steady earnings levels during the past 20 years. Which of the following is the most reasonable set of estimates for appropriate discount rates on the indicated securities of the two companies?

		Company A	Company B
1.	Debt	10%	8%
	Equity	15%	11%
2.	Debt	5%	3%
	Equity	10%	5%
3.	Debt	5%	5%
	Equity	8%	8%
4.	Debt	10%	12%
	Equity	14%	16%

Conceptual Questions 10

When a company borrows money from lenders in return for a promise to repay with interest, the interest accrued or paid is treated as an expense. When a company raises money from investors in return for an equity claim on the company, neither the dividends paid (if any) nor the opportunity cost the shareholders face are treated as an expense. Should this be changed? Should companies record as an expense on their income statement a cost of equity capital?

CHAPTER 11

VALUATION TECHNIQUES

■ ■ ■

This Chapter introduces techniques for valuing a business and ownership interests in it. It begins with a parable that presents, in an intuitive way, a variety of approaches to valuation. A more technical discussion of the methods follows, organized as balance sheet-based approaches, income statement-based approaches, and cash flow-based approaches. In each case, uses and limitations of the methods are discussed.

A. THE OLD MAN AND THE TREE

Once there was a wise old man who owned an apple tree. The tree was fine and with little care it produced a crop of apples each year which he sold for $100. The man was getting old, wanted to retire to a new climate and he decided to sell the tree. He enjoyed teaching a good lesson, and he placed an advertisement in the Business Opportunities section of *The Wall Street Journal* in which he said he wanted to sell the tree for "the best offer."

Some Red Herrings.

The first person to respond to the ad offered to pay the $50 which, he said, was what he could get for selling the apple tree for firewood after he had cut it down. "You don't know what you are talking about," the old man chastised. "You are offering to pay only the salvage value of this tree. That might be a good price for a pine tree or even this tree if it had stopped bearing fruit or if the price of apple wood had gotten so high that the tree was more valuable as a source of wood than as a source of fruit. But you are obviously not competent to understand these things so you can't see that my tree is worth far more than 50 bucks."

The next person who visited the old man offered to pay $100 for the tree. "For that," she opined, "is what I would be able to get for selling this year's crop of fruit which is about to mature."

"You are not as out of your depth as the first one," responded the old man. "At least you see that this tree has more value as a producer of apples than it would as a source of firewood. But $100 is not the right price. You are not considering the value of next year's crop of apples, nor that of the years after. Please take your $100 and go elsewhere."

The third person to come along was a young man who had just dropped out of business school. "I am going to sell apples on the Internet," he said. "I figure that the tree should live for at least another fifteen years. If I sell the apples for $100 a year, that will total $1,500. I offer you $1,500 for your tree."

"Oh, no," scoffed the old man, "you're even more ill-informed about reality than the others I've spoken with."

"Surely the $100 you would earn by selling the apples from the tree fifteen years from now cannot be worth $100 to you today. In fact, if you placed $41.73 today in a bank account paying 6% interest, compounded annually, that small sum would grow to $100 at the end of fifteen years. So the present value of $100 worth of apples fifteen years from now, assuming an interest rate of 6%, is only $41.73 not $100. Pray," pleaded the beneficent old man, "take your $1,500 and invest it safely in high-grade corporate bonds and go back to business school and learn something about finance."

Before long, there came a wealthy physician, who said, "I don't know much about apple trees, but I know what I like. I'll pay the market price for it. The last fellow was willing to pay you $1,500 for the tree, and so it must be worth that."

"Doctor," advised the old man, "you should get yourself a knowledgeable investment adviser. If there were truly a market in which apple trees were traded with some regularity, the prices at which they were sold might tell you something about their value. But not only is there no such market, even if there were, taking its price as the value is just mimicking the stupidity of that last knucklehead or the others before him. Please take your money and buy a vacation home."

A Dialogue on Assets.

The next would-be buyer was an accounting student. When the old man asked, "What price are you willing to give me?," the student first demanded to see the old man's books. The old man had kept careful records and gladly brought them out.

After examining the books, the accounting student said, "Your books show that you paid $75 for this tree ten years ago. Furthermore, you have made no deductions for depreciation. I do not know if that conforms with generally accepted accounting principles, but assuming that it does, the book value of your tree is $75. I will pay that."

"Ah, you students know so much and yet so little," chided the old man. "It is true that the book value of my tree is $75, but any fool can see that it is worth far more than that."

"Valuation based on assets cannot be limited to book value," he advised, "for that is an accounting concept not a valuation concept. An entity's book value equals total assets minus total liabilities. Business valuation may use such accounting concepts as starting points but not as end points."

Feeling that his profession had been somehow insulted, the accounting student replied: "Fair enough, but I could use this information to estimate what resources would be required to generate an equivalent business position. In the case of your tree, this would mean assessing what it would take to replicate: (1) the acreage on which the tree stands, (2) the tree itself, (3) equipment related to maintenance and production, and (4) the resources required to merchandise the apples."

The old man acknowledged this is true, but opined: "While these are not impossible judgments to make, they are very difficult. They also ask the valuation question from only one perspective, what it takes to build a business; at least as important is the question from the other perspective, what the business can do for its owner." The accounting student left.

A Dialogue on Earnings.

The last prospect to visit the old man was a young stockbroker who had recently graduated from business school. Eager to test her new skills she, too, asked to examine the books. After several hours she came back to the old man and said she was prepared to make an offer that valued the tree on the basis of the capitalization of its earnings. For the first time the old man's interest was piqued and he asked her to go on.

The young woman explained that while the apples were sold for $100 last year, that figure did not represent profits realized from the tree. There were expenses attendant to the tree, such as the cost of fertilizer, pruning, tools, picking apples, and carting them to town and selling them.

Somebody had to do these things, and a portion of the salaries paid to those persons ought to be charged against the revenues from the tree. Moreover, the purchase price, or cost, of the tree was an expense. A portion of the cost should be taken into account each year of the tree's useful life. Finally, there were taxes. She concluded that the profit from the tree was $50 last year.

"Wow!" the old man blushed. "I thought I made $100 off that tree."

"That's because you failed to match expenses with revenues, in accordance with generally accepted accounting principles," she explained. "You don't actually have to write a check to be charged with what accountants consider to be your expenses. For example, you bought a station wagon some time ago and you used it part of the time to cart apples to market. The wagon will last a while and each year some of the original cost has to be matched against revenues. A portion of the amount has to be spread out over the next several years even though you expended it all at one time. Accountants call that depreciation. I'll bet you never figured that in your calculation of profits."

"I'll bet you're right," he replied. "Tell me more."

"I also went back into the books for a few years and I saw that in some years the tree produced fewer apples than in other years, the prices varied and the costs were not exactly the same each year. Taking an average of only the last three years, I came up with a figure of $45 as a fair sample of the tree's earnings. But that is only half of what we have to do to figure the value."

"What's the other half?" he asked.

"The tricky part," she told him. "We now have to figure the value to me of owning a tree that will produce average earnings of $45 a year. If I believed that the tree was a 'one year wonder', I would say 100% of its value—as a going business—was represented by one year's earnings."

"But if I believe, as both you and I do, that the tree is more like a corporation, in that it will continue to produce earnings year after year, then the key is to figure out an appropriate rate of return. In other words, I will be investing my capital in the tree, and I need to compute the value to me of an investment that will produce $45 a year in income. We can call that amount the capitalized value of the tree."

"Do you have something in mind?" he asked.

"I'm getting there. If this tree produced entirely steady and predictable earnings each year, it would be like a U.S. Treasury bond. But its earnings are not guaranteed. So we have to take into account risks and uncertainty. If the risk of its ruin was high, I would insist that a single year's earnings represent a higher percentage of the value of the tree. After all, apples could become a glut on the market one day and you would have to cut the price thus reducing the profits from selling them."

"Or," she continued, "some doctor could discover a link between eating an apple a day and heart disease. A drought could cut the yield of the tree. Or the tree could become diseased and die. These are all risks. And we don't even know whether the costs we are sure to incur will be worth incurring."

"You are a gloomy one," reflected the old man. "There could also be a shortage of apples on the market and the price of apples could rise. If you think about it, it is even possible that I have been selling the apples at prices below what people would be willing to pay, and that you could raise the price without reducing your sales. Also, there are treatments, you know, that could be applied to increase the yield of the tree. This tree could help spawn a whole orchard. Any of these things would increase earnings."

"The earnings also could be increased by lowering costs of the sort you mentioned." the old man continued. "Costs can be reduced by speeding the time from fruition to sale, by managing extensions of credit better, and minimizing losses from bad apples. All these things would boost the relationship between overall sales and net earnings or, as the financial types say, the tree's profit margin. And that in turn would boost the return on your investment."

"I know all that," she assured him. "We will include all those things in the calculus. The fact is, we are talking about risk. And investment analysis is a cold business. We don't know with certainty what's going to happen. You want your money now and I'm supposed to live with the risk."

"That's fine with me, but then I have to look through a cloudy crystal ball, and not with 20/20 hindsight. And my resources are limited. I have to choose between your tree and the strawberry patch down the road. I cannot do both, and the purchase of your tree will deprive me of alternative investments. That means I have to compare the opportunities and the risks."

"To determine a proper rate of return," she continued, "I looked at investment opportunities comparable to the apple tree, particularly in the agribusiness industry, where these factors have been taken into account. I then adjusted my findings based on how the things we discussed worked out with your tree. Based on those judgments, I figure that 20% is an appropriate rate of return for the tree."

"In other words," she concluded, "assuming that the average earnings from the tree over the last three years (which seems to be a representative period) are indicative of the return I will receive, I am prepared to pay a price for the tree that will give me a 20% return on my investment. I am not willing to accept any lower rate of return because I don't have to; I can always buy the strawberry patch instead. Now, to figure the price, we simply divide $45 of earnings per year by the 20% return I am insisting on."

"Long division was never my strong suit. Is there a simpler way of doing the figuring?" he asked.

"There is," she replied. "We can use an approach we Wall Street types prefer, called the price-earnings (or P/E) ratio. To compute the ratio, just divide 100 by the rate of return we are seeking. If I were willing to settle for an 8% return, that would be 100 divided by 8 which equals 12.5. So we'd use a P/E ratio of 12.5 to 1. But since I want to earn 20% on my investment, I divided 100 by 20 and came up with a P/E ratio of 5:1. In other words, I am willing to pay five times the tree's estimated annual earnings. Multiplying $45 by 5, I get a value of $225. That's my offer."

The old man sat back and said he greatly appreciated the lesson. He would have to think about her offer, and he asked if she could come by the next day.

A Dialogue on Cash.

When the young woman returned she found the old man emerging from a sea of work sheets, small print columns of numbers and a calculator. "Delighted to see you," he enthralled. "I think we can do some business."

"It's easy to see how you Wall Street smarties make so much money, buying people's property for less than its true value. I think I can get you to agree that my tree is worth more than you figured."

"I'm open minded," she assured him.

"The $45 number you came up with yesterday was something you called profits, or earnings. I'm not so sure it tells you anything that important."

"Of course it does," she protested. "Profits measure efficiency and business performance."

"Fair enough," he mused, "but it sure doesn't tell you how much money you're getting. I looked in my safe yesterday after you left and I saw some stock certificates I own that never paid a dividend to me. And I kept getting reports each year telling me how great the earnings were. Now I know that the earnings increased the value of my stocks, but without any dividends I sure couldn't spend them. It's just the opposite with the tree."

"You figured the earnings were lower because of some amounts I'll never have to spend, like depreciation on my station wagon," the old man went on. "It seems to me these earnings are an idea worked up by the accountants."

Intrigued, she asked, "What is important, then?"

"Cash," he answered. "I'm talking about dollars you can spend, save, or give to your children. This tree will go on for years yielding cash."

"Don't forget the risks," she reminded him. "And the uncertainties."

"Quite right," he observed. "I think we can deal with that. Chances are that you and I could agree on the possible range of future revenues and expenses. Given our agreement that earnings averaged around $45 the last few years, I suspect we can agree on some fair estimates of cash flow over the coming five years: How about that there is a 25% chance that cash flow will be $40; a 50% chance it will be $50; and a 25% chance it will be $60?"

"That would make $50 our best guess, if you average it out," the old man figured. "Then let's just say that for ten years after that, the average will be $40. And that's it. The tree doctor tells me it can't produce any longer than that."

"Now all we have to do," he finished up, "is figure out what you pay today to get $50 a year from now, two years from now, and so on for the first five years until we figure what you would pay to get $40 a year for each of the ten years after that. Then, throw whatever we guess we could get for firewood at that time, and that's it."

"Simple," she confessed. "You want to discount to the present value future receipts, including salvage value. Of course you need to determine the rate at which you discount."

"Precisely," he concurred. "That's what my charts and the calculator are for." She nodded knowingly as he showed her discount tables that revealed what a dollar received at a later time is worth today, under different assumptions of the discount rate. It showed, for example, that at an 8% discount rate, a dollar delivered a year from now is worth $.93 today, simply because $.93 today, invested at 8%, will produce $1 a year from now.

"You could invest your money in U.S. Treasury obligations and earn say 4% interest (depending on prevailing interest rates). That looks like the risk free rate of interest to me. Anywhere else you put your money deprives you of the opportunity to earn 4% risk free. Discounting by 4% will only compensate you for the time value of the money you invest in the tree rather than in Treasuries. But the cash flow from the apple tree is not risk-free, sad to say, so we need to use a higher discount rate to compensate you for the risk in your investment. For example, putting your money in a commercial bank savings account might suggest a 5% discount rate, in high-grade corporate bonds an 8% discount rate and so on."

"Our apple tree here is riskier than these. Let's agree that we discount the receipt of $50 a year from now by 15%, and so on with the other deferred receipts. That is about the rate that is applied to investments with this magnitude of risk. You can check that out with my neighbor who just sold his strawberry patch yesterday. According to my figures, the present value of the expected yearly cash flow is $267.42, and today's value of the firewood is $2.46, for a grand total of $269.88. Let's make it $270 even. You can see how much I'm allowing for risk because if I discounted the stream at 8%, it would come to $388.61."

After a few minutes reflection, the young woman said to the old man, "It was a bit foxy of you yesterday to let me appear to be teaching you something. Where did you learn so much about finance as an apple grower?"

The old man smiled sagely: "Wisdom comes from experience in many fields."

"I enjoyed this little exercise but let me tell you something that some financial whiz kids told me," she replied. "Whether we figure value on the basis of the discounted cash flow method you like or the capitalization of earnings I proposed, so long as we apply both methods perfectly, we should come out at exactly the same point."

"Of course!" the old man exclaimed. "The wunderkinds are catching on. But the clever ones are not simply looking at old earnings, but copying managers by projecting earnings into the future. The question is which method is more likely to be misused?"

"I prefer my method of using cash rather than earnings because I don't have to monkey around with costs like depreciation of my station wagon and other long-term assets. You have to make these arbitrary assumptions about the useful life of the thing and how fast you're going to depreciate it. That's where I think you went wrong in your figuring."

"Nice try, you crafty old devil," she rejoined. "You know there is plenty of room for mistakes in your calculations too. It's easy to discount cash flows when they are nice and steady, but that doesn't help you when you've got some lumpy expenses that do not recur. For example, several years from now, that tree will need serious pruning and spraying expenses that don't show up in your flow. The labor and chemicals for that once-only occasion throw off the evenness of your calculations."

"But I'll tell you what," she bellied up, "I'll offer you $250. My cold analysis tells me I'm overpaying, but I really like that tree. I think the delight of sitting in its glorious shade must be worth something."

"It's a deal," agreed the old man. "I never said I was looking for the highest offer, but only the best offer."

Lessons.

The parable of the old man and the tree introduced a number of alternative methods of valuing productive property, whether a single asset or an entire business enterprise. The original $50 bid was based on the tree's salvage value, also sometimes called its scrap value. This valuation method will virtually always be inappropriate for valuing a productive asset, business or share of stock (though many bust-up takeover artists of the 1980s popularized the opposite claim).

The $100 bid was based only on one year's earnings and ignores the earning power over future time. The Internet apple maven's $1,500 overvaluation ignored the concept of the time value of money by simply adding together the raw dollar amounts of expected earnings over future years. Neither of these approaches even qualifies as an appropriate valuation method.

The doctor's bid drew on market-based valuation techniques by considering what other willing buyers had offered. But that technique will only ever be helpful if the property under consideration or similar properties are regularly traded in reasonably well developed markets.

Even then, it is circular because it uses the question (what's it worth?, according to others) to get the answer (what it's worth, according to others).

The deal was ultimately sealed when the buyer and the old man agreed that the two methods they used—capitalizing earnings and discounting cash flows—made most sense (noting that these two techniques if perfectly applied give the same answer). The buyer preferred to use earnings because accounting rules regarding earnings are intended to reflect economic reality pretty well. The old man held less confidence in those rules, principally because they call for deducting from revenues accounting depreciation, which he was not sure accurately reflected economic reality.

Although reasonable people can differ, both methods show that valuation is not a fool's game. The buyer and the old man both wisely and correctly acknowledge the importance of keen judgment in business analysis. Financial records track earnings and cash flows so the histories are there for all to see, but projecting them forward and then selecting the right discount rate are Herculean exercises. As the type of investment you consider becomes more uncertain, your judgment must become proportionately more razor-sharp.

Picking an index fund or even a mutual fund requires the least amount of knowledge or judgment; picking a classic stock a bit more than these; a vintage stock much more; and a rookie stock the greatest. In terms of apples, the apple tree our old man just sold is much like a classic business, an IBM say or duPont. It is mature, productive, and has an extensive track record.

At the other extreme might be a high-tech start-up business whose only record is on paper—a business plan that is the apple tree equivalent of a bag of seeds. Even if the ingredients are there, the execution is entirely in front of you. You may still have a basis for gauging the probable future—the quality of seeds, soil, fertilizer and farmer—but you are leaving more to judgment than in the case of the mature tree.

A few additional morals: Methods are useful as tools, but good judgment comes not from methods alone, but from experience. And experience comes from bad judgment. Listen closely to the experts, and hear those things they don't tell you. Behind all the sweet sounds of their confident notes, there is a great deal of discordant uncertainty. One wrong assumption can carry you pretty far from the truth.

The parable examined valuation of a business. Analogous techniques apply to determine the value of any productive asset held for financial gain (farms, patents, stocks, bonds, and so on). The value of each is a function of the net cash flows, discounted at an appropriate rate, an investor can reasonably expect it to generate during its remaining life.

Bond values are usually easiest to measure. Standard bonds bear a designated interest rate and a set maturity date. The combination defines expected cash flows and appropriate discount rate (subject to adjustment as discussed in Chapter 10).

Common stock values are usually the most difficult to measure. They have no such interest rate and there is no maturity date. An analyst thus must estimate both components in the valuation exercise.

People generally agree that the value of any productive asset held for financial gain is equal to the present value of cash it generates for its owner. But, bonds aside, disagreement arises concerning the factors used to estimate cash flows and relevant discount rate.

Debate focuses on what data most reliably indicate this value. Cash flows are pictures of the future and gauging the future can only be done by drawing on the past. Which historical indicators are the best gauges of future performance? Candidates include historical cash flows themselves, relevant earnings history, and existing asset and liability levels.

B. BALANCE SHEET BASED VALUATION

Several approaches to valuation based on examination of the balance sheet are possible. In thinking about them, however, remember that the amounts listed on a balance sheet are arrived at after application of numerous accounting principles designed to record financial history (remember the cost principle for example). Yet the question of value is rather more about the financial future. Financial history can be a useful guide for forecasting the financial future, but its limits must be recognized and the weight given to it appropriately measured.

Book Value.

Recall from Chapter 8 that the book value of an entity is the excess of its total assets as set forth on the balance sheet over its total liabilities, also as set forth on the balance sheet. In the case of BIC, that amount was $247,917,000 as of January 1, this year (see the line item for shareholders' equity on the balance sheet).

But recall that GAAP's cost and conservatism principles require assets to be reported on the balance sheet at historical cost, or in some cases at current market values if lower. The balance sheet carrying amount of assets does not reflect increases in value under current market conditions. For example, look back to Chapter 8's balance sheet for BIC. The line item for "Property, Plant and Equipment—Net" as of December 31, this year stood at $132,553,000. This amount reflects the cost of those assets but not necessarily what they could fetch if sold at current market prices. To that extent, book value has only limited significance in measuring financial value.

Liquidation Value.

Liquidation value is the net realizable amount that could be generated by selling a company's assets and discharging all its liabilities. A business liquidation conducted under or caused by adverse conditions may lead to assets such as inventory, equipment and machinery being sold at a loss compared to their balance sheet carrying amounts. Indeed, in some cases the losses on major assets such as plants or warehouses can be very great. Estimating the amounts usually requires accepting this fact for all assets (other than cash and marketable securities). Receivables require a small discount (perhaps 15% to 25% off), inventory a larger discount (perhaps 50% to 75% off), and fixed assets at least as much as inventory. Assets that cannot readily be sold should be assigned a zero value, such as goodwill and most other intangible assets as well as prepaid expenses such as for insurance or rent. What's left is available to discharge liabilities, usually listed at their fair value, and the remainder is the owners' take (the company's residual value). For going concerns, liquidation value is irrelevant.

Adjusted Book Value.

For going concerns, additional work with the balance sheet can start by adjusting all the book values to reflect such things as inflation and appreciation in market values to arrive at a more current measure of financial value. This is called *adjusted book value*. For example, the line items on the balance sheet for such assets as property, plant, and equipment could be increased to reflect current market values.

Even those sorts of adjustments may not give an accurate basis for financial valuation, however, because of another GAAP principle—the principle of economic or monetary exchange. A business enterprise may have financial value derived from intangible assets that are not recorded in the financial statements because they were not attributable to any discrete economic exchange. For example, only the cost of development of intellectual property is recorded as an asset on the balance sheet, even if the property is worth billions of dollars in the form of brand recognition or customer loyalty, and so on. You may recognize the BIC brand name, for instance, and collective consumer recognition is certainly valuable to BIC. But notice that there is no line item for the BIC brand name or associated trademarks on BIC's balance sheet.

These insights could lead one to attempt to value these sorts of intangible assets in some way in the determination of adjusted book value. One would seek to determine what it would cost to duplicate the company, buy its properties, train its employees, develop intellectual property and attract and retain a customer base. This can be part of a more elaborate valuation exercise called the reproduction cost of assets method.

Reproduction Cost of Assets.

An argument favoring using an asset-based valuation approach holds that the most reliable accounting data reside on the balance sheet, especially concerning current assets (starting with cash). Analysts may be more skeptical of bottom line income statement figures, which are the result of a number of discretionary exercises relating to the timing and measurement of reported revenue or sales and associated expenses.

To give an example of how different sorts of accounting data can be more or less reliable in a valuation exercise, consider the following assets mentioned in the order they usually appear on a balance sheet: (1) every business can use cash so a dollar held is pretty much worth a dollar; (2) accounts receivable are generally more easily collected by the company that generated them, but they can be assigned or sold and the buyer collect most of what the company could; (3) inventory can be used only by other merchandisers or manufacturers in the same or similar industries; and (4) fixed assets (property, plant and equipment) may be less adaptable, even by peers, or can be illiquid.

The reproduction cost method of balance sheet valuation establishes the value of a going concern by estimating what it would take a new entrant to its business to build it from scratch at current costs. All a target's resources and claims against it are separately assessed and netted out. Cash, marketable securities, receivables, and inventory probably can be taken at face value, as can prepaid expenses.

Investigation is required to ensure that receivables have been adequately reserved through the allowance for doubtful accounts and that inventory accounting is neither overstated (due to aging that suggests they are non-saleable for example) nor understated (due to inflation in sales prices compared to historical records concerning the cost of those goods held for sale). Fixed assets should be adjusted to reflect current market conditions, compared to historical costs (net of depreciation) at which they are carried on the books. Goodwill warrants little valuation accretion.

In addition to assets appearing on a going concern's balance sheet, numerous resources bearing value do not appear under GAAP. These so-called hidden assets include brand-name identity, product qualities, know-how, employee training, and specialized production and distribution arrangements.

For example, a new entrant might need to invest in research and development (R&D) to replicate the target company. This exact value is difficult to estimate. An informed guess can be made by estimating the resulting product's life-cycle and multiplying this by the target's average annual level of R&D expense. For a patented pharmaceutical, for example, product life could be up to the 17-year life of a patent. So if the company spends 5% of revenues annually on R&D for its patented products, an amount equal to about 85% of current revenues would be warranted (17 x 5%).

Similar estimating is appropriate to value customer relationships. These take time and resources to build. They may be judged by some multiple of the target's annual selling, general and administrative expenses (SG&A)—perhaps between 1 and 3 years' worth of these. Additional estimating goes into other hidden assets such as governmental licenses, franchise agreements, and other valuable resources which are not listed on a balance sheet under GAAP (though disclosed in footnotes).

The liabilities of a going concern, taken at face value, are subtracted from assessment in the reproduction cost method of valuation. Judgment is required for certain liability classes, however, such as for loss contingencies. A new entrant would not necessarily face such obligations. If not, they may be omitted. Debt, however, should be subtracted, either at its carrying amount or its market value, whichever is higher.

Analyzing the balance sheet includes assessing the level of liabilities and determining whether all are properly recorded. It is also prudent to examine the relationship between recorded depreciation over time and capital reinvestment levels. The former is a proxy for the latter; as a proxy, it must be tested to determine whether actual reinvestment needs are more or less than recorded depreciation expenses.

Book Values of Stocks or Bonds.

Whatever measure of book value is used, it can be refined further to specify that book value per share of common stock or preferred stock outstanding or the book value per dollar amount of bonds outstanding. For bonds issued by a corporation, since these have priority over stock upon liquidation of a corporate entity, this means book value divided by the total face amount of the bonds (usually in $1,000 increments). For preferred stock, since these are junior to bonds, the amount of the bonds outstanding are subtracted from the calculation and the per share book value determined by dividing the book value (less the outstanding amount of bonds) by the number of preferred shares outstanding. For common stock, junior to both bonds and preferred stock, both are subtracted and the result divided by the number of common shares outstanding. The amount of preferred to subtract from the calculation of book value per share of common stock is determined based on the liquidation preference given to the preferred as set forth in the entity's charter documents. Note also that if preferred stock has accumulated but unpaid dividends associated with it, the amount of those also must be deducted.

Take an example of calculating book value per common share of BIC. We'll use basic book value as set forth initially above (*i.e.*, total assets minus total liabilities, the same thing as owners' equity). Book value per common share is equal to the book value divided by the number of common shares outstanding (but if there is any liquidation preference on preferred stock that is outstanding, the amount of that preference is subtracted when calculating the book value):

$$\text{Book Value Per Share} = \frac{\text{book value}}{\text{shares outstanding}}$$

BIC's book value as of December 31 this year was $247,917,000 and it had 23,559,244 common shares outstanding (and no preferred). That implies a book value per share of $10.52. Taken alone, book value per share has limited meaning for most entities operating in the ordinary course, because at best it measures the amount of cash each share would be allocated in the event the entity were to be liquidated and thereby cease operating as a going concern. It may be of some use though in comparing how book value per share of one entity relates to the book value per share of comparable entities.

Market/Book Ratio.

Despite book value's limited utility for a single company, since comparable companies compute book value applying similar accounting principles, comparing book values across different companies can be useful. In particular, it can be useful to compare the relationship between the market price of common stock and its book value per share for groups of comparable companies. That relationship is called the *Market/Book Ratio* or *M/B Ratio* and is equal to the market price per share divided by book value per share:

$$\text{M/B Ratio} = \frac{\text{market price per share}}{\text{book value per share}}$$

Notice that BIC's financial statements do not disclose the recent prices at which the company's stock has been trading. GAAP does not require that they do. For your information, during the last year covered by the financial statements set forth at the beginning of Chapter 8, BIC's common stock traded at prices within a range between $26 and $32 per share. Its M/B Ratio during the period was therefore between 2.47 and 3.04.

That M/B Ratio can be compared with that of other publicly traded entities in the same industry to give a measure of how investors regard the subject entity compared with other entities or the industry average. Higher M/B Ratios mean that investors regard the stock more favorably.

Limitations on Balance Sheet Based Valuation.

It would be a mistake to base a valuation assessment of a business or a share in it by focusing exclusively on balance sheet valuations, even if one could overcome the limitations imposed by GAAP's cost principle, conservatism principle, or economic exchange principle. That is because, unless we are indeed valuing an entity for purposes of liquidating it, what we really want to know is not what its assets cost or what they could attract if sold.

Instead, what is usually of most interest is what those assets, and the enterprise taken as a whole, can do for us. We are interested in knowing, in other words, what it can generate in terms of returns over time. And since (as you probably have noticed or heard), valuation is an art rather than a science, the exercise should examine not only assets but also other financial information. Rather than relying on the balance sheet for the valuation exercise, therefore, we must also examine the income statement.

C. INCOME STATEMENT BASED VALUATION

Financial value can be defined as an estimate of present worth in light of past, present and prospective financial performance of an investment. This sort of value can be measured in terms of the earnings the investment generates over time. The method for assessing value this way is called *"capitalizing earnings."* Capitalizing earnings means dividing earnings by a specified rate of return, and requires an estimate of earnings and the selection of an appropriate rate of return. We consider each of these problems in turn, and return to the subject of price-earnings ratios introduced in Chapter 8.

The Earnings Estimate.

The capitalization of earnings method of valuation first requires making an estimate of earnings that will be generated in the future. In this context, the concept of earnings refers to accounting earnings as reported on the "bottom line" of the income statement. Two issues must be emphasized in employing accounting earnings in the valuation exercise: one is a timing question; the other is a reporting question.

The timing question is this: we are valuing the enterprise to assess what it can do for us in the future. But in making that assessment, we will only have available to us earnings of the present period and past periods. How can present and past earnings guide our assessment of future earnings? Consider BIC's past earnings:

BIC Corporation: Summary Earnings

	This Year	Last Year	Prior Year
Net Income	51,021,000	34,964,000	39,935,000
Per Share	2.19	1.48	1.70

Which of these is the "right" level of earnings? Perhaps we should use only this year's earnings because that is the most recent period. But notice the significant change in this year compared to the prior two years.

One issue is of course why that change occurred. Was it due to extraordinary factors that are unlikely to recur? If so, perhaps using the two prior periods would be most appropriate. On the other hand, companies sometimes bury bad news affecting multiple years into a single charge and dismiss the result as a nonrecurring episode. Adjusting for this practice requires reallocating the one-time charge across multiple periods and adjusting the current year's earnings accordingly.

Alternatively, perhaps the business is cyclical in nature and this pattern of fluctuating earnings could be expected to continue. Or the current year may be aberrational for substantive economic reasons. If the year is a cyclical down-year for the company, an upward adjustment based on earnings of prior years is indicated; if at a boom in the corporate or industrial business cycle, the reverse would be true.

Other reasons for adjusting current earnings are accounting allocations for non-cash charges such as depreciation and amortization. These are intended to serve as a proxy for how close a company's long-term assets are drawing to the ends of their useful lives and must be replaced. It is common for the required reinvestment in such assets to exceed the amount allocated in the accounting.

Recognizing these difficulties, a common practice in making an earnings estimate is to compute *normalized earnings*. It is an average of earnings over the past several years, usually three to five years. In the case of the information available to us about BIC, we can use three. BIC's three-year normalized earnings are therefore equal to the average of its earnings during the last three years:

BIC Corporation: Normalized Earnings

$$\frac{51{,}021{,}000 + 34{,}964{,}000 + 39{,}935{,}000}{3}$$

$$= \$41{,}973{,}000$$

On a per share basis given the number of shares BIC had outstanding at the end of the most recent year (23,559,244), that is $1.78. This calculation of normal earnings weights each of the last three years equally. If there is reason to believe the years are more or less representative they could be weighted accordingly. For example, the current year could be weighted three times, the prior year two times, and the year before that one time.

Related to selecting an appropriate time period for estimating earnings is the reporting question. Recall that accounting earnings are the result of subtracting from revenue all cash expenses plus all non-cash expenses such as depreciation as well as bad debt expense. Sounds simple, but also recall that the exercise entails making numerous accounting judgments. Accounting earnings are affected by the method of computing the cost of goods sold (recall from Chapter 4 the discussion of FIFO and LIFO), the method of depreciating fixed assets (recall from Chapter 5 the discussion of the straight-line method and accelerated methods), and the policies concerning allowance for bad debts (recall from Chapter 6 the discussion of the judgments that go into that exercise).

With respect to a particular entity and a particular period, GAAP's consistency principle insists that all conventions used be the same. But conventions may also be changed over time, and one must be careful to assess the impact of any such changes in earnings over time. In the case of BIC, for example, the financial statements disclose that the company changed the principles it applies with respect to accounting for postretirement benefits this year and with respect to postretirement benefits (other than pensions) last year.

In comparing a particular entity's earnings with those of other entities in the valuation exercise, care must be taken to ascertain any differences in accounting conventions that have material effects on reported earnings. And the same point holds for the question of using past, present, or normalized earnings, and how normalized earnings are computed.

Intelligent analysts eschew *pro forma* financial figures. These are pictures of performance based on making various assumptions other than those applied in preparing actual financial statements. While useful for certain exercises such as depicting how a newly-merged company would have looked if the merger had occurred some years earlier, they do not represent useful valuation resources in other contexts. *Pro forma* figures are the least reliable data in financial reporting and are invariably unreliable for a valuation exercise.

Also suspect for some analysts are assumptions about growth in future earnings extrapolated from current or past earnings. A key reason to deny estimated and unknown earnings growth is that absent sustainable competitive advantages or barriers to competitor entry, growth lacks value. If new entrants can join a company's industry as equal competitors, the effect drives a company's returns to just equal their costs—no upside is sustainable so growth adds nothing. Growing a business measured in sales requires growing the business measured in assets. Growing assets requires capital, which also poses a cost. Facing competitive entrants, the process goes nowhere (except remotely due to luck and temporarily).

The Capitalization Rate.

Once a representative earnings figure is selected, the earnings must be discounted in a conceptually equivalent way to the discounting techniques discussed in the previous Chapter. To do so, a suitable capitalization rate (referred to as the *cap rate*) must be chosen. It is the rate of return that an investor would require in order to make the investment, a rate based in part upon the risks involved in the entity and its industry, which in turn relates those risks to the risks that the expected earnings will materialize.

To broaden the point, the question an investor faces is what amount of money she is willing to pay for a specified return. Assume we have determined that BIC's expected earnings will equal its normalized earnings calculated above as $41,973,000, or $1.78 per share. The price an investor is willing to pay for the right to that level of expected earnings in the future will be a function of the rate of return necessary to compensate for the risk that the $1.78 per year will not materialize. The more risk, the greater rate of return one should insist upon; the less risk the lower the rate of return one is entitled to insist upon.

Rules of thumb help set cap rates given various levels of risk. In general, the lower the risks involved in a particular type of business, the lower the cap rate. For example, if there is a high degree of certainty that the entity will continue to perform as it has in the past, then a cap rate in the range of 8% to 10% would be appropriate. For entities that present moderate degrees of risk, a cap rate in the range of 15–25% would be more appropriate. And for particularly risky entities, those where uncertainty about sustained success is great, an appropriate cap rate could range from 30% or 40% up to 100%.

For any given entity, these rules of thumb should be tailored to address the particular risks it faces. Indeed, the cap rate would have to be adjusted depending on how the future risks the entity faces, or is likely to face, differ from historical risks. If the future risks are greater, then the cap rate would have to be increased, and vice versa.

Application.

Once an earnings estimate is made and a cap rate selected, an estimate of value can be computed by dividing the earnings estimate by the cap rate, according to the following simple formula:

$$V_e = E / R$$

where V_e is valuation based on earnings, E is the earnings figure and R is the cap rate. In the case of BIC, if we assume expected earnings (E) of $1.78 per share and an average cap rate (R) of say 7.5%, then the result would be as follows:

$$= 1.78 / .075 = \$23.73$$

This result may have an intuitive feel. If you pay $23.73 for a BIC share and it spins off $1.78 in earnings allocable to you, you are enjoying a return of 7.5%. Confirm the intuition by recalling Chapter 10's introduction to present values of annuities. We indicated that the present value of an annuity (a stream of even payments at designated intervals for a finite period of time) is $PV = x \ / \ (1 + k)^n$. Recall from that discussion that as the number of years (n) becomes larger the contributions of later years to the resulting valuation declines (they have lower present values). When applied to value corporations or shares, the stream has no definite end point (corporations have perpetual lives); it is an annuity without end, called a *perpetuity*. So the formula becomes a simpler version of the present value of annuity formula: n becomes so large—literally infinitely large—that it figuratively drops out of the picture. The result is the denominator of the formula becomes k alone, not $(1+k)^n$. Accordingly, you can understand the formula $V_e = E \ / \ R$ as the functional equivalent of the formula $PV = x \ / \ k$.

Despite the fun math, the resulting valuation figure is not necessarily the precise "answer" to the question of what a share of BIC stock is "worth", due to the judgments that were made in reaching this conclusion. Given the difficulties in selecting both a representative earnings figure and the cap rate, it would be better to make a series of calculations using a range of earnings figures and a range of cap rates. For example, we could depict various possibilities for BIC as set forth in Table 11-1.

		Various Cap Rates		
		5%	**7.5%**	**10%**
Various	**1.50**	30	20	15
Per Share	**1.75**	35	23.33	17.50
Earnings				
Estimates	**2.00**	40	26.66	20

Table 11-1
BIC Corporations: Earnings-Based Valuation Possibilities

Study the relationship between cap rates and expected earnings levels revealed by the data in Table 11-1. For any level of earnings, the value of the stock decreases at higher assumed cap rates. At first this may seem counterintuitive. But the reason is that the cap rate is reflecting a measure of risk. Higher cap rates mean greater risk that earnings will not be realized, and thus lower valuation.

Notice also that under our range of assumptions—expected earnings from $1.50 to $2.00 per share and cap rates from 5% to 10%—this approach gives us a range of values from $15 to $40 per share. This "Texas range" does not help much in pinpointing the stock's fair value. We need to be more ruthless in selecting the expected earnings or the cap rate. To do so, we can turn to public capital markets where stocks trade and determine how collective judgments about stocks are being made, either the one we are interested in directly, or others that are comparable. In particular, something can be learned both about expected earnings and implied cap rates from an analysis of P/E ratios, introduced in Chapter 8.

The Price-Earnings Ratio.

The P/E ratio reflects perceived risk by comparing the price of a share of publicly traded stock with its earnings per share. Recall that this year, the market price of a share of BIC common stock ranged between $26 and $32. Its P/E ratio, using this year's earnings per share of $2.17, ranged from about 12 to nearly 15. From this measure, we can also calculate the market's *implied cap rate*. It is the reciprocal of the P/E ratio. In BIC's case, the implied cap rate this year ranged from 1/12 to 1/15 (about 6% to 8%). The market was saying that it believed that BIC's earnings outlook was very favorable indeed.

We might agree or disagree with the market's collective judgment. If we thought the market was underappreciating BIC's business and earnings prospects, we might be inclined to regard it as a good investment and buy shares. If we thought the market was being too optimistic, we might decide to sell shares.

Indeed, the stock market frequently misprices stocks due to "investors" basing "valuation" on emotions like fear and greed rather than according to the sorts of fundamental analysis we are discussing. For example, the average common stock listed in public capital markets in the United States typically varies in price during a single year by as much as 50%. Business conditions rarely vacillate so dramatically. Hence fundamental valuation analysis is a crucial bundle of tools that should be used to help sort out when the market is offering value for investment dollars and when it is offering fool's gold. (Fuller discussion of capital market efficiency appears in Chapter 12.)

In any event, Table 11-2 translates various P/E ratios into the cap rate implied by the market's pricing.

Table 11-2	
P/E Ratios and Cap Rates	
P/E Ratio	Cap Rate (%)
100	1
50	2
25	4
20	5
12.5	8
10	10
5	20
4	25
2	50

Once the P/E ratio for a corporation is calculated, it can be compared to either the P/E ratio of a market index (such as the Dow Jones Industrial Average), a similar entity in the same industry, or the past P/E ratios of the entity in question. This comparison will show the relationship of the stock's perceived risk to the perceived risk of securities with which it is being compared.

In making such comparisons, it is important to compare apples to apples and not apples to oranges—the earnings being used for comparison between two entities should be calculated in the same way, both with respect to the timing question (past, present or normalized), and with respect to the reporting question (with respect to accounting conventions that materially affect reported earnings). For example, *The Wall Street Journal* web site may publish the P/E ratios for all stocks listed on the major exchanges. These P/E ratios are determined based upon the *current reported earnings* of the corporation. Consequently, any analysis performed using the P/E ratios given by *The Wall Street Journal* would have to be done using the current earnings-per-share figure, as reported in the entity's financial statements. Otherwise, the figures will not be comparable.

Limitations of Income Statement Based Valuation.

In the same way that balance-sheet based methods of valuation fail to give effect to the earnings potential and are therefore regarded as incomplete methods of valuation, the income statement based methods of capitalizing earnings or using P/E ratios also have significant limitations. With respect to capitalizing earnings, the determination of earnings is constrained by potentially artificial accounting conventions. Moreover, the technique is based on estimated earnings without regard to whether earnings (or any portion of them) will be paid out to shareholders in the form of dividends or be reinvested in the business.

To vary the point, what is of interest in valuation is the *future* expected stream of *payments*. With respect to P/E ratios, therefore, to provide an accurate measure of the cap rate of a stock, two conditions must be met. The first condition is that the P/E ratio must be calculated based on expected average *future* earnings and the second condition is that all such earnings must be expected to be *paid out in dividends* to stockholders rather than reinvested in the business. As a result of these limitations on income statement based valuation techniques, yet another alternative to valuation looks beyond both the balance sheet and the income statement and toward cash flows.

D. CASH FLOW BASED VALUATION

The limitations of income statement based valuation suggest considering what ultimately matters: cash. Whether valuing an entire business or a single share of stock (or other productive asset held for financial gain), cash is king. Earnings (whether of a business or per share) are a vehicle to deliver this end. Valuation of cash is generally known as *discounted cash flow* (DCF) analysis (as applied to shares of stock, it is known as the *dividend discount model* or DDM).

DCF and DDM (collectively, cash flow valuation methods) require making two key estimates, much as with the capitalization of earnings method: estimate future cash flows and then discount these to present value. To this extent, the formula resembles the form of the earnings valuation model but uses the symbols D (for cash flows, abbreviating the word dividends) and k for the discount rate:

$$V = D / k$$

Again, this is a perpetuity, the functional equivalent of the formula $V_e = E / R$ discussed above for valuation based on earnings, and both are the functional equivalent of the general formula for valuing any perpetuity $PV = x / k$. To repeat and reinforce these points, recall that an annuity (which is *finite*) is valued according to the present value of each of its payments. In formula terms:

$$PV = \frac{X_1}{(1+k)^1} + \frac{X_2}{(1+k)^2} + \frac{X_3}{(1+k)^3} + \dots \frac{X_n}{(1+k)^n}$$

This formula determines the present value for each individual payment and then adds them together. In Chapter 10 we said this expression collapses to:

$$PV = \sum \frac{x_n}{(1+k)^n}$$

In discussing valuation based on earnings, we said the perpetuity form of an annuity (which is *infinite*, lasting forever) becomes:

$$PV = x/k$$

For earnings valuation, this is customarily expressed as $V_e = E / R$. In cash flow based valuation, this is customarily expressed as $V = D / k$.

In cash flow based valuation, analysts take one additional step. They elaborate the model by making assumptions concerning expected growth rates in cash flow (or, for single shares, dividends). Three choices appear: *no growth*; growth at a steady constant rate (called *constant growth*); or growth at one rate for a short period and a different rate (usually lower) beyond that time (called *non-constant growth*). The basic formula for a perpetuity works for the no growth assumption.

What if growth is assumed? An uneven stream of future payments would involve discounting each to present value and summing them. If the stream is growing at a constant rate (call it g), the basic formula can be rewritten as:

$$V = \frac{D_0(1+g)^1}{(1+k)^1} + \frac{D_0(1+g)^2}{(1+k)^2} + \frac{D_0(1+g)^3}{(1+k)^3} + \ldots + \frac{D_0(1+g)^\infty}{(1+k)^\infty}$$

When g is the same throughout, and we are talking about a perpetuity, the formula simplifies in a way analogous to the simplification from an annuity to a perpetuity without growth:

$$V = \frac{D_0(1+g)^1}{K-g}$$

The numerator in this formula is the known amount (D_0, this year's dividend say) growing by the growth rate for one period (that is, $(1+g)^1$). Thus the formula can be simplified further to:

$$V = \frac{D^1}{k-g}$$

When nonconstant growth is assumed (growth at one rate for a finite period and a different rate to infinity), you need to take two steps. First, compute the present value of the finite stream (using the basic present value formula for an annuity that is growing); second, compute the present value of the infinite stream (using the present value formula for a perpetuity that is growing). Add the results. (Chapter 13's *Wilson* case provides an illustration of this seemingly complex but actually quite standardized method.)

Complex judgments influence whether to assume growth, at what level, and for how long. The issue is essentially the extent to which a company commands prospects and opportunities so that its net income can be redeployed to generate continual expansion and cash. If so, it grows; if not, it doesn't.

A conventional way of estimating growth draws on the relationship between a company's net income and dividends. Net income can be retained (retained earnings) or distributed (as dividends). The portion retained can drive growth. The relationship between net income and dividends can be described either as the *payout ratio* (dividends in relation to net income) or the *plowback ratio* (retained earnings in relation to net income). An estimate of growth can be made by relating the plowback ratio to the company's return on equity (ROE). Net income plowed back into the business can be expected to generate returns equal to ROE. That result is a proxy for future growth.

Estimating k is difficult. For individual stocks, one proxy for k is the *dividend yield*. This is the relationship between cash dividends per share and stock price. Notice the similarity of form to the P/E ratio when it is used as the cap rate in an earnings valuation exercise. A more general method of estimating discount rates for DCF and DDM analysis appears in the next Chapter.

Limitations on Cash Flow Valuation Methods.

DCF and the DDM are among the most popular methods for valuing common stocks and entire businesses. Despite popularity, the approach carries limitations. When valuing businesses, one reason to use or prefer balance sheet and income statement valuation techniques is that resort solely to cash flow can be deceptively simple. Cash flows alone disguise important metrics. True, cash flows drive value, but some portion of cash flows will be needed to reinvest in capital resources necessary to sustain business production and results. Thus to arrive at a cash flow figure by adjusting net income for non-cash expenditures is only a partial step. Step two is to further adjust that figure by probable future cash commitments to capital expenditures.

Suppose a company generates net income of $1,000,000. Part of the expenses recorded to generate the $1,000,000 consisted of net non-cash charges of $200,000. Cash flow is thus $1,200,000. That is step one. Then this figure must be adjusted to reflect the amount the company will need to disburse in cash to maintain its property, plant and equipment at levels sufficient to sustain business productivity. Suppose this figure is either $100,000 or $300,000. Adjusted, cash flows are now either $900,000 or $1,100,000. This is the bottom line figure, and may be called free cash flow (assuming no debt obligations or dividend plans).

Analysts sometimes fail to take this additional step of adjusting for the probable costs of required reinvestment (or do so using optimistic assumptions). It would be more accurate for these analysts simply to stick with the net income figure. After all, non-cash charges used to compute net income are at least, in part, intended as a proxy to estimate such required reinvestment. In this example, the bookkeeping allocation of non-cash charges of $200,000 may be as reasonable an estimate of required cash reinvestment as the separate estimates of either $100,000 or $300,000.

Second, in DCF models, cash flows can be measured in alternative ways. Examples are operating income (earnings before interest and taxes, called EBIT) and operating income plus the non-cash expenses of depreciation and amortization (called EBITDA). Devotees of discounted cash flow valuation analysis rarely use accounting-driven metrics such as net income.

Once cash flows are defined using one of these metrics, the discounted cash flow valuation method estimates them for a medium-term period, typically 5 to 10 years. The estimate entails examining a range of performance variables that drive cash flows, such as sales levels, profit margins and required reinvestment in the business through capital expenditures (cap-ex). With cash flows projected, the method discounts each year's estimate by a discount rate intended to reflect the subject company's cost of capital during the period. Each year's discounted result is added to all others to produce a preliminary valuation of the 5- or 10-year period.

Third, for cash flows beyond the medium-term, an additional step estimates the further cash expected in perpetuity, at some assumed growth rate. This is typically done by estimating the final year's cash flows and multiplying it by some figure to yield the perpetuity amount. The figure is determined by the relationship between the assumed growth rate and the relevant cost of capital at that horizon period. It is equal to 1 divided by the difference between these rates—so with a cost of capital of 10% and a growth rate of 5%, the multiplier is 20 determined by $1/(10\% - 5\%)$.

The fourth limitation on DDM and DCF concerns the variable of growth. Growth is not free. Its price is the cost of capital necessary to support it. Growth adds value only when the return on capital exceeds the cost of capital. Consider the following example (adapted from Bruce C. N. Greenwald, *et al.*, *Value Investing* (2001)).

Suppose that cash flow is \$32. An analyst determines it would cost \$20 to grow cash flow by 10% forever. So you can have either (a) \$32 forever or (b) \$12 growing at 10% forever. Which is better, no-growth or growth? It depends on the cost of capital. Use the valuation formula:

$$V = \frac{D}{k - g}$$

Recall that k is the discount rate (the cost of capital) and g is the growth rate.

Assume $k = 20\%$ and $g = 0$ or 10%. Then:

$$\text{(a) } V = \frac{32}{.20 - 0} = \$160$$

$$\text{(b) } V = \frac{12}{.20 - .10} = \$120$$

This shows that growth subtracts value when the cost of capital exceeds the return on capital.

Assume instead $k = 14\%$. Then:

$$\text{(a) } V = \frac{32}{.14 - 0} = \$229$$

$$\text{(b) } V = \frac{12}{.14 - 10} = \$300$$

This shows that growth adds value when the return on capital exceeds the cost of capital.

Assume finally $k = 16\%$. Then:

$$\text{(a) } V = \frac{32}{.16 - 0} = \$200$$

$$\text{(b) } V = \frac{12}{.16 - 10} = \$200$$

This shows that growth is neutral to value when the cost of capital equals the return on capital.

To summarize, growth is not free. If a company can attract capital at a cost lower than returns it generates, growth adds value. If it attracts capital at a cost higher than what it generates, growth subtracts value. If the cost of capital is the same as the return on capital, growth is neutral to value.

E. SYNTHESIS

This criticism of DDM and DCF brings this discussion of valuation techniques back to the beginning. One reason to hesitate in appraising value based on growth estimates is that growth's potential value can be ascertained using other accounting tools not requiring estimates. This involves comparing valuation estimates using earnings with those using assets.

Suppose a valuation analyst compares income statement data with balance sheet data. In particular, consider comparing earnings per share (EPS) to book value per share (BVPS). If BVPS exceeds EPS, then assets are not well-deployed—perhaps due to managerial ineptitude or intense industry competition. Growing a business like that probably *decreases* its value. But if EPS exceeds BVPS, then assets are well-deployed—perhaps due to managerial skill or competitive advantages like strong brand names. Growing a business like that probably *increases* its value.

A handy tool from Chapter 8 facilitates such comparisons: return on equity (ROE), measured as the company's net income divided by shareholders' equity (an income statement figure divided by a balance sheet figure). Companies with higher ROE probably benefit from growth and those with lower ROE are probably hurt by growth. In using DCF valuation models, therefore, it may be reasonable to assume growth for high-ROE companies but not to do so for low ROE companies. The former may be called franchise businesses.

Franchise businesses are those boasting barriers to entry and other competitive advantages that make it too costly for new entrants to compete. Strong brands can help, so long as competitors cannot match them. Examples include at least for some period of time those products bearing names synonymous with the goods, such as Coke, Kleenex, Hoover (in its day), Harley-Davidson (to some extent), Google and others. Name a few yourself.

Techniques producing franchise value include patents, exclusive licenses, know-how, and secret formulae. Generally high fixed-costs of entry also help. Common elements of franchise businesses include high costs to consumers of switching away from the target's own product in favor of competitors, high costs to consumers of seeking out such alternatives, and habits commanding consumer loyalty.

Foes of the franchise power are constraints competitors can evade. Examples are a unionized labor force, burdensome distribution arrangements, or limitations on an entity's adaptability in the face of change.

Problem 11A

Refer to the financial statements of MountainView, Inc. ("MVI") set forth at the end of Chapters Eight and Nine. MVI's financial statements were also accompanied by the following additional footnote disclosure:

1.   The land reported on the balance sheet was purchased fifteen years ago for the price shown. Comparable nearby property recently sold for $975,000.

2.   The building reported on the balance sheet has a fair market value of $100,000 in excess of the amount reported.

3.   The equipment reported on the balance sheet has a fair market value of $100,000 in excess of the amount reported.

4.   The company's common stock is listed on the New York Stock Exchange. As of December 31, Year 3, the price per share was $35.

a.   Determine the following for MVI as of the end of Year 3:

(1)   book value per share; adjusted book value per share; market to book ratio (using book value, not adjusted book value); a possible value per share assuming that the market to book ratio of comparable companies is 3;

(2)   current earnings per share; current price/earnings ratio; the implied capitalization rate based on the current price/earnings ratio; normalized earnings per share (over the past three years); the implied price/earnings ratio based on normalized earnings per share; a possible range of values per share based on the foregoing data; and

(3)   the value per share based on cash dividend streams in perpetuity, assuming zero growth, a discount rate of 7%, and an initial annual dividend of $2 per share. Evaluate whether the assumption of no growth is reasonable, considering the relationship between normalized EPS and the assumed dividend level and the level of MVI's return on equity. What valuation would this method yield if negotiators agree on an assumed growth rate of 2%?

b.   What do each of the foregoing determinations of the value of an MVI share mean? How do they relate to one another? In what ways are some measures better than others?

Problem 11B

A prosperous company shows the following dividend history during the past 7 years (starting with the earliest year and finishing with the most recent): $1.00, 1.06, 1.15, 1.25, 1.36, 1.44, and 1.59. Estimate its value using the DDM. Assume alternately (a) no growth and (b) growth of 8%. Assume in each case a suitable discount rate is 14%.

Problem 11C

A company has preferred stock that promises holders a fixed annual dividend of $8. Assuming a 12.8% discount rate based on the company's risk profile, what is the preferred stock's value?

Conceptual Questions 11

For a going concern, which is better, valuation based on reproduction cost of assets, current earnings, or discounted cash flow? Or is using them in combination the more prudent approach?

CHAPTER 12

FINANCE THEORY AND INVESTING

■ ■ ■

Finance theory was dubbed "modern finance theory" by its devotees to reflect a contemporary application of statistics and mathematical modeling to how public capital markets price securities, return relates to risk, and investors are compensated for assuming risk. This finance theory is a three-legged stool: modern portfolio theory interprets risk and offers tools to eliminate certain kinds of risk; the capital asset pricing model proposes a relationship between the residual risk and returns and provides a technique to estimate discount rates applicable to equity securities; and the efficient capital market hypothesis contends that the prices of public securities reflect this risk-return relationship.

A. INTRODUCTORY STATISTICS

Finance theory's framework for measuring risk draws on basic statistics. The principle concepts are probability distributions and standard deviations (the latter was introduced in Chapter 9). *Probability distributions* are arrangements of alternative outcomes according to the likelihood that they will occur. They can be depicted graphically. *Standard deviations* can be applied as numerical measurements of probability distributions expressed in percentages. They capture the dispersion of alternative outcomes in relation to the central tendency of the data, generally called the *expected value*. For investments, this central tendency is commonly defined as the *expected return*. It typically is a weighted average measure of the array of alternative outcomes.

Probability Distributions.

A simple dice-throwing example introduces these concepts. Consider the roll of a pair of ordinary dice, each six-sided with each side numbered 1 through 6. Possible rolls range from 2 (snake-eyes, both dies coming up 1) to 12 (both coming up 6). The probability of any given roll is a function of the number of ways that the given roll can be achieved, compared to the total number of possible rolls. For any given roll, there are a finite number of ways it can come up: there is only one way to produce a 2 (snake-eyes) and one way to produce a 12 (two 6s); there are six ways to come up with a 7 (1-6, 6-1, 2-5, 5-2, 3-4 and 4-3). The total number of possible rolls is 36. After making a complete list, you could array the possible outcomes and their associated probabilities in a table such as the following, called a probability distribution.

Table 12-1: Dice-Throwing Probability Distribution											
A. Roll:	2	3	4	5	6	7	8	9	10	11	12
B. Probability:	1/36	2/36	3/36	4/36	5/36	6/36	5/36	4/36	3/36	2/36	1/36
C. As %:	2.8	5.6	8.3	11.1	13.9	16.7	13.9	11.1	8.3	5.6	2.8

You could draw a picture of this probability distribution reflecting the likelihood of each roll. It might appear as in Figure 12-1.

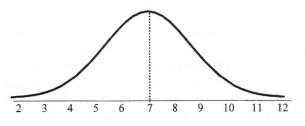

Figure 12-1: Dice-Throwing Probability Distribution Curve

You can use such pictures to answer a variety of questions about the data. For example, what's the most likely outcome? The roll of 7 comes up most often, so it is the most likely outcome. You could use these tools to determine the chances of at least a 7 coming up. It is the sum of the chances of rolling a 7 or better (these sum to 58.4%, which also tells you that there is a 41.6% chance of rolling less than a 7).

Let's confirm that 7 is the most likely outcome more formally by weighting the rolls. Do this by multiplying the decimal equivalent of the probability times the roll, and then sum the results. Table 12-2 shows how this equals 7 in this example.

Table 12-2: Dice-Throwing Weighted Expected Value											
A. Roll:	2	3	4	5	6	7	8	9	10	11	12
B. Probability as decimal:	.028	.056	.083	.111	.139	.167	.139	.111	.083	.056	.028
C. Weighted Probability (A x B)	.056	.168	.252	.555	.833	1.167	1.111	1.00	.833	.0611	.333
The probability weighted figures sum to 7. That is the weighted expected value.											

Compare a probability distribution that is not so spread out—that has a narrower range of possible outcomes or in statistical terms *less variability*. Suppose a strange pair of dice that bears only 3s and 4s on the six-sides, three of each on each die. The probability distribution of rolls appears in Table 12-3, along with its weighted expected value.

Table 12-3: Strange Dice Probability Distribution and Weighted Expected Value			
A. Result:	6	7	8
B. Probability:	9/36	18/36	9/36
C. As %:	25	50	25
D. As decimal:	.25	.50	.25
E. Probability-Weighted (A x D)	1.50	3.50	2.00
The probability weighted figures sum to 7. That is the weighted expected value.			

The most likely roll on the strange dice remains 7 and this remains the weighted expected value. But the range of possible outcomes is now curtailed from both ends. The range is from 6 to 8 rather than from 2 to 12. Those less willing to expose themselves to the extremes—the possibility of getting 2s or 12s, for example—would prefer operating in this 6-7-8 environment. There is less risk—though the expected roll remains the same. Compare stylized graphical depictions of the strange-dice scenario with the normal dice scenario, as in Figure 12-2.

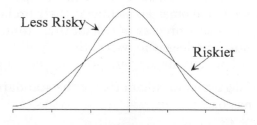

Figure 12-2
Normal Dice versus Strange Dice (Stylized)

Figure 12-2 shows a stylized image of the normal-dice scenario with a flatter peak and longer tails. There is more range or variability in it and so more risk of departure from the expected value of 7 (you can get 2 or 12). It is labeled Riskier. The stylized image of the strange-dice scenario has a sharper peak and shorter tails. There is less range or variability in it and so less risk of departure from the expected value of 7 (you can only otherwise get a 6 or 8). It is labeled Less Risky.

Standard Deviation (Revisited).

The degree to which a probability distribution is more or less risky in these terms can be measured by standard deviation. This statistic was introduced in Chapter 9. Recall that standard deviation is a numerical measure of the dispersion around the expected value. The concept, formula and key steps remain the same, with one methodological refinement as applied to probability distributions. Here are the steps to calculate standard deviation for probability distributions:

1. Calculate the expected value of the data set (EV)

2. From the expected value (EV), subtract each observation (V_i)

3. *Square each result $(EV - V_i)^2$

4. Multiply each squared result by the result's probability (p_i)

5. Sum these weighted values D

6. Take the square root of this sum $\sqrt{}$

In formula terms, the standard deviation for probability distributions is this:

$$\sqrt{\sum_{i=1}^{n}(EV - V_i)^2 \, p_i}$$

(Notice the refinement compared to standard deviations calculated in Chapter 9 for cash flow variability. There we examined data bearing equal weight—various years of cash flow—so we divided the sum of the squares by the total number of observations (less 1). If you look back to Chapter 9, you'll see that was designated as Step 5 in the process. Here we are weighting the possible outcomes according to their probabilities, in Step 4 above. Thus, Step 4 in this process of calculating standard deviations for probability distributions does the work Step 5 did in the context of calculating standard deviations for data accorded equal weight.)

Tables 12-4 and 12-5 show calculation of the standard deviation for the dice-throwing scenarios.

---

* Squaring the difference eliminates effects of negative numbers when summing the results. Squaring also implies it does not matter whether one subtracts the observation from the expected value or subtracts the expected value from the observation.

Table 12-4
Normal Dice Standard Deviation Calculation*
Step 1. Calculate Expected Value *(EV)* = 7**

Value (V)	**Steps 2 & 3.** Difference Squared $(EV\text{-}V)^2$	Probability (ρ) (Tables 12-1 & 2)	**Step 4.** $(EV\text{-}V)^2 \times (\rho)$
2	$(7 - 2)^2 = 25$	$1/36 = .028$	0.694
3	$(7 - 3)^2 = 16$	$2/36 = .056$	0.889
4	$(7 - 4)^2 = 9$	$3/36 = .083$	0.750
5	$(7 - 5)^2 = 4$	$4/36 = .111$	0.444
6	$(7 - 6)^2 = 1$	$5/36 = .139$	0.139
7	$(7 - 7)^2 = 0$	$6/36 = .167$	0.000
8	$(7 - 8)^2 = 1$	$5/36 = .139$	0.139
9	$(7 - 9)^2 = 4$	$4/36 = .111$	0.444
10	$(7 - 10)^2 = 9$	$3/36 = .083$	0.750
11	$(7 - 11)^2 = 16$	$2/36 = .056$	0.889
12	$(7 - 12)^2 = 25$	$1/36 = .028$	0.694

*Formula for SD

$$\sqrt{\sum_{i=1}^{n}(EV - V_i)^2 \rho_i}$$

**Formula for Step 1 (*see* Table 12-2)

$$\sum_{i=1}^{n}\rho_i V_i$$

Step 5. Sum the above=
5.833

Step 6. Take square root of step 5=
2.415

Table 12-5
Strange Dice Standard Deviation Calculation*
Step 1. Calculate Expected Value *(EV)* = 7**

Value (V)	Steps 2 & 3. Difference Squared $(EV\text{-}V)^2$	Probability (ρ) (Table 12-3)	Step 4. $(EV\text{-}V)^2 \times (\rho)$
6	$(7-6)^2 = 1$	9/36 = .25	.25
7	$(7-7)^2 = 0$	18/36 = .50	0
8	$(7-8)^2 = 1$	9/36 = .25	.25

*Formula for SD

$$\sqrt{\sum_{i=1}^{n}(EV - V_i)^2 \rho_i}$$

Step 5. Sum the above= .5

**Formula for Step 1(*see* Table 12-3)

$$\sum_{i=1}^{n}\rho_i V_i$$

Step 6. Take square root of step 5= 0.707

Interpret these results. The normal-dice scenario's standard deviation is 2.415 and the strange-dice scenario's standard deviation is 0.707. Which is riskier? The normal-dice scenario, by a substantial multiple.

Probability distributions that exhibit perfect symmetry are *normal distributions*. Their shape is known as a normal curve or bell curve. Standard deviations for bell curves have the following properties.

- 38.3% of all outcomes are within 1/2 a standard deviation of the expected value. In the normal dice scenario: 5.793 to 8.207 (within 1.207 of 7.00, given Y = 2.415).

- 68.27% of all outcomes are within 1 standard deviation of the expected value. In the normal dice scenario: 4.585 to 9.415 (within 2.415 of 7.00).

- 95.45% of all outcomes are within 2 standard deviations of the expected value. In the normal dice scenario: 2.170 to 11.830 (within 4.830 of 7.00).

- 99.73% of all outcomes are within 3 standard deviations of the expected value. In the normal dice scenario: 2 to 12 (obviously).

Coefficient of Variation.

Comparing risk of the dice-throwing examples is straightforward because both bear the same expected value. The relative risk is simply the comparative standard deviations, 2.415 versus 0.707. To compare relative risk of probability distributions bearing different expected values requires another tool introduced in Chapter 9: the *coefficient of variation*. Recall that this relates standard deviation to expected value. It is expressed by dividing standard deviation by the expected value, as follows:

$$= \frac{\sigma}{EV}$$

Higher coefficients of variation signify greater relative variability and thus greater relative risk. Consider two alternative investment positions offering different expected values (measured as percentage returns on investment, denoted as *EV*) and different risks (measured by standard deviation, denoted as σ):

Plan A: $EV = 15\%$ & $\sigma = 5\%$

Plan B: $EV = 20\%$ & $\sigma = 6\%$

Plan A looks nice with lower absolute risk than Plan B (5% instead of 6%) and it appears to come with a cost in return, sporting an expected value of 15% instead of Plan B's 20%. But which is riskier, taking into account both variability and expected value? Calculate the coefficients of variation:

$$CV_A = \frac{5}{15} = 33\%$$

$$CV_B = \frac{6}{20} = 30\%$$

Measured by the coefficient of variation, A is the riskier of the two. There is greater *relative* risk that returns on Plan A will deviate from its expected value than is the case with Plan B.

B. MODERN PORTFOLIO THEORY

The foregoing example, using the coefficient of variation, suggests that risks do not exist in isolation. Risks vary across items and in response to different events. An event that affects one item positively will affect a contrary one negatively.

Suppose you and a classmate form a law-firm partnership in which one of you specializes in mergers and acquisitions (M&A) and the other in bankruptcy and reorganizations (B&R). When the economy booms, the

M&A lawyer's practice soars while the B&R lawyer plays lots of golf. When the economy busts, the roles are reversed. In each case, however, the firm's cash flows are about the same and each partner draws level income. The firm is neutralized from the extreme risks associated with both booms and busts. If M&A and B&R respond in precisely opposite ways to booms and busts, then the partners have diversified these risks to zero. This is a feat unachievable with many risks, but possible with financial risks when events affect items in exactly offsetting ways.

Diversification.

Modern finance theory formalizes and elaborates these principles for the selection and assembly of investment securities, especially common stock. It says that stocks can respond differently to identical economic events and environments. Rational investors can assemble a portfolio of stocks that behave in the offsetting ways, akin to the partnership between the M&A and B&R lawyers. These investors would understand that their risk analysis should focus on the combined risk of the entire portfolio.

By assembling a portfolio of securities diversified according to their reaction to identical economic environments, overall risk can be minimized, and indeed, the peculiar risks associated with individual securities can be eliminated. Diversification cannot eliminate general systemic risks, however, such as that the lawyers face from competition in their respective specialty fields from the likes of investment bankers, accountants or auditors who may be able to pick up some of their business when doing deals or workouts.

If investors can shed specific risks, then in a properly functioning world, they should not be compensated for bearing those risks either. Imagine two investors, one who owns a single security and another who owns a dozen different ones that all behave in different ways in response to identical economic environments. The solo-holder faces more risk than the diversified-holder. Now suppose there is an auction for a new common stock on the market. Because the solo-holder faces more risk owning this or any investment, he will be constrained to bid low for the stock compared to a diversified-holder. And because he faces less risk, the diversified-holder can afford to bid more, requiring a lower return on that investment.

Risk and Return.

Another proposition enters the picture at this point: investors are risk-averse. That is, they want to avoid risks if they can and be compensated for bearing them, if they cannot. In a world like this, you should therefore expect to see strong links between risk and return. Substantial evidence supports the expectation. Consider Table 12-6. It depicts long-run average returns (indicators of expected value) to various securities and their corresponding standard deviations (measures of risk). The correlation may not be perfect, but the relationships appear robust enough to warrant theoretical development and practical attention.

Table 12-6 Long-Run Returns and Risks	Average Return	Standard Deviation
Small-Company Stocks	17.6%	33.6%
Large-Company Stocks	13.3	20.1
Long-term Corporate Bonds	5.9	8.7
Long-term Government Bonds	5.5	9.3
U.S. Treasury Bills	3.8	3.2

Correlation.

Diversification at the M&A and B&R law-firm partnership was possible because the two practices respond in (nearly) opposite ways to identical economic events, boom to bust. A two-person M&A firm, on the other hand, will share all the glory of booms and face all unhedged anxiety of busts. There is no diversification because the partners' practices are highly-positively correlated. In the M&A and B&R law firm there is some degree of negative correlation.

Diversification's power works the same way with common stocks. If you own a share of Procter & Gamble (P&G) you certainly don't shed any peculiar P&G risks by buying another P&G share. Nor would you get much diversification payoff if you bought another share of one of its arch-rivals running a similar operation, such as Colgate-Palmolive. These two stocks are more likely to respond to identical economic events in closer to identical rather than opposite ways. If you added a share of General Electric (GE) to your P&G holdings, on the other hand, you will likely shed some risk.

The correlation between stocks can be measured using an advanced application of standard deviation for probability distributions, called *covariance*. Recall that standard deviation is determined for a data set by squaring its deviations from the expected value (then weighting them, summing them, and taking the square root). Squaring is multiplying something by itself. To compare that something with something else, multiply the deviation from the expected value of the one by the deviation from the expected value of the other. (Then weight them, sum them, and take the square root). That is *covariance*.

Measuring correlation requires just one more step, relating this covariance to each item's respective standard deviation. That is, divide the covariance by the product of the respective standard deviations. That is the *correlation coefficient*.

The correlation coefficient captures correlation on a scale from +1 to − 1. Positive correlation means the two things tend to move in the same direction (up, up; down, down). *Perfect positive correlation is +1.* Negative correlation means the two things tend to move in opposite directions (up, down; down, up). *Perfect negative correlation is −1.* Two things that don't interact in systematic ways exhibit no correlation (up or down with no rhyme or reason to each other) and have correlation coefficients of 0.

Illustration.

Assume three investment alternatives under consideration, companies called Tech, Stodgy and Cig. For each, analysis indicates various probable future performances in different economic environments, from normal to boom and bust. Assume also that reliable analysis indicates an equal probability of each future economic state, a 1/3 likelihood each of normal, boom and bust. The three companies perform the same in normal economies but perform as follows otherwise:

Tech, maker of synthetic biotech materials, is phenomenal during booms but dismal during busts;

Stodgy, an old-economy car manufacturer, is strong in booms but weak in busts; and

Cig, a tobacco purveyor, does great during busts but poorly during booms.

Intuition indicates that Tech and Stodgy are *positively correlated* while Tech and Cig are *negatively correlated*. More precise details appear in Table 12-7.

Table 12-7 Tech, Stodgy and Cig Characteristics and Outlook			
Company	Boom	Bust	Normal
Tech (bio)	High-tech explodes, and Tech's returns are **phenomenal (say 20%)**	High-tech sinks, and Tech's returns are **dismal (say 4%)**	Ok **(say 12%)**
Stody (cars)	Many people buy cars, and Stodgy's returns are **strong (say 16%)**	Fewer people buy cars, and Stodgy's returns are **weak (say 8%)**	Ok **(say 12%)**
Cig (butts)	Smokers try to kick the habit, and Cig's returns are **poor (say 8%)**	Everyone despondently lights up, and Cig's returns are **great (say 16%)**	Ok **(say 12%)**

Let's examine the expected return on each investment as the probability-weighted average return and the risk of each investment measured by its standard deviation. The expected return is:

$$\sum_{i=1}^{n} \rho_i V_i$$

For Tech, this means:

$$\left(\frac{1}{3}x.20\right) + \left(\frac{1}{3}x.12\right) + \left(\frac{1}{3}x.04\right) = 12\%.$$

The others both work out to 12% as well (do this yourself). Standard deviation is:

$$\sqrt{\sum_{i=1}^{n}(EV - V_i)^2 \rho_i}$$

For Tech, this means:

Value (V)	Difference Squared $(EV\text{-}V)^2$	Probability (ρ)	$(EV\text{-}V)^2 \times (\rho)$
4	$(12 - 4)^2 = 64$	1/3 = .33	21.33
12	$(12 - 12)^2 = 0$	1/3 = .33	0
20	$(12 - 20)^2 = 64$	1/3 = .33	21.33

Sum the above
=
42.66

Square root of above =
6.53

Standard deviation for both Stodgy and Cig is 3.27% (do this yourself). Table 12-8 shows the full results.

Table 12-8
Tech, Stodgy and Cig
As Stand-Alone Investments

State & Probability	Tech	Stodgy	Cig
Bust = 33% chance	4%	8%	16%
Normal = 33% chance	12%	12%	12%
Boom = 33% chance	20%	16%	8%
Expected Return $\sum_{i=1}^{n} \rho_i V_i$	12%	12%	12%
Standard Deviation $\sqrt{\sum_{i=1}^{n} (EV - V_i)^2 \rho_i}$	6.53%	3.27%	3.27%

Consider combining these stocks. You'll see it is possible to maintain the same expected return, but with less risk. If you held Tech alone, adding an identical dollar amount of Stodgy reduces the risk of holding Tech alone, but leaves the expected return the same. The standard deviation of a 50/50 portfolio of Tech and Stodgy is 4.9% (Tech alone is 6.53%).

Moreover, if you held Tech alone, adding an identical dollar amount of Cig reduces the risk of holding either one alone, but again leaves the expected return the same. The standard deviation of a 50/50 portfolio of Tech and Cig is 1.63% (below both Tech's stand-alone risk of 6.53% and Cig's stand-alone risk of 3.27%).

Foremost, combining Stodgy and Cig gives you no risk at all (the standard deviation is 0). That means a guaranteed 12% return, no risk of being down toward the 8% level (though no reward of being up toward the 16% level either).

Table 12-9 gives the full picture.

Table 12-9
Tech, Stodgy and Cig
Combining as Portfolios

State & Probability	Tech	Stodgy	Cig	T+S	T+C	S+C
Bust = 33% chance	4%	8%	16%	6%	10%	12%
Normal = 33% chance	12%	12%	12%	12%	12%	12%
Boom = 33% chance	20%	16%	8%	18%	14%	12%
Expected Return $$\sum_{i=1}^{n}\rho_i V_i$$	12%	12%	12%	**12%**	**12%**	**12%**
Standard Deviation $$\sqrt{\sum_{i=1}^{n}(EV - V_i)^2 \rho_i}$$	6.53%	3.27%	3.27%	*4.9%*	*1.63%*	*0%*

You may infer from the data and the written conclusion that combining Stodgy and Cig into a risk-free portfolio indicates that the two are perfectly-negatively correlated stocks. Look at the outcomes. In busts, normal, and booms, respectively, Stodgy sports: 8, 12 and 16 while Cig sports 16, 12 and 8—exactly the opposite of each other. They behave in exactly opposite ways to identical economic environments. Their correlation coefficient Is –1. Figure 12-3 shows what this looks like graphically.

Figure 12-3: Perfectly-Negatively Correlated Stocks

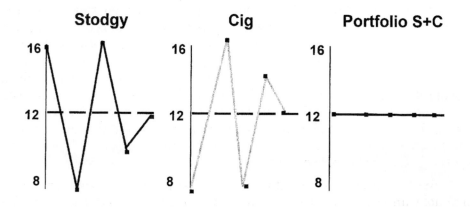

Figure 12-4 shows what two perfectly-positively correlated stocks look like alone and when combined. Imagine this as the equivalent of adding an additional share of P&G to a portfolio consisting of one share of P&G.

Figure 12-4: Perfectly-Positively Correlated Stocks

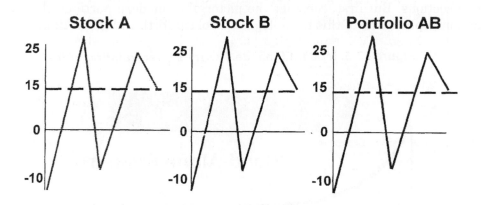

Summary and Implications.

Most stocks are positively correlated, though not perfectly so (they bear correlation coefficients approximately on the average order of .65). Combining stocks into portfolios implies reducing the risk of the overall portfolio compared to the risk of each stock on a stand-alone basis. As more stocks are added, each new one has a smaller risk-reducing effect. After adding about 10 stocks, the decline in portfolio standard deviation from diversification becomes smaller; after adding about 40 the standard deviation falls incrementally indeed (very little benefit from further diversification), meaning a basket of 40 stocks is *well-diversified*. In fact, combining stocks into a well-diversified portfolio is said to eliminate about half the risk associated with owning individual stocks.

As for practical implications, these insights of modern portfolio theory prescribe that an investor should search for that portfolio of stocks bearing a risk suitable to her appetite for risk given her taste for returns. That is, there is a relationship between risk and return and you can assemble a portfolio that maximizes one subject to the other: maximal risk for a given level of return or maximal return for a given level of risk. Finance theorists refer to this array of alternatives as the *efficient frontier*: if you are not getting the most return for your risk you are in a state of inefficiency; if you have been told you can receive return greater than the risk necessary to get it, you have been told a fairy tale.

A final point of intellectual provocation: suppose you own a one-stock portfolio. Can you expect to be compensated for bearing its risk? No. You are not well-diversified. You can diversify to eliminate the peculiar risks (those that can be diversified) so why should you expect returns for bearing what you could easily eliminate? If your market competitors are well-diversified, they'll outbid you for the stock anyway. So you can't even do it. At least, that is the story of modern finance and portfolio theory, a story that assumes this sort of investor rationality and market efficiency, subjects enhanced by the other legs of finance theory discussed in the next two sections. But first, consider the pictorial of modern portfolio theory's major implications of this three-legged stool set forth in Figure 12-5.

Figure 12-5: Modern Finance Theory's Interpretation of Risk

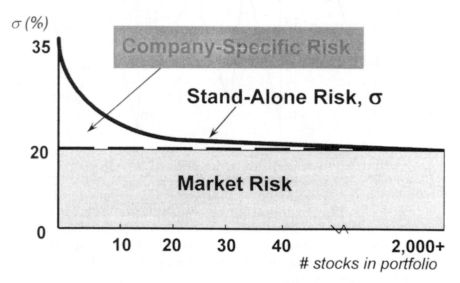

C. CAPITAL ASSET PRICING MODEL

Keep the picture of Figure 12-5 in mind as we begin this discussion of the Capital Asset Pricing Model (CAPM, pronounced *CAP-em*). It theorizes the story the picture in Figure 12-5 suggests: that stand-alone risk can be disaggregated into the company-specific risk that can be shed by diversification and the residual market risk that cannot be shed.

CAPM speaks to returns on securities being a function of how a particular stock behaves in relation to the market, or how sensitive the stock is to fluctuations in the market. It is a pricing model that predicts that stock prices should reflect returns measured this way.

In terms we've been discussing, standard deviation for a stock is a measure of its stand-alone risk (σ). Using modern portfolio theory, stand-alone risk should be unpacked into company-specific risk and market risk. So:

Stand Alone Risk = Company Specific Risk + Market Risk

Company-specific risk can be diversified away; market risk cannot. Investors shouldn't expect returns on the former, but on the latter. CAPM measures the compensation for this latter risk. It proposes that the expected return is greater for securities bearing greater sensitivity to market risk and lower for those bearing lesser sensitivity. Expected returns for assets posing like risk should be the same. Asset prices should adjust so that those with the same risk offer identical expected returns.

Beta.

CAPM measures the relationship between the risks of a particular asset with the market as a whole, called *beta* (ß). It posits that the market *beta* is equal to 1 and then defines the relative risk of other assets in relation to it. So assets bearing risks equivalent to the market have $ß = 1$, those bearing greater risks $ß > 1$ and those bearing lesser risks $ß < 1$. Expected returns follow: an asset (or portfolio) bearing $ß = 1$ has an expected return equal to the market return; those with $ß > 1$ a greater expected return than the market return; and those with $ß < 1$ a lesser expected return than the market.

In summary, CAPM proposes that the expected return on an asset or a portfolio of assets should exceed the risk-free rate of return by an amount proportional to ß. The proposition is captured in the following formula (the CAPM core):

$$ER_i = R_f + ß_i(ER_m - R_f)$$

where:

ER_i is the expected return on a particular asset or portfolio i

R_f is the risk-free rate of return (say on US Treasury bills)

$ß_i$ is the *beta* of the particular asset or portfolio i

ER_m is the expected market return (so $ER_m - R_f$ is the expected market risk premium, meaning its excess over the risk-free rate of return)

Apply this to the market itself. Assume the risk-free rate of return, R_f, is 8% and the expected market return, ER_m, is 15% (meaning an expected market risk premium of 7%). What is the market's ß?

$$.15 = .08 + ß\,(.15 - .08)$$

$$.15 = .08 + ß\,.07$$

$$ß = 1$$

Consider a wider range of examples. Suppose the risk-free rate of return, R_f, is 6% and the expected market return, ER_m, is 10% (meaning an expected market risk premium of 4%). Given various ßs, the formula shows the resulting expected return (ER):

β	CAPM	ER
0	.06 + β (.10 − .06)	.06 (U.S. Treasury Bills)
0.5		.08
1.0		.10 (the market as a whole)
1.5		.12
2.0		.14

These illustrations show the relationship stated above between β and risk. Assets or portfolios with β = 1 bear risk equivalent to the market risk. Those with β > 1 bear greater than market risk and those with β < 1 bear less than market risk.

Analysts calculate β by running a regression of past returns on a given stock versus returns on the market. The slope of the regression line is defined as the β coefficient (the market's slope or β = 1). Most stocks have β in the range of 0.5 to 1.5. Financial services firms regularly publish β-books tallying the βs of thousands of companies.

Equity Discount Rates.

CAPM can be used to estimate discount rates for equities (called the *cost of equity*, introduced in Chapter 10). Using CAPM requires knowing the risk-free rate, the expected market return (and hence the market risk premium) and β. Armed with these inputs, the calculations are simple. For example, assume a company β = 1.25, the risk-free rate from ten-year Treasury bills is 4.8% and the expected return for the market is 12.8%. What is the company's equity discount rate using CAPM?

$$ER_i = R_f + \beta_i(ER_m - R_f)$$

$$= 4.8\% + 1.25\ (12.8\% - 4.8\%)$$

$$= 4.8\% + 10.0\%$$

$$= 14.8\%.$$

Elegant though this appears, each component involves an estimate and the variables are integrated so that changes in one may indicate modification of another. For example, increases in the risk-free rate entail decreases in the market risk premium (the latter measures the difference between the risk-free rate and the expected market return).

The "market risk premium" is a guess based on history of what special inducements it takes to attract investors into stocks rather than buying U.S. Treasury securities or alternative investments. The idea is that investors must be given special compensation to bear the special risks of stocks or else they will not invest in them.

Common practice is to consult data books published by leading economists, such as the one published by a firm run by Yale University professor Roger Ibbotson called the *Ibbotson & Sinquefeld Yearbook.* The harder way is doing it yourself, which is virtually impossible for non-professionals. But it is useful to understand why, so here goes.

Market risk premium data can be calculated up-to-the-minute at any time. Three critical assumptions must be made to estimate the market risk premium. First, the estimator must choose either historical data or some measure of future performance. Second, one must define a "market" for the measure, such as the Standard & Poor's 500, the New York Stock Exchange as a whole, or some other index.

Third, the estimate is based on a specified time period. Alternatives include the period from the late 1800s (when market data were first recorded) to the time of valuation interest; from 1926 (when the University of Chicago began a data base, thought to have the virtue of including a full business cycle before the 1929 market crash) to the time of valuation interest; for the 30-year period before the time of valuation interest (reflecting business cycles exhibiting more relevant business and financial risks and factors); or for specific environments being analyzed, such as the early 2000s.

Seizing on a measure of the "market risk premium" became acutely tricky during the late 1990s because any such thing seemed to be evaporating. Any premium that once existed—*e.g.*, in the period before 1990—dwindled toward zero as the most powerful bull market in world history produced investors who needed no inducements to join. Even staunch devotees of modern finance theory lamented the declining usefulness of the "market risk premium" device during the 1990s.

Despite this well-known fact even among its fans, analysts sticking with this learning adhere to favorite benchmarks, such as 9% based on long-run historical returns on stocks dating back to the 1930s. Others respond to their gut sense that this is almost certainly wrong, and opt instead for rates of 7%, 5%, or less. Some believe it approached zero in the late 1990s.

A group of the country's leading financial economists assembled in mid-2000 to offer their measurements of the market risk premium. Eleven participated. Their estimates of the risk premium were: 0, 1–2, 3, 3–4, 4, 6, 6, and 8.1%, with three refusing to venture a guess given the concept's indefiniteness and uncertain reliability.

Reasons for the decline or evaporation include powerful forces such as: U.S. investors became more long-term oriented, U.S. business efficiency heightened, fiscal policies and monetary management improved, capitalism spread globally, wealth increased, and business fundamentals exhibited less volatility.

As for ß, it is intended to reveal what part of any "market risk premium" is borne by a particular company's stock. *Beta* determines this component of the discount rate estimate for a company's equity by using various assumptions to compare its stock price gyrations with those of the overall stock market. A stock whose price is more volatile than the market's is seen as "riskier" than one whose price gyrates less than the market as a whole. Multiplying this measure of price volatility by a "market risk premium" theoretically expresses the differential risk the particular stock poses. The result is added to the risk-free rate to give an equity discount rate.

Empirical tests of ß show mixed results. A leading study concluded that it was dead—that returns are not correlated with ß. This and other studies pointed to explanations for returns that ß did not capture. Most generally, returns varied inversely to company size measured by equity capitalization and varied proportionately to a company's book value compared to its equity capitalization. *Beta* added little or no explanatory power to returns measured in these ways. Researchers have moved to develop more elaborate multi-factor pricing models to capture the greater apparent complexity in the pricing of public securities.

Devotees recognize several assumptions as necessary to support ß and CAPM. Most generally, ß is only useful if stock prices of the subject company and of all components of the market or market index result from investor behavior that is, collectively, rational. That is, it assumes that public capital market prices are the best estimate of underlying business value. Empirical evidence concerning this is conflicting and the subject remains hotly-debated in academic finance circles. We explore this subject—the efficient capital market hypothesis—next.

D. EFFICIENT CAPITAL MARKET HYPOTHESIS

An efficient market is one where information is widely and cheaply available and all relevant and ascertainable information is reflected in prices. Markets are most likely to be efficient when characterized by the following: there are a large number of participants such that the actions of any individual participant cannot materially affect the market; participants are fully informed, have equal access to the market, and act rationally; the commodity is homogeneous; and there are no transaction costs. These are the sorts of assumptions economists use to model a range of markets; though recognized as unrealistic they are useful to develop models of markets that help to explain and predict outcomes. Of all the types of markets in the world (from real estate to labor), stock markets are the type that most-nearly bear such characteristics.

Three Forms of the EMH.

The efficient capital market hypothesis (ECMH or EMH) classifies public capital market efficiency into three hypothetical forms:

- *weak form*: prices reflect all information consisting of the record of past prices

- *strong form*: all information (public or private) is quickly reflected in prices

- *semi-strong form*: prices reflect past information and all public information and new information is rapidly incorporated into prices

Weak form efficiency hypothesizes that price changes are independent of one another. The logic proceeds as follows. Prices change *because* information changes. Information changes cannot be predicted. New information changes prices. They are therefore independent. *Q.E.D.* In more mathematical terms, this condition describes a *random walk*. Of empirical evidence, the weak form is the best-supported version of the EMH. Even so, "technical traders" doubt it, instead believing there to be patterns in price changes that can help predict the future.

Strong form efficiency is a claim about *fundamental efficiency*, a hypothesis that market price is fundamental value. The logic is nearly-theological, since it assumes all information is reflected in price, whether public or not. There is virtually no evidence supporting this heroic claim. To the contrary, insiders trading on material nonpublic information have shown that their private information is not reflected in market price (they can go to jail for this activity, when caught).

Theoretical implications of the strong-form efficiency hypothesis are as strong as the basic claim. In addition to rendering futile the technical analyst's reading of charts of price patterns, it would render meaningless the exercises of fundamental analysis. Reflectively studying business value using tools like those introduced in Chapters Ten and Eleven is meaningless given front-line traders making rapid price-determining valuation decisions. New information is rapidly digested by front-line traders whose actions drive price to equal value. An *efficiency paradox* results: there is no incentive to develop or study new valuation information. That is, if price already reflects fundamentals, there is no money in it. Investors end up rationally uninformed. But then price will not reflect value and efficiency collapses.

The semi-strong form steps in. It is a more modest, though still powerful claim, of *speculative or informational efficiency*. The hypothesis: market price rapidly reflects public information. Here the logic holds that eager arbitrageurs, traders, and investors scour the world for valuable information. Evidence here is more mixed (and a heavy debate ensues on empirical, theoretical and practical dimensions). Debaters agree that information is rapidly reflected in stock prices, but disagree on what this means. Critics divide information into two broad types: information concerning fundamentals (about economics and value) and information called noise, influenced by other factors including psychological effects. They believe both affect pricing; EMH devotees believe fundamentals squash noise.

Efficiency Hypothesis and Accounting.

The EMH makes various claims about the role of accounting information in the pricing of public securities. Bold claims are that capital markets are not influenced or tricked by any sort of accounting choice or manipulation so long as information about the actual economic effects of the convention or charade are available.

More modest claims include that the location of information within a set of financial statements does not matter. Whether transactions are expensed and run through the income statement or simply included as footnotes should have no effect on the market's assessment of a company's value.

Empirical studies testing these claims proceed as follows. If accounting conventions matter, there would be a measurable effect on price as a result of choosing one convention or another. A company's price is predicted using CAPM; a regression is run to compare the predicted price with the actual price, isolating the accounting convention of interest. If there is a discrepancy, it can be attributed to the accounting convention; absent one, the convention does not matter.

Studies supporting the EMH tended to show that a company's change from LIFO to FIFO in inventory accounting had little or no effect on its market price. They also suggested no or limited price effects from changing depreciation methods. Other evidence indicated limited market price effect as a result of rules relating to whether R&D should be expensed or capitalized.

On the other hand, some studies showed that accounting conventions do drive changes in stock price. Areas included how oil and gas companies account for drilling expenses. Casual observation, formalized in some studies, indicated that when companies announce a plan to restate their financials because they had been inaccurately rosy, the market reacts with meaningful price drops. (Chapter 16 gives examples.)

Studies aside, managers care a lot about accounting policies. Business leaders lobby intensely for or against accounting proposals. Interest ranges from changes in how to measure or classify transactions (such as concerning accounting for derivative securities or stock option compensation) to where in a report they are recorded (in the income statement, balance sheet or footnotes for example). Managerial accounting decisions reflect belief that accounting matters, as many managers opt for FIFO to maximize reported earnings despite it also reducing tax benefits. More generally, there is substantial evidence that managers attempt to manage earnings through discretionary exercises that smooth out the highs and lows in reported net income.

Behavioral Finance.

To explain observed departures from market efficiency, many finance theorists seek to develop a model of market action called behavioral finance. Its goal is to model the emerging empirical picture while adhering to professional tenets that require economists to develop stories with predictive efficacy. The general assertion is that stock market trades are routinely made on grounds other than fundamental information. It accepts that prices change rapidly in response to information, but then identifies two broad constraints on the mechanisms that otherwise might yield prices as the best estimate of value.

First, the principle of *investor sentiment* ("dumb money") means that hunch, noise, emotions, guesses, and trends drive pricing as much as fundamentals do. Memory and senses are as powerful as probability theory. Second, *limited arbitrage* ("smart money") means that correcting dumb-money errors is too risky. The upshot is that prices regularly deviate from values so EMH is undercut.

On limited arbitrage, EMH admits that dumb money exists, but asserts that smart money invariably will correct its errors and push price towards value. That is, if price is below value, arbs will buy; if price is above value, they will sell or take other positions having the effect of driving price to equal value (such as buying put options that bet on a declining price or selling a stock short, meaning a functional executory contract entailing promising to sell the stock at today's price with actual delivery made in the future using stock bought at prices prevailing at that time).

The behavioral finance challenge is that arbitrage is not risk-less. Arbs cannot be sure when price deviates from value (for example, CAPM can't reliably do it). Further, when price exceeds value, selling short is possible but costly and positions cannot be held indefinitely. In general, arbs cannot know how long price and value will deviate. In short, the real-world arbitrage capabilities are weaker than necessary to assure price-value identifies.

As for investor sentiment, the EMH fallback is that dumb money errors cancel each other, dropping out—some mistakenly believe price is above value while others mistakenly believe price is below value. The behavioral finance challenge claims that errors can be systematic. That is, investors are flawed in certain ways. Theorists point to a lengthening list of cognitive biases. Among these are:

reference point bias: investors ask not "Is price fair," but "How does it compare to my purchase price?";

frame dependence: investors do not conduct asset allocation based on defined risks but allocate more to stocks when shown long-term histories (these tend to appear smooth and upward) and less when shown short-term histories (these tend to appear jagged and dangerous);

loss aversion: investors do not sell losing stocks based on assessment of business quality but as a function of aversion to locking in the loss, keeping hope that it will "go up";

pattern seeking ("representativeness"): investors see trends unjustified by probabilities, as in the late 1990s;

status-quo bias: investors are resistant to change, exhibiting persistence towards existing trends and herding (following the crowd); and

overconfidence: 80% of drivers say they are better than average; ditto investors.

The behavioral finance struggle has led to several models, none nearly as powerful as the EMH. In the mid-1980s a *noise trading model* emerged, saying ill-informed trades are uncorrected by arbs because it is too risky (this explained more than is observed). Later a *positive feedback model* emerged, holding that momentum was a self-sustaining force where upward price pressure reinforced upward price trends and downward price pressure reinforced downward price trends (this explained persistence, but not corrections or reversals). Most recent is the *shared mistaken-beliefs model*, a theory of systematically-biased responses to new information (this maps what is often observed). Here the story says there is short-term under-and over-reaction or stickiness to the prevailing trend. For example, amid short-term upside trends, bad news gets into price late while amid short-term downside trends, good news gets into price late.

To all this, the devotees of EMH respond with an appeal to Darwinian markets. This cannot go on forever, they say. The dumb money will lose money and be wiped out. EMH will reign. Behavioral theorists agree that some dumb money traders are wiped out, others reap and run, and others give up. But they claim that some stay or new ones enter. They appeal to history, which suggests an inexhaustible supply of new dumb money. The jury is still out, but EMH is a powerful and elegant model and behavioral finance is a messy engagement with human reality. In the end, economists like to say, it takes a theory to beat a theory, and behavioral finance theory hasn't been able to beat the EMH yet.

E. PASSIVE VERSUS ACTIVE INVESTING

Modern finance theory has spawned numerous additional statistical tools that extend its analytical reach. They probe implications for basic practical questions. For one, can investment professionals add much value, after fees and expenses, to their investor clients by actively picking stocks? Or are investors better served buying an index fund holding pro rata stakes in broad market segments? The following materials consider some of these extensions and implications, beginning with a guide to certain financial products from the Securities and Exchange Commission; following with a discussion of performance measurement tools from the Office of the Comptroller of the Currency; and concluding with a critique by famed investor Warren Buffett.

Securities and Exchange Commission
Mutual Funds and Exchange-Traded Funds (ETFs):
A Guide for Investors (2017)

American investors often turn to mutual funds and exchange-traded funds (ETFs) to save for retirement and other financial goals. Although mutual funds and exchange-traded funds have similarities, they have differences that may make one option preferable for any particular investor. This [excerpt] explains the basics of mutual fund and ETF investing, how each investment option works, the potential costs associated with each option, and how to research a particular investment.

A mutual fund is an SEC-registered open-end investment company that pools money from many investors and invests the money in stocks, bonds, short-term money-market instruments, other securities or assets, or some combination of these investments. The combined securities and assets the mutual fund owns are known as its *portfolio*, which is managed by an SEC-registered *investment adviser*. Each mutual fund share represents an investor's proportionate ownership of the mutual fund's portfolio and the income the portfolio generates.

Investors in mutual funds buy their shares from, and sell/redeem their shares to, the mutual funds themselves. Mutual fund shares are typically purchased from the fund directly or through investment professionals like brokers. Mutual funds are required by law to price their shares each business day and they typically do so after the major U.S. exchanges close. This price—the per-share value of the mutual fund's assets minus its liabilities—is called the NAV or *net asset value*. Mutual funds must sell and redeem their shares at the NAV that is calculated after the investor places a purchase or redemption order. This means that, when an investor places a purchase order for mutual fund shares during the day, the investor won't know what the purchase price is until the next NAV is calculated.

Like mutual funds, ETFs are SEC-registered investment companies that offer investors a way to pool their money in a fund that makes investments in stocks, bonds, other assets or some combination of these investments and, in return, to receive an interest in that investment pool. Unlike mutual funds, however, ETFs do not sell individual shares directly to, or redeem their individual shares directly from, retail investors. Instead, ETF shares are traded throughout the day on national stock exchanges and at market prices that may or may not be the same as the NAV of the shares.

ETFs are just one type of investment within a broader category of financial products called *exchange-traded products* (ETPs). ETPs constitute a diverse class of financial products that seek to provide investors with exposure to financial instruments, financial benchmarks, or investment strategies across a wide range of asset classes. ETP trading occurs on national securities exchanges and other secondary markets, making ETPs widely available to market participants including individual investors. Some common features of mutual funds and ETFs are described below.

Professional Management. Most funds and ETFs are managed by investment advisers who are registered with the SEC.

Diversification. Spreading investments across a wide range of companies or industry sectors can help lower risk if a company or sector fails. Many investors find it less expensive to achieve such diversification through ownership of certain mutual funds or certain ETFs than through ownership of individual stocks or bonds.

Low Minimum Investment. Some mutual funds accommodate investors who don't have a lot of money to invest by setting relatively low dollar amounts for the initial purchase, subsequent monthly purchases, or both. Similarly, ETF shares can often be purchased on the market for relatively low dollar amounts.

Liquidity and Trading Convenience. Mutual fund investors can readily redeem their shares at the next calculated NAV—minus any fees and charges assessed on redemption—on any business day. Mutual funds must send investors payment for the shares within seven days, but many funds provide payment sooner. ETF investors can trade their shares on the market at any time the market is open at the market price—minus any fees and charges incurred at the time of sale. ETF and mutual fund shares traded through a broker are required to settle in three business days.

Costs Despite Negative Returns. Investors in mutual funds must pay sales charges, annual fees, management fees and other expenses, regardless of how the mutual fund performs. Investors may also have to pay taxes on any capital gains distribution they receive. Investors in ETFs must pay brokerage commissions, annual fees, management fees and other expenses, regardless of how the ETF performs. ETF investors may also have to pay taxes on any capital gains distributions; however, because of the structure of certain ETFs that redeem proceeds in kind, taxes on ETF investments have historically been lower than those for mutual fund investments. It is important to note that the tax efficiency of ETFs is not relevant if an investor holds the mutual fund or ETF investment in a tax-advantaged account, such as an IRA or a 401(k).

Lack of Control. Investors in both mutual funds and ETFs cannot directly influence which securities are included in the funds' portfolios.

Potential Price Uncertainty. With an individual stock or an ETF, an investor can obtain real-time (or close to real-time) pricing information with relative ease by checking financial websites or by calling a broker. By contrast, with a mutual fund, the price at which an investor purchases or redeems shares will depend on the fund's NAV, which the fund might not calculate until many hours after an order has been placed.

Mutual funds and ETFs fall into several main categories. Some are bond funds (also called fixed income funds), and some are stock funds (also called equity funds). There are also funds that invest in a combination of these categories, such as balanced funds and target date funds, and newer types of funds such as alternative funds, smart-beta funds and esoteric ETFs. In addition, there are money market funds, which are a specific type of mutual fund.

Hedge fund is a general, non-legal term used to describe private, unregistered investment pools that traditionally have been limited to sophisticated, wealthy investors. Hedge funds are not mutual funds and, as such, are not subject to the numerous regulations that apply to mutual funds for the protection of investors—including regulations requiring that mutual fund shares be redeemable at any time, regulations protecting against conflicts of interest, regulations to assure fairness in the pricing of fund shares, disclosure regulations, regulations limiting the use of leverage, and more.

Index-based mutual funds and ETFs seek to track an underlying securities index and achieve returns that closely correspond to the returns of that index with low fees. They generally invest primarily in the component securities of the index and typically have lower management fees than actively managed funds. Some index funds may also use derivatives (such as options or futures) to help achieve their investment objective. Index-based funds with seemingly similar benchmarks can actually be quite different and can deliver very different returns. For example, some index funds invest in all of the companies included in an index; other index funds invest in a representative sample of the companies included in an index. Because an index fund tracks the securities on a particular index, it may have less flexibility than a non-index fund to react to price declines in the securities contained in the index. Also because market indexes themselves have no expenses, even a passively managed index fund can underperform its index due to fees and taxes.

The adviser of an actively managed mutual fund or ETF may buy or sell components in the portfolio on a daily basis without regard to conformity with an index, provided that the trades are consistent with the overall investment objective of the fund. Unlike similar mutual funds, actively managed ETFs are required to publish their holdings daily. Because there is no underlying index that can serve as a point of reference for investors and other market participants as to the ETF's holdings, disclosing the specific fund holdings ensures that market participants have sufficient information to engage in activity, called *arbitrage*, that works to keep the market price of ETF shares closely linked to the ETF's underlying value.

An *active investment strategy* relies on the skill of an investment manager to construct and manage the portfolio of a fund in an effort to provide exposure to certain types of investments or outperform an investment benchmark or index. An actively managed fund has the potential to outperform the market, but its performance is dependent on the skill of the manager. Also, actively managed funds historically have had higher management fees, which can significantly lower investment returns. The shareholder is paying for more active management of portfolio assets, which often leads to higher turnover costs in the portfolio and potentially negative federal income tax consequences.

Passive investing is an investment strategy that is designed to achieve approximately the same return as a particular market index, before fees. The strategy can be implemented by replication—purchasing 100% of the securities in the same proportion as in the index or benchmark—or by a representative sampling of stocks in the index. Passive investing also typically comes with lower management fees. As discussed above, passively managed mutual funds are typically called index funds.

Most ETFs are also passively managed, although there are some actively managed ETFs on the market. Passively managed ETFs typically have lower costs for the same reasons index mutual funds do. In addition, index-based ETFs' costs and taxes can be even lower than index mutual funds' because of the manner in which ETFs operate.

Mutual funds must provide a copy of the fund's prospectus to shareholders after they purchase shares, but investors can— and should— request and read the mutual fund's prospectus before making an investment decision. There are two kinds of prospectuses: (1) the statutory prospectus; and (2) the summary prospectus. The statutory prospectus is the traditional, long-form prospectus with which most mutual fund investors are familiar. The summary prospectus, which is used by many mutual funds, is just a few pages long and contains key information about a mutual fund. The SEC specifies the kinds of information that must be included in mutual fund prospectuses and requires mutual funds to present the information in a standard format so that investors can readily compare different mutual funds.

The same key information required in the summary prospectus is required to be in the beginning of the statutory prospectus. It appears in the following standardized order: (1) investment objectives/goals; (2) fee table; (3) investments, risks, and performance; (4) management—investment advisers and portfolio managers; (5) purchase and sale of fund shares; (6) tax information; and (7) financial intermediary compensation. Investors can also find more detailed information in the statutory prospectus, including financial highlights information.

An ETF will also have a prospectus, and some ETFs may have a summary prospectus, both of which are subject to the same legal requirements as mutual fund prospectuses and summary prospectuses. While they may seem daunting at first, mutual fund and ETF prospectuses contain valuable information.

Office of the Comptroller of the Currency
Investment Performance Measurement and Analysis (2017)

The investment management industry is standardizing the presentation of investment performance and moving to disclose information fully in a fair, consistent, and understandable manner. A benefit of using a standardized method of calculating and reporting investment returns is that senior management can better monitor and evaluate each portfolio manager's performance. Standardized performance measures also enable portfolio managers to better compare their investment performance with that of external managers that use similar investment styles. Finally, standardized measurement and reporting enhances a client's ability to understand investment results and make comparisons between service providers.

The Association for Investment Management and Research (AIMR) promotes fair representation and full disclosure of investment performance for its members and the industry in general. AIMR has developed comprehensive performance presentation standards for its members that have become widely accepted and used by the industry. The standards, which include acceptable methods of calculating and reporting investment performance, provide an industry yardstick for evaluating fairness and accuracy in investment performance presentation. Some examples of questions that a performance measurement system should be able to answer are:

- What is the portfolio's total return and risk over a specified period, and did it meet or exceed the portfolio's needs and objectives?

- How does the return break down into capital gains, dividends, interest, currency fluctuations, etc.?

- To what extent does asset allocation, market timing, currency selection, industry sector, or individual asset selections explain performance?

- How does the portfolio's risk-adjusted returns compare with those of its benchmark?

- How does a portfolio manager's investment performance compare with that of a competing universe of managers?

- Is there evidence of exceptional expertise in a particular market or investment style?

- Have risk diversification objectives been achieved?

To measure investment performance, a firm periodically values a portfolio and calculates its rate of return over a specific time frame. Because performance measurement is based on transactional data, it is important that the data be accurate, reliable, and consistent. A huge amount of valuation and transaction information is synthesized into a few performance return measures. If performance measurements and risk assessments are to be useful, portfolios must be valued frequently and accurately.

A portfolio's performance can be attributed to many decisions, including the choice of instruments, markets, currencies, individual securities, and portfolio managers. Given this complexity, a detailed and frequent analysis of performance is prudent. Persons responsible for managing investment risk should periodically assess the performance of each account and portfolio manager. Evaluations of the portfolio manager should analyze the investment risks taken and should conclude whether he or she has managed these risks appropriately and professionally.

The investment management industry standard for calculating investment return is a **time-weighted, total return** measure. Time-weighted returns minimize the impact of external cash flows (over which the portfolio manager has little or no control) on the rate of return. For time periods longer than one year, the return is calculated as an annual return, or a compounded average annual return. Portfolio rates of return can be computed daily, monthly, quarterly, and annually and then compared with a portfolio's goals and objectives, which may include designated benchmarks.

A **benchmark** is the standard of comparison for investment performance analysis. It is a passive representation of the portfolio's investment strategy against which actual performance can be measured. The benchmark may be a passive market index, such as the S&P 500, a mean return of a universe of actively managed funds, or a customized portfolio of securities that closely resembles a portfolio manager's style or a client's normal portfolio strategy.

Investment risk and return measures should be analyzed to gain a true measure of relative portfolio performance. There are many risk measures used by portfolio managers and analysts. Risk-adjusted returns are used to measure the relative performance of investment portfolios and their managers. Risk-adjusted returns can also highlight investment performance that a portfolio manager achieves by incurring misunderstood, mispriced, unintended, or undisclosed risks. Risk-adjusted return measures also permit a more meaningful comparison of a portfolio manager's performance with that of an appropriate benchmark or a required rate of return.

Examples of risk-adjusted return measures are the Sharpe Ratio, the Treynor Measure, the Jensen Alpha, the Information Ratio, and the Sortino Ratio. [The note after this excerpt adds some details.] It is important that the risk-adjusted return measure used captures the appropriate performance information and relevant risks. With any risk-based return statistic, the portfolio manager must understand how it is calculated, what risk is captured, the time periods involved, and how the statistic is to be used.

Many investment management firms complete periodic **performance attribution analyses** on their portfolios. Risk managers evaluate the investment decisions that cause performance to deviate from established benchmarks. A performance attribution analysis facilitates two kinds of analysis by enabling managers to identify the separate components of return from active management and to measure the risks associated with accessing these return streams.

NOTE

1.   As the OCC excerpt notes, many techniques have been developed to measure risk-adjusted returns, including those named for researchers, such as Jensen, Sharpe, and Sortino. Such tools are premised on modern portfolio theory (MPT). Recall how it suggests that adding securities to a diversified portfolio of non-correlated securities reduces aggregate portfolio risk without reducing expected return.

For instance, the Sharpe ratio, developed by Nobel laureate William F. Sharpe, reflects a portfolio's performance relative to its riskiness. The Sharpe ratio for a portfolio is the portfolio's return less the risk-free rate, divided by the portfolio's standard deviation. As a baseline, a portfolio consisting entirely of risk-free securities has a Sharpe ratio of 0; the higher the Sharpe ratio, the more attractive the portfolio. In fact, the higher the Sharpe ratio, the more likely that a portfolio's performance is due to the manager's relative skill rather than to luck or fate.

2.   Alpha is another MPT-based tool to measure risk and performance of a fully diversified portfolio. It expresses performance relative to a broad market benchmark, such as the S&P 500, to show the degree to which the construction of the portfolio added value compared to simply buying the entire market index. In effect, alpha proxies the value added by the manager who assembled the portfolio. More loosely, the term is applied to consider the degree of outperformance of not only a portfolio but a company or stock relative to peers. For instance, an alpha of 1 means the subject outperformed the benchmark by 1% whereas an alpha of −1 means it underperformed by 1%.

Recall that beta is a measure of a security's volatility, and that a beta of 1 means it's as volatile as the market, while above 1 means it's more volatile than the market. Many investors might ideally seek high alphas and low betas—highly-skilled managers working with low-volatility securities. You might wonder whether investors really should seek such signals or would they be better off simply buying a passive index? Warren Buffett has trenchantly addressed this question, focusing on the substantial costs to investors that erode the value of professional stock picking.

Warren E. Buffett
How Your Money Finds Its Way to Wall Street
Letter to Berkshire Hathaway Shareholders (2005)

It's been an easy matter for owners of American equities to prosper over the years. Between December 31, 1899 and December 31, 1999, to give a really long-term example, the Dow rose from 66 to 11,497. (Guess what annual growth rate is required to produce this result; the surprising answer is at the end of this [excerpt].) This huge rise came about for a simple reason: Over the century American businesses did extraordinarily well and investors rode the wave of their prosperity. Businesses continue to do well. But now shareholders, through a series of self-inflicted wounds, are in a major way cutting the returns they will realize from their investments.

The explanation of how this is happening begins with a fundamental truth: With unimportant exceptions, such as bankruptcies in which some of a company's losses are borne by creditors, the most that owners in aggregate can earn between now and Judgment Day is what their businesses in aggregate earn. True, by buying and selling that is clever or lucky, investor A may take more than his share of the pie at the expense of investor B. And, yes, all investors feel richer when stocks soar. But an owner can exit only by having someone take his place. If one investor sells high, another must buy high. For owners as a whole, there is simply no magic—no shower of money from outer space—that will enable them to extract wealth from their companies beyond that created by the companies themselves.

Indeed, owners must earn less than their businesses earn because of "frictional" costs. And that's my point: These costs are now being incurred in amounts that will cause shareholders to earn far less than they historically have.

To understand how this toll has ballooned, imagine for a moment that all American corporations are, and always will be, owned by a single family. We'll call them the *Gotrocks*. After paying taxes on dividends, this family—generation after generation—becomes richer by the aggregate amount earned by its companies. Today [in 2005] that amount is about $700 billion annually. Naturally, the family spends some of these dollars. But the portion it saves steadily compounds for its benefit. In the Gotrocks household everyone grows wealthier at the same pace, and all is harmonious.

But let's now assume that a few fast-talking Helpers approach the family and persuade each of its members to try to outsmart his relatives by buying certain of their holdings and selling them certain others. The Helpers—for a fee, of course—obligingly agree to handle these transactions. The Gotrocks still own all of corporate America; the trades just rearrange who owns what. So the family's annual gain in wealth diminishes, equaling the earnings of American business minus commissions paid. The more that family members trade, the smaller their share of the pie and the larger the slice received by the Helpers. This fact is not lost upon these *broker-Helpers*: Activity is their friend and, in a wide variety of ways, they urge it on.

After a while, most of the family members realize that they are not doing so well at this new "beat-my-brother" game. Enter another set of Helpers. These newcomers explain to each member of the Gotrocks clan that by himself he'll never outsmart the rest of the family. The suggested cure: "Hire a manager—yes, us—and get the job done professionally." These *manager-Helpers* continue to use the broker-Helpers to execute trades; the managers may even increase their activity so as to permit the brokers to prosper still more. Overall, a bigger slice of the pie now goes to the two classes of Helpers.

The family's disappointment grows. Each of its members is now employing professionals. Yet overall, the group's finances have taken a turn for the worse. The solution? More help, of course.

It arrives in the form of financial planners and institutional consultants, who weigh in to advise the Gotrocks on selecting manager-Helpers. The befuddled family welcomes this assistance. By now its members know they can pick neither the right stocks nor the right stock-pickers. Why, one might ask, should they expect success in picking the right consultant? But this question does not occur to the Gotrocks, and the *consultant-Helpers* certainly don't suggest it to them.

The Gotrocks, now supporting three classes of expensive Helpers, find that their results get worse, and they sink into despair. But just as hope seems lost, a fourth group—we'll call them the *hyper-Helpers*—appears. These friendly folk explain to the Gotrocks that their unsatisfactory results are occurring because the existing Helpers—brokers, managers, consultants—are not sufficiently motivated and are simply going through the motions. "What," the new Helpers ask, "can you expect from such a bunch of zombies?"

The new arrivals offer a breathtakingly simple solution: Pay more money. Brimming with self-confidence, the hyper-Helpers assert that huge contingent payments—in addition to stiff fixed fees—are what each family member must fork over in order to really outmaneuver his relatives.

The more observant members of the family see that some of the hyper-Helpers are really just manager-Helpers wearing new uniforms, bearing sewn-on sexy names like HEDGE FUND or PRIVATE EQUITY. The new Helpers, however, assure the Gotrocks that this change of clothing is all-important, bestowing on its wearers magical powers similar to those acquired by mild-mannered Clark Kent when he changed into his Superman costume. Calmed by this explanation, the family decides to pay up.

And that's where we are today: A record portion of the earnings that would go in their entirety to owners—if they all just stayed in their rocking chairs—is now going to a swelling army of Helpers. Particularly expensive is the recent pandemic of profit arrangements under which Helpers receive large portions of the winnings when they are smart or lucky, and leave family members with all of the losses—and large fixed fees to boot—when the Helpers are dumb or unlucky (or occasionally crooked).

A sufficient number of arrangements like this—heads, the Helper takes much of the winnings; tails, the Gotrocks lose and pay dearly for the privilege of doing so—may make it more accurate to call the family the Hadrocks. Today, in fact, the family's frictional costs of all sorts may well amount to 20% of the earnings of American business. In other words, the burden of paying Helpers may cause American equity investors, overall, to earn only 80% or so of what they would earn if they just sat still and listened to no one.

Long ago, Sir Isaac Newton gave us three laws of motion, which were the work of genius. But Sir Isaac's talents didn't extend to investing: He lost a bundle in the South Sea Bubble, explaining later, "I can calculate the movement of the stars, but not the madness of men." If he had not been traumatized by this loss, Sir Isaac might well have gone on to discover the

Fourth Law of Motion: For investors as a whole, returns decrease as motion increases.

Here's the answer to the question posed at the beginning of this [excerpt]: To get very specific, the Dow increased from 65.73 to 11,497.12 in the 20th century, and that amounts to a gain of 5.3% compounded annually. (Investors would also have received dividends, of course.) To achieve an equal rate of gain in the 21st century, the Dow will have to rise by December 31, 2099 to—brace yourself—precisely 2,011,011.23. But I'm willing to settle for 2,000,000; six years into this century, the Dow has gained not at all.

Problem 12A

1.   Suppose J&J owns shares of common stock of MountainView Inc. (MVI) and this is the only common stock it owns (it sold its BIC shares years ago). The economy is "normal." Jack and Jill project total returns on the MVI shares as follows:

(i)   if the economy booms, 100;

(ii)   if the economy continues to be normal, 50; and

(iii) if we go into recession, 0.

J&J's economist reliably opines that in the relevant years ahead there is a 20% probability of a boom, a 60% probability of normal conditions and a 20% probability of a recession.

(a)   What is the expected return on MVI shares?

(b)   What is the standard deviation?

2.   To adjust its single-stock portfolio, J&J is considering adding shares of common stock of BIC (having second thoughts). Using the same forecasts for the states of the future economy set forth in Question 1, Jack and Jill project the total returns on the BIC shares as follows:

(i)   if the economy booms, 60;

(ii)   if the economy continues to be normal, 50; and

(iii) if we go into recession, 40.

(a)   What is the expected return on BIC shares?

(b)   What is the standard deviation?

3.   Following up on the foregoing Questions: Which stock is riskier, BIC or MVI, or can't you tell?

4.   Following up on the foregoing Questions: Suppose J&J combines an equal amount of BIC and MVI into a portfolio.

(a)   What is the portfolio's expected return?

(b)   What is the portfolio's standard deviation?

(c)   What do the foregoing results say about the correlation between MVI and BIC?

(d)   What do the foregoing results say about modern portfolio theory and why?

Problem 12B

The risk-free rate from ten-year Treasury bills is 5% and the expected return for the market is 12%. *Betas* have been determined for the following companies (either directly or by reference to a group of peer companies deemed sufficiently comparable to provide a reasonable basis for the conclusion). What is each company's equity discount rate using CAPM?

Company	Beta
BIC	0.8
J&J	1.1
Larry's Firm	1.25
MVI	1.5

Conceptual Questions 12

Under efficient market theory, the form of presenting accounting information does not matter (very much). Identical data can be put in the balance sheet, income statement, cash flow statement, footnotes, or MD&A and it will generate the same interpretation and result on price and thus return no matter where or how it was put—as long as it is disclosed somewhere. Does this sound right, intuitively? In addition, market price supposedly responds to cash flow effects of managerial decisions and policy, not to the effect on reported earnings per share. Companies should therefore never seek to manage earnings; investors see through it. An empirical challenge meets this theoretical point: managers do engage in "earnings management" or "income smoothing." Why? How does this matter?

PART IV

AUDITING

■ ■ ■

Introduction

For accounting data to be valuable, users must have justifiable confidence in its integrity. Forces that can jeopardize integrity include business innovation, evolution and complexity. These cannot be eliminated. The formal nature of accounting rules also creates a substantial zone of managerial discretion in financial reporting. The formal quality is difficult to avoid because it enables achieving desirable qualities of financial reporting such as comparability, consistency, and reliability.

The integrity of financial reporting can be promoted through internal control systems and by external auditor certifications. The public auditor's traditional role is to examine an entity's financial statements to ascertain whether they were prepared in accordance with GAAP and present fairly the entity's financial condition and results of operations. Such an attestation is designed to give financial statement users a credible basis for relying upon them in making investment decisions that determine capital allocation. Beginning in the mid-2000s, auditors also examine and opine on the effectiveness of internal control over financial reporting.

For investor confidence in auditor attestation to be justified, in turn, standards are necessary to assure auditor independence and integrity. This body of standards is called generally accepted auditing standards (GAAS). As with GAAP, many sources of authority constitute GAAS. Among these authorities are the SEC and the Public Company Accounting Oversight Board (PCAOB). A large dose of custom and practice also is included.

CHAPTER 13

AUDIT PRACTICE

■ ■ ■

The auditing profession is dominated by a few large firms noted in Chapter 1, but it is sprawling in size and its range of services. Standard treatments of the auditing profession distinguish between two broad types of services it renders. One is consulting, two-party arrangements exemplified by services done directly for clients such as business valuation, litigation support, computer-system design, actuarial, and tax.

The other type is assurance engagements. These are three-party arrangements offering veracity as to the quality of certain information. They include a range of matters, from verifying assertions a business makes about itself to consumers (such as testing products) to data a company makes about its financial reporting (such as "comfort letters" to underwriters of its securities and other services involving "agreed-upon procedures").

The family of attestation services includes audits, which in turn are typically distinguished into sub-categories, the most common being financial audits. A financial statement audit involves an independent auditor examining financial statements in the context of the evidence supporting them and expressing an opinion concerning whether they present fairly a company's condition and results in conformity with GAAP (or, in the case of companies or persons not required or opting to report under GAAP, in accordance with some other comprehensive basis of accounting, referred to as OCBOA, such as the cash basis system or a regulatory accounting regime).

Financial audit practice is governed by specific guidance usually referred to as generally accepted auditing standards (GAAS). It is geared toward stating an opinion as to the fair presentation of financial statements and their compliance with GAAP (or OCBOA). GAAS requires that an auditor be independent of those it audits (auditor independence is discussed in the next Chapter) and establishes a variety of recognized fieldwork standards governing audit practice introduced in this Chapter.

Understanding financial audit practice requires examining the ultimate opinion financial auditors give, introduced in Chapter 1. To give this opinion, auditors assess audit risk and examine the environment in which financial reporting is conducted, called the control environment and managed by a system of internal control.

347

After reviewing the audit report and audit risk, this Chapter introduces GAAS guidance relating to tests of controls designed to assess the necessary scope of substantive tests, and introduces these as well. It also summarizes the roles auditors play in reviewing a company's selection of accounting principles and making accounting estimates.

A. REASONABLE ASSURANCE

An auditor's opinion offers "reasonable assurance" as to the assertions covered. What this means is not entirely clear. Sources of difficulty include the relationship between GAAP and fair financial reporting and the inherent limits of auditing.

The Audit Report—"Presents Fairly" and GAAP.

The standard form of audit report expresses an opinion as to whether an examined set of financial statements *presents fairly* a company's financial position, results of operation, and cash flows, *in conformity with GAAP.* This formulation exposes a profound challenge to auditing. On its surface, the opinion cannot be given if either (a) the statements are in conformity with GAAP but do not present fairly or (b) they present fairly but not in conformity with GAAP.

The term presents fairly is not defined by law in the US or clearly in any accounting principles. This reticence reflects a sensibility familiar to the common law, of leaving to professional judgment the ultimate application of general rules to specific situations. Compliance with applicable accounting principles will presumptively but not invariably meet the standard. When they don't departures are necessary and they override literal compliance.

The meaning of "presents fairly" depends on what a system of financial reporting is designed to depict. Meeting the view may mean tracking assets, liabilities, equity, revenues and expenses using the objectives, principles, and purposes of accounting summarized in Chapter 1. The result of applying these exercises consistently should mirror external business activity—lumpy or smooth. The "presents fairly" concept entails adjustments when applying those conventions to particular events fogs the mirror.

US law generally rejects the view that compliance with GAAP satisfies the presents fairly standard, at least with respect to an accountant's exposure to liability for failing to meet it. The American classic is Judge Henry Friendly's decision in *United States v. Simon,* 425 F.2d 796, 805–06 (2d Cir. 1969), *cert. denied,* 397 U.S. 1006 (1970). It affirmed a trial court's refusal to give a defendant-accountant's proposed jury instruction that he could be found guilty of accounting fraud only if, under GAAP, the financial statements as a whole did not present fairly the company's financial condition (and then only if any departure from GAAP involved willful disregard and the accountant knew the financials were false and held an intent to deceive).

Rejecting this proposed instruction, Judge Friendly instead defined the issue as whether the financial statements, taken as a whole, present fairly the company's financial condition and results. If they do not, then the issue is whether the accountant acted in good faith. Proving compliance with GAAP evidences good faith, but is not conclusive.

The SEC certification requirements implementing Sarbanes-Oxley restated this conception of "presents fairly" and its relationship to compliance with GAAP. The regulations require certification that "the overall financial disclosure fairly presents, in all material respects, the company's financial condition, results of operations and cash flows." The SEC clarified that the certification is not limited to an attestation that the financial statements accord with GAAP, emphasizing instead the broader requirement of "overall material accuracy and completeness."

The SEC cited Judge Friendly's classic opinion in *United States v. Simon*, cautioning that "Presenting financial information in conformity with generally accepted accounting principles may not necessarily satisfy obligations under the antifraud provisions of the federal securities laws." *See* Securities and Exchange Commission, Certification of Disclosure in Companies' Quarterly and Annual Reports, Release No. 33–8124 (Aug. 28, 2002). The SEC explained that a "fair presentation" is not about results alone but also about:

> the selection of appropriate accounting policies, proper application of appropriate accounting policies, disclosure of financial information that is informative and reasonably reflects the underlying transactions and events and the inclusion of any additional disclosure necessary to provide investors with a materially accurate and complete picture of an issuer's financial condition, results of operations and cash flows.

At least prior to this SEC pronouncement made after Sarbanes-Oxley was enacted, the practice norm held that compliance with GAAP is both necessary and sufficient. In a different context, an SEC study reinforces this view. The study, required by the Sarbanes-Oxley Act, assessed debate concerning a rules-based or principles-based accounting system (recall Conceptual Questions, Chapter 6). Finding that existing GAAP is a mixture of these and favoring a similar blend which it called an objectives-based system, the study indicated that under such a system there should be very limited need ever to indulge a GAAP override. That is, following an objectives-based approach should result in a fair presentation without need for adjustments after GAAP-conforming financial statements are prepared.

Audit Risk—Confidence and Evidence.

All attestation engagements are designed to provide reasonable assurance as to covered assertions. None provides absolute assurance. In other words, *audit risk* cannot be eliminated. The best an audit practitioner can do is to hold risk to a relatively-low but statistically-acceptable level. Auditors divide audit risk into various classifications.

At the broadest level, *attestation risk* is "the probability that an auditor may unknowingly fail to modify a written conclusion about an assertion that is materially misstated." More focused is the definition of audit risk when applied to a financial audit: "the probability that an auditor may unknowingly fail to modify an opinion on financial statements that are materially misstated." Within each category, practitioners distinguish between three types of risk:

- *Inherent risk* is the susceptibility of an assertion (such as an account balance) to error that could be material, assuming there are no related internal controls.

- *Control risk* is the likelihood that error could occur and not be prevented or detected by internal controls. GAAS requires an auditor to understand an organization's internal controls and to use that understanding in estimating control risk and planning the audit.

- *Detection risk* is the likelihood that error could occur and not be detected by the auditor's procedures.

Planning an audit requires a preliminary estimate of materiality. The standard of materiality used in the auditing profession bears a similarity to the standards used in both securities law and financial accounting. All treat as material matters that a reasonable person would consider important in making a decision based on some information set.

The auditing profession publishes decision aids relating audit risk to materiality and implied requisite audit effort. It also invokes various rules of thumb. The commonest quantitative rule of thumb in financial auditing relates to an item's effect on net income. Effects less than 5% are seen as unlikely to be material and those greater than 10% are seen as likely to be material. This rule of thumb is not taken to reveal bright lines, however, and instead is seen simply as a starting point for more textured, qualitative analysis.

Throughout all audits, auditors are required to assemble *sufficient competent evidential matter* to justify their conclusions. Evidential matter consists of underlying accounting data, related accounting manuals and worksheets supporting computations, and corroborating material such as client memoranda, board minutes and other information gathered by observation, inspection and confirmation. Sufficiency is determined by professional judgment given the nature, extent, and timing of substantive tests as well as the size and complexity of the company and its business. Evidential matter is competent when it is both valid and relevant.

Auditors seal the potential gaps in assembling requisite knowledge by adopting the fundamental auditing standard of *professional skepticism.* Auditors approach the assessment and investigation process by probing. They ask questions of managers and employees, seek verification from multiple sources, and willingly engage in a second-guessing of managerial judgments on a variety of matters. The skepticism applies to both processes and outputs. It all begins with the auditor's assessment of a company's internal control over financial reporting.

B. INTERNAL CONTROL

Internal controls are processes designed to provide reasonable assurance that a company achieves its objectives. These include not only controls relating to financial reporting, but also to meeting operational and organizational goals and complying with law and regulation. In a financial audit, auditors are principally concerned with control over financial reporting, though inevitably other controls affect this area. In fact, sometimes auditors are engaged specifically to assess and opine on assertions relating to controls in other areas as well.

Internal control over financial reporting consists of interrelated components. These include communication flows for information, risk assessment, established mechanisms, and monitoring. These components together create and build upon a broader control environment. The environment, taken as a whole, defines the structure and level of discipline within the control system.

Auditors examine the control environment by evaluating factors such as manifested ethical values articulated in codes of conduct, policy statements and procedures to discipline transgression. They also consider the role played by the board of directors and its audit committee in the control process, including their interaction with accounting staff and outside auditors and overall monitoring capabilities. Assessment includes examination of business complexity; organizational structure; authority identification and delegation; hiring, training, promotion and dismissal practices; and all similar related factors.

Auditors examine the company's risk assessment practices concerning financial reporting by observing processes designed to assure transactions are recorded and that records cannot be fabricated when no transaction occurs. This examination considers various events that could enhance such risks. Among these are changes in the company's operating environment from competition, deregulation, or technological innovation; rapid rates of growth; high employee turnover; corporate restructurings; or changes in accounting principles or estimates.

Internal controls are classified as general or specific. *General controls* include those that regulate data processing centers, computer software and security over access to a company's records or assets. *Specific controls* are those geared to processing particular transactions and documents, such as invoices, checks, purchase orders and other paperwork, and assuring these are properly preserved in the company's information storage systems (such as computer memory or magnetic tape).

Internal controls are also classified as physical or procedural. Physical controls include *access security codes* and devices intended to prevent unauthorized persons from accessing data and records as well as the periodic counting of cash, inventory or other assets and comparing results with reported quantities. Procedural controls include *duty-segregation protocols* designed to reduce opportunities for a single person or small group to be in a position both to engineer and sustain improper recordkeeping. Different people are assigned responsibility for authorizing transactions, classifying and recording them, verifying them, and aggregating resulting data.

Tests of Controls.

In the preliminary stage of an engagement, auditors design tests of controls. These are audit procedures to assess the efficacy of internal controls to prevent or detect material misstatements. Tests of controls are typically performed using statistical sampling techniques. These enable auditors to examine less than 100% of the items in a population by relying upon probability theory. Despite probability theory, drawing conclusions about a total population by using samples from it expose the conclusions to the risk that a sample may not be representative of a population. This is called *sampling risk.*

While sampling risk can be reduced by increasing sample size, increased sample size carries additional costs. When designing a sampling plan, the auditor must determine what sampling risk she is willing to tolerate. In tests of controls, the ultimate risk is that the auditor may assess control risk as too low (or too high), and therefore design an audit plan with substantive testing that is too narrow (or unduly expansive).

Statistical Sampling.

In a test of controls, auditors use statistical sampling techniques. A standard method is known as an *attributes sampling technique.* This is designed to detect and measure the rate of deviations in a population. The following discussion first describes such statistical sampling techniques and then provides an illustration.

Preliminary Steps.

The first few steps in conducting an attributes sampling test of internal controls involve preliminaries. First, the test objective is determined (say a duty-segregation control that one person prepares an invoice and another person verifies its accuracy). Second, what constitutes a deviation is stated (say a verifier's failure to initial an invoice as verified). Third, the population is defined by time, item, and completeness (say all invoices for one year). Fourth, the selection technique is identified (say according to a random number generator or picking every *nth* item in the population).

Determining Minimum Sample Size.

The middle steps relate to determining the minimum sample size. It is determined according to three variables:

(1) an acceptable level *of risk that the conclusions will set the level of control risk too low* (this level is typically about 5% or 10%, meaning confidence levels of 95% or 90%);

(2) a *tolerable rate of deviation occurrence* (this level depends on professional judgment geared to how much reliance is placed on the control, and might range from deviation tolerance of 2% when substantial reliance is invested to 20% when little reliance is invested); and

(3) an *expected population deviation rate* (based on such tools as a preliminary small sample or results from prior-period applications of the test).

After finding the minimum sample size, convention is to round the minimum figure up, if necessary, to the next interval ending in 0 or 5 (rounding, say, 149 to 150; 124 to 125; 93 to 95 or 100; 36 to 40; and so on).

Auditors use tables that yield minimum sample sizes given these three inputs, as shown in the illustration that follows. Higher acceptable control risk and tolerable deviation rates imply smaller minimum sample sizes (lower thresholds imply larger minimum sample sizes); lower expected population deviation rates imply larger minimum sample sizes (higher expected rates imply smaller minimum sample sizes).

Population size has little effect on minimum sample size, at least for large populations. For example, assume an auditor settles upon a 5% risk that control risk is set too low, a 5% tolerable rate of deviation occurrence and a 1% expected population deviation rate. For the following total population sizes, the minimum sample size is indicated:

Total Population Size	Minimum Sample Size
50	45
100	64
500	87
1,000	90
2,000	92
5,000	93
100,000	93

Final Steps.

Once sample size is determined for a statistical test of controls, the final steps involve selecting the sample, running the test, and interpreting results. This entails calculating the *sample deviation rate*, done by dividing the number of observed deviations by the sample size. If you see 2 deviations from a sample size of 100, for example, the sample deviation rate is 2%.

Next, determine the *upper occurrence limit*, a way to compensate for sampling risk. This entails adding to the sample deviation rate an additional amount to reflect that the population likely contains a greater deviation rate than the sample. The additional amount is determined using tables of the kind illustrated below. As an example, if you found 2 deviations from a sample size of 100, and set an acceptable risk of assessing control risk too low of 10%, the tables will tell you that the upper occurrence limit is 5.3%. (*See* Table 13-4.) On these data, that implies the additional amount added to compensate for sampling risk is 3.3% (that is, 5.3%–2%). The upshot is that the auditor would be 90% confident that the true population deviation rate is 5.3% or less.

These final steps also require assessing whether observed deviations are due to inadvertent errors or deliberate volition. This facilitates the final step: results are interpreted according to whether the control can be relied upon. A control can be relied upon if the upper occurrence limit is below the tolerable rate and all deviations are due to error rather than volition; it should not be relied upon if the upper occurrence limit exceeds the tolerable rate; and it cannot be relied upon if the sample deviation rate is greater than the tolerable rate.

Controls that can be relied upon are deemed *effective* and enable the auditor to restrict the scope of substantive testing; those that should not or cannot be relied upon are deemed *ineffective* and require the auditor either to find and test compensating controls that are effective or expand the scope of substantive testing.

Illustration.

Suppose an auditor needs to test controls governing a company's credit department. The control calls for one person to prepare invoices and another to verify their accuracy. Verification is confirmed by the verifier initialing invoices she has verified. The auditor determines the following:

1.   The *deviation condition* is the absence of the verifier's initials on any invoice.

2.   The *population* is all invoices during the current fiscal year (of which there are a total, say, of 500, numbered sequentially from 20,001 to 20,500).

3.   Sampling will be performed using *a random number generator*.

4.   A *5% risk of assessing control risk as too low* will be used. (The standard alternative to this assumption is to use a *10% risk of assessing control risk as too low*. The former yields a confidence level of 95% and the latter a confidence level of 90%, meaning the 5% risk rate is more conservative than the 10% risk rate. Which to choose depends on professional judgment based on an assessment of the overall audit environment and engagement.)

5.   The *tolerable deviation rate*, based on judgment and past experience, is 8%.

6.   The *expected population deviation rate*, also based on judgment and past experience, is 4%.

Using these parameters, and aids such as appear in Tables 13-1 through 13-4, the auditor arrives at the following implementation conclusions. (Note that Tables 13-1 and 13-3 govern when the auditor settles upon a 5% risk of assessing control risk as too low and Tables 13-2 and 13-4 govern when the auditor settles upon a 10% risk of assessing control risk as too low.)

- The *minimum sample size* is 146. This appears by reference to Table 13-1. The auditor goes down the left column to the 4% expected population deviation rate and across the top rows to the 8% tolerable deviation rate and finds the resulting cell indicating a minimum sample size of 146. The auditor rounds this figure to 150. (Notice that with a 10% risk of assessing control as too low Table 13-2 applies and indicates a minimum sample size of 98, which the auditor would round to 100.)

- The auditor uses a computer-generated random number program to produce a total of 150 randomly-generated numbers from within the range of 20,001 to 20,500, the invoice numbers of the population. These are the invoice numbers selected as the sample for inspection.

After inspecting the indicated invoices by number, suppose the auditor finds that 6 invoices are missing the verifier's initials. This implies the following conclusions.

A.   The *sample deviation rate* is 6/150 or 4%. (Notice that using a 10% risk of assessing control as too low, the sample deviation rate on these assumptions would be 6/100 or 6%, though as explained below and should be intuitive if a sample of 150 yields 6 observed deviations then a sample of 100 from the same population would probably yield a lesser number of observed deviations such as 4 or 5).

B.   The *upper occurrence limit* is 7.8%. This is determined by reference to Table 13-3. The auditor goes down the left column to the 150-sample size and across the top rows to the 6 actual number of occurrences found to locate the cell indicating an upper occurrence limit of 7.8%. (Notice that with a 10% risk of assessing control as too low Table 13-4 applies; given a sample size of 100 and sticking with the somewhat unrealistic assumption of 6 observed deviations, it indicates an upper occurrence limit of 10.3%.)

C.   The upper occurrence limit of 7.8% is less than the tolerable rate of 8%. Accordingly, the auditor concludes that this control is sufficiently reliable. Put formally, she can conclude with 95% confidence that the true population deviation rate is less than or equal to 7.8%. Based on the procedures performed, therefore, the tolerable rate of deviation exceeds the upper occurrence limit so controls over this aspect of the credit department are considered effective in preventing or detecting misstatements. Control risk for assertions relating to invoicing can be set below the maximum level.

Notice that with a 10% risk of assessing control as too low, the opposite conclusion would be reached. Under that threshold, the upper occurrence limit of 10.3% exceeds the tolerable rate of 8%. Accordingly, the auditor would conclude that this control is not reliable. In this case, she would need either to find and test compensating controls that are effective or conduct enhanced substantive testing concerning invoices to attest to assertions made on the basis of them (such as accounts receivable balances).

As anticipated above, however, it is unlikely that the same number of observed deviations would occur in a sample of 100 versus a sample of 150 from the same population. Given that there were 6 observed deviations in the 150-sample size, you would expect more like 4 in the 100-sample size. If so, then the upper occurrence limit would be 7.9%, within the tolerable rate of 8%. (If you observed 5 deviations, the upper occurrence limit would be 9.1%, and the control would be declared ineffective.)

Table 13-1: Minimum Sample Sizes for Tests of Controls @ 5%

		Tolerable Deviation Rates								
		2%	3%	4%	5%	6%	7%	8%	9%	10%
	0%	149	99	74	59	49	42	36	32	29
	0.5%		157	117	93	78	66	58	51	46
	1.0%			156	93	78	66	58	51	46
	1.5%			192	124	103	66	58	51	46
Expected	2.0%				181	127	88	77	68	46
Population	2.5%					150	109	77	68	61
Rate	3.0%					195	148	95	84	61
Deviation	4.0%							146	100	89
	5.0%								158	116
	6.0%									179

Table 13-1 shows, for large populations, minimum sample sizes, for a 5% risk of assessing control risk as too low, under various parameters for the other inputs: expected population deviation rate (the left-hand column) and tolerable deviation rates (across the top). Table 13-2 does the same for a 10% risk of assessing control risk as too low.

Table 13-2: Minimum Sample Sizes for Tests of Controls @ 10%

		Tolerable Deviation Rates								
		2%	3%	4%	5%	6%	7%	8%	9%	10%
	0%	114	76	57	45	38	32	28	25	22
	0.5%	194	129	96	77	64	55	48	42	38
	1.0%		176	96	77	64	55	48	42	38
	1.5%			132	105	64	55	48	42	38
Expected	2.0%			198	132	88	75	48	42	38
Population	2.5%				158	110	75	65	58	38
Rate	3.0%					132	94	65	58	52
Deviation	4.0%						149	98	73	65
	5.0%							160	115	78
	6.0%								182	116

In Tables 13-1 and 13-2, the areas left blank indicate circumstances in which the sample size would be too large to be cost-effective under the constraints imposed.

Table 13-3: Sample Evaluation Upper Occurrence Limit @ 5%

		Actual Number of Occurrences Found								
		0	1	2	3	4	5	6	7	8
	25	11.3	17.6							
	30	9.5	14.9	19.5						
	35	8.2	12.9	16.9						
	40	7.2	11.3	14.9	18.3					
Sample Size	45	6.4	10.1	13.3	16.3	19.2				
	50	5.8	9.1	12.1	14.8	17.4	19.9			
	75	3.9	6.2	8.2	10.0	11.8	13.5	15.2	16.9	18.4
	100	3.0	4.7	6.2	7.6	8.9	10.2	11.5	12.7	14.0
	125	2.4	3.7	4.9	6.1	7.2	8.2	9.3	10.3	11.3
	150	2.0	3.1	4.1	5.1	6.0	6.9	7.8	8.6	9.4
	200	1.5	2.3	3.1	3.8	4.5	5.2	5.8	6.5	7.1

Table 13-3 shows, for large populations, the upper occurrence limit *as percentages*, for a 5% risk of assessing control risk as too low, under various parameters for the other inputs: sample size (the left-hand column) and actual number of occurrences found (across the top). Table 13-4 does the same for a 10% risk of assessing control risk as too low.

Table 13-4: Sample Evaluation Upper Occurrence Limit @ 10%									
	Actual Number of Occurrences Found								
	0	1	2	3	4	5	6	7	8
20	10.9	18.1							
25	8.8	14.7	19.9						
30	7.4	12.4	16.8						
35	6.4	10.7	14.5	18.1					
Sample 40	5.6	9.4	12.8	16.0					
Size 50	4.6	7.6	10.3	12.9	15.5	17.8			
70	3.3	5.5	7.5	9.3	11.1	12.9	14.6	16.3	17.9
100	2.3	3.9	5.3	6.6	7.9	9.1	10.3	11.5	12.7
120	2.0	3.3	4.4	5.5	6.6	7.6	8.7	9.7	10.7
160	1.4	2.4	3.3	4.1	4.9	5.7	6.5	7.2	8.0
200	1.2	2.0	2.7	3.4	4.0	4.6	5.3	5.9	6.5

In Tables 13-3 and 13-4, the areas left blank indicate circumstances in which the figures would be greater than 20%.

Auditing Control.

For SEC registrants, the Sarbanes-Oxley Act requires managers to certify the effectiveness of a company's internal control and auditors to express an opinion on the effectiveness of such internal control. Standards for this auditing work are promulgated by the Public Company Accounting Oversight Board (PCAOB). In turn, PCAOB references other recognized authorities that provide guidance on internal control over financial reporting and audits of such internal control. A leading reference was produced in the mid-1980s by the so-called Committee of Sponsoring Organizations of the Treadway Commission (COSO). The Treadway Commission was formally known as the National Commission on Fraudulent Financial Reporting and was sponsored by a committee of organizations: the AICPA, the American Accounting Association, the Financial Executives Institute, the Institute of Internal Auditors, and the National Association of Accountants.

PCAOB prescribes the standard form of auditor report, presented in Chapter 1, expressing auditor opinions on both financial statements and internal control over financial reporting. Look back at Chapter 1 and read the form of auditor report printed there. Notice it expresses an auditor's opinion that the company maintained effective internal control over financial reporting. An auditor may instead find internal control ineffective due to *deficiencies*. These refer to controls that do not enable preventing or detecting misstatements on a timely basis. Auditors must report any *significant deficiency* to management during the audit. A combination of deficiencies that create a *reasonable possibility* that material misstatements will not be prevented or detected on a timely basis amount to a material weakness in internal control over financial reporting. A material weakness requires the auditor to give an adverse opinion on control effectiveness.

C. SUBSTANTIVE TESTS

The auditor's goal in understanding and testing the control environment is to determine how it affects financial statement assertions. This understanding enables the auditor to plan the audit's substantive tests of financial statement assertions. Substantive tests are audit procedures designed to detect material misstatements or to identify assertions likely to contain material misstatements. They are of two types: (1) *tests of detail* are designed to detect material misstatements in accounts and (2) *analytical procedures* are evaluations of relevant trends, baselines or forecasts.

Tests of Detail.

Tests of detail can be distinguished between tests of transactions and tests of account balances. *Tests of transactions* involve searching for transactions that are not recorded or recorded transactions that did not occur. In each case, the tests involve relating underlying documents (such as invoices) to bookkeeping records and accounting reports (such as accounts receivable journal entries and T-account balances). Auditors trace underlying documents forward to assure the transactions they document are recorded; they work backwards from bookkeeping records and accounting reports to confirm that requisite documentation supports their existence or occurrence.

Tests of account balances involve exercising professional judgment to select particular accounts for scrutiny. Examples are accounts involving estimation and valuation. These include accounts relating to inventory balances, allowance for doubtful accounts, depreciation judgments, repairs and maintenance of fixed assets, and compensation expense.

Tests of account balances use statistical sampling akin to those discussed above concerning tests of controls. Additional testing techniques are often employed as well. One technique is *variables sampling* (as opposed to the attributes sampling employed for tests of controls). This means selecting a sample of items and extrapolating from it to determine whether an account balance appears to be fairly stated.

Substantive testing involves a variety of other steps, including examining underlying documentation, conducting physical inspections of property, counting inventory, interviewing company personnel, and reading minutes of an entity's board of directors.

Auditors design substantive tests for various areas of an entity's business. Convention classifies these areas into *cycles*, including:

- <u>revenue/receipt cycle</u>, concerning sales, cash, accounts receivable, and revenue recognition;

- <u>expenditure/disbursement cycle</u>, concerning purchases, cash, accounts payable, and accrued liabilities;

- <u>conversion cycle</u>, concerning prepaid expenses, inventory, and fixed assets; and

- <u>financing cycle</u>, concerning investments, debt, equity, and financial instruments.

In substantive testing of account balances across these cycles, auditors develop an *audit work program* tailored for each account to be scrutinized. GAAS requires auditors to prepare written audit work programs and to base their audit on them. They constitute a detailed listing of all procedures to be performed during the audit.

All steps throughout the audit engagement are documented in writing or on tape or film. The documentation is collectively referred to as *work papers*. They are the property of the auditor but may be subject to review and examination by regulatory authorities and susceptible to discovery in litigation.

Audit work programs for substantive testing: (1) identify the goal (such as determining whether account balances are fairly stated, but also whether requisite footnote disclosure is made); (2) state an understanding of relevant GAAP; and (3) identify required procedures involved in the applicable sampling technique and procedures such as examining documents or conducting physical inspections.

Analytical Procedures.

Auditors perform analytical procedures to test the fairness of asserted account balances. Examples of such procedures are variations on the ratio analyses discussed in Chapter 8 and parts of Chapter 9. Auditors also apply a more advanced and sophisticated set of ratios and other analytics discussed here. These tools help the auditor determine what areas require particular attention and aid in assessing whether account balances are fairly stated.

In general, the auditor examines percentage changes in line items from year to year to uncover any inconsistencies. For example, suppose entertainment expense rose from 4% of sales to 20% of sales from one year to the next. The auditor will be alert to determine reasons for this change, particularly whether it was due to sound business factors, tax law effects, or simply managerial efforts to use the company as a piggy bank to fund personal fun.

Also generally, auditors conduct ratio analytics to ascertain a company's level of *accounting risk*. Companies known for rapid earnings growth or otherwise capturing the imagination of the investment community often pose greater accounting risk than more stable or lower-profile companies.

Auditors develop an understanding of a company's industry and place the company within that context. Industry information compiled by firms such as Dun and Bradstreet and Robert Morris aid the analysis. Such firms publish more than a dozen ratios apiece on several hundred lines of business.

Asset Quality. The proper recording of assets directly relates to the eventual proper recording of earnings. *Asset quality* refers to the relationship between assets and their eventual realization into revenue. There can be a greater or lesser likelihood that particular assets will eventually drive revenue. Appraising asset quality therefore calls for assessing *asset risk* and classifying assets according to their relative risk. In general, asset quality follows the customary listing of assets on a balance sheet so that the following items are listed in order of asset quality: cash, accounts receivable, inventory, investments, fixed assets, and goodwill. Relationships auditors measure include the ratio of high-risk assets to total assets and of high-risk assets to sales. High figures indicate high asset realization risk, meaning potentially weaker future earnings.

Inventory. Inventory realization risk varies with product type. Inventory realization risk is generally lower with standardized goods, staples, and necessities such as consumer products like soap, toothpaste and peanut butter. It is generally higher with specialized items such as precision equipment, luxury merchandise such as precious gems and perishable goods such as dairy products.

Inventory realization risk can also be inferred from inventory turnover rates. Low rates compared to industry averages may indicate overstocking, product obsolescence, or marketing or product challenges. Higher rates may indicate insufficient inventory production or stocking, pointing to potential loss in sales.

Fixed Assets. Fixed assets require maintenance and repair. Depreciation expense is a proxy for the probable annual required reinvestment; accumulated depreciation is functionally a cumulative proxy. The proxy is imperfect, however, given GAAP's historical cost principle. Auditors examine the degree to which reinvestment is actually made. If such capital expenditures are not undertaken, degraded assets can threaten future productivity and hence earnings. When degraded assets are not written down in carrying value, future earnings will be overstated.

To address these issues, auditors seek to determine the age and condition of a company's major fixed assets and to ascertain the cost to repair or replace them. They assess the degree to which depreciation expense and accumulated depreciation are, in fact, good proxies for probable required reinvestment.

Auditors consider the reasonableness of depreciation assumptions. The goal is to implement the matching principle, to realistically estimate useful lives, salvage value, and an appropriate schedule (straight line or an accelerated method for example). Auditors examine the trend in depreciation expense as a percentage of both fixed assets and net sales. Declining trends suggest inadequate depreciation expense. The relationship between total depreciation expense and total capital expenditures can also reveal the reasonableness of depreciation assumptions.

Auditors examine how assumptions made for newly-acquired fixed assets compare to those made for older ones. Moving from accelerated methods to straight-line methods, for example, results in higher reported earnings in a fixed asset's early years (and in its later years the reverse effect occurs). But if not justified by realistic assessments of required reinvestment this undermines the quality of reported earnings.

Auditors examine trends in the acquisition of fixed assets to total gross assets (*i.e.*, not net of accumulated depreciation). These trends are particularly important for companies reliant on assets that become obsolete rapidly, as with many high-tech companies. Declining trends indicate failure to replace requisite infrastructure and foretell future declines in productivity.

Receivables. Relative risk realization of accounts receivable varies. High-risk receivables include those generated in politically unstable foreign countries and those due from customers experiencing financial difficulties. Receivables are higher risk when originated by a company with few rather than many customers or by companies selling principally to consumers rather than to other businesses (consumers enjoy consumer protection laws and generally face weaker reputation constraints compared to businesses).

Auditors watch for extraordinary changes in the level of accounts receivable. Large year-to-year increases may indicate increased collection risk. The company may be selling to higher-risk customers or offering more generous credit terms. Closer attention to trends in the relationship between accounts receivable to total assets and to total sales is warranted.

Also requiring greater attention are the ratios of bad debts to accounts receivable and bad debts to sales. Red flags include significant accounts receivable growth in a year's last quarter and/or substantial levels of customer returns of merchandise bought on credit in a year's first quarter.

Investments. Realization risk of investments in securities can be assessed by examining the trend in the relationship between the earnings they generate and their carrying value. Higher realization risk exists when this trend is falling, since the value of investments is in important part a function of the earnings they generate.

The range of investments held also bears on realization risk. Diversification of investments can reduce the risk associated with each individual investment, as described in Chapter 12. Auditors consider the level of a company's investment diversification to assess realization risk using tools such as correlation coefficients and standard deviations as discussed in that Chapter.

Other Assets. Asset quality can be examined line-by-line. Even cash can be examined. What is the ratio of sales to cash? A high ratio of sales to cash may indicate cash shortage problems on the horizon; a low ratio of sales to cash may indicate excess cash being hoarded. Similar examination is conducted concerning all other asset classes. Auditors investigate the level of intangible assets and the way improvements to leaseholds are handled. They review managerial judgments concerning whether acquired goodwill has been impaired in any given year. This examination typically involves a valuation of the acquired business using the sorts of techniques considered in Part III.

Liability Quality. Auditors apply similar professional skepticism to the liability side of the balance sheet. When liabilities are understated, net income is overstated. Auditors consider trends in the relationship between reported liabilities, both current and total, to baselines such as total owners' equity and/or sales. They consider whether liabilities are patient or pressing—that is, whether they could be postponed or modified if necessary or whether they must be paid when due without excuse.

Expenses. Auditors assess the levels of and changes in various categories of discretionary spending. Examples include advertising, repairs and maintenance, and research & development. Pulling back on such expenses can starve a company of needed operational sustenance. It is a quite difficult area for auditors to deploy their professional skepticism, however, for reasonable matters of corporate policy and strategy may justify substantial changes in these areas. Touchstones are the company's historical levels and changes in these items. A baseline year may be selected and prior and subsequent years compared to the baseline. Significant vacillation may indicate a company engaged in management of earnings. Auditors also examine the nature and level of deferred charges.

Particular attention is paid to the extent to which a company may try to capitalize costs that in previous periods they had treated as expenses.

Liquidity and Solvency. Auditors are particularly interested in ascertaining whether an entity is both liquid and solvent. In general, liquidity refers to the ability to meet short-term obligations as they come due and solvency to the ability to meet long-term obligations. These are of particular interest to auditors because one of their principal concerns is determining that a company is viable as a going concern. The foregoing tools, as well as the ratios presented in Chapter 8, aid in assessing both liquidity and solvency. Auditors may apply additional tests as well.

To address liquidity, auditors may use an analytical procedure to determine the approximate number of days it would take for a company's current assets to be turned into cash. The method takes the results of inventory and accounts receivable turnover calculations concerning the average number of days these are outstanding before becoming cash. It multiplies these results by their respective balances and adds the cash balance. The total compared to the balances indicates the number of days it takes for current assets to turn into cash.

For example, suppose a company has $50,000 in Cash, $200,000 in Accounts Receivable and $300,000 in Inventory, and that Accounts Receivable turn over in 25 days and Inventory in 40 days. The *liquidity index* would be calculated as follows:

	Amount		**Days**	**Total**
Cash	50,000		—	50,000
A/R	200,000	x	25	5,000,000
Inventory	300,000	x	40	12,000,000
	550,000			17,050,000

$$\text{Index} = \frac{17{,}050{,}000}{550{,}000} = 31 \text{ days}$$

Solvency can be assessed using ratios considered in Chapter 8 such as the debt-to-equity ratio and the cash-flow ratios considered in Chapter 9 assist. Auditors may supplement these tools with a more integrated method called the Z-score. It is calculated as follows.

$$= \left(\frac{WC}{TA}\right)x1.2 + \left(\frac{RE}{TA}\right)x1.4 + \left(\frac{OI}{TA}\right)x3.3 + \left(\frac{S}{TA}\right)x1.1 + \left(\frac{MVE}{TD}\right)x.6$$

where:

TA = Total Assets

WC = Working Capital

RE = Retained Earnings

OI = Operating Income

S = Sales

MVE = Market value of equity (including common and preferred stock)

TD = Total Debt

The Z-score lays out as follows, with lower scores signifying greater probability of short-term insolvency:

3 +	insolvency not likely
2.8 to 2.9	insolvency possible
1.8 to 2.7	insolvency highly probable
below 1.8	insolvency very highly probable

D. CONCLUDING AN AUDIT

Preceding Chapters show that many accounting contexts require managers to choose among accounting policies and to make estimates of various accounting quantities. Auditors review the policy choices and estimations as part of their work to enable them to conclude an audit by giving an opinion as to whether a set of financial statements accord with GAAP (or OCBOA when applicable) and present fairly a company's condition and results. Also as part of concluding an audit, auditors obtain from management a variety of representations concerning information provided to the auditor during the audit.

Policies and Estimates.

Conservatism is of overarching importance in selecting accounting policies and making accounting estimates. Conservatively determined net income is of higher quality than liberally determined net income. Auditors compare a company's judgments with those of its industry peers. The auditing profession, and individual auditing firms, regularly publish guidelines of recommended policies for particular industries in particular years.

Areas of focus concern revenue recognition timing and concerning deferral practices. The issue is the extent to which the policies and estimates are faithful to economic reality. Thus revenue should be recognized only when goods have been ordered by customers, shipped to them, and the customer sent an invoice. Costs should be reflected as expenses when incurred, not deferred to future periods by capitalizing them. The artificial shifting of revenues and costs to different periods distorts reported earnings.

Another area of concern is changes in accounting policies. When authoritative accounting principles are formally amended by standard-setters, companies must follow the guidance and make requisite changes in accounting policies. But companies may choose to change accounting policies for other reasons. This would be justified when circumstances have developed sufficiently to warrant the change. But they are not always justified. Auditors test the basis upon which managers make changes in accounting policies to determine whether the change is justified or instead seems to be an opportunistic effort to achieve desired levels of reported amounts.

Estimates are necessary in a wide variety of accounting contexts. These include relative obsolescence of inventory, estimates of useful lives and salvage value on fixed assets, allowance for doubtful accounts receivable and estimates of warranty claims, goodwill valuation, and accounting for stock options and various retiree benefits.

Auditors tend to focus on reviewing those areas where judgments are most subjective. Methods for assessing estimates with respect to bad debt and warranty reserves include comparing prior-period estimates with actual prior-period results. For estimates concerning fixed assets, methods include assessing prior-period gains or losses on the disposition of fixed assets. Substantial gains or losses suggest inaccurate depreciation estimation.

Representation Letters.

Auditors conclude the audit by obtaining from company management a representation letter confirming oral representations or assertions made during the course of the audit. It is addressed to the auditor and signed by the chief executive officer, chief financial officer, or other similar senior officer. Particulars vary with the audit engagement, but will often include the following: Management acknowledges that it is responsible for the financial statements; management has made all financial records and data available; board and shareholder minutes are complete and were made available; the financial statements are error-free and there no unrecorded transactions; information concerning inventory valuation, such as obsolescence; necessary title is held on all fixed assets; violations of law have been disclosed; gains and losses have been properly accounted for; and information concerning litigation, claims and assessments has been provided.

Management representation letters are necessary but not sufficient. That is, GAAS requires auditors to get them but they are not a substitute for substantive testing. Managerial refusal to provide a representation letter is tantamount to a scope limitation on the audit sufficient to preclude the auditor from issuing an unqualified opinion. Worse, it throws into doubt management's integrity and may lead the auditor to doubt other managerial representations or result in a disclaimer of opinion.

Critical Audit Matters (CAMs).

The PCAOB adoped rules, proposed to take effect in 2019–20, requiring public company audit reports to include the auditor's discussion of "critical audit matters" (CAMs) or state that no CAMs existed. CAMs are matters communicated or required to be communicated to the audit committee that: (1) relate to accounts or disclosures that are material to the financial statements and (2) involve "especially challenging, subjective, or complex auditor judgment."

Auditors determine whether prong (2) of this formulation is met according to various factors, including these: risks of material misstatement; the degree of auditor judgment or estimation by management; the nature and timing of significant unusual transactions; the degree of auditor subjectivity; and the nature of audit evidence obtained regarding the matter.

Auditors communicate CAMs in audit reports using the following framework: identifying the CAM; describing the principal considerations that led the auditor to make its CAM judgment and how the matter was addressed in the audit; and referring to the relevant financial statement accounts or disclosures. Auditors must develop related documentation supporting their determination and communications concerning CAMs.

E. TECHNOLOGY: AUDIT DATA ANALYTICS

Internet, cloud computing, data science, and related technologies enhance auditing capabilities. For one, they alter the geographic space. Traditional audits must be done physically, on site, with assigned local personnel, whereas tech-enhanced audits can be done remotely from multiple locations using dispersed staff. For example, analytical procedures or journal entry testing can be performed for thousands of clients globally by a single group of experts located in one office anywhere in the world. Auditors and companies can use cloud computing to plug into software and data storage/analytics to enhance statistical and probability work.

The auditing profession increasingly speaks of Audit Data Analytics (ADA) to capture tech-enhanced audit practice. An AICPA white paper, Reimagining Auditing in a Wired World (2014), explains:

> Audit Data Analytics [ADA] is the science and art of discovering and analyzing patterns, identifying anomalies, and extracting other useful information in data underlying or related

to the subject matter of an audit through analysis, modeling, and visualization for the purpose of planning or performing the audit. ADA includes methodologies for identifying and analyzing anomalous patterns and outliers in data; mapping and visualizing financial performance and other data across operating units, systems, products, or other dimensions for the purpose of focusing the audit on risks; building statistical (for example, regression) or other models that explain the data in relation to other factors and identify significant fluctuations from the model; and combining information from disparate analyses and data sources for the purpose of gaining additional insights.

Among many potential uses of ADA in GAAS financial statement audits are identifying and assessing risks associated with accepting or continuing an audit engagement, such as insolvency or fraud; performing preliminary analytical procedures and evaluating the design and implementation of internal controls and testing their effectiveness; and performing substantive analytical procedures. The authors envision ADA offering a far different future for auditing:

> The auditor's overall objective is to obtain a reasonably high level of assurance about whether the financial statements are free from material misstatement. Reasonably high is not defined, but is commonly understood to mean no less than 95 percent confidence, where degree of confidence is a measure of the auditor's degree of subjective professional belief rather than some objectively calculable probability. Technology can be used to achieve the same level of assurance but more efficiently at a lower cost, or it can be used to achieve a higher level of assurance via a more effective audit at similar cost. Technology also enables statistical techniques (for example, sampling and regression analysis) that can provide objectively quantifiable confidence levels to help build assurance.

> Economics has driven auditors to focus mostly on improving efficiency—achieving the same level of assurance but at lower cost. Less attention has been paid to increasing assurance at the same cost by improving effectiveness, even though that cost would buy the additional benefits of better meeting client and investor expectations and of reducing audit and reputational risk and liability. In medicine, physicians are expected to use better technologies as they come along if they significantly improve patient outcomes at reasonable cost. In auditing, professional standards should encourage auditors to consider and use technologies that increase assurance beyond the minimum required where economically feasible.

An example of where technology can and should be used to increase assurance is in detailed tests of transactions and balances. Traditionally, such tests were performed on a small sample of items. This was the only way to do it when items had to be selected from a printed or hand-written listing. With computerized data and file interrogation audit software, however, many tests can be performed on 100 percent of the population. It is also possible to simultaneously analyze and visualize the complete population in ways that can reveal unexpected patterns and outliers worthy of special investigation. For certain procedures, sampling is still necessary—for example, the physical inspection or third-party confirmation of assets, or the analysis of complex contracts. Nevertheless, even where sampling is necessary for certain essentials, it is often possible to increase audit assurance at little additional cost by analyzing and performing other procedures on the entire population.

Problem 13

J&J buys most component parts it uses to assemble bicycles from outside vendors. Its purchase transactions affect numerous accounts, including inventories and cost of goods sold. In connection with the annual audit of J&J's financial statements, J&J's independent auditor is assessing whether internal control over purchases can be relied upon during substantive tests of details concerning asserted balances for inventory and cost of goods sold. The issue is whether purchases have been properly approved for payment. The relevant control is a requirement that authorized personnel initial the face of each invoice the company receives for purchases. The auditor plans an attributes sampling test of purchase invoices for the fiscal year. The population is very large (more than 2,000 purchases).

a.   Preliminary assessments based on the auditor's professional experience with J&J and comparable companies indicate a variety of alternative parameters. For each set of parameters noted below, what is the minimum sample size? Assume a 5% risk of assessing control risk too low.

	Tolerable Deviation Rate	Expected Population Deviation Rate
(a)	6%	2%
(b)	7%	2.5%
(c)	8%	3%

b.   Assume the auditor established a tolerable deviation rate of 6% and an expected population deviation rate of 2.5%. Suppose that in a sample of 150 purchase invoices, the auditor found the number of deviations (absence of authorized approval initials) to be either 3 or 5. Again assume a 5% risk of assessing control risk too low. What are the respective upper occurrence limits and requisite interpretation of controls and implication for conducting substantive tests?

c.   Assuming all other controls are tested as effective, could J&J's auditor furnish an unqualified opinion on control?

Conceptual Questions 13

Under the Sarbanes-Oxley Act, auditors of public companies audit both financial statements and internal control over financial reporting. It is theoretically possible for an auditor to give an unqualified opinion on financial statements (that they present fairly in all material respects in conformity with GAAP) yet an adverse opinion on internal controls (that a material weakness exists). What does this imply?

CHAPTER 14

AUDIT POLICY

■ ■ ■

Auditing, as a discipline, is the second-guesser of accounting information. An entity's management prepares accounting reports that consumers of the information rely upon when making capital allocation and other decisions. Auditing offers reasonable assurance of the reliability of these reports.

Law increasingly regulates auditing and has placed enormous reliance upon it to promote integrity and accountability. GAAS requires that the auditor be independent of the entity whose financial statements are audited, a requirement restated in federal securities regulations applicable to public companies. The auditor is required to interact with those client executives who supervise financial reporting and auditing matters. In corporations, this usually means the audit committee of the board of directors, which in turn is usually comprised of directors otherwise independent of the corporation (not executive officers or other employees).

This Chapter surveys auditing from policy perspectives. It first considers auditing's role in corporate governance and the concept of auditor independence. It then presents a series of leading judicial opinions addressing selected legal issues concerning auditor duties and exposure to legal liability.

A. AUDIT COMMITTEES

Audits are essential to promote reliable financial reporting. Independent auditors examine internal controls and financial statements, applying a variety of tests and conducting selected reviews of management personnel, processes, and systems. Throughout, the auditor has long interfaced with the board of directors and especially the board audit committee.

The audit committee is a central feature of contemporary accounting and financial reporting. Audit committees oversee a company's financial reporting process, including internal controls. The committee is responsible for appointing, paying, and supervising outside auditors and is their chief contact point inside the company.

The audit committee also serves as the chief contact for audit matters for all parts of the company, including the full board, other committees, senior management and internal accounting and auditing staff. In addition, the committee is responsible for establishing procedures to promote employee reporting of misconduct and protect reporting employees (whistle-blowers).

As a result of audit committees bearing these substantial and vital functions, members tend to be comprised of otherwise independent directors—neither employees nor consultants of the company. They have the authority to retain the committee's own outside advisors at company expense. They adopt written charters stating their responsibilities. They also annually prepare a report on their activities to accompany annual financial statements.

Audit committee members typically have expertise in accounting and auditing, including a knowledge of GAAP. They understand the process of financial statement preparation, estimating requirements and governing principles for various accounting matters, internal control concepts and audit committee functions. Federal securities regulations and stock exchange rules encourage or require such expertise and provide alternative statements as to what financial expertise entails.

B. AUDITOR INDEPENDENCE

Auditor independence is said to be the cornerstone of a meaningful audit. The theory is simple enough: absent the kind of detachment independence affords, audit quality will sink. Defining independence in practice has proved more difficult. The difficulty seems to have increased continually during recent generations, with numerous business and demographic shifts putting additional pressure on the auditor's role. The struggle included repeated efforts by an array of professional and public bodies to define the concept of independence and specify guidelines for its application in practice.

These bodies included the AICPA, the Public Oversight Board (POB), the Independence Standards Board (ISB, 1997–2001), and most recently, PCAOB. The latter's role originated in the Sarbanes-Oxley Act of 2002. Under the Act, no audit firm is independent of a company if certain company senior officers worked at the firm and on that company's audit within the year before the start of the audit in question. To enhance the independence of individual auditors, auditors must rotate lead and reviewing partners so that neither role is performed by the same accountant for the same company for more than five consecutive years.

No current mandates compel rotation of firms, though doing so would provide some benefits. It would probably encourage more conservative accounting when choices are possible. The first thing new auditors tend to do is hunt for aggressive accounting and pressure to reverse it. The looming threat of such second guessing would ordinarily induce incumbent auditors to insist on the more conservative approach at the outset. Costs of firm rotation are the start-up burdens of firms learning peculiar systems and protocols.

Auditor independence is strongly influenced by what role auditors assume for their clients in addition to attesting to financial statements. Roles mushroomed in the past few decades as accounting firms became multi-national, multi-service conglomerates. Relationships that developed included pension management; investment advisory; broker/dealer; personal trust services for the client or its officers, directors and significant shareholders; bookkeeping; record-keeping; payroll; and executive recruiting.

Permissible roles are now restricted. Auditors are forbidden from providing any of the following services for audit clients: bookkeeping; financial information systems; appraisal, valuation or fairness opinions; actuarial; internal audit; human resources; broker/dealer, investment adviser, or investment banking services; or legal and expert services. Note that these restrictions do not encompass tax-related services.

C. LEGAL RESPONSIBILITIES

Auditors are subject to civil and criminal liability when their work fails to satisfy requisite legal standards. Numerous standards govern with multiple sources. Prominent theories of liability are breach of contract, ordinary negligence, gross negligence and fraud. Auditor engagements are routinely conducted pursuant to a written engagement agreement that can form the basis for breach of contract claims. State common law imposes on auditors the standard of care familiar from tort law applicable to professionals, the breach of which gives rise to claims for ordinary negligence. Gross negligence involves reckless departures from GAAS and fraud involves the intention to deceive and injure.

Federal statutory law imposes like obligations under specific provisions. Among these are Section 11 of the Securities Act of 1933, which exposes auditors to civil liability for negligence (usually meaning noncompliance with GAAS) and Section 10(b) of the Securities Exchange Act of 1934, which exposes auditors to civil liability for fraud. The PCAOB is empowered to impose fines and penalties and apply other disciplinary measures to auditing firms registered with it. The following cases introduce and explore some fundamental legal issues, as to scope of persons entitled to sue and some intricacies of federal securities regulation.

BILY V. ARTHUR YOUNG & CO.*

LUCAS, CHIEF JUSTICE (for the majority) . . . This litigation emanates from the meteoric rise and equally rapid demise of Osborne Computer Corporation. Founded in 1980 by entrepreneur Adam Osborne, the company manufactured the first portable personal computer for the mass market. Shipments began in 1981. By fall 1982, sales of the company's sole product, the Osborne I computer, had reached $10 million per month, making the company one of the fastest growing enterprises in the history of American business.

In late 1982, the company began planning for an early 1983 initial public offering of its stock. . . .) At the suggestion of the underwriters, the offering was postponed for several months, in part because of uncertainties caused by the company's employment of a new chief executive officer and its plans to introduce a new computer to replace the Osborne I. In order to obtain "bridge" financing needed to meet the company's capital requirements until the offering, the company issued warrants to investors in exchange for direct loans or letters of credit to secure bank loans to the company (the warrant transaction). . . .

Plaintiffs in this case were investors in the company. They include individuals as well as pension and venture capital investment funds. Several plaintiffs purchased warrants from the company as part of the warrant transaction. Others purchased the common stock of the company during early 1983. . . .

[Defendant auditing firm] Arthur Young issued unqualified or "clean" audit opinions on the company's 1981 and 1982 financial statements. Each opinion appeared on Arthur Young's letterhead, was addressed to the company, and stated in essence: (1) Arthur Young had performed an examination of the accompanying financial statements in accordance with the accounting profession's "Generally Accepted Auditing Standards" (GAAS); (2) the statements had been prepared in accordance with "Generally Accepted Accounting Principles" (GAAP); and (3) the statements "present[ed] fairly" the company's financial position. . . . The 1982 financial statements included a "Consolidated Statement of Operations" which revealed a modest net operating profit of $69,000 on sales of more than $68 million. . . .

As the warrant transaction closed on April 8, 1983, the company's financial performance began to falter. Sales declined sharply because of manufacturing problems with the company's new "Executive" model computer. When the Executive appeared on the market, sales of the Osborne I naturally decreased, but were not being replaced because Executive units could not be produced fast enough. In June 1983, the IBM

---

*   834 P.2d 745 (Cal. 1992).

personal computer and IBM-compatible software became major factors in the small computer market, further damaging the company's sales. The public offering never materialized. The company filed for bankruptcy on September 13, 1983. Plaintiffs ultimately lost their investments.

Plaintiffs' principal expert witness, William J. Baedecker, reviewed the 1982 audit and offered a critique identifying more than 40 deficiencies in Arthur Young's performance amounting, in Baedecker's view, to gross professional negligence. In his opinion, Arthur Young did not perform its examination in accordance with GAAS. He found the liabilities on the company's financial statements to have been understated by approximately $3 million. As a result, the company's supposed $69,000 operating profit was, in his view, a loss of more than $3 million. He also determined that Arthur Young had discovered material weaknesses in the company's accounting controls, but failed to report its discovery to management.

Although most of Baedecker's criticisms involved matters of oversight or nonfeasance, *e.g.*, failures to detect weaknesses in the company's accounting procedures and systems, he also charged that Arthur Young had actually discovered deviations from GAAP, but failed to disclose them as qualifications or corrections to its audit report. For example, by January 1983, a senior auditor with Arthur Young identified $1.3 million in unrecorded liabilities including failures to account for customer rebates, returns of products, etc. . . .

The case was tried to a jury for 13 weeks. . . . The jury exonerated Arthur Young with respect to the allegations of intentional fraud and negligent misrepresentation, but returned a verdict in plaintiffs' favor based on professional negligence. No comparative negligence on plaintiffs' part was found. The jury awarded compensatory damages of approximately $4.3 million, representing approximately 75 percent of each investment made by plaintiffs. The Court of Appeal affirmed the resulting judgment in plaintiffs' favor with respect to all matters relevant to the issue now before us.

Although certified public accountants (CPA's) perform a variety of services for their clients, their primary function, which is the one that most frequently generates lawsuits against them by third persons, is financial auditing. . . . In a typical audit, a CPA firm may verify the existence of tangible assets, observe business activities, and confirm account balances and mathematical computations. It might also examine sample transactions or records to ascertain the accuracy of the client company's financial and accounting systems. . . . The end product of an audit is the audit report or opinion. . . .

The complex nature of the audit function and its economic implications has resulted in different approaches to the question whether CPA auditors should be subjected to liability to third parties who read and rely on audit reports. Although three schools of thought are commonly recognized, there are some variations within each school. . . .

A substantial number of jurisdictions follow the lead of Chief Judge Cardozo's 1931 opinion for the New York Court of Appeals in [*Ultramares Corp. v. Touche*, 255 N.Y. 170 (1931)], by denying recovery to third parties for auditor negligence in the absence of a third party relationship to the auditor that is "akin to privity." In contrast, a handful of jurisdictions, spurred by law review commentary, have recently allowed recovery based on auditor negligence to third parties whose reliance on the audit report was "foreseeable."

Most jurisdictions, supported by the weight of commentary and the modern English common law decisions cited by the parties, have steered a middle course based in varying degrees on Restatement Second of Torts section 552, which generally imposes liability on suppliers of commercial information to third persons who are intended beneficiaries of the information. [The] federal securities laws have also dealt with the problem by imposing auditor liability for negligence-related conduct only in connection with misstatements in publicly filed and distributed offering documents. [This opinion adopts the Restatement Second of Torts approach.]

[Under the privity rule, rooted in *Ultramares*, auditors owe no duty to third parties for issuing erroneous opinions. A privity relationship may be inferred from the relationship between an auditor and a designated class of persons, including partners of a partnership where the latter engaged the auditor. *White v. Guarente*, 43 N.Y.2d 356 (1977); *see also Credit Alliance Corp. v. Arthur Andersen & Co.*, 65 N.Y.2d 536 (1985), which states as follows:] "Before accountants may be held liable in negligence to noncontractual parties who rely to their detriment on inaccurate financial reports, certain prerequisites must be satisfied: (1) the accountant must have been aware that the financial reports were to be used for a particular purpose or purposes; (2) in the furtherance of which a known party or parties was intended to rely; and (3) there must have been some conduct on the part of the accountants linking them to that party or parties, which evinces the accountants' understanding of that party or parties' reliance."

[A]t least nine states purport to follow privity or near privity rules restricting the liability of auditors to parties with whom they have a contractual or similar relationship. In five states, this result has been reached by decisions of their highest courts. In four other states, the rule has been enacted by statute. Federal court decisions have held that the rule represents the law of three additional states whose highest courts have not expressly considered the question. The more recent of the cited cases generally follow the New York rule as reformulated in *Credit Alliance*.

[Under the foreseeability approach, auditor liability becomes a question of fact to investigate whether an auditor should reasonably have foreseen reliance by a particular party or a class of parties of which a particular party is a member. Only Wisconsin and Mississippi endorse it. Four state supreme courts have rejected it.] The foreseeability approach has also encountered substantial criticism from commentators, who have questioned, among other matters, its failure to consider seriously the problem of indeterminate liability and its prediction of a significant deterrent effect that will improve the quality of audit reporting. . . .

Section 552 of the Restatement Second of Torts covers "Information Negligently Supplied for the Guidance of Others." It states a general principle that one who negligently supplies false information "for the guidance of others in their business transactions" is liable for economic loss suffered by the recipients in justifiable reliance on the information. (*Id.*, subd. (1).) But the liability created by the general principle is expressly limited to loss suffered: "(a) [B]y the person or one of a limited group of persons for whose benefit and guidance he [or she] intends to supply the information or knows that the recipient intends to supply it; and (b) through reliance upon it in a transaction that he intends the information to influence or knows that the recipient so intends or in a substantially similar transaction." (*Id.*, subd. (2).) To paraphrase, a supplier of information is liable for negligence to a third party only if he or she intends to supply the information for the benefit of one or more third parties in a specific transaction or type of transaction identified to the supplier.

Comment (h) to subdivision (2) of section 552, Restatement Second of Torts, observes that the liability of a negligent supplier of information is appropriately more narrowly restricted than that of an intentionally fraudulent supplier. It also notes that a commercial supplier of information has a legitimate concern as to the nature and scope of the client's transactions that may expand the supplier's exposure to liability. . . .

Under the Restatement rule, an auditor retained to conduct an annual audit and to furnish an opinion for no particular purpose generally undertakes no duty to third parties. [The Restatement provides an Illustration. "A [client corporation] uses the financial statements and accompanying auditor's opinion to obtain a loan from [a particular] bank. Because of [the auditor's] negligence, [the auditor] issues an unqualifiedly favorable opinion upon a balance sheet that materially misstates the financial position of [the client] and through reliance upon it [the bank] suffers pecuniary loss. . . . [The auditor] is not liable to [the bank]." . . .

Although the parties debate precisely how many states follow the Restatement rule, a review of the cases reveals the rule has somewhat more support than the privity of relationship rule and much more support than the foreseeability rule. At least 17 state and federal decisions have endorsed the rule in this and related contexts. Whatever the exact number of states that have endorsed it, the Restatement rule has been for many, if not most, courts a satisfactory compromise between their discomfort with the traditional privity approach and the [foreseeability rule's] "specter of unlimited liability." (*Briggs v. Sterner* (S.D. Iowa 1981) 529 F.Supp. 1155, 1177.) . . .

Viewing the problem before us in light of the factors set forth above, we decline to permit all merely foreseeable third party users of audit reports to sue the auditor on a theory of professional negligence. Our holding is premised on three central concerns: (1) Given the secondary "watchdog" role of the auditor, the complexity of the professional opinions rendered in audit reports, and the difficult and potentially tenuous causal relationships between audit reports and economic losses from investment and credit decisions, the auditor exposed to negligence claims from all foreseeable third parties faces potential liability far out of proportion to its fault; (2) the generally more sophisticated class of plaintiffs in auditor liability cases (*e.g.*, business lenders and investors) permits the effective use of contract rather than tort liability to control and adjust the relevant risks through "private ordering"; and (3) the asserted advantages of more accurate auditing and more efficient loss spreading relied upon by those who advocate a pure foreseeability approach are unlikely to occur; indeed, dislocations of resources, including increased expense and decreased availability of auditing services in some sectors of the economy, are more probable consequences of expanded liability. . . .

An auditor is a watchdog, not a bloodhound. As a matter of commercial reality, audits are performed in a client-controlled environment. The client typically prepares its own financial statements; it has direct control over and assumes primary responsibility for their contents. The client engages the auditor, pays for the audit, and communicates with audit personnel throughout the engagement. Because the auditor cannot in the time available become an expert in the client's business and record-keeping systems, the client necessarily furnishes the information base for the audit. . . .

Moreover, an audit report is not a simple statement of verifiable fact that . . . can be easily checked against uniform standards of indisputable accuracy. Rather, an audit report is a professional opinion based on numerous and complex factors. [T]he report is based on the auditor's interpretation and application of hundreds of professional standards, many of which are broadly phrased and readily subject to different constructions. Although ultimately expressed in shorthand form, the report is the final product of a complex process involving discretion and judgment on the part of the auditor at every stage. Using different initial assumptions and approaches, different sampling techniques, and the wisdom of 20-20 hindsight, few CPA audits would be immune from criticism.

Although the auditor's role in the financial reporting process is secondary and the subject of complex professional judgment, the liability it faces in a negligence suit by a third party is primary and personal and can be massive. The client, its promoters, and its managers have generally left the scene, headed in most cases for government-supervised liquidation or the bankruptcy court. The auditor has now assumed center stage as the remaining solvent defendant and is faced with a claim for all sums of money ever loaned to or invested in the client. Yet the auditor may never have been aware of the existence, let alone the nature or scope, of the third party transaction that resulted in the claim. . . .

Investment and credit decisions are by their nature complex and multifaceted. Although an audit report might play a role in such decisions, reasonable and prudent investors and lenders will dig far deeper in their "due diligence" investigations than the surface level of an auditor's opinion. And, particularly in financially large transactions, the ultimate decision to lend or invest is often based on numerous business factors that have little to do with the audit report. The auditing CPA has no expertise in or control over the products or services of its clients or their markets; it does not choose the client's executives or make its business decisions; yet, when clients fail financially, the CPA auditor is a prime target in litigation claiming investor and creditor economic losses because it is the only available (and solvent) entity that had any direct contact with the client's business affairs.

The facts of this case provide an apt example. Although plaintiffs now profess reliance on Arthur Young's audit report as the sine qua non of their investments, the record reveals a more complicated decisionmaking process. As a group of corporate insiders and venture capitalists who were closely following the Cinderella-like transformation of the company, plaintiffs perceived an opportunity to make a large sum of money in a very short time by investing in a company they believed would (literally within months) become the dominant force in the new personal computer market.

Although hindsight suggests they misjudged a number of major factors (including, at a minimum, the product, the market, the competition, and the company's manufacturing capacity), plaintiffs' litigation-focused attention is now exclusively on the auditor and its report. Plaintiffs would have us believe that, had the Arthur Young report disclosed deficiencies in accounting controls and the $3 million loss (on income of over $68 million),* they would have ignored all the other positive factors that triggered their interest (such as the company's rapid growth in sales, its dynamic management, and the intense interest of underwriters in a public offering) and flatly withheld all their funds. Plaintiffs' revisionist view of the company's history, the audit, and their own investments, suggests

---

　　* [Students reading this book should recognize that the court obviously meant sales revenue, not income. Ed.]

something less than a "close connection" between Arthur Young's audit report and the loss of their invested funds.

In view of the factors discussed above, judicial endorsement of third party negligence suits against auditors limited only by the concept of forseeability raises the spectre of multibillion-dollar professional liability that is distinctly out of proportion to: (1) the fault of the auditor (which is necessarily secondary and may be based on complex differences of professional opinion); and (2) the connection between the auditor's conduct and the third party's injury (which will often be attenuated by unrelated business factors that underlie investment and credit decisions). . . . [S]uch disproportionate liability cannot fairly be justified on moral, ethical, or economic grounds. . . .

Courts advocating unlimited auditor liability to all foreseeably injured third parties often analogize the auditor's opinion to a consumer product, arguing that the demise of privity as a barrier to recovery for negligence in product manufacture implies its irrelevance in the area of auditor liability as well. Plaintiffs advance similar arguments. The analogy lacks persuasive force for two reasons. Initially, as noted above, the maker of a consumer product has complete control over the design and manufacture of its product; in contrast, the auditor merely expresses an opinion about its client's financial statements—the client is primarily responsible for the content of those statements in the form they reach the third party.

Moreover, the general character of the class of third parties is also different. Investors, creditors, and others who read and rely on audit reports and financial statements are not the equivalent of ordinary consumers. Like plaintiffs here, they often possess considerable sophistication in analyzing financial information and are aware from training and experience of the limits of an audit report "product" that is, at bottom, simply a broadly phrased professional opinion based on a necessarily confined examination. . . .

As a matter of economic and social policy, third parties should be encouraged to rely on their own prudence, diligence, and contracting power, as well as other informational tools. This kind of self-reliance promotes sound investment and credit practices and discourages the careless use of monetary resources. If, instead, third parties are simply permitted to recover from the auditor for mistakes in the client's financial statements, the auditor becomes, in effect, an insurer of not only the financial statements, but of bad loans and investments in general.

Courts and commentators advocating auditor negligence liability to third parties also predict that such liability might deter auditor mistakes, promote more careful audits, and result in a more efficient spreading of the risk of inaccurate financial statements. . . . We are not directed to any empirical data supporting these prognostications. From our review of the cases and commentary, we doubt that a significant and desirable improvement in audit care would result from an expanded rule of liability. Indeed, deleterious economic effects appear at least as likely to occur.

In view of the inherent dependence of the auditor on the client and the labor-intensive nature of auditing, we doubt whether audits can be done in ways that would yield significantly greater accuracy without disadvantages. Auditors may rationally respond to increased liability by simply reducing audit services in fledgling industries where the business failure rate is high, reasoning that they will inevitably be singled out and sued when their client goes into bankruptcy regardless of the care or detail of their audits. [T]he economic result of unlimited negligence liability could just as easily be an increase in the cost and decrease in the availability of audits and audit reports with no compensating improvement in overall audit quality.

In light of the relationships between auditor, client, and third party, and the relative sophistication of third parties who lend and invest based on audit reports, it might also be doubted whether auditors are the most efficient absorbers of the losses from inaccuracies in financial information. Investors and creditors can limit the impact of losses by diversifying investments and loan portfolios. . . . In the audit liability context, no reason appears to favor the alleged tortfeasor over the alleged victim as an effective distributor of loss. . . .

For the reasons stated above, we hold that an auditor's liability for general negligence in the conduct of an audit of its client financial statements is confined to the client, *i.e.*, the person who contracts for or engages the audit services. Other persons may not recover on a pure negligence theory. . . . The sole client of Arthur Young in the audit engagements involved in this case was the company. None of the plaintiffs qualify as clients. Under the rule we adopt, they are not entitled to recover on a pure negligence theory. Therefore, the verdict and judgment in their favor based on that theory are reversed.

[Negligent misrepresentation is a theory of liability distinct from general negligence.] Under certain circumstances, expressions of professional opinion are treated as representations of fact. [W]hen a party possesses or holds itself out as possessing superior knowledge or special information or expertise regarding the subject matter and a plaintiff is so situated that it may reasonably rely on such supposed knowledge, information, or expertise, the defendant's representation may be treated as one of material fact. There is no dispute that Arthur Young's statements in audit opinions fall within these principles. [But those entitled to rely on the representations are limited to those to or for whom the misrepresentations were made.]

. . . Restatement Second of Torts section 552, subdivision (b) is most consistent with the elements and policy foundations of the tort of negligent misrepresentation. The rule expressed there attempts to define a narrow and circumscribed class of persons to whom or for whom representations are made. In this way, it recognizes commercial realities by avoiding both unlimited and uncertain liability for economic losses in cases of professional mistake and exoneration of the auditor in situations where it clearly intended to undertake the responsibility of influencing particular business transactions involving third persons. The Restatement rule thus appears to be a sensible and moderate approach to the potential consequences of imposing unlimited negligence liability which we have identified. . . .

The Restatement Second of Torts approach is also the only one that achieves consistency in the law of negligent misrepresentation. Accountants are not unique in their position as suppliers of information and evaluations for the use and benefit of others. Other professionals, including attorneys, architects, engineers, title insurers and abstractors, and others also perform that function. And, like auditors, these professionals may also face suits by third persons claiming reliance on information and opinions generated in a professional capacity. . . .

KENNARD, JUSTICE (dissenting, with whom MOSK, JUSTICE, concurred) . . . The majority concludes that defendant owed plaintiffs no duty. Rummaging in the archives of legal history, amidst the debris of discarded dogmas, the majority retrieves and revives, as an element of a cause of action for negligence, the requirement of privity, which this court had described more than 20 years ago as "virtually abandoned in California." Under the strict version of the privity rule that the majority adopts, an accountant's liability for professional negligence in the conduct of an audit "is confined to the client" who retained the accountant to audit its financial statements.

Turning to plaintiffs' cause of action for negligent misrepresentation, the majority adopts a rule that is equally arbitrary in operation and only slightly less restrictive than the rule it adopts for negligence liability. The majority holds that an accountant is liable to a third party for negligent misrepresentation in an audit report only if the third party relied on the misrepresentation in a transaction that the accountant intended to influence. The effect of these holdings is to give negligent accountants broad immunity for their professional malpractice in rendering audit opinions.

In defining the scope of duty in negligence cases, courts must balance competing concerns. The burden imposed by the duty should bear some reasonable relation to the moral fault of the negligent party and should not be so onerous that those held liable are unwilling or financially unable to engage in socially beneficial activity. On the other hand, tort liability is itself socially beneficial to the extent that it provides both an incentive for due care, thereby preventing avoidable injuries, and compensation for those who have been injured. Courts should not define a legal duty so narrowly as to preclude these positive effects of tort liability, as the majority has done in this case.

Lenders and investors use the reports prepared by independent auditors so widely, and rely on them so heavily, that it is difficult to conceive how our complex modern capital markets would function if they were no longer available or no longer able to inspire confidence. In weighing the competing policy considerations that factor into a decision defining the scope of the accountant's duty in this context, a court must seek to fashion a rule that, without making the provision of auditing services prohibitively risky, ensures that the quality of those critically important services will be maintained at a high level. Such a rule is necessary so that lenders and investors will continue to have confidence in audited financial reports and so that the usual and foreseeable users of audit reports will receive fair compensation when they have been victimized by the occasional failure of an accountant to meet prevailing professional norms.

In my view, the law that has existed in this state until today strikes the proper balance. Until today, California law had recognized that accountants owe a duty of care to all persons who reasonably and foreseeably rely on accountants' professional opinions. Extending the duty to all such users provides a necessary incentive for due care in the conduct of audits and in the preparation of audit reports, and ensures fair compensation to innocent victims of auditors' negligence. Unlike the majority, I am not persuaded that the duty so defined has excessively burdened the accounting profession, or that it has caused or is likely to cause a significant reduction in the availability of auditing services. Even if these unfortunate consequences could be demonstrated, the remedy should come in the form of carefully crafted legislation, not wholesale curtailment of legal duty.

Unlike the majority, I would not adopt one rule for negligence liability and a different rule for liability under the conceptually distinct but factually related theory of negligent misrepresentation. Under these two liability theories, essentially the same standard of care is applied to the same conduct by the accountant. Given this overlap, it is anomalous to hold that the class of persons to whom the accountant owes a duty varies depending on which legal theory has been pleaded. . . .

ERNST & ERNST V. HOCHFELDER*

POWELL, JUSTICE. The issue in this case is whether an action for civil damages may lie under § 10(b) of the Securities Exchange Act of 1934 (1934 Act), 15 U.S.C. § 78j(b), and Securities and Exchange Commission Rule 10b–5, in the absence of an allegation of intent to deceive, manipulate, or defraud on the part of the defendant.

Petitioner, Ernst & Ernst, is an accounting firm. From 1946 through 1967 it was retained by First Securities Company of Chicago (First Securities), a small brokerage firm . . . to perform periodic audits of the firm's books and records. . . .

Respondents were customers of First Securities who invested in a fraudulent securities scheme perpetrated by Leston B. Nay, president of the firm and owner of 92% of its stock. Nay induced the respondents to invest funds in "escrow" accounts that he represented would yield a high rate of return. Respondents did so from 1942 through 1966, with the majority of the transactions occurring in the 1950's. In fact, there were no escrow accounts as Nay converted respondents' funds to his own use immediately upon receipt. These transactions were not in the customary form of dealings between First Securities and its customers. The respondents drew their personal checks payable to Nay or a designated bank for his account. No such escrow accounts were reflected on the books and records of First Securities, and none was shown on its periodic accounting to respondents in connection with their other investments. Nor were they included in First Securities' filings with the Commission. . . .

This fraud came to light in 1968 when Nay committed suicide, leaving a note that described First Securities as bankrupt and the escrow accounts as "spurious." Respondents subsequently filed this action for damages against Ernst & Ernst. . . . The complaint charged that Nay's escrow scheme violated § 10(b) and Commission Rule 10b–5, and that Ernst & Ernst had "aided and abetted" Nay's violations by its "failure" to conduct proper audits of First Securities. As revealed through discovery, respondents' cause of action rested on a theory of negligent nonfeasance. The premise was that Ernst & Ernst had failed to utilize "appropriate auditing procedures" in its audits of First Securities, thereby failing to discover internal practices of the firm said to prevent an effective audit. The practice principally relied on was Nay's rule that only he could open mail addressed to him at First Securities or addressed to First Securities to his attention, even if it arrived in his absence. Respondents contended that if Ernst & Ernst had conducted a proper audit, it would have discovered this "mail rule." The existence of the rule then would have been disclosed in reports to . . . the Commission by Ernst & Ernst as an irregular procedure that prevented an effective audit. This would have led to an

---

*   425 U.S. 185 (1976).

investigation of Nay that would have revealed the fraudulent scheme. Respondents specifically disclaimed the existence of fraud or intentional misconduct on the part of Ernst & Ernst. . . .

We granted certiorari to resolve the question whether a private cause of action for damages will lie under § 10(b) and Rule 10b–5 in the absence of any allegation of "scienter"—intent to deceive, manipulate, or defraud. We conclude that it will not. . . .[12]

Federal regulation of transactions in securities emerged as part of the aftermath of the market crash in 1929. The Securities Act of 1933 (1933 Act) . . . was designed to provide investors with full disclosure of material information concerning public offerings of securities in commerce, to protect investors against fraud and, through the imposition of specified civil liabilities, to promote ethical standards of honesty and fair dealing. The 1934 Act was intended principally to protect investors against manipulation of stock prices through regulation of transactions upon securities exchanges and in over-the-counter markets, and to impose regular reporting requirements on companies whose stock is listed on national securities exchanges. Although the Acts contain numerous carefully drawn express civil remedies and criminal penalties, Congress recognized that efficient regulation of securities trading could not be accomplished under a rigid statutory program. As part of the 1934 Act Congress created the Commission, which is provided with an arsenal of flexible enforcement powers.

Section 10 of the 1934 Act makes it "unlawful for any person . . . (b) [t]o use or employ, in connection with the purchase or sale of any security . . . any manipulative or deceptive device or contrivance in contravention of such rules and regulations as the Commission may prescribe as necessary or appropriate in the public interest or for the protection of investors." 15 U.S.C. § 78j. In 1945, acting pursuant to the power conferred by § 10(b), the Commission promulgated Rule 10b–5. . . .

Although § 10(b) does not by its terms create an express civil remedy for its violation, and there is no indication that Congress, or the Commission when adopting Rule 10b–5, contemplated such a remedy, the existence of a private cause of action for violations of the statute and the Rule is now well established. *Blue Chip Stamps v. Manor Drug Stores*, 421 U.S. 723, 730 (1975). . . . Courts and commentators long have differed with regard to whether scienter is a necessary element of such a cause of action, or whether negligent conduct alone is sufficient. . . .

---

[12] . . . In this opinion the term "scienter" refers to a mental state embracing intent to deceive, manipulate, or defraud. In certain areas of the law recklessness is considered to be a form of intentional conduct for purposes of imposing liability for some act. We need not address here the question whether, in some circumstances, reckless behavior is sufficient for civil liability under § 10(b) and Rule 10b–5. . . .

Section 10(b) makes unlawful the use or employment of "any manipulative or deceptive device or contrivance" in contravention of Commission rules. The words "manipulative or deceptive" used in conjunction with "device or contrivance" strongly suggest that § 10(b) was intended to proscribe knowing or intentional misconduct.

In its amicus curiae brief, however, the Commission contends that nothing in the language "manipulative or deceptive device or contrivance" limits its operation to knowing or intentional practices. In support of its view, the Commission cites the overall congressional purpose in the 1933 and 1934 Acts to protect investors against false and deceptive practices that might injure them. The Commission then reasons that since the "effect" upon investors of given conduct is the same regardless of whether the conduct is negligent or intentional, Congress must have intended to bar all such practices and not just those done knowingly or intentionally. The logic of this effect-oriented approach would impose liability for wholly faultless conduct where such conduct results in harm to investors, a result the Commission would be unlikely to support. But apart from where its logic might lead, the Commission would add a gloss to the operative language of the statute quite different from its commonly accepted meaning. The argument simply ignores the use of the words "manipulative," "device," and "contrivance"—terms that make unmistakable a congressional intent to proscribe a type of conduct quite different from negligence. Use of the word "manipulative" is especially significant. It is and was virtually a term of art when used in connection with securities markets. It connotes intentional or willful conduct designed to deceive or defraud investors by controlling or artificially affecting the price of securities. . . .

It is thus evident that Congress fashioned standards of fault in the express civil remedies in the 1933 and 1934 Acts on a particularized basis. Ascertainment of congressional intent with respect to the standard of liability created by a particular section of the Acts must therefore rest primarily on the language of that section. . . .

The 1933 and 1934 Acts constitute interrelated components of the federal regulatory scheme governing transactions in securities. *See Blue Chip Stamps*, 421 U.S., at 727–730. As the Court indicated in *SEC v. National Securities, Inc.*, 393 U.S. 453, 466 (1969), "the interdependence of the various sections of the securities laws is certainly a relevant factor in any interpretation of the language Congress has chosen. . . ." Recognizing this, respondents and the Commission contrast § 10(b) with other sections of the Acts to support their contention that civil liability may be imposed upon proof of negligent conduct. We think they misconceive the significance of the other provisions of the Acts.

The Commission argues that Congress has been explicit in requiring willful conduct when that was the standard of fault intended, citing § 9 of the 1934 Act, 15 U.S.C. § 78, which generally proscribes manipulation of securities prices. . . . From this the Commission concludes that since § 10(b) is not by its terms explicitly restricted to willful, knowing, or purposeful conduct, it should not be construed in all cases to require more than negligent action or inaction as a precondition for civil liability.

The structure of the Acts does not support the Commission's argument. In each instance that Congress created express civil liability in favor of purchasers or sellers of securities it clearly specified whether recovery was to be premised on knowing or intentional conduct, negligence, or entirely innocent mistake. For example, § 11 of the 1933 Act unambiguously creates a private action for damages when a registration statement includes untrue statements of material facts or fails to state material facts necessary to make the statements therein not misleading. Within the limits specified by § 11(e), the issuer of the securities is held absolutely liable for any damages resulting from such misstatement or omission. But experts such as accountants who have prepared portions of the registration statement are accorded a "due diligence" defense. In effect, this is a negligence standard. An expert may avoid civil liability with respect to the portions of the registration statement for which he was responsible by showing that "after reasonable investigation" he had "reasonable ground[s] to believe" that the statements for which he was responsible were true and there was no omission of a material fact. § 11(b)(3)(B)(i). *See, e.g., Escott v. BarChris Constr. Corp.*, 283 F.Supp. 643, 697–703 (S.D.N.Y. 1968). The express recognition of a cause of action premised on negligent behavior in § 11 stands in sharp contrast to the language of § 10(b), and significantly undercuts the Commission's argument.

We also consider it significant that each of the express civil remedies in the 1933 Act allowing recovery for negligent conduct is subject to significant procedural restrictions not applicable under § 10(b). Section 11(e) of the 1933 Act, for example, authorizes the court to require a plaintiff bringing a suit under § 11, § 12(2), or § 15 thereof to post a bond for costs, including attorneys' fees, and in specified circumstances to assess costs at the conclusion of the litigation. Section 13 specifies a statute of limitations of one year from the time the violation was or should have been discovered, in no event to exceed three years from the time of offer or sale, applicable to actions brought under § 11, § 12 (2), or § 15. . . . We think these procedural limitations indicate that the judicially created private damages remedy under § 10(b)—which has no comparable restrictions—cannot be extended, consistently with the intent of Congress, to actions premised on negligent wrongdoing. Such extension would allow causes of action covered by §§ 11, 12(2), and 15 to be brought instead under § 10(b) and thereby nullify the effectiveness of the carefully drawn procedural restrictions on these express actions. . . .[31]

BLACKMUN, JUSTICE (dissenting, with whom BRENNAN, JUSTICE, joins). Once again—*see Blue Chip Stamps v. Manor Drug Stores*, 421 U.S. 723, 730 (1975)—the Court interprets § 10(b) of the Securities Exchange Act of 1934 and the Securities and Exchange Commission's Rule 10b–5, restrictively and narrowly and thereby stultifies recovery for the victim. This time the Court does so by confining the statute and the Rule to situations where the defendant has "scienter," that is, the "intent to deceive, manipulate, or defraud." Sheer negligence, the Court says, is not within the reach of the statute and the Rule, and was not contemplated when the great reforms of 1933, 1934, and 1942 were effectuated by Congress and the Commission.

Perhaps the Court is right, but I doubt it. The Government and the Commission doubt it too, as is evidenced by the thrust of the brief filed by the Solicitor General on behalf of the Commission as amicus curiae. The Court's opinion, to be sure, has a certain technical consistency about it. It seems to me, however, that an investor can be victimized just as much by negligent conduct as by positive deception, and that it is not logical to drive a wedge between the two, saying that Congress clearly intended the one but certainly not the other.

No one questions the fact that the respondents here were the victims of an intentional securities fraud practiced by Leston B. Nay. What is at issue, of course, is the petitioner accountant firm's involvement and that firm's responsibility under Rule 10b–5. The language of the Rule . . . seems to me, clearly and succinctly, to prohibit negligent as well as intentional conduct of the kind proscribed, to extend beyond common-law fraud, and to apply to negligent omission and commission. This is consistent with Congress' intent, repeatedly recognized by the Court, that securities legislation enacted for the purpose of avoiding frauds be construed "not technically and restrictively, but flexibly to effectuate its remedial purposes." *SEC v. Capital Gains Research Bureau*, 375 U.S. 180, 195 (1963); *Superintendent of Insurance v. Bankers Life & Cas. Co.*, 404 U.S. 6, 12 (1971); *Affiliated Ute Citizens v. United States*, 406 U.S. 128, 151 (1972).

On motion for summary judgment, therefore, the respondents' allegations, in my view, were sufficient, and the District Court's dismissal of the action was improper to the extent that the dismissal rested on the

---

[31] Section 18 of the 1934 Act creates a private cause of action against persons, such as accountants, who "make or cause to be made" materially misleading statements in reports or other documents filed with the Commission. 15 U.S.C. § 78r. We need not consider the question whether a cause of action may be maintained under § 10(b) on the basis of actions that would constitute a violation of § 18. Under § 18 liability extends to persons who, in reliance on such statements, purchased or sold a security whose price was affected by the statements. Liability is limited, however, in the important respect that the defendant is accorded the defense that he acted in "good faith and had no knowledge that such statement was false or misleading." . . .

proposition that suit could not be maintained under § 10(b) and Rule 10b–5 for mere negligence. The opposite appears to be true, at least in the Second Circuit, with respect to suits by the SEC to enjoin a violation of the Rule. *S.E.C. v. Management Dynamics, Inc.*, 515 F.2d 801 (2nd 1975); *SEC v. Spectrum, Ltd.*, 489 F. 2d 535, 541 (1973); *SEC v. Texas Gulf Sulphur Co.*, 401 F. 2d 833, 854–855 (1968), *cert. denied sub nom. Coates v. SEC*, 394 U.S. 976 (1969). I see no real distinction between that situation and this one, for surely the question whether negligent conduct violates the Rule should not depend upon the plaintiff's identity. If negligence is a violation factor when the SEC sues, it must be a violation factor when a private party sues. And, in its present posture, this case is concerned with the issue of violation, not with the secondary issue of a private party's judicially created entitlement to damages or other specific relief. *See Rondeau v. Mosinee Paper Corp.*, 422 U.S. 49 (1975).

The critical importance of the auditing accountant's role in insuring full disclosure cannot be overestimated. The SEC has emphasized that in certifying statements the accountant's duty "is to safeguard the public interest, not that of his client." *In re Touche, Niven, Bailey & Smart*, 37 S.E.C. 629, 670–671 (1957). "In our complex society the accountant's certificate and the lawyer's opinion can be instruments for inflicting pecuniary loss more potent than the chisel or the crowbar." *United States v. Benjamin*, 328 F. 2d 854, 863 (CA2), *cert. denied sub nom. Howard v. United States*, 377 U.S. 953 (1964). In this light, the initial inquiry into whether Ernst & Ernst's preparation and certification of the financial statements of First Securities Company of Chicago were negligent, because of the failure to perceive Nay's extraordinary mail rule, and in other alleged respects, and thus whether Rule 10b–5 was violated, should not be thwarted.

But the Court today decides that it is to be thwarted, and so once again it rests with Congress to rephrase and to re-enact, if investor victims, such as these, are ever to have relief under the federal securities laws that I thought had been enacted for their broad, needed, and deserving benefit. . . .

HERMAN & MACLEAN V. HUDDLESTON*

MARSHALL, JUSTICE. These consolidated cases raise two unresolved questions concerning § 10(b) of the Securities Exchange Act of 1934 (1934 Act). The first is whether purchasers of registered securities who allege they were defrauded by misrepresentations in a registration statement may maintain an action under § 10(b) notwithstanding the express remedy for misstatements and omissions in registration statements provided by § 11 of the Securities Act of 1933 (1933 Act). The second question is

---

*   459 U.S. 375 (1983).

whether persons seeking recovery under § 10(b) must prove their cause of action by clear and convincing evidence rather than by a preponderance of the evidence.

In 1969 Texas International Speedway, Inc. (TIS), filed a registration statement and prospectus with the Securities and Exchange Commission offering a total of $4,398,900 in securities to the public. The proceeds of the sale were to be used to finance the construction of an automobile speedway. The entire issue was sold on the offering date, October 30, 1969. TIS did not meet with success, however, and the corporation filed a petition for bankruptcy on November 30, 1970.

In 1972 plaintiffs Huddleston and Bradley instituted a class action in the United States District Court for the Southern District of Texas on behalf of themselves and other purchasers of TIS securities. The complaint alleged violations of § 10(b) of the 1934 Act and SEC Rule 10b–5 promulgated thereunder. Plaintiffs sued most of the participants in the offering, including the accounting firm, Herman & MacLean, which had issued an opinion concerning certain financial statements . . . that were contained in the registration statement and prospectus. Plaintiffs claimed that the defendants had engaged in a fraudulent scheme to misrepresent or conceal material facts regarding the financial condition of TIS, including the costs incurred in building the speedway.

[The District Court concluded that liability could be found only if the defendants acted with scienter, proven by a preponderance of the evidence, and found this to be so proven. The Appellate Court] held that a cause of action may be maintained under § 10(b) of the 1934 Act for fraudulent misrepresentations and omissions even when that conduct might also be actionable under § 11 of the 1933 Act. However, the Court of Appeals disagreed with the District Court as to the appropriate standard of proof for an action under § 10(b), concluding that a plaintiff must prove his case by "clear and convincing" evidence. . . . We granted certiorari to consider whether an implied cause of action under § 10(b) of the 1934 Act will lie for conduct subject to an express civil remedy under the 1933 Act, an issue we have previously reserved [in *Blue Chip Stamps v. Manor Drug Stores*, 421 U.S. 723, 752, n. 15 (1975)], and to decide the standard of proof applicable to actions under § 10(b). We now affirm the Court of Appeals' holding that plaintiffs could maintain an action under § 10(b) of the 1934 Act, but we reverse as to the applicable standard of proof.

The Securities Act of 1933 and the 1934 Act "constitute interrelated components of the federal regulatory scheme governing transactions in securities." *Ernst & Ernst v. Hochfelder*, 425 U.S. 185, 206 (1976). The Acts created several express private rights of action, one of which is contained in § 11 of the 1933 Act. In addition to the private actions created explicitly by the 1933 and 1934 Acts, federal courts have implied private remedies under other provisions of the two laws. Most significantly for present purposes, a private right of action under § 10(b) of the 1934 Act and Rule 10b–5 has been consistently recognized for more than 35 years. The existence of this implied remedy is simply beyond peradventure.

The issue in this case is whether a party should be barred from invoking this established remedy for fraud because the allegedly fraudulent conduct would apparently also provide the basis for a damages action under § 11 of the 1933 Act. The resolution of this issue turns on the fact that the two provisions involve distinct causes of action and were intended to address different types of wrongdoing.

Section 11 of the 1933 Act allows purchasers of a registered security to sue certain enumerated parties in a registered offering when false or misleading information is included in a registration statement. The section was designed to assure compliance with the disclosure provisions of the Act by imposing a stringent standard of liability on the parties who play a direct role in a registered offering [including accountants]. If a plaintiff purchased a security issued pursuant to a registration statement, he need only show a material misstatement or omission to establish his prima facie case. Liability against the issuer of a security is virtually absolute, even for innocent misstatements. Other defendants bear the burden of demonstrating due diligence.

Although limited in scope, § 11 places a relatively minimal burden on a plaintiff. In contrast, § 10(b) is a "catchall" antifraud provision, but it requires a plaintiff to carry a heavier burden to establish a cause of action. While a § 11 action must be brought by a purchaser of a registered security, must be based on misstatements or omissions in a registration statement, and can only be brought against certain parties, a § 10(b) action can be brought by a purchaser or seller of "*any* security" against "*any* person" who has used "*any* manipulative or deceptive device or contrivance" in connection with the purchase or sale of a security. 15 U.S.C. § 78j (emphasis added). However, a § 10(b) plaintiff carries a heavier burden than a § 11 plaintiff. Most significantly, he must prove that the defendant acted with scienter, *i.e.*, with intent to deceive, manipulate, or defraud.

Since § 11 and § 10(b) address different types of wrongdoing, we see no reason to carve out an exception to § 10(b) for fraud occurring in a registration statement just because the same conduct may also be actionable under § 11. Exempting such conduct from liability under § 10(b) would conflict with the basic purpose of the 1933 Act: to provide greater protection to purchasers of registered securities. It would be anomalous indeed if the special protection afforded to purchasers in a registered offering by the 1933 Act were deemed to deprive such purchasers of the protections against manipulation and deception that § 10(b) makes available to all persons who deal in securities. . . .

This conclusion is reinforced by our reasoning in *Ernst & Ernst v. Hochfelder*, which held that actions under § 10(b) require proof of scienter and do not encompass negligent conduct. In so holding, we noted that each of the express civil remedies in the 1933 Act allowing recovery for negligent conduct is subject to procedural restrictions not applicable to a § 10(b) action. 425 U.S., at 208–210. We emphasized that extension of § 10(b) to negligent conduct would have allowed causes of action for negligence under the express remedies to be brought instead under § 10(b), "thereby [nullifying] the effectiveness of the carefully drawn procedural restrictions on these express actions." *Id.*, at 210. In reasoning that scienter should be required in § 10(b) actions in order to avoid circumvention of the procedural restrictions surrounding the express remedies, we necessarily assumed that the express remedies were not exclusive. Otherwise there would have been no danger of nullification. Conversely, because the added burden of proving scienter attaches to suits under § 10(b), invocation of the § 10(b) remedy will not "nullify" the procedural restrictions that apply to the express remedies. . . .

A cumulative construction of the securities laws also furthers their broad remedial purposes. In enacting the 1934 Act, Congress stated that its purpose was "to impose requirements necessary to make [securities] regulation and control reasonably complete and effective." 15 U.S.C. § 78b. In furtherance of that objective, § 10(b) makes it unlawful to use "any manipulative or deceptive device or contrivance" in connection with the purchase or sale of any security. The effectiveness of the broad proscription against fraud in § 10(b) would be undermined if its scope were restricted by the existence of an express remedy under § 11.[22] Yet we have repeatedly recognized that securities laws combating fraud should be construed "not technically and restrictively, but flexibly to effectuate [their] remedial purposes." *SEC v. Capital Gains Research Bureau, Inc.*, 375 U.S. 180, 195 (1963). We therefore reject an interpretation of the securities laws that displaces an action under § 10(b).

Accordingly, we hold that the availability of an express remedy under § 11 of the 1933 Act does not preclude defrauded purchasers of registered securities from maintaining an action under § 10(b) of the 1934 Act. To this extent the judgment of the Court of Appeals is affirmed.

---

[22] Moreover, certain individuals who play a part in preparing the registration statement generally cannot be reached by a § 11 action. These include corporate officers other than those specified in 15 U.S.C. § 77k(a), lawyers not acting as "experts," and accountants with respect to parts of a registration statement which they are not named as having prepared or certified. If, as Herman & MacLean argues, purchasers in registered offerings were required to rely solely on § 11, they would have no recourse against such individuals even if the excluded parties engaged in fraudulent conduct while participating in the registration statement. The exempted individuals would be immune from federal liability for fraudulent conduct even though § 10(b) extends to "any person" who engages in fraud in connection with a purchase or sale of securities.

[Turning to the standard of proof, in] a typical civil suit for money damages, plaintiffs must prove their case by a preponderance of the evidence. Similarly, in an action by the SEC to establish fraud under § 17(a) of the 1933 Act, we have held that proof by a preponderance of the evidence suffices to establish liability. *SEC v. C. M. Joiner Leasing Corp.*, 320 U.S. 344, 355 (1943). "Where . . . proof is offered in a civil action, as here, a preponderance of the evidence will establish the case. . . ." *Ibid.* The same standard applies in administrative proceedings before the SEC and has been consistently employed by the lower courts in private actions under the securities laws.

The Court of Appeals nonetheless held that plaintiffs in a § 10(b) suit must establish their case by clear and convincing evidence. The Court of Appeals relied primarily on the traditional use of a higher burden of proof in civil fraud actions at common law. 640 F.2d, at 545–546. Reference to common-law practices can be misleading, however, since the historical considerations underlying the imposition of a higher standard of proof have questionable pertinence here. *See Blue Chip Stamps v. Manor Drug Stores*, 421 U.S. 723, 744–745 (1975) ("[The] typical fact situation in which the classic tort of misrepresentation and deceit evolved was light years away from the world of commercial transactions to which Rule 10b–5 is applicable"). Moreover, the antifraud provisions of the securities laws are not coextensive with common-law doctrines of fraud. Indeed, an important purpose of the federal securities statutes was to rectify perceived deficiencies in the available common-law protections by establishing higher standards of conduct in the securities industry. We therefore find reference to the common law in this instance unavailing.

Where Congress has not prescribed the appropriate standard of proof and the Constitution does not dictate a particular standard, we must prescribe one. In doing so, we are mindful that a standard of proof "serves to allocate the risk of error between the litigants and to indicate the relative importance attached to the ultimate decision." *Addington v. Texas*, 441 U.S. 418, 423 (1979). . . .

A preponderance-of-the-evidence standard allows both parties to "share the risk of error in roughly equal fashion." *Addington v. Texas*, *supra*, at 423. Any other standard expresses a preference for one side's interests. The balance of interests in this case warrants use of the preponderance standard. On the one hand, the defendants face the risk of opprobrium that may result from a finding of fraudulent conduct, but this risk is identical to that in an action under § 17(a), which is governed by the preponderance-of-the-evidence standard. The interests of defendants in a securities case do not differ qualitatively from the interests of defendants sued for violations of other federal statutes such as the antitrust or civil rights laws, for which proof by a preponderance of the evidence suffices. On the other hand, the interests of plaintiffs in such suits are significant.

Defrauded investors are among the very individuals Congress sought to protect in the securities laws. If they prove that it is more likely than not that they were defrauded, they should recover. . . .

CENTRAL BANK V. FIRST INTERSTATE BANK*

KENNEDY, JUSTICE (for the majority). [The Court decides that private civil liability under § 10(b) does not extend] to those who do not engage in the manipulative or deceptive practice, but who aid and abet the violation [a question the Court left unanswered in] *Herman & MacLean v. Huddleston*, 459 U.S. 375, 379, n. 5 (1983); *Ernst & Ernst v. Hochfelder*, 425 U.S. 185, 191–192, n. 7 (1976). [The Court addresses the question in the context of claims against an indenture trustee for an issue of public building authority bonds. The authority defaulted on the debt and bondholders sued it and the underwriter for direct violations of § 10(b) of the Securities Exchange Act of 1934 and the trustee as "secondarily liable under § 10(b) for its conduct in aiding and abetting the fraud." The District Court granted summary judgment for the trustee, the Tenth Circuit reversed, and the Supreme Court reversed again, deciding that the text of Section 10(b) does not encompass liability for aiding and abetting. The holding appears to extend to accountants.]

Like the Court of Appeals in this case, other federal courts have allowed private aiding and abetting actions under § 10(b). The first and leading case to impose the liability was *Brennan v. Midwestern United Life Ins. Co.*, 259 F. Supp. 673 (ND Ind. 1966), *aff'd*, 417 F.2d 147 (CA7 1969), *cert. denied*, 397 U.S. 989 (1970). The court reasoned that "in the absence of a clear legislative expression to the contrary, the statute must be flexibly applied so as to implement its policies and purposes." 259 F. Supp. at 680–681. Since 1966, numerous courts have taken the same position.

After our decisions in *Santa Fe Industries, Inc. v. Green*, 430 U.S. 462 (1977), and *Ernst & Ernst v. Hochfelder*, 425 U.S. 185 (1976), where we paid close attention to the statutory text in defining the scope of conduct prohibited by § 10(b), courts and commentators began to question whether aiding and abetting liability under § 10(b) was still available. . . . We granted certiorari to resolve the continuing confusion over the existence and scope of the § 10(b) aiding and abetting action. 508 U.S. 959 (1993). . . .

With respect [to] the scope of conduct prohibited by § 10(b), the text of the statute controls our decision. In § 10(b), Congress prohibited manipulative or deceptive acts in connection with the purchase or sale of securities. It envisioned that the SEC would enforce the statutory prohibition through administrative and injunctive actions. Of course, a private plaintiff now may bring suit against violators of § 10(b). But the private plaintiff may not bring a 10b–5 suit against a defendant for acts

---

*   511 U.S. 164 (1993).

not prohibited by the text of § 10(b). To the contrary, our cases considering the scope of conduct prohibited by § 10(b) in private suits have emphasized adherence to the statutory language, " 'the starting point in every case involving construction of a statute.' " *Ernst & Ernst, supra,* 425 U.S. 185 at 197 (quoting *Blue Chip Stamps,* 421 U.S. at 756 (Powell, J., concurring)). We have refused to allow 10b–5 challenges to conduct not prohibited by the text of the statute.

In *Ernst & Ernst,* we considered whether negligent acts could violate § 10(b). We first noted that "the words 'manipulative or deceptive' used in conjunction with 'device or contrivance' strongly suggest that § 10(b) was intended to proscribe knowing or intentional misconduct." 425 U.S. at 197. The SEC argued that the broad congressional purposes behind the Act—to protect investors from false and misleading practices that might injure them—suggested that § 10(b) should also reach negligent conduct. We rejected that argument, concluding that the SEC's interpretation would "add a gloss to the operative language of the statute quite different from its commonly accepted meaning." *Id.,* at 199. . . .

Adherence to the text in defining the conduct covered by § 10(b) is consistent with our decisions interpreting other provisions of the securities Acts. . . . Our consideration of statutory duties, especially in cases interpreting § 10(b), establishes that the statutory text controls the definition of conduct covered by § 10(b). That bodes ill for respondents, for "the language of Section 10(b) does not in terms mention aiding and abetting." Brief for SEC as Amicus Curiae 8. To overcome this problem, respondents and the SEC suggest (or hint at) the novel argument that the use of the phrase "directly or indirectly" in the text of § 10(b) covers aiding and abetting.

The federal courts have not relied on the "directly or indirectly" language when imposing aiding and abetting liability under § 10(b), and with good reason. There is a basic flaw with this interpretation. According to respondents and the SEC, the "directly or indirectly" language shows that "Congress . . . intended to reach all persons who engage, even if only indirectly, in proscribed activities connected with securities transactions." *Ibid.* The problem, of course, is that aiding and abetting liability extends beyond persons who engage, even indirectly, in a proscribed activity; aiding and abetting liability reaches persons who do not engage in the proscribed activities at all, but who give a degree of aid to those who do. A further problem with respondents' interpretation of the "directly or indirectly" language is posed by the numerous provisions of the 1934 Act that use the term in a way that does not impose aiding and abetting liability. . . .

Congress knew how to impose aiding and abetting liability when it chose to do so. *See, e.g.,* Act of Mar. 4, 1909, § 332, 35 Stat. 1152, as amended, 18 U.S.C. § 2 (general criminal aiding and abetting statute). If, as respondents seem to say, Congress intended to impose aiding and abetting liability, we presume it would have used the words "aid" and "abet" in the statutory text. But it did not. *Cf. Pinter v. Dahl*, 486 U.S. at 650 ("When Congress wished to create such liability, it had little trouble doing so"); *Blue Chip Stamps*, 421 U.S. at 734 ("When Congress wished to provide a remedy to those who neither purchase nor sell securities, it had little trouble in doing so expressly").

We reach the uncontroversial conclusion, accepted even by those courts recognizing a § 10(b) aiding and abetting cause of action, that the text of the 1934 Act does not itself reach those who aid and abet a § 10(b) violation. Unlike those courts, however, we think that conclusion resolves the case. It is inconsistent with settled methodology in § 10(b) cases to extend liability beyond the scope of conduct prohibited by the statutory text. To be sure, aiding and abetting a wrongdoer ought to be actionable in certain instances. *Cf.* Restatement (Second) of Torts § 876(b) (1977).The issue, however, is not whether imposing private civil liability on aiders and abettors is good policy but whether aiding and abetting is covered by the statute. . . .

STEVENS, JUSTICE (dissenting, with whom BLACKMAN, SOUTER and GINSBURG, JUSTICES, join). The main themes of the Court's opinion are that the text of § 10(b) of the Securities Exchange Act of 1934 (Exchange Act) does not expressly mention aiding and abetting liability, and that Congress knows how to legislate. Both propositions are unexceptionable, but neither is reason to eliminate the private right of action against aiders and abettors of violations of § 10(b) and the Securities and Exchange Commission's (SEC's) Rule 10b–5. Because the majority gives short shrift to a long history of aider and abettor liability under § 10(b) and Rule 10b–5, and because its rationale imperils other well-established forms of secondary liability not expressly addressed in the securities laws, I respectfully dissent.

In hundreds of judicial and administrative proceedings in every Circuit in the federal system, the courts and the SEC have concluded that aiders and abettors are subject to liability under § 10(b) and Rule 10b–5. While we have reserved decision on the legitimacy of the theory in two cases that did not present it, all 11 Courts of Appeals to have considered the question have recognized a private cause of action against aiders and abettors under § 10(b) and Rule 10b–5. The early aiding and abetting decisions relied upon principles borrowed from tort law; in those cases, judges closer to the times and climate of the 73d Congress than we concluded that holding aiders and abettors liable was consonant with the Exchange Act's purpose to strengthen the antifraud remedies of the common law. . . .

The Courts of Appeals have usually applied a familiar three-part test for aider and abettor liability, patterned on the Restatement of Torts formulation, that requires (i) the existence of a primary violation of § 10(b) or Rule 10b–5, (ii) the defendant's knowledge of (or recklessness as to) that primary violation, and (iii) "substantial assistance" of the violation by the defendant. If indeed there has been "continuing confusion" concerning the private right of action against aiders and abettors, that confusion has not concerned its basic structure, still less its "existence." Indeed, in this case, petitioner assumed the existence of a right of action against aiders and abettors, and sought review only of the subsidiary questions whether an indenture trustee could be found liable as an aider and abettor absent a breach of an indenture agreement or other duty under state law, and whether it could be liable as an aider and abettor based only on a showing of recklessness. These questions, it is true, have engendered genuine disagreement in the Courts of Appeals. But instead of simply addressing the questions presented by the parties, on which the law really was unsettled, the Court *sua sponte* directed the parties to address a question on which even the petitioner justifiably thought the law was settled, and reaches out to overturn a most considerable body of precedent.

Many of the observations in the majority's opinion would be persuasive if we were considering whether to recognize a private right of action based upon a securities statute enacted recently. Our approach to implied causes of action, as to other matters of statutory construction, has changed markedly since the Exchange Act's passage in 1934. At that time, and indeed until quite recently, courts regularly assumed, in accord with the traditional common-law presumption, that a statute enacted for the benefit of a particular class conferred on members of that class the right to sue violators of that statute. . . .

As framed by the Court's order redrafting the questions presented, this case concerns only the existence and scope of aiding and abetting liability in suits brought by private parties under § 10(b) and Rule 10b–5. The majority's rationale, however, sweeps far beyond even those important issues. The majority leaves little doubt that the Exchange Act does not even permit the SEC to pursue aiders and abettors in civil enforcement actions under § 10(b) and Rule 10b–5. Aiding and abetting liability has a long pedigree in civil proceedings brought by the SEC under § 10(b) and Rule 10b–5, and has become an important part of the SEC's enforcement arsenal. Moreover, the majority's approach to aiding and abetting at the very least casts serious doubt, both for private and SEC actions, on other forms of secondary liability that, like the aiding and abetting theory, have long been recognized by the SEC and the courts but are not expressly spelled out in the securities statutes. The principle the Court espouses today—that liability may not be imposed on parties who are not within the scope of § 10(b)'s plain language—is inconsistent with long-established SEC and judicial precedent. . . .

NOTES

1.   The logic and statutory analysis in *Central Bank* extend to deny private rights of action to investors arguing that a third party, such as an accountant or lawyer, facilitated another's fraudulent scheme. *See Stoneridge Investment Partners v. Scientific-Atlanta, Inc.*, 552 U.S. 148 (2008) (concerning vendors and customers).

2.   The Private Securities Litigation Reform Act of 1995, 15 U.S.C. § 78u–4, modified the prevailing federal securities law regime of joint and several liability by replacing it, to a substantial extent, with a regime of proportionate liability. Imposing joint and several liability requires a specific finding that a person "knowingly" violated the securities laws. Others found liable are responsible only for the portion of a judgment corresponding to their percentage of responsibility, as the fact finder determines it. Accounting firms are important beneficiaries of this shift.

3.   The dissent's concern about the SEC's authority to pursue aiders and abettors in civil enforcement actions was resolved by subsequent Congressional action giving the SEC this power. Dodd-Frank Wall Street Reform and Consumer Protection Act of 2010, § 929. That legislation empowered the SEC to bring such cases, and obtain monetary penalties, under all parts of the federal securities laws. It also made "recklessness" the standard of proof that the SEC must meet, overturning judicial interpretations which had held that proving "actual knowledge" was required.

Problem 14

The following appeared on the op-ed page of *The New York Times* in the wake of a broad scandal that erupted concerning Enron Corp. (more on that case in Chapter 16). It is written by Harrison J. Goldin, comptroller of New York City from 1974 to 1989, and adjunct professor at Cardozo Law School. The piece is dated February 1, 2002, and called "Auditor Term Limits."

> The question of auditor independence is at the heart of the Enron fiasco. Although many of the current proposals to ensure this independence are worth considering, the best of them is one borrowed from the world of government and politics: term limits.

> Like elected officials in New York City and elsewhere, auditors of publicly held companies should be allowed to serve the same company for only a set number of years. An auditing firm

that knew that its contract had a defined time horizon—say, five years—would have far less incentive to compromise its standards to accommodate a management whose accounting practices were questionably aggressive or problematic.

Other suggestions designed to assure auditors' independence have serious limitations. Preventing a company from hiring the same accounting firm as auditor and consultant might lessen conflicts. Yet accounting firms might be even more desperate to retain clients, and even more reluctant to buck top management, if they had only an auditing contract and no consulting function. Requiring more complete financial disclosure from corporations would surely be helpful. But with business practices changing so quickly—and becoming increasingly subtle and complex— auditors need the guidance of comprehensive, and often necessarily ambiguous, standards. Creating a new oversight mechanism, not tied to the accounting industry, might promote independence. Still, whatever its composition, such a board would likely embody many of the inherent limitations of its predecessors.

Term limits for auditors is the most sensible and practical option. The Securities and Exchange Commission could simply require that all auditing contracts for public companies be for a limited duration, after which they would not be subject to immediate renewal. (The same accounting firm could return to audit a company after a suitable period of time had passed.) Not only would this promote the general goal of greater independence, but it would also provide an incentive for auditors to improve their performance. Since each accounting firm would know that it would be succeeded by a competitor, it would do whatever it could to ensure that its work was above reproach. The new firm, in turn, would have an interest in disclosing and disclaiming responsibility for any questionable practice allowed by its predecessor. What better way to ensure that the original auditor—and those that come after it—adhere to the highest professional standards?

The cost of requiring the regular replacement of auditors may be high. And there is value in continuity, familiarity and efficiency. But the cost, as the Enron debacle dramatizes, is one the marketplace must bear to preserve—or recapture—the public confidence on which our free market system depends.

Questions: Are term limits the best way to promote auditor independence? Audit reports beginning in 2017 must disclose the auditor's tenure, as noted in Chapter 1. Do you expect such disclosure to contribute significantly to audit effectiveness?

In the wake of the Enron debacle of 2002, each of the largest auditing firms announced an intention to refuse to do any consulting business for audit clients (except for tax and compliance services). Some large companies announced they would not use their audit firms for consulting advice. Do such steps promote auditor independence? Which are likely to be more effective? Are other alternatives available?

Consider the following table of concerns about audit integrity and possible responses. Most of those listed were adopted in some form in the Sarbanes-Oxley Act of 2002. The mandatory firm rotation proposal made above was not. Instead, the Act directed that the Government Accountability Office (GAO) conduct a study of the concept. The GAO's study concluded, after examining associated costs and benefits, that the scores of other changes the Act mandated should be allowed time to work before pursuing the mandatory audit firm rotation concept. It does not appear that the time has yet come.

Concern About Audit Integrity
Causes and Cures

Dual role as auditor and consultant posing *conflicts of interest*	Prohibit, curtail, refrain
Dual role as internal and external auditor posing *conflicts of interest*	Prohibit, curtail, refrain
Internal audit firm oversight inadequate	Create supervisory board or include independent directors on audit firm boards
External audit firm oversight inadequate	Create or strengthen profession review board, to include members from outside the auditing profession
Corporate governance oversight inadequate	Use audit committee, composed entirely of outside directors, with the power to hire and fire audit firms
Deterring knowing audit failure	Heighten penalties for auditor negligence, loosen plaintiff/shareholder burden in suing auditors
Deterring corporate managerial deception	Criminalize lying to auditors
Deterring providing an incomplete picture	Establish audit rules that express the character of a corporation's accounting, ranging from conservative to aggressive and specifying areas of each
Erasing financial incentives to "look the other way"	Require corporations to pay full audit fees and other amounts due when auditor is fired

---

Conceptual Questions 14

Auditor work papers are ordinarily discoverable in litigation (a limited accountant-client privilege exists under some state laws and under federal law for communications relating to tax matters, *see* Internal Revenue Code § 7525, but these are generally narrower than the attorney-client privilege and attorney work-product doctrine). As you may know (and Chapter 15 considers), lawyer work papers are ordinarily protected from discovery in litigation under either the attorney-client privilege or the work-product doctrine. Why shouldn't auditors have an auditor-client privilege? Why should not their work papers be protected under a work-product doctrine?

CHAPTER 15

PERSPECTIVES ON THE LAWYER'S ROLE

■ ■ ■

Lawyers regularly interact with auditors, as well as managers and accountants, on a wide variety of transactions in which many professionals are involved. Each professional serves a particular function and operates in a culture defined by a set of norms and expectations unique to that profession. Even when all professionals are interested in the same ultimate objectives for a client—say raising financing, closing an acquisition and so on—the professional roles may come into conflict. Those conflicts can be more acute when professionals work on different sides of a transaction or are otherwise formally adverse, as in litigation.

A. LOSS CONTINGENCIES AND LAWYERS' LETTERS

The most striking accounting context in which a lawyer's and auditor's role may conflict concerns loss contingencies, introduced in Chapter 6. At any time, most substantial entities will be involved, or be at risk of involvement, in legal proceedings in which the entity's position is not clear. For example, entities can be the subject of lawsuits or administrative proceedings in which, while no present liability is known, the potential for liability is real. Sometimes entities retain lawyers in other capacities, such as to investigate the integrity of internal controls designed to promote legal compliance. Auditors would want to know what risks of legal liability exist but are not ordinarily in a position to know of their existence or appraise their significance.

For this purpose, auditors typically inquire of the entity's general counsel for an assessment of the entity's legal positions. But even the general counsel may not be in the best position to gauge the materiality of potential exposure to legal claims if, as is often the case, outside counsel is handling the matter. As a result, general counsel typically rely on the entity's outside counsel handling a matter and request them to respond to the auditor's inquiry.

In all these circumstances, tension arises because outside counsel risk (among other things) waiving the attorney-client privilege or work-product doctrine with respect to information provided to auditors concerning potential exposure. Such disclosure could be damaging in certain contexts, such as pending litigation in which the entity vigorously denies claims against it. In response to the tension between counsel's need to preserve privileges and the auditor's need to understand and provide disclosure with respect to contingent legal liabilities, the American Bar Association (ABA) and the AICPA, in the 1970's, jointly promulgated a policy statement to delineate the proper form and scope of an auditor's inquiry and counsel's response.

As to legal loss contingencies, that statement identifies three categories: *pending or overtly threatened litigation* (whether or not specified by the entity in its request to counsel); *contractual obligations* upon which the entity specifically requests the counsel to comment; and *unasserted possible claims* upon which the entity specifically requests the counsel to comment. While neither the ABA/AICPA Statement nor anything else obligates counsel to respond in any particular way, its failure to do so, or in any event to satisfy the inquiry, poses the risk that the auditor will be forced to issue some sort of qualified audit report. Because of the seriousness of such a position, efforts are usually made to reach a reasonable accommodation, though the tensions are ultimately unavoidable. Consider the following discussion of lawyers' letters for auditors.*

When auditors ask lawyers to help them decide if a client's financial statements should reflect possible litigation losses, the lawyer's response may be of limited use. This is because of potential misunderstandings between the two professions. Among the central issues, two stand out. First, when auditors receive lawyer letters saying litigation losses are neither "probable" nor "reasonably possible," is it safe to conclude that financial statement disclosure is not required under accounting standards? Second, will a standard unqualified opinion meet audit requirements?

These questions are difficult to answer because lawyers' interpretations of their responsibilities in replying to auditors differ from auditor expectations. To preserve privileges and due to professional conservatism, lawyers are reluctant to provide auditors with estimates of the likelihood and dollar amounts of losses. For the auditor, this means any information lawyers provide must be evaluated carefully before it is used.

Accounting and Auditing Requirements.

Proper accounting and auditing for litigation loss contingencies present numerous practical problems. The accounting and auditing standards for these contingencies—which result from litigation, claims, assessments and unasserted claims against a client—are general and require the exercise of considerable professional judgment.

---

* Adapted from Bruce K. Behn & Kurt Pany, "Auditing: Limitations of Lawyers' Letters," *Journal of Accountancy* (Feb. 1995) at 61.

Both the financial statement treatment and the impact on the audit report are affected by whether the likelihood of loss is remote, reasonably possible or probable. Under GAAS, litigation information is obtained from a client, presented in a letter of audit inquiry to the client's lawyer and corroborated and expanded upon in the reply from the lawyer (who has devoted "substantive attention" to the matters). While lawyers are not required to supplement the list for omitted unasserted claims, where assertion is likely, they should so inform the client. When auditors receive lawyers' replies with insufficient information, a "scope limitation" on the audit occurs that may result in a qualified opinion or a disclaimer of opinion.

The Legal View.

The lawyer is the expert on litigation, yet differences in the responsibilities of lawyers and auditors with respect to common clients have resulted in contentious difficulties. While auditors are responsible for determining that there is "adequate disclosure" and when an explanatory "scope limitation" paragraph should be added to an audit report, lawyers are responsible for advancing their client's interests in litigation. Since information provided by lawyers may affect a case adversely, these responsibilities may conflict.

Many lawyers believe that, despite a client's request that they provide the auditor with information, they should remain cautious in letters to auditors out of concern their replies may (1) impair the client-lawyer confidentiality privilege; (2) disclose a client confidence or secret; (3) prejudice the client's defense of a claim; and/or (4) constitute an admission by the client. ABA guidance for lawyers in this situation advocates lawyerly caution in communications with auditors, a point emphasized in the first sentence of an ABA position statement: "The public interest in protecting the confidentiality of lawyer-client communications is fundamental."

The ABA statement also says lawyers normally should refrain from expressing judgments on outcome—either likelihood or amount of loss. The result of these principles is that auditors generally can obtain relatively complete responses on the existence of litigation and the dates when the underlying cause occurred but less complete responses on the likelihood of an unfavorable outcome and the amount of potential loss.

In addition to an implicit hesitancy to provide evidential matter on likelihood and amount of loss, the ABA defines the terms "probable" and "remote" in ways at odds with auditing's definitions of similar terms. Consider the variations in these definitions in Table 15-1.

Table 15-1

ABA Definitions	Auditing Definitions
Remote: An unfavorable outcome is remote if the prospects for the client not succeeding in its defense are extremely doubtful and the prospects of success by the climant are slight.	**Remote:** The chance of the future event or events occurring is slight.
Probable: An unfavorable outcome for the client is probable if the claimant's prospects of not succeeding are extremely doubtful and the client's prospects for success in its defense are slight.	**Reasonably possible:** The chance of the future event or events occurring is more than remote but less than likely.
	Probable: The future event or events are likely to occur.

Financial Reporting and Audit Difficulties.

What is the significance of these differences? Will lawyers interpret remote, reasonably possible and probable according to the auditing formulation? Presumably auditors will prepare the inquiry with that standard in mind. While it may be desirable for lawyers to follow suit for clarity of communication, plenty of lawyers adhere to the ABA definitional guidelines.

Does it matter whether lawyers use the auditing definitions? If lawyers use the ABA definitions in making their reply, the issue becomes one of determining whether the definitions differ significantly from those auditing offers. This calls for a bit of parsing nearly as mind-bending as considering such questions as what the meaning of the word is is!

The definitions of "remote" are similar in that both use the term slight. The ABA definition adds that the prospects of not succeeding are extremely doubtful. Even if the ABA definition is more stringent, resulting in fewer "remote" characterizations, auditors are likely to decide to perform additional audit procedures to determine if further disclosure, as by a footnote, is necessary. Accordingly, differences in how the auditing and legal professions view remote may have limited real-world significance.

The definition of "probable" seems substantively different. The auditing "likely-to-occur" requirement seems less definitive than the ABA's "extremely doubtful" or "slight." Thus, for example, a loss contingency could meet the FASB requirements for loss accrual (likely to occur) and still not meet the ABA definition of probable (extremely doubtful or slight chance of succeeding).

Assume, for example, an auditor believes a likelihood of 70% or greater should be considered probable. The lawyer's definition is more stringent—say, 95%. The lawyer considers cases in terms of probabilities and believes it is 85% likely a loss will occur. Under these circumstances, the lawyer will not consider the event probable and will not report it to the auditor. Thus, even when both agree the likelihood is 85%, the auditor will not be informed that the likelihood of loss is probable and the amount, if it can be reasonably estimated, will not be recorded in the financial statements as auditing standards seem to require.

Consider the term "reasonably possible," which the auditing definitions use but the ABA does not. When material, auditing standards require that "reasonably possible" loss contingencies be disclosed in financial statement footnotes. Auditors define the term to mean "more than remote but less than likely." Presumably that means probable. While the ABA approach not only does not use the term, its structure hints that in most situations an unfavorable outcome will be neither "probable" nor "remote."

It is possible to locate the concept of "reasonably possible" somewhere on the ABA continuum between remote and probable in the same manner as the auditor's continuum. You could, for example, array the different probability standards applied by auditors and lawyers in the following graphic, inferring "reasonably possible" in the case of the ABA.

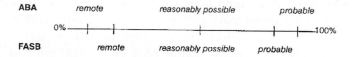

On the other hand, it can be credibly argued that the ABA's failure to acknowledge reasonably possible is deliberate, making a probabilistic continuum inappropriate. Proponents of this view emphasize that the results of litigation against clients generally are unpredictable until a final non-appealable judgment is rendered or a case settled or litigation otherwise abandoned. This does not make the results reasonably possible—they simply are unpredictable.

The general nature of auditing's definitions has led to studies asking auditors and others to interpret the meanings of "reasonably possible" and "probable." Replies showed significant variation within the profession. Average responses for reasonably possible differ by study and are between 15% and 42%. Slightly less variation exists for probable, with various studies reporting mean responses of approximately 60% to 70% likely.

A lawyer's letter describing a potential loss as probable (and for which the likely loss can be measured) in most circumstances requires financial statements to be adjusted for the loss. When the lawyer does not include an estimate of the likelihood of an unfavorable outcome, the problem is more difficult since accrual of a loss may or may not be necessary. It is unlikely the letter will include what auditing standards describe as reasonably possible situations. When lawyers do not provide a specific likelihood, auditors must try to determine whether auditing's definition of probable (likely to occur) has been met.

Must a lawyer who believes a litigation loss is probable under the ABA statement inform the auditor? As indicated, the ABA definition of probable suggests a higher likelihood than auditing's definition. However, the problem is even more severe if lawyers believe that level has been met and don't report it. The ABA statement suggests a lawyer "may" choose to report a probable outcome. Indeed, the professional auditing literature includes an interpretation of the auditing standards as suggesting that the lawyer "is not required to use those terms in communicating his evaluation to the auditor." The ABA statement says the suggested approach can be modified.

Accordingly, a lawyer's letter that fails to characterize a likelihood of loss as probable is not sufficient to determine whether auditing requirements have been met by a footnote (or by no) disclosure. Auditors appeal to guidance on the terminology often included in lawyer's letters, a version of which is set forth in Tables 16-2 and 16-3.

Lawyers sometimes consider examples like those in each Table in settling upon particular language to be used in communicating with auditors. Table 15-2 gives examples of ambiguous language contained in lawyer's letters that auditors may construe as signaling that an unfavorable outcome is remote. Table 15-3 gives examples of somewhat more ambiguous language that would reasonably lead auditors to request further information from the lawyer to clarify what is being communicated.

Table 15-2

Lawyer Opinion Language Auditors See
Signaling Unfavorable Outcomes Is Remote

- We are of the opinion that this action will not result in any liability to the company.
- It is our opinion that the possible liability to the company in this proceeding is nominal in amount.
- We believe the company will be able to defend this action successfully.
- We believe that the plaintiff's case against the company is without merit.
- Based on the facts known to us, after a full investigation, it is our opinion that no liability will be established against the company in these suits.

> **Table 15-3**
>
> *Lawyer Opinion Language Auditors See
> Requiring Auditor to Request Clarification*
>
> - It is our opinion that the company will be able to asset meritorious defenses to this action.
>
> - We believe the action can be settled for less than the damages claimed.
>
> - We are unable to express an opinion as to the merits of the litigation at this time. The company believes there is absolutely no merit to the litigation.
>
> - In our opinion, the company has a substantial chance of prevailing in this action.
>
> - The facts are unique and the applicable law uncertain but we believe the plaintiff will face substantial difficulty establishing the company's liability.

In light of lawyer hesitancy to furnish such clarification or to be more precise, auditors are sometimes tempted to think they can consult a different lawyer to generate likelihood and amount estimates. This probably is not feasible because of the confidential relationship between lawyer and client. Also, it is doubtful another lawyer could provide additional insight into the problem because of the difficulty of predicting the results of litigation, especially without knowing the manner in which the client's lawyers intend to defend against the action.

Given the difficulties auditors may face in obtaining the necessary information from lawyers, how are audit reporting requirements being met? Some are concerned that they are not—*i.e.*, that the rules are being ignored for material litigation loss contingencies that require footnote disclosure for those deemed "reasonably possible" and require adjusting entries for those deemed "probable."

Where that leaves the legal profession is not entirely clear either. The joint ABA/auditing statement, for example, expressly permits counsel's formal response to an auditor's inquiry to include some discussion of counsel's professional responsibility in responding to the inquiry. As set forth in that statement:

> The auditor may properly assume that whenever, in the course of performing legal services for the client with respect to a matter recognized to involve an unasserted possible claim or assessment which may call for a financial statement disclosure, the lawyer has formed a professional conclusion that the client must disclose or consider disclosure concerning such possible claim or assessment, the lawyer, as a matter of professional responsibility to the client, will so advise the client and will consult with the

client concerning the question of such disclosure and the applicable requirements concerning accounting for loss contingencies.

It is customary for lawyer's responses to auditor's inquiry letters to refer not only to the lawyer's professional responsibility in responding to the inquiry, but also to the limitations of the lawyer's duty to make disclosure. Consider the following case.

TEW V. ARKY, FREED, ET AL.*

Defendant Arky, Freed, Stearns, Watson, Greer, Weaver & Harris, P.A. ("Arky Freed") has moved pursuant to Fed. R. Civ. P. 56 for partial summary judgement on Counts II and III of the Amended Complaint as to any liability resulting from the events of January 21, 1985, a date upon which plaintiff claims that Stephen Arky, a former member of Arky Freed, learned of the insolvency of [a number of corporate entities for which plaintiff is acting as receiver]. . . .

The court has considered the briefs, affidavits, deposition testimony, and exhibits submitted by the parties, as well as the arguments of counsel. The court finds that there is no genuine issue of material fact and that Arky Freed's motion for partial summary judgement must be granted as a matter of law.

Arky Freed owed no legal duty to disclose to ESM's auditors, Alexander Grant & Co. ("Grant"), Stephen Arky's alleged knowledge of ESM's financial condition purportedly obtained in a meeting attended by Mr. Arky on January 21, 1985, approximately six weeks prior to ESM's collapse.

An attorney's responsibilities with respect to responses to auditor's inquiries is governed by the American Bar Association "Statement of Policy Regarding Lawyer's Responses to Auditor's Request for Information" ("ABA Statement"). The preamble of the ABA Statement reads: "The public interest in protecting the confidentiality of lawyer-client communications is fundamental." As concerns this case, "that is the whole law; the rest is mere commentary." Hillel, Pirke Avot (Ethics of the Fathers), quoted in 14 Encyclopedia Americana 197 (1984).

The ABA Statement provides that an attorney is authorized to disclose information to his client's auditors only where the client has both "specifically identified" "in the [audit] inquiry letter or supplement thereto" a particular unasserted claim or assessment, and has "specifically requested" comment by the attorney on that unasserted claim or

---

*   655 F.Supp. 1573 (S.D.Fla. 1987), aff'd, 846 F.2d 753 (11th Cir. 1988).

assessment. ABA Statement, Paragraph 2. The requirement that the client both specifically identify and specifically request comment on the unasserted claim or assessment in the audit inquiry letter is predicated on the ABA Statement's fundamental concern with preserving the confidentiality of attorney-client communications. Under the ABA Statement, an attorney has no duty "to investigate legal problems of the client, even when on notice of some facts which might conceivably constitute a legal problem nor should [he or she] include information concerning the client which the lawyer receives in another role." ABA Statement, Commentary to Paragraph 2.

There is no genuine issue of material fact that ESM ever identified its financial problems in its auditor's inquiry letters to Arky Freed, or requested Arky Freed to comment thereon. In fact, the ABA Statement's limitations on an attorney's duties were expressly contained in both ESM's audit inquiry letters to Arky Freed, and Arky Freed's audit responses. Furthermore, Mr. Arky was not consulted or retained by ESM at the January 21, 1985 meeting, but rather was consulted concerning [the personal affairs of an individual associated with ESM]. Failure to disclose under these circumstances does not constitute either negligence or breach of contract.

[The court also rejected the plaintiff's contention that Disciplinary Rule 7–102(B) of the Florida Code of Professional Responsibility created any legal duty upon Arky Freed.]

Accordingly, the court hereby enters judgment in favor of Arky Freed dismissing with prejudice plaintiff's claims in Counts II and III of the Amended Complaint which arise out of the events of January 21, 1985.

The *Arky, Freed* case seems to say that a lawyer's compliance with the ABA Statement provides a legal defense for a lawyer against claims of failure to disclose information to the auditor. Would a lawyer's noncompliance constitute a breach of a duty to disclose? Suppose ESM's auditor's inquiry letter specifically identified and specifically requested comment on ESM's financial problems as unasserted claims. Would Arky, Freed have had a legal duty to disclose them? How does the public interest in protecting the confidentiality of lawyer-client communications bear on that question? *See generally*, James J. Fuld, Lawyers' Responses to Auditors—Some Practical Aspects, 44 *Bus. Law.*159 (1988).

An Accounting Solution?

Continuing tensions between the legal and auditing professions led FASB to offer an accounting solution. It began a project in 2008 to update accounting standards governing litigation loss contingencies. It contemplates expanded disclosure to enable financial statement users more reliably to assess the likelihood, timing and amount of future cash flows that such contingencies may absorb. It envisions more quantitative and qualitative disclosure. Quantitative disclosures would include tabular comparisons of year-to-year changes in total amounts recognized on balance sheets for loss contingencies. Qualitative disclosure would describe factors bearing on a contingency's likely outcome and assumptions used in making quantitative estimates of outcomes and amounts.

FASB appreciates that such disclosure can compromise an entity's litigation strategy. It offers to prevent that by authorizing aggregation of disclosures to avoid enabling adversaries to identify particular cases or, if that is infeasible, to allow entities simply to withhold the information. Lawyers express concern over such expanded disclosure. They note both litigation strategy impairment and risks of waiving the attorney-client privilege or work-product doctrine.

Internal Control Auditing Difficulties.

As auditors began to undertake direct audits of internal control over financial reporting after Sarbanes-Oxley, they appeared to seek more extensive information from lawyers than in the past. One result was an ABA resolution in 2006 urging the SEC, PCAOB and AICPA to assure preservation of the attorney-client privilege and work-product doctrine. It proposed limiting auditor access to privileged information to circumstances where it is "clearly necessary" for an audit, not where it "merely would be convenient" or "provide additional confirmation or comfort." These developments may jeopardize the traditional lawyer-auditor accommodation, reached in the 1970s, given that auditors' basis for seeking information is now federal statutory law and related regulatory enforcement, no longer simply a matter of professional auditing standards established by the AICPA.

B. THE PROBLEM OF PRIVILEGES

A free flow of information from lawyers to auditors reduces the risks of an adverse audit report, but it increases the risks of exposing confidential information by stripping it of the protection provided by the attorney-client privilege or the work-product doctrine. Consider the following case.

IN RE WILLKIE FARR & GALLAGHER[*]

Plaintiffs in this securities fraud class action, currently pending in the Southern District of Florida, move this Court for an order compelling non-party Willkie Farr & Gallagher ("Willkie") to produce documents relating

---

[*]   1997 WL 118369 (S.D.N.Y. 1997).

to an investigation Willkie conducted on behalf of the Audit Committee of Sensormatic Electronics Corporation ("Sensormatic").

I.   FACTUAL BACKGROUND

The current dispute forms but a small portion of a complex securities fraud action alleging that Sensormatic's senior management had a longstanding practice of improperly recognizing revenue before it was actually earned in violation of generally accepted accounting principles. On July 10, 1995, two securities class action complaints were filed against Sensormatic, immediately following the company's public announcement that its financial results for the fiscal year ending June 30, 1995 would not meet earning estimates. Also during that summer the Securities and Exchange Commission ("SEC") advised Sensormatic that it had commenced an informal inquiry concerning accounting-related issues and trading activity of the Company's securities.

At about the same time the Audit Committee of Sensormatic's Board of Directors was advised by its outside auditors, Ernst & Young, that in the course of its audit of the Company's financial statements for the 1994–95 fiscal year, it encountered some irregularities in the Company's income recognition. Ernst & Young advised the Committee that it was expanding the scope of its audit and advised the Board to retain independent counsel to investigate these practices. The Audit Committee consulted with its regular outside counsel, decided to obtain independent legal advice and hired Willkie to conduct an investigation of the Company's accounting practices, policies and procedures, and to provide legal advice to the Audit Committee regarding these issues.

Willkie conducted a comprehensive investigation during late August and early September of 1995, interviewing over 40 officers, directors and employees of Sensormatic and reviewing extensive documentation regarding the Company's accounting practices. Ernst & Young then informed the Audit Committee that it could not provide Sensormatic with an unqualified audit opinion unless it had unrestricted access to the results of Willkie's investigation. Both Willkie and Sensormatic expressed concern about waiving any privileges by disclosing to Ernst & Young the results of Willkie's investigation.

In his deposition by the SEC, Lou Pugliese, a partner at Ernst & Young, explained the procedure used to reveal the results of the Willkie investigation. Willkie met with Ernst & Young to give them hypothetical results from their investigation. Willkie orally paraphrased statements from the employee interviews and told Ernst & Young who they believed was credible. Once Ernst & Young confirmed that these hypotheticals would enable the outside auditors to issue an unqualified opinion, Willkie confirmed that the hypotheticals were in fact the actual situation.

At issue before this Court is whether the documents in Willkie's control—the result of work commissioned by Sensormatic and disclosed to Ernst & Young in order to obtain an unqualified audit opinion—are protected by either the work product doctrine . . . or the attorney-client privilege.

Plaintiffs are not moving to compel Willkie to produce any documents that can be obtained from parties to this action and plaintiffs' subpoena is limited to documents specifically related to Willkie's Audit Committee Investigation. . . .

II. DISCUSSION

A. Work Product Doctrine

The work product doctrine shields from discovery material prepared by an attorney, or under his supervision, in anticipation of litigation. *United States v. Nobles,* 422 U.S. 225 (1975). It may only be invoked if the party claiming the privilege proves that the withheld documents "were prepared principally or exclusively to assist in anticipated or ongoing litigation." *United States v. Constr. Prod. Research, Inc.,* 73 F.3d 464, 473 (2d Cir. 1996). The fact that Sensormatic foresaw litigation is not, in and of itself, enough. *In re Kidder Peabody Sec. Litig.,* [168 F.R.D. 459] (S.D.N.Y. 1996); *In re the Leslie Fay Comp. Sec. Litig.,* 161 F.R.D. 274, 280 (S.D.N.Y. 1995).

In this case, Willkie cannot meet its burden of proving that the work product doctrine applies. The record indicates that the Audit Committee hired Willkie to undertake the investigation in order to deal with a serious business problem. Although this problem might have involved litigation, this was clearly not the motivating force behind the Audit Committee's decision to retain Willkie. The investigation was necessary to maintain the integrity of the financial reports of a publicly-held corporation and the documents were prepared primarily for business purposes. Where primary motivation for the creation of work product is other than litigation, the work product doctrine does not apply. *Binks Mfg. Co. v. Nat'l Presto Indus., Inc.,* 709 F.2d 1109, 1118–19 (7th Cir. 1983) (citing 8 Wright & Miller, Federal Practice & Procedure, § 2024).

B. Attorney-Client Privilege

Willkie argues that even if the material is not protected by the work product doctrine, it is protected by attorney-client privilege. The attorney-client privilege protects from disclosure communications between an attorney and a client, made in confidence, for the purpose of rendering or obtaining legal advice. *In re Grand Jury Subpoena Duces Tecum,* 731 F.2d 1032, 1036 (2d Cir. 1984). The burden is on Willkie to both prove the privilege and to prove non-waiver of the privilege. *von Bulow v. von Bulow,*

811 F.2d at 144; *Nikkal Indus., Ltd. v. Salton, Inc.,* 689 F. Supp. 187, 191 (S.D.N.Y. 1988).

Plaintiffs argue that the attorney-client privilege never attached to these documents because the Audit Committee never intended to keep them confidential. It is clear, however, that the attorney-client privilege did attach to these documents before they were produced to Ernst & Young. *See Upjohn Co. v. United States,* 449 U.S. 383 (1981). The Audit Committee, whether on the advice of Ernst & Young or on its own accord, hired Willkie to represent them before the Securities and Exchange Commission and to get advice about how to conduct their affairs in light of Ernst & Young's findings. The individuals interviewed by Willkie were employees of Sensormatic, and they were assured by the Willkie attorneys that their communications would be kept confidential, were covered by attorney-client privilege, and could only be waived by Sensormatic.

As evidenced by the Audit Committee's dealings with Ernst & Young, Sensormatic hoped to keep the investigation confidential. Once it became clear, however, that the cost of that confidentiality was the inability to get from Ernst & Young an unqualified audit opinion, Sensormatic made a strategic decision to waive the privilege. Once the Audit Committee disclosed to Ernst & Young the substantive and detailed results of the Willkie investigation, including paraphrased statements of what Sensormatic employees had stated in confidence to Willkie attorneys, Sensormatic waived its privilege. *In re John Doe Corp.,* 675 F.2d 482, 488 (2d Cir. 1982). In *In re John Doe,* the court stated that:

> A claim that a need for confidentiality must be respected in order to facilitate the seeking and rendering of informed legal advice is not consistent with selective disclosure when the claimant decides that confidential materials can be put to other beneficial purposes.

Id. at 489.

Because the Court finds a waiver of the attorney-client privilege with respect to the information disclosed to Ernst & Young, the Court must also determine the scope of that waiver. While the Audit Committee has certainly waived the attorney-client privilege with respect to the material divulged to Ernst & Young, they have not necessarily waived the privilege with respect to every single document underlying the disclosed material. Whether such a waiver has taken place depends on the "fairness doctrine," and what "prejudice to a party and distortion of the judicial process . . . may be caused by the privilege-holder's selective disclosure during litigation of otherwise privileged information." *In re von Bulow v. von Bulow,* 828 F.2d 94, 101 (2d Cir. 1987).

The waiver of underlying materials or a complete subject matter waiver applies when a party seeks to use the privilege selectively, as both a sword and shield in litigation. See *In re Leslie Fay,* 161 F.R.D. at 282; *In* *re Kidder*, [168 F.R.D. 459]; *cf. Carter v. Rosenberg & Estis,* 1996 WL 695866 at *2 (S.D.N.Y. Dec. 4, 1996). In this case Sensormatic did just that when it argued to the Florida court that plaintiffs' complaint should be dismissed because Ernst & Young's audit, which relied on Willkie's investigation, showed that the alleged irregularities in the financial statement were not material.

Willkie's reliance on *von Bulow* to argue that the privilege has not been waived is misplaced. von Bulow, 828 F.2d at 102. Although the Second Circuit found that the attorney-client privilege did not apply to all underlying material disclosed when the attorney published some of his client conversations in a book about his representation of Claus von Bulow, that holding was based on the extra-judicial nature of the material. *Id.* In this case, the results of the Willkie investigation are not extra-judicial and have been put at issue in this litigation through defendant's motion to dismiss.

In these circumstances, it is appropriate to find a waiver of the attorney-client privilege. Such a waiver under the fairness doctrine, however, requires that the remedy be narrowly tailored to address the potential prejudice to the parties attacking the privilege. *In re Leslie Fay,* 161 F.R.D. at 284 (citing *Brock Equities, Ltd. v. Josephthal Lyon & Ross, Inc.,* 1993 WL 350026 at (S.D.N.Y. Sept. 9, 1993)).

In this case, plaintiffs suffer prejudice to the extent that Sensormatic relies on the results of the Ernst & Young audit to disclaim liability, but does not reveal the facts uncovered by Willkie that made that audit possible. Plaintiffs have shown that Sensormatic disclosed to Ernst & Young which employees Willkie believed were "credible" and paraphrased statements of what these employees said. Therefore, plaintiffs' motion is granted with respect to all notes of interviews with Sensormatic employees and notes of meetings with the Audit Committee at which Ernst & Young was present, as well as all evidence relied upon in determining which employees were credible.

Plaintiffs did not show, however, that Willkie disclosed to Ernst & Young other legal advice or analysis that they were providing to Sensormatic, or that protecting the privilege with respect to other legal analysis visits any unfairness on plaintiffs. Willkie may, therefore, assert the attorney-client privilege for portions of other documents that plaintiffs request which contain legal analysis or advice that was never disclosed to Ernst & Young. . . .

For the foregoing reasons plaintiffs' motion is granted in part and denied in part.

In ordinary dealings between auditors and lawyers the work-product doctrine does not apply because the lawyer's work is not conducted in anticipation of litigation but in the hopes of enabling the auditor to deliver a clean audit report. Was *Willkie Farr* such an "ordinary case"? Does it matter that, as the court notes in part II.B of its opinion, the Audit Committee had retained Willkie to represent it before the SEC? Does it matter whether the SEC's action at the time was an "informal inquiry"? What if it had been, or became, an administrative enforcement action?

Note the manner by which Willkie Farr disclosed the information to Ernst & Young. Suppose that Willkie Farr's hypothetical investigation results had not satisfied Ernst & Young sufficiently to enable the auditors to deliver a clean audit letter and therefore the law firm never confirmed to the auditors that the hypotheticals were the actual situation. Would Sensormatic have been deemed to waive the attorney-client privilege then?

Do you agree with the court that Sensormatic used the attorney-client privilege selectively by supporting its motion to dismiss on the grounds that Ernst & Young had issued a clean audit letter? Is the fact that Ernst & Young relied upon the Willkie investigation to deliver that letter dispositive?

C. INTERNAL REPORTING

Pursuant to the Sarbanes-Oxley Act of 2002, the SEC issued rules establishing standards of professional conduct for attorneys appearing and practicing before it. Rules require that lawyers report evidence of material securities or fiduciary law violations by the company or its agents when a lawyer becomes aware of them. The report must be made either to (1) the company's chief legal officer (CLO, typically the general counsel), (2) a pre-existing *qualified legal compliance committee* (QLCC) established to receive such reports, or (3) the board audit committee, another committee comprised of independent directors, or the full board.

Upon receiving a report, a CLO can either conduct an inquiry or refer the matter to a pre-existing QLCC and must advise the reporting lawyer. If there is a basis for the report, the CLO (or QLCC or other body) must ensure that the company responds appropriately. If an appropriate response is not forthcoming, the reporting lawyer is obliged to carry the report up the corporate ladder (from the CLO/QLCC, to the CEO, a board committee, and so on up to the full board). The rules are not definite concerning what a reporting lawyer should do if the full board does not respond appropriately. One possibility, not adopted, would require the lawyer to withdraw from the representation in a public fashion (the so-called *noisy withdrawal* concept).

State court rules traditionally regulate lawyers, often pursuant to codes established by the American Bar Association (ABA). These SEC rules under Sarbanes-Oxley represent a federal incursion into that territory, prompting controversy. The ABA observed that lawyers serve both a public function ("officers of the court") and an advocacy function and that state rules strike a balance to reconcile the two. The SEC rules create an overlay that risks confusion, according to the ABA.

Commentators offered mixed views, recognizing some uncertainty but suggesting that the ABA and state rules lagged behind in addressing the specific circumstances Sarbanes-Oxley addresses. Their view was that such rules never required lawyers to take any specific action upon becoming aware of securities or fiduciary law violations within an organizational client. A particular point of sensitivity in lodging this power in the SEC, however, is that the SEC often faces lawyers practicing before it as adversaries in enforcement proceedings and litigation.

D. LAWYERS AS PART-TIME ACCOUNTANTS

Lawyers owe their clients various ethical obligations, including a basic duty of competence. Does a business lawyer's duty of competence require understanding basic accounting and auditing? Though experienced business lawyers understand such knowledge to be essential to the competent practice of business law, the professional literature concerning legal ethics is equivocal as to what the duty of competence requires. Even so, a good case can be made that a business lawyer's professional ethics should command him or her to master accounting and auditing basics.

Lawyers are fiduciaries for their clients. The principal justification for this designation is that clients seek from their lawyers the exercise of "professional judgment." That, in turn, requires the client to repose trust and confidence in the lawyer. In exercising professional judgment, the lawyer must advance the client's interests as the client would define them if fully informed. A wellspring of duties flow from the fiduciary obligation, including undivided loyalty and avoiding conflicts of interest, preserving client confidences and secrets, representing a client zealously, safeguarding client property, and—of greatest importance here—the duties of competence, diligence, and candor.

Lawyers think of competency in terms of "general technical proficiency." Competency means ability, in fact, to accomplish objectives with the capacity of an ordinarily able professional in similar circumstances. This ordinarily concerns legal knowledge, skill, and preparation, in light of the legal and factual context of a representation. Knowledge relates to identifying, assessing, and dealing with legal problems; skill relates to advising, negotiating, and planning a course of action; and preparation is the thinking through on both lines of professional activity.

The professional literature and ethics codes speak of legal competence. On its face, therefore, competency in distinctly non-legal areas of accounting or auditing would not be required. Yet law often overlaps with accounting and auditing. Mixed questions of law and fact arise. The facts or factual context of a business law representation include financial realities and the manner of their reporting and attestation. Competence encompasses an understanding of that relationship and an analysis of the degree to which differences exist that affect legal positions.

Reinforcing this common-sense view are prudential factors that stem from two kindred duties, the duty of diligence and the duty of candor. The duty of diligence may compel business lawyers, as a matter of legal ethics, to gain a little accounting and auditing competency. Advising a corporate client concerning the disposition of 60% of its "net book assets" may require brushing up on the meaning of the terms assets, sales, and earnings. Failing that, the duty of candor probably compels lawyers to inform clients of limited capabilities.

As an outer limit, lawyers must advise clients so that they avoid any violation of law and may not "counsel . . . or assist a client, in conduct that . . . is criminal or fraudulent." Lawyers cannot further a client's criminal or fraudulent purpose nor continue representation that is known to assist the client in the design. These mandates call for active rather than passive attention to client actions and purposes. They encompass the capacity to address non-legal matters, in the business law setting including ways accounting and auditing facts may indicate when fraud or criminality is afoot. Cynicism is obviously not required, but healthy professional skepticism and curiosity is.

One distinguishing feature of business law is the frequent presence of an organizational client, such as a corporation or partnership. Lawyers' duties in such representations can run in numerous directions, depending on who is identified as the client. Candidates are the entity itself, plus its board of directors, individual directors, committees, individual executives, and all others. A business lawyer urged to act on a manager's behalf when the corporate client's interest would be harmed must not act. Perceiving how the managerial and corporate interests diverge in these ways may require accounting and auditing knowledge.

If a business lawyer's duty of competence encompasses matters of accounting and auditing, however, this by no means requires direct or prior knowledge. That is only one way to discharge the duty. Lawyers may discharge the duty of competence by learning on the spot. Lawyers can also meet their duty of competence by leaning on other lawyers with the requisite expertise. So the duty of competence can be discharged by knowing, learning, or affiliating. In the case of affiliation, moreover, relying upon trained accountants and auditors would ordinarily discharge the duty.

Even if the duty of competence can be met by associating with professionals possessing the core competency, there remains a need for business lawyers to have a working knowledge of relevant standards. This view of the duty of competence means only that failure of business lawyers to understand accounting and auditing issues involved in deals they are structuring and advising do not, as a technical matter, breach their professional responsibility or constitute malpractice.

This is not saying much. In practice, after all, enforcement of competency standards by professional discipline is rare, limited to the "blatant bungler." Legal malpractice claims can be defeated even for failure to master legal principles taught in basic first-year law classes, such as the rule against perpetuities. Failure to master accounting matters, even in the intersection of law and financial reporting, is less likely to result in successful malpractice claims. For these, a good defense would be the hardy "mere error in judgment" doctrine, strong so long as a lawyer can show good faith.

Should this excuse business lawyers from the effort? All lawyers know that just because something is legal does not mean it is right. In the area of legal ethics, just because a duty can be technically discharged in a painless way, does not mean client interests are served. This is particularly true when rival lawyers are masters of the competency. Clients without such lawyers are twice disadvantaged.

Rather than examining the technical content of the duty of competence and doing the bare minimum to meet it, the more ethical and prudential question is how best to meet client needs in the realistic context of business law practice. The answer is akin to the knowledge lawyers in other fields must command though no formal legal or ethical demand is imposed on the lawyer: environmental lawyers knowing a little geology; medical malpractice lawyers knowing a little medicine; constitutional lawyers knowing some political theory; agents who are lawyers knowing something about publishing, music, or sports; and criminal defense lawyers having some street smarts.

E. FORENSIC ACCOUNTING

The incidence of accounting machinations increased in the past several decades. Formal restatements of financial data reached an annual average of about 150 by the late 1990s, three times greater than the decade as a whole. Though this level remains low in the overall scheme of things (fewer than 1% of public companies), the trend is unappealing and the number of innocent people hurt in the process significant. In this midst, an entire industry called forensic accounting has emerged. Consisting of both lawyers and accountants, these sleuths seek to understand the causes of accounting scandals once they are uncovered.

The term "forensic" means "belonging to courts of justice." Branches of knowledge implicated in legal disputes have long been designated by the term. Forensic pathology, for example, is the branch of medicine dealing with diseases of the body in relation to legal principles and cases (such as whether someone who is brain dead can have testamentary capacity) and forensic psychiatry is the branch of medicine dealing with disorders of the mind in that relation (such as fitness for trial or insanity as a defense in a criminal prosecution).

The continental European word for this is *forensis* which in turn derives from the Latin term *forensis homo*, indicating an advocate or a pleader of causes, one who practices in court. Specialized disciplines have practiced in this intersection with law for centuries, including forensic medicine, forensic linguistics and forensic engineering.

Forensic accounting, a relative newcomer, is the branch of the public accounting profession dealing with dysfunctional financial reporting in relation to criminal and civil law. This Section introduces forensic accounting, starting with a few case studies adapted from reports of the international accounting firm of RSM (formerly McGladrey & Pullen); this is followed by a description of the forensic practice at another such firm, Grant Thornton; and concludes with the report of an AICPA survey of attorneys and accountants about what it takes to be a successful forensic accountant.

RSM Case Studies in Forensic Accounting

Bank Regulatory.

In 2012, a community bank in the southern United States, with 10 branches and more than 75 years of service to local customers, was under scrutiny by the Office of the Comptroller of the Currency (OCC). The OCC evaluated the bank very closely, and through a series of examinations, several suspect transactions came to light. After a review, the OCC determined that the bank's president and CEO made fraudulent transactions and misappropriations from the institution.

The OCC mandated the removal of the president and CEO from his position and prohibited any further dealings with the bank. An independent forensic investigation was ordered of the leadership team, senior officers and several other areas within the bank.

RSM was retained to provide the independent investigation, based on a cross-functional proposal highlighting financial advisory and risk advisory capabilities, as well as depth of experience with similar investigations and positive relationships with regulators. The team developed a step-by-step work plan, which was approved by the OCC. The plan included fact-finding and informational interviews with board members, directors, senior executives and employees, as well as public records background investigations on employees of interest to the OCC.

The OCC designated areas for evaluation, and the RSM team expanded the scope and planned testing in other areas, in order to ensure a comprehensive examination. A significant amount of work concentrated on the bank's accounts payable and fixed assets due to accusations of capitalizing personal expenses into the institution's fixed asset ledgers. RSM traced the bank's accounts and affiliated accounts of targeted individuals, looking at loans senior officers took out. In addition, the team evaluated bank transactions and monies obtained through the Troubled Asset Relief Program (TARP), evaluating how those funds were used.

The team extracted emails from the bank's senior executive officers and CEO, and imaged and searched computer hard drives. Other real estate owned (OREO) and their dispositions were scrutinized, including how they were sold, to what entities and what loans were made by the bank. Personnel records were investigated after accusations were made that the former bank CEO had family members on the payroll. This was found to be the case; therefore, their expense reimbursements were evaluated.

RSM investigated a significant sum borrowed by the bank against a bank-owned life insurance policy, where the money was misappropriated by the president and CEO and deposited into an entity he controlled. The bank was owned by the president and CEO, but while under an OCC directive and accepting TARP funds, excess compensation is prohibited. RSM found significant evidence of attempts to circumvent regulations, and fraudulent representations as a part of TARP compliance and required reporting due to directives.

The RSM team of fraud investigators, regulatory compliance and computer forensic professionals kept in constant contact with the OCC, and issued a final report that was ultimately subpoenaed by federal authorities as evidence in a criminal investigation to recover bank funds. The findings helped the new administration's stability and developed stronger goodwill with regulators. After a period of significant pressure against the bank, the OCC is comfortable with the project's results and new management. The institution has corrected the issues that led to self-dealing and financial malfeasance by senior executives, and recognized the losses on its financial statements and call reports moving forward.

Credit Union Fraud Discovery.

In 2014, a local credit union uncovered fraud while investigating a stale-dated $20,000 reconciling item in a general ledger account. The employee responsible was quickly identified, but that was just the beginning. As the credit union investigated the employee's activities, the investigation spread from $20,000 and a single fraud to dozens of acts over a period of years. As losses reached the $100,000 mark and continued to grow, the credit union became overwhelmed by the scope of the investigation and turned to RSM for help. The credit union wanted to ensure that all of the culprit's fraudulent activities were uncovered, to accurately quantify its loss and, most importantly, to ensure it understood exactly how the fraud had been committed so that it could adjust its controls accordingly.

RSM's investigators went to work and found a familiar story. The perpetrator was a well-liked and trusted administrative assistant with strong relationships with both the credit union's staff and with its customers. Because of this trust and the credit union's small size, she was trusted with a wide range of functions, which led to a breakdown in the appropriate segregation of duties. She had system access to perform all of the following functions: opening member accounts and loans; transferring funds between member accounts; cutting cashier's checks, including access to check stock; initiating automatic clearing house (ACH) transactions; posting to general ledger accounts; and making data changes to member accounts, such as names, addresses, statement codes and Social Security numbers.

As is often the case, the employee had committed a small original fraud due to a financial hardship in her personal life, with the intention of returning the money. However, because the first fraudulent act was so easy to commit and went undiscovered, her activities quickly snowballed into years of fraudulent acts. Here is an overview of the scope of the fraud:

- The perpetrator opened a fake account in the name of a credit union member with health issues that the perpetrator knew would prevent that member from identifying unusual activity in the member's accounts. She then changed the last name on the account by a single letter, changed the Social Security number by two digits and changed the mailing address to a post office box.

- The perpetrator would change this data back to the accurate member data at the statement cutoff date to keep the discrepancies from being identified, then immediately change it back to the false data once the date had passed. She used this account for most of her fraudulent activity. For example, as her fraud deepened, she would use this account to make payments on a variety of fictitious loans that she opened. Eventually, she also began to make withdrawals from this member's IRA account.

- The perpetrator created a number of fictitious loans using the false member account and deposited advances from those loans into the account, which she then transferred via ACH to her own personal accounts at other financial institutions, usually keeping the transfers at or below the $10,000 ACH limit.

- The perpetrator took over other member accounts that were dormant, but still open with minimal balances. She then created fictitious loans to these members. Again, the funds were transferred to her personal accounts via ACH or sometimes with fraudulent checks. Using the date change module in the credit union's system, she would move money back and forth between the various accounts and loans she controlled to kite loan payments and cover her tracks. These date changes and the outgoing ACH transfers were also done through this module. Neither were identified by teller number, making her activities difficult to track back to her.

- The perpetrator used general ledger entries through suspense accounts to purchase cashier's checks payable to other banks. She would handwrite her personal account information on the memo line of the checks so that her account information was not recorded in the credit union's systems. These entries eventually showed up on reconciliation reports as stale-dated items. However, the perpetrator herself was the one charged with researching those items. She cleared them using funds from the various fake accounts she controlled.

The credit union began to make some changes to its controls, which included limiting the ability to open new loans. This cut off the perpetrator's main source of fraudulent funds, limiting her to the general ledger activity that eventually led to her discovery. When the credit union asked for help, it had uncovered approximately $100,000 in fraudulent activity dating back about one year. By the time we concluded our investigation, we had uncovered a series of frauds totaling more than $300,000, dating from 2009 to 2014, and had exposed the full range of tactics the perpetrator had used to commit them. Our report was also provided to the credit union's regulatory body to explain the institution's losses and supported the credit union's claim to its insurance carrier. The credit union subsequently submitted our report to authorities to assist in prosecuting the perpetrator.

Proactive Fraud Detection.

In 2016, the new chief financial officer (CFO) of a publicly traded manufacturer was concerned that its rapid growth and highly diversified business lines may have created opportunities for fraud. The client sought a proactive review of the entire population of payments, invoices, vendors and employees over the last three years in order to identify weaknesses in internal controls and gauge the company's fraud risk.

The company hired RSM to use our proprietary forensic data analytics platform and process, to review more than 3,000 employee and 6,000 vendor records, more than 100,000 invoices and more than 40,000 payment transactions. Our analysis, which included more than 50 forensic tests, targeted: duplicate payments and invoices; payments and invoices with unusual characteristics that can indicate fraud; ghost vendors and employees; invalid vendors and employees; duplicate vendors; potential conflicts between employees and vendors; Benford's Law analysis, which identifies unlikely frequencies of numbers within a data set that can indicate fraud.

As a result of this engagement, the manufacturer validated and strengthened its ethics and anti-fraud approach and was able to move forward with its integration with confidence. We provided a summary of all areas of concern, including a risk score and exceptions for each vendor and employee. Specific findings included:

- Invoices representing hundreds of thousands of dollars that gave strong indications of being duplicates.

- A small subset of payments and invoices representing more than $1 million in payments whose questionable frequency of occurrence made them suspicious. Some of the vendors associated with these transactions had been identified as high priority through our risk scoring methodology.

- Hundreds of invoices with sequential numbers from the same vendors, which bore further examination.

- A vendor with two active vendor records in the system, one which had received millions of dollars in payments and a second that had received a highly questionable payment of $800,000.

By combining the risk scores and payment amounts associated with each employee and vendor, we helped the client prioritize and focus its attention on investigating transactions with high value and significant risk characteristics. Using these findings, the client will be able to translate our findings into stronger policies and controls.

NOTE

Forensic accounting services are but one of a set of often-interrelated professional forensic services offered by firms providing expertise in legal aspects of financial practice. Specifically, forensic accounting may encompass or closely relate to issues concerning accounting irregularities and restatements; asset tracing; board investigations; corporate compliance, including with the Foreign Corrupt Practices Act or regulations of the U.S. Treasury's Office of Foreign Assets Control; and measures to counter bribery, corruption, fraud or money-laundering.

Lawyers may draw upon professionals at such service firms for assistance in arbitration or litigation for advice or expert testimony concerning accounting as well as economics, insurance, intellectual property, tax, or valuation. Technological skills are often essential in all such settings, and lawyers as well as accountants and other professionals benefit from commanding expertise in such fields as e-discovery; data analytics (i.e., predictive coding); records and risk management; incident response and data breach investigations; and computer forensics—a burgeoning field unto itself.

Consider the following description of Grant Thornton's "forensic advisory services," which includes forensic accounting along with kindred offerings.

<h3 style="text-align:center">Grant Thornton
Forensic Advisory Services</h3>

When risk turns into reality, you need a team of professionals that can react quickly and bring clarity to the situation so decision-makers can determine the best course of action. Whether you are facing whistleblower allegations, regulatory scrutiny, complex litigation or corruption across the globe, our Forensic Advisory Services professionals can help bring the clarity you need to manage adversity, protect value and return to normal operations.

Investigations. Combining highly technical forensic accounting skills, investigative prowess, state-of the-art technology and deep industry knowledge, our professionals assist clients and their legal counsel in investigating allegations of fraud, waste or abuse and whistleblower claims, as well as responding to shareholder or regulatory inquiries. Our diverse Forensic Advisory Services team is made up of CPAs, Certified in Financial Forensics designees, Certified Fraud Examiners, Certified Anti-Money Laundering Specialists, computer forensic specialists and former senior law enforcement and regulatory officials. We are trained to help uncover corporate crimes such as embezzlement, money laundering, financial statement fraud, kickback schemes and tax scams, among others.

Our consultants can help organizations understand the myriad rules and regulations across all industries that affect compliance efforts today. Whether your concerns are related to the Foreign Corrupt Practices Act (FCPA), anti-money laundering rules, Office of Foreign Assets Control (OFAC) issues, HIPAA or any other compliance mandate, our advisers can help. We assist clients in developing compliance programs, conducting gap analysis and executing compliance testing. Various regulators have approved Grant Thornton to serve as an independent monitor on consent orders, settlement agreements and other administrative agreements.

Litigation. When it comes to complex litigation, the stakes are high and getting higher. Now more than ever, early case assessment, solid strategies, and clear and insightful analytical strength are pivotal to prevailing in business disputes. Our litigation and dispute team can support experienced litigators with meaningful financial and economic analysis, dispute resolution and professional services that can help unravel complex business disputes. Our experienced professionals are especially helpful during the discovery phase of litigation and the determination of economic damages.

Forensics. Our forensic technology professionals utilize state-of-the-art hardware and software—along with advanced discovery processes, methodologies and proprietary analytical routines—to identify, collect, recover, reconstruct and preserve electronic evidence. This sophisticated protocol of testing complete data populations allows our team to reach accurate and defensible conclusions, whether those conclusions represent simple control deficiencies or are indicators of potential corruption, waste or abuse.

Corporate intelligence. Leveraging local offices and multilingual data sources our corporate intelligence services are designed to gather information needed to assess such areas as "know your customer" and anti-money laundering background checks, adversary party background checks, deep-dive integrity background checks, third-party vendor background checks, and asset tracing on companies and individuals.

AICPA White Paper
Characteristics and Skills of the Forensic Accountant
by Charles Davis, Ramona Farrell & Suzanne Ogilby

The marketplace requires the forensic accountant to possess a different skill set from the traditional accountant. The authors surveyed attorneys, CPAs and academics and received responses from 126 attorneys, 603 CPAs and 50 accounting/auditing professors to better understand the current perceptions of what it means to be an effective forensic accountant.

The respondents were asked to choose the Top 5 items for each question from a larger number of attributes. For example, the first of the three questions was: "Please identify the five essential traits and characteristics for a forensic accountant." Perhaps the most striking finding in the traits and characteristics results is the highest frequency of choosing "Analytical" for all three groups in the Top 5 with the "Detail-oriented" choice close behind for attorneys and CPAs. Complementing the analytical characteristic is the "Inquisitive" trait and the "Persistent" trait. These highly ranked traits suggest the need for the forensic accountant to seek out all relevant information for an engagement, as well as be able to process it and solve the problem at hand.

The need to be analytical in a forensic accounting engagement may be the initial and most important overall characteristic, without which other traits and abilities would be difficult to develop. The importance of analytical traits and abilities is supported by earlier studies as well. . . After analytical or problem-solving traits, "softer" or more interpretive and interpersonal traits were ranked next highest. For example, the "Intuitive" trait was ranked in the Top 5 only by CPAs, at rank "5." CPAs also chose the "Inquisitive" and "Skepticism" traits that support "Intuitive," second and fourth highest overall, respectively. In addition, "Ethical," was ranked third by those in the field, with academics ranking it second. The high ranking of "Ethical" is consistent with the mission of the forensic accountant. Also, "Responsive" and "Skepticism" were chosen frequently. This second tier of interpretive traits may build on the more analytical and individual skills that form the basis for the ability of the forensic accountant to provide value-added services.

[Concerning "Core Skills," the results] indicate that communication skills are key to the effectiveness of the forensic accountant and should be emphasized. Compared with the essential traits and characteristics results, there was less agreement across the three groups of respondents on core skills. Attorneys chose "Effective oral communicator" most frequently on average, reflecting the need to effectively represent verbally a position in a court of law. CPAs concurred by choosing it third most frequently in the Top 5 and "Effective written communicator" second, perhaps indicating the importance of preparing internal reports and documentation for review by colleagues, or the submission of a written report to the court. Similarly, the ability to simplify the information (ranked second most important by attorneys) becomes more critical when giving oral testimony before a jury or providing demonstrative evidence in a court of law.

Academics and CPAs chose "Critical/strategic thinker" most frequently in the Top 5 core skills. This is consistent with the high frequency of choosing the analytical trait. Interestingly, academics chose "Auditing skills" second most frequently whereas this skill did not make it into the Top 5 for CPAs, most of whom have such skills. Attorneys rated "Auditing skills" along with "Investigative ability" fifth most frequently in the Top 5 core skills. Closely related to the analytical trait is "Synthesize results of discovery and analysis," in fourth place for academics. Similarly, "Organize an unstructured situation" was fairly high-ranked by all three groups of respondents.

Those core skills in the middle of the overall ranking, such as "Think like the wrongdoer," "Understand the goals of the case," "Tell the story" and "See the big picture" are core skills one would initially believe to be important in forensic accounting, but their specific wording may have caused the somewhat lower ranking (although academics did rate "think like the wrongdoer" fifth). More generalized skills appear to be favored by the respondent groups. Being an effective oral communicator and having the ability to simplify the information are core skills that, if possessed, would enable the forensic accountant to do some of these more specific skills such as "Tell the story" and "Synthesize results." . . .

[A]ttorneys and CPAs agreed on "Analyze and interpret financial statements and information" as the most important enhanced skill. Their agreement is consistent with the fact that the attorneys in the sample hire forensic accountants with great frequency. The high ranking for this enhanced skill may also reflect the current dominance of this specific type of engagement. The frequency for attorneys was 91%, the highest percentage by a large margin—nearly all attorneys chose this enhanced skill in the Top 5.

The second most highly chosen enhanced skill for attorneys is "Testifying," whereas for academics and CPAs their second choice was "Interviewing skills." There is a similarity among these skills, both of which involve oral communication and thinking on one's feet. Interviewing is more highly ranked than "Fraud detection," and "Knowledge of relevant professional standards," which suggests the importance of interviewing as a means of obtaining pertinent information for a case. The image of the forensic accountant as a detective again is suggested by this finding.

"Knowledge of relevant professional standards" was rated in the Top 5 enhanced skills with the third highest frequency for attorneys, a result consistent with attorneys' top choice. This enhanced skill was ranked fifth for academics but did not make the Top 5 for CPAs who ranked "Analyze and interpret financial statements and information" first. Again, the response by the attorneys could be directly related to services performed, i.e., defense of CPAs in tax malpractice or accountancy malpractice engagements.

Fraud detection, considered by many to be one of the most important aspects of forensic accounting, made the Top 5 for each group with attorneys at rank "4," academics at rank "1" and CPAs at rank "3." This finding places fraud detection among the more important activities in the forensic accounting field. The ratings were only slightly below those for the previous question about specialty areas (ratings of 3 for attorneys and 1 for academics and CPAs). Academics were completely consistent about their view that fraud detection is the most critical enhanced skill and activity in forensic accounting. These results may also indicate that academics view the field of forensic accounting through a narrower lens or think "forensic accounting" is fraud detection rather than through a wider lens that sees the breadth of specialized forensic accounting services available.

Rounding out the Top 5 ranked enhanced skills for attorneys is "Asset tracing." Essentially the same percentage of CPAs also chose this enhanced skill as one of the Top 5. Also for CPAs, their fifth most frequent pick was "General knowledge of rules of evidence and civil procedure," indicating their increasing service in legal proceedings as it involves accounting. This reflects one of the more general views or definitions of forensic accounting.

Problem 15

A company faces a lawsuit with a 50/50 chance of success and a range of damages if it loses running from reducing owners' equity by 20% to wiping out owners' equity entirely. Auditor inquiry letters are sent. The lawyer reasonably forms a professional opinion that he cannot disclose details of the lawsuit, including probabilities and magnitudes, without waiving the attorney-client privilege. He understands that this may cause the company to omit disclosing the matter in its financial statements, violating GAAP. He also understands that this may lead the auditor to issue an unqualified opinion on the company's financial statements and that these financial statements may therefore be publicly released in a materially misstated manner. Does the Sarbanes-Oxley Act require the lawyer to report this to the company's chief legal officer (CLO) or other corporate agent? When would the lawyer "become aware" of a violation? What would constitute an appropriate response?

Conceptual Questions 15

Do the lawyer-reporting rules under Sarbanes-Oxley retain the traditional professional conception of the lawyer or do they move it toward that of the traditional professional conception of the auditor? Consider the audit report. No one wants other than a clean audit opinion. Adverse and qualified opinions are rare. They are not necessarily rare because auditors are supine. The statements are revised until the auditor can give an unqualified opinion. That means auditors go up the ladder until an appropriate response is received. When lawyers become aware of fraud they must go up the ladder until an appropriate response is received.

CHAPTER 16

SHENANIGANS

■ ■ ■

Beyond the hard questions posed by the auditor-lawyer relationship in the financial reporting process are a number of hard questions for the lawyer trained as a lawyer and not trained as an accountant, financial analyst or auditor. What contributions can such a lawyer nevertheless make through some familiarity with accounting, finance and auditing? This closing Chapter suggests ways.

Accounting shenanigans have plagued bookkeeping since it was codified by Luca Pacioli in 1494. There is no reason to expect that the next 500 hundred years will stray from history's pattern. No amount of rule-making—from accounting, auditing or elsewhere—can insure the integrity of financial reporting. Rules cannot eliminate managerial discretion and there will always be the possibility of imaginative, unorthodox, creative, and even fraudulent financial reporting. Lawyers should be sensitive to this.

A. TESTING THE LINE

The non-fraudulent cases are often the harder to deal with. They consist of a variety of so-called *income smoothing techniques* and *off-balance sheet financing*. Income smoothing, also sometimes known as earnings management, involves taking advantage of the flexibility of GAAP to classify transactions or to allocate them by time period to achieve favorable financial reporting. Off-balance sheet financing refers to structural techniques that enable one entity to draw resources from another entity without burdening its own balance sheet with the consequences. Some examples of both types are given below.

The techniques are not always unlawful and do not always violate GAAP. Often, however, they impair the integrity of financial reporting. Worse, a corporate or financial reporting culture that condones aggressive practices presents the risk of degradation of financial reporting: what starts as merely aggressive can create pressure that leads reporting over the line and into the fraudulent.

When, inevitably, the mischief is uncovered the fallout is severe. Scores of corporate professionals get embarrassed, investigated, fired, and, in some cases, jailed. Hundreds of corporate employees are put at risk as

433

their employers face insolvency or worse. Multimillion dollar lawsuits loom and substantial capital is misallocated.

In the wake of accounting scandals, people commonly ask, where were the auditors? The boards? Financial analysts? Auditors can be fooled or co-opted, and board-designed internal controls can be circumvented. Financial analysts digest financial information as reported, and a long time can pass between use and detection of improper financial reporting.

A rarely asked question is how lawyers can help avert financial reporting scandals that ultimately are in no one's interest, even those tempted to perpetrate or condone them. Lawyers are frequently positioned to help, given their proximity to the situation; too often they cannot help, however, due to inadequate training in accounting and bookkeeping fundamentals. When a scandal rocks a client, many lawyers get crash courses in advanced accounting. But lawyers who are sensitive to some basic accounting principles can add value by deterring aggressive accounting positions in the first place, promoting the integrity of the financial reporting process and avoiding client turmoil.

There is almost always some pressure to engage in accounting shenanigans. Many scandals suggest that pressure to use irregular accounting is especially acute at businesses with poor economic characteristics or facing tough competitive conditions. An entity's contractual profile may increase pressure for aggressive or irregular accounting. Many loan agreements, for example, contain promises by the borrower to maintain certain financial ratios such as those discussed in Chapter 8 (*e.g.*, minimum inventory turnover or interest coverage ratio or maximum debt to equity ratio).

Incentive compensation agreements triggered by meeting sales or earnings targets may also encourage accounting games. Similar pressures can emerge from settlement agreements, consent decrees, or other legal obligations an entity faces. Planning for additional financing can add pressure to paint pretty pictures of dismal performance. For public companies, motives include maintaining a high stock price to use in paying for acquisitions. More generally, in an investment climate obsessed with short-term results, there is invariably pressure to sustain steady increases in earnings growth.

Lawyers may not be in a perfect position to understand these pressures or to assess the incentives they create for fabricated reporting. But attuned lawyers can watch for aggressive accounting, and underscore for auditors and managers the enormous legal and public relations risk it poses. Lawyerly reminders of the numerous massive jury verdicts against, and multimillion dollar settlements by, big accounting and auditing firms can motivate supine auditors. Reminding managers that many managers who cooked the books also did jail time can thwart managerial temptation, as can highlighting the dozens of annual SEC enforcement actions charging fraudulent financial reporting.

To convince participants to heed these warnings, however, lawyers must know basic accounting. Grasping most problems requires only a rudimentary understanding of simple bookkeeping rules and their relationship to financial statements. A major purpose of this book has been to introduce these basics, and to suggest that the bookkeeping rules are inviolate but that the accounting principles necessarily give plenty of room for judgment in classification. Indeed, short of making up or not recording transactions, the tricks are played in classifying them. An expense (say for advertising) can instead be treated as an asset (capitalizing it); or a liability (say a commitment to render future services) can instead be booked as revenue (ignoring the accrual system).

Yet what eventually is called fraudulent or scandalous does not always begin as gaming. Difficult judgments are often necessary in deciding how or when to account for a transaction. In making a judgment, though, managers and auditors may be tempted to make the call most favorable to the reporting company, even if it is aggressive. A lawyer aware of special pressures to do so and sufficiently conversant with accounting to understand a judgment's dubiousness can often make the difference between nurturing the roots of an accounting scandal and nipping one in the bud.

The techniques are as old as accounting itself and have been used to full advantage (sometimes appropriately, often not) by managers over the centuries. Yet the contemporary problems may be heightened due to managerial obsession to meet consensus earnings estimates formulated by the increasingly influential profession of financial analysts. This dizzying obsession with "making one's numbers" is well documented. About 1 in 10 managers facing small declines and about 4 in 10 facing negative earnings managed to report positive earnings!

There are lots of techniques for aggressive accounting and lots of circumstances that call for difficult judgments and it would be surprising for any two scandals to be identical. Yet many accounting scandals share common characteristics worth being aware of. Among the major areas singled out for special concern are these:

• *"Big Bath."* Big bath accounting is a particularly aggressive version of earnings management that is a sort of financial facelift. It lumps major events adversely affecting income to current periods to facilitate improved financial appearances in succeeding periods. It is particularly common in, but by no means limited to, costs occasioned by acquisitions, divestitures, reorganizations, and other extraordinary organic business change.

These transactions call for numerous accounting judgments as to both timing and classification. Managers often expense as much of the potential costs of the transaction at the time it is consummated as possible. It's also tempting to give current earnings such a "big bath" in one year to create a brighter looking future when the year is so dismal anyway that financial analysts have written it off (this happens all the time, even at some otherwise reputable companies).

- *"Cookie Jar Reserves."* This entails the overestimation or underestimation of things like sales returns by publishers or probable loan losses of lending institutions or warranty obligations for manufacturers. The incorrect estimation enables managers to adjust and smooth out earnings as the actual earnings vary from expected earnings period to period.

- *"It's Not Material."* The materiality principle requires reporting of items that are material and allows non-reporting of items that are not. Materiality is not an absolute concept but rather entails making judgments. A standard legal formulation for public corporations under federal securities laws is whether the item would be important to a reasonable investor in making an investment decision about a security (the accounting rule similarly asks whether it would influence a reasonable person's judgment).

Judgments concerning materiality are often guided by rough rules of thumb. One rule of thumb accountants and auditors often use in determining materiality is whether a particular item entails more than say a 5% impact on a company's earnings. But applying such a simple rule could lead to excluding things that are meaningful to a user of the financial statements in a qualitative sense.

- *"Wine Before Its Time."* This image of popping open a bottle of wine before it matures reflects the premature recognition of revenue. For instance, a toy manufacturer tagging goods in a warehouse as "sold," even though they are not and might never be sold. Or a distributor of cell phones recording revenue for merchandise it shipped and received payment for but which is subject to free return and full refund for a period of say 90 days.

- *"Off-Balance Sheet Financing."* This describes a category of practices, some of which are legitimate, to engage in transactions that produce desirable benefits without undesirable reporting burdens. Events or transactions not required by GAAP to appear on a balance sheet are among the obvious for both their appeal and their legitimacy, underscoring the importance of maintaining accounting rules with integrity. To give some examples raised in Chapter 6, investments can be structured to be accounted for using the equity rather than the consolidation method, deals can be structured to obtain desired lease accounting treatment and, until not long ago, neither derivative financial instruments nor commitments to cover retiree benefits needed to be recorded on a balance sheet.

B. CROSSING THE LINE

Accounting judgments that err on the side of conservative not only respect the FASB principle mandating conservatism. They also help steer clear of the snowball effect in accounting. This refers to the phenomenon that a stretch of the accounting imagination on day one will invariably need to be followed up by another one a month later, two more the next time, three more down the road and so on. That is, if an accountant boosts profits this quarter with a wink of the eye, to sustain that level next quarter he'll have to do it again—and then some.

Likewise, small matters of aggressive accounting build into broader cultural toleration for larger matters of aggressive accounting. In all events, the temptation arises to cross the line. The conservatism principle in part is defensible as a prudential mechanism to rein in the temptation. Take a range of examples of accounting judgments from modestly aggressive to clearly objectionable and see how in each case ultimately the judgment produced a blow up.

Pearson/Penguin.

Start with Pearson's accounting for book sales through its Penguin division, for example. Sales made on credit require two entries in equal amounts: a debit (a left-side entry) to Accounts Receivable, the asset account; and a credit (a right-side entry) to Sales, the revenue account. Subsequent receipt of the cash payment calls for a debit to Cash and a credit to Accounts Receivable.

Penguin began granting 10% discounts off its list price to selected buyers who paid their accounts early—say, within 30 days instead of the usual 90 days. Following bookkeeping's simple rules, receipt of those early cash payments called for a credit to Accounts Receivable equal to 100% of the list price; the debit would be to Cash for 90% of the list price and to an expense account—say, Discount Expense—for the other 10%. That expense would reduce reported earnings.

Instead of doing that, Pearson apparently recorded receipts of early payments as a debit to Cash for 90% of the list price. So the 10% discount never showed up as an expense. It simply remained part of the asset account, Accounts Receivable—and artificially inflated reported earnings.

Why Penguin buried the discounts remains unclear, although independent bookstores not given discounts later suggested that the selective discounts violated a consent decree binding Penguin not to favor bookstore chains with discounts that are not given to independent bookstores.

While Penguin's individual discounts given on a per-customer basis may have seemed like small change, it is astonishing that auditors did not detect the aggregate amount, which grew over six years to $163 million. Pearson management eventually discovered the buried discounts when evaluating the integration of Penguin and Pearson's recently acquired Putnam Berkley publishing house.

In the course of its sale to Pearson, Putnam Berkley's lawyers might have noticed this irregularity had they examined Penguin's operations more thoroughly. With the law of looting in desuetude, the seller's lawyers perhaps had little incentive to do so. But especially in light of the consent decree and the lawsuits about discount practices leading up to it, those lawyers might have asked about discount policies and then wondered about the bookkeeping. Asking simple questions might have enabled detection at least a year or two earlier, significantly lowering the stakes.

Mercury Finance.

Many attorneys were involved in major deals with Mercury Finance, a lender to borrowers with weak credit quality, during a period when it apparently treated as assets what should have been expenses. Some commentators correctly noted that many companies in high-risk businesses (like lending to people with bad credit ratings) use "aggressive accounting techniques;" others said—unhelpfully and incorrectly—that accounting in finance companies is "extraordinarily complex." It is not all that complex.

To lenders, loans are assets. Some loans are unlikely to be repaid. Bad loans are a cost of doing business—an expense. Expenses reduce net income. Estimating the amount of bad loans may involve complex judgments, but the accounting is simple. The portion of loans deemed uncollectible is recorded as an expense—as a debit (left-side entry) in bookkeeping terms. The credit (right-side entry) is made to Allowance for Doubtful Accounts.

Instead of treating all bad loans as expenses, Mercury Finance apparently decided that even if a borrower was not going to pay, somehow the company would recover—by repossessing the related car, for example. In the bookkeeping, a debit was apparently made to an asset account called Other Assets to reflect the right to repossess, rather than to an expense account—to reflect that the loan probably was never going to be paid. With far fewer reported expenses, Mercury Finance reported far higher earnings.

Just as detecting the buried discounts in Pearson's Accounts Receivable should not have been tricky, a bright red flag existed on Mercury Finance's financial statements. The Other Assets account on its balance sheet rocketed from $24.6 million to $121 million a year later. Maybe that account really included assets other than repossession rights.

But the increase does seem peculiar, at least to a business lawyer with a little accounting sense, and at least in hindsight. One of the many corporate lawyers on the scene with enough sense to ask good questions about bad loans and Other Assets might have eased managerial aggressiveness and strengthened the auditor's spine.

America Online.

America OnLine's (AOL) asset and expense flipping imbroglio followed from treating disbursements for developing a subscriber base not as a cost of doing business (an expense) but as an investment in the business (an asset). There was a judgment to make here. One could liken on-line services to newspapers and follow that industry's practice of expensing these costs; or one could analogize it to direct mail-order companies and follow that industry's practice of capitalizing them—treating them as assets whose cost is allocated over future accounting periods. In choosing between these treatments, the accounting issue is whether the disbursements would contribute reliably to revenue generation in future periods. As it turned out, America Online could not say that they would do so, because it could not gauge for how long its new subscribers would remain customers.

Maybe it was reasonable for AOL's managers and auditors to make the judgment they did. Following the horrible press coverage and class-action shareholder lawsuit that resulted, however, you can be sure they would like to have that decision to make again. Lawyers—had they been effective participants in the judgment-making process—could have helped them see that the public relations and legal risks were real. Lawyers are trained in analogical reasoning, after all, and could have helped draw useful analogies.

As with Mercury Finance, a telltale red flag existed: AOL's balance sheet showed an unusual asset called Deferred Subscriber Acquisition Costs. Mushrooming to $385 million in just over one year, it became the largest single asset on AOL's balance sheet. Angry shareholder agitation led AOL to abandon the practice and restate its earnings, wiping out about 80% of owners' equity.

Rent-Way.

A similar problem of expensing-versus-capitalizing plagued Rent-Way Inc., the second-largest operator of rent-to-own stores in the country. For a company with $500 million in revenue, the amounts involved in its accounting scandal were important and got more so: the misstatements were first announced at $30 million; raised to $60 million; and ultimately $110 million.

The pressure to manipulate the books in this case came from the combination of a Mercury Finance-like business model and an ambitious plan for growth. The rent-to-own business caters to low-income clientele.

Customers acquire the products Rent-Way markets, such as televisions and furniture, by making weekly rental payments until they've paid enough to own and keep the merchandise outright.

Founded by a former manager of one such store, a decade later Rent-Way owned over a dozen stores. The founder and a partner thereafter set out to grow the business, by buying existing stores, bringing the total to 1000 in a few years. Revenue shot up from $8 million to nearly $600 million in seven years. Costs for acquisitions amounted to $35 million in one year alone. These included the costs of buying shabby stores carrying shoddy inventory.

With the CEO on the road buying stores to grow the business at this frenetic pace, the bean counters back at the home office had to contend with endless streams of new data and integration questions, along with thousands of accounting judgments. The boss was buying growth— sometimes making costly commitments—while financial analysts were cheering him on with excitement about the growth.

Using a bookkeeping trick that should be quite familiar at this point, Rent-Way recorded as an asset what should have been an expense. There is a choice to be made between treating 100% of a disbursement as a current expense (with an immediate hit to income) or capitalizing it (allocating it as an expense over numerous future accounting periods).

At Rent-Way, some disbursements for automobile maintenance were apparently done this way. This can be a close call. The basic rule is that ordinary maintenance and repairs on fixed assets are expensed when incurred; for disbursements of a more substantial kind that lengthen the asset's useful life, capitalizing them is permitted.

Rent-Way also kept on its books as assets worn out, crummy furniture that should have been written off as an expense. This is what finally tipped superiors off: a comparison between the company's books relating to inventory and the reports of inventory held in the stores. Stores were reporting lower levels than the balance sheet indicated.

Sunbeam.

Sunbeam committed a distinct but all too common type of accounting fraud. Its widely-publicized accounting machinations boiled down to a series of so-called "bill-and-hold" transactions. During the winter months, it recorded charcoal grill sales even though the grills were not to be shipped until the spring. This manipulative maneuver enabled it to report higher sales in the winter.

The accounting shenanigans took place near the end of the reign of self-proclaimed business turnaround king Al Dunlap. Upon taking the helm at Sunbeam—floundering from a substantial business downturn— Dunlap fired half its workers and closed or consolidated more than half its facilities. Boasting that he aimed to "attack" his company, Dunlap declared that his plan was as carefully plotted as the invasion of Normandy. (Alas, Dunlap is no Churchill, and all his plans for Sunbeam failed miserably.) Driven by that kind of siege mentality, accounting irregularities may not have been inevitable, but they were certainly made more likely.

Rite Aid.

Rite Aid, owner of a chain of drug stores, announced disappointing earnings results. One factor was increased interest costs associated with debt used to make a recent acquisition. That debt needed to be refinanced or else the company faced the risk of bankruptcy. On the news, Rite Aid's stock price fell 40%, slashing $4 billion off its market capitalization. Shareholder lawsuits followed, though the worst was yet to come.

Later that year, Rite Aid announced that its previous three years of financial statements would have to be restated, reducing by $500 million the company's previously reported pre-tax earnings. One accounting trick apparently played was that when the company sold 189 stores, it had a gain on the sale of $82.5 million. GAAP calls for such a gain to be recognized when received. Instead, Rite Aid's top managers apparently created a special asset of $82.5 million as a reserve that could then be drawn on in the future to offset future operating expenses.

A few days later, the Rite Aid Board's Finance Committee met. With most directors present, the issue under discussion was refinancing the acquisition debt. One director suggested that Rite Aid could improve the terms of the refinancing by pledging as collateral stock it held in a recently-acquired company called PCS. At that point, Rite Aid's general counsel stated that the PCS stock was already pledged, explaining that weeks earlier, Rite Aid's CEO had met with the company's bankers on his own. Rite Aid needed about $800 million to pay off some commercial paper that was coming due in three days. The bankers offered to furnish the $800 million in short term credit if Rite Aid would pledge assets. The CEO agreed and pledged the PCS stock. So the stock was unavailable to help with the long-term refinancing.

The directors regarded this unilateral CEO action as beyond the CEO's power to effect and felt at a minimum that he should have consulted the board and may even have been obliged to disclose the pledge publicly. The CEO resigned, being given no severance package. The audit committee of Rite Aid's board conducted an internal investigation and retained outside lawyers and forensic accountants and, cooperating with law enforcement authorities, found further evidence of breach of fiduciary duties and other accounting deceptions.

Fabri-Centers.

Managers can persuade a lot of people—auditors and even directors—to accept their position when they emphasize the judgment they are making in choosing to expense or capitalize a transaction, or to make other accounting decisions. But even when the managerial judgment is made, lawyers can and should insist that full disclosure about the judgment be included in footnotes to financial statements or in MD&A.

The need for such disclosure detailing difficult judgment calls is the story behind the settlement of SEC charges against Fabri-Centers, operator of over 900 retail stores, including the JoAnn Fabrics chain. Fabri-Centers knew the daily sales figures at its stores, but could not determine the cost of goods sold or profit margin until it conducted an annual inventory. So it estimated them, using the so-called gross profit method of applying the prior year's actual profit margin to estimate quarterly profits the succeeding year. During several quarters, however, heavy price competition substantially eroded the margin. Before the erosion had been reported or publicly disclosed, the company effected a public debt offering. The SEC charged Fabri-Centers with inadequate disclosure about price competition and its estimation practice in that offering.

Under the company's inventory system as it existed (it has since been modernized), a judgment about quarterly profit margins was obviously necessary. But lawyers involved in the debt offering—aware both that the quarterly financial statements were unaudited and that they just might have been prepared in anticipation of the offering—could have paid greater attention to the role that accounting estimates were playing. At a minimum, fuller disclosure about pricing and estimating practices would have been proper. True, the company's financing cost might have been higher, but it would have been far lower than the subsequent public relations and settlement costs—as well as legal and accounting fees—Fabri-Centers incurred defending against SEC charges.

Cendant.

Footnote or other narrative disclosure must be very clear in order to tell the complete story of a business. This is one of the scores of lessons to take from the notorious accounting scandal that unfolded at Cendant Corporation, an entity formed by the merger of CUC International and HFS Inc.

These entities operate discount shopping services for members only and generate revenue through membership dues payments. On average, membership clubs such as these generate greater profits from longer-term members than from shorter-term members. Indeed, the tendency is to make no profit from members having been enrolled for less than a year partly because members are typically entitled to a refund of dues upon cancellation of membership.

CUC had met with some accounting embarrassment for its practice of recognizing as revenue the total amount of each membership payment in the period it was received while expensing amounts allocable to each membership over a three-year period. Although CUC backed down from that position in the face of criticism by financial analysts and others, it continued to practice aggressive accounting in other areas. One example was its practice of reporting its membership flows and annual renewal rates, important information to gauge company prospects given that newer members contribute little or nothing to the bottom line while the real value is in the long-term member.

Of new members enrolled at the end of a given year, 70% renewed, but the way CUC had reported this in its footnote and narrative disclosure it was possible to understand it to mean that of all members who joined during the year 70% renewed. So if 100 members had been in and out during the year but 10 remained members at year end, the 70% figure meant that 7 renewed but could have been understood to mean that 70 renewed—a difference of night and day to the company's prospects.

This misleading disclosure was just one example of numerous irregularities at the company, as a subsequent forensic accounting report made clear. That report emphasized that these sorts of irregularities were part of an overall culture of aggressive or irregular accounting practices that also included such machinations as manipulation of the books relating to the level of membership dues that were subject to refund, how cash was managed, and, ultimately, how the combined Cendant accounted for the merger between CUC and HFS that created it.

The red thread of that report is that the corporate and financial reporting culture created for the company by top management permitted this kind of behavior. One lesson for lawyers is that they as a professional group participating in the financial reporting process by drafting and reviewing footnote and other narrative disclosures can help shape corporate culture toward integrity rather than in its face.

It is not only in the area of alertness to incubating financial scandals, of course, that lawyers may find the lessons of accounting valuable. Indeed, for transactional lawyers these lessons will prove valuable in drafting the sorts of loan and other agreements mentioned at the beginning of this section. That activity is an important part of what many lawyers do, and is a valuable art to master.

C. AUDIT FAILURE

All cases discussed in the preceding section involved accounting deceptions undetected by auditors. No audit can guarantee detecting all materially false or misleading or non-compliant financial statements. Audits fail to do so either because of inherent risks associated with audits or an auditor fails to comply with GAAS. Telling the difference is difficult and highly-fact intensive. Some additional perspective on audit failure can be gleaned by considering the cases discussed in this section.

*Phar-Mor, Inc.**

Michael Monus was sentenced to 19 years and 7 months in prison for accounting fraud at the deep-discount retail chain called Phar-Mor, Inc. He was the chief operating officer at the company and, along with other managers, engineered a six-year scheme that inflated owners' equity by $500 million at a company that went bankrupt upon revelation of the fraud. During a seven-year period, Phar-Mor grew from 15 stores to 310 stores, reporting sales of $3 billion.

As a deep-discount retailer, Phar-Mor's strategy was to beat its competitors' prices. It apparently got carried away with this business model, engaging in accounting chicanery that artificially enabled it to sell at cut-throat prices. In other words, its prices were so low that it was losing money. But its accounting was so creative that this was never apparent from its financial statements. Key tricks were altering accounting records to understate the cost of goods sold and overstate inventory (as well as accounts receivable).

Numerous factors contributed to enabling Monus and his conspirators to deceive both its auditors and the market place. Apart from the collusion, the company had weak internal controls, including a deliberately porous management information system that kept key information from managers outside the conspiracy group.

Strikingly, the fraud's masterminds included several former auditors, including one from the auditing firm that conducted Phar-Mor's audits. They boasted that one reason they got away with the fraud for so long was they knew what the auditors would be looking for! (The Sarbanes-Oxley Act subsequently provided that, as a matter of law, audit firms are not independent of companies when former audit firm employees become company employees.)

Phar-Mor's outside auditor recognized the client as a high-risk audit. The auditor observed apparent exaggeration in inventory levels and accounts receivable, the company's primary assets. Evidence in a lawsuit against the auditor suggested that the lead audit partner on the engagement faced pressure to bring in additional non-auditing business from Phar-Mor.

Investor lawsuits against the auditor seeking $1 billion in damages resulted in a jury verdict for the investors. Subsequently, the parties reached a settlement without disclosing terms. Plaintiffs acknowledged

---

* This discussion is based upon Mark S. Beasley *et al.*, *Auditing Cases* (Prentice Hall 2d ed. 2002), case 6.

that the fraud alone did not indicate auditor culpability. They observed that the issue was not whether the auditor could have detected the fraud. Rather, they submitted that the issue was whether the auditor conducted a proper GAAS audit. If so, it was not liable; if not, then it committed fraud in falsely and misleadingly stating that it had conducted such an audit.

A principal area in which the investors claimed the auditor did not conduct a GAAS audit concerned inventory. In one illustration, Phar-Mor bought inventory from an affiliated party (one owned by Phar-Mor's controlling shareholder). The affiliate shipped goods to Phar-Mor, partly filling orders but fully-billing for them. Phar-Mor and the affiliate were uncertain of the discrepancy's amount and after discussions agreed that the affiliate would pay $7 million to make up for the shortage.

Phar-Mor booked receipt of this sum as a reduction to its purchases account. This reduced cost of goods sold under the formula, discussed in Chapter 4, $COGS = BI + P - EI$. That move converted the year's net income from a loss of $2 million to a profit of $5 million. The investors argued that this move was, in fact, a disguised capital contribution from the affiliate to Phar-Mor not inventory transactions. In court, investors alleged that the auditor did not gather sufficient evidence to confirm that the settlement amount was based on the difference between goods shipped and goods billed.

A second area arose from a problem akin to that in the Fabri-Centers case described in the previous section. Like Fabri-Centers, Phar-Mor maintained a periodic inventory system rather than a perpetual system and conducted an annual physical inventory count. It then adjusted inventory in its records based on the physical count. When counted inventory was below booked inventory, proper bookkeeping entails reducing the inventory account with a right-side entry (a credit) and increasing the cost of goods sold account with a left-side entry (a debit).

Taking this opportunity to manipulate the figures, the fraudsters recorded the offsetting amount to what they called "bucket accounts," not to the cost of goods sold. These bucket accounts were given strange-sounding names like "Accounts Receivable Inventory Contra." The effect was to reduce inventory but to leave cost of goods sold artificially low. At year-end, these bucket accounts would be reduced with an offsetting entry to some other asset account, often one called "Accrued Inventory." It would then be incorporated back into the inventory account, boosting it artificially. Here the claim against the auditors was that their review of the inventory adjusting entries was inadequate, both in terms of sampling performed in reviewing the entries and in failing to investigate the suspicious names given to bucket accounts.

This process raised a third issue in the investor's claim against the auditors. As former auditors, the perpetrators knew that auditors apply a lower level of scrutiny to accounts bearing zero balances at period ends than those with balances. So they emptied the bucket accounts into other asset accounts before the period-end closing process, a sort of account-laundering process akin to the efforts money-launderers undertake when shifting cash through a series of bank transactions to disguise origins and impair tracing. In this case, all the entries had been run through the general ledger, using the strange names like Accounts Receivable Inventory Contra and Accrued Inventory, but ended up in other asset accounts with normal names like Inventory.

The allegation against the auditor was that it should have reviewed the general ledger more carefully, not rely on the final T-account balances. The auditor defended itself saying it had taken a sufficient sample of adjusting entries at period end to meet GAAS. It pointed out there is no requirement in GAAS to review every general ledger entry line by line. The ledgers they reviewed were consolidated ledgers in which the bucket accounts had already been filled and emptied. The fraudsters perceived these cracks in the auditing process and exploited them. Whether the auditor was outsmarted or inclined to skirt GAAS to gain Phar-Mor's non-audit business is unclear and presumably unknowable given the undisclosed settlement.

Andersen.

Professor Arthur Andersen taught accounting at Northwestern University in the early 20th century. Integrity was his hallmark. He parlayed this trait into a public accounting firm seen through most of that century as a faithful steward of the public's trust. A well-known firm motto held that "there's the Andersen way and the wrong way." His firm died amid the Enron Corp. scandal that rocked corporate America in the early 2000s, one of three other big frauds at companies Andersen audited during this heady financial period.

Amid Enron's collapse, Arthur Andersen employees engaged in a flurry of illicit efforts to destroy documents relating to the firm's work with the imploding company. These actions, taken after it was known that investigations by the SEC and others were underway and that they included subpoenas, constituted obstruction of justice. The fallout in a jury trial in Texas was the collapse of the once-venerable accounting firm. Following are abstracts of some of the stories that reduced the Big Five accounting firms to the Big Four and spawned the Sarbanes-Oxley Act of 2002.

Enron.

Enron through the 1980s was a natural gas drilling and pipeline company. It morphed through the financial boom of the late 1990s into a fiction, doing phony internal trading and recording false revenues. The company engaged in volatile trading activity and housed it in special purpose entities (SPEs) to insulate the company's earnings and hence stock price from resulting short-term gyrations. Using SPEs is legitimate and lawful as matters of accounting and commercial and securities laws, so long as rules are observed.

To obtain off-balance treatment, SPEs must satisfy general well-known rules of consolidation accounting and particular arcane rules applied to these entities. The general rule provides that to avoid full consolidation of an entity, a third-party must control a majority of that entity's equity (discussed in Chapter 6); the arcane rule says that at least 3% of the SPE's total capital must be equity (capping the debt equity ratio at approximately 97:3 or about 32:1).

In early transactions, Enron followed both rules, capitalizing SPEs with a debt: equity ratio no greater than 32:1 and placing a majority of the equity with a third party. In subsequent deals, however, one or both requirements went unmet. In most of these, either Enron, an affiliate or an Enron executive held the equity. This meant that all the deals constituted related-party transactions and all should have been disclosed and/or consolidated on Enron's books. None was. Debt housed in these controlled entities ran to billions of dollars, and the security was often Enron's own stock. When business conditions turned adverse, its stock price weakened and the debts came home to roost in cascades, leading to bankruptcy.

Much trading activity to be housed in the SPEs and much of Enron's direct activity centered on the risk management business pursued through the development and trading of financial instruments. Fair value accounting (Chapter 6) applied, requiring Enron to assign values to these instruments. The tendency was for Enron to use excessively rosy assumptions and aggressive allocation judgments. Managers assigned high asset values to trades and listed those amounts on the balance sheet and correspondingly high, theoretical profits in the income statement. In other cases, managers treated borrowed funds as sale-and-purchase transactions not loans—a modern version of a classic trick from the accounting fraud cookbook.

The immediate consequences were staggering, and worsened. The first inkling of trouble came in a conference call with financial analysts, when management disclosed a reduction in equity of $1.2 billion (about 10%) due to losses at the SPEs. A few weeks later, the greater gravity of the situation emerged, with the company announcing that 20% of its equity was wiped out—$2.2 billion worth. The company restated its financials for the preceding four years, producing a 20% reduction to reported cumulative net income of nearly $600 million. On the balance sheet, consolidation increased debt by billions of dollars.

The blow was so severe that Enron shopped itself around to other corporate buyers, agreeing to be sold to an erstwhile arch-rival in the energy business, Dynegy. Yet as the avalanche of terrible accounting news continued to flow, even that deal blew up, with Dynegy terminating the agreement. Ultimately, Enron filed for voluntary bankruptcy protection under Chapter 11. The board appointed a special committee to investigate, as shareholders filed lawsuits against it, top managers, and Enron's outside auditors. The SEC also conducted an investigation, as did numerous arms of Congress and other governmental agencies. Some Enron executives received prison sentences.

WorldCom.

WorldCom's fiasco typifies classic cases of fraudulent accounting accompanied by audit and internal control failure. Once the nation's second largest long-distance telecommunications carrier (marketed under the MCI brand), WorldCom's business was in tatters. To disguise this, it turned to accounting fraud, shifting expense accounts to asset accounts.

WorldCom's internal controls failed to prevent these shifts because they allowed senior financial executives to jigger ledger entries without immediate detection. The mischief was finally detected by an internal auditor conducting a spot check of the capital expenditure (cap-ex) records. One entry related to "line costs," disbursements made to local telecom networks to make phone calls and other connections. These would normally be characterized properly as routine business expenses, as the cost of generating current revenue. Such disbursements should have been recorded as current operating expenses, not capitalized.

And it wasn't just that the figures were listed in the asset accounts rather than the expense accounts. Apparently the journal entries properly recorded line costs as expenses. But during the closing process, they were transferred to the asset accounts—and indeed sprinkled across these. Internal controls should have prevented the deception. Specific protocols should have ensured automatic posting of entries from the journal to the ledger T-accounts and finally into the financial statements. Allowing managers to override those systems during the closing process is an internal control failure.

The controller, in charge of the closing process, rationalized that these line charges would contribute reliably to future earnings, and there was some evidence that this belief was shared in the telecom community. Several billion dollars of these disbursements were recorded in the cap-ex accounts, as assets on the balance sheet (not affecting the income statement), rather than in the expense accounts burdening net income.

As reported, line costs tallied about $15 billion, but should have been recorded at $22 billion. The result changed a year's worth of large losses into apparent paper profits. Also of interest was the fact that in prior years line costs were expensed; the change to cap-exing them thus also required some explanation.

Following control procedures for an internal audit, internal auditors subsequently discovered these overrides and reported them to the company's audit committee chair, who was soon fired along with its CFO and controller. Wrath, ire, and wrenching ensued throughout the company, media, regulatory agencies, and Congress. Anguish reached all the way to the Oval Office where President George W. Bush condemned the bookkeeping stunt as "outrageous."

Treating operating expenses as capital expenditures is an age-old move and there is an age-old tendency for the abuser to overdo it, festooning the balance sheet with a bright red flag. A cap ex account increasing by several billion dollars in a year stands out, even in a company WorldCom's multi-billion dollar size. After the controller made the overriding adjustments during the account closing process, additional internal controls should have raised a question about the size of these items, another case of internal control failure.

For internal controls to work, however, the company's senior management must want them to work. When the CFO and controller, along with the chairman of the board audit committee, wish to evade internal controls, it becomes far easier to do so. Proper internal controls must be designed to thwart collusion among senior management that could undermine them. Defects in internal controls should be discovered during a company's external audit, and the external audit should discover override capabilities and related concealment. WorldCom's external audit, performed by erstwhile Big Five accounting firm Arthur Andersen, did neither.

Parmalat Finanziaria SpA.

Global companies incorporated outside the US are not immune from accounting scandals. Consider Parmalat Finanziaria SpA, a large Italian multinational maker of foods including Sunnydale Farms milk and Archway cookies. An accounting scandal several years in the making resulted in Italy's largest-ever bankruptcy. Aggressions apparently were wide-ranging but uniting them was the use of numerous subsidiaries and divisions throughout the world.

Parmalat said it owned more than 200 subsidiaries operating in more than 50 countries. Together, the family of companies issued €6.4 billion in bonds over six years (averaged during that period, this amount in Euros is about the equivalent amount in US dollars). Where the money went is a mystery, with at least €2 billion of it unaccounted for, part of the €8 billion that disappeared. One way its disappearance was apparently hidden: a company bank account at Bank of America listed as having a balance of $4.9 billion was a fiction. A chain of transactions facilitated such fabrications, including inflating earnings, fabricating assets and hiding losses through a global web of shell companies.

Chicanery included asset transfers. A Luxembourg unit reported gains and losses on sales of various African operations reportedly sold to various parent divisions. These transfers should have been recorded on the unit's books but would have been eliminated in the parent's consolidated financial statements. (See Chapter 6.) Apparently valuations assigned to the transactions by separate units of the family differed, however. A selling unit might indicate a low sales price to generate a loss beneficial for tax purposes and a buying unit might indicate a high sales price to generate a high asset value on its books (or the opposite could be desirable, a high sales price to sport gains and thus high earnings and a low purchase price to sport low depreciation expenses on the asset). Either way, the differences would not neatly net for elimination on the parent's books. Aggressions at each unit would magnify rather than neutralize each other.

Parmalat's auditors noted some problems. Their notes accompanied reports only of the operating units, not the consolidated parent. Auditors of the parent apparently did not review them. If they had, these consolidated statements (called *group accounts* in European accounting) would have shown red flags. These audit reports indicated the company provided inadequate evidence to support claimed asset values for ownership interests in other business units. These values were created using a variety of phony asset transfers. The audit notes were not disclosed to investors who bought Parmalat bonds based on accompanying offering documents.

This reveals a governance problem for large global auditing firms. Some operating units were audited by other firms entirely and other operating units by affiliates of the parent's auditor. Auditors ideally operate as global entities that are integrated. In fact, operations are highly decentralized. Often the parent auditor relies on work by service units and sometimes other audit firms altogether. The units and the work are not integrated with the parent auditor and its work.

For global companies, this creates opportunities to run transactions through Byzantine webs of operating units. These units can be governed by different accounting rules in different countries and reports can even be prepared in different languages. International auditing standards increasingly place on parent auditors primary and independent responsibility for audits of units. They meet this obligation by verifying the reliability of the other audits, steps apparently not taken in Parmalat's case.

D. SATIRE

In the mid-1930s, noted investor and Columbia University business school teacher Benjamin Graham satirically hypothesized a phantom US Steel Corporation adopting "advanced bookkeeping methods" to report "phenomenally enhanced" earnings without any cash outlays or changes in operating conditions or sales. To update that illustration of accounting chicanery, consider how a phantom company might today achieve the same results using techniques like those discussed earlier in this Chapter. Its press release and accompanying disclosure might appear as follows.

A Satire on Financial Reporting Shenanigans

E-America Dot.Com Announces Higher-than-Expected Earnings

E-America Dot.Com today announced record earnings, stunning Wall Street analysts whose consensus view estimated continued losses for the start-up that went public last year. Its stock price shot up 40% on the news. Though this response is usually reserved for companies that report losses, we believe it is justified for the same sort of reasons—none.

Rather than taking any action to increase sales or improve its products, marketing strategy, distribution channels, or customer service, the earnings increase was due to improvements in the manner in which the company's economic activity is recorded in its books. These new bookkeeping methods report profits of $50 per share instead of the $25 per share loss that otherwise would be reported. The accounting improvements consist of the following steps:

- Modifying revenue recognition policies
- Adjusting reserves and treatment of returns
- Recording the value of market share as an asset
- Recording the amount of cash we "burn" as an asset
- Reporting in a fictitious currency
- Refining the concept of materiality

The Board of Directors of E-America Dot.Com, in collusion with their independent outside auditors, reached the following conclusions in adopting this program in a resolution unanimously approved at its board meeting this week:

The Board of Directors and its Independent Outside Auditors, after careful study and review, determined that the accounting policies and practices it used since its recent initial public offering 10 months ago are outdated and do not reflect the performance managers of the company expect or predict.

The Board and its Auditors, aided and abetted by a special audit committee, determined that many other companies obtain a competitive advantage in the capital markets by reporting accounting results in terms of innovative, cutting-edge techniques. Moreover, the company was penalized for failing to follow these best practices, referred to as the "New Accounting."

Adopting the New Accounting will neutralize this disadvantage and enable the company to increase its market capitalization without the need for disbursing cash or changing any of its operating activities. The changes adopted by the Board, with the attestation of its Auditors, are as follows:

• <u>Modifying revenue recognition policies</u>. Competitive conditions in our industry lead us to give generous credit terms to our customers. These include giving them the right to return goods to us for a full refund if they cannot resell them to the ultimate consumer within 180 days. We formerly deferred recognizing the revenue in connection with such transactions until after that 180-day period passed on the grounds that no sale was complete until then.

But this Old Economy policy substantially reduced the amount of reported sales reflected on our income statement. The Board decided to treat those transactions as sales immediately, on the grounds that our sales team put tireless effort into generating them and should get credit. (We can make adjustments for returns later, but for now, we would rather report the good news in the short-term and defer the bad news for the long-term.)

In particular, we will occasionally "park" inventory with our customers to whom we give unconditional return rights, either orally or in "side letters" kept separate from the sales documents. As a result of this scheme, we will report much higher sales revenue and dramatic increases in earnings. If adjustments must be made to smooth those earnings, we will restate past earnings in subsequent quarterly reports and disclose that these are one-time events.

In some of our highly evolving businesses, when finished product is not available for shipment to satisfy our order flow, unfinished product is shipped to a freight forwarder's warehouse to be held until recalled by us for final assembly. This is necessary in order to sustain our time-to-customer cycles, and we increasingly ship products that are not fully assembled and not fully functional. In some cases, we are unable to ship products to customers that submitted purchase orders, and in others we ship products before customers want delivery. In each case, we believe that it is better to record the sales when the unfinished product is shipped and the purchase order is received rather than when we get around to delivering it.

• <u>Adjusting reserves and treatment of returns</u>. In the financing arm of our business, we intend to reduce the amount of reserves we record for delinquent and uncollectible accounts by reporting them as current. To do so, we will in some cases simply extend the due dates of our customers' obligations. In others, we will assume that we can repossess the items secured by these delinquent loans, whether or not that is feasible. This enables us to record far lower reserves in our allowance for credit losses, thus increasing our net income.

Similarly, in all of our businesses, we will record customer returns of merchandise as purchases of goods, rather than charging them against our reserves for returns. Another benefit of this new policy is to increase our receivable turns, making our operations look speedier and more efficient.

- <u>Recording the value of market share as an asset</u>. A hot trend in the marketplace for traders and speculators is to assign a value to Internet companies based on their market share. This is necessary to justify the stratospheric prices being paid for stocks of these companies in initial public offerings and in exchange trading. After all, most of these companies do not generate any earnings or even positive cash flows. Staying ahead of the stampede, we are moving one logical step further by listing the value of this market share on our balance sheet as an asset.

Every quarter we will gauge the amount of value the market is giving us based on our market share and record that in an asset account called market share. This may seem like a "belts-and-suspenders" policy given that our other New Accounting changes will enable us to report actual earnings and actual cash flows which otherwise would be negative. Nevertheless, we believe that this is what shareholders and market players want, and we are just trying to be responsive.

- <u>Recording the amount of cash we "burn" as an asset</u>. Companies with negative cash flows sometimes get credit for the amount of cash they raise and spend on researching new products. This is especially true in the biotechnology industry. We see no reason why the logic of that approach should not extend to our businesses as well. Speculators and traders give substantial valuation credit for this cash burn.

Beginning today, we will treat the amount of our cash burn as an asset on the balance sheet rather than as an expense on the income statement. On the other hand, because of the significant impact that the treatment of disbursed cash as an expense or an asset has on our earnings, we reserve the right from time to time to alternate between these treatments depending on the trend in reported earnings from quarter to quarter.

- <u>Reporting in a different currency</u>. We sell many of our products and conduct a clearinghouse operation for other businesses in a barter exchange web-site on the Internet. In lieu of trading (or bartering) such goods and services directly, however, exchange members use our trademarked "dotcom dollars," issued to them by us for bartering. These dotcom dollars have a face value far greater than the US dollar and we propose to record certain of our assets and sales transactions in dotcom dollars rather than US dollars, thereby substantially increasing the magnitude of reported assets and income (we are not fools, however, so expenses and liabilities, of course, will continue to be reported in US dollars).

- Refining the concept of materiality. Lawyers and auditors often place great weight on whether some economic event is material to our company or not. They define materiality in terms of what a reasonable investor thinks about its impact on the company's business or financial condition. In the past, this led us to report in our financial statements details that don't really seem to matter very much to the managers at our company or to other owners of options on our stock.

To reconcile managerial needs with the requirements of financial reporting, the board adopted a New Rule of materiality. Under it, no economic activity is material to the company unless it impacts our earnings by at least 5%. This rule is more definitive and reliable than the Old Rule and will result in greater certainty in our bookkeeping department. Applying this approach to materiality, we can ignore a variety of burdensome reporting questions, thus saving (material) basketfuls of money.

As satire, the report from E-America Dot.Com reveals how atrocious and distorted aggressive accounting and earnings management can be. (Most of the examples are based on actual cases.) Yet you will never see the kind of candor expressed in this news release coming out of corporations. That kind of honesty is inconsistent with the goals underlying the shenanigans.

Problem 16

Each of the following cases poses an issue that may be labeled ethical in that it involves a judgment concerning whether posited accounting action is right or wrong. In each case, identify the ethics issue and evaluate the position you would take in confirming it.*

a.   New FASB standards are ordinarily issued with the requirement that they be implemented within one year of the issue date, with earlier implementation encouraged. Suppose that a chief financial officer (CFO) believes early implementation of a new standard would better reflect economic reality at his company but also sees that it would result in his company's reported net income being lower than otherwise. He asks your advice as to whether he should implement the new standard this year or wait until next year.

---

*   Problems are adapted from Donald E. Kieso, Jerry J. Weygandt & Terry D. Warfield, *international Accounting* (10th ed. 2001, John Wiley & Sons), which in turn draw from actual CPA examinations.

b.   A nuclear power generating company determines that one of its reactors will be shut down at the end of its estimated useful life 15 years from now at great expense. Recall the matching principle that commands accountants to match revenue and expense. Two internal accountants at the company debate whether to (1) allocate the shut-down costs evenly over the next 15 years or (2) await the shut down to record any expense. They ask you to settle their debate.

c.   Computer Trader Inc. sells computer software and uses the LIFO method of inventory reporting. Sales were up substantially this year and forecasts for next year are grim due to a highly inflationary economic environment. To even things out, the President tells the controller to tell the purchasing department to load up on inventory just before year end at prices so high the carrying amount of purchased inventory will have the effect of reducing net income this year. You overhear the order. Thoughts?

d.   Varsity Sports is a merchandising company that in the past has recorded an allowance for doubtful accounts on its receivables of 4% of net credit sales, which the CFO believes is appropriate in light of past history. The President tells the CFO this year to increase the allowance to 6%, arguing that the consequent reduction in net income this year will enable superior growth rates in earnings next year. What is the CFO to do?

e.   Jack Smith runs a small medical services and supply company, owned by 10 doctors who lack financial backgrounds, and whose books Jack has kept on a cash basis since founding it 10 years ago. Business is booming, with increasing complexity in and levels of inventory, accounts receivable and fixed assets. With these complexities, Jack knows that accrual basis financials would show net income at lower levels than the cash basis. The doctors are eager to continue to grow the business and encourage Jack to get financing from banks, which seek accrual statements. Jack would prefer not to hand over the accrual statements to the doctors because he fears they may conclude his performance is slipping. Jack asks for your advice.

f.   Brainiacs Inc. is a biotech drug research outfit that is poised for a major breakthrough. It will produce a revolutionary cancer drug. Substantial profits should result. But the research will incur huge expenses that GAAP requires to be recognized immediately rather than capitalized over time. To avoid the earnings hit, the controller hatches a plan to create a separate partnership in which Brainiacs would have a 49% interest and several other co-investors would each hold smaller stakes. When the partnership finishes its work and procures patent protection on the drug, Brainiacs will buy the patent, which it can record on its books as an asset. Good idea?

Conceptual Questions 16

What's a better system to reduce the incidence of accounting fraud, audit failure, and misallocation of investment capital? More capitalism or less? More rules or more standards? In standard-setting, more responsibility allocated to the private sector or more towards government? From a systemic standpoint, is there a tolerable level of fraud via financial reporting?

GLOSSARY

■ ■ ■

Note: This is an informal selection and specification, intended as an aid to studying this introductory text rather than a complete or nuanced lexicon. Readers may wish to add terms or modify definitions provided.

A

Accelerated depreciation: A method of depreciation that expenses more of a fixed asset's depreciable base in the early years of its useful life and less in the later years rather than evenly as under straight-line depreciation.

Account: A record in which change in a designated financial item is recorded.

Account payable: An obligation to pay, typically to a supplier, not evidenced by a note, this is a current liability. Plural: accounts payable.

Account receivable: A right to be paid, typically by a customer, not evidenced by a note, this is a current asset. Plural: accounts receivable.

Accounting equation: *See* fundamental equation.

Accounting income: Also called book income, income determined in accordance with accounting principles as contrasted with income determined in accordance with tax law or regulations.

Accounting period: Also called a reporting period, the period of time covered by a set of financial statements, usually a year, quarter or month.

Accounts receivable turnover ratio: An expression of the number of times per period accounts receivable were totally replaced, indicating their relative liquidity and collectability, and computed as credit sales divided by average accounts receivable.

Accrual accounting (or accrual basis of accounting): The standard method of accounting, calling for recording revenues in the period they are earned and expenses in the period they are incurred. *Compare* cash accounting (or cash basis of accounting).

Accruals: Revenues that have been earned and expenses that have been incurred by the end of a given accounting period but which will not be collected or paid until a subsequent accounting period.

Accrued expense: Also called accrued liability, an obligation arising when expense is incurred prior to making the related cash payment, this is a current liability.

Accrued revenue: Also called accrued asset, a right arising when revenue is earned prior to receiving the related cash payment, this is a current asset.

Accumulated depreciation: A contra account showing the aggregate amount of a fixed asset's depreciation since its acquisition. When subtracted from the fixed asset's historical cost this yields the asset's book value.

Acid test ratio: Also called the quick ratio, a stringent test of liquidity determined by dividing the most liquid current assets (such as cash, marketable securities and accounts receivable but usually excluding inventory) by current liabilities.

Additional paid-in-capital: The amount equity investors paid in excess of the par value of a corporation's stock.

Adjusting entries: Journal entries made during the closing process to reflect non-transactional items such as depreciation expense and accruals and deferrals.

Adverse opinion: In a financial statement audit, an auditor's opinion stating that financial statements do not fairly present the financial position, results of operations, or cash flows in conformity with generally accepted accounting principles. In an audit of internal control over financial reporting, an auditor's opinion that a company did not maintain effective control over financial reporting.

AICPA: American Institute of Certified Public Accountants, a professional trade association of accountants in the United States and an influential standard setter for both GAAP and GAAS.

Alpha: A measure of risk and performance of an investment portfolio or business compared to a market index or benchmark, reflecting the relative economic value of the manager of the portfolio or business.

Allowance for doubtful accounts: Also called allowance for bad debts, a contra account showing the amount of estimated bad debts associated with accounts receivable. It is subtracted from accounts receivable listed on a balance sheet.

Amortization: In accounting, the process of writing off or allocating the cost of intangible assets such as goodwill, copyrights, patents and trademarks (the term has different meanings in other contexts).

Analytical procedures: Method of obtaining evidence in an audit and determining additional areas requiring auditing attention, examples include comparing actual financial statement figures with budgets.

Annual percentage rate: Nominal annual rate of interest assuming interest is compounded annually.

Annual percentage yield: Also called effective annual yield, a rate of interest after taking account of compounding more frequently than annually.

Annualize: To convert non-yearly figures into yearly figures by adjusting from the non-yearly period to a yearly period.

Annuity: A series of equal periodic payments or receipts over time, *ordinary annuities* involve payments or receipts at period-end and *annuities due* involve payments or receipts at the beginning of a period.

Articulation: The interrelationships among components within a set of financial statements, characterized by like measurement principles facilitating the interrelationship.

Asset: *1. Informal*: An item bearing value, owned or controlled, and acquired at a cost measurable in money. *2. Formal* (FASB): "probable future economic benefits obtained or controlled by an entity resulting from past transactions or events."

Asset intensive (or intensity): Signifying an entity heavily reliant upon fixed assets or current assets for the generation of its revenue.

Audit committee: Committee of a corporate board of directors charged with overseeing accounting, auditing and other financial matters, usually composed of members otherwise independent of the company.

Audit data analytics (ADA): Tech-enhanced methods to discover and analyze patterns and anomalies in financial records, used to enhance the planning and performance of an audit.

Audit report: *1.* An opinion accompanying a set of financial statements expressing the view of an independent auditor as to whether the financial statements fairly present the financial position, results of operations, and cash flows of an entity in conformity with generally accepted accounting principles. *2.* A similar opinion concerning the effectiveness of internal control over financial reporting.

Audit risk: The possibility that an auditor unknowingly fails to appropriately modify his/her opinion on financial statements that are materially misstated.

Audit sampling: The application of an audit procedure to less than 100% of the items within an account balance or class of transactions for the purpose of evaluating some characteristic of the balance or class.

Auditing: The process of examining and opining upon assertions made by third-parties, financial auditing entails examining financial statements and increasingly an associated examination and opinion concerning the effectiveness of internal control over financial reporting.

Average-cost method: A method of measuring the cost of goods sold by computing the average cost of beginning inventory plus purchases, this also drives the reported amount of ending inventory.

B

Bad debt: An account receivable that will not be collected.

Bad debt expense: Also called uncollectible accounts expense, the estimated portion of accounts receivable generated during an accounting period unlikely to be collected.

Balance sheet: A component of financial statements showing the assets, liabilities and equity at a moment in time and capturing the fundamental equation.

Beginning inventory: The balance in the inventory account as of the first day of an accounting period, which is equal to the balance in the inventory account as of the last day of the previous accounting period.

Beta (β): In modern finance theory, a statistical expression of the volatility of the price of a security measured against the volatility of the overall market.

Book income: *See* accounting income.

Book value: *1.* For assets, also called the carrying value, the net amount shown on a balance sheet (*e.g.*, for a fixed asset, the difference between its historical cost and accumulated depreciation; for accounts receivable, the difference between gross receivables and allowance for doubtful accounts). *2.* For an entity, the difference between total assets and total liabilities.

Bookkeeping: A support function for accounting, tending to involve routine implementation steps rather than judgments of classification or measurement that accounting addresses.

C

Capital: Generally funds provided by investors in the form of loans (debt) or shareholdings (equity), though the term has a variety of uses and meanings in numerous contexts.

Capital accounts: A collection of accounts comprising owners' equity in a business (divided variously for different forms of business organization).

Capital asset: *See* fixed asset.

Capital asset pricing model (CAPM): In modern finance theory, a theory of pricing publicly-traded investment securities in which the relationship between systemic risk and expected return is proportional to *beta* and there is no return for diversifiable risk.

Capital expenditure: Often referred to as *cap-ex*, outlays to acquire or improve fixed assets with the costs capitalized as part of the acquired or improved asset.

Capital lease: An asset giving functional control over a property for substantially the property's entire useful life.

Capital stock: An equity account showing the amount shareholders contributed when purchasing shares of a corporation. This plus retained earnings amounts to total equity.

Capital structure: The mix and design of long-term capital resources employed by an entity, chiefly the mix of debt and equity capital.

Capitalization of earnings: Valuation method involving estimate of earnings and appropriate discount rate (in this context called the capitalization rate or cap rate for short).

Capitalize: To charge an expenditure to an asset account because it benefits periods exceeding one year. (Capitalizing is the process thereof; *compare* expensing).

Cash: Money, whether in currency, bank accounts, or equivalent instruments bearing maturities typically less than three months.

Cash accounting (or cash basis of accounting): Not a recognized method of accounting under GAAP, a system of accounting that records transactions when cash is paid or received. *Compare* accrual accounting, recognized under GAAP, which allocates items of revenue and expense to periods independent of when cash is paid or received.

Cash flow statement: A component of financial statements showing the sources and uses of cash during an accounting period.

Certified public accountant (CPA): A designation awarded by states in the US to persons meeting stringent professional qualifications, passing rigorous examination, and meeting experience requirements, these persons are licensed to render opinions concerning auditing services. (In British Commonwealth countries, the designation is called chartered accountant (CA)).

Closely-held corporation: A corporation whose capital stock is owned by a small number of shareholders and/or which is not publicly-traded.

Closing entries: Journal entries used at the end of an accounting period to transfer balances in income statement accounts (chiefly revenue and expense) to the owners' equity portion of the balance sheet (as retained earnings).

Closing process: The steps taken at the end of an accounting period to prepare financial statements from underlying accounts.

Coefficient of variation: Standard deviation divided by expected value, a measure of relative risk of two populations (such as portfolios or securities under modern finance theory) bearing different expected values.

Common stock: The ownership interest in a corporation, representing the residual claim on assets after liabilities are discharged and any preferred stock paid, the return on which is a function of dividends and appreciation in value as opposed to fixed promises to pay, and owners of which typically hold legal rights to elect the corporation's board of directors.

Compound entry: A journal entry involving more than one debit, one credit or both, it does not change the fact that the respective left-and right-side amounts equal each other.

Compound interest: Interest paid on interest earned in prior periods (in addition to interest earned on principal). *Compare* simple interest.

Compounding: In finance, the process of converting from present value to future value. *Compare* discounting.

Comprehensive income: *See* other comprehensive income.

Conservatism principle: A general attitude to prefer understating revenues and assets and overstating expenses and liabilities when choices are possible, with particular emphasis on the recognition of equity increases only when reasonably certain and equity decreases when reasonably possible.

Consistency principle: Uniformity of accounting procedures, classifications and measurements within a set of financial statements and from period to period.

Consolidated statements: Financial statements prepared for an entire corporate family as if it were a single entity, with the family consisting of the parent and its subsidiaries.

Consolidation method: Means of accounting used by an entity owning more than 50% of the voting power of another entity or otherwise possessing effective control, it calls for the parent to prepare consolidated statements.

Contingent liability: A potential obligation, dependent upon the future outcome of a past event, such as lawsuits or administrative proceedings, requiring footnote disclosure for possible losses (and recording an estimated liability when losses become probable).

Contra account: An account whose balance is subtracted from that of its corresponding account. Examples: accumulated depreciation is a contra account for fixed assets; allowance for doubtful accounts is a contra account for accounts receivable.

Contributed capital: *See* paid-in-capital.

Conversion cost: Also called production cost, the labor, materials and overhead costs associated with converting raw materials into finished goods.

Correlation: The degree to which two variables move together.

Correlation coefficient: As applied in modern finance theory, a statistical measure of the degree to which two variables, such as stocks or portfolios, move together; always between −1 and +1.

COSO: The Committee of Sponsoring Organizations of the Treadway Commission on Fraudulent Financial Reporting, whose 1985 report includes guidance for auditor responsibilities relating to internal control over financial reporting, generally recognized as authoritative in the United States, including by PCAOB.

Cost: A monetary measure of the amount of designated resources such as that of a fixed asset or a good held for resale.

Cost accounting: A system for determining and recording measurements of the cost of manufactured goods.

Cost method: Means of accounting used by an investor owning less than 20% of the voting power of another entity or otherwise lacking significant influence, it calls for recording the investment at cost without periodic recognition of its share of profit or loss.

Cost of goods sold (COGS): An expense, the cost of products contributing to sales during an accounting period, determined by the formula: BI + P − EI (that is, beginning inventory + purchases or production − ending inventory).

Cost principle: Transactions are recorded at historical costs or exchange prices on the transaction date.

Coupon: *Informal*: The interest rate on the face amount of a debt security.

Credit: *1. Noun*: The right-hand side of an account, journal or ledger or the amount entered there. *2. Verb*. The act of entering an amount on the right side of an account, journal or ledger.

Credit sales: Sales generated by extending credit to customers, classified into accounts receivable.

Critical accounting policies: As used in MD&A regulations requiring narrative disclosures, these concern judgments and choices an entity makes in classifying and measuring transactions that pose particularly significant effects on data presented in financial statements.

Critical audit matters (CAMs): matters communicated or required to be communicated by auditors to audit committee relating to material financial statement matters and involving especially challenging, subjective, or complex auditor judgment.

Current assets: Cash and assets reasonably expected to be converted into cash or otherwise sold or consumed within a short period of time, usually one year.

Current liabilities: Obligations due within a short period of time, usually one year.

Current ratio: The ratio of current assets to current liabilities, offering a measure of liquidity (the capacity to meet short-term debts as they come due).

D

Debit: *1. Noun*: The left-hand side of an account, journal or ledger or the amount entered there. *2. Verb*. The act of entering an amount on the left side of an account, journal or ledger.

Debt: *1*. Funding generated by borrowings, including bonds and notes. *2*. Also called debt capital, the capital supplied by lenders.

Debt-to-equity ratio: An expression of the relationship between the amounts of debt and equity in a capital structure, usually calculated as average or total debt divided by average or total owners' equity.

Deferrals: Previously recorded assets, liabilities, revenues or expenses that must be adjusted at the end of an accounting period to reflect earned revenues or incurred expenses.

Deferred expense: Also called prepaid expense, an asset account showing the amount paid to others in respect of goods or services not yet enjoyed and which when enjoyed will become expenses. *Examples*: Prepaid Insurance or Prepaid Lease.

Deferred revenue (or deferred income): Also called unearned revenue (or unearned income), a liability account showing the amount received from clients or customers for services or goods in advance of delivery.

Depletion: The process of writing-off or allocating the cost of wasting assets such as mines, timberland, and oil fields over their useful lives.

Depreciation: The process of writing-off or allocating the cost of fixed tangible assets such as buildings and equipment over their useful lives.

Depreciation expense: The portion of a fixed asset's depreciable base allocated as an expense during an accounting period.

Depreciable base (or cost): Also called net cost, the difference between a fixed asset's historical cost and its estimated salvage value, the amount to be allocated over its expected useful life.

Derivatives: Financial instruments, such as futures, options and swaps, which derive their value from other securities or benchmarks such as bonds, currencies, equities, interest rates or currency exchange rates.

Discount rate: The percentage rate (usually annual) used to make present value calculations for future cash flows, reflecting both the time value of money and relevant risks.

Discounted cash flow (DCF) analysis: A particular application of present value principles, a valuation method involving estimating future cash flows and discounting them to present value at a suitable discount rate or rates.

Discounting: In finance, the process of converting from future value to present value. *Compare* compounding.

Diversifiable risk: In modern finance theory, the risk associated with an investment security that can be eliminated by combining it with other risky investments.

Diversification: In modern finance theory, the process of assembling a mix of investment securities to produce a portfolio in which company-specific risk can be eliminated and overall risk reduced without reducing expected return.

Dividend: Distributions to shareholders of a corporation upon the declaration of the corporation's board of directors. Cash and property dividends are a return of capital to shareholders and treated as direct reductions to owners' equity (retained earnings), not an expense; stock dividends require rearranging the capital accounts.

Dividend discount model (DDM): A particular application of present value principles, including discounted cash flow analysis, for valuing common stocks based on expected future dividend payments.

Dividend yield: A stock's annualized cash dividend divided by its market price, expressed as a percentage, an estimate of per share cash return.

Double-declining balance: An accelerated method of depreciation, whereby the rate of depreciation is determined by doubling the rate that would apply using straight-line depreciation (and the rate is applied to the full historical cost, with scrap value netted at the end of the depreciation period).

Double-entry bookkeeping: A characteristic of accounting systems in which every transaction requires at least two entries in the records because there are at least two changes in the accounts, this concept is essential to maintaining the balance sheet in balance.

E

Earnings: A synonym for net income or profit, each measures the difference between revenue and expense (including any gains or losses).

EBIT: Earnings before interest and taxes.

EBITA: Earnings before interest, taxes and amortization.

EBITDA: Earnings before interest, taxes, depreciation and amortization.

Earnings per share (EPS): Earnings for an accounting period divided by the weighted average number of common shares outstanding during the period. In complex capital structures, earnings allocable to the common shareholders would be determined by subtracting amounts allocable to preferred shareholders, convertible debt holders and holders of options.

Efficient frontier: In modern finance theory, that combination of securities in a portfolio such that changing the portfolio could not reduce risk given an expected return or increase expected return given risk.

Efficient capital market hypothesis (ECMH or EMH): In modern finance theory, proposition that prices of publicly-traded securities reflect all relevant and ascertainable information, further specified in three forms: weak (past price information), semi-strong (all public information) and strong (all information).

Ending inventory: The balance in the inventory account as of the last day of an accounting period, and constituting beginning inventory for the succeeding accounting period.

Entity principle (or separate entity principle): A general principle holding that accounts are kept for a discrete entity rather than for the persons who own or operate it.

Entry: The accounting record made for a single transaction in a journal or posted to a ledger.

Equity (or owners' equity): *1.* The residual interest in an entity, determined by subtracting total liabilities from total assets. *2.* Also called equity capital, the capital supplied by (a) the owners of an entity plus (b) retained earnings.

Equity method: Means of accounting used by an investor owning 20% to 50% of the voting power of another entity or where though more than 50% is held the position does not give the investor control, it entails the investor recognizing a percentage interest in the net income of the investee.

Expectations gap: The difference between what users of financial statements expect and what the accounting and auditing professions can deliver.

Expected return: In finance, the weighted average of an investment's possible returns, measured as the sum of all possible returns each multiplied by its chance of occurrence.

Expected value: In statistics, usually the weighted average of a variable's possible values, weighted according to the chance that the variable takes each given value.

Expense: *1. Informal*: A decrease in equity resulting from using up or consuming resources during an accounting period. *2. Formal* (FASB): A decrease in equity from asset decreases or liability increases by virtue of delivering goods or services or carrying out activities constituting an entity's ongoing major or central operations.

Expensing: The process of charging the cost of an asset to an expense account. *Compare* capitalizing.

F

Fair Value Accounting: A method of measuring assets by reference to prevailing fair (market) values as opposed to measuring assets using historical cost, based on the amount of cash at which an asset could be exchanged in an assumed arm's-length transaction between a willing buyer and willing seller in an active functioning market (or, if no such market is available, according to reliable assumptions about one). *See also* mark-to-market accounting.

FASB (pronounced *faz-bee*): Financial Accounting Standards Board, established in the early 1970s as the leading official standard setter for GAAP in the United States.

Fee revenue (or service revenue): Revenue from the delivery of services to paying clients.

FIFO (First-In-First-Out): A method of measuring the cost of goods sold by assuming that the oldest goods (those first in) are the first to be sold (the first out), this also drives the reported amount of ending inventory.

Financial leverage: *See* leverage.

Financial statements: Together, the balance sheet, income statement, and statement of cash flows, and also tending to include the statement of changes in equity, accompanying footnote disclosure and auditor's report.

Fiscal year: An entity's accounting year, often a calendar year but can be another period, usually selected according to when an entity's operations tend naturally to draw to a low level.

Fixed assets: Tangible (*i.e.*, physical, touchable), non-current assets, often referred to collectively as "property, plant and equipment" and by some as "plant" for short.

Free cash flow: Operating cash flow after subtracting amounts for required reinvestment, debt payments, and dividends, this suggests cash available to cushion adversity and/or exploit opportunities.

Fundamental analysis: Approach to valuation entailing examination of an entity's financial statements and related information.

Fundamental equation: Also called the accounting equation, this is the bedrock of accounting and double-entry bookkeeping and underpins the balance sheet, of the form: Assets = Liabilities + Owners' Equity. It is sustained by the rule that debits always equal credits (left-side entries always equal right-side entries).

Future value: The amount of cash at a given future time and a specified discount rate that is equivalent to a specified sum on the date of valuation.

G

GAAP (pronounced *gap*): Generally accepted accounting principles.

GAAS (pronounced *gas*): Generally accepted auditing standards.

Gain: An increase in equity from a peripheral or incidental transaction.

General ledger: The main group of accounts.

Going concern principle: Assumption that an entity will continue to operate indefinitely.

Goodwill: *1. Accounting sense*: an intangible asset measured as the amount paid for an acquired business in excess of the value of its identifiable net assets. *2. Economic sense*: the value associated with operating a business as a going concern arising from customer and employee loyalty, brand-name recognition and similar factors.

Gross: An amount expressed before subtracting some other designated item or items.

Gross profit: Also called gross profit on sales, net sales minus cost of goods sold.

Gross profit margin: Also called gross margin, gross profit on sales divided by net sales.

H

Historical cost: *See* cost.

Hybrid instrument: Generally a reference to a wide class of investment securities that have attributes of both debt and equity, such as a debt instrument convertible into common stock or an equity security that is subject to mandatory redemption by its issuer.

I

IASB: International Accounting Standards Board, established in the late 1990s and early 2000s as a private organization to set universal global accounting standards, called International Financial Reporting Standards (IFRS).

IFRS: International Financial Reporting Standards, promulgated by the International Accounting Standards Board (IASB) and intended to offer a universal global alternative to GAAP (and the many national variants in accounting worldwide).

Income: Revenue minus expenses, the amount by which owners' equity increases as a result of operations during an accounting period.

Income statement: A component of financial statements showing the revenue and expenses and difference between them for an accounting period.

Inflation: A general rise in the price level of goods and services in an economy.

Insolvency: Either or both (a) inability to meet obligations as they come due (called equity or income statement insolvency); (b) condition under which assets are less than liabilities (called bankruptcy or balance sheet insolvency).

Intangible assets: Non-monetary assets lacking physical substance other than on paper, such as copyrights, trademarks, patents, franchise arrangements, goodwill and acquired in-process research and development.

Interest coverage ratio: *See* times interest earned ratio (TIER).

Internal control: Also called internal controls, processes or systems designed to promote advancement of managerial policy and entity objectives, including the preparation of proper financial statements (called internal control over financial reporting).

Inventory: Goods held for sale and raw materials or partly finished materials to be sold upon completion.

Inventory entries: Entries required during the closing process when using the periodic inventory system to compute and post cost of goods sold.

Inventory turnover ratio: An expression of the number of times per period inventory was totally replaced, indicating its relative liquidity, and computed as cost of goods sold divided by average inventory. (Note: a minority of analysts use sales as the numerator in computing this ratio, requiring caution in relying on data for comparison.)

Invoice: The original document issued by an entity for the sale of goods on credit (a sales invoice) or received by an entity for goods bought on credit (a purchase invoice).

J

Journal: A record in which transactions are recorded in chronological order, showing the accounts to be debited (left-side entries) and credited (right-side entries) and the amounts thereof.

Journal entries: The transactions recorded in a journal.

L

Lawyer's letter: Letter from auditor to lawyer seeking verification of management's assertions concerning lawsuits and claims.

Ledger: A group of accounts, including the T-accounts, to which journal entries are posted.

Legal capital: The amount of stockholders' equity in a corporation that may not lawfully be reduced by paying dividends.

Leverage: The comparison of a company's long term debt to its total capital, total equity, or total assets (and in some applications net income), it reflects the idea that adding debt to a capital structure can enhance returns on equity.

Liability: *1. Informal.* An obligation owed to a third party, including short-term funding from suppliers, long-term loans from banks, and other debt instruments. *2. Formal* (FASB): "probable future sacrifices of economic benefits arising from present obligations to transfer assets or render services in the future."

LIFO (Last-In-First-Out): A method of measuring the cost of goods sold by assuming that the goods most recently bought or made (those last in) are the first to be sold (the first out), this also drives the reported amount of ending inventory.

Limited liability: A feature of US corporation and partnership law providing that ordinarily shareholders of a corporation and limited partners of a partnership are not liable for the entity's obligations beyond their investment.

Liquidity: *1.* Capacity to meet obligations short-term, often measured by the current ratio or quick ratio. *2.* The relative ease and speed with which a non-cash asset can be converted into cash.

Liquidity index. Analytical tool often used in auditing to indicate number of days current assets require to be converted to cash.

Long-lived assets (or long-term asset): *See* fixed assets.

Long-term liability (or debt): obligations with due dates beyond one year.

Loss: *1.* Negative net income (opposite of profit). *2.* A decrease in equity from a peripheral or incidental transaction (opposite of gain).

Lower of cost or market (LCM): A valuation principle based on conservatism, requiring that certain assets, including inventory, appear on the balance sheet at the lower of their historical cost or replacement (market) cost.

M

MACRS (modified accelerated cost recovery system): Federal tax code innovation concerning method of accelerated depreciation for tax purposes.

Management's discussion and analysis (MD&A): Narrative accompanying financial statements furnishing an insider's assessment of condition, performance, liquidity, critical accounting policies and other matters.

Managerial accounting: system of accounting designed to provide information for internal users (as opposed to financial accounting, designed to provide information for external users).

Mark-to-Market Accounting: A term more commonly used in tax accounting than financial accounting, financial accounting's equivalent term is fair value accounting, both referring to the method of measuring assets by reference to prevailing fair (market) values as opposed to measuring assets using historical cost. *See also* fair value accounting.

Market risk premium: In modern finance theory, the payoff to investors for having held investments in the form of equity securities across the entire equity market compared to the payoff on risk-free assets such as U.S. Treasury securities.

Marketable securities: Investments in the debt or equity of another entity expected to be converted into cash within a year (a current asset).

Matching principle: Costs associated with the revenue of an accounting period are expenses of that period.

Mean: measure of central tendency or average.

Median: mid-point variable when a data set is arranged in ascending or descending order.

Minority interest: *See* Non-controlling interest.

Modern finance theory (MFT): Collectively, modern portfolio theory, the capital asset pricing model, and the efficient capital market hypothesis.

Modern portfolio theory (MPT): Assuming investors are rational and risk-averse, they will assemble portfolios of securities bearing different correlations such that the combination has the effect of diversifying company-specific risk to zero and resulting in expected return only in relation to market risk.

Monetary transactions principle: Accounting records report only on transactions measurable in money.

N

Net: An amount remaining after some other designated item or items have been subtracted.

Net income: A synonym for earnings or profit, each measures the difference between revenue and expense (including any gains or losses), also informally called the "bottom line" on an income statement.

Net loss: The amount by which expenses exceed revenue during an accounting period.

Net profit margin: Operating income divided by net sales.

Net sales: Sales minus returns, discounts, allowances and the like.

Net worth: A term used to designate owners' equity, though it is slightly misleading in that owners' equity is an accounting concept not a valuation (worth) concept.

Nominal accounts: Accounts serving an administrative function as opposed to corresponding to actual transactional activity, such as the profit and loss account and the components thereof. Some accountants consider the income statement accounts to be nominal accounts in the sense that they are closed at the end of each accounting period.

Non-controlling interest: The portion of the equity of a consolidated subsidiary held by parties other than the parent, reported as an equity item on the parent's consolidated financial statements. In financial statements prepared before 2008, the term "minority interest" was used.

Normal curve (or normal distribution): The familiar "bell curve," symmetric around its mid-point, and bearing properties relating the range of outcomes to various multiples of standard deviation.

Note payable: An obligation to pay evidenced by a written instrument.

Note receivable: A right to receive payment evidenced by a written instrument.

O

Off-balance sheet financing: A manner of obtaining long-term funds not requiring reporting on a balance sheet, as through a long-term lease accounted for as an operating lease rather than a capital lease, these arrangements must be disclosed in notes to financial statements in most circumstances.

Operating cycle: The average time required for an entity to procure its inventory, sell it, and collect cash for sales.

Operating income: Total revenue less expenses applicable to normal operations, including cost of goods sold, SG & A, and depreciation; but excluding interest, taxes, extraordinary items, and incidental or peripheral items.

Other comprehensive income: Comprehensive income consists of the total amount of income from both operating and other activities recorded in the income statement *plus* activities not recorded directly in the income statement such as the effects of foreign currency translation changes and changes in accounting principles applied; the latter is called other comprehensive income.

Overhead: Product costs other than direct labor and direct material costs, including supervision, maintenance and utilities.

Overhead rate: A rate used in cost accounting to allocate overhead to inventory.

Owners' equity (or equity or shareholders' equity): *1.* Residual interest in a business entity, determined by subtracting total liabilities from total assets. *2.* Also called equity capital, the capital supplied by (a) the owners of an entity plus (b) retained earnings.

P

Parent: A corporation that controls another corporation, as by owning more than 50% of its stock.

PCAOB: *See* Public Company Accounting Oversight Board.

Paid-in-capital: The amount equity investors paid to buy a corporation's shares (the excess of this amount over the par value is additional-paid-in-capital), shown as a section of the owners' equity portion of a corporation's balance sheet.

Par value: A nominal figure assigned to equity shares, now substantively anachronistic for accounting but carrying legal significance to limit lawful distributions to shareholders.

Payout ratio: cash dividends per share divided by earnings per share.

Periodic inventory system: Method of bookkeeping for inventory in which a period-end physical count is necessary to determine inventory quantities and cost of goods sold, and requiring related inventory entries during the closing process.

Permanent account: All balance sheet accounts are permanent accounts, meaning they are not closed at the end of the accounting period.

Perpetual inventory system: Method of bookkeeping for inventory in which inventory quantities and related costs of goods sold are recorded throughout the accounting period, dispensing with the need for inventory entries during the closing process necessary in a periodic inventory system.

Perpetuity: Annuity that continues indefinitely.

Plant: Short-hand term for property, plant and equipment; also, fixed assets.

Portfolio theory: *See* modern portfolio theory.

Posting: The process of transferring entries from the journal to the ledger, including the process of transferring balances in inventory accounts to the cost of goods sold account.

Preferred stock: Corporate equity ranking senior to common stock and junior to debt, governed by corporate documentation designating preferences over common stock such as concerning dividend payments.

Prepaid expense: Also called deferred expense, a current asset account showing the amount paid to others in respect of goods or services not yet enjoyed and which when enjoyed will become expenses. *Examples*: Prepaid Insurance or Prepaid Lease.

Present value: As of a valuation date, the amount of cash that is the equivalent of a sum to be received at a given future time (or times) at a given discount rate (or rates).

Price-earnings (P/E) ratio: The price of a share of stock divided by earnings per share.

Probability distribution: A complete specification of the chances of alternative outcomes or values a variable will take.

Profit: A synonym for earnings or net income, each measures the difference between revenue and expense (including any gains or losses).

Profit and loss account (P & L Account): The nominal account used during the closing process to compute income.

Profit and loss statement: Another name for the income statement.

Profit margin: This can refer either to *gross* profit margin (gross profit on sales divided by net sales) or *net* profit margin (operating income divided by net sales); when neither adjective is used, it usually refers to the latter. Sometimes the terms gross operating profit margin and net operating profit margin are used.

Property, plant and equipment (PP & E): A common designation for fixed assets, both in presenting financial statements and in conversation.

Public Company Accounting Oversight Board (PCAOB): Body created by the Sarbanes-Oxley Act of 2002 to establish generally accepted auditing standards in the United States and to oversee the profession of independent public accounting firms engaged in rendering auditing services.

Publicly-held company: Also often called a public company, an entity whose ownership interests (such as stock in a corporation) are held by members of the public and listed on a public securities exchange.

Q

Quality of income ratio: Cash flow provided by operating activities divided by operating income, a measure of the degree to which income generation corresponds to cash generation.

Quick ratio: Also called the acid test ratio, a stringent test of liquidity determined by dividing the most liquid current assets (such as cash, marketable securities and accounts receivable but usually excluding inventory) by current liabilities.

R

Realization principle: Recognize revenue when goods or services are delivered, in an amount reasonably certain to be realized.

Receivables: *See* accounts receivable.

Recognition: The act of recording revenue or expense items as allocable to a particular accounting period (note that revenue recognition is governed by the realization principle).

Retail inventory method: A specialized procedure used to estimate ending inventory in the retailing industry, determined by converting ending inventory at retail prices to a cost basis using a ratio based upon the retailer's ordinary profit margin.

Retained earnings: The portion of a corporation's owners' equity resulting from operations and not distributed to its shareholders, shown on the balance sheet as a separate section in owners' equity.

Return on assets (ROA): An overall measure of performance determined by dividing earnings before interest and taxes (EBIT) by total or average assets. Some analysts use net income in the numerator.

Return on equity (ROE): A measure of performance focused on returns driven by shareholder capital determined by dividing net income by total or average owners' equity.

Return on investment (ROI): A measure of performance focused on returns driven by shareholder and other long-term capital determined by dividing earnings before interest and taxes (EBIT) by the sum of total or average owners' equity and total or average long-term liabilities.

Revenue: *1. Informal*: An increase in equity resulting from operations during an accounting period, usually from the sale of goods or the rendition of services. *2. Formal* (FASB): An increase in equity from asset increases and/or liability decreases by virtue of delivering goods or services or carrying out activities constituting an entity's ongoing major or central operations.

Revenue recognition: A critical judgment in any accounting system that determines the top line of the income statement, focused on depicting the consideration expected from customers in exchange for the transfer of goods or rendition of services.

Reverse stock split: The combining of a number of shares into a smaller number of shares, this has no effect on anything substantive except the number of shares outstanding (the number of slices into which a corporate pie is cut decreases).

Risk-free rate: The return paid on securities deemed to pose no investment risk, principally U.S. Treasury securities.

S

Sales: Revenue from the delivery of goods to paying customers.

Salvage value: Also called scrap value, the estimated residual value of a fixed asset upon disposition at the end of its useful life, a judgment necessary to perform most depreciation exercises.

Sarbanes-Oxley Act of 2002 (abbreviated and pronounced by some as SOX): United States federal legislation creating PCAOB, reforming structural features of FASB, requiring senior officers of SEC-registered entities to prepare certifications of internal control effectiveness and making numerous other changes in provisions relating to accounting, auditing and corporate governance concerning SEC-registered entities.

Securities and Exchange Commission (SEC): United States governmental agency created in 1934 to administer federal securities laws that relate to matters of disclosure, the SEC has plenary power to promulgate requisite accounting standards though it generally defers to and sanctions those established by FASB and its predecessors.

Selling, general & administrative (SG & A): Expenses relating to the operation of an entity's business otherwise unclassified.

Separate entity principle (or entity principle): A general principle holding that accounts are kept for a discrete entity rather than for the persons who own or operate it.

Service revenue (or fee revenue): Revenue from the delivery of services to paying clients.

Shares (or stock): The instruments representing equity interests in a corporation.

Shareholders (or stockholders): The owners of a corporation.

Shareholders' equity (or equity or owner's equity): *1.* Residual interest in a business entity, determined by subtracting total liabilities from total assets. *2.* Also called equity capital, the capital supplied by (a) the owners of an entity plus (b) retained earnings.

Sharpe ratio: A measure of a portfolio's performance relative to its riskiness, expressed as the portfolio's return less the risk-free rate, divided by the portfolio's standard deviation.

Simple interest: The interest rate times the original principal, not including interest on interest. *Compare* compound interest.

Solvency: The capacity to meet obligations long-term.

Specific identification method: A method of measuring the cost of goods sold by tagging and tracking each specific item, this also drives the reported amount of ending inventory.

Stand-alone risk: In modern finance theory, the total risk of a security, consisting of both company-specific risk (non-systemic) and market (systemic) risk.

Standard deviation: Numerical measurement of the dispersion of possible outcomes or values of a data set, commonly used as a measure of investment risk and earnings or cash flow variability; higher standard deviations indicate higher risk or variability.

Stated capital: Par value times shares outstanding.

Statement of financial condition (or position): Other names for the balance sheet.

Stock, stockholders, stockholders' equity: *See* shares, shareholders, shareholders' equity.

Stock dividend: A dividend paid in the form of shares.

Stock split: A division of existing shares into a greater number of shares, this has no effect on anything substantive except the number of shares outstanding (the number of slices into which a corporate pie is cut increases).

Straight-line depreciation: A method of depreciating fixed assets whereby the rate of depreciation is determined by dividing the depreciable base by the useful life, yielding an even amount of annual depreciation expense.

Subsidiary: A corporation controlled by another corporation (its parent), as by the parent owning more than 50% of its stock.

Sum-of-the-years' digits: An accelerated method of depreciation whereby the rate of depreciation is a fraction whose numerator is the remaining useful life and whose denominator is the sum of digits from 1 to the estimated useful life. For n years, a short-cut to determine the sum of these digits is $n\ (n+1)\ /\ 2$.

Systematic risk: In finance theory, also called market risk or non-diversifiable risk, the portion of an investment security's risk that cannot be eliminated by diversification.

T

T-account: The simplest version of an account and contained in the ledger, it receives postings of transactions from the journal to enable depiction of each transaction affecting that account during an accounting period and the summation of these transactions.

Tangible assets: Assets that can be touched, bearing physical qualities such as buildings, motor vehicles, plant and equipment, fixtures and fittings.

Temporary account: All income statement accounts are temporary accounts, meaning they are closed at the end of the accounting period.

Test of transactions: Auditing procedures related to examining specified transactions and supporting documents.

Times interest earned ratio (TIER): Also called the interest coverage ratio, earnings before interest and taxes (EBIT) divided by interest expense.

Transaction: An event recorded in accounting records, always having at least two elements.

Treadway Commission: *See* COSO.

U

Uncollectible accounts expense: Also called bad debt expense, the estimated portion of accounts receivable generated during an accounting period unlikely to be collected.

Unearned revenue: Payment received in advance of providing a good or service, this is a liability.

Units-of-production method: Procedure for depreciating fixed assets by allocating costs in proportion to the asset's use in operation.

Unrealized gain (or loss): Gains or losses not yet realized because the related asset has not yet been disposed of.

Useful life: Also called service life, an estimate of the period of time a fixed asset will contribute to revenue-generating capacity, a judgment necessary to perform most depreciation exercises.

V

Variability: A measure of risk expressing the degree of a data's deviation from expected returns, expected values or trends.

W

Wasting assets: Natural resources deemed subject to literal physical exhaustion, including mines, timberland, and oil fields.

Working capital: Current assets minus current liabilities, net short-term resources.

Write-down: Reduce the carrying amount of an item to market value, typified by inventory when obsolete or damaged.

Write-off: Reduce the carrying amount of an item to zero, typified by accounts receivable amounting to bad debts.

Z

Z-Score: A solvency or bankruptcy prediction model sometimes used by auditors as an analytical procedure, computed by weighting various financial statement ratios.

BIBLIOGRAPHY

■ ■ ■

Anthony, Robert N., *Rethinking the Rules of Financial Accounting* (McGraw Hill 2004)

Anthony, Robert N. & Leslie K. Breitner, *Essentials of Accounting* (Prentice Hall 8th ed. 2003)

Ayer, John D., *Guide to Finance for Lawyers* (LEXIS 2001)

Beasley, Mark S., *Auditing Cases* (Prentice Hall 2nd ed. 2003)

Bernstein, Leopold A. & John J. Wild, *Analysis of Financial Statements* (McGraw Hill 5th ed. 2000)

Bodie, Zvi & Robert C. Merton, *Finance* (Prentice Hall 2000)

Bradford, C. Steven & Gary Adna Ames, *Basic Accounting Principles for Lawyers* (Andersen 1997)

Bratton, William W., *Corporate Finance: Cases and Materials* (Foundation Press 6th ed. 2007)

Brealey, Richard A. & Stewart C. Myers, *Principles of Corporate Finance* (McGraw Hill 4th ed. 1991)

Briloff, Abraham, *More Debits than Credits* (Harper & Row 1976)

Copeland, Tom *et al.*, *Valuation* (John Wiley & Sons 3rd ed. 2000)

Cox, James D., *Financial Information, Accounting and the Law* (Little, Brown 1980)

Cunningham, Lawrence A., *Law and Accounting: Cases and Materials* (West 2005)

Dauber, Nicky A. *et al.*, *The Vest-Pocket CPA* (Prentice Hall 2nd ed. 1996)

Droms, William G., *Finance and Accounting for Nonfinancial Managers* (Perseus 5th ed. 2003)

Epstein, Barry J., *Handbook of Accounting and Auditing* (Warren, Gorham & Lamont 2004)

Estes, Ralph, *Dictionary of Accounting* (MIT Press 2nd ed. 1985)

Faris, E. McGruder, *Accounting for Lawyers* (Michie 4th ed. 1982)

Fiflis, Ted J., *Accounting Issues for Lawyers* (West 4th ed. 1991)

Finkler, Steven A., *Finance & Accounting for Nonfinancial Managers* (Prentice Hall 1992)

Graham, Benjamin, *The Interpretation of Financial Statements* (Harper & Row 1937)

Graham, Benjamin & David L. Dodd, *Security Analysis* (McGraw Hill 2nd ed. 1940)

Greenwald, Bruce C.N. *et al.*, *Value Investing* (John Wiley & Sons 2001)

Haas, Jeffrey J., *Corporate Finance in a Nutshell* (West 2004)

Hardesty, David E., *Practical Guide to Corporate Governance and Accounting: Implementing the Requirements of the Sarbanes-Oxley Act, 2004* (Warren, Gorham & Lamont 2003)

Herwitz, David R. & Matthew J. Barrett, *Accounting for Lawyers* (Foundation Press 4th ed. 2006)

Jackson, Howell E. *et al.*, *Analytical Methods for Lawyers* (Foundation Press 2003)

Kieso, Donald E. *et al.*, *Intermediate Accounting* (John Wiley & Sons 10th ed. 2001)

Klein, William A. & John C. Coffee, Jr., *Business Organization and Finance: Legal and Economic Principles* (Foundation Press 10th ed. 2007)

Libby, Robert *et al.*, *Financial Accounting* (McGraw Hill 3rd ed. 2001)

Lipsky, David & David Lipton, *A Student's Guide to Accounting for Lawyers* (LEXIS 3rd ed. 1998)

Logue, Dennis E., ed., *Handbook of Modern Finance* (Warren, Gorham & Lamont 2003)

Meigs, Robert F. & Walter B. Meigs, *Accounting: The Basis of Business Decisions* (McGraw Hill 9th ed. 1993)

Meyer, Charles H., *Accounting and Finance for Lawyers in a Nutshell* (West 2nd ed. 2002)

Michael, Douglas C., *Legal Accounting: Principles and Applications* (West 1997)

Mundstock, George, *A Finance Approach to Accounting for Lawyers* (Foundation Press 1999)

O'Reilly, Vincent M. *et al.*, *Montgomery's Auditing* (John Wiley & Sons 12th ed. 1998)

Previts, Gary John & Barbara Dubis Merino, *A History of Accountancy in the United States: The Cultural Significance of Accounting* (Ohio St. U. Press 1998)

Riahi-Belkaoui, Ahmed, *Accounting Theory* (Thomson 4th ed. 2000)

Ricchiute, David N., *Auditing and Assurance Services* (South-Western 7th ed. 2003)

Shleifer, Andrei, *Inefficient Markets: An Introduction to Behavioral Finance* (Oxford U. Press 2000)

Siegel, Joel G. & Jae K. Shim, *Dictionary of Accounting Terms* (Barron's 1987)

Siegel, Stanley & David A. Siegel, *Accounting and Financial Disclosure* (West 1983)

Wolk, Harry I. *et al.*, *Accounting Theory: Conceptual Issues in a Political and Economic Environment* (South-Western 6th ed. 2004)

Wright, Charles R., *Understanding and Using Financial Data: An Ernst & Young Guide for Attorneys* (John Wiley & Sons 2nd ed. 1996)

Young, Michael R., ed., *Accounting Irregularities and Financial Fraud: A Corporate Governance Guide* (Aspen Law & Business 2nd ed. 2002)

INDEX

References are to Pages